Cultural Anthropology

Cultural Anthropology

TRIBES, STATES, AND THE GLOBAL SYSTEM

Third Edition

JOHN H. BODLEY

Washington State University

Mayfield Publishing Company
Mountain View, California
London • Toronto

Library of Congress Cataloging-in-Publication Data

Bodley, John H.
    Cultural anthropology : tribes, states, and the global system /
John H. Bodley.—3rd ed.
      p. cm.
    Includes bibliographical references and index.
    ISBN 0-7674-1194-3
    1. Ethnology. I. Title.
GN316.B63 1999
306—dc21   99-12137
                                   CIP

Manufactured in the United States of America
10 9 8 7 6 5 4 3 2 1

Mayfield Publishing Company
1280 Villa Street
Mountain View, California 94041

Sponsoring editor, Janet M. Beatty; production, Strawberry Field Publishing; manuscript editor, Tom Briggs; art manager, Jean Mailander; text designer, Joan Greenfield; cover designer, Linda Robertson; illustrators, Joan Carol and K. M. Bodley; manufacturing manager, Randy Hurst. The text was set in 9/11 Aster by Thompson Type and printed on 45# Highland Plus by Malloy Lithographing, Inc.

Cover photo: Medford Taylor NGS/Image Coll.

Text and illustration credits continue at the back of the book on pages 473–474, which constitute an extension of the copyright page.

 Printed on acid-free, recycled paper.

Preface

Given the interconnections among cultural groups on the current world stage (and the rapidity with which those dynamics change), it is imperative that we learn as much as we can about world culture, history, and geography in order to lead informed, productive lives in our global village. What better way to start than by applying the traditional methods of anthropology to a modern view of the world? With this as my underlying goal, I've presented the basic concepts of cultural anthropology in this introductory text by comparing cultures of increasing scale and focusing on specific universal issues. The end result, I hope, is a stimulating, culturally integrated alternative to topically arranged and encyclopedic texts.

To demonstrate the vitality of fieldwork and to generate enthusiasm for the discipline, Chapter 1 begins with a personal account of my fieldwork with the Ashaninka of Amazonia. Not only does it explain why I was inspired to approach anthropology from a humanistic, culture-scale perspective, but it also introduces the field methods employed by cultural anthropologists. Ensuing chapters examine a representative sample of cultures in sufficient depth to maintain cultural context and to provide students with a sound understanding of the world's major cultural areas and dominant civilizations.

The book is designed to provide balanced coverage of three dramatically different cultural types. After Part I's introduction to fieldwork, Part II examines domestic-scale, autonomous tribal cultures. Part III presents politically organized, class-based civilizations and ancient empires, and Part IV surveys global, industrial, market-based civilizations. Scale is used as an organizing principle in order to provide a basis for comparison; however, I've avoided the implicit value judgments that are part of popular ideas about evolutionary progress. The following universal issues about the human conditions are explored from a comparative, anthropological perspective: What is "natural" about humans? What is "cultural" about humans? Which human *inequalities* are natural? Which are cultural? Is *population growth* natural or cultural? Is *economic growth* natural or cultural? What are the human costs and benefits of socioeconomic growth? The ethnographic material will focus on the influence of culture scale and the distribution of social power on such basic matters as quality of life, domestic organization, intergroup relations, and relationship to the environment. The text devotes special attention to how anthropological explanations themselves have developed and where controversies have arisen over interpretation. The causes and consequences of changes in culture scale are central themes.

Ethnographic case studies are used to describe the functional interconnections between the material bases and the social and ideological systems of representative cultures at each scale. The cultures selected as case studies are those that are best described in ethnographic films and monographs, and they are the subject of abundant analytical materials. Australian aborigines, Amazonian villagers, and East African pastoralists represent domestic-scale cultures and are treated in separate chapters. Political-scale cultures are represented by Pacific Island chiefdoms and the ancient and modern great civilizations of Mesopotamia, the Inca, China, Islam, and Hindu India. The commercial cultures of the United States, the British empire, contemporary indigenous peoples, and the rural peasantry are examined as part of the global system. The text shows cultures in depth—as adapting, integrated systems—and as part of regional, continental, and global systems, as appropriate.

Throughout the text, I've challenged students to consider the big questions about the nature of cultural systems: How are cultures structured to satisfy basic human needs? What is it like to be human under different cultural conditions? Are race, language, and environment determinants of culture? Are materialist explanations more useful than ideological ones? What are the major turning points in human history?

The culture-scale perspective highlights the unique problems of the present world system. Roughly one-third of the text is devoted to issues of current concern, especially the problem of inequality and how to make our world sustainable. A wide range of global humanitarian issues such as ethnocide, genocide, and ecocide also are considered, along with a variety of more narrow theoretical and methodological issues. My hope is that understanding how tribes, states, and global systems work and how they differ might help citizens design a more secure and equitable world.

To further strengthen the thought-provoking nature of this text, I've included a number of critical thinking and learning aids. End-of-chapter study questions highlight and reinforce important issues and arguments. Timelines of the prehistory and early history of the major sociocultural systems are included. Key terms are set in bold type and are defined on the spread where they first appear. Suggested readings at the ends of chapters, coupled with an extensive bibliography, encourage students to pursue specific case materials and issues in greater depth.

Because many anthropology courses are organized by standard topics such as subsistence, social organization, and religion, the Instructor's Manual provides an alternative course outline that breaks up the integrated cultures covered in the text and sorts their components into their respective topical categories. A topical classroom presentation can enhance cross-cultural comparisons and draw attention to cultural institutions, while the organization of the book will ensure that the fundamental integration of individual cultures and the significance of differences in culture scale will not be overlooked.

NEW IN THIS EDITION

The most conspicuous changes in the third edition reflect an attempt to simplify and sharpen the theoretical focus around the interconnected themes of culture, cultural process, growth, and social power. *Culture scale* remains the key comparative concept, representing the evolution of culture as measured by orders-of-magnitude difference in levels of socioeconomic growth. In this third edition, I examine why culture scale changes, who benefits from such change, and who pays. In a world where scale change accelerates daily, these are certainly among the most crucial questions for anthropology. The objective is to provide students with stronger tools to analyze ethnographic data in ways that will help them understand the cultural forces that shape the quality of life for people in all human societies.

The *small-*, *large-*, and *global-scale* labels that previously were used to structure the book have been emended to *domestic-*, *political-*, and *commercial-scale* to emphasize that different ways of organizing social power are the crucial distinction that limits the scale of cultures. Students will be challenged to consider the extent to which individual power-seeking elites may actually direct, and differentially benefit from, the process of cultural evolution. Culture change thus can be seen as ultimately falling under human control and serving human ends, rather than as a "natural" and "inevitable" process that just happens. The exciting question becomes, *Who* controls culture growth and the distribution of social power? These revisions simplify the theoretical background and provide a consistent, readily grasped framework for interpreting the rich ethnographic detail that is presented throughout the text.

Several revisions in Chapter 1 improve the treatment of the culture concept and focus attention more closely on the concept of cultural process, defined as cultural actions producing an outcome. Social power, growth, and scale are more carefully defined and are directly linked to the material in later chapters.

Culture is introduced as the unique means by which human societies satisfy human needs, regulate size and social power, and manage natural resources. This revised discussion of culture stresses the utility of treating culture as socially inherited ideas that guide human behavior, as well as the specific aspects, functions, and features of culture that make culture distinctively human. This dual emphasis on biology and culture reflects recent developments in biocultural evolutionary theory that recognize biology and culture as dual inheritance systems (Boyd and Richerson 1985, Durham 1991).

Chapter 3 now includes a case study of Mundurucú headhunting to demonstrate the utility of biocultural evolutionary theory for understanding Amazonian tribal warfare. The discussion of the emergence of politically organized societies in Chapters 6 and 7 has been revised to focus directly on the politicization process, stressing the role of elites and change in scale in the emergence of government. Chapter 11 has been thoroughly revised to treat the emergence of capitalism in Europe in greater ethnohistorical depth. Rich ethnographic material has been added on European cosmology, feudalism, peasant farming systems, specific mercantile capitalists, and the London poor in the nineteenth century. Chapter 12 also has been extensively revised with new ethnohistorical material,

with a special focus on New York City. Chapter 15 highlights positive approaches for solving global problems, including development alternatives that empower local communities.

After reading this book, students should be able to differentiate meaningfully between domestic-, political-, and commercial-scale cultures and be able to refer to specific cultural processes and ethnographic examples using some of the terminology of cultural anthropology. I hope students will recognize that growth and the cultural distribution of social power are among our most crucial human problems as we enter the new millennium. I also hope students will recognize that anthropology has utility, and will be motivated to learn more about anthropology.

ACKNOWLEDGMENTS

This book began as a one-page outline in the spring of 1981, and over the years it has benefited greatly from discussions with my colleagues and suggestions from numerous readers. I'm very grateful to all who offered me advice and support.

I'd like to thank especially Jan Beatty, Gerald Berreman, Geoffrey Gamble, and Thomas Headland, who wrote in support of my sabbatical leave from Washington State University in 1990, which enabled me to complete much of the primary research and writing in one concentrated effort. In July 1991, I made the first public presentation of the culture-scale approach in a paper entitled "Indigenous Peoples vs. the State: A Culture Scale Approach," which I gave at a conference called "Indigenous People in Remote Regions: A Global Perspective," organized by historian Ken Coates at the University of Victoria, British Columbia.

My students and colleagues at Washington State University who listened to my ideas and offered suggestions and materials were particularly helpful; I'd like to thank Robert Ackerman, Diana Ames-Marshall, Michael Blair, Mark Fleisher, Lee Freese, Chris Harris, Fekri Hassan, Barry Hewlett, Barry Hicks, Tim Kohler, Grover Krantz, William Lipe, Robert Littlewood, Nancy McKee, Peter J. Mehringer, Jr., Frank Myka, Margaret Reed, Allan Smith, and Linda Stone.

At the risk of omitting someone, I also want to thank those who provided me with materials that found their way into the book: Mary Abascal-Hildebrand, Clifford Behrens, Diane Bell, Gerald D. Berreman, Jean-Pierre Bocquet-Appel, Cecil H. Brown, Stephen B. Brush, John W. Burton, Gudren Dahl, Shelton H. Davis, Paul L. Doughty, Nancy M. Flowers, Richard A. Gould, Brian Hayden, Thomas Headland, Howard M. Hecker, L. R. Hiatt, Arthur Hippler, Betty Meehan, Peter G. Roe, Nicholas Thomas, Norman B. Tindale, and Gerald Weiss.

I am grateful to the reviewers of the third edition, whose thoughtful comments contributed much: Jeffrey H. Cohen, Texas A&M University; Robert Dirks, Illinois State University; Michael P. Freedman, Syracuse University; Susan A. Johnston, University of Rhode Island; Adrian S. Novotny, Long Beach City College; and Lars Rodseth, University of Utah.

For the second edition, I owe special thanks to Bill Lipe and Linda Stone in my department for directing me to new material on the global culture. Also thanks to Barry Hicks of the Health Research and Education Center, Washington State University, Spokane, for assistance with my state- and county-level research. Kevin Norris in the Information Systems Department of Spokane County, Washington, provided me with data on Spokane County land ownership. Zoltan Porga, system analyst, and Gilbert A. Pierson, Information Technology, at Washington State University, guided me through the intricacies of SAS. The staff in my department, especially LeAnn Couch and Joan Pubols, provided important support as I served as department chair while preparing this revision.

I am especially indebted to the reviewers of the second edition and the many users of the first edition who provided me with invaluable comments, especially James Armstrong, State University of New York, Plattsburgh; Diane Baxter, George Washington University; Michael P. Freedman, Syracuse University; Josiah McC. Heyman, Michigan Technological University; David T. Hughes, Wichita State University; Ronald R. McIrvin, University of North Carolina, Greensboro; David McMahon, Saint Francis College; Richard K. Reed, Trinity University; and William Stuart, University of Maryland, College Park. I have tried hard to respond to their suggestions, and they definitely shaped the result.

I remain grateful to the reviewers of the first edition manuscript for their many incisive comments and helpful suggestions: Gerald D. Berreman (University of California, Berkeley), Peter J. Bertocci (Oakland University), Daniel L. Boxberger (Western Washington University), Jill Brody (Louisiana State University), Thomas E. Durbin (California State University, Stanislaus), James F. Eder (Arizona State University), James F. Garber (Southwest Texas State University), James W. Hamilton (University of Missouri, Columbia), Patricia Lyons Johnson (Pennsylvania State University), Arthur C. Lehmann (California State University, Chico), Fran Markowitz (DePaul University), David McCurdy (Macalester College), Michael D. Olien (University of Georgia), Mary Kay Gilliland Olsen (Pima Community College and University of Arizona), Aaron Podolefsky (University of Northern Iowa), Scott Rushforth (New Mexico State University), and Daniel J. Yakes (Muskegon Community College).

Many people at Mayfield worked very hard on this project. I'd particularly like to thank Jan Beatty for providing editorial guidance and Melanie Field and April Wells-Hayes for shepherding the project through production. Copyeditor Tom Briggs gave the entire manuscript a careful edit.

Finally, I'd especially like to thank Kathi, Brett, and Antonie for their encouragement and patience. Kathi helped create the index and offered her support throughout the entire project.

Contents

3 Native Amazonians: Villagers of the Rain Forest

4 African Cattle Peoples: Tribal Pastoralists

5 Body, Mind, and Soul: The Quality of Tribal Life

PART THREE
Political-Scale Culture: The End of Equality

6 Pacific Islanders: The Ranked Chiefdoms

7 Early States: The Near East and the Andes

I

Understanding Other Cultures

Human problems like military conflict, public health, social disorder, and environmental deterioration are best treated as sociocultural, not specialized technological, issues. Cultural anthropology can help us think about these problems creatively because it offers a view of many alternative ways of living. We need to understand and respect the diverse cultures that operate at local, regional, and global levels while at the same time safeguarding the increasingly vulnerable biosphere that we all depend on and share. Familiarity with only a single cultural tradition leaves one ill-equipped to cope with perplexing issues arising even within multiethnic states. Internationally, efforts to solve global problems may require a broad theoretical understanding of cultural systems, as well as practical knowledge about major regional civilizations and specific local cultures.

The primary concern in this book is with understanding the significance of cultures for the security and well-being of humanity. We will examine many representative cultures in depth to gain insight into the different ways in which people in different cultures relate to one another and to the natural environment. By better understanding the internal logic of cultural practices that might initially seem

irrational, we can learn tolerance and respect for the world's cultures.

The first part of the chapter draws on my field experiences in South America to show what it is like to actually do anthropology and to explain why I use culture scale as an organizing principle. The chapter then introduces the key concepts of culture and ethnocentrism, and discusses how culture scale, growth, and process will be used throughout the book. Here, we review some major turning points in human history and demonstrate that anthropology has enormous practical significance and is directly concerned with the great public issues of our time.

DOING ANTHROPOLOGY

Adventures in the Field

How did background knowledge about a particular culture help the author size up a difficult and potentially dangerous situation?

Doing cultural anthropology is a continuous adventure. It means exploring the unknown to gain a better understanding of other peoples and cultures.

1

Such understanding can be obtained indirectly from books and class work, but it is most exciting and vivid when it comes directly from real-life experiences—sometimes in unexpected ways. For example, my richest understanding of native Amazonian political leadership was gained during a 2-day encounter with Chonkiri, a proud and independent Ashaninka **bigman,*** who lived with his small band in the rugged foothills of the Andes along the headwaters of the Peruvian Amazon (see Figure 1.1). Bigman leadership is based entirely on force of personality, and Chonkiri displayed this quality admirably (see Figure 1.2).

In 1969, my wife, Kathleen, and I were exploring the remote interior of the Ashaninka homeland to assess the living conditions of those Ashaninka still maintaining a self-sufficient way of life. A bush pilot flew us to Obenteni, a tiny frontier outpost in the Gran Pajonal, 5 days by mule trail from the nearest truck road and 50 air miles from the nearest town. At that time the Gran Pajonal was an unmapped maze of savanna-covered ridges and deep forested canyons. It was a vast wilderness, inhabited by the isolated, still fiercely independent Ashaninka.

After a hard day's walk from Obenteni, we spotted a column of four Ashaninka men on the skyline of an intersecting ridge. Carrying bows and arrows and shotguns, they were an awe-inspiring sight in their long brown cotton robes (*cushmas*) and bright red face paint. They approached briskly and then halted astride the trail a few paces in front of us. With potentially hostile strangers meeting, there was fear and uncertainty on both sides. But the Ashaninka were armed and on their home ground, so they controlled the situation. Their leader Chonkiri, obviously a traditional bigman, stepped forward, struck a defiant pose, and shouted a tirade of angry questions at me. The same scene might have greeted the first European explorers to enter Ashaninka territory in 1673.

Chonkiri demanded to know where we were going, why we had come, and whether we were bringing sickness. These were legitimate questions, and, although I knew his hostile manner was a formal ritual, I was still uneasy because the Pajonal Ashan-

*Key terms are set in bold italic type and are defined on the page spread where they first appear.

inka had every reason to resent outsiders. Recent measles epidemics had killed many Ashaninka, and colonists and missionaries were appearing in ever greater numbers. In isolated areas such as this, Ashaninka often fled at the approach of strangers. However, Chonkiri betrayed no fear. He was playing the role of a powerful and supremely self-confident bigman. (His impressive demeanor was in striking contrast to the timidity of an Ashaninka man we had met earlier, who had been almost too shy to speak.)

Satisfied with my answers, Chonkiri became a generous host (see Figure 1.3). He led us to his house and offered his hospitality—cooked manioc and taro tubers along with handfuls of live ants, which he and his sons had just collected. (I knew that insects are an important food throughout the Pajonal, because game is scarce, but I was amazed to see children sorting through heaps of corn husks to extract fat, inch-long white grubs and pop them, still wiggling, into their mouths.) I declined to sample this delicacy, although I enjoyed the roast manioc from Chonkiri's cooking fire.

After dinner, Chonkiri and his well-armed men followed us back to our camp. They were eager to see what we had brought, and Chonkiri insisted that we unload our backpacks for his inspection (see Figure 1.4). Smiling broadly, he immediately took possession of the box of shotgun shells that I had tucked into my pack for trading purposes. "These are mine!" he announced, handing the shells out one at a time to his men. I nodded my approval, hoping that he would be satisfied with such a lavish gift but feeling more and more uneasy at his brashness.

The next morning, Chonkiri returned with a gift basket of corn and bananas. This was simple sharing, giving and receiving, with no monetary score-keeping. Intellectually, I recognized his gesture as a textbook example of *generalized reciprocity* in a *nonmarket economy.* His generosity reminded me that yesterday Chonkiri had behaved like a tribal bigman by giving away things, even if they were my things.

My instinctive distrust of Chonkiri's real motives was immediately justified. With no further preliminaries, he began to root through our possessions, snatching up whatever he wanted—clothing, trade goods, medical supplies, food, and utensils. In my

FIGURE 1.1 *Map of the territory of the Ashaninka in the Peruvian Amazon.*

culture, this was armed robbery, and we were outnumbered, unarmed, and virtually defenseless. An earlier warning that some Pajonal bigmen were killers suddenly flashed to mind, and I graciously allowed Chonkiri's followers, including his sons, to share my entire assortment of little mirrors and all the rest of my trade goods, even though this would leave me in an awkward position (see Figure 1.5).

Chonkiri betrayed his own nervousness when he ripped open a box of unexposed film and started to unreel it, but dropped it with a start when my wife, Kathleen, blurted, "Stop!" He quickly regained his composure, and his boisterous demands soon became so outrageous that we were forced to call his bluff. He was turning our encounter into a test of will. First, he demanded the hunting knife that Kathleen wore in a sheath on her belt. She refused, insisting that it belonged to her father. Becoming frustrated, Chonkiri picked up my *cushma*, which I used as my only blanket, announcing loudly that it was newer than his and that he intended to take it. When I said, "No!" he flung it to the ground, angrily stomping his feet in a display of temper befitting a true bigman. I cautiously assumed that this outburst was for show and would not escalate to violence.

I had a general understanding of the rules. Normally, one was expected to show generosity by giving away anything that was asked for, but now, clearly, Chonkiri was asking for too much. He was showing his bigman status by pushing the limits. I was obliged to refuse his request with no show of fear, although I had no idea how the game would end. The final test came when Chonkiri appropriated the fat roll of cash (50 Sole bills worth approximately $2 each) hidden in my pack. He triumphantly peeled off the bills and handed them out to his men. Using unmistakable gestures, I responded with my most emphatic "No!" If I had not shown personal strength at that moment, it would have been a humiliating, perhaps even dangerous, defeat. To my considerable relief, he promptly collected the money and restored it to my pack. Chonkiri and I had reached an understanding based on mutual respect. In this situation, familiarity with

bigman A self-made leader in a domestic-scale culture. His position is temporary, depending on personal ability and the consent of his followers.

generalized reciprocity The distribution of goods and services by direct sharing. It is assumed that in the long run, giving and receiving balances out, but no accounts are maintained.

nonmarket economy Goods and services distributed by direct exchange or reciprocity in the absence of markets and money.

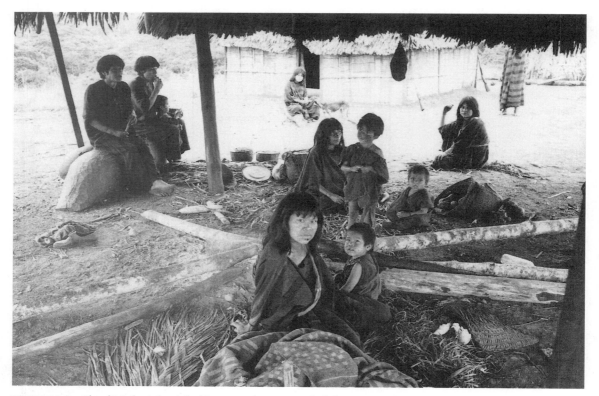

FIGURE 1.2   *Chonkiri, the Ashaninka bigman, at home—on the left, sitting on the beer trough.*

the culture was as important as courage. I realized that Chonkiri's bravado and bluster betrayed his personal vulnerability as a bigman. If he failed to command the respect of his followers, they could simply walk away. A bigman had no means of coercing loyalty in a culture in which every household could be economically self-sufficient.

After our standoff, Chonkiri became the generous host again. He gave us a grand tour of his house and garden, and provided one of his sons to serve as a trail guide. However, he continued to emphasize his dominance by firmly kicking aside Kathleen when she sat on the overturned beer trough that he wanted to occupy. I chose not to consider that gesture a personal affront, but it helped me decide that we would cut short our visit. We parted on friendly terms.

This episode gives a brief glimpse into the daily politics in an autonomous *domestic-scale culture* beyond the reach of government control. However, the apparent isolation was illusory, for Chonkiri and his band were part of the global market economy, even though its direct influence was slight. Several of Chonkiri's men were wearing factory-made pants under their *cushmas*. There were steel axes and metal pots lying about. Obenteni had been a Franciscan mission since the 1930s, and the entire region had been briefly missionized in the eighteenth century. Chonkiri's house was located near an abandoned cattle ranch that 3 years earlier had served as a temporary base for Marxist guerrillas. Nevertheless, we were inspired to witness the vitality and autonomy of Ashaninka culture after three centuries of European pressure.

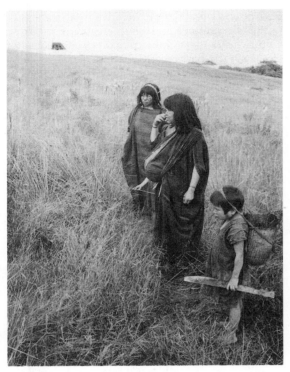

FIGURE 1.3   *Women and children in Chonkiri's group.*

FIGURE 1.4   *Chonkiri, the Ashaninka bigman, seated, investigating the contents of my backpack. The ears of corn in the left foreground are his reciprocal gift. The boy in shirt and pants is the son of one of my Ashaninka field assistants.*

Anthropological Research in Amazonia

What field research methods did the author use to answer his research problem? How did his findings lead him to challenge some conventional anthropological wisdom? What striking contrasts between Ashaninka culture and our own culture emerged?

During my first visit to the Peruvian Amazon in 1964, my experience with the Ashaninka led me to question many fundamental assumptions about the place of domestic-scale cultures in the contemporary world. I developed a profound respect for the Ashaninka and their ability to live so well and so self-sufficiently in their rain forest environment. I also recognized that even though the Ashaninka were one of the largest indigenous groups in the entire Amazon basin, outsiders seeking to exploit Ashaninka resources were threatening their independence and their culture. I learned that although some Ashaninka were avoiding all contacts with the colonists who were invading their territory, others were attempting to adjust to their changing circumstances by establishing economic relationships with the intruders.

According to conventional anthropological theory, the Ashaninka were undergoing rapid ***acculturation,*** and their culture would soon disappear

---

acculturation   Culture change brought about by contact between peoples with different cultures. Usually refers to the loss of traditional culture when the members of domestic-scale cultures adopt elements of commercial-scale cultures.

FIGURE 1.5 *Chonkiri's sons eagerly snatching up all of my trade goods.*

as Ashaninka society was absorbed into the dominant Peruvian national society. I was disturbed by the obvious negative aspects of this process and wanted to learn how their increasing involvement with the global system was affecting the Ashaninka and Ashaninka culture. My knowledge of the long history of Ashaninka resistance to foreign intrusion convinced me that, contrary to popular wisdom, there was nothing inevitable about acculturation. Furthermore, the neutral term *acculturation* seemed to disguise the harsh fact that the Ashaninka were being forcibly conquered and dispossessed. This did not seem to be a natural process and was perhaps neither fair nor beneficial. But no one had gone to the trouble of asking the questions that would illuminate the process. I hoped that my research findings would contribute to new government policies that would allow the Ashaninka and similar peoples to maintain their independent lifestyle.

Altogether I spent some 15 months working on this problem on three separate visits to Peru over a 5-year period. I wanted to understand how specific changes in Ashaninka economic adaptation were reflected in changes in their society. I collected most of my data by directly observing and participating in the daily life of Ashaninka settlements. This basic anthropological field method, called

participant observation, involves total immersion in the alien culture and a suspension of one's own cultural judgments about appropriate behavior. However, the participant observer never loses his or her own cultural identity, and can never become a full member of the other culture. I never pretended to be an Ashaninka, although I lived in their houses, studied their language, ate their food and drink, accompanied them to their gardens and on foraging expeditions, and listened to their nightly stories and songs. This allowed me to *see* Ashaninka economy and society in ways that would never have been possible if I had remained a complete outsider. Participant observation also generates empathy and respect for the other culture, especially when it is used as a method of learning, rather than as a means to induce others to change their way of life.

Effective participant observation is combined with the ***ethnographic method.*** That is, the anthropologist observes everyday activities and asks informal questions, often working closely with a few ***key informants,*** rather than relying entirely on formal interviews or impersonal survey questionnaires. The key informant may be one's host in the community or a hired guide, translator, or teacher. Because cultures are integrated in complex, often unexpected ways, at first I could not be sure what Ashaninka activities had economic or social implications. Thus, it was critical that I observe with an open mind and record as much as possible. I kept a daily journal in which I recorded all my observations and interviews with informants. Even the most obscure observations might have eventually proved useful. For example, it turned out that knowing the native names of the palm trees used for roof thatch became a clue to the intensity with which forest resources were being used in a given area.

Anthropologists often work intensively in a single village, with one or two key informants, but my research required a broader approach. Relying on photos taken from aircraft to locate isolated settlements, I worked in four different regions, collecting detailed census data on more than four hundred Ashaninka households living in some forty local groups and speaking four dialects. Altogether, six men, one 12-year-old boy, and one woman were my primary Ashaninka assistants.

The key to much of my work was the **genealogical method.** This involved sitting down with the senior man in a group or household and asking him to name his wife or wives and all his children by relative age. I would ask where everyone was born and determine where they were living or where and how they had died. If possible, I would compile similar information on more distant kin. Then I would draw a sketch map of the village, numbering each house and identifying the occupants by name (see Figure 1.6). I also worked intensively with many individuals to outline their life histories in greater detail. All this material allowed me to begin recognizing culturally meaningful social patterns. Without knowing who people were by name, where they lived, and who their relatives were, I would have remained an outsider. This information allowed me to analyze settlement and household structures, migration patterns, marriage and kinship terms, and fertility and mortality rates, and it proved indispensable for understanding the impact of changing economic patterns.

What emerged from these data was a shocking pattern of Ashaninka depopulation and exploitation. For example, I found that diseases spread by uncontrolled contact with colonists had dramatically elevated Ashaninka mortality. In some areas, the Ashaninka were indeed disappearing. Many had died violently or been taken captive to work for colonists. Local groups and families were fragmented and scattered, and subsistence activities suffered as people were drawn into virtual debt slavery. Opportunities for individual Ashaninka to participate successfully in the market economy were extremely limited. Many joined mission communities in hopes of escaping exploitation, but living conditions at the missions often were poor because the concentrated population quickly depleted local resources. Furthermore, the missionaries disapproved of many Ashaninka cultural practices. It was a discouraging picture; however, Ashaninka culture was extremely resilient, and vast areas of their traditional lands remained undisturbed. I was certain that both people and culture could survive if given the chance.

Eventually, I presented my findings in a doctoral dissertation (Bodley 1970) and in a series of published papers (Bodley 1972a, 1972b, 1973, 1981a).

Some of my Ashaninka ethnographic material illustrates important aspects of independent, domestic-scale cultures as they existed in the **ethnographic present** before they were seriously disrupted by intruders from commercial-scale, market-based, politically organized cultures (see Chapters 3 and 5). Of course, anthropology involves much more than ethnographic description. It can also provide insights on critical issues of national and international policy. For example, my research led me to recommend that the Peruvian government legally recognize and respect the political and economic autonomy of the Ashaninka on the lands that they traditionally occupied (see Chapter 14).

My research on the Ashaninka also forced me to ask questions about my own culture. I was impressed by the contrast between the precariousness and inequality of our market-based, industrial way of life and the ability of the Ashaninka to provide for all of their material needs—food, clothing, and shelter—while maintaining a high-quality environment and high levels of social equality. In this respect, their culture seems to be more effective than our own, and its integrity deserves to be safeguarded from uninvited intrusion. This realization launched me into a much larger research project to systematically compare domestic-scale tribal cultures, like the Ashaninka, with larger-scale cultures in politically organized states and modern, industrial cultures whose influences span the globe. Understanding how tribes, states, and global systems work and how they differ might help policymakers design a more secure and equitable world. This book is a product of this ongoing investigation.

---

participant observation   Field method in which the observer shares in community activities.

ethnographic method   Reliance on direct participant observation, key informants, and informal interviews as a data-collecting technique.

key informant   A member of the host culture who helps the anthropologist learn about the culture.

genealogical method   Tracing the marriage and family relationships among people as a basis for identifying cultural patterns in a community.

ethnographic present   An arbitrary time period when the process of culture change is ignored in order to describe a given culture as if it were a stable system.

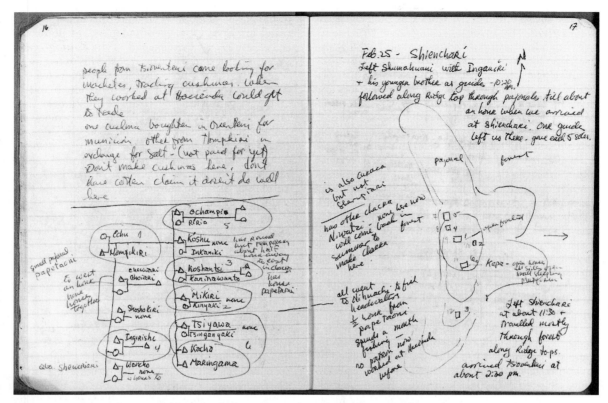

FIGURE 1.6   *A page from my field notebook showing an Ashaninka local group and genealogical relationships.*

Before further exploring the global implications of cultural understanding, let us examine several basic anthropological concepts.

CULTURE AND ETHNOCENTRISM: THE KEY ANTHROPOLOGICAL CONCEPTS

Culture: The Human Way of Life

What is culture? How do anthropologists define it? What is the most productive way to think about culture in order to solve human problems?

Culture is the most basic concept in anthropology, yet there is remarkable variation in how anthro-

pologists define culture and what aspects of culture they think are important. The modern technical definition of culture, as socially patterned human thought and behavior, was originally proposed by pioneering British anthropologist Edward Tylor:

Culture . . . is that complex whole which includes knowledge, belief, art, law, morals, custom, and any other capabilities and habits acquired by man as a member of society. (Tylor 1871)

Virtually all anthropologists take Tylor's definition as a starting point. Tylor assumed that culture was a uniquely human trait, but he distinguished between biologically inherited and socially transmitted human traits. It is useful to consider humans as the product of this dual inheritance (biological and cultural) because, as a learned inheritance, culture can be unlearned and modified to help solve human problems. If all aspects of culture were biologically inherited, we would need to resort to genetic engineering to solve certain human problems.

Although early anthropologists acknowledged the close biological kinship between humans and the great apes—especially gorillas and chimpanzees—they maintained that it was *culture* that produced a uniquely human way of life. They also assumed that culture requires superior, biologically based mental abilities, which for Tylor were best demonstrated by the powerful symbolism of human speech:

To use words in themselves unmeaning, as symbols by which to conduct and convey the complex intellectual processes in which mental conceptions are suggested, compared, combined, and even analyzed, and new ones created—this is a faculty which is scarcely to be traced in any lower animal. (Tylor 1875)

This emphasis on words and symbols certainly identifies one of the most important features of culture, but Tylor left unanswered many questions concerning how to make sense of the rest of culture. Anthropologists since Tylor have debated the most useful attributes that a technical conception of culture should stress. How particular anthropologists define culture is important because the definition influences their choice of research problems, their methods and interpretations, and their positions on public policy issues. At one extreme, culture may be considered a thing in itself that simply evolves as an abstract system. This view may be helpful for understanding the impact of cultures on the physical environment, but it fails to consider the decision making of individual human actors. Some contemporary anthropologists (the postmodernists) emphasize that culture itself, as well as every ethnographic description of culture, is constructed and interpreted by individuals. In this sense, there is no absolute cultural reality. Rather, culture consists of the narratives and symbolic dialogues that individuals construct—a view that emphasizes the fluidity and dynamism of culture. The postmodern view is a humbling reminder of the difficulties involved in sorting out cultural meanings. It is also a valuable anthropological tool for learning how people construct and manipulate culture to gain power over others.

As used in this text, there are three *aspects* of culture: (1) *mental*, or what people think, (2) *behavioral*, or what people do, and (3) *material*, or what people produce (see Table 1.1) Thus, just as Tylor originally proposed, mental processes, beliefs, knowledge, and values all can be considered part of culture, but human actors and actions also are important. In this respect, culture is the socially transmitted information that shapes human action. Some anthropologists would define culture entirely as mental rules guiding behavior, although they would recognize as well the often wide gap between the acknowledged rules for correct behavior and people's actual conduct. Consequently, some researchers focus on human behavior and its material products, rather than on the underlying mental information producing them.

In addition to these aspects, culture has several important *features*. As already noted, culture is socially transmitted and shared, symbolic and patterned. Culture is conservative, yet it changes, it has a history, and it tells people what is best and proper. The shared aspect of culture means that it is a social phenomenon; idiosyncratic behavior is not cultural. Culture is learned, not biologically inherited, and as Tylor noted, it involves arbitrarily assigned, symbolic meanings. For example, Americans are not born knowing that the color white means purity, and indeed this is not a universal **symbol** for purity. (In East Asia, white often symbolizes death.) The human ability to assign arbitrary meaning to any object, behavior, or condition makes culture enormously creative and helps distinguish culture from animal behavior. This also means that people can change cultures in positive ways.

Culture also has primary *functions*. Culture exists to guarantee human survival and reproduction. Culture is the unique means by which people in a given **society** satisfy their human needs, regulate the size of their society and the distribution of

culture Socially transmitted, often symbolic, information that shapes human behavior and that regulates human society so that people can successfully maintain themselves and reproduce. Culture has mental, behavioral, and material aspects; it is patterned and provides a model for proper behavior.
symbol Anything with a culturally defined meaning.
society An interacting, intermarrying human population sharing a common culture.

TABLE 1.1   *Key Aspects, Features, and Functions of Culture*

Aspects	Features	Functions
Mental	Patterned	Regulation
Behavioral	Symbolic	Maintenance
Material	Shared	Survival and reproduction
	Socially transmitted	Fitness-enhancement
	Ethnocentric	
	Conservative	
	Normative	
	Dynamic	
	Historical	

social power, and manage natural resources. Culture gives people power to produce and distribute resources in ways that can make entire groups prosper or decline. How culture is used as a means of power over the natural environment is clearly one of the keys to human survival and well-being. Effective adaptation to the natural environment means more than mere survival; it involves establishing a sustainable balance between resources and consumption while maintaining a satisfying and secure society. Because environments change constantly, adaptation is an ongoing process.

Tylor's basic definition of culture has served anthropology well, but in his day, little was known about the behavior of chimpanzees, our closest nonhuman relatives. Recent research with chimpanzees suggests that many aspects of culture may not be unique to humans.

Chimpanzee Culture?

How is human culture distinctive? Do chimpanzees that speak in sign language and make tools have humanlike culture? Are there both qualitative and quantitative differences between chimpanzee culture and human culture?

Twentieth-century American anthropologist Leslie White (1949) echoed Tylor's views on the uniqueness of human culture in a widely reprinted article attributing the origin of culture to the human ability "to symbol." Unquestionably, speech is the key human feature that greatly facilitates the production and transmission of culture. However, more recent research with "cross-fostered" chimpanzees—raised by humans and enculturated like children—demonstrates that chimpanzees can learn to communicate symbolically. Although their vocal anatomy prevents chimpanzees from speaking effectively, they can be taught to use ASL (American Sign Language), a gesture language created for those with hearing impairments. The most famous experimental work with cross-fostered chimpanzees was begun in 1966 by R. Allen Gardner and Beatrix Gardner (Gardner and Gardner 1994a, 1994b) and continued by Roger Fouts (1994). This research began as Project Washoe, named for Washoe, a 10-month-old wild chimpanzee who was cross-fostered and intensively taught ASL over a 4-year period. Washoe and the other chimpanzees in these experiments proved able to learn up to 150 ASL signs over 5 years of training. They signed to themselves, to one another, and to humans, producing novel phrases such as "ICECREAM HURRY GIMME." They also taught signs to one another, thereby reproducing symbolic, shared, learned behavior (which certainly could be called culture), but they did not construct new signs. Although the limits of chimpanzee language ability under human fosterage have not been established, such symbolic constructions clearly are not prominent in free-ranging chimpanzees.

During the first half of the twentieth century, conventional anthropological views of human evolution identified toolmaking as the earliest evidence for human culture. Anthropologists argued that toolmaking is a uniquely human trait, functionally connected to increased brain size and upright posture, or **bipedalism,** which freed the hands. Field research with free-ranging chimpanzees—especially primatologist Jane Goodall's work in Tanzania—demonstrated that chimpanzees make and use simple tools fairly extensively, which suggests the presence of shared, learned cultural behavior. As many as nineteen different tool uses have been identified for wild chimpanzees, including stones used as hammers and missiles, and sticks and branches used as clubs, flails, probes, extractors, and carrying devices. Chimpanzees also use leaves for sponges, napkins, grooming implements, and even medicine (McGrew 1992).

Many anthropologists and primatologists do not hesitate to speak of chimpanzee "culture," "cultural traditions," and "chimpanzee politics" (Goodall 1986, McGrew 1992, de Wall 1982). Humans and chimpanzees appear to differ only in the quantity of culture that they produce. Humans do make many more types of tools. In addition, human speech permits vast increases in the scale of human culture and in the ways that it can be produced, reproduced, and accumulated. Human culture is more complex, with more parts and subparts, and with many culturally defined roles that support much larger societies. Indeed, humans have elaborated culture to such a degree that they are unique in the animal world in their total dependence on culture (Slurink 1994).

Given that most human behavior is socially, rather than biologically, motivated, we still cannot neatly separate human behavior from animal behavior. Learned and shared "cultural traditions" have even been attributed to mountain sheep, as when all the animals in particular herds shared distinctive behaviors (Geist 1994). However, important distinctions between human and animal culture can be made. Michael Tomasello (1994) observes that human cultural behavior is highly uniform, whereas chimp learned behavior often is idiosyncratic and individually produced. A particular chimp may learn a very efficient way to crack open a nut, but it might never be copied by any other chimp. Human culture always involves numerous behaviors that are uniform and universally shared by all members of a given cultural tradition. For example, all adult Ashaninka share the learned behaviors of wearing the *cushma*, applying red face paint, and believing that the forest is populated by dangerous spirit demons. In contrast, only a few of the thirty-six known groups of African chimpanzees display any specific, universally shared, learned behaviors such as using sticks to dig for termites.

Tomasello suggests that chimpanzees may be limited in their ability to produce and transmit culture because they tend to *emulate* rather than *imitate* the behavior of their fellows. That is, they may be inspired to achieve the results that others produce, but they do not precisely copy their behavior. Learning by imitation requires the ability to understand the intentions of others and to make careful observations. Both observation and imitation are greatly enhanced by the rich conceptualization and symbolism encouraged by human speech.

Universal People and Original Culture

What social and sexual relationships do humans and chimpanzees have in common? Is there a biologically inherited male supremacy complex in humans? What do we mean by Universal People?

Humans display both uniquely human social patterns and universal features that link them to chimpanzee societies and to even more distant primate relatives. Both chimpanzees and humans, and presumably their common ancestor, are distinct from other primates in their tendency for male kin to remain in local groups (*patrilocality*) while females disperse, or marry out (*exogamy*). Related males may cooperate in hunting and scavenging and jointly defend their common territory. As discussed in later chapters, some anthropologists consider such "male supremacy" to be a human universal and argue that it has a genetic basis. For example, male sexual jealousy might confer a selective advantage because it helps men ensure that their genes are passed on. However, these issues are controversial, and we will see that different cultures handle gender relations in very different ways.

Lars Rodseth and his colleagues (1991) observe that the human pattern of maintaining lifelong (often polygynous) pair bonds, such as between married couples, is unusual among primates. When

---

bipedalism   Walking upright on two legs.
patrilocality   A cultural preference for a newly married couple to live near the husband's parents or patrilineal relatives.
exogamy   Marriage outside a culturally defined group.

resources are scarce, this strategy might be favored by a **hominid** species with prolonged infant dependency that was preadapted for cooperative male hunting. It would be advantageous for females to rely on supplemental food provided by their consorts (Slurink 1994). Archaeological evidence suggests that as early as a million years ago, human ancestors were establishing home bases and distinctively human patterns that would favor the development of speech.

Donald Brown points out in his book *Human Universals* (1991) that all humans share many cultural traits that must date back to the earliest people. However, learned behavior is not always easily separated from biologically determined behavior. Some human behavior, such as the facial expressions that universally signify basic emotions, may be genetically, not culturally, inherited. Brown creates a "Universal People" (UP) category and draws up a lengthy list of the biological and cultural traits that all people share. Most UP traits are not surprising because they are universal, but it is important to acknowledge how much all people have in common. For example, UP make elaborate use of highly symbolic speech that allows them to communicate about things that are remote in time and space. UP language is rich in metaphor, poetics, and deception. It includes a basic vocabulary for colors, emotions, body parts, gender, flora, fauna, and weather, and it invariably includes words for *mother* and *father*. All peoples distinguish the self from others and recognize normal and abnormal mental conditions.

Contemporary peoples have fully developed languages. Modern human languages have probably existed for at least 30,000 years. At that time, near the end of the last ice age, art, clothing, ornamentation, rituals, and complex tools suddenly appeared worldwide. This explosion of cultural activity suggests that all the elements of human culture were finally in place.

Viewing Other Cultures: The Problem of Observer Bias

Why is it so difficult to understand another culture? How can anthropologists suspend their own cultural biases to gain cultural under-standing yet still make value judgments about other cultures? What are the limitations of a functionalist approach?

It is impossible to really know any culture except from the inside, as a native member. Even the most skilled anthropologist will always be an outsider when viewing a different culture. The problem for anthropologists is how to overcome, or at least become aware of, their own cultural biases, while attempting to understand other cultures from the inside. Translation of symbols from a given culture into categories that will be meaningful to outsiders will always be imprecise. The problem is compounded by the fact that cultural insiders may be quite unconscious of the underlying meanings of their own cultural categories.

One of anthropology's most important contributions toward the understanding of other cultures is its recognition of the problem of **ethnocentrism**— the tendency to evaluate other cultures in reference to one's own presumably superior culture (see the box entitled "An Ethnocentric Look at Australian Aborigines"). Ethnocentrism contributes to internal social solidarity, but it can seriously distort one's perception of others and hinders cross-cultural understanding. For example, some Christian missionaries disapproved of Ashaninka shamans, disregarding their valuable skills as curers and herbalists. In addition, outsider developers mistakenly regarded indigenous shifting cultivation in the tropical rain forest as backward and wasteful "slash and burn." But when anthropologists actually examined the internal logic of these practices, they found that Amazonian cultivation patterns, like the Ashaninka's, were sustainable, productive, and energy efficient.

Anthropologists must constantly strive to recognize their own ethnocentrism and consciously suspend it when attempting to understand other cultures. As an alternative to ethnocentrism, anthropologists often advocate **cultural relativism**— the position that other cultures have intrinsic worth and can only be usefully evaluated or understood in their own terms. The ideal of cultural relativism can be applied to anthropological research using functionalist methods. **Functionalism** is the belief that particular cultural traits may play a role in maintaining the culture. It is a powerful analytic tool to help anthropologists view each culture as an interconnected system of parts and subparts, and look for the function of each part. Even loathsome practices such as infanticide may in some way contribute to the survival of the total culture. However, identifying the *functions* of particular customs does not explain why they exist or whether they should exist. Anthropologists are interested in evaluating the impact of specific cultural practices on individuals, households, communities, nations, and ecosystems. Making such evaluations in a systematic and unbiased way is one of anthropology's great strengths.

Acknowledging one's own ethnocentrism and applying cultural relativism does not mean abandoning judgments and values. For example, when I compiled my first life history of an Ashaninka man, I learned that when he was orphaned as a child, a shaman had called him a witch. He would have been burned to death if he had not escaped to a mission. Many Ashaninka themselves condemn witch burning, but killing witches was understandable within the Ashaninka belief system, just as it was in Salem, Massachusetts, in 1692. I, however, consider killing witches, children or not, to be repulsive. Such practices are also a gross violation of internationally recognized human rights standards. Ashaninka bigmen organized intergroup raids—killing men and kidnapping women and children. I found abundant evidence of these practices in my genealogies and life histories, and I understood them to be part of a complex of cultural practices centered on the bigman in the absence of centralized political authority. Both witchcraft and raiding no doubt were intensified by the intrusion of outsiders.

From a functionalist, nonethnocentric perspective, cultures can be seen to form logical wholes, but they need not be viewed as discrete, static, perfectly balanced systems. Cultures are open-ended networks of ideas, objects, and people that constantly change as their circumstances change. A major part of understanding culture is evaluating how successfully different cultures meet basic human needs.

Ethnocentrism can influence both what an observer sees and how observations are interpreted. Ethnocentrism also can influence a researcher's choice of research problem and the mode of expla-

nation adopted. The problem of ethnocentrism is now a standard part of modern anthropological training, but at the height of colonial expansion in the nineteenth century, European anthropologists were convinced of their own cultural superiority and were blissfully unaware of the concept of ethnocentrism.

Beyond Ethnocentrism: Emic and Etic Views

What are the obstacles to gaining a native understanding of another culture?

One way to move beyond ethnocentric bias is to self-consciously try to view another culture through the eyes of a cultural insider. This requires the use of insider cultural categories. Anthropologists use the terms **emic/etic** to refer to the inside/outside perspective on a culture (Headland, Pike, and Harris 1990). For example, an insider emic understanding of Ashaninka leadership would start with the Ashaninka term *pinkatsari,* literally, "big man." I learned that a *pinkatsari* was a prominent person with a forceful personality. If I had applied the outsider etic category "chief" to Chonkiri, I would have completely misunderstood his cultural role. As a *pinkatsari,* Chonkiri could harangue and persuade, but he held no coercive authority over his followers. He did not inherit his position and could not automatically pass it on to his sons. In fact, the Ashaninka reject the kind of central political authority implied by the outsider word *chief.*

This distinction between *emic* and *etic* is based on the use of these terms in linguistics to refer to phon*emic* and phon*etic* transcription, following

---

hominid A member of the human family, distinct from the great apes.

ethnocentrism Evaluating other cultures from the perspective of one's own presumably superior culture.

cultural relativism Understanding other cultures by their own categories, which are assumed to be valid and worthy of respect.

functionalism The assumption that particular cultural traits may have a role in maintaining the culture.

emic Cultural meanings derived from inside a given culture and presumed to be unique to that culture.

etic Cultural meanings as translated for cross-cultural comparison.

An Ethnocentric Look at Australian Aborigines

Ethnocentric distortion is well illustrated by an outrageous paper on Australian aborigines read before the Anthropological Institute in London in 1871 by the institute's director, Charles Staniland Wake (1872). (Chapter 2, which is entirely devoted to Australian aboriginal culture, will demonstrate how misleading Wake's views were.) The language of Wake's paper is so offensive that it is difficult to imagine that it was presented as objective science. Wake's ethnocentrism is readily betrayed by his derogatory references to "moral defects" and the "barbarity" and "absurdity" of aboriginal customs, which he claimed were founded on "unmitigated selfishness." Such ethnocentrism had its origins in the assumptions of racial and cultural superiority that supported European colonialism.

In Wake's view, aborigines, with their simple material culture, were living examples of the earliest stage of human evolution. He sought to describe their mental characteristics but felt that it was inaccurate to speak of their "intellectual" abilities, because aborigines operated almost by instinct, barely above the animal level. They had "no aim in life but the continuance of their existence and the gratifications of their passions, with the least possible trouble to themselves."

Their technological achievements, such as the boomerang, were derided as accidental discoveries, while their art was likened to "the productions of children." Even aboriginal languages and complex marriage systems were treated as mere unconscious developments, reflecting no particular intellectual ability.

Morally, aborigines were described as children, who enjoyed song and dance and became "extremely indolent" when food was abundant. The aboriginal mind was "saturated with superstition," but the aborigines had no religion. In Wake's view, they also had no abstract concept of morality, could not form any idea of death, and routinely mistreated women, the young, and the weak. They cannibalized their children and beat, speared, and enslaved their wives. Wake even had doubts about whether aboriginal mothers had "natural affection" for their children, although he also accused them of being overindulgent parents.

In regard to their relations with Europeans, Wake found the aborigines to be haughty, insolent, cunning, and treacherous—thieves and liars who unpredictably

Kenneth Pike (1954). **Phonemes** are the unique sounds recognized as significant by speakers of a given language. For example, the words *pray* and *play* are distinguished by speakers of English because *r* and *l* are different phonemes and are thus heard as different sounds. Speakers of another language might not hear any difference between *pray* and *play*. A phonetic transcription records the sounds as heard by a nonspeaker of the language who does not know which sound distinctions are meaningful. Phonetic transcriptions may be clumsy approximations of the "real" sounds of a language.

killed strangers. He made no connection between these negative personality traits and the obvious facts of colonial invasion, yet he did attribute their treachery to suspicion. Wake's interpretation of aboriginal culture did not go beyond his original assumption that aborigines represented the very "childhood of humanity." They were moral and intellectual children, not degenerates from a higher state. Given Wake's assumptions that European culture was the most highly evolved and that Europeans would inevitably dominate the world, his ethnocentrism is hardly surprising. Wake never actually saw an aborigine, and his knowledge of the culture apparently did not go beyond the superficial stereotypes of unsympathetic European explorers and settlers.

Not even modern anthropologists have been immune from this kind of ethnocentrism. In 1978, American anthropologist Arthur Hippler published a remarkably similar characterization of Australian aboriginal personality. Hippler deprecated the aboriginal personality and worldview as "infantile." Aborigines were "superstitious" and had difficulty separating reality from fantasy. They routinely mistreated women. Aboriginal parents were thoughtless, selfish, inconsistent, harsh, and lacking in empathy toward their children.

Hippler's work is not typical of contemporary anthropology and was promptly condemned by outraged aboriginal specialists. Nevertheless, it illustrates how easily the ethnocentrism of an earlier century can be repeated. Hippler only briefly visited the aboriginal community he described and relied heavily on other sources. His research was based on his prior theory that the child-rearing practices of tribal cultures are inferior and thus produce inferior adults. Hippler deliberately rejected the anthropological standard of cultural relativism—that one at least attempt to view other cultures in their own terms. Furthermore, he began with the openly ethnocentric assumption that "there is no question that Euro-American culture is vastly superior in its flexibility, tolerance for variety, scientific thought, and interest in emergent possibilities to any primitive society extant" (Hippler 1981:395).

Similarly, the meanings of unique words, symbols, rituals, and institutions may be difficult to translate cross-culturally. Even a trained observer can only watch what people do and record native explanations. Observations must be selectively screened through the observer's own cultural categories; then, in effect, an interpretation of the culture must be created.

---

phoneme   The minimal unit of sound that carries meaning and is recognized as distinctive by the speakers of a given language.

CULTURE SCALE, GROWTH, AND PROCESS

The past century of astounding material and technological progress has produced a global middle class of some 1.4 billion well-off people—one-fourth of humanity whose private cars, comfortable homes, and abundant consumer goods reflect a standard of prosperity absolutely unprecedented in human experience. Paradoxically, the bottom 70 percent of the global population, more than 4 billion people, are now poor, if not totally destitute. When uneven development leaves this many people disempowered, the potential for social upheaval is large. Furthermore, human activities are disturbing natural processes on a scale that may threaten everyone's future well-being through undesirable ecosystem modification, species extinctions, and global climate change. How could cultural development have become such a mixed blessing? Does gross inequity and massive social and environmental stress inevitably flow from human nature? Is growth in human population and cultural complexity a natural process, or can individuals and societies shape culture for their own benefit? A knowledge of cultural anthropology can help today's global citizens understand the cultural processes that produce growth and distribute social power.

This book explores what is "natural" and what is "cultural" about human behavior by using the basic concepts of cultural anthropology to examine the full range of cultural diversity, worldwide and throughout history and prehistory. The nature–culture question is crucial because if extreme poverty and environmental degradation are indeed natural, we can only seek to mitigate their most severe consequences. But if poverty and environmental deterioration are under cultural control, they could be significantly reduced, or even eliminated, by cultural design and change. Culture growth and the distribution of social power in different cultural settings are important variables, because growth in the scale of human activities has the potential to produce both wealth and poverty. If growth is a purely natural process, we remain spectators; but if growth is a human-directed process, then as empowered global citizens, we can consciously shape growth to meet our human needs.

The Sapienization Process: Reproducing and Maintaining People

What is the most important function of culture? Why is the household the most crucial social unit?

Culture, conceived of as the socially transmitted information that shapes human behavior, is part of a biocultural evolutionary process that produced and sustains *Homo sapiens*, the human species. Biocultural theorists Robert Boyd and Peter Richerson (1985) and William Durham (1991) point out that our genes and our culture are interdependent, and have coevolved as a dual inheritance. Genes and culture must be reproduced and transmitted to the next generation. However, there is a crucial difference between natural selection operating on genes and cultural selection operating on culture: People often quite deliberately guide cultural selection. Genes and culture are connected because people are likely to adopt and transmit cultural patterns that they think will improve their *genetic fitness*, or the degree to which their genes are reproduced.

Cultural ideas constitute the templates for a series of human actions that produce outcomes chosen by individual human actors. These actions can be called *cultural processes*. The most important cultural process is **sapienization**—the production and maintenance of people, societies, and cultures. Sapienization involves a tightly integrated series of subprocesses that collectively define a uniquely human way of life centered on marriage, the family, and the household (see Table 1.2). The most crucial sapienization subprocess is the human ability to conceptualize and thereby produce the abstract concepts and symbols, such as father, mother, son, and daughter, that define the family as a social unit and the foundation of human society. Speech, or the ability to verbalize concepts, makes it possible for people to store and efficiently transmit vast quantities of cultural information. Cultural concepts also are frequently given physical form, or materialized, when people build shelters and make tools and ornaments or art objects, or when they act out their beliefs in rituals or stories. For culture to exist, it must be stored and transmitted, or reproduced in the next generation. Cultural transmission

TABLE 1.2   *Domestically Directed Sapienization Subprocesses*

Conceptualization	Producing abstract concepts and symbols that shape behavior
Materialization	Giving physical form to concepts
Verbalization	Producing human speech
Socialization	Producing permanent human societies
Cultural transmission	Reproducing culture
Subsistence intensification	Producing more food
Sedentization	Maintaining village life

can occur in many ways, including by observation and borrowing, but transmission from parents to children within the household is the most basic transmission process.

The Cultural Regulation of Social Power

What is social power? What are the different types of social power? How does the way social power is organized relate to the scale of society and culture?

This book emphasizes one of the most important and interesting functions of culture: *the way people use culture to produce **social power** to achieve their goals in relation to other people and the natural environment.* Social power is not easily defined or measured, but it is a familiar feature of daily life. Broadly, it is a measure of a person's ability to get what he or she wants, even when others might object. From a biocultural perspective, individuals are naturally predisposed to seek social power in order to improve their genetic fitness. However, individuals need social support. Therefore, social power must be culturally regulated, because if individuals gain too much power or misuse their power, they can weaken the social cohesion necessary for successful biological and cultural reproduction. Social power also must be regulated when it is applied to other societies and to the natural environment, because all societies depend to some degree on neighboring societies and on nature. Social power also must be regulated when it is applied to other societies and nature, because cultural and biological interchange between societies is too important to be permanently disrupted by all-out conflict, and natural resources are too vulnerable to overexploitation.

Following the lead of historical sociologist Michael Mann (1986), in this book we will distinguish among four types of social power: ideological, economic, military, and political (see Table 1.3). *Ideological power* refers to people's cultural beliefs about supernatural forces. Such beliefs may be materialized, or physically represented in rituals, in artwork like statues and sculptures, and in monumental architectural constructions like temples and cathedrals. Power seekers can use religious beliefs to generate strong emotional support among their followers for their personal projects. *Economic power* involves the ability to direct the labor of other people to one's own advantage and to gain control over material resources. The members of every household must have sufficient economic power to maintain themselves and to reproduce a viable household in the succeeding generation. *Military power* refers to the ability to employ organized violence against other groups. *Political power* is the ability to direct people beyond one's own household.

The diverse ways that people in a given society organize social power are perhaps the most important cultural variables for anthropological analysis, because the organization of power limits the scale of society and shapes all aspects of culture. Every successful society is a system of social power based on shared cultural understandings. People must agree to organize and distribute power in

---

sapienization   The production and maintenance of human beings, human societies, and human cultures, based on social power organized at the household, or domestic, level.

social power   An individual's ability to get what he or she wants, even when others might object.

TABLE 1.3 *Social Power: How People Achieve Their Goals in Relation to Others*

Types of Social Power
Ideological   Military
Economic   Political

Cultural Organization of Social Power
By kin in domestic-scale cultures
By rulers in political-scale cultures
By entrepreneurs and financiers in commercial-scale cultures

particular ways. They must believe that the power structure will work to their advantage or that they are making the best available choices. The tremendous diversity of world cultures is a result of creative people designing and transmitting cultural understandings acceptable to others. Cultures change when people are persuaded to accept new ideas about power or when they withdraw their consent from existing power systems.

The societies discussed in this book are grouped into at least one of three power systems: domestic, political, or commercial. Each system involves distinctive social structures, ideological foundations, types of cultural transmission, and production and distribution systems. And corresponding cultures reflect differences in population, intensity of technology, and form of economy, society, polity, and ideology related to different modes of organizing social power (see Table 1.4). At the most basic level, these differences can be illustrated by the different ways food is treated under each system of social power and **culture scale,** producing different costs and benefits for society (see Table 1.5).

Domestically organized societies disperse social power at the household level in order to optimize household well-being and to enable individuals to focus on the sapienization process. Each household enjoys access to the material resources it requires and has approximately equal social power, depending on the size and shape of individual families and their kinship support networks. When social power is domestically organized, individuals have neither the cultural incentive nor the cultural ability to gain permanent power beyond their own local kinship group or village. Virtually every adult is in charge of daily decision making.

Politically organized societies are directed by rulers rather than by household heads. Thus, in the cultural process of **politicization,** social power is concentrated in a relatively few hands, and the needs of individual households are subordinated to the needs of the rulers. At least four cultural subprocesses typically accompany politicization: taxation, specialization, militarization, and urbanization. Individual households must provide taxes or tribute in the form of labor or goods so that the ruler can support an expanded elite household with specialist servants, priests, artisans, and bodyguards concentrated in an urban center; they also must provide military service in confrontations with neighboring rulers. The power inequity inherent in the politicization process means that rulers must devise and transmit new cultural beliefs and behaviors that will coerce or persuade people to accept their authority. This is not an easy task because politicization competes directly with the sapienization process and the interests of individual households. Domestically organized power systems still operate in politically organized societies, but households must be subservient to the interests of political rulers.

Commercially organized societies feature a new set of power elites who control the production and distribution of goods and services by means of the business enterprises they own and the financial capital they direct. Commercial power depends on the cultural institutions of private property, contractual agreements, and monetary systems, which are legitimized and protected by centralized political power. Commercial power expands as food, land, labor, and an increasing range of goods and services that were previously managed by households for domestic use are converted into commercial products. As commercial elites gain greater power, they may become the dominant power holders in a society, and they may promote technological changes that will speed the rate and volume of production and exchange to further increase their economic power. The contemporary world is shaped by commercial power under the capitalist system. Capitalism has produced truly amazing levels of material progress for millions of people, but these benefits have not been evenly distributed, and capitalism also has generated many seemingly intractable human problems.

TABLE 1.4   *The Scale of World Cultures*

	Domestic Scale	Political Scale	Commercial Scale
Examples	Australian aborigines Amazon villagers Ashaninka Mundurucú Yanomami East African pastoralists Nuer Maasai	Pacific Islanders Micronesia Ulithi Polynesia Tikopia Hawaii Mesopotamia Andeans: Inca China Shang Ch'ing South Asia Hindu Islam	Medieval England Early industrial England British Empire America (U.S.A.) Brazil Bangladesh Peru
Characteristics			
Population	500–1000 Low-density	10,000 or more High-density	1 million or more Urban
Technology	Foraging Gardening Herding	Intensive Agricultural	Industrial Fossil fuel Monocrop
Economy	Subsistence Display Recriprocal exchange	Tribute tax Wealth Specialists	Markets Corporations Capitalism Consumerism
Society	Egalitarian Kin-based Age-graded	Ranked Class-based Caste	Class-based Literate
Polity	Acephalus Bigman *headman* Descent groups	Chiefdoms Kingdoms Empires	Nation-states Supranationalism
Ideology	Animism Shamanism Ancestor cults	High gods Divine kings	Patriotism Monotheism Progress

Sociocultural Growth and the Scale of Culture

What is the relationship between the organization of social power and the growth trajectories of particular societies and cultural systems? How does this growth increase the power of elites?

Each cultural system of social power produces a different growth trajectory and scale of culture, and a distinctive distribution of social power

and household living standards. When any sociocultural system grows larger, it can be expected to undergo organizational and technological changes simply because it is larger. The quality of everyday

---

culture scale   Order-of-magnitude differences among cultures on various socioeconomic dimensions, based on different modes of organizing social power.
politicization   The production and maintenance of political power.

TABLE 1.5   *Social Power, Culture Scale, and Food Objectives*

Culture Scale	Culture Process	Food Objective	Cost/ Benefit
Domestic	Sapienization	Nutrition	Stability Equality
Political	Politicization	Taxable surplus	Instability Inequality
Commercial	Commercialization	Profit-making commodity	Inequality Instability Poverty

life and human relationships will necessarily change. Most people will have less control over their daily affairs; new, more powerful leaders will emerge; and the familiarity characteristic of village life will disappear. Direct participatory democracy is impossible in a large nation. Likewise, when every household cannot be self-sufficient, production systems must become larger, more energy-intensive, and more centralized. When households lose control over production, they may have more difficulty meeting their basic material needs, and poverty may emerge.

Ethnographic analysis reveals that as societies adopt larger-scale power systems, order-of-magnitude differences appear in the quantity and concentration of social power as measured on various socioeconomic dimensions. As the case studies in the following chapters will demonstrate, when social power is organized exclusively at the domestic level, the largest politically autonomous social unit seldom exceeds five hundred people. But when power is centralized and politically organized power becomes dominant, millions of people can be politically integrated. Likewise, maximum household wealth, measured by the number of people the richest household could support in a year, can be millions of times greater in commercially organized societies than in domestically organized societies, where wealth is not accumulated. Differences of this magnitude, and the cultural changes that make them possible, are so striking that cultures that organize power differently have come to constitute distinctive scales of culture.

Domestic-scale cultures are small-scale societies with domestically managed production and distribution systems, and networks of kin that provide systems of social support for households. ***Political-scale cultures*** are relatively large-scale, autonomous societies with centrally managed, relatively energy-intensive production systems necessarily geared to the needs of the ruling elite. ***Commercial-scale cultures*** are integrated by impersonal market exchanges and transnational commercial enterprises. National societies throughout the world now are dependent on centrally managed, mass-industrialized production and distribution systems, and they participate in a global culture characterized by common cultural understandings. The differences for human social life between domestic-, political-, and commercial-scale cultures are a fertile ground for anthropolitical analysis, as we will see in the following chapters.

Sociocultural growth, and accompanying changes in the scale of culture, has been neither a steady nor a totally predictable process. The anthropological record shows a very long, relatively stable era, from approximately 50,000 to 8000 years ago, when all societies were organized as domestic-scale cultures. During this phase of cultural development, humanity spread in great migrations around the globe and diversified into thousands of ethnolinguistic groups adapted to innumerable local ecosystems. They lived exclusively in small-scale, self-sufficient local and regional societies based initially on mobile foraging and later on sedentary village life (see Figure 1.7). All the major domestic technologies, including ceramics, textiles, farming, and herding, were invented and disseminated during this time. These technologies uniformly improved the quality of daily life because they were equally available to every household. Regional pop-

FIGURE 1.7   *The world of tribal villagers (domestic-scale cultures), showing independent centers of plant and animal domestication and the areas where farming or pastoralism had spread by approximately 5000 BP.*

ulations remained small, and densities were low; the global population in 8000 BP (before the present) probably did not exceed 85 million people. Limits were established by the optimum size of households and kinship groups and by the population density that local ecosystems and domestic technologies could sustain, as will be discussed in the following chapters.

Under the influence of the politicization process, which began perhaps 8000 years ago, chiefdoms, small agrarian kingdoms, and then larger political empires emerged wherever more energy-intensive production systems could be developed and populations enlarged (see Figure 1.8). Global population peaked at some 200 million people by AD 200 and then receded as various empires proved unsustainable. After a series of sociocultural collapses, another cycle of cultural development peaked in the thirteenth century and global population reached

360 million, but political disorder and plagues again caused decline.

Cultural changes associated with the ***commercialization*** process, beginning about AD 1400, led to increased economic activity culminating in a new wave of technological development that per-

---

domestic-scale culture   A cultural system characterized by small, kinship-based societies, often with only 500 people, in which households organize production and distribution.

political-scale culture   A cultural system characterized by centrally organized societies with thousands or millions of members and energy-intensive production directed by political rulers.

commercial-scale culture   A cultural system organized by impersonal market exchanges, commercial enterprises, contracts, and money, and potentially encompassing the entire world.

commercialization   The production and maintenance of private profit-making business enterprises.

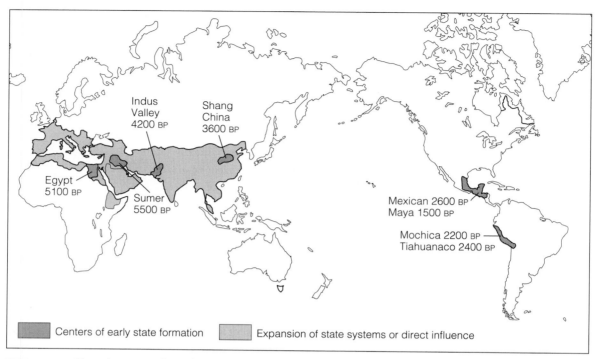

FIGURE 1.8   *Six early centers of state formation (commercial-scale cultures) from 1500 to
5500 BP and the regions that they influenced.*

mitted faster and larger-scale production and distribution systems. World population rapidly soared to 1 billion by 1825 and to 2 billion by 1925, but along with growth and change came enormous social upheaval and widespread impoverishment. Resource consumption rates grew rapidly, but dramatic improvements in living standards did not become widespread in the industrialized nations until the 1950s. Influenced by the bustling money economy and the use of cheap fossil fuels, growth accelerated exponentially, unfettered by cultural limits.

The emergence of commercial-scale cultures is a challenging anthropological problem. Socioeconomic growth is difficult to explain because it produces few immediate benefits for most people and creates obvious new burdens such as taxes, wars, insecurity, and dependency. Throughout this book, we will examine the possibility that cultural developments, as measured by population growth and increased economic indicators, are caused not by popular demand, but by individual power seekers striving to increase their immediate personal power. Elites can attain more power only by having more people to control and more economic resources to exploit, and this necessarily requires growth. Elites may gain the power to direct culture change in their own short-term interests. However, they cannot predict the long-term consequences of their actions, nor can they necessarily control the events that they set in motion, including the counterforces of popular social movements led by disaffected people.

The diverse selection of world cultures presented in the following chapters will allow us to test the hypothesis that socioeconomic growth is an elite-directed process that concentrates social power in direct proportion to increases in culture scale. This hypothesis runs counter to the conventional understanding of how economic growth works in the contemporary world: Everyone supposedly benefits from growth, and growth supposedly is natural and inevitable. If the power-elite hypothesis proves correct, then larger-scale cultural systems should have more concentrated social power, and people may be disproportionately impoverished and disempowered by certain growth processes. This analysis raises important questions about the relative benefits of different cultural systems, and it can provide an informed basis for the argument that growth itself may be the biggest human problem and that development without growth may be a solution.

Culture Scale and the Quality of Life: Evaluating Cultures

Recent technological innovations and economic growth undoubtedly have improved the lives of many people, especially since the 1870s. Electric power, antibiotics, water and sewage systems, telephones, personal computers, home appliances, mechanized transportation, printing—all certainly have enhanced our lives in many ways. These technologies were produced by commercial-scale cultures in which commercial elites also came to dominate the sources of social power, but they now are part of the cultural heritage of all of humanity. However, it is an open question what cultural arrangements can best produce, maintain, regulate, and distribute these technologies and their by-products to ensure that their benefits are most widely shared and that they remain available to future generations.

Many anthropologists theorize that technology determines social organization and that social organization determines ideology. According to this misleading simplification, technology is the supreme cultural determinant. But technologies are *human* creations. They are tools that are directed and controlled by human agents motivated by cultural information and by innate drives. Technology need not dictate the distribution of social power and thereby determine the form of our societies and the quality of our daily lives. Quite possibly, advanced technologies and their benefits can be best sustained by smaller-scale cultural systems based on an equitable balance between domestic, political, and commercial power structures. To discover the best balance, we must first understand how power, growth, and scale are culturally regulated in different societies, and then carefully evaluate the

human impact of these differences. Cultural evaluation of this sort is perhaps anthropology's most important function, but it must be done objectively to avoid the pitfalls of ethnocentrism.

Throughout this book, the effectiveness of different cultures will be evaluated according to five universal variables: (1) human health and well-being, (2) social cohesion, (3) population stability, (4) natural resources and ecosystems, and (5) cultural continuity. These variables are objectively measurable and directly related to the effectiveness of the sapienization process. There is cross-cultural consensus that health and social cohesion are universally desirable goals, because they directly support household well-being. However, population stability and sustained-yield resource management are not recognized as desirable by all members of all cultures, because they might limit the route to individual power.

Human societies can maintain themselves and successfully reproduce only when all of these variables remain within viable limits, but their acceptable ranges will vary widely because people can tolerate great adversity. The five variables listed here are interrelated in complex ways. Social cohesion is closely related to equitable distribution of social power: Societies that are more equitable are likely to be more cohesive, and they may generate fewer incentives for destabilizing growth. Conspicuous concentrations of wealth can create a maladaptive, runaway growth process when people support and emulate elite cultural patterns, because they believe that by copying the elite, they will improve their own life chances. Significantly, health and well-being in industrialized societies, as measured by life expectancy, have now been found to be improved more by social equality and social cohesion than by absolute increases in wealth. The distribution of wealth and power thus may be the most important cultural pattern determining the success of the sapienization process. The following chapters will explore these issues in depth.

SUMMARY

Culture, the most important concept of cultural anthropology, refers to the socially transmitted, often symbolic, information that shapes human behavior. Culture has mental, behavioral, and material aspects. It is patterned and provides a model for proper behavior, and it regulates human society so that people can successfully maintain themselves and reproduce. The goal of cultural anthropology is to increase cultural understanding. Cultural anthropology's most important research technique, the ethnographic method, relies on participant observation and key informants, and strives to achieve a sympathetic, nonethnocentric view of other cultures from an inside, or emic, perspective.

A major objective of cultural analysis is to sort out the different ways people use culture as a source of social power to achieve their goals in relation to other people and the natural environment. Although not all aspects of culture are unique to humans, humans are unique in their emphasis on linguistically patterned symbolic meanings. All people have the same potential to create culture, and all cultures share many universal features. The most important cultural differences concern the three distinctive ways that people can organize social power: (1) domestically by households, (2) politically by rulers, or (3) commercially by business enterprises. Each method of organization involves its own dominant culture process, whether sapienization, politicization, or commercialization, and each requires distinctive ideologies and progressively larger-scale societies, more complex polities, and more intensive technologies. Sapienization is the most crucial cultural process, because it is centered on the household and involves the maintenance and reproduction of individual humans, human society, and human culture. Cultures can be grouped according to their dominant mode of organizing social power: (1) domestic-scale cultures (tribes), (2) political-scale cultures (nation-states), and (3) commercial-scale cultures (the global system).

STUDY QUESTIONS

1. Discuss the great divides of cultural development in relation to culture scale. Refer to sapienization, politicization, commercialization, sedentization, domestication, state formation, and industrialization, and to domestic-, political-, and global-scale cultures.

2. What are the principal components and aspects of culture as traditionally viewed by anthropologists?

3. Use the encounter with Chonkiri to illustrate emic and etic interpretations, ethnocentrism, and cultural relativity.

4. In what nonethnocentric respect might it be argued that domestic-scale tribal cultures were more or less successful as cultural systems than political-scale chiefdoms and states?

5. What is social power and why is it important? What are the different ways it can be organized?

6. Why does culture scale matter? Discuss the human costs and benefits of socioeconomic growth.

SUGGESTED READING

DeVita, Philip R. 1990. *The Humbled Anthropologist: Tales from the Pacific*. Belmont, Calif.: Wadsworth. A collection of personal accounts of fieldwork experiences in the Pacific written by twenty anthropologists.

Fagan, Brian. 1992. *People of the Earth*. New York: Harper-Collins. An overview of world prehistory.

Gamst, Frederick C., and Edward Norbeck. 1976. *Ideas of Culture: Sources and Uses*. New York: Holt, Rinehart & Winston. An extensive examination of the culture concept.

2

Australian Aborigines: Mobile Foragers for 50,000 Years

The Australians have been the historical, evolutionary and sociological prototype for the study of hunter-gatherers and for the relations between man and nature. From the onset of modern anthropology they have inspired, challenged or provided the limiting case for nearly every view of man's behavior.... (Peterson 1986:v)

Australia, the only continent in the modern world to have been occupied exclusively by tribal foragers, has always been central to anthropological theories about domestic-scale cultures. The 40,000–50,000-year prehistory of aboriginal culture raises major questions about cultural stability and change, carrying capacity and population regulation, quality of life, and the inevitability of cultural evolution. Furthermore, Australian aborigines are justly famous for their elegant kinship systems and elaborate ritual life, supported by one of the world's simplest known material technologies. The Australian aboriginal culture also raises important questions about the function of initiation rituals and the meaning of equality in a tribal society in which, according to the standard view, the old men appear to control much of the ideological system. The extent to which such cultures can be considered affluent, egalitarian, and "in balance with nature" is also

an issue for debate. All of these issues are discussed in this chapter.

The discovery and successful colonization of the Australian continent by foraging peoples and its continuous occupation for 50,000 years is surely one of the most remarkable events in human history. It clearly demonstrates the tremendous potential of mobile foraging technology and egalitarian social systems, which adapted to diverse, and often unpredictable, environments and to long-term climatic change. The foraging way of life is certainly one of the most successful human adaptations ever developed and persists in scattered locations throughout the world.

It is estimated that at the time of European contact in 1788, Australia was occupied by at least 300,000 people and perhaps a million or more, representing some 600 culturally distinct groups and speaking some 200 languages (Tindale 1974). Throughout the millennia, the aborigines intensified their subsistence techniques and managed and shaped their natural resources, but they never resorted to farming or sedentary village life. Australia was, in fact, the largest world area to avoid domestication and social stratification and the associated burdens of agriculture. The pervasive and authoritarian religious system of the aborigines seems to be the central integrative key to the entire culture.

CONSTRUCTING A SUSTAINABLE DESERT CULTURE

Imagine yourself with 500 other people of all ages—men, women, and children—naked and empty-handed on the shore of an uninhabited desert continent. You are all participants in a great human experiment. Your collective challenge is more than mere survival. The experiment requires you to design a fully self-sufficient culture that will satisfy everyone's human needs while guaranteeing the same security for all future generations. Without machines, metal tools, or libraries, you need to find food and shelter in your strange surroundings. This task requires extensive, highly specialized knowledge and skills, which need to be acquired, stored, and reproduced. Perhaps even more difficult, you need to establish rules to regulate marriage, prevent conflict, and reproduce the culture. Whatever culture you create will need to provide enough human satisfaction that the majority supports it. There will be no chance to start over. This *was* the challenge that faced the first Australians, and they solved it brilliantly.

The great achievement and continuity of aboriginal culture took on a personal meaning for me in 1988 when I visited Nourlangie Rock and the rock shelter of Ubirr in Kakadu National Park on the edge of the great Arnhem Land escarpment. Both of these sites contain richly painted galleries with pictures of people, mythological figures, fish, and animals, many in the unique x-ray style of contemporary Arnhem Land bark painting. Some of the most recent paintings date to the 1960s, but there are multiple layers of increasingly faded red ochre and white line drawings that shade into the remote past. There are also stenciled hand prints, hauntingly reminiscent of those seen in Ice Age cave paintings in France. Archaeological excavations show that people lived in the Kakadu more than 20,000 years ago. Aborigines living in the Kakadu today assert their traditional ownership over these sites and are extremely protective of these direct links to their land and culture. Later, I went on a foraging expedition on the floodplain of the South Alligator River escorted by members of the Murrumbur clan. I saw wallabies, saltwater crocodiles, goannas (lizards), and cockatoos in this game-rich country, and watched my guides gather wild tomatoes and edible waterlilies. They made fire by twirling a stick, and we dined on roast magpie geese and long-necked turtles that the women extracted from the muddy bottom of a shallow lake.

The Earliest Australians

When and how did the first settlers reach Australia? What special problems did the Australian environment pose for the earliest human settlers?

The first major event in Australian prehistory was the original settlement of the continent (see Table 2.1). Archaeologists have obtained absolute dates—ages of objects given in years rather than less precisely—of 50,000–60,000 BP for human occupation in northern Australia using thermoluminescence—a technique for directly calculating the age of certain minerals (Roberts, Jones, and Smith 1990). Genetic evidence suggests that the ancestors of Australian aborigines must have come from Southeast Asia, but it will never be known precisely how they crossed the 70-kilometer (44-mile) stretch of open water that separated the closest Asian islands from Australia. Because this must have occurred during the Ice Age when Australia and New Guinea were connected by the Sahul Shelf, any evidence of these earliest pioneers would have been obliterated by rising sea levels (see Figure 2.1).

The suitability of Australia for occupation by foraging peoples, those who use no domesticated plants or herd animals, is determined by the availability of wild plants and animals, which in turn is shaped by the complex interaction of geological history and geography. Remarkably, the Australian continent, which has the same land area as the lower forty-eight United States, is almost totally lacking in major rivers and mountains, and has been called the driest continent in the world. Australia is situated in the dry latitudes astride the temperate and tropical zones, and rainfall is low and extremely variable. Aridity is the principal factor

TABLE 2.1   *Australian Prehistory, 60,000 BP–AD 1788*

AD 1500–1788	1788	European colonization
	1500	Indonesian fishermen visit
5000–6000 BP	5000	Small Tool Tradition; spear points, backed-blade microliths, spear-thrower; dingo; subsistence intensification
	6000	Sea level stabilizes
8000–15,000 BP	8000	Cape York separated from New Guinea
	10,000	Earliest dated wooden implements: spear, digging stick, firestick, boomerang; Kangaroo Island isolated; desert interior fully occupied
	12,000	Tasmania cut off from mainland; bead ornaments (Devil's Lair)
	15,000	Sea levels begin to rise
20,000–60,000 BP	20,000	Widespread occupation; rock art; heavy "horse hoof" core tools, choppers, ground-stone axes, ochre; low sea levels
	26,000	Cremation (Lake Mungo)
	30,000	Earliest human remains (Lake Mungo)
	38,000	Earliest dated cultural remains (Upper Swan site)
	12,000–50,000	Pleistocene extinctions of megafauna
	40,000–60,000	Initial settlement

SOURCES: Flood (1983), Lourandos (1987), and White and O'Connell (1982).

limiting the density and diversity of organisms, including foraging humans, throughout the continent (see Figure 2.2).

Biologically, Australia is famous for its unique flora and fauna, which developed in relative isolation. The zoological uniqueness of Australia is recognized by its designation, together with New Guinea, as the Australian Region; this is one of the world's six major faunal regions or zoogeographic realms, distinguished by its egg-laying mammals, numerous marsupials (like kangaroos and opossums), and unique birds (see Figure 2.3). Biological productivity, food energy stored by green plants and animals, can be reflected by the density and diversity of plants and animals. Biological productivity is the best overall predictor of basic survival resources, or subsistence potential, for foragers. In Australia, human population densities varied directly with rainfall and were greatest in the biologically rich coastal regions, especially in the tropical north and east. Population densities remained extremely low in the dry interior.

In the arid center of Australia, water is certainly the most critical factor shaping the availability of both plant and animal foods, and determining human population movements and density. Conditions are most extreme in the Western Desert, where there is no real seasonality or predictability

in rainfall and drought conditions may continue for years. In the open country, distant rainstorms can be observed for up to 50 miles (80 km), and people watch the clouds and rely on their detailed knowledge of the locations of specific rock holes and soaks to plan their nomadism. Population densities there were among the lowest for foragers in the world, averaging less than 0.01 person per square kilometer (Gould 1980).

Population Stability and Balance with Nature?

What is the evidence that aboriginal Australians regulated their populations and did not deplete natural resources?

Given the vast time period that people have lived in Australia and the relatively low total population when Europeans arrived, many anthropologists have wondered whether aborigines achieved a balance between population and resources. Joseph Birdsell (1957) believed that aborigines rapidly reached the maximum potential population that could be supported by their foraging technology throughout Australia and then maintained a constant balance between population and resources. Others suggest that aborigines very gradually ex-

FIGURE 2.1   *Map of Australia showing principal geographic features and locations of groups and sites. (SOURCE: Adapted from Lourandos 1987, Figure 2.)*

panded their population and elaborated their technology over many thousands of years (Bowdler 1977, Lourandos 1985, 1987). In either case, the aboriginal achievement is impressive.

During the Pleistocene geological epoch, which ended some 10,000 years ago, Australia contained many giant animals, or megafauna, including giant flightless birds, kangaroos 10 feet (3 m) tall, and

FIGURE 2.2
Desert landscape in the Olga National Park, Australian Northern Territory. The luxuriant vegetation followed an unusually wet year.

FIGURE 2.3
Gray kangaroos, one of Australia's largest marsupials. Australia's unique animals are a result of its biological isolation from the world's other major faunal areas.

other large marsupials, which disappeared by 12,000 BP. This coincides with the disappearance of the mammoths, mastodons, and other megafauna in Eurasia and the Americas, and was originally attributed to overkill, or overhunting, by humans (Martin 1967, Merrilees 1968).

Australian aborigines did coexist with these giant animals, but there is little evidence for overkill in this case. Not all of the Australian megafauna disappeared, and several very large kangaroos survived; it has been suggested that many large species persisted in dwarfed forms. There are few indisputable examples of human exploitation of the megafauna and no evidence of a specialized big game–hunting adaptation in Australia. Modification of the vegetation by deliberately lit fires might have caused problems for some of the megafauna, but not enough is known about their ecological requirements to be certain. It has also been argued that the megafauna, because of its large size, was especially vulnerable to drought and may have been more stressed than smaller species by changes in vegetation. The precise causes of the extinctions must have been varied and may never be known in detail.

Global sea levels dropped to lows of 328–492 feet (100–150 m) below present levels during the Ice Age. As the ice retreated at the end of the Pleistocene, sea levels began to rise, inundating the Sahul Shelf and cutting New Guinea and Tasmania off from the mainland. It is estimated that the sea advanced across the Sahul by as much as 3 miles (5 km) in a single year and 62 miles (100 km) in a generation (Flood 1983). These events have been enshrined in aboriginal myths. It is a tribute to the foraging technology of the aborigines that they were able to adjust to this enormous reduction in resources without adopting farming and settling into village life.

Australian aboriginal society offers an interesting test case for the proposition that foraging peoples were more "in balance" with the environment than village farmers or large-scale societies. The archaeological record shows that the foraging way of life has existed vastly longer than any other, and there is no evidence that foraging peoples experienced periodic population crashes or depleted their resources (except in the most extreme cases,

as in the Arctic). The implication is that stationary populations, in which births exactly replace deaths, must have been the norm. Some culturally regulated population controls must have operated because even the smallest deviation from balanced fertility and mortality rates operating over thousands of years would have led either to extinction, overpopulation, and hardship or to drastic cultural change. Aboriginal societies had optimum sizes, but it is not certain how population actually was regulated.

Carrying capacity is the term anthropologists use to describe the number of people who could, in theory, be supported indefinitely in a given environment with a given technology and culture. Birdsell (1973) estimated that tribal territories were optimally populated at 60 percent of their carrying capacity to allow for random fluctuation in resources. He assumed that intentional infanticide involving up to 50 percent of births was the primary mechanism limiting population. It is known that babies were sometimes killed at birth, but there is little direct evidence for the actual rate. Infanticide was most likely carried out by women who were motivated by their desire either to eliminate deformed children or to space out their families in order to have only one child at a time under 3 or 4 years of age to carry and nurse. This kind of family planning increased the likelihood that a given child could be raised to maturity. Given the relatively high "natural" infant mortality rates and overall low life expectancy that probably characterized tribal demography, spacing births every 4 years could produce a stationary population.

Infanticide was related to foraging conditions because both mobility and the burden of carrying children increase when resources are scarce. Similarly, given existing food sources and preparation techniques, there was no baby food other than mothers' milk; thus, nursing would be prolonged, often for 4 years or more. The balance between population and resources was also under unconscious biological control because extended lactation and nutritional deficiencies can lower fertility by causing hormonal changes in a woman's reproductive cycle.

Infanticide reflected the autonomy that women maintained in reproductive decision making, and it also gave them some covert political leverage in a society that was publicly dominated by men. Gillian Cowlishaw (1978) has argued that some women expressed their resentment over arranged marriages by killing their firstborn, although this type of infanticide would not be a response to resource depletion.

It has sometimes been suggested, on the basis of census data showing sex ratios skewed in favor of boys, that girls were more likely to be killed than boys, thereby making infanticide a more powerful means of population control. However, these data are suspect because girls may have been hidden from census takers, and a careful review of completed families in Australia shows no evidence that girls were selectively killed (Yengoyan 1981). Computer simulation studies also suggest that, if systematically applied, even very low rates of selective female infanticide would lead to population extinction. The concept of selective female infanticide, which is related to theories about a widespread male supremacy cult in domestic-scale societies, will be discussed further in Chapter 3.

The Dreaming and the Structure of Aboriginal Society

How do the beliefs and rituals focused on the Dreaming integrate virtually all aspects of aboriginal culture and social life?

The key element of aboriginal culture is the complex, multidimensional concept aborigines call the Dreaming, which recognizes the interdependence and vitality of all parts of the cosmos. Humans are actors along with other species in a balanced living system whose goal is the continuity of life and the maintenance of the cosmos itself. Regardless of what anthropologists decide about the balance and stability of aboriginal culture, aborigines themselves believe their culture to be fundamentally changeless and in balance with nature.

The emic term *Dreaming* refers variously to creation, the moral order, an ancestral being, people, a spirit, the origin point of a spirit, a specific topographic feature, and a *totem* species, object, or phenomenon. Furthermore, all of these can be thought of as the same, whereas in Western thought they would be sharply distinguished. Outsiders have treated the Dreaming as aboriginal religion, but it is a profound concept that permeates all aspects of the culture and defies easy categorization. Aborigines identify themselves completely with their culture and their land through the Dreaming in a way that nonaborigines have difficulty comprehending. For an aborigine to say, "I am a kangaroo," might sound like nonsense, but within the Dreaming context such a statement carries special significance.

As a philosophy of life, the Dreaming provides both a *cosmogony* to account for the origin of everything and a *cosmology* to explain the fundamental order of the universe. The Dreaming thus answers the basic meaning-of-life questions; offers a detailed charter for day-to-day living, including basic social categories and ritual activities; and ascribes cultural meanings to the natural environment (see Figure 2.4).

When regarded as a mythic cosmogony, the Dreaming is sometimes imprecisely called the Dreamtime, referring to the creation time when a series of heroic ancestor beings crisscrossed the landscape and transformed specific topographic features as a permanent record of their activities. The problem with referring to creation as the Dreamtime is that aborigines are not really concerned with origins as historical events; instead, origin myths are timeless explanations. Time, culture, and nature are viewed as cyclical and changeless. The Dreamtime ancestors followed the same cultural rules that are practiced today, and their influence is still so vital that it is more reasonable to refer to the Dreaming as the Everywhen, or the Eternal Dreamtime, than to place it

---

carrying capacity   The number of people who could, in theory, be supported indefinitely in a given environment with a given technology and culture.

totem   In Australia, specific animals, plants, natural phenomena, or other objects that originate in the Dreaming and are the spiritual progenitors of aboriginal descent groups. Elsewhere, refers to any cultural association between specific natural objects and human social groups.

cosmogony   An ideological system that seeks to explain the origin of everything: people, nature, and the universe.

cosmology   An ideological system that explains the order and meaning of the universe and people's places within it.

FIGURE 2.4
*A functional model of
aboriginal culture.*

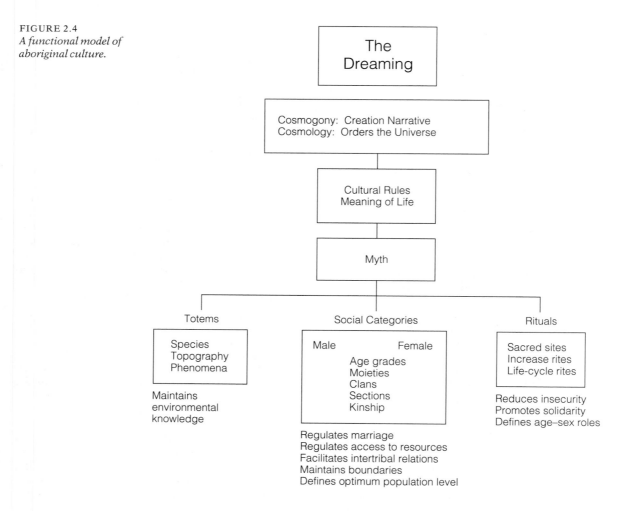

in the Dreamtime past (see the boxes entitled "An Aboriginal Woman Explains the Dreaming" and "Functionalism, Structuralism, and the Illusion of Totemism").

When the Dreaming is referred to as the moral authority for behavior, it may be called simply the *Law*, or the *Dreaming Law*, and in this respect it is beyond question. Stability is thus a fundamental feature of the culture.

The aboriginal cosmos differs in striking ways from the religions of larger-scale cultures. There is no all-powerful god and no rank order in the Dreaming. Similarly, there is no heaven or hell, and the distinctions between sacred and profane,

natural and supernatural, are blurred. Aborigines experience the mystical as a perpetual unity with the cosmos as they follow the Dreaming Law in their daily life. For example, a seemingly mundane activity, such as seasonally burning grass, can be considered a religious act because it perpetuates life and the cosmic balance between sun and rain, people and game.

Sacred Sites and Dreamtime Pathways at Uluru

How does Dreamtime symbolism directly connect aborigines with specific places in the land?

An Aboriginal Woman Explains the Dreaming

During an Australia-wide conference of aboriginal women held in Adelaide in 1980, Nganyintja Ilyatjari, a Pitjantjatjara woman from central Australia, interpreted the Dreaming and related it to the land. Ilyatjari drew a series of small circles on a map of Australia and explained in Pitjantjatjara:

I am drawing the places all over Australia where our Dreamtime started a long long time ago— Listen! . . . This is Dreaming, Dreaming of the kangaroo, the goanna, the wild fig and lot of other different ones—a long time ago the Dreaming was there, a very long time ago.

This is what all people have always listened to, this Dreaming is ours. . . . In all these different places all over Australia lots of aboriginal people have always lived since the beginning. If I could speak English well I would tell you in English.

Our country, the country out there near Mt. Davies, is full of sacred places. The kangaroo Dreaming has been there since the beginning, the wild fig Dreaming has been there since the beginning, many other women's Dreamings are also there. In other places men and women's Dreaming were together from a long time ago. . . .

These places have been part of the sacred Dreamtime since the beginning of time. They were made then by our Dreamtime ancestors—like the kangaroo. Our country is sacred, this country is sacred. (Ilyatjari 1983:55–57)

How do these places help people remember Dreamtime events?

Misunderstanding of aboriginal culture began with the British colonization of Australia in 1788. Because they saw no aboriginal farms or permanent houses, British authorities mistakenly concluded that the aborigines had no fixed relationship to the land. Australia was declared *terra nullius,* an empty wasteland, free for the taking, and so aboriginal land was appropriated. Nineteenth-century evolutionary anthropologists did little to help the situation. Lewis Henry Morgan (1877) considered aborigines to be living representatives of middle savagery, elevated one step above the subhumans of lower savagery. Only over the past hundred years have anthropologists begun to appreciate the subtle complexities of the aborigines' enduring ties to their land. The anthropological debate over government policies toward aborigines is explored in Chapter 14, as part of the broader discussion of the place of domestic-scale cultures within the global system.

The Dreamtime ancestors, or totemic beings, make a direct link between people and their land by means of the sacred sites, which are the physical remains of the ancestors or their activities. The role of these beings is dramatically illustrated at Uluru, or Ayers Rock, a giant monolith in central Australia (see Figure 2.6). Uluru is a weathered dome, some 5 miles (8 km) around and rising more than 1100 feet (335 m) from the desert plain. As the largest such monolith in the world, it was designated as a national park and biosphere reserve in 1985, and is administered jointly by the aboriginal owners and the Australian National Park and Wildlife Service. More importantly for aborigines, Uluru is a perpetual Dreamtime monument crammed with cultural meaning.

The north side of the rock belongs to the clan of hare wallabies, rabbit-sized kangaroos, while the south side belongs to the carpet boa clan. A series of stories recounts the activities of ten totemic beings and their relatives, including various snakes, reptiles, birds, and mammals, who created the existing landscape and established the clan boundaries. Charles Mountford (1965), who recorded some of these myths from the Pitjantjatjara people between 1935 and 1960, published some 200 photographs detailing specific rock outcrops, stains,

Functionalism, Structuralism, and the Illusion of Totemism

The special association between aborigines and their Dreamings was called *totemism* by anthropologists and became the subject of widespread theoretical speculation. Sir James Frazer (1910) attributed the origin of Australian totemism to the supposed aboriginal ignorance of the physiological basis of conception.

Functionalist interpretations rooted totemism in the need for social order. Clan solidarity and identity were reinforced by the positive feelings of belonging and group pride and legitimacy generated by ritual activities, which in turn required totems as visible symbols or emblems (see Figure 2.5a). British functionalist A. R. Radcliffe-Brown (1929) argued that aborigines first adopted a ritual attitude toward species that were "good to eat," and then these species became group emblems or totems. The functionalist line of argument proved inconclusive because not all valuable species were totems, whereas some highly nonutilitarian species, such as mosquitoes and diseases, often were considered totems.

French structuralist anthropologist Claude Lévi-Strauss (1963) contended that totemism is an illusion as a single anthropological category because it merges too many diverse phenomena. Lévi-Strauss (1963, 1966) observed that totemism can profitably be considered an example of *complementary opposition*, the tendency for people to create mental sets of paired opposites such as day and night, male and female, nature and culture (see Figure 2.5b). Natural species represent social units, "not because they are 'good to eat' but because they are 'good to think'" (Lévi-Strauss 1963:89). This is a structuralist argument because cultural meaning is derived from the way different elements, species, and clans can be combined like elements in a code that convey a message.

This mental game draws an analogy between nature and human society in a way that makes cultural patterns seem natural. Things that are naturally different, such as male and female, can thus be seen to create an integrated pair.

The advantage of this mental classification process is that opposition can create social integration. Clan **A** differs from clan **B** in the same way that a kangaroo differs from an emu. There are two homologous systems of differences, one operating in nature and the other in culture. Species are "naturally" different, whereas totemic clans are distinguished by the "cultural illusion" of the ritual functions thought to perpetuate the totemic species. Exogamy means that women who are "naturally" similar because of their sex are culturally differentiated into marriageable and nonmarriageable categories. The result is that totemic social groups can be integrated by intermarriage. The social groups opposed by totemic classification are made complementary because one clan cannot reproduce without the other.

In the end, it seems that Lévi-Strauss would agree that totemism is simply a way in which people conceptualize society in order to create solidarity.

FIGURE 2.5
Theories of totemism: (a) British functionalism, (b) French structuralism.

(a)

FIGURE 2.6   *Uluru, or Ayers Rock. Rising from the desert center of Australia, this giant monolith contains many important Dreamtime sacred sites.*

caves, and pockmarks that represent the bodies, camps, and physical signs of these totemic beings.

The same totemic beings who created sites at Uluru traveled widely across the country, leaving permanent Dreaming paths. During their travels, they interacted with other beings and created similar sites elsewhere. Specific Dreaming pathways can stretch for hundreds of miles, crossing the territory of different clans and tribes.

Dreaming locations, or sacred sites, such as those at Uluru, are centers for ritual activity and help define territorial boundaries and regulate use of resources. Some sites contain the spirit essence of their creators and are the places where special "increase ceremonies" are performed to perpetuate particular species. For example, control of a kangaroo increase site means ritual control over the supply of kangaroos. Entry to or even knowledge of such sites often is restricted, and unauthorized intrusion may be severely punished. Other sites contain especially dangerous substances and must be avoided by everyone. To avoid the risks of trespassing, people must seek permission before entering unfamiliar areas. Since 1976, many of these sacred sites have been officially protected by federal legislation, and fines can be levied for trespass.

The spirit essence localized at certain sites also completes the direct link between people and

their individual Dreamings, because this animating power is believed to be an essential but not an exclusive element in human conception and reproduction. Pregnancy is identified with the totemic "soul stuff" emanating from a specific Dreaming site, and this soul stuff returns to the site at death. Thus, in a real sense, an individual is a physical part of the Dreaming, and this spiritual connection is a more important cultural fact than biological paternity.

An added value of the Dreaming tracks is that they serve as mnemonic devices to help fix in memory the location of permanent waterholes, which are critically important. The Dreaming myths and related rituals are dramatic reminders of specific geographic details and preserve them in people's minds as accurately as would any large-scale printed map. The Dreaming also takes on visible form in body paint, sand drawings, rock art, and paintings or carvings on ritual objects, all of which may incorporate an elaborate iconography (Munn 1973) (see Figure 2.7).

Aboriginal Band and Clan: Equality and Flexibility

What factors influence the structure of foraging camps and ownership groups? How does band

FIGURE 2.7 *A Dreamtime kangaroo in a rock painting from the Northern Territory.*

organization allow everyone access to natural resources while minimizing resource depletion? How does band organization reduce conflict and encourage social equality?

Australian society is based on highly flexible, multi-family foraging groups or **bands,** and a ritual **estate,** or religious property, which is tied to the land. Band and estate are functionally interconnected in the range, which is the territory defined by Dreaming sacred sites and occupied by the band. This band–estate system serves a resource management function and helps space out and define the optimum limits for local populations, thus contributing directly to long-term stability.

The aborigines' own view of their social system corresponds in general to the anthropological categories of "band" and "range" (Hiatt 1984a, Peterson 1986), but not to Julian Steward's **patrilocal band** of anthropological theory, which was thought to be based on a cluster of functionally interconnected anthropological concepts including **exogamy, patrilocality, patrilineal descent, patrilineages,** and **clans** (see the box entitled "The Band–Horde Controversy"). For aborigines, *band* refers to the families that camp and forage together (see Figure 2.8). Different native terms may distinguish the camp, the residents of the camp, and the country they occupy, but these terms have multiple meanings. For example, depending on the context, *country* may refer to land as a religious estate or as a foraging territory. Band members may be referred to as "people of" a particular place, whereas individuals may claim affiliation with several countries. The band is not exclusively patrilocal and may change composition frequently as individual families visit relatives in other areas. Nevertheless, the band is an important social group, and individual bands retain their unity during temporary multiband encampments.

The range over which the band forages is a discrete territory containing the critical resources that sustain the band during normal years. Band territorial boundaries are recognized but not directly defended. Visitors must observe special entry rites upon arrival at a camp. They also must ask permission before they can forage within band territory. Under this system, the "owners" of the country operate as resource managers. Permission to forage would rarely be denied, but knowing who is foraging where makes resource exploitation much more efficient and minimizes potential conflicts.

It is important to distinguish between use rights to band territory as a range and ownership rights to the land as a religious estate. All band members and those asking permission can use range resources, but only those qualified to be estate owners can give permission and act as managers. The legal nature of the aboriginal land-holding system was formally recognized by an Australian judge who presided over a court hearing in 1970 in which the Yolngu people tried to prove their traditional ownership of their land. The 3 weeks of direct testimony about clans, spirit beings, and the land included the following exchange between the court and a man from the Manggalili clan about permission to use clan land:

> Q: *Before you went hunting kangaroos, did you talk to anyone?*
> A: *Yes, we would talk together.*
> Q: *Who would you talk to?*
> A: *If I was living with the Rirratjingu [clan], I would talk to those Rirratjingu people.*
> Q: *And what did you say to them?*
> A: *I am going to get animals—kangaroos.* (Williams 1986:171)

The judge found that the Yolngu land tenure system was "highly adapted to the country" and "remarkably free from the vagaries of personal whim or influence" (Justice Blackburn, cited in Williams 1986:158).

Many sorts of overlapping claims are recognized, both to the right to ask to use a range and to

---

band A group of twenty-five to fifty people who camp and forage together.

estate Property held in common by a descent group, perhaps including territory, sacred sites, and ceremonies.

patrilocal band A theoretical form of band organization based on exogamy and patrilocal residence.

exogamy Marriage outside a culturally defined group.

patrilocality A cultural preference for a newly married couple to live near the husband's parents or patrilineal relatives.

patrilineal descent Descent traced through a line of men to a male ancestor.

patrilineage A lineage based on descent traced through a line of men to a common male ancestor and sharing a joint estate.

clan A named group claiming descent from a common but often remote ancestor and sharing a joint estate.

The Band— Horde Controversy

The first anthropological interpretation of the aboriginal band was by A. R. Radcliffe-Brown (1913, 1918), who described a formal, highly structured system based on *patrilineal descent*, group membership assigned through males. Married couples practiced *patrilocality*, living near the husband's parents or relatives, creating localized *patrilineages*. Radcliffe-Brown saw the band, or "clan-horde" as he called it, as a rigid, patrilineal, patrilocal, landowning organization. Radcliffe-Brown speculated that men needed to stay on familiar ground, where their detailed local knowledge of resources would be most useful. Calling Australian bands "clans" confused the band—actually a *land-using* group containing members recruited through a variety of means—with the *clan*, a descent-based group that at best could only be a *landowning* unit.

Radcliffe-Brown's clan-horde was reinterpreted as the "patrilocal band" by cultural ecologist Julian Steward (1936) and for decades served as the anthropological model of the social organization of foraging peoples worldwide. Steward thought the band was produced by the scarcity of wild-food resources, which kept the human population at very low levels and prevented larger, more permanent social groups from forming. At the same time, it was advantageous for related men to use and defend a common territory. Band *exogamy*, or out-marrying, resulted from the universal incest taboo that prohibited the intermarriage of close kin.

More recent field research led to the surprising discovery that real bands were much more flexible than originally thought (Lee and DeVore 1968). Men actually spent much of their time living away from their clan land. Rigid adherence to the patrilineal band model would be an unreliable organizational strategy for foragers in an unpredictable desert environment. Furthermore, bands were not defended by armed force, and resource use was regulated by a policy of open admission to social groups. Even the notion that hunting required patrilocality has been questioned because foraging by women also requires detailed local knowledge.

the right to estate ownership. Patrilineal descent invariably provides the strongest claim, but a person also has special claims on a mother's estate and use rights in a spouse's country. Extended residence also can provide a claim, as can one's place of conception and birth and the burial place of kin. Under this system, ownership and use are distributed in a way that discourages any concentration of social power. Households always have many places to go during droughts or famines. An owner can also be sure that visitors will return to their own countries where their Dreaming connections are strongest.

The ease with which people can move among bands helps reduce conflict because people who are not getting along can simply move apart.

As Steward (1936) pointed out, the size and density of the band is in part determined by environmental, demographic, and cultural factors. Worldwide, band populations average twenty-five to fifty people. Because food, especially game, is pooled among families within the band, the minimum average of twenty-five is probably determined by the number required to maintain foraging security by ensuring that enough adult food producers

An aboriginal camp—an Aranda family in Alice Springs, 1896. The man is smoothing a spear shaft and a woman is grinding corn. Families that camp and forage together make up the band.

are available. There are strong reasons for people to hold down the upper limits of band size. Given fixed territories, increased numbers above minimum levels would soon result in a reduction in leisure and more frequent moves as resources became depleted.

The minimum size of bands also may be shaped by the need to maintain marriage alliances that would reduce the likelihood of interband conflict. Bands tend to space themselves uniformly across the landscape in roughly hexagonal territories, such that each band is surrounded by five or six neighboring bands. The cultural requirement of band exogamy is a good excuse for marrying otherwise potentially hostile neighbors.

Social Interaction Networks and Vanishing Tribes

Given that there are no permanent political offices or government in domestic-scale cultures, what is the nature of aboriginal social networks above the band?

While the band is a clearly defined unit in aboriginal society, the existence of the tribe is not so obvious, even though the term *tribe* was used as a descriptive label by generations of anthropologists. (Tribal names often only mean "people" in a local dialect.) Many authorities rightly question the utility of *tribe* as an analytic concept, and in Australia the term has virtually vanished from contemporary

anthropological writing. Domestic-scale societies are not tribal political units; that is, there is no permanent leadership above the band or village, although "tribes" have been artificially created by colonial governments for administrative purposes. Nevertheless, politically independent bands and villages do share a common culture with their neighbors, and this connection is recognized by the people themselves. For Australia, Joseph Birdsell (1973) called this common culture the dialect tribe, because language or dialect difference is often the most distinctive cultural difference between the largest permanent aboriginal groups. He described it as a minimal breeding population, a collection of adjacent bands who interact frequently enough through marriage alliances, joint ceremonies, and visits that they maintain a common language and culture. Birdsell suggested that such tribes fluctuate in size around 500 people. In theory, when dialect tribes fall below 200 people, members will have difficulty finding mates and will be absorbed by larger neighbors, whereas tribes growing to 1000 or more people will be expected to split as interaction between remotely situated bands becomes diffused.

Dialect tribes are interaction networks that, like bands, tend to occupy hexagonally shaped territories and seem to vary in area according to the productivity of the environment, while the total number of people in the tribe remains relatively constant. Birdsell found a predictable inverse relationship between rainfall, as a measure of biological productivity, and population density, such that in areas with higher rainfall, tribal territories became smaller.

The problem with the dialect tribe is that language boundaries are not as distinct as the maps imply. Aborigines are multilingual, and intermarriage and joint ceremonies between people speaking different languages and dialects are common. Language groups often are associated with territories, but such territories are probably de facto artifacts of the aggregated territorial estates when viewed from the outside. There are few, if any, occasions when the members of a dialect tribe would act as a unit, and joint defense of tribal territory must have been a rare event. However, there is often a strong sense of "tribal" identity reflecting shared language, territory, and culture.

Aboriginal Australia comprises overlapping networks of social interaction that span the entire continent. Aboriginal material culture is the simplest of any ethnographically known people. In the next section, we examine how they remain well fed and comfortable in the desert, with nothing more than fire and a few implements of wood and stone.

MAKING A LIVING WITH FORAGING TECHNOLOGY

Foraging technology is a brilliant human achievement based on mobility and the productivity of natural ecosystems, interconnected communities of plants and animals. Foraging allows an appropriately organized and culturally outfitted regional population of a mere 500 people to maintain itself indefinitely in virtually any environment with no outside assistance. Human survival under such conditions is an impressive achievement. It is unlikely that a contemporary urban population of 500 people, including families with dependent children and elderly, could survive if placed empty-handed in a wilderness. Foraging requires a vast store of knowledge about plants and animals, specialized manufacturing and food-processing techniques, and hunting-and-gathering skills, as well as assorted material implements and facilities.

Foragers ultimately are constrained by the level of food resources produced by the natural ecosys-

tems they occupy, but many options exist for adjusting subsistence output to meet basic human needs, including the tools used, the species eaten, and the organization of labor. Most important is the ability to move as resources decline.

For optimum efficiency and sociability, foragers in temperate and tropical areas typically organize themselves into camps of twenty-five to fifty people, based on a flexible division of labor by gender: Women collect plant food and small animals within a 3-mile (5-km) radius of camp, and men hunt within a 6-mile (10-km) range. These distances are generalized averages based on the assumption that people will be able to return easily to camp each day. Except as compensation for severe seasonal shortages, food storage is rare, and camps are moved as soon as food yields decline. The degree of mobility is directly related to the size of camps and resource availability. As long as the human population density remains low, there is little danger of serious resource depletion.

Lizards and Grass Seeds: Aboriginal Food Resources

Without domestic livestock and cultivated crops, what do aborigines eat? How does their food supply vary in different parts of the country?

Virtually every edible plant and animal has been part of the aboriginal diet somewhere in Australia. The list would include insects, lizards, whales, birds, mammals, turtles, fish and shellfish, and nuts, fruits, greens, and grass seeds. Aborigines commonly distinguish between plant and animal foods, with the latter usually ranked higher. Animal fat, rather than meat as such, is often the food most desired by foragers.

Although animal food might be preferred, there is great variation throughout Australia in actual consumption patterns (see Figure 2.9). The Anbarra and Oenpelli aborigines, who live in the tropical monsoon north, have enjoyed the greatest abundance of animals, especially when they have had access to marine ecosystems (see Figure 2.10). Foragers have considerable difficulty maintaining a high intake of meat in the desert, where species diversity and abundance are low, and they rely heavily on lizards as a staple, supplemented with insects.

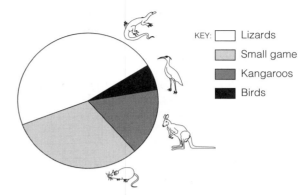

FIGURE 2.9   *Food consumption patterns, in percentage by weight, of plants and animals by three aboriginal groups: Western Desert (Gould 1980), Anbarra (Meehan 1982), and Oenpelli (McArthur 1960).*

FIGURE 2.11   *Meat consumption pattern, in percentage by weight, of lizards, small game, kangaroos, and birds by desert aborigines. (SOURCE: Gould 1980.)*

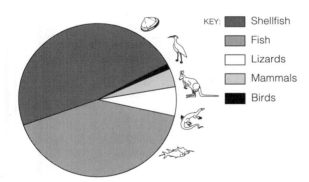

FIGURE 2.10   *Meat consumption pattern, in percentage by weight, of shellfish, fish, reptiles, mammals, and birds by Anbarra (coastal) aborigines. (SOURCE: Meehan 1982.)*

The importance of lizard meat in the Western Desert is striking (see Figure 2.11). Lizards made up nearly half, by weight, of the total meat animals brought in by a group of ten aborigines observed in the 1960s (Gould 1980). Lizards represent one of the most efficient desert resources considering the time and energy needed to collect and process them in relation to their food value (O'Connell and Hawkes 1981). It takes only 15 minutes to capture and cook 2.2 pounds (1 kilogram [kg]) of lizard, which yields more than 1000 kilocalories (kcal) of food energy. Kangaroos, though highly desired, are not so easy to secure and contributed only 16 per-

cent to the total meat supply. The famous Witchetty grub, actually a wood-boring moth larva extracted from the roots of certain desert trees, is also quite energy-efficient. The grubs, which weigh a little over 1 ounce (30 g) each, are almost pure fat and protein. Aborigines can extract 1 kilogram of grubs in 30 minutes (O'Connell and Hawkes 1981, Tindale 1981).

Desert aborigines have relatively few plant foods available to them, but they use them intensively. In the Central Desert, more than one hundred plant species are consumed, especially grasses and seeds, which are among the most costly food resources. Seed collecting and grinding requires up to 6 hours of work per kilogram produced (O'Connell and Hawkes 1981:123). The use of seeds is a testimony to the skill and resourcefulness of the desert foragers.

Throughout Australia, the primary concern traditionally was to maintain long-term food security, because unpredictable fluctuations and shortages of key staples could occur even in the richest areas. Techniques of food storage were known, but they were used only to address short-term emergencies or to sustain temporary aggregations of people. Rather than stockpiling food, the basic strategy was to maintain access to resources over a wide area through kinship ties and social networks. In the desert, a combination of rain and an unusual abundance of kangaroos might provide the occasion for a joint encampment of a hundred or more people for feasting, performing rituals, and arranging marriages. The most remarkable food bonuses were the great masses of moths that congregated in the summer on the rock walls of the Great Dividing Range (Flood 1980, 1983, Gould 1980). A rich source of fat, the moths could be eaten immediately or ground to a paste and shaped into cakes. The moth feast supported aggregations of up to 700 aborigines at specific campgrounds.

Aboriginal Tools: Digging Stick, Firestick, and Spear

How do aborigines make their simple tools? How important is fire? What are the multiple uses for the spear-thrower? Have any changes occurred in aboriginal technology over 50,000 years?

The diverse foraging activities of the aborigines have been supported for 50,000 years by a remarkably sparse toolkit of simple stone, bone, and wood implements, which expanded only about 4000–5000 years ago. The oldest and most universal food-getting tools in Australia are the digging sticks used by women to collect roots and small animals, the men's wooden hunting spear, and the firestick.

This division of tools by gender is symbolically valid, but in practice the aborigines are much more pragmatic than anthropological stereotypes suggest. For example, a group of women from Borroloola, on the Gulf of Carpentaria, declared:

We are Aboriginal women. We talk for our hunting business, ceremony business. We used to go hunting. We can't wait for the men. We are ladies, we go hunting and feed the men too. . . . Sometimes we use that shovel spear—kangaroo, emu and fish, all that with the spears. . . . Sometimes camping out, leave husbands, just the women go hunting. (Gale 1983:70–71)

The tools themselves are simple, but they can be manufactured, maintained, and used only in combination with a vast store of specialized environmental knowledge. Aborigines on the move always carry glowing firesticks. Students schooled in the dangers of forest fire and the value of systematic fire suppression usually are shocked by the seemingly casual manner in which aborigines in ethnographic films light brush fires and leave them

burning. Such practices, however, are neither reckless nor destructive. Besides its obvious use for cooking and keeping warm, fire is a vital resource management tool used extensively to drive game, to keep the country open for easy travel, and to facilitate the growth of valuable food plants. Many plants will not reproduce without periodic burning, and frequent burning prevents the accumulation of plant litter that might fuel destructive fires. Signal fires also help widely scattered groups keep track of one another.

About 5000 years ago, a technological change known as the Small Tool Tradition spread throughout Australia. It was distinguished by the mounting of small stone flakes on spear shafts, the use of the spear-thrower, and the appearance of the dingo, a semidomesticated dog. These new developments may have increased hunting efficiency and made possible increased ritual activities and the expansion of social networks.

The *woomera*, or spear-thrower, increases the power and accuracy of the spear. It is a long, thin, curved piece of wood with a hook on one end and a chipped-stone blade, or adze, mounted on the other end (see Figure 2.12). This multipurpose tool also can be used as a shovel, fire starter, or percussion musical instrument (Gould 1970).

In much of Australia, very simple stone-flaked tools satisfied all aboriginal cutting needs. However, where boomerangs and throwing clubs were frequently used, as Brian Hayden (1977) notes, it made sense to use edge-ground rather than chipped-stone tools. Grinding an edge is more work than chipping, but a ground tool can be resharpened many times. Furthermore, because they are so durable, edge-ground tools can be mounted on handles to make a stone ax with twice the striking force of a hand-held tool (Dickson 1981). The edge must be carefully aligned and painstakingly ground on sandstone with water. Crafting the head shape is not easy, and the hafting technique requires much skill. The haft must be rigid enough to keep the head in place while maintaining enough handle flexibility to cushion the shock of chopping blows. The head usually is grooved to receive a wrap-around, heat-treated, wooden handle, which is glued with vegetable gum and tied in place. Stone axes can be very sharp and efficient tools, but they take longer for a given cutting task than steel axes

FIGURE 2.12 *The spear-thrower, or* woomera, *a tool that has been in use in Australia for at least 5000 years. (a) Side and top views—note the gum-mounted, chipped-stone blade and wooden hook on the ends; (b) an aboriginal man launching a spear using a spear-thrower.*

because the stone blade is thicker and more wood must be removed to cut to a given depth (Dickson 1981).

The Original Affluent Society

How effective is aboriginal foraging? How hard do people work? Do they live well?

Evaluating the effectiveness of the foraging way of life has not been an easy task for anthropologists. At first, the general assumption was that all foragers lived a precarious existence. Without farming and storage, they were thought to have little control over their resources. This view began to change when detailed studies of modern foragers began to appear in the 1960s. Marshall Sahlins (1968) drew on a 1948 study of Arnhem Land aborigines (McCarthy and McArthur 1960) to conclude that foragers in fact, represented "the original affluent society" because men and women worked no more than 4–5 hours a day to collect and process enough food to keep themselves well nourished and healthy (see Figure 2.13). They appeared to have plenty of leisure time and were in that sense more highly "evolved" than agricultural peoples. Sahlins pointed to the absence of food storage and the apparent underutilization of resources as further indication of the "affluence" of aboriginal foragers.

Other researchers found conditions only slightly less affluent in the desert interior. Richard Gould (1969, 1980), who studied self-sufficient Pitjantjatjara foragers in the Western Desert in 1966–1970 during a period of moderate drought, found that women were putting in 5–7 hours a day collecting and processing food. They relaxed 5 hours a day during the heat of the afternoon and were still able to provide 80 percent of the household diet.

This affluence view has been challenged by more recent studies rating women's foraging as significantly less productive than previously thought (Hawkes and O'Connell 1981, O'Connell and Hawkes 1981). These new findings, however, are not convincing refutations of forager affluence. The aboriginal groups involved in these studies had largely replaced the bush food collected by women with store-bought food, and they were not fully nomadic and thus probably not as skilled as full-time foragers. Some researchers point to the low birth weights and slow childhood growth rates found in some modern forager populations as evidence of food shortages (Hill and Hurtado 1996). Foragers in difficult environments may work harder and face more shortfalls than Sahlins thought.

FIGURE 2.13   *Aboriginal men spearfishing in the coastal waters of the tropical north. They have speared a stingray.*

Other critics of forager affluence have noted that most modern aborigines permanently abandoned the desert interior during periods of severe drought. However, drought is nothing new in Australia. In earlier times, people likely abandoned certain areas temporarily when the environment became uninhabitable, relied on their social support network in more favorable areas, and then returned to their homelands when conditions improved. The European invasion disrupted this support system.

Perhaps the strongest evidence for the affluence view is the fact that aborigines did not become farmers. Earlier anthropologists attributed the absence of farming in aboriginal Australia to isolation and extreme conservatism, if not ignorance and backwardness. These explanations can be easily rejected. Aboriginal technology was sophisticated and required high-level skill and knowledge. Ab-

origines certainly understood how plants grew and, in some cases, deliberately left cuttings to regrow. Some technological items, such as ground-stone axes and boomerangs, appeared in Australia earlier than anywhere else in the world. The spear-thrower apparently was independently invented in Australia. Many cultural traits were borrowed from New Guinea, but not New Guinea farming, domesticated pigs, pottery, or the bow and arrow. It can be inferred that aborigines simply did not consider these technologies to be an improvement.

William Lyons (1995) identifies an adaptive advantage of forager affluence, arguing that foragers store time rather than food. Maximizing leisure means that extra effort can be expended during times of resource scarcity. Sahlins suggested that foragers were affluent because they limited their needs to match their limited production means. Thus, they were responding to ecological constraints. In addition, Nurit Bird-David (1992) proposes that forager affluence is a culturally constructed metaphorical model of a "cosmic economy of sharing." Foragers recognize a direct kinship with spirit beings who socialize and share food with people as part of the natural order of existence. This is the essence of Dreamtime symbolism. In this mutual sharing relationship, people only ask of nature what nature can give. There is no cultural incentive for storage or increased production.

Aborigines as "Stone Age" Peoples

Because aboriginal technology relies heavily on stone tools, should aborigines be considered Paleolithic peoples?

Australian aborigines often were considered to be "Stone Age" or "Paleolithic" peoples by earlier anthropologists who followed an evolutionary-stage approach. Aborigines did not use metal, but the view of the Stone Age as an inferior evolutionary stage contributes little to our understanding and implies that aboriginal culture must be obsolete.

Aside from the political implications of labeling any contemporary people Paleolithic, there are many logical difficulties with evolutionary-stage categories based on tool types. Tools are poor indicators of economic productivity because even very simple tools, as the Australian case shows, can be very productive and efficient. Furthermore, tool types that are supposed to be indicative of Paleolithic, Mesolithic, and Neolithic stages often overlap in unexpected ways. For example, aborigines who seemed to lack Upper Paleolithic stone blades were assigned to the Middle Paleolithic, along with Neanderthals, whereas aborigines who used Neolithic ground-stone axes were considered Paleolithic because they did not farm. The notions of inevitability and directionality in tool types also are problematic, especially given how long certain tool types have been in use. Rather than reflecting differences in mental ability or ingenuity, it is more likely that the tools used by a particular people reflect their culturally defined needs.

The foraging technological subsystem provides the energy, nutrients, and raw materials needed by the population, but the technology depends on a much more complex social and ideological system.

Domestic-scale cultures generate social status and power only through marriage and the family. In the next section, we look at how these social networks are organized and how power is obtained.

KINSHIP, AGE, AND GENDER: DAILY LIFE IN FORAGER SOCIETY

Australian aboriginal society, although rooted in antiquity and sustained by simple technology, is a fully developed and dynamic system. It would be a serious distortion to treat it as either a fragile relic of the Paleolithic or a temporary step on the way to political centralization. The basic challenge for aborigines is the circular problem of maintaining a domestic-scale cultural system that will perpetuate their population and, in turn, reproduce the culture. Understanding how aborigines solve this problem has preoccupied anthropologists for more than a century and has generated a continuing debate.

Anthropological interpretations of aboriginal culture have shifted dramatically over time as theoretical perspectives have changed and as new data have become available. This debate has helped establish many of the most basic concepts of cultural anthropology while gradually revealing the genius of aboriginal culture. The broadest theoretical issues concern how the culture actually works: the role of the belief system and the way the culture relates to environmental and demographic factors. Important humanistic issues concern how much social equality there is and whether women and young men are being exploited by old men.

A Kinship-Based Society

How do aborigines use kinship relationships to organize their society?

Aboriginal society is highly decentralized and egalitarian, with people in overlapping and interdependent roles that minimize the possibility that divisive interest groups will come into serious conflict. The social system allows us to sort the 500 or so people that we might encounter into a workable number of social categories that specify appropriate interpersonal behavior, especially in the critical areas of marriage and access to spiritual property. The totemic estate groups are among the most important social categories. In a given aboriginal society, there might be dozens of totemic estate groups, or clans, that regulate rights in spiritual property and indirectly provide access to natural resources. Who one marries is partly determined in reference to the totemic groups of one's parents, and marriage establishes access to territory associated with one's spouse's totemic estates.

All social interaction takes place between people who can place themselves in specific kinship categories. Kinship terms—mother, father, uncle, sister—define an individual's personal network of culturally significant categories that are conceptually based on the relationships arising from the **nuclear family** of mother, father, and dependent children. Aboriginal **kinship terminology** systems typically distinguish some fifteen to twenty relationship pairs such as father/daughter, brother/sister, and so on. Kin terms may distinguish sex and relative age or generation, and whether one is a **consanguine** (related by a common ancestor) or an **affine** (related by marriage). Aboriginal kin terms also indicate marriageability and relative totemic estate group affiliation. Because everyone must be fitted into a "kinship" category, most people are not necessarily what nonaboriginals would consider "real kin," but aborigines *do* treat them as kin. The terms reflect shared understandings of social status, and they become basic guides for expected behavior.

Kinship in aboriginal society is not strictly a system of consanguinity and affinity as early anthropologists believed. Kinship terms represent cultural categories, and their specific application varies considerably cross-culturally. For example, in a given system, someone might refer to several women using the same term applied to mother. The term *mother* might then mean "woman of mother's generation who belongs to mother's totemic estate group (clan)." The biological facts of motherhood might be irrelevant in this context. When the biological relationship needs to be designated, a modifier such as *true* or *real* might be attached to the term. Similarly, a man might refer to several women as "wife's mother," yet not be married to any of their daughters. From an aboriginal viewpoint,

what is most important is potential marriageability and relationship to totemic estate groups.

The complexity inherent in kinship terminologies and estate groups is reduced by another system of categories in aboriginal society known as moieties and sections. **Moieties** sort people into two sides by estate groups, or from the viewpoint of a specific individual, they may divide the entire society into "own group" and "other group." In some aboriginal societies, all people, totems, and natural phenomena are assigned to a specific moiety. For example, one-half of a society might be associated with the color black, kangaroos, acacia trees, and goanna lizard Dreaming sites, whereas the other half is white, emus, gum trees, and rainbow serpent Dreaming sites. Membership may be assigned through mother (matrimoiety) or father (patrimoiety) or by generation level.

Moiety groupings help organize ritual activities and can be used to specify roles in initiation ceremonies, marriages, and funerals. For example, one moiety may "own" a particular ritual, while the other moiety actually carries out the ritual. This is a form of **complementary opposition** because the ceremony could not be performed without the cooperation of both groups.

The **section system** simply extends the number of summary social categories from two moieties to four sections and sometimes eight subsections. Because a given society may be crosscut by overlapping moiety systems, sections can significantly simplify social status and help determine whom people can marry (see the boxes entitled "Cross-Cousins and Marriage Sections" and "Kinship and Mother-in-Law Avoidance"). People belong to the same section category in relation to everyone, unlike the case of kinship terms that depend on each person's unique network of kin. Thus, sections serve as convenient identifying labels, especially because aborigines often consider it rude to use personal names in public. Knowing someone's section would allow one to make reasonable inferences about more specific social categories. Furthermore, because sections are recognized intertribally, strangers can quickly fit into a local social network.

Moieties, sections, totems, and kinship terms all work together in a neatly integrated system to guide people in their daily interaction with one another and in their relationships to their countries and spiritual properties. It is a remarkably successful system that significantly reduces the potential for conflict and makes authoritarian rule unnecessary.

Polygyny, Gerontocracy, and Social Equality

In what way is polygyny a central feature of aboriginal society? Do polygynous old men exploit women and young men? How can aboriginal society be considered egalitarian?

Many aspects of aboriginal society are related to the widespread practice of *polygyny* (plural wives). Polygyny automatically creates a scarcity of potential wives, which is partially alleviated by the large age difference between men and women at marriage. Girls may be promised in marriage long before they are born, and men might be well beyond 30 years of age before their first marriage, perhaps to a much older widow, while a 12-year-old girl might marry a 50-year-old man. If one assumes an even sex ratio, then the only way in which some men could have more than one wife would be for women to marry at a younger age than men. The wider the age differential at marriage, the more polygynous marriages can take place. A recent study in Arnhem Land found that nearly one-half of the men over 40 years of age had more than one wife, and one-third had three or more (Shapiro 1981). More than one-third of the men ages 20–40 were still unmarried.

Many anthropologists (Bern 1979, Godelier 1975, Meillassoux 1981) have called aboriginal society a polygynous *gerontocracy.* They argue that the old men occupy the upper "class" and use polygyny and Dreamtime ideology to control women and the labor supply. In this view, women as a class are mystified and subordinated by the secret ritual life of men, and they are oppressed by arranged marriages and polygyny. The young men are deprived of wives and kept subservient by the male initiation system (explained in the next section). In this interpretation, aboriginal society resembles the rank-and-class systems of larger-scale societies and may reflect the perceptions of some of the old men, particularly when they are describing the system to male anthropologists, but it is an inadequate and misleading generalization. Emphasis on male gerontocracy ignores the important role of women both in the ritual system and in domestic life, and it obscures the essentially egalitarian nature of aboriginal society.

Although the marriage age differential facilitates polygyny, the existence of polygyny itself remains to be explained. It may appear to be the direct result of manipulation by self-interested and influential older men, but this is a narrow view. Polygyny also offers important benefits for the entire society. Polygynous households may provide childbearing women with greater security. An older man is more likely than a young man to have a thorough knowledge of the territory and a wider network of kinship connections, which will benefit his entire household, especially in times of resource shortage. Similarly, delaying marriage provides the young men with an opportunity to learn the intricacies of the totemic landscape and the locations of critical waterholes while they remain free of domestic responsibilities.

The way in which aboriginal marriage customs are discussed by anthropologists, as with the terms *wife-givers* and *wife-receivers*, often implies male domination where it is not present. The terms *wife bestowal* and even *mother-in-law bestowal* are sometimes applied to the spouse selection process.

---

nuclear family   The primary family unit of mother, father, and dependent children.

kinship terminology   An ego-centered system of terms that specifies genealogical relationships of consanguinity and affinity in reference to a given individual.

consanguine   A relative by culturally recognized descent from a common ancestor; sometimes called a "blood" relative.

affine   A relative by marriage.

moiety   One part of a two-part social division.

complementary opposition   A structural principle in which pairs of opposites, such as males and females, form a logical larger whole.

section system   A social division into four (sections) or eight (subsections) intermarrying, named groups, which summarize social relationships. Members of each group must marry only members of one other specific group.

polygyny   A form of marriage in which a man may have more than one wife.

gerontocracy   An age hierarchy that is controlled or dominated by the oldest age groups.

Aboriginal marriage practices provide an important key to understanding many aspects of the social system. Marriages, normally arranged by the elders, fit within precisely defined cultural categories, which vary in detail from group to group. Frequently, the ideal mate for a man (Ego in Figure 2.14) would be the daughter of someone he would refer to as "wife's mother" (WM). WM might also be a woman of the father's totemic clan and in the "father's sister" (FZ) category. WM might be married to a man whom ego would place in the "mother's brother" (MB) category. MB could be any man who was a member of the same totemic clan to which ego's actual mother belonged. Of course, several men could be in this category, and they would not need to be the actual brother of ego's actual mother. Also, an appropriate spouse often will be someone in the kinship category of *cross-cousin* (the daughter of mother's brother or father's sister—MBD or FZD) because these women could not belong to ego's descent group.

A person would be expected to marry within a certain range of ego-based kin and in reference to specific clan, moiety, and section categories. One would always marry outside of one's own clan and might even refer to one's own-generation fellow clan members as brother and sister, emphasizing the incestuous nature of clan *endogamy*—marriage within a culturally defined group. Where societywide moieties exist, spouses would be drawn from opposite moieties, and the moiety groups could be called exogamous.

Appropriate marriages also can be described in relation to the section system. With a four-section system, there are four named sections, and an individual can marry into only one specific section (see Figure 2.15). Siblings always belong to the same section but belong to different sections from their parents, reflecting the fact that marriage within parent–child and sibling categories would be incestuous. Sections only indirectly regulate marriage because not all women in the appropriate section will be in the marriageable MBD category. Knowing someone's section identity simply narrows the search.

Claude Lévi-Strauss (1949) described aboriginal society as a series of groups tied together by marriage alliances based on cross-cousin marriage. He used this as a model of the essential structure of many domestic-scale societies throughout the world. In this model, society is divided into wife-giving and wife-receiving localized descent groups, and women are exchanged between them as "gifts." Such a scheme may provide an intellectually satisfying view for outsiders, but it is a distinctly male-centered view and may be far removed from the realities of the system, as either experienced or imagined by aborigines. Women do not simply move as objects between groups at the whim of men. The members of the totemic estates act as a group only on ritual occasions; even then, nonmembers would also play important roles. Marriages do create "alliances," but these are expressed through overlapping ego-based networks.

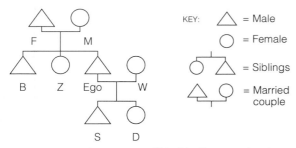

KEY:
△ = Male
○ = Female
○—△ = Siblings
△—○ = Married couple

FIGURE 2.14 *Conventions of kinship diagramming. Anthropologists find it useful to describe all kinship terms using combinations of standard abbreviations based on the following eight primary relationship categories: F = father, M = mother, S = son, D = daughter, B = brother, Z = sister, H = husband, and W = wife. Thus, FB = father's brother, MB = mother's brother, FF = father's father, FBD = father's brother's daughter, MBD = mother's brother's daughter, and so on. Ego, always the reference point in any kinship diagram, is the person who applies the terms shown. These designations are culturally specific social categories; they need not represent actual biological relationships. Even primary terms such as* mother *can be applied to several people who are not one's biological mother.*

Mother-in-law bestowal refers to a ceremony in which a young girl is publicly designated as wife's mother to a young man. The term *bestowal*, rather than the more neutral term *betrothal*, may suggest that a father is "giving away" a daughter, when, in fact, the girl's mother or mother's brother is more likely to make the arrangements. Furthermore, the term suggests that the marriage might never take place. Given a man's age at marriage, he might not even be around when his daughter actually marries, although he might have had some involvement in her prenatal betrothal.

The place of women in aboriginal culture has been interpreted in many different ways. Ethnocentric European travelers mistakenly described these women as degraded and passive servants of the men. The seemingly sharp gender divisions in the activity spheres of aboriginal culture made it difficult for anthropologists to obtain a balanced picture. Early anthropologists were mostly men who necessarily observed male culture and talked to male informants. These male anthropologists were also quite comfortable with the male superiority view because it corresponded closely to their own Victorian biases. Victorian anthropologists considered women in general to be spiritually inferior and even described them as "profane," whereas men were seen as "sacred." More recent fieldwork by female anthropologists working with aboriginal women has broadened the picture by showing that these women have a very active secret ritual life and exercise considerable autonomy in domestic affairs.

Australian anthropologist Diane Bell (1983, 1987) spent many months living in aboriginal communities in northern Australia. As a divorced woman with children, she was treated as an adult widow, given a kinship status, and included in public ceremonies. When her female hosts were satisfied that she would respect their secrecy, she was allowed to participate in women's secret rituals. From this perspective, she discovered that aboriginal women share joint and complementary responsibility with men for maintaining their spiritual heritage. Whereas men's rituals emphasize creative power, women's rituals focus on the nurturing role of women, health, social harmony, and connections with the land.

Women also play a major role in subsistence, may arrange marriages, control family size by means of infanticide, and can influence the choice of conception totems. Some anthropologists still consider aboriginal men "superior" but would grant women the status of "junior partners." However, the notion of rank by sex is probably not a culturally significant issue for aborigines. Throughout the world, foraging peoples that are characterized by high mobility and low population density are the most egalitarian societies known. Equality is reflected in the conspicuous absence of differences in material wealth among individuals, in the availability to each household of the resources needed to secure its existence, and in the absence of permanent political leaders with coercive power over others. However, social equality does not mean that everyone is alike. Obvious differences exist between men and women, between young and old, and between individuals with different personalities and physical characteristics.

Foragers, like the aborigines, who operate with immediate-return systems, provide little basis for people or corporate groups to maintain coercive power over others (Lee 1981, Woodburn 1982).

FIGURE 2.15
Australian aborigine
marriage systems:
(a) cross-cousins,
(b) a simple two-section
moiety system,
(c) a four-section system,
alternate generations.

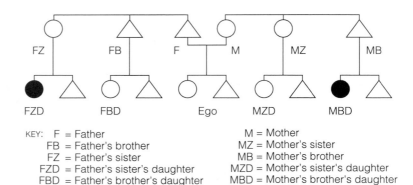

KEY: F = Father
      FB = Father's brother
      FZ = Father's sister
      FZD = Father's sister's daughter
      FBD = Father's brother's daughter

      M = Mother
      MZ = Mother's sister
      MB = Mother's brother
      MZD = Mother's sister's daughter
      MBD = Mother's brother's daughter

(a)

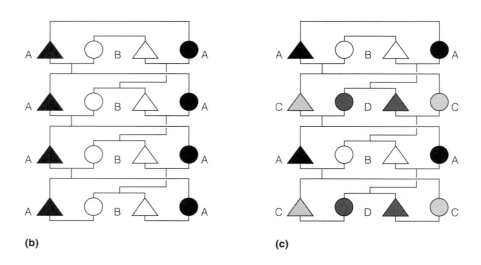

(b)   **(c)**

With immediate-return systems, there is no invest-ment of labor in fixed structures, gardens, or herds that will produce a delayed-return system and that might require long-term storage. Thus, there is no particular advantage in long-term control of a labor force. When basic production is left to nature and food is harvested and consumed on a daily basis, population densities must remain low, and social groups must be highly flexible and mobile to re-spond to natural fluctuations in supply. Reciprocity, especially pooling and sharing of food, levels out individual variation in production and operates among all households in a camp. In immediate-return production systems, every household has freely available the productive tools and natural re-sources that it requires. Mobility reduces the poten-tial for social domination and exploitation by discouraging wealth accumulation and making it easy for people to walk away from adverse interper-sonal situations.

Social equality also is closely related to the "openness" of aboriginal society. Open societies derive their special characteristics from their mo-bility and the absence of permanent houses, tombs,

Kinship and Mother-in-Law Avoidance

One striking form of aboriginal kinship behavior is the extreme avoidance operating between a man and any woman whom he calls wife's mother (WM). In some aboriginal groups, a man cannot look at, remain near, or speak directly to his WM. She is considered to be a source of "shame," and he must avoid any sexual references in her presence and may even use a special form of avoidance speech full of circumlocutions to avoid embarrassment. Early observers thought such customs were absurd, but in cultural context, they make a great deal of sense.

L. R. Hiatt (1984b) points out that in Australia, a man often may live in close proximity to his WM and may provide her with meat as a form of bride-service, even before marrying his WMD. Given the often great age differential at marriage, a man may be nearly the same age as his WM and could find her attractive, while the WM might find a young daughter's husband more attractive than the old man who would be her husband. Meat giving also has sexual implications and takes place between husband and wife. Under these circumstances, extreme avoidance would certainly reduce the possibility of conflict between a man and his wife's father (WF). Avoidance also would prevent the possibility of father–daughter incest because if a man did have an affair with his WM, he could be his own WF.

---

temples, and institutionalized leadership. Domestic life takes place in the open, where people can pay close attention to one another (Wilson 1988). Under these conditions, there are few secrets and few sources of conflict. Furthermore, with weapons always at hand, the use of force is available to everyone and is less likely to become a means for domination.

Outsiders may be struck by the apparent frequency of conflict in aboriginal society, the violence of domestic quarrels, and the charges of infidelity or failure to share. Conflicts of this sort apparently are more common under the crowded conditions of modern settlements. Furthermore, any conflict is a public event in an open society and cannot be hidden behind walls as may be the case in other societies. Victoria Burbank (1994) recorded hundreds of incidents of verbal and physical aggression between individuals during 18 months of research in an aboriginal community in Arnhem Land. Contrary to the way Americans view domestic conflict in their own culture, she found that aboriginal women were not passive victims of male aggression. Women initiated fights nearly as often as men,

sometimes physically assaulting men. Burbank emphasizes that for aborigines, aggression is culturally constructed as an often-legitimate expression of anger. Its openness means that kin may intervene to prevent serious injuries. The cultural support for aboriginal women taking an aggressive stance toward men is a way of balancing the otherwise unequal physical differences between men and women that could be expressed as unequal social power.

The religious life in open societies is primarily concerned with healing, love magic, and natural fertility rather than with witchcraft. Individual souls are recycled and may exist briefly as ghosts, but they are not permanently commemorated in ancestor cults. Groups, even those based on kinship, are not rigidly bounded corporate entities. Both individual friendships and kinship categories define social relationships; they are not exclusively determined by genealogical criteria.

Paradoxically, aboriginal society is at the same time intensely egalitarian and religiously authoritarian (Hiatt 1987). Although aboriginal society is sometimes described as a society without politics because of the absence of formal chiefs, elders do have moral authority, based on the Dreaming, over their juniors, both men and women. Relationships among individuals at different generation levels are hierarchical and may be expressed as a kinship responsibility to "hold" or "look after" or "raise" the junior (Myers 1980). This is considered nurturing and guiding behavior, not domination or exploitation. In aboriginal English, one's elder may be referred to as a "boss" who has control over one's marriage and ritual advancement. Such an elder–junior system extends throughout the society so that everyone but the youngest child would be responsible for a junior, but the context is always specific. No one has generalized power over all others.

An age hierarchy is different from a government bureaucracy because, in the age system, status is always relative, everyone at a given level is equivalent, and everyone moves up. No one is permanently excluded from access to basic resources or political power by membership in a lower social class. As they mature, everyone—men and women alike—move to positions of greater decision-making ability in society.

For aborigines, the ideological foundation of their society is the Dreaming, which defines and is perpetuated by the generational hierarchy. Knowledge of the Dreaming is concentrated in the elders, who are obligated to transmit it to the juniors. Holding and transmitting such knowledge can be considered an exercise of political power, but it is a very special kind of power that cannot be directly compared with the political power in large-scale, nonegalitarian societies.

There often are aboriginal "bigmen" or "men of high renown" who stand out because of their vast ritual knowledge or oratorical skills, but their range of action is limited. They may have considerable influence in the ceremonial life and may be able to manipulate certain social relationships to their advantage with threats of supernatural punishment. However, in the larger society, even such powerful individuals can take little political action without broad popular consensus.

Male Initiation: The Terrible Rite

How have anthropologists explained the painful rituals of circumcision and subincision practiced by aborigines? How do aborigines understand these practices?

The physical ordeals of scarification, nose piercing, bloodletting, tooth evulsion, genital mutilation, and fingernail extraction associated with aboriginal male initiation rituals have been a continuing source of amazement for outsiders and have generated endless speculation about their origins and persistence. These rites occur throughout Australia, but not all groups share the same specific forms. For males, the rituals mark different age grades in social maturity and acquisition of ritual knowledge. Women and girls pass through similar maturation grades but with few physical ordeals.

The obvious functionalist interpretation of these rituals is that they are **rites of passage** publicly marking an individual's change of status. For example, a boy must be circumcised before he can marry. The pain makes the new status more valuable and increases one's pride of membership, thus contributing to social solidarity. The value of body mutilation, especially where little clothing is worn, is that the change in status is permanently visible and unlikely to be faked; genital mutilation is also performed only on males. These rituals are part of the formal instruction in ritual lore and make the ritual more valuable and more memorable. The initiates must accept the discipline of the older men, and they owe respect and gifts of meat to their tutors.

The most dramatic male ordeal is subincision, which follows circumcision and involves slitting the underside of the penis lengthwise to open the urethra. The operation is performed by the initiate's MB or WF, who uses a very sharp stone knife. The initiate must remain passive and show no signs of experiencing pain. After healing, the incision remains open, but infection or reproductive impairment does not normally occur.

Subincision appears to have been a recent invention and was actively spreading from tribe to tribe when Europeans arrived. Young men willingly submit to the ordeal because it admits them to the privileges of manhood in a society in which other tests of strength and courage such as warfare are of little importance. As psychologist S. D. Porteus (1931) explained, "It is the price that must be paid for tribal membership, and all must pay. . . . that the price is high puts an enhanced value on these bonds of tribal union" (280–281).

From the aboriginal viewpoint, subincision requires no special explanation beyond the fact that it originated in the Dreaming. Aborigines may point to the physical resemblance between the subincised penis and the genitals of kangaroos and emus as confirmation of the Dreaming connection (Cawte 1974).

Psychoanalysts have suggested that subincision is a subconscious way for aboriginal men to deal with oedipal fears, castration anxiety, or their supposed envy of female reproductive powers. In opposition to the aboriginal interpretation, the subincision would represent a woman's vagina, not a totemic kangaroo penis. The best support for the psychoanalytic view is that the initiates are symbolically killed in the ritual and reborn as men. However, because men already have a culturally acknowledged role in fertility through totemic increase ceremonies, vagina envy seems unnecessary. A conflicting psychological argument is that boys who grow up too closely associated with their mothers need a painful initiation to affirm their identity as males.

We may never know how rituals such as subincision originated in the first place. But they play an important role in the culture and are best understood as expressions of the overwhelming importance of the Dreaming.

SUMMARY

Australian aborigines demonstrate that a domestic-scale culture can remain egalitarian and in balance with its resource base indefinitely as long as it is not invaded by larger-scale neighbors. For over 50,000 years, gradual adjustments in aboriginal technology occurred as environmental conditions changed, and the ritual system and social organization underwent continuous elaboration; aboriginal culture, however, retains its fundamental character as a domestic-scale system. This is clearly a dynamic, responsive, and highly creative system, but it appears to have changed in such a way that the most fundamental cultural elements remain in place. The Dreaming itself, and all its associated features, seems to be the key element in understanding this remarkable cultural stability.

STUDY QUESTIONS

1. In what sense could the aboriginal subsistence system be considered an affluent economy?

2. Discuss the role of women in aboriginal society. Are they really oppressed and exploited by the old men as some suggest?

3. Demonstrate the connections between religion and society *or* between religion and adaptation to the natural environment in aboriginal Australia.

4. Discuss explanations for the remarkable initiation practices of the aboriginals, distinguishing between how aborigines view these practices and how anthropologists and other outsiders see them.

5. Describe the marriage practices of aborigines.

6. In what sense can aboriginal society be considered egalitarian? What cultural mechanisms contribute to equality?

7. What is the evidence for or against long-term stability in aboriginal culture?

SUGGESTED READING

FLOOD, JOSEPHINE. 1983. *Archaeology of the Dreamtime.* Honolulu: University of Hawaii Press. A comprehensive overview of the prehistory of Australia.

GOULD, RICHARD A. 1980. *Living Archaeology.* Cambridge, Eng.: Cambridge University Press. An engaging work by an archaeologist who studied contemporary aborigines in the Western Desert to help understand the prehistoric remains.

SAHLINS, MARSHALL. 1968. "Notes on the Original Affluent Society." In *Man the Hunter,* edited by Richard B. Lee and Irven DeVore, pp. 85–89. Chicago: Aldine. A short section that compares foraging and market economies.

TONKINSON, ROBERT. 1991. *The Mardudjara Aborigines: Living the Dream in Australia's Desert,* 2nd ed. New York: Holt, Rinehart & Winston. A well-rounded ethnography of aboriginal culture in the Western Desert.

rite of passage A ritual marking culturally significant changes in an individual's life cycle, such as birth, puberty, marriage, old age, and death.

3

Native Amazonians: Villagers of the Rain Forest

Since early in the sixteenth century, European accounts of the native inhabitants of Amazonia have fueled the myth of the "noble savage." The earliest European explorers correctly described the relative social and political equality and the communalism of the rain forest villagers, but they mistakenly equated the prevailing nudity of the natives with the innocence and perfection of the biblical Eden. Native Amazonians were not perfect peoples, but their cultures still fascinate outsiders because they continue to offer a dramatic contrast to life in political-scale states and commercial-scale cultures.

Amazonia is the last large area of the world where autonomous tribal cultures continued to function within regional intertribal worlds. Amazonia also is home to the world's largest tropical rain forest, which is now receiving international attention from environmentalists and humanitarians because of the global implications of deforestation and the related issue of the destruction of traditional cultures. Furthermore, an important and still independent Amazonian people, the Yanomami, are the subject of one of the most widely used ethnographic monographs and are vividly portrayed in several ethnographic films. As sedentary villagers, the native peoples of Amazonia offer a striking contrast to the Australian aborigines and raise further

questions about social equality, political power, balance with resources, and the role of ideological systems in domestic-scale cultures. This chapter focuses on an ethnographic present that assumes political and economic independence of tribal Amazonia. (Chapter 14 examines the problems created by the intrusion of commercial-scale culture.)

LIVING IN THE TROPICAL RAIN FOREST

The Fragile Abundance of the Rain Forest

What physical conditions produce tropical rain forests? How do tropical forests differ from temperate forests? What special challenges does the rain forest present to human settlers?

Amazonia contains one of the world's great ecosystems, combining the largest continuous stand of tropical rain forest with the greatest river system in the world (see Figure 3.1). The Amazon River drains an area of 2.25 million square miles (mi²) (5.87 million square kilometers [km²]) and discharges four times the volume of water carried by the Congo, the next largest river in the world. The

FIGURE 3.1
Map of the Amazonian culture area showing the culture groups discussed. Note that the Amazon basin proper covers only part of the culture area.

rain forest stretches for some 2000 miles (3218 km) east to west across the center of South America. This warm, wet region is an ideal climate for plant growth and serves as a veritable treasury of biological diversity (see Figure 3.2).

Amazonia is a land without winter. In the coolest month, the temperature does not drop below 64°F (18°C), and no month receives less than 2.4 inches (6 centimeters [cm]) of rain. Amazonia is entirely in the tropics, mostly within 10 degrees of the

FIGURE 3.2   *A high waterfall, one of many that can be found in the Guyana highlands and along the Andean foothills, and that feed into the Amazon River.*

equator, so there are 12 hours of daylight every day and the sun's rays strike the region with maximum intensity. Rainfall is abundant throughout the region, usually averaging over 80 inches (203 cm) a year. Daytime high temperatures reach 90°F (32°C), and nighttime lows about 70°F (21°C). This daily range is greater than the seasonal variation in temperature.

The basic biological productivity of tropical rain forest is three to five times that of most temperate forests, and the total biomass (weight of plants and animals) is among the highest of any terrestrial ecosystem. The forest is composed predominantly of woody plants, and small, familiar temperate plants such as violets and grasses are represented here as trees. Rain forest trees are usually straight and tall, their interlocking limbs forming a closed canopy laced with woody vines.

The number of plant and animal species in Amazonia is remarkable. It is not unusual to find twenty to eighty or more species of trees per acre, whereas temperate forests might have only four tree species per acre (Richards 1973). A study from central Amazonia reported some 500 plant species over 4 feet (1.2 m) high in a plot of less than half an acre (Fittkau and Klinge 1973). Amazonian rivers may contain as many as 3000 fish species (Goulding 1980), whereas only 60 species occur in the rivers of western Europe, and only 250 species occur in the Mississippi system. There are probably more species of birds in Amazonia than in any other area of similar size in the world. More than 500 species were found in one 2-mile^2 (5-km^2) area in the Peruvian Amazon, whereas only 440 species are known in the entire eastern half of North America.

The biological wealth of the rain forest hides some curious paradoxes. High productivity does not mean high human carrying capacity because much energy goes to the production of inedible forest litter. Marketable timber seems to be produced at about the same rate as in temperate forests, but there is a heavy output of small branches and leaves. Soil fertility often is very low and quickly depleted. There are few easily harvested carbohydrates in the woody vegetation, and 90 percent of the animal biomass is composed of ants, termites, and other small invertebrates that can eat leaves and wood. Large vertebrates are relatively scarce, and animal protein is difficult for hunters to secure because game often is nocturnal or hidden in the forest canopy. Natural food resources for people are so scarce that some authorities argue that no full-time foraging peoples have been able to live in the rain forest unless they have had access to aquatic resources or been able to obtain garden produce from village farmers (Bailey et al. 1989).

The infertility of Amazonian soils is due to the combination of heavy humidity and warm temperature, which fosters both luxuriant growth and the rapid breakdown of forest litter. The top humus layer of the soil is actually very shallow, and most tree roots are near the surface where they can quickly take in the nutrients liberated by decomposition. Trees recycle litter so efficiently that more nutrients are held in the forest itself than in the soil.

The forest also regulates the water cycle, contributing directly to the daily thundershowers through transpiration and moderating the potential for erosion by cushioning and dispersing the heavy downpours. The forest also sustains the Amazon's wealth of fish, because many species are specialized to feed on fruit on the floor of seasonally flooded forests (Goulding 1980). The scientific community still has a poor understanding of the extreme complexity of the Amazonian ecosystem, but it is apparent that successful long-term human utilization of this region requires maintaining the forest.

The First Amazonians

How long have people lived in the Amazon? What major changes led to the development of tropical rain forest culture based on settled village life and domestication? What environmental factors shaped these changes? Why was domestication such a momentous change?

The physical evidence of teeth, bones, and blood indicates that people reached the New World from Asia by at least 12,000 BP (see Table 3.1). Periods of

TABLE 3.1 *Prehistory of Amazonia, 32,000 BP–AD 1542*

Floodplain Chiefdoms and Autonomous Forest Villagers (AD 1542–2000 BP)

AD 1542	Orellana expedition—European invasion
1150 BP	Incised pottery in central Amazonia
1400	Incised pottery on Orinoco
1800	Polychrome pottery in central Amazonia
2000	Varzea chiefdoms

Spread of Tropical Forest Culture (2000–5000 BP)

2800	Maize on Orinoco
3500	Maize in coastal Brazil
3000–5000	Zoned hachure pottery style, earliest ceramics in South America
4000	Manioc griddles, manioc beer vessels

Sedentism and Domestication (5000–9000 BP)

5000–7000	Domestication of manioc inferred
7000	Maize domesticated in Central America

Foragers and First Settlers (12,000–32,000 BP)

12,000	Earliest widely accepted entry into the New World
17,000	Rock paintings in northeast Brazil
32,000	Rock shelter hearths in northeast Brazil

lowered sea levels during the Ice Age created a land bridge between Asia and America, which facilitated the first settlement of the New World. There is no archaeological record of the occupation of the Amazonian rain forest by mobile foragers, but people may have lived in that region for many thousands of years, without leaving a trace, before becoming settled village farmers. Even if the rain forest itself was not easily exploited by foragers, they might have remained near the rivers. It is also likely that the rain forest was not always as extensive and continuous as it was in AD 1500. Studies of soils, fossil pollen, and the distribution of plants and animals suggest that during the Ice Age, the climate of Amazonia fluctuated between wetter and drier periods. The forest perhaps retreated during the coldest, driest periods, to be temporarily replaced by scrub forest or savanna that would have provided more food resources for foraging peoples. We can only speculate about the living patterns of these early groups, but they must have remained in very small and highly mobile bands, except where abundant coastal or riverine resources permitted larger, more permanent settlement.

Beginning about 9000 BP, a steady intensification of subsistence activities must have occurred in Amazonia, paralleling similar events that occurred throughout the world, including Australia, at the end of the Ice Age in response to global changes in climate, vegetation, and fauna. Rising sea levels reduced productive coastal zones, and many big game animals disappeared. People had to work harder to make a living and expanded their food base to include not only the smaller, more numerous species, such as fish and shellfish, but also a broad range of plant species. These changes meant more careful scheduling of seasonal activities and more work in food acquisition and processing, but they resulted in greater food production per unit of territory and more permanent settlement at greater densities. This process has been called ***subsistence intensification.***

In Amazonia, and worldwide, subsistence intensification marked the transition from mobile foraging to settled village life and plant domestication.

---

subsistence intensification Technological innovations that produce more food from the same land area but often require increased effort.

However, it is important to recall, as noted in Chapter 2, that Australian aborigines apparently managed to remain in balance with their resources during this time without turning to domestication. Anthropologists at first considered domestication to be a remarkable invention or discovery that occurred in very few places. But, in fact, there were many centers of domestication, and domestication was a gradual process, not an instant discovery (see Figure 1.7). It must have been compelled by intractable imbalances between population and resources. Paradoxically, domestication represented a response to the need to increase food production, but it promoted further population growth by reducing the incentives for family planning encouraged by mobile foraging and by making further increases in food production readily achievable. Thus, village farmers were more likely to experience gradual population growth and had to work harder to maintain a balance with natural resources than did mobile foragers. They also were prone to migrate into territories formerly occupied exclusively by foragers.

Richard Adams (1988) points out that domestication was a form of co-evolution in which people, plants, and animals became dependent on one another. Humans and domesticates (plants and animals) formed a single two-sector system that evolved together under human direction. People intensified their subsistence efforts and sacrificed freedom of mobility, but they gained the selective advantage of greater short-term control over their energy sources. The problem was that villagers, living in large sedentary settlements sustained by permanent agriculture, had difficulty restraining the growth of political power. By contrast, mobile foragers could readily abandon oppressive leaders. Thus, domestication ultimately prepared the way for further increases in culture scale. However, the first, and most crucial, cultural change was the loss of domestic control over political power, which resulted in a loss of domestic control over technology.

Domestication requires drastic changes in human activities because, even as plants become dependent on people for their care and reproduction, people become increasingly specialized and dependent on the plants. People made major sacrifices in personal freedom to till their new gardens.

In its earliest stages, domestication is not distinguishable from the careful management of wild resources or the simple transplanting of wild plants to more convenient locations. The transition from dependence on wild to genetically altered, domestic plants, and from mobile foraging to relatively permanent villages, must have occurred over several thousand years. This transition did not occur everywhere, and some village farmers, such as those in Amazonia, never became dependent on domesticated animals.

Archaeologist Donald Lathrap (1977) speculated that early plant domestication in Amazonia resulted from efforts to intensify fishing production, in response to the decline in the amount of game as the forest expanded. Increased use of nets and fish poisons would have encouraged people to selectively cultivate cotton (for nets and lines), bottle gourds (for floats), and poisonous plants in easily tended house gardens near their settlements. Cultivation would have been an advantage because in the tropical forest, most plant species are widely dispersed and might be unavailable in the quantity needed.

The domestication of manioc (genus *Manihot*), the most important food plant in Amazonia, probably took place more than 5000 years ago. Manioc is a woody shrub that grows readily from cuttings, and the tuber can be stored in the ground until needed. Although deficient in protein, manioc is very rich in carbohydrates, is highly productive even in poor soils, and is an ideal complement to the fish and game of Amazonia. It can also be fermented to produce a nutritious, mildly alcoholic drink, which may have been an important incentive for its domestication. Manioc likely was domesticated in Amazonia, rather than spreading there from elsewhere. As a *root crop*, it represents a distinctive cultivation system from maize, the major New World *seed crop* that originated in Mesoamerica and spread to Amazonia.

By at least 2000 BP, the tropical forest cultural pattern of small, autonomous tribal villages—based on shifting cultivation, hunting, and fishing—was established throughout Amazonia. With average population densities of perhaps 0.4 persons per square mile, the total population may have exceeded 1 million people. At least five major language groups—Tupi, Carib, Arawak, Panoan, and

Ge—diversified into some 200 languages (Migliazza 1982). People lived in small, widely separated villages of up to 500 people, sometimes in large communal houses (*malocas*). The bow and arrow was the most common weapon. Dugout canoes provided river transport, while an impressive array of implements of wood, stone, basketry, and pottery were used in food processing. Cotton was used to make hammocks and clothing, while colorful plumes were made into elaborate headdresses and other ornaments. Diverse regional culture patterns, or culture areas, can be distinguished based on variations in material culture and details of social organization and religion, but the broad pattern is the same.

Within the past 2000 years, political-scale cultures developed along the Amazon and Orinoco rivers and the Bolivian lowlands. These groups were politically organized chiefdoms, distinguished archaeologically by distinctive pottery styles, and had dense populations presumably based on maize cultivation in alluvial soils and fishing. They were quickly destroyed by invading Europeans after the first Spanish expedition descended the Amazon in 1542 under the direction of Francisco de Orellana and will not be examined in this chapter. Domestic-scale cultures continued to occupy most of the rain forest and Amazon tributaries.

Rain Forest Gardening and Manioc Processing

What features of shifting cultivation make it well suited to the rain forest environment? What are the costs and benefits of manioc as a staple food crop?

Manioc production, the key to successful human occupation of Amazonia, depends on a specialized system of shifting cultivation that minimally disrupts the forest ecosystem. It is the forest that ultimately maintains soil quality, regulates the local climate, recycles nutrients and water, and sustains fish and game resources. With shifting cultivation, as still practiced by native peoples throughout Amazonia, food is harvested from small, temporary forest clearings containing mixed gardens.

In comparison with the large monocrop farms and plantations that have recently been introduced in Amazonia for commercial purposes, native gardens, or *swiddens*, rely on a diverse mix of crops. The overlapping layers of different plant species minimize erosion and losses to insects and disease while making efficient use of the space. Sweet potato vines and beans quickly cover the ground, then are shaded by maize and manioc, which in turn are shaded by bananas and various fruit trees.

This gardening system is sometimes called **slash and burn** because it is based on an apparently simple technology of cutting the forest, and then burning the dry slash (see Figure 3.3). The burn is usually incomplete, and many trees survive and quickly regrow. Some plants may even be deliberately protected. The burning concentrates nutrients in the ash, thus eliminating the need for additional fertilizer. Unburned logs provide an easy source of wood for cooking fires.

Shifting cultivation requires a great deal of specialized knowledge, which has an elaborate vocabulary. Native Amazonians distinguish several different types of soil and forest, and they take into account the special characteristics of each when selecting a garden site. Because many varieties of manioc require more than 6 months to produce large tubers, manioc must be grown on land that is not seasonally flooded; thus, manioc gardens cannot take advantage of the annually renewed alluvial soils along the major rivers. Gardens typically are about an acre in size. Although they are seldom carefully tended for more than 1 year, they may yield manioc for up to 3 years. New gardens might be made each year, so that at a given time every household has gardens at different stages of production. In this **forest fallow system,** a plot usually would not be replanted for at least 25 years to allow ample time for forest regrowth. Actually, full forest regrowth might require 50–100 years or more, but as long as gardens remain small and widely scattered, a 25-year cycle can adequately protect the forest.

---

slash and burn   A farming technique in which forest is cleared and burned to enrich the soil for planting; a forest fallow system depending on forest regrowth.

forest fallow system   A system of cultivation in which soil nutrients are restored by allowing the forest to regrow.

(b)

(a)

FIGURE 3.3   *Shifting cultivation in Amazonia: (a) an Ashaninka mother and child rest in the shade in a newly cleared swidden; (b) an Ashaninka man plants manioc cuttings.*

Native peoples prefer the forest fallow system to more intensive cultivation for several reasons. Gardens are abandoned in part because rapid forest regrowth makes weeding a burdensome task. In most forest soils, continuous replanting would soon lead to a decline in fertility and yield. Reclearing of old garden sites is avoided because, during the early stages of forest succession, the vegetation is very dense and difficult to clear with hand tools. Village sites themselves may be shifted every few years to reduce conflict or to find better hunting ground.

The productivity of manioc is truly impressive and readily explains its importance in the subsistence system. A single garden belonging to an Ashaninka household in the Peruvian Amazon potentially could produce some 30,000 pounds of manioc in a year. This is more than double the household's consumption requirements and disregards replanting. Such apparent overproduction provides an important security margin. Other researchers found that the nearby Machiguenga peo-

ple obtained more than two-thirds of their food by weight from manioc, which was produced at roughly 10 percent of the labor cost by weight of food produced by hunting, foraging, and fishing (see Table 3.2). The recent use of metal axes has no doubt increased the relative advantage of manioc by making tree felling easier, but even with stone tools, manioc cultivation would have been very attractive. The Machiguenga allocated just over half of their total subsistence effort to gardening, which produced over 90 percent of their total food by weight (Johnson and Behrens 1982). But manioc alone does not provide an adequate diet, so the Machiguenga raise a dozen other important crops and cultivate some eighty named plant varieties for various purposes (Johnson 1983).

Most Amazonians grow a dozen or more varieties of manioc, carefully distinguishing them based on characteristics of tuber and leaf. The Kuikuru on the upper Xingu River in Brazil can name 46 manioc varieties, while the Aguaruna and Huambisa of Peru recognize more than 100 (Boster 1983,

TABLE 3.2   *Machiguenga Subsistence per Household per Year*

	Production (kg)	(%)	Energy Cost (kcal/kg)	Subsistence Effort (%)
Gardening*	6755	93	80	55
Fishing	298	4	740	22
Hunting/ gathering	194	3	1151	22
Total	7247	100	1971	99

SOURCE: Johnson and Behrens (1982).

*Manioc alone = 4887 kg, or 67 percent of total production weight.

Carneiro 1983). Such diversity suggests that long-term selective breeding is taking place.

All manioc tubers contain potentially toxic substances. In "sweet" varieties, they can be eliminated merely by peeling and cooking, but the "bitter" varieties require more elaborate processing. The quality of the starch in bitter manioc is especially suitable for flour, which is made by an elaborate, labor-intensive process of squeezing, sifting, and roasting the grated pulp. The Waiwai of Guyana have developed at least fourteen types of bread and fourteen beverages based on bitter manioc and its by-products (Yde 1965). The flour may be sifted in various ways, baked in bread, toasted, or used in soups and stews. The juice is used directly in soups, and there are several uses for the tapioca starch extracted from the juice (see Figure 3.4).

Manioc may be stored in the ground until it is used, or it can be stored as processed flour or bread as long as it is kept dry. Potentially, it could provide an important *surplus* that could help support a political-scale society, but as will be shown, a variety of other factors—both cultural and ecological—keep this surplus only potential.

Village Limits: Gardens, Protein, or Autonomy?

Do Amazonian villagers tend to maximize population size at the expense of leisure or to maximize leisure at the expense of population size?

It is a striking fact that rain forest villages usually remain small, averaging less than 100 people and seldom exceeding 300 people. These villages are relatively impermanent, as villagers relocate every few years. Anthropologists often have assumed that environmental factors in Amazonia must set upper limits on village size. Unfortunately, posing the problem in such terms may imply that political-scale cultures are somehow more "natural" and desirable than domestic-scale cultures and that the environment is the only limiting factor. A closer look at Amazonia suggests that the rewards of life in domestic-scale society may encourage people to resist pressures for increasing village size and permanence.

The most obvious limiting factors in Amazonia are poor soils and the scarcity of animal protein. At first, theorists viewed Amazonia as a uniform environment that could not support political-scale cultures because it was assumed that infertile forest soils could not support the intensive agricultural systems needed to maintain higher population densities (Meggers 1954). Robert Carneiro (1960) was quick to demonstrate that manioc gardening could produce enough calories to support permanent villages of 500 people, as long as they could get enough animal protein from fish and game (see the box entitled "Carrying-Capacity Calculations").

If garden production does not set the upper limit of village size, then perhaps animal protein is the critical factor. Further research led to the distinction between the *riverine* environments—known as the Varzea, or flood forest zone, in Brazil—and the *interfluvial* environments—the terra firma zone (Lathrap 1970, Meggers 1971). The riverine areas generally have larger, more permanent villages

---

surplus Subsistence production that exceeds the needs of the producer households and that is extracted by political leaders to support nonfood-producing specialists.

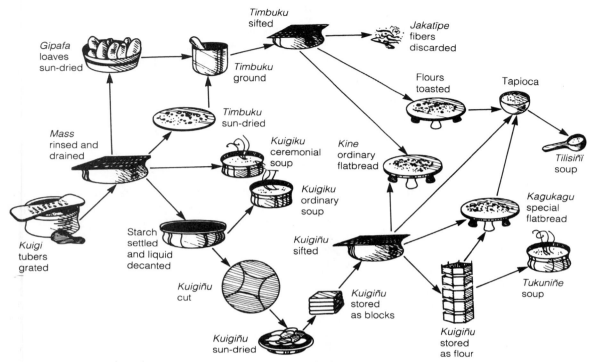

FIGURE 3.4   *Steps in the preparation of manioc among the Kuikuru. (SOURCE: Adapted from Dole 1978.)*

whose occupants exploit the abundant supplies of fish and other aquatic animals such as manatees, turtles, and caiman. Furthermore, fast-growing crops such as maize can be grown on the seasonally exposed alluvial soils and are significantly richer in protein than manioc. Villagers in the terra firma zone must rely more on hunting for their protein, and generally villages are smaller and densities lower. Protein availability does seem to be a critical limiting factor, but many purely cultural factors also must be considered.

Protein is a basic human nutritional requirement; people need an average of about 2 ounces (50 grams [g]) of protein daily with a correct balance of amino acids. In both the riverine and the interfluvial forests of Amazonia, however, this figure usually is exceeded by a healthy margin, especially when plant protein is included (Gross 1975). Apparently, villages could be larger throughout Amazonia if people were willing to either hunt and fish more

intensively, rely more on plant protein, maintain domestic animals, or accept a nutritionally lower standard of living and/or the higher levels of political authority that such changes might require. Cultural factors connected with the advantages of domestic-scale society must encourage people to halt gardening, hunting, and fishing production at levels well below what would be theoretically sustainable. Cultural preferences for large game animals, maximum leisure, and household-level autonomy seem to be more important objectives than supporting the largest possible villages.

Biodiversity and Ethnoecological Knowledge

What do Native Amazonians know about their rain forest environment? How do they differ from commercial-scale cultures in their treatment of biodiversity?

*Carrying-
Capacity
Calculations:
Manioc Starch
Versus Animal
Protein*

———

Robert Carneiro devised a formula to specify the critical variables that determine the maximum size of a village as limited by the productivity of manioc under shifting cultivation (see Figure 3.5). The amount of arable land is set by the maximum distance women choose to carry produce from the garden—usually about 3 miles (5 km), yielding 18,000 acres (7290 hectares). Assuming Carneiro's modest figure of 13,350 acres (5468 hectares) of arable land, gardens cultivated for 3 years, and a 25-year fallow, a village of 2043 people could meet its manioc needs without ever moving. This is more than six times the observed upper limit for Amazonian villages. Extending the fallow to 100 years would reduce the potential size of the village to 561 people, well above average for Amazonia. These figures demonstrate that manioc shortages do not limit village size.

Village size limits based on the productivity of rain forest hunting are more difficult to estimate because we do not have accurate figures for game populations. Figure 3.6 lists some of the variables that must be taken into account, along with a formula for calculating the number of people who theoretically could obtain 2 ounces (50 g) of protein from game per year per 0.4 mile^2 (1 km^2) on a sustained basis. The most critical value is the *biomass* (the total weight of biological organisms living in a given area) of the game, but this can be estimated based on zoological surveys of rain forest mammals (Eisenburg and Thorington 1973, Walsh and Gannon 1967), allowing for cultural definitions of edibility, technology, and sustainability. These calculations predict a potential village size remarkably close to that seen ethnographically. The high estimate for biomass suggests that up to 300 people could supply their protein needs within a 6 mile (10 km) hunting radius of a permanent village.

The hunting efficiency of different groups can vary considerably (see Figure 3.7), but total hunting effort is unlikely to exceed an average of about 4 hours a day. Hunting production might be increased by changing technology and the cultural definition of edibility. The formula in Figure 3.6 includes both large and small species, but hunters might intensify production by trapping rodents. Most hunting is done by single men using a bow and arrow, but the blowgun and poison darts can harvest birds very efficiently. Economies of scale might also be gained if large groups organized game drives or used nets. Nevertheless, there is a clear preference for large game. Native Amazonians never took the obvious step of domesticating animals, even though they made pets of wild pigs and large rodents such as agoutis and pacas, which enjoy manioc.

Dennis Werner (1983) suggests that villagers seek optimal diets while holding their work loads at moderate levels. This means that they must vary their village size or mobility to balance these goals as resource availability varies. It is remarkable that average daily intake of animal protein per person invariably remains within nutritionally acceptable ranges, whether based on fish or game, while total work load averages about 50 hours a week (see Table 3.3).

Basic Formula:

$$P = \frac{[T/(R + Y)]Y}{A}$$

Where P = village population, T = arable land, R = years in forest fallow, Y = years garden cultivated, and A = garden area per person.

If T = 13,350 acres, R = 25 yr, Y = 3 yr, and A = .7 acres, then P = 2043 people.

If R = 100 yr, then P = 561 people.

FIGURE 3.5   *A formula for environmental gardening limits on Amazonian villagers.* (SOURCE: *Carneiro 1960.*)

Basic Formula:

$$P = \frac{BHSCN}{R}$$

Where P = people/km^2, B = mammal biomass, H = mammals hunted, S = sustainable harvest, C = carcass weight, N = protein content, R = protein required per person per year.

If B = 5300 kg/km^2, H = .43, S = .10, C = .50, N = .16, and R = 50 g × 365 days = 18 kg, then P = 1 person/km^2.

Therefore, a 10-km hunting radius covering an area of 314 km^2 supports 314 people.

FIGURE 3.6   *A formula for estimating the number of people who could be supported by hunting within a 6-mile (10-km) radius of a rain forest village.*

One evening, I loaned my portable tape recorder to a small group of Ashaninka who were visiting my camp. They immediately created a word game in which they excitedly passed the microphone back and forth until the tape was filled with a steady stream of Ashaninka words. They were spontaneously reciting a seemingly endless list of animal names, playing with their working knowledge of rain forest biological diversity. The Ashaninka not only knew the names of the animals but understood many details of their natural history and imbued

many species with rich cultural significance. Biological diversity is the foundation on which the Ashaninka way of life depends. They are, in effect, treating biodiversity as natural capital; it is their investment for the future. In contrast, in our commercial-scale culture, we relegate biological diversity to the concern of a handful of specialized

FIGURE 3.7
Hunting-and-fishing time and efficiency for twelve Amazonian societies. (SOURCE: *Hames 1987.*)

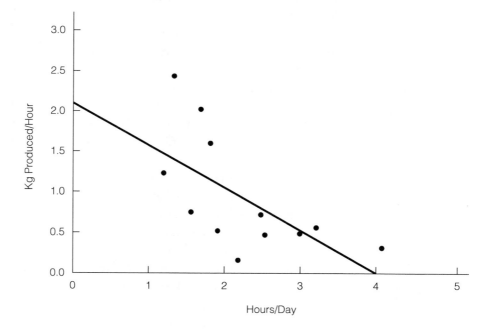

TABLE 3.3   *Average Daily Work Load in Amazonia, in Hours*

	Food Production*		Other Work[†]		Total Work	
	Men	*Women*	*Men*	*Women*	*Men*	*Women*
Machiguenga	5.9	2.2	1.6	4.4	7.5	7.8
Yanomami	2.8	2.4	—	—	—	—
Mekranoti	2.5	2.7	3.2	4.2[‡]	5.7	6.9
Shipibo	1.6	0.3	0.8	3.9	2.4	4.2
Xavante	3.9	3.2	1.1	5.2[‡]	5.0	8.4
Average	3.3	2.2	1.7	4.4	5.2	6.8

SOURCES: Machiguenga (Johnson 1975); Yanomami (Lizot 1977); Mekranoti (Werner 1983); Shipibo (Bergman 1974); Xavante (Flowers 1983).
*Includes gardening, forest clearing, hunting, fishing, and gathering.
[†]Includes food preparation, miscellaneous household maintenance, and manufacturing.
[‡]Includes child care.

ecologists, biologists, and industrial technicians. We also make biodiversity a commercial product to be bought and sold for private gain, and in policy debates we wonder if we can "afford" to maintain natural diversity in parks and nature preserves as a public good where it does not produce direct monetary profits.

I later found that the Ashaninka's knowledge of rain forest animals was matched by their knowledge of useful cultivated plants. I found dozens of named varieties of manioc and bananas in Ashaninka gardens. This genetic diversity was produced without the incentive of commercial markets or tax-supported research grants. People experimented with new varieties and were eager to discuss their different qualities. Most adults in these domestic-scale cultures can readily name 500–1000 plants, whereas few urban Americans are likely to know more than 50–100.

The breadth of indigenous knowledge of Amazonian biodiversity also is indicated by the detailed work of Berkeley anthropologists Brent and Elois Berlin (1983), who collected 875 animal names from the Jivaroan-speaking peoples near the Ecuadorean border. Carneiro (1978a) elicited 187 tree identifications from the Kuikuru in Brazil and obtained 45 named trees in a 0.17-acre (0.07-hectare) tract and 43 plants from a 10-foot² (0.9-m²) tract. He even found that the Kuikuru could identify 45 plant varieties based on the decomposing leaves collected from 1 foot² (0.09 m²) of forest floor. They also had an intimate understanding of the relationships between specific animals and specific plants.

It is hardly surprising that rain forest peoples are interested in biological diversity, because it is the very source of their existence. In 1976–1977, I documented some thirty-five species of forest palm trees that the Shipibo in Peru used to produce roofs, floors, and walls for houses, as well as basketry, bows and arrows, foodstuffs, and cosmetics (Bodley and Benson 1979). In the 1960s, I visited isolated Ashaninka household groups that, with the exception of a few metal pots, knives, and axes, were entirely self-sufficient, drawing all that they needed from the forest and their gardens. They made their own houses, food, medicine, and clothing directly from the raw materials that they personally extracted from their local environment. The important point about Ashaninka self-sufficiency is that they live well. They are well fed, comfortably housed and clothed, healthy, and self-confident. They are not impoverished and do not need to be "developed." Like many indigenous peoples, they secure most of their livelihood directly from the biological diversity that they produce and maintain.

Rain Forest Affluence

How do rain forest peoples spend their time? How do their work loads and leisure time compare with the routines of foragers and commercial-culture peoples?

Amazonian villages clearly demonstrate some striking advantages of life in domestic-scale societies. The villagers have developed an equitably balanced subsistence system. Men do the heavy work of garden clearing in seasonally concentrated bursts of effort, and women carry out the bulk of routine cultivation, harvesting, and food processing. Men, women, and children forage for wild plant food, insects, and small animals. Everyone may join large-scale fishing expeditions, but men provide most of the daily animal protein by hunting and fishing. Meat and fish are pooled and distributed to each household in the village to smooth out the variation in productivity between households. All of these activities are individually directed, and everyone controls the necessary tools. There are no inequalities here.

This production system guarantees that each household can meet its nutritional needs with relatively moderate work loads while maintaining a reasonable labor balance between the sexes. It also provides strong incentives for maintaining low population densities because, as densities increase, work loads quickly accelerate due to game depletion and the increasing distances that women must walk to their gardens. Work loads also would be increased dramatically if people needed to produce food to support the nonfood-producing specialists, who inevitably accompany increases in societal scale. Thus, an incentive to maintain social equality is also the foundation of domestic-scale societies.

Several recent extensive investigations show that subsistence work loads in Amazonia are not significantly different from those reported earlier for Australian aborigines. In both cases, there is abundant leisure time. The figures presented in Table 3.3 indicate that, on average, all food production needs can be met with just 2–3 hours of work a day. Men average about 3 hours and women about 2 hours. Total work loads, including everything that must be done around the house, require only 5–7 hours daily and would be unlikely to exceed 8 hours. This means that if the workday begins at 6 AM, with the equatorial sunrise, one can possibly spend the whole afternoon lounging in a hammock.

These data must be interpreted with caution because they were collected by different researchers who did not always classify activities in the same way. Some researchers did not regard child care as work. There is also the basic problem of the cross-cultural validity of the concept of "work." For example, should hunting, which is often an exciting and enjoyable activity, be considered work? Researchers also used different techniques for recording time expenditures. Roland Bergman (1974), for example, relied on self-reporting by the Shipibo, whereas Allen Johnson (1975) used a system of randomly scheduled spot checks of activities. All of these studies were continued for several months and thus minimized seasonally induced biases. When taken together, they do show a consistent tendency, which is difficult to refute, to limit work loads to immediate household needs.

Johnson (1985) made a useful comparison of the work load of the Machiguenga, which is heavy by Amazonian standards, with the way modern urban French people spend their time (considering women working both in and outside the home). He showed that although both the Machiguenga and the French get about 8 hours of sleep a night, the Machiguenga work about 2 hours less a day than the French to satisfy their basic needs. The Machiguenga have fewer other demands on their time than the French and enjoy 5 hours more of free time a day, which they spend resting and visiting. Data such as these tend to confirm the idea of affluence in domestic-scale societies, lending credibility to the early reports from frustrated colonial plantation owners that Native Amazonians were "lazy" and hated to work. In fact, they do work, but only until their basic needs are satisfied, and their society is structured so that no one works for an overlord.

It would be a mistake to view these systems as underdeveloped technological stages that will inevitably evolve into something better. These are already highly developed systems that elegantly solve the problems posed for them. They would be difficult to improve upon, given their culturally defined objective of equitably meeting the physical needs of small communities.

VILLAGE LIFE IN AMAZONIA
Gender, Ideology, and Politics

What are the general organizational features of Amazonian societies? How do they compare with Australian aboriginal societies?

Local settlements in Amazonia resemble the bands of Australian aborigines in that both are usually

Domestic Residence and Descent Groups in Amazonia

Some anthropologists (especially Murdock 1949) argue that descent organization is determined by the residence pattern followed by newly married couples. This is because residential groupings create alignments of people who may share enough common interests to become cross-generational groups based on descent. Figure 3.8 illustrates the domestic groupings that are created by patrilocality and matrilocality; other possible residence patterns include bilocality and neolocality. Patrilocality and matrilocality create de facto patrilineages and matrilineages, respectively. There are also interesting cases, such as the Mundurucú, in which residence matrilocality occurs with patrilineal descent groups. However, if de facto descent groups are not culturally named or otherwise operationally significant, then the society would best be described as bilateral, or non-unilineal. This is clearly the predominant situation in Amazonia (see Table 3.4).

In Amazonia, the emphasis on manioc gardening seems to encourage matrilocal residence patterns, in which a husband lives with or near his wife's family. This may be because mothers, daughters, and sisters often form cooperative work groups when gardening, processing manioc, or making ceramics. More than 80 percent (31) of a sample of thirty-seven Amazonian societies either are listed as matrilocal (17) or show matrilocality as a temporary or alternative pattern (14) (see Table 3.4). With temporary matrilocality, a newly married couple will remain near the wife's mother until after their first child is born so that the new mother has help from her mother. Given the prevalence of matrilocality, it is interesting that matrilineality is rare in Amazonia. In part, this must be due to the relative infrequency of descent organization. The high frequency of patrilocality may be related to the common pattern of revenge raiding in Amazonia, which makes it advantageous for closely related men to remain close together.

exogamous groups. Amazonian villages, however, may be larger than Australian bands, and they are much more sedentary. Because rain forest villages are frequently moved, individual houses and landholdings are not inherited. Ordinarily, gardens are only owned by those who clear and cultivate them until they are abandoned to the forest. In addition, there are no Australian-like sacred sites, and whereas clan groupings may have ritual functions, clans and formal **descent groups,** especially **unilineal descent groups,** are not common (see the box entitled "Domestic Residence and Descent Groups in Amazonia"). Genealogical reckoning is shallow and even discouraged by frequent taboos on speaking the names of dead ancestors. This prevents ancestor cults or invidious ranking of descent lines. The result is a highly egalitarian social system that encourages easy access to natural resources. Larger social groups often are named after rivers, but territories frequently overlap and generally seem much more flexible than in Australia.

---

descent group A social group based on genealogical connections to a common ancestor.
unilineal descent group Membership based on descent traced through a line of ancestors of one sex to a common ancestor.

FIGURE 3.8
Residence patterns and descent groups.

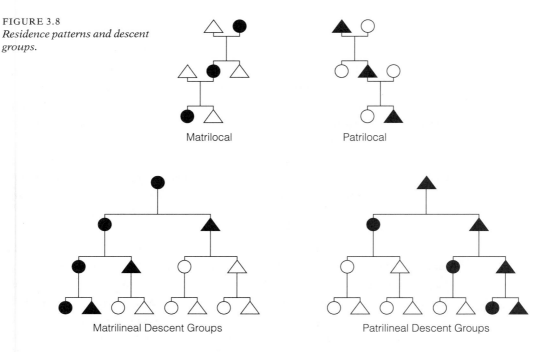

Matrilocal   Patrilocal

Matrilineal Descent Groups   Patrilineal Descent Groups

TABLE 3.4   *Residence and Descent in Amazonia*

| Residence | Descent | | | |
	Patrilineal	Matrilineal	Bilateral	Total
Patrilocality	6	0	10	16
Matrilocality	2	2	13	17
Bilocality/Neolocality	0	0	4	4
Total	8	2	27	37

SOURCE: Murdock (1981).

Because Native Amazonians typically spend most of the year at a permanent residence, they could be considered "domesticated" societies, as opposed to "Paleolithic" mobile foragers, according to the evolutionary theories proposed by Peter Wilson (1988). Life in houses has the potential to change the relationships among people and between people and place. Mobile foragers are likely to be socially more open and less territorial than sedentary villagers, because the privacy of houses creates a potentially closed society in which suspicion can thrive and a social hierarchy can arise. The house itself can be treated metaphorically in the cosmology as the foundation for ancestor cults, tombs, and hierarchical descent groups. However,

except for the chiefdoms along the Amazon itself, most Native Amazonians have not taken this route. The communal *maloca* (large common household) certainly minimizes household privacy, and the requirements of rain forest hunting and shifting horticulture make hierarchical organization distinctly unattractive. Native Amazonians clearly prefer low-density, domestic-scale societies and minimize the disadvantages of domesticated society.

Men and Women
in the Mundurucú Village

How are the relationships between men and women shaped by the physical structure of the

Mundurucú village, their residence patterns, and their cultural construction of gender and descent?

Gender roles are critical for understanding how rain forest cultures work because age and sex, not wealth and class, are the primary differences between people in these domestic-scale cultures. The Mundurucú illustrate how the antagonisms between men and women are played out in the daily life of village cultures in Brazilian Amazonia. In 1953, anthropologists Yolanda and Robert Murphy spent a year with 350 Mundurucú, who lived in small villages of 50–100 people in the savannas and forests of the upper tributaries of the Tapajos River (Murphy and Murphy 1974). As a husband and wife team, the Murphys could observe Mundurucú culture from both sexes' viewpoint.

The world of Mundurucú men and women is sharply divided. Men are primarily hunters, although they also do the heavy work of garden clearing. Women cultivate, harvest, and process bitter manioc. Mundurucú men assume public roles, which is symbolically reflected in the physical structure of the village. Adult males and older boys sleep communally and spend much of their time in the *eksa*, an open-walled men's house, whereas all females and young boys sleep in individual, close-walled domestic houses.

As is common in Australian aboriginal society, the Mundurucú are divided into exogamous moieties. Mundurucú moieties are color-coded "red" and "white," and membership in them is allocated through males. People marry their **cross-cousins,** who belong to opposite moieties. The moieties are subdivided into 38 patrilineal clans (16 red, 22 white), each with an animal founder, like the Australian Dreaming ancestors. Clan loyalties are strong, and ancestral spirits are symbolically present in sacred flutes, which are hidden in the men's house. The potential for intervillage conflict is reduced by the Mundurucú practice of **matrilocality,** which contrasts significantly with the patrilocality of Australian aborigines. Matrilocality requires that a young man, who must marry outside of his clan and moiety, leaves his own village and moves into the men's house in his new wife's village. The result is that village residence crosscuts clan loyalties such that the men of a given village, who

cooperate daily, are unlikely to fight their fellow clansmen in another village.

According to the Murphys, men consider themselves to be the superior sex, and they frequently draw on symbolic support for this position, but the women reject this male understanding. The entire mythic charter for the male view is enshrined in the central myth of the phallic sacred flutes. The myth tells how women originally possessed mysterious flutes that reversed normal gender roles. As long as women had the flutes, they occupied the men's house, relegating the men to the domestic houses to cook, carry water and firewood, and be seduced by aggressive women. The downfall for the women was that the flutes demanded meat, but only men could hunt. Eventually, the men grew impatient with this arrangement and threatened to stop hunting, thereby forcing the women to surrender the flutes and restoring normal gender roles. The myth explains why men are both sexually and publicly dominant. Men are superior to women—not because they are inherently superior, but because gender roles differ and male hunting is culturally the most important gender role. Hunting and meat are thus critical to anthropologists for understanding Amazonian cultures.

The sacred flute myth highlights a central human problem: Men are sexually attracted to women and physically dependent on them, but they fear their power. Patrilineality gives men rights over the status of children, but only women can produce children. The myth suggests that men know their vulnerability and must constantly assert themselves, or women will overcome them. The mythic flutes are symbolically embodied in the 4-foot-long hollow wooden tubes, which are stored and regularly played in the men's house. Sometimes the flutes are paraded about the village, but the women are never supposed to view them; women who do see them can expect to be gang raped. The flutes reinforce the male role in patrilineality and hunting because they contain the spirits of the *patriclan* (a named descent group with membership assigned

---

cross-cousin The son or daughter of one's mother's brother or father's sister, and often considered to be in a marriageable category.
matrilocality Residence near the wife's kin, normally near her parents.

The Basics of Ashaninka Society and Kinship

Ashaninka villages consist of a few individual houses (see Figure 3.9)—often only two and usually located in the same ridgetop clearing—occupied by closely related individual nuclear families (husband, wife, and dependent children). A village, or household group, is either an extended family or households connected by sibling ties (see Figure 3.10). Extended families are formed when married children reside near their parents, either matrilocally or patrilocally. Each household is an independent domestic unit with its own kitchen and garden, but there is daily economic cooperation between the households, and fish and game are pooled. Household groups might be an hour's walk from any neighboring groups, but such groups might periodically socialize over manioc beer and sing and dance. They also might combine to form raiding parties.

The Ashaninka recognize three categories of people: kin, formal trading partners, and strangers who are potential enemies. If friendly interaction is to take place, strangers are immediately placed in a kinship category and treated appropriately. For example, men who wanted to request a favor from me would address me as "brother." When they wanted to show deference, they called me "father-in-law."

The Ashaninka kinship terminological system is of the Iroquois type, which is the most common system throughout Amazonia (see Figure 3.11). (This system is called Iroquois because it was first described by Lewis Henry Morgan [1851] for the Iroquois tribe in New York State.) The distinctive feature of these systems is that one's immediate kin are sorted into just two groups: (1) parents and siblings, or stepparents and stepsiblings, who are close family and thus not marriageable, and (2) those who are potential in-laws and spouses. As is common in Australian

through male lines), and they must be offered meat. The phallic symbolism of the flutes is explicitly recognized by the Mundurucú, and men openly joke about penis power and vaginas with teeth.

Mundurucú male dominance is a male ideology of gender roles. Publicly, women remain in the background, actively maintaining their separation from men, but in practical terms, they have real power in their daily lives. Regardless of male ideology, Mundurucú women are in charge of their **households.** Each house contains a single cooking hearth to serve an **extended family,** with twenty to twenty-five people in four to five **nuclear families.** Senior women direct household activities and control food distribution, handing out both manioc

and meat. Given matrilocality, households are centered predominantly on sisters, mothers, and daughters. Kin ties between women are very strong and are expressed in the question, "How would a girl manage without her mother to help her?" (Murphy and Murphy 1974:122). Thus, women are likely to be supported by close kin in any domestic struggle. Women also gain solidarity by routinely working together in the manioc flour shed. Women carry out all their daily activities in groups, because a woman alone is assumed to be sexually available. Thus, women are effectively united in their resistance to male ideological domination.

The Mundurucú women questioned Yolanda Murphy about her daily home life (Murphy and aboriginal society, one marries someone who can be called a cross-cousin, and the parents of cross-cousins are called in-laws. Parallel cousins, the children of one's father's brother and mother's sister, are often treated as siblings, and their parents are treated like one's own parents.

Figure 3.12 illustrates some of the actual terms that are used in one Ashaninka language. Father is called *Pawa*, and one's father's brother is called *Pawachori*, which might be translated as "step" or "potential" father. *Pawachori* might, in fact, marry one's mother if one's father died (a practice known as the *levirate*), and his spouse would be called *Nanayni*, or mother's sister.

When an Ashaninka man seeks a spouse, he must find someone whom he can call *Ingyayni*, or cross-cousin. The terms need not refer to actual biological relationships. Any unrelated woman might be placed in that category if everyone agrees, but this is an important decision because it has obvious sexual implications. A man's lover will almost certainly be called *Ingyayni*. The parents of someone called *Ingyayni* would be called *Kongki* and *Iyoeni* (in-laws). A husband would show respect for his in-laws and would be expected to work for them during the initial, often matrilocal, phase of his marriage.

Although the Iroquois kin system reflects cross-cousin marriage, it can also be characterized as a sibling-exchange system. Figure 3.13 illustrates how the Ashaninka terms accommodate both forms of marriage. Cross-cousin marriage could be conceptualized as the continuation of sibling exchanges in consecutive generations, and with the Ashaninka, sibling-exchange marriages are more common than marriages of "biological" cross-cousins.

Murphy 1974:219). Recognizing the apparent social isolation of American women, they asked, "But if you don't go with the other women to get water and to bathe, aren't you lonely?" Yolanda responded, "Yes, we are."

Although in Mundurucú society the nuclear family is not the primary domestic unit, marriage and nuclear families perpetuate moieties, clans, and the kinship roles that structure everything. The Ashaninka of the Peruvian Amazon provide an example of the specific kinship categories that are functionally connected to simple moiety systems and cross-cousin marriage, which is so common in domestic-scale cultures (see the box entitled "The Basics of Ashaninka Society and Kinship").

The Headman and Village Politics: Society Against the State

What are the key political features of domestic-scale cultures? What is the role of leaders in village society? What prevents leaders from taking too much power?

household   A social unit that shares domestic activities such as food production, cooking, eating, and sleeping, often under one roof, and is usually based on the nuclear or extended family.

extended family   A joint household based on a parent family and one or more families of its married children.

nuclear family   The primary family unit of mother, father, and dependent children.

FIGURE 3.9
An Ashaninka house. Each household usually occupies a single palm leaf–thatched house constructed of posts and beams, with slats peeled from palm trunks as flooring: (a) construction details; (b) a photograph of the house in the diagram.

(a)

(b)

One of the most distinctive features of domestic-scale cultures is the way they preclude any concentration of political power that might threaten the autonomy of households and communities. Village leaders serve the people and are granted no undue power. Christopher Boehm (1993) calls this distinctive political arrangement in domestic-scale cultures a ***reverse dominance hierarchy.***

The largest local settlement in Amazonia is a politically autonomous unit, even if it contains only twenty-five people. Political autonomy in this context means that villagers can move the village whenever they choose, can kill intruders, and can control their natural resources. Given exogamy,

there cannot be complete village autonomy, because spouses must be drawn from other settlements. A leader, or ***headman,*** often is recognized and may even be called a "chief" by outsiders, but his authority is extremely limited. A headman's responsibilities increase with the size of the village, but normally he is a powerless coordinator who formally announces what everyone had already decided to do, such as clean the village plaza or begin a group fishing expedition. Such a headman cannot force anyone to do anything against his or her will.

As the French ethnologist Pierre Clastres (1977) observed, an Amazon village is essentially a "society against the state" in that it is designed to prevent

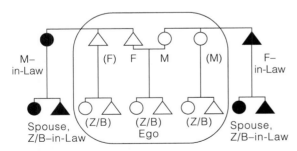

FIGURE 3.10 *Ground plan of an Ashaninka extended-family household group situated on a ridgetop clearing. Curaca is the Quechua (Inca) term for headman. House numbers correspond to the circled household members in the genealogical diagram.*

FIGURE 3.11 *Iroquois kinship system.*

FIGURE 3.12 *Ashaninka kinship terminology.*

FIGURE 3.13 *Sibling-exchange marriages and cross-cousin marriages as reflected in Ashaninka kinship terminology.*

lygyny, which is more likely to be practiced by a headman. But he also frequently works harder than everyone else and is denied real power. Polygyny is not an exclusive prerogative of headmen and should not be construed as payment for the headman's leadership services. Rather, it is a requirement of the job because more wives are needed to help brew the extra manioc beer expected from a generous headman. Society is not paying for his services, but he can hold his position only as long as he serves the community. As Claude Lévi-Strauss (1944) has argued, leadership in this system is its own reward, and only a few would take on the responsibility.

A good headman must be a good public speaker and be especially generous, giving things away on request, but he is not distinguished by special dress

the concentration of political power that would allow anyone to gain control of the economy for his own benefit. In some respects, the headman is held hostage by the community. He is granted a certain degree of privileged status, often indicated by po-

reverse dominance hierarchy System whereby the members of a village or community intentionally limit the power of leaders, keeping them subservient to the group will.

headman A political leader who coordinates group activities and is a village spokesman but who serves only with the consent of the community and has no coercive power.

or insignias of office. The importance of the head-man's oratorial skills further shows that he cannot use coercive violence. He must be verbally persua-sive at settling intravillage conflicts; but if he fails as a peacemaker, the village simply breaks apart. Society's refusal to grant political power to the headman may be the most critical limit on the size of villages in Amazonia. Amazonian political or-ganization relates to game resources because dis-putes over meat distribution increase as villages become larger. When a headman's powers are lim-ited to verbal persuasion, he may be unable to keep the peace in a community larger than 200–300 people.

Janet Siskind (1973) argued that the underlying source of village conflict is the shortage of game and the related competition between village men for access to women, which in the absence of a powerful headman can lead to village fragmenta-tion. Sexual competition is intensified by the rela-tive scarcity of women created by exogamy and by even a limited practice of polygyny. Throughout Amazonia, hunting success is equated with virility, and the successful hunter can support wives and lovers through gifts of meat. Successful hunters also have free time to engage in infidelities while less skilled hunters are still in the forest. This leads to conflict, and villages break apart before poten-tially irreversible game depletion sets in (see Figure 3.14). When game is really abundant, Siskind ar-gued, individual differences in hunting abilities are less prominent, and men may turn to raiding other villages to capture women. Successful raiding would increase village size, raise the pressure on hunters, and result in village fragmentation.

The Spirit World: Sexual Symbols, Shamans, and Forest Demons

How do Amazonian peoples use myths and symbols to shape their understandings of the mysteries of daily life, the relationships be-tween men and women, village politics, and their place in nature?

The Amazonian equivalent of the Australian Dream-time is found in a rich body of myth, beliefs, and ritual practices concerned with the meaning of life

FIGURE 3.14   *A group of Yanomami men armed with bows and arrows embarking on a peccary hunt. White-lipped peccary roam in large herds, and hunters can some-times kill many at one time.*

and subsumed under the anthropological concept of cosmology. Of central concern are the universal human problems of creation, life and death, and the relationship between nature and culture.

In domestic-scale societies, there are no priests, no full-time professionals to formalize the belief system, and nothing codified in writing. And de-spite considerable fluidity in individual beliefs, there are underlying uniformities. E. B. Tylor (1871) called the unifying ideological theme **ani-mism,** a belief in spirits. The spirit world is ani-mated with human, animal, and plant souls and a wide variety of anthropomorphic beings with su-perhuman characteristics. These beings can intrude directly in the affairs of humans and control natural resources. **Shamans** are religious specialists who, by training and self-selection, are particularly adept at communicating with the spirit world—curing illnesses and dealing with misfortune. In the absence of centralized political authority, shamans often play a key role in the politics of village life by using their spirit power to enforce social control. Shamans can also use their supernatural powers to counterbalance the political power of village headmen.

Gertrude Dole (1964) provided a dramatic example of the political role of a Kuikuru shaman on the upper Xingu in central Brazil. When a house unexpectedly burned down, the villagers asked Metse, their most skilled shaman, to use spirit divination to determine the cause. Metse went into a tobacco-smoke-induced trance and announced that three mysterious strangers had started the fire with a flaming arrow, as the villagers suspected. He added that they were attempting to plant a magical lightning rod in his house in order to kill him. Remarkably, within 3 weeks Metse's house was struck by lightning. His house burned, and Metse was injured. Metse went into a trance again and accused another village's shaman of being the sorcerer responsible for the fires and the lightning attack. Shortly thereafter, a spontaneous avenging party ambushed and killed the accused shaman. It turned out that Metse's kinsmen had good reason to fear their victim, because the rival shaman had created resentment among the villagers after breaking an agreement to marry a local woman. People suspected him because the fire broke out in the woman's house as soon as Metse's younger brother had arranged to marry her. Given their belief in Metse's spirit powers, the villagers had little difficulty in accepting his interpretation of events, and they felt fully justified in killing a potentially dangerous sorcerer. The lightning strike enormously enhanced Metse's prestige as a powerful shaman.

The fear of being accused of sorcery is a powerful means of enforcing social control and strengthening kin ties in a small community. Behaving aggressively or doing anything that deviates from social norms can bring one under suspicion of sorcery. The shaman whom Metse accused not only had behaved inappropriately but also had little support in the village. His only brother was considered weak, and he had also left the village. Kin ties are critical because individuals who are surrounded by supportive kin rarely are accused of sorcery.

Amazonian ideology is part of a highly elaborated, logical, and consistent philosophy of life. Spirit beings normally are invisible, but they can assume visible form and freely transform from human to animal form and back again. In Ashaninka thought, any unusual animal or otherwise unexplained event may be attributed to a spirit (Weiss 1975). The Ashaninka recognize and name scores of specific spiritual entities; some include the souls of their own ancestors, which are ordinarily considered harmless. Malevolent spirit beings may appear as blue butterflies, tapirs, jaguars, hairy red humanoid dwarfs, or hoof-footed human impersonators. They are found in the deep forest, and they frequent whirlpools and rocky cliffs. Human contact with or even sight of malevolent spirit beings may cause illness or death.

A central feature in Amazonian cosmology is the theme that women in animal form were originally the possessors of culture, which was wrested from them by men who humanized them and took control of culture in the form of fire and cultivated plants. This theme is present in the Mundurucú myth of the sacred flutes and in related rituals. The entire cosmology is permeated by sexual antagonism; it is primarily a male construction, relegating women to a negative role, as in their symbolic association with sickness and death. The principal actors in the **myths** and their spirit representatives in the forest and rivers invariably are oversexed demons seeking to seduce people, especially vulnerable women.

Amazonian myths consistently focus on the cosmic issues of reproduction and fertility, the

---

animism A belief in spirits that occupy plants, animals, and people. Spirits are supernatural and normally invisible but may transform into different forms. Animism is considered by cultural evolutionists to be the simplest and earliest form of religion.

shaman A part-time religious specialist with special skills for dealing with the spirit world; may help his community by healing, by divination, and by directing supernatural powers against enemies.

myth A narrative that recounts the activities of supernatural beings. Often acted out in ritual, myths encapsulate a culture's cosmology and cosmogony and provide justification for culturally prescribed behavior.

An Anaconda Myth

The following myth was recounted to archaeologist Peter Roe by my Shipibo assistant Manuel Rengifo in 1971. It shows that the anaconda can be a source of noxious pests and illustrates how spirit beings take on human form and can influence hunter success.

One day a man who was a very bad hunter set out once more to pursue the game of the forest with his blowgun. He had had no luck, as usual, until he approached the shores of a lake. There he noticed a man wearing a decorated cushma *[woven cotton robe]. The man greeted him and asked him if he would like to accompany him so that the strange man could show the hunter his "real* cushma*." The hunter agreed, and they set off, only to finally encounter a huge coiled "Mother of All Boas," the anaconda. This, the man informed the hunter, was his real* cushma*. The hunter was very frightened, but the man reassured him and said that he would show him how to be a good hunter. The anaconda man first blew through his blowgun but out came only a horde of stinging, poisonous animals like mosquitos, black biting flies, stingrays, scorpions, and spiders. When the stranger blew again, hosts of deadly vipers as well as all the other evil snakes of the jungle poured forth from the tip of his blowgun. He then handed his blowgun to the hunter, whom he instructed to do as he had done. The hunter blew through the instrument and immediately killed a monkey. From that day on the hunter, thanks to his friendship with the anaconda man, always enjoyed success as a great hunter. (Roe 1982:52)*

relationship between the sexes, the origin of culture, and illness and death. The dominant characters are drawn from especially powerful **natural symbols** found in the rain forest, such as the anaconda, jaguar, tapir, caiman, and harpy eagle (see the box entitled "An Anaconda Myth"). To introduce novelty, Amazonian storytellers might explore the classic themes using a complex series of character transformations based on logical chains of association that may depend on specific knowledge of the animal in question. For example, the anaconda, caiman, tapir, king vulture, and frog may all be associated as feminine symbols. Hollow bee hives may replace gourds as a feminine symbol, while the giant anteater may replace the anaconda as a masculine symbol because he introduces a long, phallic tongue into the hive (see the box entitled "Mythic Jaguars and Anacondas").

Roe relates this sexual antagonism in the cosmology to the striking gender division in Amazonian society, which often physically separates men and women, as demonstrated by the Mundurucú. The vivid sexual imagery also can be attributed to the fact that sex is one of the only activities that men and women engage in together and thus is a major preoccupation. Furthermore, men seem to be jealous of women's role in reproduction, and in the myths masculine characters sometimes assume important creative roles. This jealousy is reflected in the special vulnerability of women to assaults by demons when their biological role is especially evident at puberty, menstruation, and pregnancy. During these times, women may be secluded and may observe specific food taboos.

Gerardo Reichel-Dolmatoff (1971, 1976), who analyzed the cosmology of the Tukano of the Colombian Amazon, has called attention to the similarity between Tukano cosmology and basic ecological principles. He notes that the Tukano believe in a circuit of solar sexual energy that fertilizes the earth and flows through both people and animals. They assume that a balance must be maintained between a finite supply of fish and game and the human population that depends on them. People threaten that balance through overhunting and through uncontrolled sexual behavior, which leads to overpopulation. Sexual repression through observation of the rules of exogamy and basic restraint helps maintain the energy cycle. The game animals are protected by a spirit being, the Keeper of the Game, who is identified with the jaguar in Roe's model but who can exist in many forms. The Keeper of the Game regulates the supply of animals and may release them to be hunted at the request of the shaman who communicates with him while in a hallucinogenic, drug-induced trance or with the aid of tobacco smoke. This explains the obsessive concern of the Keeper of the Game with the sex life of humans. He may withhold game or send sickness if he feels that people are being irresponsible. Hunting itself is replete with sexual imagery: It is literally seen as making love to the animals and, in preparation for hunting, people must practice sexual abstinence and observe other specific requirements.

There is no doubt a connection between the belief systems of Native Amazonians, as seen in their cosmologies, and sexual behavior, food taboos, and hunting patterns—all of which can have important adaptive significance. Examining dietary restrictions in sixty-nine Amazonian societies, David McDonald (1977) has shown, for example, that the strongest food taboos tend to be applied to larger animals, which would be more vulnerable to overhunting (see Table 3.7). Evidence such as this and Reichel-Dolmatoff's ecological argument shows the mutual compatibility of structuralist and materialist interpretations. Both interpretations lend meaning and understanding to the otherwise bewildering complexity of religious belief and practice in domestic-scale societies, but neither interpretation is completely satisfactory in itself.

WAR IN THE TRIBAL ZONE

Understanding the Yanomami

How does intergroup conflict in domestic-scale cultures differ from wars waged by political- and commercial-scale cultures? Are domestic-scale cultures more likely to be peaceful or warlike? What are the causes of war in domestic-scale cultures?

Domestic-scale cultures are characterized by chronic intervillage conflict because they have no overall political authority to enforce peace. Of course, centralized political authorities are also prone to wage war in their own interests and do not always guarantee peace. Certainly, conflict occurs between autonomous villages, and whenever groups of men fight one another, it can be called "war." However, wars waged by states are both qualitatively and quantitatively different. States have complex, authoritarian military command hierarchies. They mobilize vast armies and wage extended campaigns for political conquest. In Amazonia, intervillage conflict is carried out for personal reasons—to avenge previous wrongs, to prevent future attacks, to capture wives, to gain individual prestige, and to obtain material benefits. The objective is not political conquest; domestic-scale conflict is better characterized as raiding and/or *feuding*.

In the absence of any legal authority such as a police force, people must resort to self-help in the event of serious trouble. A single homicide can set off a chain of revenge killings, which can go on for years because there are few mechanisms for making peace. This is a situation of political anarchy in the sense of an absence of formal government, but it does not mean that total chaos reigns. There is great variability in the frequency and intensity of such conflict, but normally the loss of life is not great. Exogamy works to reduce the potential for conflict by creating in-law/kinship relationships between people in different villages. Formal trading partnerships and feasting can prepare the way for marriage ties. Everyday objects such as arrows may be traded on the basis of *deferred exchanges* in which the initial gift giving will not be reciprocated for several months or even years. In this way, a continuing relationship is maintained, and there is always an excuse for further visits.

natural symbols Inherent qualities of specific plants and animals used as signs or metaphors for issues that concern people.

feuding Chronic intergroup conflict that exists between communities in the absence of centralized political authority. It may involve a cycle of revenge raids and killing that is difficult to break.

deferred exchange A form of trade in which gift giving is reciprocated with a return gift at a later time, thus providing an excuse for maintaining contacts and establishing alliances between potentially hostile groups.

Mythic Jaguars and Anacondas: A Structuralist View

French anthropologist Claude Lévi-Strauss has demonstrated that many South American myths are concerned with the opposition between nature and culture (1969, 1973, 1978). Lévi-Strauss assumes that myths function to help people deal with life's basic contradictions by publicly restating them in different ways. He derives the meaning of myths from the structural relationships and symbolic oppositions between major elements of myths, as illustrated in his famous reduction of the Oedipus myth to an algebraic formula (see Figure 3.15). He views the Oedipus myth as an encoded restatement of the logical dilemma in the fact that the first people must have had a single origin, implying original incest, which is a universal taboo. The contradiction is resolved through the story because it is shown to be part of a larger whole, with the opposed parts belonging to each other.

Peter Roe (1982) takes the structuralist approach further by analyzing the universal meanings of the natural symbols that are the key actors in Amazonian myths. Roe sifted through hundreds of myths to construct a simplified descriptive model, a "metacosmology," as a way to understand the diverse beliefs of different cultural groups throughout Amazonia (see Figure 3.16). His model is abstract and not necessarily applicable to any particular group. It codifies what is otherwise an inherently dynamic and fluid system, and many of the relationships shown would not be consciously recognized by individual believers.

Roe employs the logical structures and the algebraic formulas of Lévi-Strauss (see Tables 3.5 and 3.6), but he assumes that people pick particular natural symbols, such as the jaguar and the sun, as characters in their myths because they are drawing analogies between the symbols and specific human concerns. Particular features of natural symbols make them obvious signs or metaphors for something

---

Whatever its extent, even the possibility that such conflict might occur has consequences for the pattern of life in Amazonia. For example, villages may be located on easily defended ridgetops, or they may be encircled by stout log palisades. There may also be pressures to maintain larger villages for defense. Where raiding is especially common, extensive "no-man's lands" may develop between hostile groups and can serve as de facto game reserves to replenish adjacent hunting territories.

Amazonia has been a fertile area for anthropological theorists interested in domestic-scale warfare. Because extensive tribal areas have remained beyond effective government control and various

native groups have maintained their political autonomy, anthropologists have been able to collect fresh material on conflict. The Yanomami (also called Yanomamo and Yanoama) of the Orinoco headwaters along the Brazil–Venezuela frontier have been a major focus for anthropological research on domestic-scale warfare, beginning with the work of Napoleon Chagnon in 1964. With their vigorous culture and thousands of people living in hundreds of autonomous villages, the Yanomami provide textbook examples of endemic tribal warfare, explained as either an adaptive response to environmental constraints by the cultural materialist perspective (Harris 1974, 1984) or in socioelse. For example, an anaconda may represent a male figure, while a hollow gourd may represent a womb.

Roe's basic model depicts a three-tiered cosmos of earth, celestial world, and underworld, centered on the communal house, and joined together by a world tree rooted in the underworld (see Figure 3.16). Some Amazonian groups recognize more than three layers to the cosmos, but three is the minimum needed to explain the daily cycle of sun and moon. The house is surrounded by a cleared plaza that represents culture in opposition to the surrounding forest, which is savage nature inhabited by demons. The underworld is a source of death and disease and has many feminine associations, whereas the celestial world is dominated by male symbols. The underworld is represented in the night sky as the Milky Way, which is also associated with the rainbow and the multicolored anaconda.

The dominant symbol in the cosmology is the world tree represented by the kapok or silk cotton tree (Ceiba) and its relatives. This tree has predominantly feminine associations because it is soft, hollow, and filled with water. It is considered to be a source of life and culture and may appear in myths in varied form, sometimes as a dragon tree, a fish woman, a tree with fish and frogs inside, and so on.

Two primary opposing associations center on the dragon and the jaguar. The dragon, usually represented by the caiman, is a sinister underworld being. The jaguar has both male and female associations and is an ambiguous figure, mediating between oppositions. The most striking natural features of real jaguars are that they are active day and night, they are at home in the water and on land—in trees and on the ground—and they are dangerous to humans. It is not surprising, then, that powerful shamans may transform themselves into jaguars.

biological terms as an aspect of tribal politics that enhances the reproductive success of individual warriors (Chagnon 1979, 1983, 1988). This difference in perspective influences our understanding of many key features of domestic-scale village cultures.

The Fierce People:
Reproductive Striving or Protein Scarcity?

Does Yanomami warfare confer selective advantage to an individual? How might Yanomami warfare be an adaptation to resource scarcity?

Chagnon entitled early editions of his text *Yano-mamo: The Fierce People*, declaring in his first edition that "that is the most accurate single phrase that describes them" (1968a:1). He suggested that the entire Yanomami culture fosters violent behavior, and he found that the recent history of the villages he studied consisted of a succession of raids and counterraids. According to Chagnon, the ideal Yanomami man is "sly, aggressive, and intimidating" (1968a:9). Wife beating is common, and men goad one another into contests marked by escalating levels of violence—from chest pounding, to side slapping, to club or machete fights; up to 30 percent of adult men die violently (1988). Women expect to

FIGURE 3.15
Lévi-Strauss' structural interpretation of the Oedipus myth.

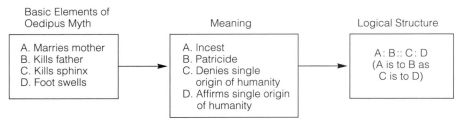

Basic Elements of
Oedipus Myth

A. Marries mother
B. Kills father
C. Kills sphinx
D. Foot swells

Meaning

A. Incest
B. Patricide
C. Denies single
   origin of humanity
D. Affirms single origin
   of humanity

Logical Structure

A : B :: C : D
(A is to B as
C is to D)

Incest is to patricide as denying the single origin of humanity
is to affirming it; they are both logical opposites.

FIGURE 3.16
Schematic rendering of the Roe (1982) model of Amazonian metacosmology.

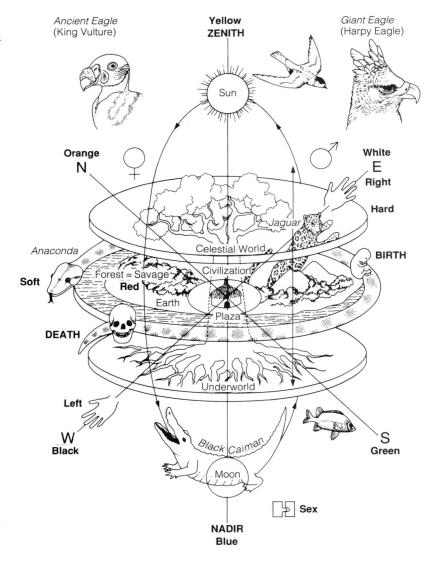

TABLE 3.5   *Male–Female Oppositions in Amazonian Cosmology*

Male	Female
Hard	Soft
Virtue	Corruption
Order	Chaos
Aggressiveness	Passivity
Life	Death
Marriage rules	Incest, promiscuity
Culture	Nature
Right hand	Left hand
Red, yellow	Blue, green
White	Black
Sun	Moon
Closed	Open
Land	Water
Dry	Wet

SOURCES: Riviere (1969) and Roe (1982).

be mistreated and live in constant fear of abduction (1983). The general editors of the series in which the first edition appeared noted in their foreword that the Yanomami reversed the conventional meanings of "good" and "desirable" by condoning "brutal, cruel, and treacherous behavior."

This is certainly not a flattering picture, and it has been severely criticized, but Chagnon has defended his basic characterization of Yanomami culture and the scientific merit of his emphasis on Yanomami violence. In later editions of his text (1977, 1983), he has attempted to "balance the image of fierceness" by stressing the basic humanity of the Yanomami, and in 1992 he abandoned the subtitle *The Fierce People*. Initially, Chagnon (1968b) explained Yanomami "fierceness" as a cultural com-

plex that was an expression of village autonomy. He found that wife stealing, and not a struggle for territory or material resources, was the proximate cause of conflict. The Yanomami, by their own admission, were fighting over women, and this was aggravated by an apparent scarcity of women, which Chagnon attributed to polygyny and selective female infanticide.

Chagnon's later interpretations (1979, 1983, 1988) are based on sociobiological theory and stress the value of violent, and even homicidal, behavior to Yanomami men. Yanomami war is thus ultimately caused by the "reproductive strivings" of Yanomami men. Chagnon argues that gaining a reputation for fierceness by swift retaliation against aggressors makes a Yanomami man a more attractive mate and makes it easier for him to prevent others from stealing his wives. Thus, his individual ***inclusive fitness,*** or the proportion of his genetic material that will be contributed to succeeding generations, is increased. To support this contention, Chagnon presents figures showing that men who are culturally designated as "killers" have more wives and children than those who do not. Sociobiological theory predicts that competitive behavior will be genetically selected for when the genetic benefits to individuals are greater than the costs. Therefore, Yanomami men are simply following the genetically favored goals of their culture,

---

inclusive fitness   A biological concept referring to the degree to which individuals are successful in passing on a higher proportion of their genes to succeeding generations.

TABLE 3.6   *Structural Equations and Associations in Amazonian Cosmology*

Chains of Association	Structural Equations
Sun = bird = jaguar	Sun : moon :: life : death
Moon = fish = caiman (dragon)	Up : good things :: down : bad things
Yellow jaguar = master of animals	Wasps : dragon :: birds : yellow jaguar
Black jaguar = master of fish	
Master of fish = dolphin = forest ogre = dragon	
World tree = dragon tree = fish woman	
Rainbow = Milky Way = anaconda	
Woman = poison = death	
Menstrual blood = fish poison = death = night	

SOURCE: Roe (1982).

TABLE 3.7   *Food Taboos and Animal Size**

| Taboos | Animal Size | | Total |
	Large[†]	Small	
Strong[‡]	20	13	33
Weak	10	26	36
Total	30	39	69

SOURCE: McDonald (1977).

*Food taboos practiced by eleven Amazonian groups, representing sixty-nine different cases in which a specific cultural group restricted their food use of a particular game animal. Each case is sorted by size of animal and strength of restriction (or taboo).

[†]Large animals = 35 lb (16 kg) and over.

[‡]Strong taboos = 10 percent or greater reduction in potential demand based on length of the restriction and segment of the population to which it applies.

although they may not be consciously attempting to improve their inclusive fitness.

R. Brian Ferguson (1995) has challenged Chagnon's data and his conclusions. Ferguson notes that Chagnon's figures are skewed toward counting older men as the fiercest. But these men, because they are older, are also likely to have more children and to practice polygyny. Ferguson observes further that Chagnon did not include the many fierce men who died violently and who may have left few offspring. Fierceness might prove to be reproductively disadvantageous.

Critics of Chagnon's interpretations have also attacked the applicability of sociobiology to culture and have presented alternative historical and ecological explanations for Yanomami violence. The weakest link in the sociobiological interpretation is that it is difficult to demonstrate a specific genetic basis for any complex cultural behavior such as revenge killing. Genes determine only the broadest parameters of human behavior. Culture can vary and change independently of human genetics. Furthermore, abundant evidence indicates that culturally defined kinship categories and cultural definitions of parentage are only marginally concerned with biology (Sahlins 1976c).

Fierceness is only one aspect of Yanomami culture (see Figure 3.17). Many Yanomami groups appear to be peaceful. Other observers have presented ethnographic portrayals of the Yanomami that are so strikingly different that they are powerful reminders that anthropological writing is not pure observation or pure science (Ramos 1987). For

example, Jacques Lizot (1985) focuses on the romantic adventures that fill the daily life of the Yanomami, and Bruce Albert (1985) explores their intellectual life, symbolic systems, and related beliefs about illness.

The most vocal foe of Chagnon's genetic interpretations of Yanomami warfare has been cultural materialist Marvin Harris (1971b), who considers war in domestic-scale societies to be a cultural adaptation that functions to balance population and resources. Harris' basic argument is that the high standard of living of domestic-scale societies depends on female infanticide, warfare, and a ***male supremacy complex.*** Harris originally thought that warfare in domestic-scale societies regulated population directly through war deaths and dispersal of members of defeated groups. Later (Harris 1974), he incorporated the suggestions of William Divale that a tradition of warfare encourages people to selectively raise boys to become warriors while systematically neglecting and even killing girls. This practice, in turn, increases hostilities by unbalancing the sex ratio and making wives scarce, but it has the adaptive advantage of limiting population growth more directly than by killing males. Drawing on cross-cultural survey data correlating unbalanced sex ratios with warfare, Divale and Harris (1976) argued that ***selective female infanticide*** and war are related to a series of "male supremacy" traits in domestic-scale societies, including patrilocality, polygyny, inequitable sexual division of labor, male domination of headmanship and shamanism, and ritual subordination of women.

Referring specifically to the Yanomami, Harris suggested that they had already exceeded the carrying capacity of the forest and were suffering from protein deficiencies. Yanomami women would recognize that it was in their best interests to kill their newborn daughters because only boys would grow up to be hunters and ultimately provide more meat to eat. But as further data on actual rates of protein consumption began to confirm that deficiencies were, in fact, rare among any Amazonian groups, including the Yanomami (Gross 1975, Lizot 1977), Harris revised his theory. He replaced the carrying-capacity argument with the view that ***diminishing returns*** in protein production was the critical mechanism to call up female infanticide and warfare (Harris 1984). (See Figure 3.18 for a schematic

(a)   (b)

FIGURE 3.17 *Yanomami daily life: (a) people
resting inside the communal* shabono *and (b)
women grooming.*

interpretation of the various explanations of Yanomami feuding.)

Harris' theory suffers from the deficiencies of
most functionalist arguments. That is, the functions identified for warfare may be perfectly reasonable, but it is difficult to prove that they actually
work in the way proposed. The theory also does not
explain why warfare was selected for when other
traits might "function" equally well, nor does it explain the widespread variation in homicide rates,
even in Amazonia. The Yanomami do appear to be
an extreme case. It is also important to note that
diminishing returns, conflict, and village fissioning
(splitting) are not necessarily equated with violence
and warfare. Villages can split with hard feelings
but no loss of life.

One can accept Harris' general argument, acknowledging many of the potential functions of

hostilities, while questioning the specifics. For example, selective female infanticide may not be the
principal means of population regulation, and
warfare may not always occur at high rates. What
is significant is that the threat of conflict always

---

male supremacy complex A functionally interrelated
series of presumably male-centered traits, including patrilocality, polygyny, inequitable sexual division of labor,
male domination of headmanship and shamanism, and
ritual subordination of women.

selective female infanticide According to cultural materialist theory, a cultural pattern in which infant girls are
selectively killed or neglected in favor of boys who will
become hunters and warriors.

diminishing returns A decline in output for each increase in effort that accompanies an attempt to increase
total production beyond a certain point. Overhunting often produces diminishing returns.

FIGURE 3.18
Interpretations of Yanomami feuding: (a) as an adaptation to the cultural environment (Chagnon 1968b); (b) as an improved inclusive fitness (Chagnon 1979, 1988); (c) as an expression of cultural materialism (Harris 1984).

(a)

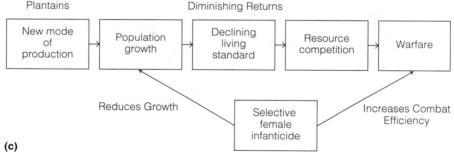

(b)

(c)

exists, and the threat itself, rather than its realization, can contribute to the environmental regulating functions attributed to warfare. This argument closely parallels Harris' own argument that actual protein deficiency need not occur, as long as there are diminishing returns from hunting and the implied threat of a shortfall.

Yanomami History: Commercial Culture, Inequality, and Conflict

How might Yanomami warfare be related to historical pressures from commercial cultures?

How does this highlight the contrasts between domestic- and commercial-scale cultures?

Reproductive striving and protein scarcity are not the only ways to understand Yanomami conflict. Historical factors may be far more decisive. Both Chagnon and Harris explain Yanomami warfare as a purely indigenous cultural pattern. Chagnon is emphatic on this point, stating that it is remarkable that the Yanomami "retain their native patterns of warfare and political integrity without interference from the outside world" (1992:1). But Ferguson (1995) rejects this "pristine war" view of the Yanomami and makes a convincing case that their high rate of violence is caused by the introduction of exotic manufactured goods, especially steel axes and machetes, and the related disruptions of commercial culture. Ferguson and Neil Whitehead (1992) designate regions such as the Yanomami homeland as tribal zones. In these tribal zones, unregulated contacts between the commercial culture and autonomous domestic-scale cultures dramatically increase violence.

The high Yanomami rate of violent death has no documented parallels in Amazonia and stands out as an extreme case, although a certain level of violence is to be expected in domestic-scale societies that reject political authority. Several historical factors may have amplified Yanomami violence. For example, some Yanomami areas appear to have been experiencing very rapid population growth due to the recent introduction of bananas and plantains, both highly productive Old World food crops, and steel tools, which suddenly elevated their gardening productivity. This might have resulted in dramatic increases in village size and sedentism, placing unprecedented stresses on both the sociopolitical system and game resources (Colchester 1984).

In his detailed historical analysis, Ferguson shows that the Yanomami have been subjected to slave raiding and other forms of direct and indirect intrusion from the commercial culture for at least 250 years. He argues that the most politically destabilizing factor was the introduction of steel tools. The Yanomami greatly desired axes and machetes because they made their daily activities so much easier. Ferguson shows that warfare increased as different groups altered their marriage patterns, trading networks, and political alliances in order to improve their access to manufactured goods. The simultaneous introduction of axes, machetes, and, more recently, shotguns made all conflicts more violent and provided further motives for raiding. Ferguson's most convincing argument is that Yanomami warfare declines when such trade goods are either unavailable or equitably distributed. The problem thus is not the tools themselves, but the way they are acquired and distributed. Imported manufactured goods are replacing the tools that households could produce directly for their own use. Because economic equality is such a fundamental principle of domestic-scale culture, with everyone allowed the same access to the means of production, it is not surprising that sudden inequality in a key economic resource can be devastating. The Yanomami are experiencing in microcosm the material inequality, relative deprivation, insatiable demand, and inherent conflict of the commercial culture.

Europeans began to have a more direct impact in Yanomami territory after about 1950, and this could also have elevated Yanomami violence. The spread of epidemic diseases such as influenza and measles into Yanomami territory has caused mortality rates to skyrocket. Chagnon's (1974) own figures show that approximately 60 percent of all male deaths, including those attributed to sorcery, were due to illness. Because the Yanomami attribute all deaths to malevolent human intention and are obligated to seek revenge, any increase in mortality likely would be accompanied by an increase in revenge killings. Clearly, there are important historical factors associated with the violence in Amazonian societies (Davis 1976, Ross 1984).

Unfortunately for the Yanomami, outside intrusion and violence have increased since the 1960s, as miners, missionaries, and anthropologists have entered Yanomami territory in greater numbers. In many areas, local Yanomami groups are threatened with extermination. In one widely publicized incident in 1993, Brazilian gold miners killed sixteen Yanomami and destroyed their village. International cooperation is needed to stop illegal interventions and to distribute crucial economic resources to the Yanomami without aggravating internal conflict.

Mundurucú Headhunting and Resource Competition

How can the "cultural fitness" of Mundurucú headhunting be explained from a biocultural evolutionary perspective?

William Durham's (1991) analysis of the persistence of Mundurucú warfare provides a biocultural evolutionary perspective on Yanomami violence, demonstrating the utility of diverse approaches. From the time they were first encountered by Europeans in the 1760s until well into the twentieth century, the Mundurucú were feared throughout the

FIGURE 3.19   *Mundurucú trophy head.*

central Brazilian Amazon because they conducted long-distance raids against neighboring tribes to take heads and capture children. Robert Murphy (1957, 1960) originally considered Mundurucú headhunting to be a "safety valve" that diffused potential aggression among unrelated men living in the same village. However, such a functionalist explanation is hard to defend, because many other cultural patterns might serve equally well to reduce internal tensions. More recently, Durham has proposed that the cultural ideas behind Mundurucú headhunting, and the practice itself, persisted because the Mundurucú themselves believed that it effectively reduced intertribal competition for game animals.

The Mundurucú told Murphy that they fought because they thought it was fun and exciting. They also liked to barter captives for European trade goods, and they enjoyed the increased social status

that warriors received because of the ritual value of the trophy head (see Figure 3.19). Durham accepts that these personal motives certainly helped perpetuate headhunting. But he argues that historically the practice probably preceded the arrival of European manufactured goods and is best explained as part of a complex of cultural beliefs related to hunting. Like many other Amazonian peoples, the Mundurucú were constantly threatened by game shortages, and they explicitly linked head-taking with improved game supplies. Successful Mundurucú headhunters were given the honorific title of *Dajeboishi*, or "mother of the peccary," and the trophy head was thought to magically guarantee general hunting success by promoting animal fertility. More directly, the head also effectively demonstrated that they had eliminated a competing hunter who might have invaded Mundurucú hunting territory. The Mundurucú explicitly compared warfare to hunting, and it seems likely that at one time they ate their victims, like game animals; after all, their close relatives, the Tupinamba, and many other Tupi speakers, were enthusiastic cannibals. Durham argues that the Mundurucú remained headhunters because the practice worked well for them. All the men shared in the risks, the entire society enjoyed the perceived benefits that it produced, and better hunting improved everyone's genetic fitness. Thus, Durham's all-inclusive biocultural explanation takes into account history, food resources, cultural meanings, personal motivations, and reproductive success.

SUMMARY

Amazonia provides a background for discussing a variety of theories on the causes and consequences of sedentary village life based on domesticated plants. Sedentary living is certainly a great divide, and it undermines many of the mechanisms that promote social equality and stability among mobile foragers. Major issues for villagers include resolving conflict, limiting individual acquisition of political power, and maintaining access to resources as density increases. Ecological factors, in combination with cultural preferences for wild game and a desire to maintain light work loads, help keep villages small and population densities low. The Ashaninka–Iroquois kinship system shows how kin terms are used to define social relationships and are related to marriage and family patterns.

Structuralist interpretations of Amazonian life use examples of Amazonian myth and symbolism and related ritual practices, which express an underlying pan-Amazonian cosmology. This cosmology illustrates symbolic patterns that are virtually universal, but it also distinctly reflects tribal culture in the rain forest environment and provides an important point of comparison and contrast with the cosmology underlying the Inca empire to be described in Chapter 7. In functional terms, Amazonian cosmology works to resolve important logical contradictions while contributing to the basic adaptation of the culture.

Important cultural ecological issues in Amazonia include the contrasts between the river and the forest environments, the success of shifting cultivation, and the controversy over the cultural importance of animal protein. Conflicting sociobiology and cultural materialist interpretations of infanticide and raiding in Amazonia have been advanced. The Yanomami territory also can be seen as a tribal zone, experiencing heightened conflict due to commercial-culture intrusions. Finally, a biocultural interpretation of Mundurucú headhunting helps synthesize many diverse interpretations of these issues.

STUDY QUESTIONS

1. Why might protein be considered a population control factor in Amazonia? What other factors also influence village size?

2. How is shifting cultivation adapted to the special conditions of the tropical rain forest environment?

3. Describe the kinship terminology system of the Ashaninka, and show how it is related to marriage practices.

4. Discuss the sociobiological, historical, and materialist interpretations of Yanomami conflict.

5. In what ways do the religious beliefs and practices of Native Amazonians relate to social and ecological conditions?

SUGGESTED READING

CHAGNON, NAPOLEON. 1992. *The Yanomamo*, 4th ed. New York: Holt, Rinehart & Winston. Well-rounded ethnography, but focused on the issue of conflict.

HAMES, RAYMOND B., AND WILLIAM T. VICKERS (eds.). 1983. *Adaptive Responses of Native Amazonians*. New York: Academic Press. A collection of detailed cultural ecological studies of different Amazonian groups.

REICHEL-DOLMATOFF, GERARDO. 1971. *Amazonian Cosmos: The Sexual and Religious Symbolism of the Tukano Indians*. Chicago: University of Chicago Press. Very detailed analysis of an Amazonian belief system covering ritual and myth and relating it to rain forest adaptation.

4

*African Cattle Peoples:
Tribal Pastoralists*

The Nuer, Karimojong, Maasai, and other Nilotic-speaking peoples in East Africa have fascinated casual European observers and anthropologists for more than a century. The pride and arrogant self-confidence of these peoples were so striking, and their warriors were so brave and numerous, that they commanded the immediate respect of the first European colonialists. The Maasai were viewed with special awe, because their warriors made a contest out of killing lions with spears and wore their manes as a badge of courage. It was even more impressive that these peoples could support themselves almost entirely from their cattle in an environment that Europeans considered virtually useless. In fact, cattle dominated all aspects of their culture, to a degree that outsiders thought irrational and obsessive. However, these East Africans, who may be respectfully called "cattle peoples," have survived droughts and epidemics, and they have retained much of their autonomy despite many government-imposed changes.

After the Ice Age ended, animals were domesticated in many parts of the world. This opened up new possibilities for people while creating many new problems. In the absence of animal domesticates, the population density of farming peoples was limited by the availability of fish and game, as

was discussed in Chapter 3. But cattle are a valuable source of protein and can serve as a mobile food surplus and a reproducible source of wealth. Cattle also can be stolen and thus must be defended. They can make social equality more difficult to maintain, and they may be handled in ways that alter the relations between men and women and the structure of domestic groups.

Ethnographic material illustrates how East African herders manage their animals for subsistence needs in an unpredictable environment. Cattle are so important in these Cattle Complex cultures that they provide ideal case material for illustrating functionalist interconnections and for making comparisons between the explanatory power of idealist, values interpretations of cultural patterns and materialist, cultural ecological interpretations. Cattle cultures are also useful for introducing such important anthropological concepts as segmentary lineage systems, bride-wealth, age-class warrior systems, animal sacrifice, and acephalous politics. In societies such as these, in which status is so closely tied to ownership of animals and success in raiding, the potential for both social inequality and environmental deterioration through overgrazing is significant. A major issue we will explore is the extent to which poverty and desertification, which are certainly problems in contemporary East Africa, are intrinsic features of traditional pastoral cultures. A related issue is the compatibility of pastoral nomadism with wildlife in Africa.

MAKING A LIVING WITH COWS

Cattle Herding and Tropical Grasslands

What special advantages do cattle offer peoples living in the East African savanna? How does subsistence herding differ from commercial ranching?

East Africa is part of the tropical savanna ecosystem, but it is topographically a highly diverse region (see Figure 4.1). Much of the area occupied by the Nilotic pastoralists in Kenya and Tanzania straddles the equator along a zone lying 3000–7000 feet (914–2134 meters [m]) in elevation and consisting of arid plains and wetter, grassy uplands. Today this region includes some of the most famous game parks in the world, such as the Amboseli and Serengeti national parks in Kenya and Tanzania,

FIGURE 4.1 *Map of savanna regions of Africa showing the Nilotic-speaking East African cattle cultures discussed.*

respectively. It is also home to many domestic-scale cultural groups involved in a wide range of subsistence economies.

The tropical savanna ecosystem is a grassland zone, which may have a few trees and shrubs, separating tropical rain forests from arid deserts (see Figure 4.2). Fire and grazing play an important role in maintaining and extending savannas. But savannas result primarily from climate, soil, and topographic conditions, especially a pronounced wet and dry season. In striking contrast to the diversity and stability of tropical rain forests, savannas are dominated by very few species and exist in an unstable, dynamic equilibrium. Drought cycles or changes in grazing pressure caused by livestock disease can rapidly change the inventory of plant species and shift the balance between trees and grasses. Biological productivity in the savanna is high in relation to biomass, but plants are short-lived in comparison to rain forest species. Nutrients are turned over, or cycled, much more rapidly

in the savanna. There are proportionately more leaves and grass and less wood in the savanna, and the foliage is more palatable because it contains fewer resins and other chemical defenses. Extreme seasonal variations in rainfall create periodic pulses of primary production resulting in brief food surpluses that are best exploited by nomadic grazers (Bourliere and Hadley 1983).

Pastoralism in East Africa, like the savanna itself, exists along a rainfall continuum from wet to dry, showing greater dependence on animals and greater nomadism as rainfall declines (see the box entitled "The Origins of African Pastoralism"). In areas where the average annual rainfall exceeds approximately 25 inches (650 millimeters [mm]) per year, people are likely to be village farmers, relying on grains such as millet, with livestock raising a minor subsistence activity. Where rainfall drops lower than 25 inches, pastoralism becomes increasingly attractive, nomadism increases, and people become more and more dependent on their ani-

FIGURE 4.2   *The East African savanna ecosystem, a complex product of the interaction of human activity and natural conditions.*

mals, while farming becomes supplemental. In extreme cases, as with some Maasai groups, people may subsist almost entirely on animal products, although some may exchange animal products for grains from their settled neighbors.

The great advantage of domestic livestock is that they convert otherwise inedible plant material into meat, blood, and milk for human consumption, in areas where farming would be at best a marginal activity. The use of domestic animals also permits dramatic increases in human population density over that supported in the same environment by foraging. East Africa can support up to 22,076 pounds (10,000 kilograms [kg]) of wildlife biomass per square kilometer (km^2) with some fifty species of large grazing mammals. The Hadza of Tanzania, who forage in this hunter's paradise, take only a small fraction of the game and maintain themselves at typically low population densities of just 0.4 persons per square kilometer. The Maasai, their pastoral neighbors, support 2–6 people per square kilometer. Pastoralism permits precise control over reproduction and harvesting of the animals and leads to large increases in food production per unit of land. However, successful pastoralism is a complex, delicately balanced system that poses many difficult problems and requires major adjustments in the organization of society and labor.

East African cattle peoples, operating within domestic-scale cultures, manage their cattle and relate to their grassland ecosystem in radically different ways from market-oriented ranchers operating within the commercial culture. The first objective of subsistence pastoralists is to extract the maximum food value from their animals for direct consumption as efficiently as possible, while emphasizing self-reliance and long-term security (Dyson-Hudson and Dyson-Hudson 1969). African cattle may appear scrawny in comparison with the hefty beef cattle of North American rangelands and feedlots, but range-fed African cattle do not require an enormous subsidy of fossil fuel energy, and they are well adapted to survive seasonal drought and disease (see the box entitled "Cattle Carrying Capacity"). American cattle are raised with the least human labor possible. They must gain weight quickly so they can be sold for the maximum financial profit. They thrive on water pumped from deep wells; special food that is planted, processed, stored, and trucked to their feeding troughs and feedlots; and expensive antibiotics, growth hormones, and appetite stimulants (see Chapter 12). Furthermore, American beef goes through a chain of processors, wholesalers, and retailers to be processed, packaged, advertised, stored, and marketed before being consumed. By contrast, no remote shareholders who did not participate in raising them profit from African cattle. African cattle are ritually sacrificed, butchered, and eaten by the same people who care for them.

The Cattle Complex: Obsession or Adaptation?

Why do African pastoralists focus so much of their culture on cattle? Is it an irrational cultural obsession, or do they make rational use of their animals? Is herding a sustainable adaptation in this environment?

Historically, East African pastoralists have been seriously misunderstood by anthropologists, development planners, and conservationists. Many observers concluded that they irrationally overemphasized cattle in culturally determined ways, leading to overgrazing and poor-quality animals. American anthropologist Melville Herskovits (1926) apparently was the first to refer to the East African cattle area and to describe the Cattle Complex as an irrational cultural value on cattle for nonutilitarian purposes. According to Herskovits, Cattle Complex peoples used cattle more for social and ritual purposes than for subsistence. Cattle were treated as wealth objects and sources of prestige. People rarely ate cattle; instead, they exchanged cattle at marriage, used them to settle disputes, and sacrificed them on ritual occasions. Besides these noneconomical uses, East Africans seemed to have an exaggerated and personal attachment to their animals. When range management professionals later found that pastoral cattle were underweight and less productive than their counterparts in the American West, they accused the pastoralists of overgrazing and blamed them for desertification, the process by which a savanna is converted to arid desert by overgrazing.

British anthropologist E. E. Evans-Pritchard conducted one of the first and most detailed studies

The Origins of African Pastoralism

African food-producing systems based on pastoralism and farming probably arose some 10,000 years ago. Developments in Africa roughly paralleled those in the Middle Eastern Neolithic; in both areas, developments were due to a combination of still poorly understood factors involving both resource constraints and new opportunities.

Domestication of animals involves a process of mutual changes in the behavior of both people and animals, which offers certain benefits to both. It should not be thought of as a remarkable discovery or invention. The question is, Why did people decide to raise animals, and why did they choose the animals they did? Cattle, sheep, and goats are ideally suited for domestication for two reasons. First, as herd animals, they can be easily controlled. Second, because they have multichambered stomachs, they can digest cellulose that humans cannot, which converts to animal protein that humans can digest. Animal domestication may have been undertaken as a gradual process of increasing control over game animals to make up for the shortfall in animal protein that accompanied population growth after the Ice Age.

As cultural control, animal domestication involves any systematic human intervention that makes the animals more available for human exploitation. The process can move from seasonal culling of wild herds to increase their growth rates, to corralling and maintaining herds year-round, to selective breeding (Hecker 1982). Such activities were probably underway with sheep, goats, and cattle in the Middle East by 9000 BP and quickly resulted in physical changes in the animals. Archaeological evidence of domestication includes such things as reduction in the size of animals; specific changes in morphology, such as horn shape in goats; and an increase in the skeletal remains of young animals slaughtered as a result of selective culling (Stein 1986).

Pastoralism, as a full-time specialization in domestic animals, probably has been practiced in Africa as long as anywhere in the world. Sheep and goats likely were brought into North Africa from the Middle East, whereas wild cattle may have been locally domesticated by 7000 BP or earlier (Smith 1984). The Zebu, or hump-backed cattle, apparently reached Africa from India about 4000 BP (see Figure 4.3). Because the cattle, sheep, or goats have no known wild ancestors in

of a cattle culture among the Nuer of Sudan between 1930 and 1936. This study (Evans-Pritchard 1940), which became a classic in ethnographic literature, showed the social, ritual, and emotional value of cattle but also demonstrated their utilitarian function.

Evans-Pritchard called the Nuer "pre-eminently pastoral." He reported that they considered them-sub-Saharan Africa, it is assumed that they were introduced to East Africa from elsewhere as domesticates.

The spread of pastoralism depended on environmental conditions. Over the past 10,000 years, small changes in rainfall have made the Sahara environment fluctuate abruptly between conditions favoring and discouraging pastoralism. The first favorable period began about 7000 BP and presented an open niche for pastoralist expansion. After pastoralism became established as a basic way of life in the Sahara, people apparently carried it south into appropriate environments in sub-Saharan Africa as they became available. The primary barrier to the spread of pastoralism in sub-Saharan Africa was the tsetse fly, which transmits trypanosomiasis, a form of sleeping sickness often fatal to cattle. The tsetse fly flourishes in forested and brushy vegetation and effectively precludes raising cattle in large areas of Africa.

Pastoralism first became established in East Africa in the central Sudan by 5400 BP and then in the arid zone of northeast Kenya by 5200 BP, where it was presumably introduced by early Cushitic-speaking peoples from Ethiopia (see Table 4.1). The higher savannas of East Africa apparently were not occupied by pastoralists, because of tsetse flies, until 3300 BP., when changes in climate and vegetation made conditions more favorable. Shortly thereafter, by 2500 BP, Nilotic-speaking ancestors of the modern Maasai and Turkana peoples arrived (Ambrose 1984). Therefore, African pastoralism was a well-established human adaptation and can reasonably be considered a basic component of the savanna ecosystem.

Anthropologists often group the "cattle peoples" of East Africa into a single culture area stretching from Sudan to South Africa, but they are a diverse group of cultures organized at different scales of social complexity and united only by their common interest in cattle. The most famous cattle cultures, such as the Nuer, Dinka, Karimojong, Turkana, and Maasai, all belong to the Nilotic branch of Nilo-Saharan. (*Nilotic* also refers to the very tall physical type of Nilotic speakers.) These peoples occupy the swampy plains along the White Nile in southern Sudan, the high savannas of the Rift Valley system, and the areas south and east of Lake Victoria to the Serengeti plains of Tanzania. The Nilotic peoples are the primary focus of this chapter.

selves herdsmen above all else and only grudgingly resorted to farming when they didn't have enough animals. They looked contemptuously on people without cattle, as he discovered on his arrival in Nuerland, when the Nuer refused to carry his baggage. He found that they had "the herdsman's outlook on the world" and considered cattle "their dearest possessions." Cattle were ornamented and

FIGURE 4.3
Samburu Maasai warriors preparing to slaughter a Zebu ox at a wedding. Hump-backed Zebu cattle may have been in Africa for 4,000 years.

TABLE 4.1   *Prehistory of East Africa, 200,000–1000 BP*

1000–2000 BP	Expansion of Bantu-speaking, iron-using village farmers
Pastoral Neolithic in Kenya (2500–5200 BP)	
2500	Southern Nilotic speakers from southern Sudan enter highlands as mixed farmer/pastoralists with livestock, millet, and sorghum
3300	Modern climate and vegetation established
	Savanna pastoral Neolithic in highlands
4500	Domestic camels reach Horn of Africa from southern Arabia
3000–5600	Climate drying after wet phase; tsetse bushes in highlands inhibit pastoralists
	Scattered foragers in highlands
5200	Savanna pastoral Neolithic introduced in lowlands by Cushitic speakers bringing domestic livestock and ceramics
Saharan Pastoralism (4000–8000 BP)	
4000–5400	Domestic livestock and ceramics in central Sudan
7000–8000	Local domestication of cattle in Sahara
	Domestic sheep and goats reach North Africa from Near East
***Homo Sapiens* Foragers (40,000–200,000 BP)**	
200,000	Middle Stone Age; core tools, flake points, scrapers

SOURCES: Ambrose (1984), Clark (1984), Phillipson (1985), Smith (1984), and Wendorf and Schild (1984).

named, and their genealogies were remembered. Boys received an "ox-name" at birth, men were addressed using names that referred to their favorite oxen, and women were named after the cows they milked. And, to Evans-Pritchard's dismay, they always talked about their animals:

I used sometimes to despair that I never discussed anything with the young men but livestock and girls, and even the subject of girls led inevitably to that of cattle. Start on whatever subject I would, and approach it from whatever angle, we would soon be speaking of cows and oxen, heifers and steers. (Evans-Pritchard 1940:18–19)

Cattle Carrying Capacity

Comparative analysis of subsistence herders requires several types of data and concepts, which are outlined in Figures 4.4 and 4.5. Calculating the carrying capacity for herd animals and the number of people who could be supported by pastoralism is a deceptively simple theoretical problem. One need only know the amount of plant biomass that animals can consume in a given area each year on a sustained basis and the amount of human food that the herds can produce. Range management specialists usually assume that 50 percent of the annual new plant growth can safely be consumed by herbivores without degrading the grazing resources. Carrying capacity is rated in TLUs (tropical livestock units of 250 kg [552 lb] of biomass)/km²/year and varies according to the AGNPP (aboveground net primary production), which in turn depends on rainfall. It is assumed that each TLU will consume approximately 3105 kilograms (6854 lb) of dry forage annually.

In practice, none of these figures can be precise, and the formula is not so easily applied. This explains why there is so much professional disagreement over whether pastoralists are managing their herds rationally and maintaining the quality of their pastures. The primary problem is that AGNPP, the most critical value, varies dramatically in time and space in the pastoral zones. Successful pastoralists must plan for long-term, minimum carrying-capacity values, taking into account the frequency of droughts. Actual productivity rates of human food will depend on the particular mix of animals in use and the specific pattern of herd management.

For Evans-Pritchard, this "pastoral mentality" took on the appearance of an "over-emphasis," a "hypertrophy of a single interest." As further indication of Nuer obsession with cattle, he pointed to the "linguistic profusion" of cattle terminology. He found ten terms for describing cows of one solid color and hundreds of possible permutations of terms based on combinations of white with various patterns and associations with natural objects. Further Nuer terminological distinctions are based on horn shape, ear cropping, and age and sex categories. In all, the Nuer had thousands of ways of describing cattle and composed poetry and songs using their names. A. B. C. Ocholla-Ayayo (1979) has listed 125 terms applied by the Luo, Nilotic neighbors of the Nuer, to cattle anatomy, both internal and external, covering bones and internal organs in great detail (see Figure 4.6).

Evans-Pritchard recognized that this extreme interest in cattle had a utilitarian basis. He noted that the Nuers' flat, clay-soiled, seasonally flooded environment was deficient in such basic raw materials as stone and wood and was a difficult area to grow crops, but it provided excellent pasturage. The Nuer therefore lavished seemingly extravagant care on their animals, such that the cattle enjoyed a "gentle, indolent, sluggish life" (Evans-Pritchard 1940:36). He described the virtually symbiotic relationship between the Nuer and their cattle, in which each depended on the other. The Nuer extract an impressive array of material resources from cattle. Milk is the primary product, and it may be consumed fresh or sour, or processed as cheese. Blood is drawn from veins in the neck and then boiled or allowed to coagulate and roasted in a block. An animal ordinarily is slaughtered only for

FIGURE 4.4
Energy flow in a pastoral production system, the Turkana. (SOURCE: Coughenour et al. 1985.)

Savanna Ecosystem
Annual Production
2375 GJ AGNPP

KEY: AGNPP = Above-ground net primary production
GJ = 1 billion joules, or 466,061 kcal

Plants

Grass and Herbs
108

Consumption by Livestock GJ/yr

Trees and Shrubs
141

Livestock

| Donkeys 0.03 | Cattle 0.37 | Sheep 0.14 | Camels 0.95 | Goats 0.29 |

Food Production by Livestock GJ/yr

Food Products

Milk 1.19   Meat 0.14   Blood 0.14

Exchange

Grain

People
1.47 GJ

Approximately 962 kcal/capita/day Directly from Livestock

ritual purposes, but then it is butchered and the parts distributed. Dung is a critical fuel for cooking, and dung fires help drive off biting insects. Dung is also used as a construction plaster, as well as for medicinal and cosmetic purposes. Cattle urine is used in cheese making and tanning, while skin and bones have many uses in the manufacture of various artifacts such as containers and ornaments. Without cattle and their products, life would be very difficult in Nuerland.

Pastoralists have been widely accused of irrationality for supposedly raising far more poor-quality animals than they need for mere subsistence in order to achieve the prestige and social value of large numbers of cattle. They have been accused of overstocking their ranges and degrading their environments, thus contributing to desertification. This is sometimes seen as a classic tragedy of the commons situation (destruction of a communal resource to serve self-interests), because

grazing lands are communal property and an individual herder would have no incentive to hold down the size of his herd. Planners often recommend that pastoralists would do better to raise beef for the market as private ranchers. Actually, little firm evidence supports the view that domestic-scale pastoralism is inherently prone to overstocking, while abundant evidence suggests that outside development pressures do contribute to overgrazing (Homewood and Rodgers 1984). Domestic-scale subsistence pastoralists operating outside of the market economy are unlikely to find any conflict between individual self-interest and their social responsibility to maintain range quality (McCay and Acheson 1987).

Whether African pastoralists are self-conscious conservationists, their traditional subsistence practices include important limiting factors that reduce the likelihood of overgrazing. First, the subsistence needs of a household determine herd size (see Ta-

Basic Formulas:

$$CC = (AGNPP/.5)/C$$
$$P = CC/R$$

_ _ _ _ _ _ _ _ _ _ _ _ _ _ _ _

Carrying-Capacity Variables:

Where CC = Carrying capacity, the number of animals in TLU that can be supported/km²/year on a sustained basis

$AGNPP$ = Above-ground net primary productivity in kilograms of DM (dry plant matter)/ km²/year (new plant biomass produced each year)

DM = 19 mJ/kg, or 4500 kcal/kg

TLU = Tropical livestock units, 250 kg of animal biomass

C = kg of DM consumed/TLU/year

R = TLU required for human subsistence/ person/year

P = Number of people supported/km²/year

FIGURE 4.5 *A formula for estimating environmental limits on African pastoralists.*

bles 4.2 and 4.3), and the labor supply and the declining feeding efficiencies that arise as herds grow set its upper limits. Second, in the absence of trucks, pumps, and deep wells, the frequency that animals must be watered and the distance they can travel between grazing areas and water severely limit grazing during the dry season.

African cattle under traditional nomadic pastoralism do appear to be of lower quality when compared with U.S. beef and dairy cattle (see Table 4.4). African animals convert less of their forage into human food and produce less body weight because the frequent droughts cause animals to channel more of their energy into biological maintenance than into meat production. They must adjust their metabolisms to cycles of periodic thirst and starvation followed by recovery (Coughenour et al. 1985, Western and Finch 1986). Low production is thus a long-range adaptation to severe environmental constraints. U.S. cattle achieve their high biological efficiencies thanks to a significant fossil fuel energy subsidy, which is not counted in these calculations but which is required to produce and distribute

tractors, farm chemicals, feed, and agricultural research.

Pastoral Subsistence: Meat, Blood, and Milk

How are different animals used by pastoralists for food? How do they manage their animals for maximum food security?

To design a reliable food system based on domestic animals, a subsistence herder must solve several problems: which animals to use, what food products to produce, how many animals to herd, what age and sex categories to maintain in the herds, when to slaughter, when to time breeding, how to feed and water the herd, and how to protect the herd from disease and predators. Whereas hunters let nature take care of most of these matters, herders must constantly attend to the needs of their animals.

Most East African pastoralists are considered, and consider themselves, to be cattle peoples because of the dominant cultural role that cattle are assigned, but they actually depend on several functionally distinct domesticates, including cattle, camels, sheep, and goats (see Table 4.5). Cattle play major social, ritual, and subsistence roles while providing important material products. Camels become increasingly important as rainfall declines or pastures become overgrazed. The small stock (sheep and goats) may provide more of a household's meat requirements than cattle and can be a significant source of milk. Small stock also are useful to speed recovery after a serious drought because they reproduce more quickly than cattle. Reliance on animal domesticates makes for a situation that is the reverse of the protein limitation situation in Amazonia. East African pastoralists have an abundance of protein but have some difficulty producing adequate carbohydrates and calories except where they can grow grain or obtain it by barter with neighboring farmers.

Complementarity between domesticates is a striking aspect of pastoral systems. Maintaining mixed herds of large and small grazers and browsers makes for more efficient utilization of available forage and, in a simple way, duplicates the complexity of the natural savanna ecosystem. As

FIGURE 4.6
Approximately half of the 125 anatomical terms applied to cattle by the Nilotic-speaking Luo (Ocholla-Ayayo 1979).

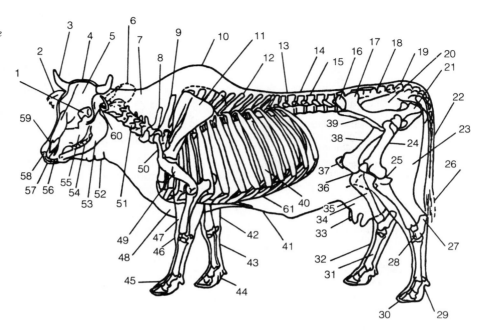

1. Chokndorro	22. Ip	43. Ogwala
2. It	23. Ring em maoko	44. Ofunjtielo or n̄guttielo
3. Tuṅg	24. Odiere machien	45. Witielo
4. Tatwich	25. Fuond odire gi ogwala	46. Choṅg
5. Sihanga or patwich	26. Orengo	47. Bat korjachien
6. It (omwot it)	27. Fuond ogwala	48. Agoko
7. Ṅgut	28. Nyapoṅg tielo	49. Chokbat mar oriere
8. Chok ṅgutmachiek	29. Odofuny tielo	50. Chokrangach (colar bone)
9. Chok ṅgutmabor	30. Okak tielo	51. Choke ṅgudi
10. Kuom	31. Chok oluko	52. Jund dhiaṅg
11. Opal	32. Ogwala	53. Choklem mapiny
12. Ariedi lihumblu	33. Thuno	54. Nyiponge
13. Giko nyakmeru	34. Dagthuno	55. Choklem mamalo
14. Dierṅgech	35. Chok em	56. Lep
15. Giko nyakmeru	36. Fundodiere	57. Leke mamon
16. Wichok oguro	37. Nyapoṅg odiere	58. Um
17. Chokoguro	38. Odiere	59. Chok um
18. Choktie ip	39. Chokbam	60. Tiend it
19. Oguch dhiaṅg	40. Ṅgede	61. Chokagoko
20. Ringsarara	41. Pinyich	
21. Dhokisonga	42. Bat korachich	

grazers, cattle and sheep feed primarily on grasses and herbaceous vegetation; as browsers, goats and camels rely on woody shrubs and trees. Utilization of diverse domesticates also helps level out seasonal fluctuation in food production: Camels often produce milk year-round, cows produce only during the wet season, and sheep and goats produce most milk during the dry season.

The diverse animal products that pastoralists consume also have the advantage of complementarity, and they maximize sustainable subsistence yield. Rather than emphasizing meat production, which obviously represents a onetime use of an animal, herders are concerned primarily with milk production. Milk maximizes biological efficiency because the calories in milk can be produced four

TABLE 4.2   *Minimum Estimated Herd Size to Support One Household**

	Camels	Cattle	Sheep	Goats
kcal	28	64	116	205
Protein	11	28	64	74

SOURCE: Dahl and Hjort (1976).

*These figures represent the number of animals of each type that the reference household would require to meet all of its needs for either calories or protein. Reference household assumes six people, including husband and wife, boy age 18 years, girl age 15 years, and two small children, ages 3 and 8 years. Total daily nutritional needs of 318 g of protein and 13,800 kcal.

TABLE 4.4   *Ecological Efficiency of African Nomadic Subsistence Cattle in Comparison with U.S. Cattle**

	Ecological Efficiency	Production/ Biomass
African nomadic	0.9	0.2
U.S. beef	5.5	0.78–1.1
U.S. dairy[†]	17.0	0.8–2.6

SOURCE: Coughenour et al. (1985).

*Ecological efficiency = production/energy consumed by animal.
[†]U.S. dairy production refers only to milk.

times more efficiently in terms of energy costs than the calories in meat. Blood and milk can be produced without harm to the animal, and they complement each other in that blood is a major source of iron and can be drawn from animals that are not producing milk. This is especially important for cows when their milk production drops during the dry season. Cattle are not as efficient as goats at meat production, so cattle are rarely slaughtered except ritually, although they will be eaten when they die naturally.

Traditional herding is a labor-intensive activity. Individual herds may be subdivided to better reflect the abilities and requirements of different types of animals. Herds are moved seasonally to take advantage of the best pasture, and in some areas, a regular altitudinal ***transhumance*** (moving herds for optimum grazing) may be practiced. Pastoralists manage their herds to maximize the number of female animals to keep milk yields and growth potential high. Given the natural mortality rates of cattle and their reproductive biology, a herd is unlikely to contain more than about 30 percent fertile cows, and only half of these will be producing milk.

The actual number of animals needed to satisfy household nutritional requirements can be theoretically estimated, based on calculations of the

transhumance   Seasonal movement of livestock herds to maintain optimum grazing conditions; often involves altitudinal shifts.

TABLE 4.3   *Average Reported Household Herd Size and Composition**

	Camels	Cattle	Sheep	Goats
Rendille				
TLU/household[†]	12	11	40	61
kcal (%)	19	16	11	15
Protein (%)	50	33	23	32
Karimojong				
TLU/household	—	33	—	—
kcal (%)	—	34	—	—
Protein (%)	—	—	—	—
Turkana				
TLU/household	—	—	—	—
kcal (%)	43	14	17	—
Protein (%)	—	—	—	—

SOURCES: Rendille (Field 1985); Karimojong (Little and Morren 1976); Turkana (Coughenour et al. 1985).

*All based on average family of 8 people, counted as 6.5 adult equivalents.
[†]TLU = tropical livestock unit.

TABLE 4.5   *A Functional Comparison of East Africa Livestock* *

	Camels	Cattle	Sheep	Goats
Vital Statistics				
Weight/kg	453	250	45	45
Feeding	Browser	Grazer	Grazer	Browser
Calves or kids/female/year	0.5	0.7	1.5	2
Herd growth, %/year	1.5	3.4	18	33
Subsistence Production/Animal				
Milk (kg/day)	4	2	0.01	0.03
Blood (liters [L]/year)	60	6	—	—
Carcass/(kg)	226	125	10–25	10–25
Production/Herd of 100 Animals/Year				
Milk				
kcal[†]	17,374	5497	2340	1847
Protein (kg)	918	245	131	91
Blood				
kcal[†]	163	108	—	—
Protein (kg)	38	27	—	—
Meat				
kcal[†]	664	4536	2017	608
Protein (kg)	142	278	50	65
Fal (camel hump)				
kcal[†]	527	—	—	—

SOURCE: Dahl and Hjort (1976).

*These figures are estimates; actual figures can vary widely. Annual production for herd reflects average age and sex distributions and natural mortality, as well as intentional slaughtering. Milk production represents the human share after the needs of calves and kids are satisfied.

[†]In thousands.

annual production of a standard herd; however, there are many variables, and published estimates range from thirty to ninety or more head of cattle per household. Different researchers may use different estimates of household size and daily per capita minimum caloric requirements. The widely accepted figure of 2300 minimum daily kilocalories (kcal) is probably too high because it is based on Euro-American standards. East African cattle herders are smaller people and should have correspondingly lower energy needs. Furthermore, use of the high-calorie figure inflates minimum herd requirements. Although the production of milk per animal under pastoral nomadism is lower than on European dairy farms, pastoral milk is more concentrated, and its nutritional value is 30 percent higher than that of European milk. Given the archaeological record of pastoralism in East Africa

and the incredible resilience of the system under the impact of colonial invasion and recent forces for change, traditional herders seem to be operating quite rationally. Their herding strategies contribute to the long-range survival of their families in a very difficult environment.

DAILY LIFE IN EAST AFRICA

Virtually all aspects of East African pastoralist society are in some way connected with the need to maintain cattle. The examples that follow are drawn from the Nuer and related Maasai peoples and demonstrate close connections between cattle and marriage arrangements, residence patterns, descent groups, age and gender roles, religious beliefs, and ethnic identity.

How Do Nuer Men View Women?

Anthropologist John Burton (1980) asked several Atuot (Nuer) men and women to respond to this question: "What are the relations of a wife and husband, and how do they come to quarrel?" He felt that their answers closely matched what he observed. Mayan Akuot, a father of six children, answered as follows:

In our land, it is for a woman to give birth to children. Women are not good or bad—they are in between. Their badness is that even if you are married with one hundred cows, she may still leave. Even if you cultivate much grain, she may still leave you. This is because some women have no heart. If it is a good woman she will bear many children. If there were no women, how would all the people be here? She is the one who created the land. There is the wife of the black people, of the animals, of the cows, of the fish—all of them have this land. If it were not for women, how would people be so many? Women are good—they make children and food and beer. The woman has the land. If a man stays in this land without a woman, he will not go ahead [that is, his progeny will never be realized]. (Burton 1980:717)

Nuer Society: Bride-Wealth, Lovers, and Ghosts

How do cattle provide a central focus of marriage, kinship, ritual, and politics in the daily life of cattle people? What role do cattle play in Nuer marriage? How does the distinction between biological and social paternity influence Nuer marriage arrangements and concepts of sexual morality in this patrilineal society?

Apart from their obvious utilitarian value, the Nuer told Evans-Pritchard that the "supreme value" of cattle came from their use as **bride-wealth,** which was the basic requirement for establishing a fully legitimate household (Evans-Pritchard 1951:96). (I avoid the use of the term *legal* to refer to marriage or household in this context because it implies formal law, supported by courts and an enforcement structure that did not exist in Nuer society.) Nuer marriage involves rights over cattle and women and is an agreement between the families of the bride and groom (see the box entitled "How Do Nuer Men View Women?"). It requires a lengthy series of negotiations, public and private ceremonies, and transactions, which are not complete until children are born to the couple. Because Nuer marriage is so complex and involves so many different rights, it is an ideal case from which to examine the meaning of marriage, family, and household as cross-cultural concepts.

The process of Nuer marriage is initiated by preliminary talks between the two families in order to specify the animals that can be transferred. The bride's family can demand cattle for six different categories of claimants by order or precedence: the bride's grandparents or their ghosts, the bride's parents, her uncles, her aunts, the spirits of her father and mother, and her brothers and half-brothers (see Figure 4.7). Ideally, some 40 head of cattle ultimately are transferred to the bride's father, who is then obligated to distribute them to each of the claimants on his side of the family and to the bride's mother's family. In a typical distribution, 20 animals would go to the bride's immediate family, with her father getting the largest share, and 10 animals would go to each set of uncles and aunts (see Figure 4.8). Each category of claimant receives a specific number and type of animal. For example, the bride's full brother can receive 3 cows, 2 oxen, and 1 cow with its calf, 7 animals in all. In the negotiations, animals are promised by name to specific people.

The preliminary negotiations are formalized in the betrothal ceremony, which is the first public marriage ritual. Betrothal is marked by the sacri-

---

bride-wealth Goods, often livestock, that are transferred from the family of the groom to the family of the bride in order to legitimize the marriage and the children of the couple.

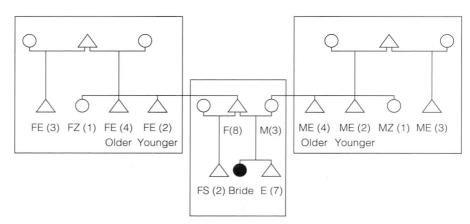

FIGURE 4.7
Order of precedence of claimants on Nuer bride-wealth cattle: (1) grand-parents or their ghosts; (2) father (F) and mother (M); (3) father's brother(s) (FB) and mother's brother(s) (MB); (4) father's sister(s) (FZ) and mother's sister(s) (MZ); (5) spirits of father (F) and mother (M); (6) brother(s) (B) and half-brother(s) (FS). (SOURCE: Evans-Pritchard 1951.)

FIGURE 4.8
The distribution of Nuer bride-wealth cattle; the numbers in parentheses indicate the number of cattle received. (SOURCE: Evans-Pritchard 1951.)

fice and distribution of an ox by the bride's father to the groom's family. The first installment of bride-wealth cattle also is transferred to the bride's father. Several weeks later, at the wedding ceremony, negotiations are finalized and more cattle transferred, but the transfer and the marriage are not considered official until a later consummation ceremony with its own series of rituals. After this, the groom's family can demand compensation in the event of his wife's infidelity, but the couple does not establish a joint homestead until after their first child is weaned. Until then, the wife remains in her parents' homestead, and her husband is a visitor who must maintain a ritual distance from his in-laws.

Once completed, the "ordinary" Nuer marriage creates a simple nuclear family household based on husband, wife, and child. Such a household is headed by the husband and draws its subsistence

from his herd and from the wife's garden. The homestead contains a *byre* (a cattle barn) and its *kraal* (corral), a cooking hearth, and a small sleeping house for the wife. In a polygynous marriage, each wife has her own house. Several such homesteads belonging to a group of brothers or a father and his sons might cluster around a common *kraal* as a composite homestead.

Many other domestic arrangements are possible (see Figure 4.9). For example, a woman, especially if she were infertile, might become a "husband" and have children by marrying another woman who then takes a male lover who becomes the biological father, or **genitor,** of the female husband's children. In this case, the female husband is the legitimate father, or **pater,** of the children, as well as the husband, and her family transfers cattle as bride-wealth to the family of her wife. In a "ghost

FIGURE 4.9
Nuer forms of marriage.
(*SOURCE: Evans-Pritchard 1951.*)

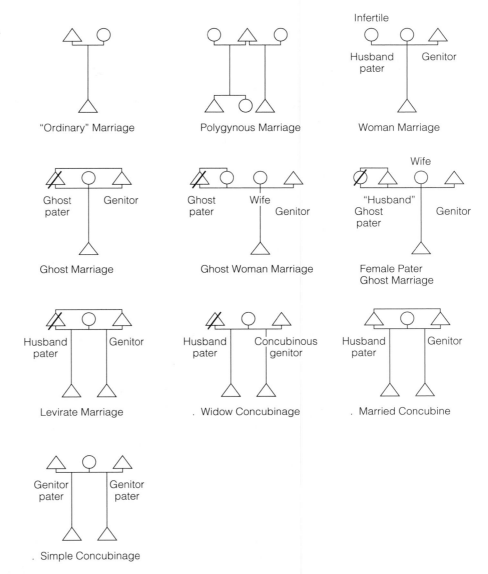

"Ordinary" Marriage

Polygynous Marriage

Woman Marriage

Ghost Marriage

Ghost Woman Marriage

Female Pater
Ghost Marriage

Levirate Marriage

. Widow Concubinage

. Married Concubine

. Simple Concubinage

marriage," someone marries in the name of a sibling or other relative who has died without having completed a marriage and who thus has left no descendants. In all such cases, cattle are transferred to the bride's family, while the deceased, male or female, becomes the pater; the stand-in relative lives with the wife as "husband" and genitor but has no rights over the children. **Levirate** marriage, in which a man marries his deceased brother's wife,

resembles ghost marriage except that the dead husband was already married and the bride-wealth had been transferred. The original, now dead, husband

---

genitor   The biological father of a child.
pater   The culturally legitimate, or sociological, father of a child.
levirate   A cultural pattern in which a woman marries a brother of her deceased husband.

Cattle and Kinship Terminology

The importance of bride-wealth exchanges is also seen in the kinship terminologies of cattle peoples. The Nuer, and related northern Nilotic groups, are noted for using highly descriptive kinship systems (sometimes called *Sudanese*) that place each of ego's cousins in a distinctive category based on terms that are combinations of terms applied to primary relatives, as in the English expression "father's sister's daughter." This makes sense given the different positions these kin take with respect to bride-wealth cattle and the fact that none of them are marriageable. It is important for people to distinguish between kin on the mother's side and the father's side and between distinct groups of kin related through males, because that is the primary line through which cattle and rights in cattle are inherited. Cattle, as movable property with important social, ritual, and economic significance, make all the difference. The Iroquois kinship systems of Australian aborigines and Native Amazonians (see Chapters 2 and 3) need to make fewer distinctions and can merge kin on the father's and the mother's sides.

The Maasai kinship system represents another type commonly associated with groups that emphasize the rights of kin related through males and in which complex property relations also must be distinguished. In this system, which is usually called *Omaha*, ego groups mother's agnates (kin related through males) into a single category regardless of generation (see Figure 4.10). A. R. Radcliffe-Brown (1941) originally interpreted this as the operation of the principle of the unity of the lineage group, inferring that males of the mother's patrilineage were treated as a single group, which reflects the fact that ego did not actually belong to the group but was still connected to it in important ways. Such an interpretation is not an adequate explanation for why the Maasai have Omaha terminology, but it does make the system understandable.

is still considered the husband, and the brother who stands in his place has less control over his wife than the "husband" in a ghost marriage.

Women have considerable freedom in Nuer domestic arrangements, even though all marriages are officially arranged by the families involved. Instead of remarrying, widows sometimes live with lovers, who may father children by them. However, the original legitimate family, established by bride-wealth, remains intact, and her children will all belong to her original husband, who is always their pater. Evans-Pritchard (1951) called such arrangements "widow concubinage." In some cases, a woman may move in with a lover while she is still married. She will be a "married concubine," and again her children will all belong to her husband because of the bride-wealth.

For the Nuer, the concept of paternity, or "belonging to," is far more important than biological parentage or the details of domestic arrangements. Paternity is established by bride-wealth cattle, thereby providing one with claims to cattle that may, in turn, be used for bride-wealth. Marriage also links one to a set of ancestor ghosts and spirits that must be ritually acknowledged. Maintaining such claims is more important than whether a "father" is living or dead, male or female, or with whom one's mother cohabits.

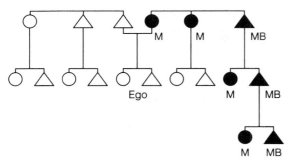

FIGURE 4.10 *The Omaha kinship terminology system,
which emphasizes mother's patrilineage.*

The use of bride-wealth, such as cattle, to formalize marriage has so many ramifications throughout the culture that some anthropologists recognize societies based on bride-wealth and those based on **bride-service** as distinctive societal types (Collier 1988). These two marriage systems create different culturally defined systems of domestic relations, organizing the inequalities of age and sex in different ways. Young men in bride-service societies, such as in aboriginal Australia and Amazonia, do not incur long-term debt obligations when they marry and need only hunt or provide other services to their in-laws during the early stages in their marriage. In bride-wealth societies, the exchange of bride-wealth valuables between male heads of families sharply defines the social statuses of husband, wife, parent, and child. The social importance of bride-wealth cattle gives a man more of a vested interest in the marriages of his brothers and sisters than he might have in a bride-service society.

Bride-wealth has sometimes been called *bride-price* by anthropologists, who may even refer to wife markets, but these terms are better avoided because they imply purchase and incorrectly suggest that women are chattels in cattle societies. With the Nuer, this is certainly *not* the case because women have the final say over whom they marry. It would be foolish for a father to force his daughter into a marriage against her wishes because bride-wealth cattle would have to be returned in the event of a divorce before children were born to the marriage. There are, however, inequalities of age and sex built into the system. The marriage transaction gives a man, or a woman acting as a man, the right to establish paternity, to demand cattle as an indemnity for adultery, and to claim cattle when his wife's daughters marry. Men in this system sometimes explicitly equate women with cattle because, when women are "given" in marriage, they bring cattle in exchange (see the box entitled "Cattle and Kinship Terminology").

From a Marxist perspective, marriage in such systems is considered an instrument of political power that allows men to gain rights to exploit women's reproductive powers (Meillassoux 1981). In Nuer society, through marriage, a man gains the labor not only of his wife but also of his sons, who will work as herdsmen, and his daughters, who will be gardeners and milkmaids along with their mothers until they move to their husband's household. Furthermore, young men are exploited, because it is the male elders who ultimately control the cattle that the young men need to marry, just as in aboriginal Australia the old men control ritual knowledge and the initiation process that are the requirements for adulthood. There are explicit dependency relationships here between men and women, and young and old. But equating this with the domination and exploitation that produces poverty in commercial-scale societies and divides households by social class is misleading because households in domestic-scale societies have relatively equal access to strategic resources such as food and shelter.

Understanding Nuer Descent Groups

*How did outsiders' views of Nuer descent
groups differ from the Nuer interpretation of
their social divisions?*

Evans-Pritchard devised an ingenious model to describe the political organization of Nuer society. The Nuer, with a population of some 300,000 in the 1930s, were said to be organized by clans, lineages, and territorial groups into an **acephalous,** or headless, political system, which operated in the absence of formal political offices (Evans-Pritchard 1940). The clans and lineages were descent groups

bride-service The cultural expectation that a newly married husband will perform certain tasks for his in-laws.

acephalous A political system without central authority or permanent leaders.

thought to be based on an ***agnatic*** principle, which meant that they recruited members exclusively through males by means of patrilineal descent, or ***filiation.*** In Evans-Pritchard's scheme, the highest descent-based unit was the clan, which was composed of maximal, major, minor, and minimal lineages. These units corresponded to the territorial units, with the tribe at the top and primary, secondary, and tertiary tribal sections down to the village community at the lowest territorial level (see Figure 4.11a).

As the figure shows, this system can be represented in a tidy diagram, but the Nuer themselves may well understand it differently, as Michel Verdon (1982) suggests. The Nuer apparently have no term in their own language for clan or lineage; when Evans-Pritchard pressed them for lineage affiliations, they did not understand what he wanted to know. He was able to obtain names for lineage segments, but these were merely the names of particular ancestors. When he asked the Nuer to draw their lineages, they came up with lines radiating from a center, not the branching trees and pyramids that he preferred (see Figure 4.11b). He also observed that "lineages" did not, in fact, form discrete localized groups. That is, the members of a lineage often did not live in the same village, nor were they strictly patrilineal. He found that lineages often incorporated children filiated through women or through adoption.

Despite the inconsistencies, Evans-Pritchard (1940) declared that clans and lineages appeared on ritual occasions when people made sacrifices to their ancestors, when groups mobilized to settle disputes, or when groups conducted raids. Such ephemeral descent groups acquired their own reality in the anthropological literature—especially in the work of British functionalists in Africa, where they became standard descriptive devices, and in major comparative studies. However, regardless of whether the Nuer linguistically identify clans and lineages, they do divide their society into nested levels of inclusiveness, based on their assumptions about relations to ancestors and territory. Perhaps most importantly, they successfully organize large numbers of people without central political authority.

When it became obvious that the natives were not very concerned with the purity or even the existence of their descent groups, some argued that descent was simply "ideology." Sahlins (1965) observed that different ideological models of descent organization could be projected onto the same arrangement of people. A given group might, for example, consider themselves to be patrilineal, matrilineal, or even bilateral, without making any changes in individuals. Descent thus became a cultural fiction that people adopted for whatever purpose and then imposed on themselves.

As anthropological models, lineages and clans grew out of nineteenth-century evolutionary theories that viewed them as stages on the way to statehood, according to Adam Kuper (1982). A clan-based society was thought to represent an evo-

FIGURE 4.11　*The segmentary lineage of Nuer society as devised by (a) Evans-Pritchard (1940) and (b) the Nuer themselves.*

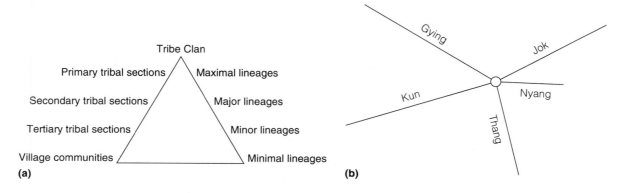

(a)

(b)

lutionary advance over societies organized only by families, but because they were still based on kinship or biological descent, clan societies were considered to be more "primitive" than territorially organized states. Lineages and clans were seen as equivalent to corporate legal entities that, like business corporations, existed in perpetuity apart from their individual members. However, in case after case, critical examination showed that clans and lineages did not form consistent, culturally recognized units. East African pastoralists do remember ancestors, and they marry outside of specific categories of kin; but, like Australian aborigines, they seem not to organize themselves into corporate descent groups. Instead, their lives are organized around politically autonomous villages, households, and overlapping networks of kinship. The Nuer categories that Evans-Pritchard called **patrilineages** have also been described as interest groups concerned with claims in cattle (Verdon 1982). Ranked descent lines may be traced to elite persons in hierarchically organized societies; in such cases, "royal" or "noble" clans and lineages may be culturally significant, but such is not the case with the Nuer, or the other African pastoralists considered here.

Leopard-Skin Chiefs and Politics in Headless Societies

How do the Nuer organize themselves politically in the absence of centralized political authority? What were the roles of cattle, locality, and the leopard-skin chiefs?

Before his 1965 critique of descent theory, Marshall Sahlins (1961) suggested that the Nuer were a critical "type specimen" of the **segmentary lineage system** operating as a political mechanism for "predatory expansion" by tribal societies against other tribal societies contesting a common ecological niche. Thus, segmentary lineages made a sort of ordered anarchy possible in acephalous (headless) societies lacking a permanent ranking system, formal political offices, or government institutions. In his early reading of Nuer ethnography, Sahlins ignored multiple evidence that lineages were not culturally recognized and that local residential groups did not represent descent groups. He accepted Evans-Pritchard's contention that local villages were organized around lineages and lineage principles and argued that sociability increased with spatial and genealogical proximity. The lineage structure determined how severe conflict would be and what groups would mobilize.

If the Nuer were not really organized around segmentary lineages, how did they handle conflict without resorting to political hierarchy? This is no small problem because we are talking about relatively large societies that make Australian aboriginal and Native Amazonian societies seem insignificant in comparison. Government census figures for 1955–1956 list some 460,000 Nuer and 1.152 million Dinka, a closely related group (Southall 1976). Organizing this many people into a vast network of politically autonomous villages, each with no more than a few hundred people, is a major achievement.

The key feature of the Nuer segmentary system was complementary opposition, or what Sahlins called the "massing effect," which means that political alliances form according to the affiliation of individual combatants. Thus, for example, if a conflict developed between two villages, members of other villages would not join in; but if someone stole a cow from another district, then neighboring villages might form a temporary alliance against the perceived common enemy. Similarly, all members of an ethnic group might move against a different ethnic group. All of this was very similar to the type of conflict described for Amazonian groups, but on a larger scale.

Evans-Pritchard (1940) described a political system with increasing levels of violence as social distance increased. Within a village, men might fight with clubs, but serious disputes would be settled quickly. Between villages, men might fight with

---

agnatic   Kin who are related through male links.
filiation   A parent–child relationship link used as a basis for descent-group membership.
patrilineage   A lineage based on descent traced through a line of men to a common male ancestor and sharing a joint estate.
segmentary lineage system   A system in which complementary opposition and genealogical principles of unilineal descent are used by residential groups as a basis for political mobilization in the absence of centralized political leadership.

spears, and blood feuds were possible, but cattle could be accepted as compensation for homicide. Raiding for cattle routinely occurred between more distant groups of Nuer villages, which Evans-Pritchard designated as tribes but which were probably shifting alliances of adjacent villages. Women and children and granaries were spared in "intertribal" raiding, but they might not be spared in raids against non-Nuer groups such as the Dinka, even though they developed from a common culture.

Conflicts seemed to arise primarily over cattle, either from cattle raiding or from disputes over unpaid bride-wealth transfers. Homicides could lead to feuds between kin groups, which could lead to further vengeance killings as in Amazonia, but among the Nuer there was a mechanism for mediation. Specific individuals, whom Evans-Pritchard (1940) called leopard-skin chiefs, served as mediators and attempted to persuade the conflicting parties to settle the dispute by means of compensation in the form of cattle transfer (see Figure 4.12). Leopard-skin chiefs were respected as ritual practitioners and as mediators, but they were not chiefs with political authority. In his mediator role, the chief was expected to threaten to curse a reluctant party with supernatural sanctions but, in fact, had no coercive power.

Although cattle are a major cause of conflict, they also provide an incentive for reducing conflict. Intervillage feuding would disrupt bride-wealth transfers because wide extension of incest restrictions, which reduces confusion in bride-wealth transfers, means that villages are usually exogamous. This divides the loyalties of people who might feel obligated to support one another in blood feuds as co-villagers, as close kin, or as claimants to bride-wealth cattle. It is thus in virtually everyone's self-interest to keep feuding to an absolute minimum. By crosscutting village membership in this way, domestic-scale societies create what has been called the peace in the feud (Gluckman 1956). It appears both that cattle made possible increased population densities and that their cultural use provided an incentive and a mechanism for limiting the feud.

Viewed in its own terms, Nuer politics makes perfectly good sense for a domestic-scale society of autonomous villages maximizing equality and eco-

FIGURE 4.12   *A Nuer leopard-skin chief. The individuals serve as mediators rather than as political leaders.*

nomic self-sufficiency. The advantage of the segmentary system was that it came into effect only when it was needed. It seems to have given the Nuer a decisive advantage in their raids for Dinka cattle and allowed them to steadily gain territory at the expense of the Dinka. Some observers have called Nuer expansion a "conquest" and "tribal imperialism" (Kelly 1985), but such terms are more applicable to war conducted by a central authority. It is important to distinguish between wars of conquest as state policy and raids and feuds between domestic-scale societies. Nuer expansion, a relatively gradual process over many decades, involved steady incorporation of the Dinka through intermarriage and adoption, with relatively little loss of life. Because the Nuer and Dinka are such close cultural relatives, the issue of the Nuer encroachment raises the question of ethnic identity in domestic-scale societies (see the box entitled "Ethnic Identity: Who Are the Nuer? Who Are the Maasai?").

Nuer Spirits, Symbolism, and Sacrifice

How do the Nuer construct their collective religious beliefs around the concept of Spirit? In what respects is their religion egalitarian? What is the symbolic religious role of cattle?

The religious beliefs of African pastoralists such as the Nuer and Maasai are primarily expressed in life cycle rituals or during other crisis events, such as drought and disease, and often feature the sacrifice of animals. The most basic distinctions in Nuer cosmology are made between Spirit and Creation, or between the immaterial and material worlds, which exist in complementary opposition (Beidelman 1966, 1971). When people show proper respect (*thek*) for these distinctions, their lives can normally be expected to go smoothly; misfortune occurs, however, when these categories intrude on each other, either in natural events or due to immoral human actions involving natural categories or human society. Failure to observe incest restrictions, for example, can bring illness. Confusion of categories causes ritual pollution, or contamination by "dirt," as "matter out of place" (Douglas 1966:35). Sacrifice and ritual can restore the previous order by mediating between the opposing principles of Spirit and Creation.

In Evans-Pritchard's (1953) analysis of the Nuer concept of Spirit (his translation for the Nuer word *Kwoth*), he described a hierarchy of spirit manifestations ranked from high to low and with distinctions based on their location and social associations (see Table 4.6). He felt that all of these different spirits were simply different "refractions" of a single unitary Spirit concept. The highest level is called God and is considered to be a pure spirit who is located in the sky and is associated with humanity in general. Genealogically, he may be referred to as father, but his involvement with human affairs is indirect. The air spirits occur at a lower level, in the atmosphere, and are represented by charismatic religious specialists known as prophets who are thought to communicate directly with these spirits. They may help warriors prepare themselves spiritually for cattle raiding and may be instrumental in organizing relatively large-scale military expeditions. Lower-level spirits may be manifest in animals and objects and are associated with kin groups and individuals. There are many

ritual specialists including earth priests, cattle priests, and grass priests, to name a few, and a wide range of curers and diviners, all of whom maintain special relationships with these spirits. According to T. O. Beidelman's (1966, 1971) analysis, Nuer religious specialists demonstrate their association with Spirit by assuming the ambiguous characteristics of confused categories. Prophets have long hair and beards, wear clothing, and appear unkempt, when ordinary Nuer would be unclothed, clean-shaven, and neat. They accomplish their role as mediators between Spirit and Creation because they partake of both categories and thus are in a position to realign them. When anyone performs a ritual sacrifice, he, in effect, helps restore the cosmic order.

The preferred sacrificial animal is an ox (a bull, castrated at maturity), and every sacrifice is called an ox even when a sheep or goat is used. Because cattle are slaughtered only on ritual occasions and because herds are managed for maximum growth potential and milk production, it is reasonable on strictly utilitarian grounds that male animals would be sacrificed. However, Beidelman (1966) argued that oxen are chosen for sacrifice because of their close symbolic association with men and because oxen are male animals but sterile—thus, in an ambiguous category, making them ideal mediators between Spirit and Creation. Nuer cows are equated with women. Nuer women are allocated cows from bride-wealth, and women may be named after the cows that they milk. Men have ox names and a favorite ox, which is "initiated" with cuts on its horns that duplicate the deep incisions that are made on the foreheads of Nuer young men at their initiations. Young men marry after their initiation, but their oxen (technically bulls until that point) are then castrated. Beidelman stresses the parallels between marriage and restrained sexual morality for men and castration as moral domestication of the animal. Some men are called bulls, but, like real bulls, they are seen as aggressive and troublesome.

Even with the ethnographic reports of high gods, priests, and prophets for cattle pastoralists, these ideological systems are essentially egalitarian. There is no codified religious system and no fraternity of religious specialists. Spirit possession is available to anyone. Individuals retain a brief identity after death in relation to cattle and

Ethnic Identity: Who Are the Nuer? Who Are the Maasai?

The distribution map of Nilotic-speaking ethnic groups in the upper Nile does suggest that a rapid military conquest of the Dinka by the Nuer occurred along the "predatory expansion" lines suggested by Marshall Sahlins (1961) and Raymond Kelly (1985) (see Figure 4.13), especially given the Nuer predilection for raiding Dinka cattle and their negative stereotype of the Dinka. Kelly even suggests that the Nuer motive for expansion was their higher bride-wealth rates. The conquest theory originated with early British administrators and explorers, who were themselves members of a conquest society, and it is hardly surprising that they were quick to see evidence of imperialism among peoples they were themselves conquering. Peter Newcomer (1972) challenged the conquest theory and initiated the debate over Nuer identity. Newcomer asserted that the Nuer were, in fact, originally a Dinka subgroup who were lucky enough to develop the segmentary system as a social mutation that gave them an advantage over other Dinka in competition for finite pastoral resources. In this view, the Nuer were simply Dinka who became more successful raiders.

Newcomer's argument, which was elaborated by Maurice Glickman (1972), is that the Nuer became more effective cattle raiders because herders from different Nuer villages were forced to interact amicably in dry-season cattle camps and found it easy to form intervillage raiding parties. By contrast, the Dinka occupied more favorable grazing lands, made less extensive seasonal moves, and consequently did not need to develop the elaborate social network that formed the basis of Nuer "segmentation." Thus, ecological factors related to cattle herding might account for the superior organizational ability of the Nuer (Glickman 1972).

This discussion still leaves unanswered the question of who the Nuer are. A careful reader of Evans-Pritchard's *The Nuer* (1940) might be surprised to learn that the Nuer do not call themselves "Nuer." They are "Nath" or "Naath." In a footnote, we find that "the word 'Nuer' is sanctioned by a century of usage" and is what the Naath are called by the Dinka, and by all other outsiders, we might add. The Dinka, in turn, call themselves "Jieng." In both cases, as so often occurs with ethnic self-appellations, the words *Naath* and *Jieng* mean "people" (Southall 1976). When both Nuer and Dinka speak of an individual person, they use the same term, *Raan.* Linguists refer to the "Nuer" and "Dinka" languages, but they are closely related, and both are divided into many dialects such that the differences between any two Dinka dialects might be greater than between two Nuer and Dinka dialects. Thus, even treating Nuer and Dinka as two distinct languages is somewhat of a "convenient fiction" to facilitate communication among linguists, missionaries, anthropologists, and government administrators (Southall 1976).

Calling the Nuer Naath only shifts the question to, Who are the Naath? The Nuer become as difficult to pin down as their phantom segmentary lineages. Because there is no permanent Nuer tribal entity, it follows that there is no Nuer "tribe." Indeed, anthropologist John Burton declares, "Such ethnic designation as 'Nuer' and 'Dinka' . . . are at best marginally indicative of observable interethnic relations and associations" (1981:157). The only consensus, apparently shared by the Nuer and the Dinka and their observers, is that the Nuer raid cattle from the Dinka.

The absence of fixed boundaries between Nuer and Dinka frustrated British administrators for years. The Nuer and Dinka freely intermarry, and cattle move between them as booty and as bride-wealth. Someone might grow up as a Dinka and be initiated as a Nuer. There are other rituals that convert adult Dinka into Nuer. Indeed, the two apparent ethnic categories share so many cultural traits that in mixed camps, they may tell each other apart most easily by referring to physical differences in their cattle. In the final analysis, it seems that "true Nuer" are those who are the most successful herders in a given community. In this case, not only are the Nuer and Dinka people, but as Burton observes, "They are first of all pastoralists rather than antagonistic representatives of supposedly pure ethnic groups. . . . Ethnicity therefore moves on the hoof" (1981:160, 161).

John Galaty (1982) examined the problem of ethnic identity from the viewpoint of another Nilotic people, the Maasai of Kenya and Tanzania. According to Maasai ethnosociology (how a society views its own cultural identity), the Maasai are speakers of the Maa language who belong to any of a number of named tribal sections of a single Maasai "nation," which has no formal political organization. The term *Maasai* literally means "I will not beg" and is a frequently used polite expression associated with the dominant Maasai values of bravery and arrogance. In their self-designation, Maasai also call attention to the beads that are featured in their dress and, most prominently, to their association with cattle. In their own eyes, the Maasai are "people of cattle." However, as the term *Maasai* is used, it has multiple meanings that shift depending on context. Galaty has represented this as a series of three nested triangles of three sets of contrasting identities, based on distance from a central Maasai identity (see Figure 4.14). In the widest context (triangle A in the diagram), Maasai speakers see themselves as pastoralists distinguished from other people who emphasize hunting or farming for their subsistence. Non-Maasai-speaking pastoral peoples, such as the Somali, may be considered "Maasai" in deference to their herding and are treated with special respect. At a second level, encompassing all Maasai speakers, there are specific categories based on dominant economy, such that Maasai who hunt are called *Torrobo*, those who farm are *Ilkurrman*, and "other Maasai" herders are *Iloikop*. Thus, at this level, common descent from mythical Maasai ancestors is invoked to verify one's Maasai identity even when herding is not practiced. Closest to the center, Maasai blacksmiths are *Ilkunono*, diviners are *Iloibonok*, and ordinary herders are called *Ilomet* by the blacksmiths and diviners. Because the specific meaning of Maasai and the nine related social categories are so dependent on the context in which the terms are used, the confusion experienced by colonial-era Europeans when they attempted to elicit East African "tribal" names is understandable. They were looking for discrete, territorially based, politically organized "tribes," led by "chiefs" with whom they could sign treaties, and that they could "administer" as colonial dependencies. In reality, things were not that simple.

children, but there is no ancestor cult. Any man can perform sacrifices, and the political roles that prophets and leopard-skin chiefs play are strictly limited. These roles do not give them control over strategic resources or allow them to extract labor or tribute. At least one especially charismatic nineteenth-century Nuer prophet gained enough influence to convince people to erect a dirt-mound pyramid shrine, but he was unable to convert it into permanent political power or an enduring ancestor cult.

FIGURE 4.13   *The Nuer and neighboring peoples, in central Sudan.*

KEY: ■ Shilluk ■ Dinka ▨ Nuer ■ Anuak

The Maasai Age-Class System

How does age organize Maasai society? How do age classes contribute to social solidarity?

The Maasai pastoral system has remained viable even after years of colonial rule, cycles of drought and disease, persistent penetration by the market economy, and political control by the modern independent states of Kenya and Tanzania. African pastoralism has proved to have remarkable resilience, not only to the natural environment but also to the wider political economy surrounding it. The Maasai demonstrate that a domestic-scale culture based on subsistence herding organized at a family level can maintain a high degree of social equality and autonomy while coexisting with larger-scale social systems. Anthropologist Paul Spencer (1988) argues that perhaps the principal reason for the success of Maasai pastoralism is not the pervasiveness of "cattle complex values," but the personal rewards offered by the **age-class system** common to many East African cattle peoples.

Maasai pastoralism, in its ideal form, represents the extreme in subsistence dependence on herding by African cattle peoples. As described by Spencer, the Maasai system depends on three critical social roles: the elders, who control normal herding activities; the wives, who do the milking and take care of the animals within the domestic compound; and the *moran*, unmarried warriors who until recently raided for cattle. The Maasai settlement pattern re-

FIGURE 4.14
The Maasai ethnosociological system.

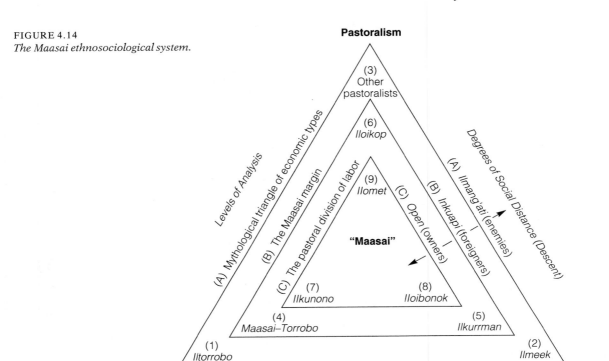

TABLE 4.6   *The Nuer Concept of Spirit* (Kwoth)

Spirit Type	Location	Social Association	Manifestation	Genealogy	Rank
God	Sky	Humanity	Pure spirit	Father	Aristocratic
Air spirits	Air, clouds, breezes	Political movements, raiding	Prophets	Upper: God's children Lower: God's grandchildren	—
Totemic spirits	Earth	Kinship groups	Animals	Children of God's daughters	Dinka-like
Nature spirits, fetishes	Earth, underworld	Individuals	Things	Children of daughters of air spirit	Foreigners

SOURCE: Evans-Pritchard (1953).

sembles the Nuer pattern described previously. Family herds are managed by the male heads of households, which are ideally polygynous. A man's married sons live in the same homestead compound, with their individual corrals grouped around

age-class system   A system in which individuals of similar age are placed in a named group and moved as a unit through the culturally defined stages of life. Specific rituals mark each change in age status.

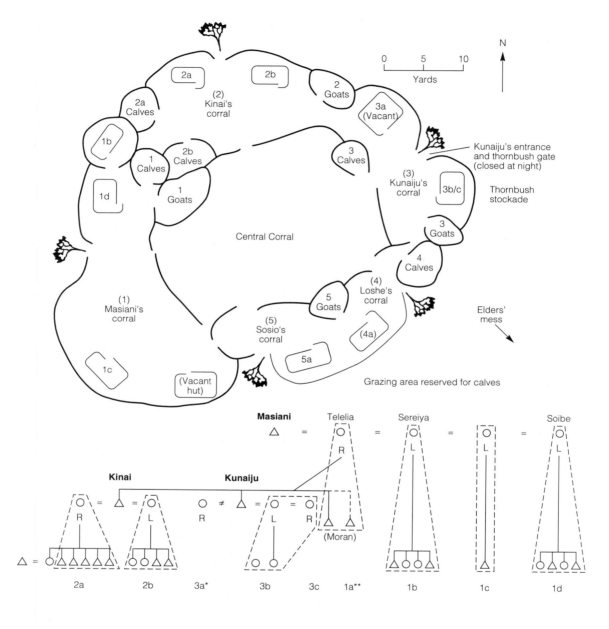

FIGURE 4.15   *A Maasai homestead, showing houses, household composition, and livestock corrals. (SOURCE: Spencer 1988.)*

a common corral (see Figure 4.15). Control by the older men over the wives and children is a more overt cultural pattern with the Maasai than among the Nuer and is perhaps a reflection of the subsistence dominance of herding for the Maasai. Marriages are entirely arranged by a girl's father, who selects a future husband for her from among her suitors. It is also assumed that men will make the important decisions concerning the cattle, and they may beat wives who flout their authority.

As is frequently the case with polygynous societies, women marry at a very young age, whereas men marry significantly later. This arrangement makes polygyny possible and makes it the prerogative of the older men, as in aboriginal Australia. With the Maasai surveyed by Spencer (1988), only 16 percent of the young men ages 18–25 years were married, and none polygynously, whereas 60 percent of the men over 40 (ages 41–70 years) had more than one wife. Polygyny offers direct advantages to the herd manager because it increases his labor force and allows him to subdivide responsibility for his animals.

The age-class system, with its associated rituals, helps balance the social stresses created by polygyny and patriarchy. Life stages and generation levels are marked by a series of rituals that occur throughout an individual's lifetime (see Table 4.7). Step by step, prepubescent children are named, their heads are shaved, their lower incisors are removed, and their ears are pierced and stretched. Each ceremony indicates increasing maturity. Removal of the lower incisors, for example, means that a young boy is old enough to herd livestock near the homestead, but he does not go far afield with the animals until he is old enough to tolerate large incisions in his ear lobes. A calf is ritually slaughtered at the first stage of adulthood, but this must occur after the father has been ritually inducted into his status as a full elder by having an ox slaughtered and after the mother has ritually completed the process of her marriage. The spacing of these two ceremonies thus marks a generation. Ceremonies surrounding initiation make the initiation process a ritual rebirth, and the initiate symbolically becomes a dependent child. Initiation itself is marked by genital mutilation—clitoridectomy for girls and circumcision for boys. Shortly after the operation, girls are led to their new hus-

TABLE 4.7   *Maasai Age Grades*

Grade	Age*	Features
Senior elder	50+	Religious and ritual power, charisma of old age assumed
Great Ox Ceremony—Precedes Son's Initiation		
Junior elders	35–50	Incest avoidance of daughters of the age class, not expected to fight, have power to curse, sponsor new age class
Olngesher Ceremony—*Moran* Become Elders, Age Class United and Named		
Senior *moran*	20–35	Preparation of elderhood, may marry, meat and milk avoidances lifted
Eunoto Ceremony		
Junior *moran*	15–20	Wear red ochre, braid hair, dance with girls, have distinctive spears, perform ritual rebellion, form *manyata* warrior village, avoid meat and milk
Initiates	12–15	Age mates begin to associate distinctive regalia
Circumcision Ceremony		
Boyhood	10–12	Earlobes cut and stretched, work as herdboys
Childhood	0–10	Naming, lower incisors removed

SOURCE: Spencer (1965, 1988).
*Age intervals overlap because the actual age of specific individuals in a particular grade will vary widely.

band's homesteads as brides, and boys move through other ceremonies that ritually separate them from their status as children and prepare them for *moran*-hood. Only males participate in the age-class system. Age groupings are sometimes described using a variety of terms, but in this discussion, which follows the definitions employed by Bernardo Bernardi (1985), *age class* refers to the group of people who are promoted together through the same sequence of **age grades,** or culturally designated stages. Thus, for example, males of roughly the same age move as a group sequentially through a series of subgrades from boyhood, to warriorhood (or the *moran* grade), to elderhood,

age grade   A culturally defined stage of an age-class system such as childhood, adolescence, parenthood, and old age.

and, finally, to retirement. Age classes are named, and the members of each class carry a distinct style of hand-forged iron spear and form a fraternity (Larick 1986).

Each tribal section independently operates its own age-class system. A new class is formed roughly every 15 years under the sponsorship of the elders, who are two classes ahead of them, or approximately 30 years their senior, and who will serve as patrons of the new class. The recruitment period for each class is ritually closed by the elders in the class immediately senior to it. Each class is, in effect, forced up the age-grade ladder by the demands of the youths below who do not want to be the last to join a class that is about to advance. Late recruits experience a foreshortened time period in the favored warrior grade. The extended time during which a given age class can recruit means that there will be a relatively wide spread of ages within a given class; some Maasai set up junior and senior subsets within a single class, granting each different privileges and moving each subset through their own ritual stages of maturation. When the youngest subset of a class enters the grade of elderhood, the entire class assumes a single name.

The highlight of the entire age sequence is the *moran* grade, which young men enter after going through ceremonies that ritually separate them from their natal families. As *moran*, they become the warrior protectors of their communities; at the same time, however, these young men form their own egalitarian communities of age mates united by special bonds of loyalty and shared experience. Freed from domestic routines and still unmarried, the novice *moran* are expected to dress in special finery, wear their hair in braids, dance and display, and carry on with young girls. Traditionally, they conducted raids to capture cattle and defended the local herds against raiders and lions. The most important privilege of the *moran* is the few years they spend in segregated warrior villages, known as *manyat* (singular, *manyata*), which are set up to defend individual districts. The *moran* flaunt their independence and live the communalistic ideals of *moran* brotherhood in their *manyat*. The supreme ideal of the *manyata* is represented by individual warriors, known as "diehards," who pledge themselves to die in combat rather than retreat (see Figure 4.16).

To establish a *manyata*, the *moran* conduct raids on their parental homes and carry off their mothers and small herds of cattle, sometimes against the protests of their fathers. As Spencer (1988) points out, this is clearly a ritual rebellion against the fa-

FIGURE 4.16   *Maasai warriors.*

ther's patriarchal control and has obvious Freudian overtones. The *manyat* villages of the *moran* are organized around egalitarian and communalistic principles in direct opposition to the age hierarchy and individualism of the domestic homestead.

The midpoint of *moran*-hood is ritually marked by an extended ceremony known as *eunoto*, which begins 5 years into the grade and initiates a 10-year series of steps leading to elderhood. After this ceremony, a *moran* may be expected to marry. In the *eunoto*, the *manyat* villages are disbanded, and the combined age class is formally launched. This ceremony involves a spectacular display of massed warriors that even attracts fee-paying European tourists and film crews.

Although many ceremonial phases of the Maasai age-class system incorporate ritualized rebellions against parental authority, the excesses of the *moran* are held in check, and they are guided through the maturation process by their elder patrons, who maintain ultimate control by their power to curse their charges. It could certainly be argued that the age-class system constructively channels the otherwise potentially disruptive energies of young men who grow up as subservient herdboys and must wait at least 10 years before they can marry. Spencer (1988) suggests that the age system diverts the stresses that are inherent in the family system away from the senior male household heads to elders in general. In some respects, the *manyata* phase place the *moran* in what Arnold van Gennep (1909) would call a **liminal phase.** It is a rite of transition in which the *moran* are ritually suspended in the space between being herdboys and elders.

The age-class system is functionally related to incest avoidance and marriage practices in a mutually reinforcing way. Spencer (1988) points out that Maasai incest restrictions are more elaborated toward daughters and mothers-in-law than mothers and sisters. This is apparently because a system of age-class exogamy operates in which the men of one age class marry the daughters of the men in the class senior to them, rather than marrying the daughters of their own age mates. The age classes thus are linked by marriage alliances, such as might operate between exogamous clans. This reinforces the respect that must obtain between junior and senior classes if the age-class system is to survive, because the junior class members will find their fathers-in-law in the senior class. Age-class exogamy also means that men will tend to marry much younger women, thereby creating the age differential that makes frequent polygyny possible.

The persistence of the Maasai as a society up to the present day is evidence of the importance of their age-class system. It is significant that while the population of Kenya as a whole has recently experienced extremely high population increases that threaten the economic viability of the entire country, settled farming groups are growing at twice the rate of the Maasai and other pastoralists (4 percent versus 2.2 percent or less). Isaac Sindiga (1987) suggests that the traditional Maasai practices of polygyny, postpartum taboos on sexual intercourse, and prolonged lactation, which are all linked to patriarchy and the age-class system, are significant child-spacing and fertility-dampening factors.

Although the position of Maasai women usually is described by both men and women as relatively inferior, Maasai women seem to accept this, or at least attempt to make the best of it (see the box entitled "Maasai Women"). Within the age-class system, young men also are subject to the authority of the elders who control bride-wealth cattle and marriages. Women do not become elders, but they clearly do have a stake in their society and work to maintain the system, especially as they grow older. Senior wives may welcome polygyny because it lightens their domestic routine. Women themselves perform the clitoridectomy, and they accept it as a precondition of marriage. Divorce is an option, especially early in an unhappy marriage. After women have children, they gain more autonomy, and because they marry young, they usually outlive their husbands. Abused wives may appeal to the elders for help; men who commit serious offenses against women may be perceived as a threat to all women; they may be assaulted and beaten and have their cattle slaughtered by a large group of enraged women acting in a publicly sanctioned role as enforcers of community morality. Women also conduct their own rituals of rebellion against patriarchal authority.

---

liminal phase   An ambiguous phase of ritual transition in which one is on the threshold between two states.

Maasai Women

In the film *Maasai Women*, anthropologist Melissa Llewelyn-Davies, who speaks the Maasai language and has years of research experience with the Maasai, engages several Maasai women in a free-ranging discussion about their experiences as women. In their own words, these Maasai women define and accept as a given the gender roles of their culture. Women milk cows, bear children, and build their own houses. A woman "has nothing." Women care for animals and have milking rights but no ownership rights over them. Men make the decisions about herds. Yet in this discussion with a sympathetic and knowledgeable nonnative woman, the Maasai women are quick to place their own cultural roles in a positive light. Clitoridectomy (female circumcision), which is strongly condemned by international feminists, is defended as something "we've always done." One woman explains, "It is something God began long ago. A girl wants to hurry up and be circumcised. It is a very good thing." When Llewelyn-Davies asks if the initiate is happy about the experience, she is told emphatically that she is "very happy" because the girl will then be thought of as a woman and will be able to marry soon.

Female circumcision may not be fully supported by all Maasai women, regardless of what they say about it. It may not even be a functionally irreplaceable part of their culture. In this case, women themselves perpetuate customs that may not be in their best interests.

In the film, the women tell Llewelyn-Davies that although they accept arranged marriages to old men, they are not always happy about it and may select young warriors as lovers even though their husbands would be angry if they found out. When Llewelyn-Davies raises the possibility of women being jealous over young co-wives in this polygynous society, a Maasai woman declares:

We're not jealous like you Europeans. . . . To us a co-wife is something very good because there is much work to do. When it rains, the village gets mucky and it's you who clears it out. It's you who looks after the cows. You do the milking, and your husband may have very many cows. That's a lot of work. You have to milk and smear the roof and see to the calves. . . . So when you give birth and it rains, who will smear the roof if you have no co-wife? No one. Who will clear the muck from the village? No one. So Maasai aren't jealous because of all this work.

However, the film also shows women greeting new co-wives with open, "ritualized" hostility.

It is a hard life, but there are rewards. After a girl's initiation, a group of women in the film sing,

Listen God to what suits women. It suits us to prepare charms for the initiates, to be busy with our children's circumcisions, to have celebrations, which are lavish in honey beer and milk and meat and butter. It suits us when our sons go out herding. It suits us to sit resting in the shade. It suits us when we suckle children. God, nursing mother, remember what suits us.

In some respects, the age-class system can be considered a highly egalitarian form of political organization used by stateless societies to regulate rights, privileges, and responsibilities between men who might otherwise find themselves in frequent conflict (Bernardi 1985). The division of labor places women outside the public political arena as is often the case in domestic-scale societies. The underlying principle of male age classes is that every male enjoys the same potential to be a warrior, marry, raise a family, officiate at rituals, and so on, and these potentials are realized in orderly sequence by virtue of his membership in an age class in which these rights are jointly shared. Conflicts do arise in the system, but they occur primarily over the timing of promotions. Political struggle takes place between groups, not individuals. Political power thus is widely distributed and strictly regulated. The system is not simply a gerontocracy with power concentrated at the top.

SUMMARY

East African cattle peoples have certainly developed a highly successful system that makes effective use of a difficult environment. Age hierarchy and apparent male dominance in many spheres exist alongside basic equality between households. Individual households maintain considerable self-sufficiency. To be poor in such a system is to have too few animals for subsistence and bride-wealth, but social support systems normally take care of both problems. There is little overt poverty in that cattle are widely loaned or shared between households according to need, regardless of their actual ownership. The effects of variation in herd composition are leveled out such that people are likely to go hungry only under the most severe drought conditions, when people would be forced to draw on their small stock; but then, everyone would go hungry. Sharing cattle between households also reduces the possibility that all of one's animals would be lost to raids or disease and makes the most efficient use of unpredictable and highly variable grazing and water resources. Raiding served to redistribute animals and allowed young men to build their herds rapidly. People who find themselves cattleless might opt out of the system by becoming foragers or sedentary farmers.

STUDY QUESTIONS

1. Describe the subsistence uses East African pastoralists make of their cattle.

2. What are the most critical limiting factors to which African pastoralists must adapt?

3. Why is it difficult to determine how many cattle African pastoralists actually need and to establish the carrying capacity of the range?

4. Describe the marriage process for the Nuer, including the concepts of bride-wealth, household, husband, wife, pater, and genitor.

5. How does the Maasai age-class system relate to gerontocracy and patriarchy, and how does it contribute to the resilience of Maasai society?

6. Describe the social and ritual uses of cattle in East Africa.

SUGGESTED READING

EVANS-PRITCHARD, E. E. 1940. *The Nuer: A Description of the Modes of Livelihood and Political Institutions of a Nilotic People.* New York and Oxford, Eng.: Oxford University Press. The most famous early ethnography of East African cattle people; vividly describes their dependence on cattle, emphasizing ecological relationships.

SPENCER, PAUL. 1988. *The Maasai of Matapato: A Study of Rituals of Rebellion.* Bloomington and Indianapolis: Indiana University Press. An excellent modern ethnography that focuses on social organization, life cycle, and ritual.

5

Body, Mind, and Soul:
The Quality of Tribal Life

The thought, beliefs, and health practices of domestic-scale cultures raise many important, intriguing, and critical questions related to cross-cultural understanding. The basic issue is how to evaluate the mental, emotional, and physical well-being of tribal peoples in order to assess the overall effectiveness of their cultures. This is an important problem because welfare intervention programs undertaken on behalf of tribal peoples by missionaries, government educators, and health workers often assume that these people must be ignorant and backward. Members of wealthy industrial nations easily equate hospitals, schools, and sewage treatment plants with health and intelligence and look down on anyone lacking these standards. Such ethnocentric views are reinforced by the seemingly bizarre and irrational elements in tribal shamanism, witchcraft, and magic. Whereas earlier chapters showed these aspects of religion and ideology within their cultural context, this chapter considers their significance for individuals.

We will review some of the classic interpretations of tribal religion and "primitive mentality" by such historically prominent anthropological theorists as Edward Tylor, Sir James Frazer, Franz Boas, Lucien Lévy-Bruhl, and Bronislaw Malinowski, along with the more recent views of Claude Lévi-Strauss and C. R. Hallpike. Because racist beliefs have clouded many views of tribal peoples, we will review the facts of human biology to affirm the fundamental unity of humankind, before considering the issues of language and culture, religious practice, and health. We will place special emphasis on Australian and Amazonian examples because full cultural context has been established in previous chapters.

THE MENTAL ABILITIES OF TRIBAL PEOPLES

Collective Representations and Primitive Mentality

How have anthropologists evaluated the mental abilities of tribal peoples, and what are the difficulties of this cross-cultural research? Do tribal peoples think differently than other people?

The rapid European colonial domination of Africa, which was in full swing by the late nineteenth century, made it imperative for the new European administrators and petty colonial officials to understand the peoples that they were attempting to control. Because it was so difficult for foreigners to predict the behavior of natives, it was widely believed that native thought processes were inferior to those of Europeans. And because explicitly racist evolutionary theories were used to justify colonialism, Europeans readily assumed that people living in domestic-scale societies must be physically and culturally underdeveloped and therefore childlike in their thinking.

American anthropologists under Franz Boas distanced themselves somewhat from such interpretations. Boas rated Euro-American civilization as the highest human cultural achievement, but he was firmly antiracist and believed that there were no significant differences in basic mental faculties between "uncivilized primitives" and "civilized" peoples. In his book *The Mind of Primitive Man* (1911), he easily refuted a list of presumably inferior mental features that were widely attributed to tribal people, including their supposed inability to inhibit their emotions, their shortened attention spans, and their limited powers of original thought. Boas found that natives were impulsive and improvident when it was culturally appropriate but showed remarkable restraint when necessary. He noted that the supposed inability of natives to focus their attention was most likely to be reported by frustrated ethnographers who found it difficult to get reluctant informants to answer a long series of irrelevant questions. Likewise, within their own cultural context, natives showed plenty of creativity. Boas certainly acknowledged differences in forms of thought between tribal and civilized peoples, but these he attributed to social, or cultural, differences, not racial factors. He concluded that tribal peoples simply classified experiences differently and merged concepts in ways that appeared peculiar to us.

British anthropologist E. B. Tylor (1871) argued in *Primitive Culture* that seemingly bizarre tribal religious beliefs and rituals developed out of what he called *animistic thinking,* in which intellectually curious people attempted to explain dream experiences and death by attributing a detachable animating soul to people, animals, plants, and "inanimate" objects. Tylor felt that the soul concept was the basis of all religion, shamanism, and witchcraft and that tribal people arrived at it by logical

mental processes, which were basically like our own. Sir James Frazer elaborated this intellectualist approach in *The Golden Bough* ([1890] 1900) when he identified the laws that he thought underlay magical practices. His *law of sympathy* held that things such as hair, which were once part of someone, could still influence that person even after they were separated. Therefore, a man's hair clippings might be used by shamans to harm him. Like Tylor, Frazer argued that primitives were crude logicians who thought like Englishmen but simply made mistakes.

French positivist philosopher Lucien Lévy-Bruhl was one of the first scholars to systematically examine the thought processes of tribal peoples with the practical purpose of showing how they differed from those of "civilized" peoples. He applied the concept of *collective representations,* or group ideas, developed by French sociologist Emile Durkheim. According to Lévy-Bruhl ([1922] 1923, 1926) collective representations, like culture in general, are emotion-laden thoughts, or ideas, that are shared by the members of a specific society and transmitted across generations. These thoughts are collective in that they are not the unique property of specific individuals, and therefore they cannot be understood according to the principles of individual psychology. He insisted throughout that primitive mentality was not inferior and that natives were not childlike; their thinking was simply different. However, this point was easily overlooked when he referred to primitive mentality as "prelogical," not "illogical," and when he declared that the collective representations of "undeveloped peoples" could not be understood by studying the categories and logical principles used by "adult, civilized, white man" (1926:13). Lévy-Bruhl agreed with

---

animistic thinking   The soul concept used by tribal individuals as an intellectual explanation of life, death, and dream experiences; part of Tylor's theory of animism as the origin of religion.

law of sympathy   Frazer's explanation for the logic underlying magic, sorcery, and shamanism. He thought that tribal peoples believed that anything ever connected with a person, such as hair or blood, could be manipulated to influence that person.

collective representations   Ideas, or thoughts, and emotions common to a society as a whole, especially in reference to the supernatural.

Boas that thought was culturally conditioned, but he emphatically departed from Boas, as well as from Tylor and Frazer, by declaring that the mental processes of "primitives" are distinctively different and can be understood only by their own "laws." He rejected animist, intellectualist explanations because they were based on individual, not collective, thought.

The most critical aspect of primitive thought, Lévy-Bruhl argued, was that it assumed a "mystic" reality—it was based on a socially conditioned belief in imperceptible forces. This was *prelogical thinking*, based on a *law of participation*, under which contradictions were ignored and something could be two things at once. Thus, primitives saw nothing contradictory in a shaman being a man and a tiger at the same time. Of course, all peoples have this ability. For example, Christians, who may be members of political- and commercial-scale cultures, have no apparent difficulty considering Jesus Christ to be both a man and a god.

Lévy-Bruhl declared, "Primitives perceive nothing in the same way as we do" (1926:43), even though their brains and their senses are the same as ours. In primitive thought, according to Lévy-Bruhl, the causes of natural events like disease and accident might be sought in what we would call the supernatural. Physical causes were irrelevant in collective representations, even though individuals were certainly logical enough to know when to come in out of the rain and could successfully manage their daily affairs. Prelogical natives formed concrete impressions that they felt and lived emotionally, whereas civilized people worked with abstract, conceptual thought. In his own contradictory terms, Lévy-Bruhl suggested that primitive thought was thus "concrete," whereas civilized thinking was abstract and conceptual. This misleading distinction still plagues anthropological theorists.

Despite the difficulties Lévy-Bruhl experienced in grappling with cross-cultural understanding, he correctly observed that barriers to emic understanding were in a sense insurmountable. Translation problems are critical because categories are seldom precisely the same even when superficial resemblances exist. For example, traditional exchange objects, which often are called "money," are not actually money as it exists in a market econ-omy. Although the difference in meaning may not be accurately characterized as that between concrete and abstract, Lévy-Bruhl was correct in calling for in-depth linguistic knowledge because it was perfectly possible to have a minimal speaking knowledge without really being able to think in another language.

Claude Lévi-Strauss (1966) began his work on primitive thought by calling into question the entire distinction between abstract and concrete words by relating it to differences in level of attention and interest, not to differences in method of thought. Lévi-Strauss argued that tribal people, like civilized people, use many abstract words and pursue objective knowledge about the environment for its own sake. People name things, not simply because these are objects of immediate utilitarian interest, but because they find it aesthetically pleasing to impose order on the world through careful observation and cataloguing. Such attention to detail was well illustrated in our previous discussion of the ethnoecological knowledge of Native Amazonians and the Dreaming maps of Australian aborigines. According to Lévi-Strauss, it is this common drive for order that underlies all human thought and that makes unfamiliar thought patterns understandable.

The view that folk biological taxonomies (the way people classify plants and animals) may be an intellectual pursuit reflecting what is "good to think" as much as an interest in what is "good to eat" or that they may be useful has been challenged by Robert Randall and Eugene Hunn (1984, Hunn 1985). They argue that in many cases, labeling is directly utilitarian. For example, some peoples carefully name caterpillars that are significant as food or as pests while paying little attention to otherwise conspicuous adult butterflies and moths.

Lévi-Strauss did not find it particularly mystical that people identify with totemic animals. Natives are not confused by a law of participation into thinking that they are their totems. There is no contradiction in holding empirical and emotional knowledge about a single object. Instead of speaking of a prelogical mentality, Lévi-Strauss maintained that magical thought, or what he preferred to call *mythical thought*, differs from formal scientific thought in method and purpose, but not in logic. Mythical thought is scientific in that it produced the important technological developments of the Neolithic, such as domestication, pottery, and weaving. However, the "Neolithic paradox" for Lévi-Strauss is the difficulty in explaining why technological development seemingly stagnated after the scientific achievements of the Neolithic until the establishment of formal science. To resolve the paradox, Lévi-Strauss argued that there are two distinct but opposite types of scientific thought, each equally valid and neither a stage in the development of the other: the *science of the concrete,* which is based on perceptions and signs, and formal science, which works with concepts.

Mythical thought works with a culturally limited set of signs, including significant images and events, which it orders into structured relationships that provide aesthetic satisfaction while helping people understand reality (see Figure 5.1). Lévi-Strauss is here referring to the structured sets of logical associations and complementary oppositions that are so characteristic of myths and the ritual beliefs and practices that are related to them. These were discussed in some detail in the Amazonian cosmology examined in Chapter 3. Formal scientific concepts remain as close to natural reality as possible. They are derived from structured theories and hypotheses and are used to expand the total cultural inventory and to make changes, or create events, in the external world.

Cross-Cultural Intelligence Testing

How have arguments that tribal peoples are cognitively retarded been challenged? Why is cross-cultural intelligence testing unreliable?

Anthropologist C. R. Hallpike (1979) carries on Lévy-Bruhl's argument that "primitives" think differently than civilized peoples by substituting the term *preoperatory* for *prelogical*. Hallpike's theories deserve attention because, even though they are not a major influence in anthropology, they could be uncritically used to support the view that tribal peoples are mentally inferior and thus in need of improvement by more enlightened outsiders.

Primitives, for Hallpike, are the rural illiterate and unschooled, as well as the members of the domestic-scale societies dealt with in Chapters 2–4 of this book. Their thinking is not actually different from our own — it is merely incomplete and less developed. Hallpike uses the stages devised by Swiss psychologist Jean Piaget to describe the acquisition of cognitive abilities by children in order to catalogue the cognitive abilities of tribal adults (see Table 5.1). The Piagetian sensorimotor, preoperational, concrete operations, and formal stages are assumed to be biologically determined levels of intellectual development through which individuals progress as they mature. The stages were based on a variety of performance tests applied to European children. Preoperational children are assumed to be incapable of realizing that a liquid conserves its original quantity when poured into a taller glass. This implies that although they may understand comparatives such as taller and shorter, preoperational children do not yet grasp the abstract concept of volume. Their cognitive abilities also are inferior to the operational and formal thinking of older children in many other ways.

Hallpike finds resemblances between the collective representations of tribal peoples, such as the mystical thinking identified by Lévy-Bruhl, and thinking characteristics of children at the preoperational stage. Hallpike infers that this means that the majority of primitive adults are incapable of what Piaget defined as adult thought. They are mentally equivalent to 7-year-old European children, but because they are grown up, they are, in effect, retarded. Such retardation, Hallpike argues, is caused by the absence of schools and literacy. He softens this conclusion by noting that although primitives may be cognitive children, as adults they nevertheless have acquired enough knowledge and experience to make them smarter than children.

prelogical thinking Lévy-Bruhl's characterization of the collective representations of tribal peoples, which he thought reflected concrete thought and a mystic reality unique to domestic-scale cultures.

law of participation The assumption that a thing can participate in or be part of two or more things at once; identified by Lévy-Bruhl as the principle underlying his concept of prelogical thought.

mythical thought Lévi-Strauss' term for the thinking underlying myth and magic; logically similar to scientific thought but based on the science of the concrete and used to serve aesthetic purposes and to solve existential problems.

science of the concrete Thought based on perceptions and signs, images, and events, as opposed to formal science based on concepts.

FIGURE 5.1 *The Pokot, East African pastoralists, dancing to celebrate a male initiation cere-mony. Ritual activities like these are rich in symbolic associations, connecting mind, body, and soul.*

TABLE 5.1 *Piaget's Stages of Mental Development*

Stage	Description
Sensorimotor	Age 0–2 years: nonverbal, private learning from experience through concrete objects
Preoperational	Age 2–7 years: objects represented by words
Concrete operations	Age 7–12 years: objects classified by similarities and differences; coordination of multiple dimensions of length, number, weight, area, volume
Formal (scientific)	Age 12–adult: formal logic; propositional, deductive reasoning

However, such a distinction would probably be lost on anyone wishing to limit the political rights of tribal people by treating them as legal minors.

Hallpike (1979) cites a variety of psychological tests performed on "primitives" to support his con-clusions. These tests seem to show that primitives cannot verbally sort objects into classes by obvious differences, cannot sort the events of a narrative into a logical sequence, cannot grasp the argument of simple syllogisms, and so on. Hallpike makes a careful point-by-point comparison of primitive thought with our presumably more developed formal thought and finds primitive thinking profoundly inadequate (see Table 5.2). However, both the validity and the reliability of the cross-cultural tests of cognition that Hallpike relies on are open to serious question. For example, Hallpike decided that a 37-year-old Russian peasant was cognitively preoperational because he refused to tell a psychological fieldworker that the bears in Novaya Zemlya must all be white when he was presented with a logical syllogism emphatically declaring that Novaya Zemlya was in the far north, where it always snows, and that in the far north where it always snows, all the bears are white. The subject might have been displaying rational cynicism toward bureaucratic authority when he declared, "What I know, I say, and nothing beyond that." Hallpike interpreted this test as further demonstration that primitives lack the cognitive ability to handle the hypothetical in a logical problem.

As Richard Shweder observes (1982, 1985), Hallpike is vulnerable on a number of issues. In the first place, Piagetian stage theory has come under increasing attack by developmental psychologists who stress that the boundaries between the stages are not as sharp as once thought. Young children may be quite capable of operational and formal thinking at much earlier ages than previously be-

TABLE 5.2   *Primitive, Preoperational Thought Versus Operational Thought*

Primitive	Operational
Contextual	Generalizable
Concrete	Abstract
Nonspecialized	Specialized
Ethnocentric	Objective
Dogmatic	Relativistic
Simple	Complex
Incomplete	Complete
Inexplicit	Explicit
Personal	Impersonal
Percept based	Concept based
Animistic	Causal
Purposeless	Utilitarian
Undifferentiated	Differentiated
Tacit	Reflective

SOURCES: Hallpike (1979:126) and Shweder (1982:356).

lieved; they may simply not often use these abilities and may have difficulty verbalizing about them. Furthermore, Hallpike (1979) infers too easily that collective representations result from the cognitive abilities of the majority of the individuals in a society, when collective representations, such as literacy, themselves may encourage certain types of thinking, as Hallpike acknowledges. Hallpike also infers that an apparent similarity in thinking between children and primitives must be due to the same cause, that is, a shared absence of certain cognitive skills.

Hallpike's developmentalist view is in opposition to both *universalist* and *relativist* approaches to thought. In Lévi-Strauss' view, the mental processes that people use to construct classification systems and that would, in Piagetian terms, be considered operational are a human universal shared by all peoples. The relativist position would emphasize the priority of language in the development of thought, suggesting that individuals do not invent their own mentalities but take on the mental processes that their language hands them. Such a view is not incompatible with a universalist interpretation to the extent that linguistic universals are recognized.

Failure to identify higher cognitive skills in children or "primitives" may tell us more about deficiencies in testing techniques and our concepts of cognition than about their thought processes. Many cross-cultural psychologists have questioned the validity of applying test procedures developed in one culture to people in an entirely different culture, especially where there is no practical context, content, or experience for the procedure or any familiarity with the concept of an intelligence test. Language is an obvious barrier in cross-cultural testing, and even when interpreters are used and in-depth interviews attempted, questioning will still be an impersonal, out-of-context ritual, which subjects likely will treat as irrelevant, if not as an unwelcome invasion of their privacy. Test subjects also may be quite justified in objecting to testing because it has often had practical implications for people and has seldom been carried out as pure science. For example, early in the twentieth century, the Stanford-Binet IQ test was extensively used in the United States to identify the "feeble-minded" and to influence policies concerning immigration, eugenics, education, institutionalization, and military service (Gould 1981).

The most significant differences in thought patterns between the members of domestic-scale societies and urban, industrial peoples probably do relate to basic lifestyle differences. But this does not necessarily imply that such differences reflect developmental stages or absolute superiority of one culture over the other. Perhaps the most serious problem with earlier attempts to assess the cognitive abilities of peoples living in domestic-scale societies is that they have focused on a rather narrow, culture-specific concept of pure intelligence. Surely, intelligence must mean more than scores achieved on a test that might relate to academic achievement or some other performance in commercial-scale societies.

Cross-cultural psychologists J. W. Berry and S. H. Irvine (1986, Irvine and Berry 1988) stress that for test scores to be meaningful, the tests must be conducted within the cultural and ecological context of the people being assessed. They categorically reject the validity of tests that are applied outside the culture for which they were originally devised. Taking a firmly cultural-relativist position on cognitive ability, Irvine and Berry have formulated a *law of cultural differentiation,* which states:

Cultural factors prescribe what shall be learned and at what age; consequently different cultural environments lead to the development of different patterns of ability. (Irvine and Berry 1988:4)

They prefer to speak of cognitive abilities rather than "intelligence" because there is no agreement on a global theory of human intelligence. Few researchers have even asked, What does intelligence mean to a particular people? Too often, intelligence testing has shown what people do not do but has not examined the cognitive skills, or the "practical intelligence," that is required for the successful performances of everyday life. In the following section, we consider this kind of intelligence for Australian aborigines.

The Cognitive Abilities of Australian Aborigines

Why have cognitive tests of Australian aborigines yielded such contradictory results?

The European invaders of Australia were convinced of the intellectual inferiority of aborigines from the very beginning. This ethnocentric assessment found frequent "scientific" support, as the selection from Staniland Wake (1872) in Chapter 1 demonstrated. The first formal test of the cognitive abilities of aborigines was conducted in 1915 using the Porteus Maze Solving Test, which could be taken by illiterates. S. D. Porteus (1917) first applied his maze test to a control group of forty-two delinquent and criminal white Australian boys to make sure the test would identify a lack of foresight, prudence, and general mental deficiency, which he assumed would accompany social deviancy. When he applied the test to twenty-eight aboriginal children at a mission, he discovered that they actually performed better than the white delinquents and criminals, but he attributed this to the assumed rapid physical maturation of aborigines. He argued that aboriginal mental development occurred rapidly and then stopped. Unshaken in his belief in the racial inferiority of aborigines, he concluded that by early adolescence, "the common racial characteristics of indolence, shiftlessness, and lack of foresight become apparent" (Porteus 1917:38).

Porteus recognized the difficulties of cross-cultural testing and granted that within their own culture, aborigines exhibited considerable "social intelligence." He attempted to make his tests more culturally relevant by using photographs of footprints, for example, but he still considered aboriginal mentality to be relatively inferior, and not merely different.

Psychological testing in Australia, as elsewhere, is used by the state to diagnose mental health, educational problems, and vocational potential; thus, for aborigines, the tests may have significant implications. During the period from 1960 to 1980, as the government became increasingly concerned with the social problems of aborigines, some 280 separate cognitive studies were conducted on aborigines (Klich 1988). This research often yielded contradictory results. Considerable debate ensued over whether the diagnosed aboriginal "inferiority" was due to culture or genes, but the prevailing view that aborigines were somehow mentally inferior seemed unshaken. For example, Piagetian tests applied to aborigines showed performance levels consistently lower than the European standard. Because the aboriginal environment was assumed to be the problem, some researchers concluded that aboriginal children should be removed from their retarding environments so that they could develop "normally" (see reviews by Keats and Keats 1988 and Klich 1988).

A modern study of aboriginal mentality by psychoanalytic anthropologist Arthur Hippler (1978) takes a Freudian twist and ethnocentrically attributes assumed aboriginal mental deficiencies to "inferior" child-rearing practices. Hippler rejects racist explanations but explicitly retains the biased evolutionist position that peoples can usefully be ranked by cognitive and emotional ability according to a Euro-American standard. As a self-styled "psychocultural evolutionist," Hippler believes that all people are born with equal mental potential but that primitive cultures stifle this potential by faulty child rearing. Following a modified Piagetian-stages approach, he argues that primitives are retarded at the preoperational level and thus as adults allow the magical fantasies of childhood to cloud their perception of the real world. This retardation occurs because primitives are frozen at a correspondingly low stage in the evolutionary development of child-rearing practices. According to Hippler (1977), primitives practice an "infanticidal and abandoning" evolutionary stage of child rearing, which is so cruel and inconsistent that children are unable to repress their sexual impulses and childish fantasies and are thus unable to reach their cognitive potentials.

Hippler paid a brief visit to aboriginal communities in Arnhem Land where he administered a few Rorschach inkblot tests and, as expected, concluded that the Yolngu people were "impulse-ridden, sexually anxious, jealous and fearful." They had difficulty separating fantasy from reality. They lacked imagination, were impulsive yet rigid, and had cognitively "lesser" capacities than Western norms. He considered sacred sites to be a "cultural pathology" because they overvalued land forms. In remarkable detail, he pointed out the shortcomings of Yolngu child rearing, which he felt accounted for their cognitive problems. He found parents to be "infantile, thoughtless and selfish," and their child rearing was characterized by such "neglect and harshness," and such "anger and hostility," that the physical welfare

of children was in constant peril and they were left with "emotional and cognitive scarring."

Australian anthropologists who were familiar with the Yolngu people were outraged by Hippler's assessment, both theoretically and substantively, and found it a totally unfounded distortion (Hamilton 1979, Reser 1981). They had no difficulty presenting respectable and convincing evidence based on in-depth field experience to refute Hippler's ethnocentric stereotypes. In response, rather than defending his specific interpretations, Hippler (1981) reiterated his view that traditional culture was "incredibly repressive" and argued for the complete abandonment of cultural relativism. Such a move would make serious cross-cultural understanding unlikely and would represent a return to the Eurocentrism of the nineteenth century. If Hippler's work had not appeared in a serious professional journal in the last quarter of the twentieth century, it might be shrugged off as representative of the lunatic fringe; as it is, however, it offers a textbook example of how theoretical preconceptions can influence one's "scientific" observation.

Belatedly, researchers began to examine the cognitive skills that aborigines actually used in their daily lives and found that they consistently rated higher than Europeans. For example, aborigines excelled on visual memory and spatial tests, which were skills that served them well in route finding, tracking, hunting, and gathering (Klich 1988). Earlier anthropological observers also had been impressed by the superior visual acuity and observational abilities of aborigines; but in line with their racist and evolutionary biases, they devalued them as instinctive survival skills and "lower" mental functions. D. Lewis (1976) found that aborigines routinely kept detailed mental track of the topographic features that they passed when traveling across country that to him seemed virtually featureless. In random tests in which he used a compass, Lewis found that aborigines could point with great precision in the direction of sacred sites that were 77 or more miles (200 km) away. Such accu-

---

law of cultural differentiation A statement of the cultural relativity of cognitive ability or basic intelligence. It assumes that no single culture-bound test can adequately test cognitive ability because different cultures produce different cognitive abilities in individuals.

racy required them to constantly update a mental map of their movements, and they were able to do this even in unfamiliar country. These spatial abilities are well supported by the aboriginal language and the Dreamtime cosmology. A European would have rated as feebleminded in such a test.

RACISM

The Origins of Humanity

What is racism? How does our evolutionary history demonstrate the essential biological unity of humankind?

Ethnocentrism is one of the most prevalent sources of cross-cultural misunderstanding, and it becomes even more problematic when it is combined with racism—the belief that certain groups of people are genetically superior or inferior in basic human capabilities. These beliefs can be extremely destructive, especially when policymakers and opinion leaders use racial classifications to the disadvantage of supposedly inferior groups. In this section, we briefly review the principal scientific findings of physical anthropology and archaeology demonstrating the common origins of humanity, the genetic basis of human unity and diversity, and the failures of recent attempts to explain economic performance in genetic terms.

The archaeological record confirms that for the past 30,000 or so years, all *Homo sapiens* populations have shared the same biological capacity to produce rich, linguistically based cultures. This means that all peoples have the same overall human potential. About 2 million years ago, our closest humanlike fossil ancestor, *Homo erectus*, moved definitively in the human direction. *Homo erectus* did not look fully modern—they had thick skulls with receding foreheads and chins and heavy brow ridges and jaws—but their brains approached modern size. Even more significantly, *Homo erectus* used culture to adaptive advantage. They probably made fires, built shelters, lived in caves, and used relatively sophisticated stone tools for butchering and woodworking. It also seems likely that they had some form of "protolanguage" (Bickerton 1990) to propel these cultural developments, thus making it possible for *Homo erectus* to spread beyond Africa

to Europe and Asia perhaps 1 million years ago. This began the evolutionary process of sapienization that simultaneously produced human culture and physically modern *Homo sapiens*.

Fossil evidence and DNA analysis of contemporary peoples suggest that physically modern humans can be traced to a common origin in Africa some 200,000 years ago. Citing this evidence, some physical anthropologists take a monogenesis position, arguing that *Homo erectus* first evolved into *Homo sapiens* in Africa and then quickly spread throughout the Eastern Hemisphere, eliminating and replacing all earlier humanlike populations. Anthropologists who take a polygenesis position hold that there were multiple human origins. They point to physical traits found in modern regional populations in Europe and Asia that were also found in *Homo erectus* populations living in the same regions much earlier than 200,000 BP. Polygenesis suggests that *Homo erectus* may have evolved into *Homo sapiens* in several different regions at approximately the same time. Given the likelihood of continuous genetic exchange between populations, these two theories may not be incompatible. Rather, they may suggest that humans have constituted a single polymorphic species, characterized by considerable genetic diversity, since the very dawn of humanity.

Facts of Life and the Culture of Race

In what respects are popular American racial categories cultural constructions rather than biological realities? Why are racial categories unscientific? What is the genetic basis of human diversity? What inherited human traits are shaped by the environment? How do human descent groups based on selectively neutral traits compare with populations defined by environmentally selected genetic traits?

Popular racial classifications are primarily *cultural* constructions, not biological realities. For example, the five categories—black, white, American Indian–Alaskan Native, Asian–Pacific Islander, and Hispanic—used by the U.S. Census in 1980 and 1990 are culturally produced legal fictions that have no scientific validity. Culturally defined racial categories mix legal citizenship and ethnicity with naive assumptions about skin color and blood, but they ignore the genetic facts of life. For example, the U.S. government follows a blood quantum rule and recognizes "American Indians" as legal tribal members only if they can demonstrate ancestry of at least one-fourth "full blood." But "full blood" is itself a legal fiction based on previous tribal enrollments. Thus, "American Indian" is legally declared to be a biological category. Similarly, an American with a single black grandparent is likely to be classified "black." The underlying myth of such racial categories is that genetically "pure" races exist. Nazi attempts to "purify" an Aryan super-race during World War II were equally misguided and caused enormous human suffering.

In Latin America, there are many racial classifications that explicitly reflect culture rather than biology. For example, in Andean Peru, individuals who look exactly alike will self-identify and be classified as "Indios" (Indian) if they wear distinctive Indian clothing and speak Quechua (an indigenous language). As small shopkeepers fluent in both Quechua and Spanish, they might be "Cholos." More affluent Spanish speakers might be either "mestizos" or "criollos." The cultural aspect of these categories is demonstrated by the ability of individuals to move from one to another depending on their success in the market economy.

Human racial classifications are scientifically inappropriate for several reasons. Humans constitute a global, polymorphic, continuously interbreeding population. For the past 30,000 years, no peoples, other than a handful of tiny populations on remote islands, have been isolated long enough to produce more than a relatively small genetic distance from any other human populations. Therefore, any scientific classification of people into genetic populations must necessarily be an arbitrary exercise based on variations in gene frequencies. The U.S. Census fivefold classification cannot be validated scientifically with gene frequency tests. A careful observer could distinguish thousands of "races" based on particular traits.

The human genome consists of 23 pairs of chromosomes, carrying 50–100,000 genes, each represented by unique segments of DNA (see the box entitled "Human Genetics"). The genetic information encoded in the sequences of the four DNA nucleotides (A, C, G, T) in human chromosomes provides virtually infinite potential for human diversity. Human geneticist Luigi Cavalli-Sforza (Cavalli-Sforza and Cavalli-Sforza 1995:255) notes that it would take some 3000 volumes of 300 pages each to print the ACGT codes making up the 3 billion nucleotides of the human genome.

Many genetic differences between peoples do have important health implications, but these real differences do not have any relation to popular racial stereotypes. For example, the blood sickle-cell allele found originally in certain West African tropical forest populations provides resistance to malaria. Another allele, present in descendants of herding peoples, produces lactase, an enzyme that digests lactose, or milk sugar. People lacking this allele can suffer from lactose intolerance. Knowing that the U.S. Census considered someone to be an "Asian–Pacific Islander" would not be a reliable predictor of lactase deficiency, and knowing that a person was categorized as "black" would not identify the sickle-cell allele.

Geneticists and anthropologists (Cavalli-Sforza and Cavalli-Sforza 1995; Cavalli-Sforza, Menozzi, and Piazza 1994; Krantz 1980) sort human genetic variation into two broad types: classical adaptive traits and neutral polymorphisms. Classical traits are highly visible features, such as skin, hair and eye color; body build; and the shape of the face. These traits are the basis of popular racial stereotypes, but they are not discrete variables. They are produced in complex ways by the interaction of multiple genes, and they vary continuously among individuals and populations, as shades of skin color along a gradient from light to dark. For example, populations can be described using fine distinctions in average skin reflectivity along a scale of 1 to 100. Classical traits are actively selected for by climate, and they often correlate with latitude. For example, darker—rather than lighter—skin, eyes, and hair provide better protection from intensive solar radiation. Natural selection, the differential survival of various phenotypes under differing environmental conditions, means that populations that are not closely related may come to resemble one another in classical traits if they move into similar environments. Blood types, proteins, enzymes, and mitochondrial DNA provide a rather precise way of establishing human descent groups, but these traits are not readily observed without sophisticated testing techniques.

Human Genetics

allele   A variant form of a gene, produced by mutation.

chromosome   A single strand of DNA; twenty-three pairs in humans.

DNA   Deoxyribonucleic acid. A long double-helix molecule composed of a sequence of nucleotides.

gene   A segment of DNA producing a particular protein controlling some aspect of an individual's development.

gene frequency   The percentage of individuals in a population with a particular gene.

genetic distance   A statistical measure of the difference in gene frequencies between two or more populations.

genetic drift   Changes in gene frequencies caused by random factors.

genetic polymorphism   Multiple alleles for a particular trait. On average, 1 nucleotide per 500 is likely to vary, between the same chromosome in a given pair or between individuals.

genotype   The genetic composition of an individual, including each half of each chromosome pair contributed by each parent.

human genome   All the genetic material that makes up an individual.

migration   Population movements that can produce changes in gene frequencies.

mitochondrial DNA   Small organs within cells that have metabolic functions. They possess small chromosomes containing some 16,500 nucleotides; they are transmitted to the next generation only by the mother's egg cell.

mutation   A change in a nucleotide. On average, 1 in 200,000,000 nucleotides mutate per generation.

natural selection   Differential survival of varying phenotypes under differing environmental conditions, producing changes in gene frequencies.

nucleotide   The amino acids adenine (A) and guanine (G), thymine (T) and cytosine (C), which combine in a sequential chain to form the DNA molecule. There are some 3 billion chromosomal nucleotides in each half of the DNA molecule.

phenotype   The actual expression of genetic traits in an individual as shaped by environmental factors.

SOURCE: Derived in part from Cavalli-Sforza and Cavalli-Sforza (1995) and Cavalli-Sforza, Menozzi, and Piazza (1994).

Family Trees and the Myth of Racial Purity

How do family trees based on DNA analysis of contemporary peoples demonstrate the essential biological unity of humanity? What genetic processes make racial purity a misleading concept?

The complexity of actual genetic relationships among peoples, in contrast to simplistic racial ste-

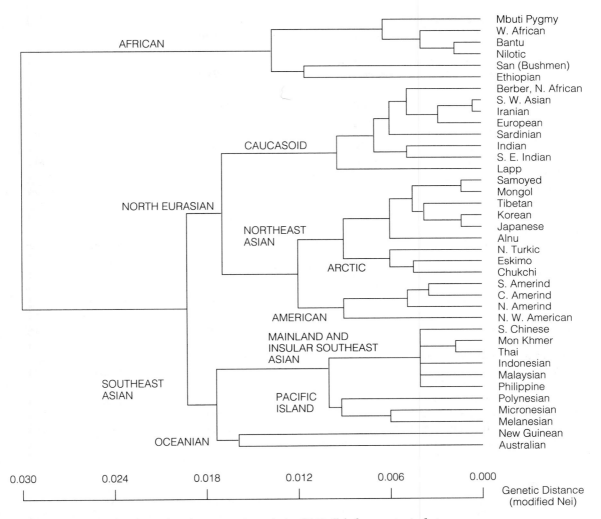

FIGURE 5.2   *Global family tree based on a genetic analysis of 142 allele frequencies in forty-two populations. (SOURCE: Cavalli-Sforza et al. 1994, Figure 2.3.2.A.)*

reotypes, is illustrated by human family trees based on sophisticated genetic testing. Although enormously complex, Allan Wilson and R. L. Cann's (1992) family tree of 182 diverse individuals (based on mitochondrial DNA) ultimately connects everyone to a common African ancestress. Cavalli-Sforza and his associates (1994) have produced a global family tree for forty-two local populations based on 120 neutral allele frequencies (see Figure 5.2).

These populations were pooled from a much larger sample of nearly 2000 "indigenous" populations whose ancestors presumably were living in the same location before AD 1500. Branches in this diagram reflect the major population movements of the past 30,000 years up to AD 1500, including the pioneer occupations of the major land masses and the migrations associated with domestication and cultivation. The Cavalli-Sforza tree also roughly corresponds to major language classifications and, like Wilson and Cann's tree, suggests a common African origin for humanity.

Popular racial classifications fail because they falsely assume purity and stability of genetic inheritance. Not only is racial purity improbable, it would be extremely maladaptive. All the processes of biological evolution—including mutation, genetic drift, migration, and natural selection—are constantly changing the genetic composition of every population. The genetic characteristics of populations are not discrete bundles of features; they overlap in complex ways, and the frequencies of particular genes vary gradually along geographical gradients, or *clines*. By AD 1500, many local populations had the necessary stability for natural selection to produce superficial adaptations in skin and body form to regional climates. However, since 1500, the dramatic increases in migration and travel and the demographic disturbances initiated by the emerging global commercial culture have introduced tremendous genetic diversity into formerly indigenous populations. Any European or American is likely to have ancestors drawn from many formerly indigenous gene pools. For example, someone born in 1975 theoretically would have 510 ancestors, assuming 25-year generations and counting back eight generations to great-great-great-great-great-great-grandparents born in 1775. Counting back nineteen generations to AD 1500 would include more than a million ancestors! Only extremely naive racists could pretend that each and every one of their ancestors came from the same discrete gene pool.

Race, IQ, and Economic Achievement

What are the scientific weaknesses and logical flaws in the argument that some groups in the United States are poor because they are genetically inferior?

Several recent authors have used racial categories and notions of racial inferiority, based on the intervening variable of IQ scores, to explain different levels of economic achievement in the United States. The modern argument began with an article by Berkeley, California, educational psychologist Arthur Jensen (1969), who claimed that black IQs averaged 15 points lower than white IQs, that this

difference was primarily genetic, and that it explained poor academic achievement by black children. Psychologist Richard J. Herrnstein (1971) quickly pushed these misleading conclusions to another level, arguing that IQ, economic achievement, and social standing were all significantly determined by genetics.

Anthropologists, biologists, and geneticists promptly refuted Jensen's and Herrnstein's theories as unscientific (Bodmer and Cavalli-Sforza 1970, Cavalli-Sforza and Feldman 1981, Gould 1981), but they reappeared 25 years later in the 1994 bestseller *The Bell Curve: Intelligence and Class Structure in American Life*, co-authored by Herrnstein and political scientist Charles Murray. This time the term *ethnic* often replaced the more emotional *race*, but the underlying genetic argument has remained unchanged. At its starkest, *The Bell Curve* argues that blacks have inferior genes for basic intelligence and so score poorly on IQ tests; thus, they are unable to attain the high-paying jobs that lead to economic achievement in America. Crime, welfare dependency, and broken homes are all portrayed as inherited-IQ problems. This argument requires the improbable assumption that American society is structured to reward people strictly on the basis of their genetic endowment. The "cognitive elite" are successful, good citizens primarily because their genes are superior. The obvious policy implication is that federal money for social services would be wasted on the poor because they are too genetically inferior to improve.

Critical reviewers of *The Bell Curve* again have pointed out the numerous logical and scientific flaws in this racist argument (Cavalli-Sforza and Cavalli-Sforza 1995, Kamin 1995, Marks 1995). Anthropologists' exasperation with this revival of "pseudo-scientific racism" led to a resolution at their 1994 annual meeting declaring that biologically defined "races" were "meaningless and unscientific as a way of explaining variation (whether in intelligence or other traits)" (*Anthropology Newsletter* 1995).

It is both arrogant and ethnocentric to assume that the designers of IQ tests know what human intelligence is and that they can measure it for all people. IQ scores are cultural products that measure a relatively narrow range of cognitive skills, skills that have only recently been elevated in status in commercial-scale culture. There are many human intellectual qualities, such as wisdom and creativity, that IQ does not measure.

Herrnstein and Murray maintain that 60–70 percent of IQ is genetically determined, yet the heritability of intellectual qualities of whatever sort cannot be accurately separated from cultural factors, and especially from parental influences. Luigi and Francesco Cavalli-Sforza (1995:280) suggest that only 33 percent of an IQ score might be attributable to genetic inheritance. Furthermore, the racial classifications underlying arguments of racial inferiority are as problematic as the IQ scores themselves. Given that "blacks" and "whites" are cultural categories that do not represent discrete gene pools, it is meaningless to attribute black/white IQ differences to genetics.

Attributing differences in economic success to IQ scores confuses correlation with causation. How can Herrnstein and Murray be so certain that genetics, and not poverty, causes low scores? It is more reasonable to speculate that people who are enculturated in impoverished households and communities with poorly equipped schools and fewer cultural resources will exhibit both lower IQ scores and lower economic achievement. Physical anthropologist Jonathan Marks (1995) points out that an earlier American impoverished underclass from central and southern Europe—including ancestors of present-day Italian Americans, Polish Americans, Czech Americans, Jewish Americans, and so on—was branded as genetically inferior by the "cognitive elites" of the time (to use Herrnstein and Murray's invidious and arrogant term), but they and their descendants successfully raised their IQ scores and joined the overclass. It is self-serving and disingenuous for elites to deprecate the intellectual abilities of the underclass. The primary forces shaping human destiny are now cultural, not biological. The cultural organization of social power, not genetics, is the primary determinant of human well-being.

LANGUAGE AND CULTURE

A major point of theoretical debate in anthropology is between the extreme relativists, who insist that each culture can only be understood in its own terms, and those who are more interested in comparison and seek cultural universals or stages of development. This debate was introduced in Chapter 1 with the emic/etic distinction and was discussed again in the first section of this chapter. In this section, we view the issue from the perspective of language. The goal here is to assess the tendency of people who speak different languages to see the world in fundamentally unique ways and then examine the ways in which linguistic classification is constrained by the limits of the physical world. Linguistic and ethnoscience material on biological classification systems and color terminologies will help to illuminate these intriguing questions.

Linguistic Relativity and the Sapir-Whorf Hypothesis

Are language categories human universals, perhaps even biologically determined, or are they cultural constructions? What evolutionary interpretations of linguistic development were rejected in favor of linguistic relativity?

The relativist view of language, as it developed in American anthropology under Franz Boas and his student Edward Sapir, was a direct response to the extreme Eurocentric evolutionary schemes that were developed by nineteenth-century linguists who maintained that Indo-European languages were the most highly evolved in the world. German linguist Max Müller constructed a scale of linguistic evolutionary development based on an earlier grammatical classification of languages into isolating, agglutinating, and amalgamating types. The most primitive types were called *isolating* because they were thought to use words that were unaltered roots. *Agglutinating* languages made composite words from previously isolated roots, and *amalgamating* languages, such as Indo-European, changed the meaning of words by inflection. In Müller's scheme of evolutionary progress, the appearance of amalgamating languages corresponded to the rise of civilization in the Near East and thus was identified with civilization and progress, whereas more primitive languages were associated with nomadism (see Figure 5.3).

FIGURE 5.3
Stages of evolutionary progress in the development of languages, according to Müller.
(SOURCE: *Bunsen 1854.*)

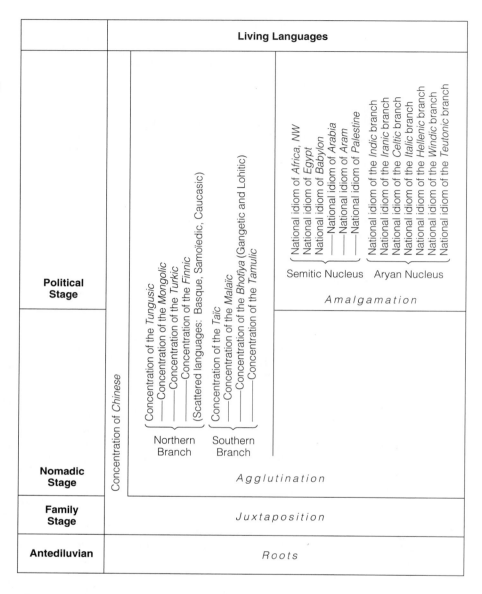

As non-Indo-European languages became better known, it quickly became apparent that Müller's evolutionary scheme had little empirical foundation. Using Native American languages, Boas argued that with language, as with mentality generally, there was no basis for ranking into higher and lower stages of evolutionary progress. Although Boas recognized many specific differences in languages, he felt that all were equally capable of expressing complex ideas and did so as the need arose. Boas also implied that linguistic categories were characterized by a certain arbitrariness. For example, he observed that although many hues of color could be distinguished, a given language might name only a few, and in ways that were not readily translatable into the color terms of another language (Boas 1911). Ruth Benedict (1934) adopted this position when she argued that each culture was built from behaviors arbitrarily selected from the spectrum of possible behavior. Edward Sapir, a linguistic student of Boas, and Sapir's student Benjamin Whorf carried these ideas further and implied that linguistic categories defined the reality that the speakers of a given language perceived. In effect, the speakers of different languages live in different perceptual worlds. This general view that language somehow shapes perception became known as the **Sapir-Whorf hypothesis**, although Sapir and Whorf never formulated their views as a single testable hypothesis (Kay and Kempton 1984).

Color Classifications and Folk Taxonomies

What do color terms reveal regarding the argument that the speakers of different languages live in different perceptual worlds? How do biological taxonomies differ between cultures of different scale?

The most famous examination of the issues implied by the Sapir-Whorf hypothesis was the comparative analysis of color terms by Brent Berlin and Paul Kay (1969). These researchers collected color terms from speakers of twenty widely diverse languages by placing a transparent sheet over a chart of 329 color chips arranged by degree of hue and brightness. Native speakers were asked to mark with a grease pen the focal point of each color term or the chip that best represented it, as well as the total range of chips to which each term could refer. Basic color terms could not be composites or narrowly applied, so terms like *blue-green*, *pinkish*, and *apple red* were excluded.

The researchers found that among all the languages, only eleven basic color terms were recognized (*white, black, red, green, yellow, blue, brown, purple, pink, orange,* and *gray*), and there was remarkable agreement on the focal points of each term (see Figure 5.4). This was a surprising blow to those who felt that color terms were not constrained by nature. But even more surprising was

the discovery that the set of terms used by any particular language was limited and to a certain extent predictable. Although, in theory, there were 2048 possible combinations of the 11 basic color terms, only 22 sets or combinations actually occurred. Furthermore, these combinations could be grouped into seven stages, which implied an evolutionary sequence because they appeared to correspond to levels of cultural complexity (see Figure 5.5).

By searching the literature, Berlin and Kay (1969) expanded their sample to include ninety-eight languages and confirmed their original findings. No language had fewer than two color terms, and these two were *black* and *white* (see the box entitled "An Aboriginal Color System"). When there were three terms, *red* would be added to *black* and *white*. Next, *green* and *yellow* were added in either order, then *blue* and *brown* in sequence. Finally, *purple, pink, orange,* and *gray* would be added in any order. Languages associated with domestic-scale cultures had fewer color terms than those spoken by industrial societies. Presumably, the increase in color terms was in response to increased cultural needs, but the precise sequence of color terms could not be explained beyond the possibility that they represented levels of distinctive physical contrast, which were perceptual universals.

The search for universals in linguistic classification and their possible evolutionary implications quickly expanded to other domains. Berlin and his associates turned their attention to ethnobiology and established a hierarchy of folk taxonomic terms that appeared to resemble the color term sequence. They first inferred (Berlin 1972; Berlin, Breedlove, and Raven 1973) that languages potentially could recognize five taxonomic categories: generic, life form, specific, intermediate/varietal, and unique beginner (see Figure 5.6).

In an inferred developmental sequence of plant taxonomies, a language first acquires generic terms, such as *oak* and *pine*, before differentiating between them with specific terms, such as *black oak*, or generalizing by adding a few life-form terms, such as

---

Sapir-Whorf hypothesis Suggests that one's view of the world is shaped by language, such that the speakers of different languages may live in different perceptual worlds.

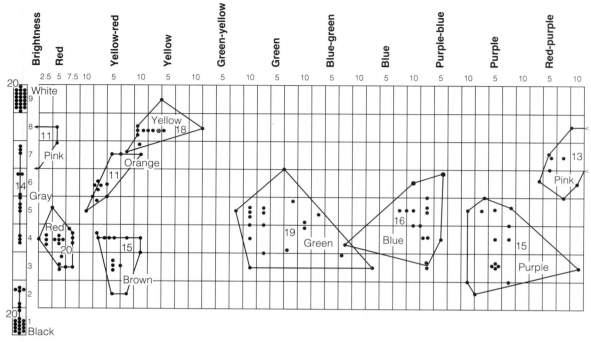

FIGURE 5.4 *Normalized foci of basic color terms in twenty languages. Numerals appearing along the borders of the chart refer to the Munsell system of color notation, distinguishing hue, brightness, and color strength. Numerals appearing in the body of the chart refer to the number of languages in the sample of twenty that encode the corresponding color category. The smallest possible number of lines are used to enclose each color area.* (SOURCE: *Berlin and Kay 1969.*)

FIGURE 5.5 *Developmental sequence for the acquisition of basic color terms.* (SOURCE: *Berlin and Kay 1969:4.*)

$$\begin{bmatrix} \text{White} \\ \text{Black} \end{bmatrix} \longrightarrow [\text{Red}] \begin{smallmatrix} \nearrow \\ \searrow \end{smallmatrix} \begin{matrix} [\text{Green}] \longrightarrow [\text{Yellow}] \\ [\text{Yellow}] \longrightarrow [\text{Green}] \end{matrix} \begin{smallmatrix} \searrow \\ \nearrow \end{smallmatrix} [\text{Blue}] \longrightarrow [\text{Brown}] \longrightarrow \begin{bmatrix} \text{Purple} \\ \text{Pink} \\ \text{Orange} \\ \text{Gray} \end{bmatrix}$$

tree. Varietal terms are most likely to be applied to cultivated plants. Most peoples find little need to recognize the unique beginner term *plant.*

Cecil Brown (1977) suggested that six globally distributed life-form terms for plants—*tree, grass, herb, "grerb"* (grass and herb), *bush,* and *vine*— were added to a language in a predictable sequence, like basic color terms (see Figure 5.7). The six life-form terms could in theory occur in sixty-four different combinations. However, in a survey of 105 languages, Brown found that only eleven patterns actually occurred, and these could be grouped into six stages. A language might have no life-form terms, or it might only recognize the *tree*

life form. In Stage 3, a single life-form term was added, *"grerb,"* which might refer to either grass or herbs, or both. By Stage 6, all six life-form terms would be recognized. The first three stages of development thus used no more than two life-form terms and were thought to be associated with domestic-scale societies. Brown (1979a) also identifies five animal life-form terms: *fish, bird, snake, "wug"* (small insectlike creatures, bugs, and worms), and *mammal,* which follow similar sequential stages (see Figure 5.8).

Brown (1979a) infers that the actual sequence of life-form terms reflects the universal tendency for classification to be based on simple binary opposi-

An Aboriginal Color System

That any culture could function with no more than two basic color terms is difficult to imagine, but an Australian aboriginal example of such a system shows how feasible it is. Based on their fieldwork, Rhys Jones and Betty Meehan (1978) have provided a detailed description of the use of color terms by the Anbarra aborigines of Arnhem Land. They found two basic terms in use as adjectives: *-gungaltja* (light) and *-gungundja* (dark). Only a few of the very lightest colors were called *-gungaltja*—just 10 percent of the Munsell chips used by Berlin and Kay (1969), including bright red. All objects could be described using these two terms. For example, storm clouds, the sky, granite, and aborigines were "dark," while other clouds, the sea, sandstone, newborn babies, Europeans, and sunsets were "light." Four mineral pigments were used as paints and were distinctively named: white clay, black charcoal, red ochre, and yellow ochre. These pigments are very ancient in Australia and have great symbolic significance. Objects painted with these pigments, or that resemble their color, could be described in reference to the pigment. Thus, a sunset might be described as "light, red ochre present within it," but such restricted use would seem to disqualify such pigment terms for recognition as basic color terms as defined by Berlin and Kay. A gray-green-colored, waterborne algal scum was also treated as a paint pigment term. The restricted nature of pigment terms was apparent as well from the fact that each belonged to a specific moiety, whereas the basic color terms, *light* and *dark*, had no moiety affiliation. Many plant dyes were in use, and dyed objects were described by reference to the specific plant used, but such terms were not generalized further. In recent years, the Anbarra have readily applied English color terms to the brightly colored European objects that have entered their region.

tions and the fact that biological groupings share natural features that make them conspicuous to human perception. The sequence also seems to reflect the order in which children learn to classify nature.

This analysis has interesting implications for the debate about primitive mentality. If life-form and unique beginner terms are considered more abstract and generic terms more concrete, then this undermines some expectations about cultural progress because increased abstraction coincides with a general devolution in knowledge of nature as cultural scale increases. Terms seem to disappear from the bottom of the taxonomic hierarchy as increasingly urbanized and industrialized people become less directly dependent on nature. It is not uncommon for individuals in domestic-scale societies to be able to name 500–1000 plants, whereas urban people may know barely 50–100 plants. Based on detailed linguistic reconstructions within specific language groups, Brown (1979b) infers that life-form terms have been added largely within the past

FIGURE 5.6 *Universal taxonomic categories of folk biological taxonomies. (SOURCE: Berlin 1972.)*

Generic → { Life form / Specific } → { Intermediate/ varietal } → Unique beginner

$$\begin{bmatrix} \text{No life} \\ \text{forms} \end{bmatrix} \longrightarrow [\text{Tree}] \longrightarrow \begin{bmatrix} \text{(Grerb)} \\ \text{Grass + Herb} \\ \text{or} \\ \text{Grass} \end{bmatrix}$$

[Bush] → [Vine] → [Grass]   Path 1

[Bush] → [Grass]   Path 2

[Vine] → [Grass] → [Bush]   Path 3

Stages   1   2   3   4   5   6

"Grerb" is realized as *herb* when *grass* is encoded at Stage 5 or 6.
Herb refers to herbaceous plants excluding grasses.

FIGURE 5.7   *Lexical-encoding sequence for folk botanical life forms (showing three possible paths for adding life-form terms). "Grerb" is realized as* herb *when* grass *is encoded at Stage 5 or 6.* Herb *refers to herbaceous plants excluding grasses. (SOURCE: Brown 1977.)*

2000–4000 years in step with the increase in political complexity, while use of generic terms has sharply declined.

Randall and Hunn (1984, Hunn 1985) are critical of the life-form concept used by Brown, arguing that there is no justification for defining it by morphological criteria. They point out that some life-form terms, such as *bird*, are distinctive biological categories, whereas others, such as *tree*, are neither natural nor very distinctive as categories, although they are important for people to distinguish for utilitarian reasons. Randall and Hunn suggest that languages judged to be more primitive because they lack life-form terms actually may group generic taxa (taxonomic groups or entities) into many abstract utilitarian categories, such as by edibility or method of extraction. There are also serious methodological issues in Brown's work, especially the possibility that folk taxonomies may be altered by schooling and translation problems. Biological categories are inherently more difficult to work with than color, which has relatively few dimensions to control.

Basic color terms do appear to be genuine cultural universals, and they are a challenge to strict cultural relativists, who maintain that cultures can define physical reality in completely arbitrary ways. But cultural determinism still can be seen to operate. Marshall Sahlins (1976a) argued that cultures systematically make symbolic use of the natural distinctions that people can most readily perceive in color, just as natural sounds are used for linguistic purposes. Berlin and Kay (1969) pointed out

Stages   1–3   4   5

FIGURE 5.8   *Lexical-encoding sequence for folk zoological life forms. (SOURCE: Brown 1979a.)*

that languages add new color terms in a way that maximizes the efficiency of perceptible contrasts, which parallels the order in which children learn to articulate phonemic distinctions as they acquire speech. However, as Sahlins stressed, even given that color differences are naturally perceptible, it is still important to ask what cultural uses, or meanings, are made of these differences. What was important for Sahlins when new color terms are added is the new relations between terms, the new meanings, that become possible.

Sahlins observed that Stage 1 color terms, which distinguish only two colors, light and dark, are used for simple dualistic symbolic oppositions, such as between life and death, male and female, or sacred and profane. The addition of red creates a mediated opposition in which red can variously be opposed to either dark or light, like the ambiguous jaguar mediating between the complementary opposites of male and female in Chapter 3. The further addition of either green or yellow in Stage 3 creates a pair of analogous opposition, as in the familiar $a : b :: c : d$ pattern. These perceptual structures can be created using jaguars, caimans, and anacondas, as well as with colors, and they can then be made to carry a variety of cultural meanings.

MAGIC, BELIEF, AND THE SUPERNATURAL

Shamanism and Psychopathology

How do shamanistic trances differ from psychopathologies?

Shamans are part-time religious specialists and healers who personify the most extreme elements of so-called primitive mentalities and magical thinking in domestic-scale societies. Early missionaries often called shamans witch doctors, attributing their supernatural powers to the devil, and confronted them as enemies of Christianity. Government authorities often disapproved of shamans because they sometimes used their powers within the community to organize resistance to government programs and because shamanistic curing practices frequently were considered to be contrary to modern medical science, if not actually dangerous. Even anthropologists have had difficulty being objective about shamans. For example, Alfred Kroeber, a prominent Boas-trained anthropologist, suggested in the 1948 edition of *Anthropology*, long a standard textbook, that modern civilization's rejection of shamanism and related beliefs was a measure of scientific progress. He observed that people in our own society recognize as abnormal or insane anyone who talks to the dead or who thinks they can turn into a bear, whereas "backward people" consider such behavior socially acceptable and even admirable. Kroeber regarded shamanism as a psychopathology and emphatically declared:

When the sane and well in one culture believe what only the most ignorant, warped, and insane believe in another, there would seem to be some warrant for rating the first culture lower and the second higher. Or are our discards, insane, and hypersuggestibles perhaps right and the rest of us wrong? (Kroeber 1948:298)

Shamanism does involve a striking collection of phenomena, including various trance states, magical flight, and spirit possession (Peters and Price-Williams 1980), all of which may be difficult to understand outside of the cultural context in which they occur. Shamans induce trances using rhythmical chanting, dancing, deprivation, and psychoactive drugs. Anthropologist Michael Harner (1980), who conducts popular workshops and seminars on shamanism, has demonstrated that under the proper conditions, virtually anyone can induce such trance states. Shamanism may well be tens of thousands of years old, judging from parallels between the distinctive lines and grid patterns scratched on European cave walls during the Ice Age and similar designs characteristic of rock art associated with shamans in many parts of the world. Some researchers infer that these images are entoptic phenomena, images that tribal shamans see with their mind's eye during trance states. In ecstatic trance, shamans contact the otherwise invisible spirit world and perform amazing feats, including the magical killing of enemies and transformations into animals. Using their spirit helpers to cure, shamans massage their patients and dramatically suck out intrusive objects thought to be the causes of illness; or they shoot invisible darts into the bodies of enemies to harm them. Australian aboriginal shamans reportedly have killed people simply by pointing a bone in their direction.

I was impressed by the cultural reality of Amazonian shamanism while I conducted a routine residence pattern survey in an Ashaninka village. I was surprised to encounter a man who maintained a separate house from his wife. It is common for young unmarried Ashaninka men to build separate houses, but this case was unusual enough for me to question further. I discovered that this man was a powerful jaguar shaman who could cure people and transform himself into a jaguar to magically attack his enemies. He explained to me matter-of-factly that it sometimes upset his wife when he became a jaguar at night, so he often slept in his own house.

Ashaninka shamans are called "tobacco-eaters," after the bamboo tubes they carry containing a thick, tarlike tobacco paste that is licked from a stick to help induce shamanistic visions. Jaguar shamans are widely respected and feared by the Ashaninka, and their exploits are well known. I heard accounts of someone shooting an intruding jaguar at night and then discovering that he had killed a shaman. Another incident demonstrated the social context of shamanistic curing. My Shipibo field assistant developed a chronic leg infection that refused to heal. He consulted a shaman who attributed the problem to the otter spirit, which had been sent by another villager who was a bitter personal enemy of my assistant. The cure was effected when the two reached a reconciliation.

Many observers have questioned the authenticity of shamanistic performances, pointing to incidences in which the shaman does not seem to be in a genuine trance or when a curer has hidden in his mouth the object that he intends to suck from his patient. Deliberately hidden objects of this sort simply add drama to the curing performance. Some shamans may indeed pretend to be in trance, but most suspicions of fraud may be due to a misunderstanding of the nature of shamanism, especially the fact that shamanistic trances often differ from other forms of spirit possession. A shaman typically is in a "lucid trance" or a "waking dream" in which he communicates with both the spirits and his audience, and he will usually be able to remember the events later (see Figure 5.9). This is not the same as pathological hysteria, and it does not mean that the shaman becomes totally dissociated. The shaman trance is a temporary reduction of normal reality testing in which dream images are treated as if real within a specific cultural context and are then used for social purposes (Peters and Price-Williams 1980).

The psychopathological view of shamanism by anthropologists was in favor for a long time. For example, Julian Silverman (1967) emphasized the parallels between acute schizophrenics who behave in bizarre fashion and shamans who experience cognitive disturbances, or altered states of consciousness, as an apparent reaction to a major personal crisis involving guilt or failure. In Silverman's view, like Kroeber's, the most significant difference between schizophrenics in our society and shamans in domestic-scale societies is that schizophrenics find no social support for their behavior, and it is consequently maladaptive, whereas shamans are culturally accepted. Thus, in this view, shamanism can be considered a therapeutic psychological adjustment to a psychopathology.

The connection between schizophrenia and shamanism is also implied in the authoritative *Diagnostic and Statistical Manual of Mental Disorders* (*DSM-III*), the guidebook published by the American Psychiatric Association (APA) for use by clinicians. According to *DSM-III*, "magical thinking" is seen "in children, in people in primitive cultures, and in Schizotypal Personality Disorder, Schizo-

FIGURE 5.9 *A Yanomami shaman in a "lucid trance" during a feast.*

phrenia, and Obsessive Compulsive Disorder" (APA 1980:363). The belief that the members of domestic-scale cultures are sick and childlike dies hard, even among scientists!

The clinical concept of schizophrenia has been refined considerably since Silverman's analysis was published, and even using the definition of schizophrenic disorders contained within *DSM-III*, striking differences between schizophrenics and shamans now seem evident. As Richard Noll (1984) points out, attributing shamanistic experiences to an altered state of consciousness implies out-of-control hallucinations and other paranoid delusions that we tend to view negatively but that, in fact, are not characteristic of shamanism. Noll speaks of the **shamanic state of consciousness (SSC),** which he distinguishes from the altered state of consciousness (ASC) as it is usually recognized. The ASC of the schizophrenic is obviously maladaptive. It comes unbidden, and the schizophrenic hears uncontrollable mocking voices, whereas the shaman can enter the SSC virtually at will, remains aware of his state, sees visions, uses them for socially beneficial purposes, and then freely returns to his normal consciousness. A successful shaman achieves a balance between his spiritual experiences and the demands of everyday life, but there is no reason to view the SSC as a psychopathology.

Aboriginal Voodoo Death and Culture-Bound Syndromes

What physical and psychological factors are involved in the dramatic pathologies that are sometimes related to particular cultural beliefs about the spirit world?

Anthropologists and medical researchers have been fascinated by reports of mysterious deaths and illnesses in tribal societies that are culturally attributed to supernatural causes and that have not always been readily explainable in purely physical terms. A prime example from aboriginal Australia are cases of so-called voodoo death, such as the bone pointing referred to previously, in which people are killed by sorcery. The long-established anthropological interpretation of such incidents was that the victim died from shock, caused by intense fear of death combined with an absolute belief in

the reality of sorcery (Cannon 1942). More extensive observations in recent years by medically trained individuals have clarified both the physical and cultural basis of such deaths. Harry Eastwell (1982), who conducted periodic psychiatric clinics in aboriginal communities in Arnhem Land between 1969 and 1980, treated thirty-nine patients for a variety of physical and emotional symptoms that he called "fear of sorcery syndrome." In nearly all cases, some specific event—such as the death or illness of close kin, interpersonal conflicts, or a ritual violation—led to suspicions of supernatural danger. Patients showed the typical symptoms of extreme fear: bulging eyes, dilated pupils, sweating, agitation, and sleeplessness. Two of the patients died, one with an abnormality of the adrenal glands, which may have made him more vulnerable to stress, and the other from kidney and heart failure.

Because so few deaths actually occurred in these cases, Eastwell began to suspect that more than merely fear was involved in voodoo death. This suspicion was further supported when two patients thought to be dying from sorcery were found to be severely dehydrated and were saved by prompt medical intervention. Additional analyses of the process of dying experienced by elderly aborigines revealed a regular cultural pattern in which both dying person and kin decide that death is imminent and mutually facilitate the process—the dying person refuses to drink and the kin withhold water so that death by dehydration occurs within 24–48 hours.

The parallels between aboriginal patient-assisted euthanasia and voodoo death are striking. In both cases, the actual mechanism of death is probably dehydration, but it occurs because the patient and the community agree that the patient is dying. Water is withheld at the same time that wailing and formal funeral rituals are begun. It is believed that only the totemic spirit animates the dying person,

---

shamanic state of consciousness (SSC)   An interpretation of the shamantic trance phenomenon that distinguishes it from the altered state of consciousness of schizophrenics. A shaman may enter and leave the SSC at will, remains aware of his surroundings, and uses the SSC for socially beneficial purposes.

and it does not need to drink. At death, this spirit returns to the ancestral well.

Psychiatrist John Cawte (1976) describes another Australian culture-bound syndrome, *Malgri*, from the Wellesley Island aborigines in the Gulf of Carpentaria. In this case, violation of ritual restrictions on keeping land foods and seafoods separate causes local totemic spirits to afflict a person with severe abdominal swelling and pain. The condition apparently is not fatal, and sufferers usually respond to specific ritual treatment. To observers trained in psychoanalysis, *Malgri* suggested hysterical "displacement" of oedipal conflicts, but Cawte felt that it was more understandable as part of the totemically regulated system of territoriality based on the Dreaming. He noted that *Malgri* was most likely to affect people outside of their own estate territories, and the most dangerous spirits were those controlling the richest resource zones, where foraging pressure was the greatest. Furthermore, *Malgri* did not occur on the nearby mainland, where population densities were lower and resources thus less critical.

The Healing Power of Myth and Symbols

How do people draw healing and self-confidence from their myth and symbol systems?

Medically trained observers generally agree that shamanistic healers can successfully treat people suffering from a variety of psychiatric complaints, such as *Malgri*, using ritual techniques. Native curers may also be adept at treating injuries and illnesses with herbal remedies that have empirically identifiable chemical properties. Researchers further concede that shamanistic rituals may involve important psychotherapeutic techniques including the power of suggestion, the restructuring of social relations, catharsis, and the stimulation of neurochemicals (Dow 1986).

Whatever the specific healing mechanism might be, James Dow suggests that shamanistic ritual works because culturally defined symbols are manipulated to influence the body–mind relationship by helping people to alter their self-perceptions. Symbols, whether they involve totemic spirits or psychoanalytic concepts such as guilt and repression, are drawn from cultural myths that condense important truths about the human experience in

society. For psychotherapy to succeed, the patient and practitioner must establish a working relationship, and the shaman may facilitate this through what Dow calls the "shamanic paradox." That is, the patient must suspend any disbelief about the validity of the empirically unbelievable supernatural powers claimed by the shaman—he must implicitly believe in the authenticity of the therapeutic process before it can be effective. When the patient fully participates in the curing process, through belief or the suspension of disbelief, he may be able to reevaluate his own experiences and gain control over his feelings. These therapeutic principles help explain the persistence and apparent success of many ritual symbols.

Australian material illustrates the effectiveness of symbols, again from Arnhem Land. In this area, the central Dreamtime myth, which is reenacted in a major series of rituals including circumcision ceremonies, concerns the Wawilak sisters, two Dreaming ancestors who created the local cultural landscape during their Dreamtime travels. The myth details the creative activities of the Wawilak sisters and recounts how they lose ritual power to men when they are swallowed by the Rainbow Serpent, who is attracted when the sisters' menstrual blood contaminates the snake's pool. The Wawilak sisters, and women in general, are associated with the fertile dry season. The Rainbow Serpent rising up to eat the Wawilak sisters has obvious male associations and creates the widespread flooding of the lowlands during the Arnhem Land wet season (see Figure 5.10).

The Wawilak myth parallels the sacred flute myths found in Amazonia and deals with the same classic issues of life and death, reproduction, and gender roles. Although the Wawilak ritual complex does not directly involve shamanistic curing, according to the analysis of Nancy Munn (1969), participants in the rituals consciously identify with the characters in the myth, and as they enact it they convert their personal fears of death into more positive outcomes and satisfying images of health and community well-being. For example, circumcision of a boy is metaphorically compared to the swallowing of the sisters, only in this case he is ritually reborn. In other ceremonial reenactments, women happily avoid being eaten by the serpent. Bloodletting conducted in connection with circumcision

FIGURE 5.10   *Rock painting of the Rainbow Serpent, an important mythic figure central to ritual performances that strengthen community well-being in many areas of northern Australia.*

ceremonies is equated with the menstrual blood of the Wawilak sisters and is converted to ritual use as body paint, thus transferring symbolic strength and actual positive feelings to the participant. As one aboriginal man explained,

It makes us feel easy and comfortable and it makes us strong. It makes us good.... We have that ... strength from that blood. It goes inside when we put that blood on. (Munn 1969:195, citing Warner 1958)

Interpreting the meaning of many other specific practices that we identify as "magical" because we assume they have no empirical basis is equally challenging. Michael Brown (1984) has examined ritual songs that the Aguaruna of the Peruvian Amazon use to improve their hunting, especially when they go after spider monkeys with blowguns. The songs may be sung before a man goes hunting or sung silently as the hunt is in progress, and they contain complex allusions to myths and images of hunting success. Brown argues that the Aguaruna consider these songs to be as instrumental for their hunting success as the technical quality of their blowguns and stalking skills. In his view, the Agu-

aruna are right because these "magical" songs help them focus their energy on the hunting task. They alter their internal mental states, giving them confidence, in the same way that ritual symbols can have a psychotherapeutic effect. This line of argument is similar to Bronislaw Malinowski's functionalist theory that magic helps people deal with the uncertainties that lie beyond the limits of their technical capabilities.

HEALTH AND NUTRITION IN TRIBAL SOCIETIES

Many well-meaning people who are neither racist nor unusually ethnocentric may mistakenly assume that tribal peoples must have a low quality of life because their sanitation standards seem lower and they lack the advantages of modern medicine. This is not a simple issue, because public health programs and modern medicine associated with industrialization have improved life expectancy for many people; nevertheless, independent tribal societies have enjoyed a high quality of life. Perhaps what tribal peoples have, and what we have lost, is an equitable distribution of social power, giving everyone the feeling of control over their daily lives. Tribal peoples living in autonomous, domestic-scaled cultures seldom experience material impoverishment. In this section, we consider specific evidence on tribal health and well-being bearing on these important questions.

Myth and Reality of the "Noble Savage"

What factors contribute to the excellent physical condition of many autonomous tribal peoples?

Most early visitors to undisturbed tribal societies were impressed with the health and vigor of the peoples they saw. These first impressions likely were basically accurate, but they were confused and embellished with unnecessary pronouncements about morality and human perfection that became the myth of the "noble savage." For example, some of the first Europeans to visit Brazil reported that the Indians "naturally follow goodness" and "live together in harmony, with no dissension" (Hemming 1978:15). From such glowing descriptions, it was easy to conclude that "savages" were superior human beings living idyllic lives in Eden-like innocence. The comfortable nudity of most Native Amazonians that astonished Europeans certainly contributed to this noble savage image.

Most anthropologists have been careful to disassociate themselves from such noble savage romanticism. Members of domestic-scale cultures clearly are no more superior or inferior as people than any other group of humans. Tribal peoples can be selfish and cruel. They quarrel and kill one another, just like people who live in cities. Tribal culture is also not perfect. Tribal societies are not perfectly egalitarian, nor are they perfectly balanced with nature. And dietary and medical practices, as well as many aspects of tribal culture, may sometimes be harmful, as Robert Edgerton (1992) emphasizes. It is not unusual for tribal therapy to conflict with accepted practices in the medical community. For example, I witnessed a snake-bite victim being treated with herbal hot compresses, which would have accelerated the spread of the venom. Individuals must sometimes pay high personal costs for tribal membership, as people must to live in any human society. Nevertheless, generally good health and vigor seem to be two advantages of life in domestic-scale cultures for those who reach adulthood.

Evidence for the overall high quality of life in relatively independent tribal societies appears in a report by geneticist James Neel (1970). He summarized the findings of 8 years of biochemical and health research among Native Amazonians, carried out by an interdisciplinary team of more than a dozen researchers using sophisticated techniques. Neel reported that, in general, they found the Xavante, Yanomami, and Makiritare, whom they examined in Brazil and Venezuela, to be in "excellent physical condition" (see the box entitled "Health Report on the Waorani"). Infant and childhood mortality rates were higher than in fully industrialized countries, but the general pattern of life expectancy was better than in colonial India at the end of the nineteenth century.

Neel concluded that these tribal peoples were well adjusted to the viruses, bacterial diseases, and internal parasites naturally occurring in their terri-

tory. The Yanomami and Xavante were found to have twice the levels of gamma globulin, the blood protein containing infection-fighting antibodies, found in civilized populations. Yanomami babies are born with a high degree of passive immunity acquired from their mothers. These immunities are maintained by prolonged breast feeding. Yanomami infants then quickly develop active immunities because they are continuously exposed to all the local pathogens. The most significant diseases, including malaria and measles, were assumed to be post-Columbian introductions to which people were not yet well adjusted.

Theoretically, there are many reasons the quality of life should be high in domestic-scale societies. The most important are their generally low population densities and relative social equality, which help ensure equal access to basic subsistence resources so that everyone enjoys good nutrition. Furthermore, low densities and frequent mobility significantly reduce the occurrence of epidemic diseases, and natural selection—in the absence of the antibiotics, immunizations, surgery, and other forms of medical intervention—develop high levels of disease resistance. Healthy people are those who survive. Tribal societies, in effect, maintain public health by emphasizing prevention of morbidity rather than treatment. The healthiest conditions likely exist under mobile foraging and pastoralism, whereas there might be some health costs associated with the increased densities and reduced mobility of settled farming villages.

Dental Health and Tribal Diets

What accounts for the generally superior dentition of tribal peoples?

Health researchers have increasingly recognized that the typical diet found among domestic-scale subsistence foragers and farmers, which is low in fat, salt, and refined sugars and high in fiber and vitamin C, is actually an ideal human diet. Skeletal evidence suggests that archaeologically, the shift from foraging to farming frequently was accompanied by a decline in overall health and human nutrition (Cohen 1989). Significant epidemiological evidence suggests that many forms of cancer are

Health Report on the Waorani

A detailed assessment of the health status of the Waorani of Ecuador, a Native Amazonian group, was conducted in the field by a seven-person medical team in 1976. At that time, the Waorani were living independently as manioc gardeners and hunters and maintained only limited contacts with outsiders. In all, 293 people received thorough medical exams. On the positive side, more than 95 percent of the sample appeared to be "very robust" and in "excellent health" (Larrick et al. 1979). There was no malnutrition, no obesity, no high blood pressure, and no cardiovascular disease. Everyone had excellent eyesight, with no color blindness, and no one was deaf.

There were some negatives: Many children had scalp infections, but these were attributed to contacts with outsiders; some two-thirds out of a sample of sixty-three people showed evidence of light intestinal parasite infestation; two old women had pneumonia; three people were blind in one eye due to accidents; and there were many scars from spears and jaguar and peccary bites. Six people were described by the Waorani themselves as mentally deficient, and most of these cases were readily attributed to head injuries, fevers, or genetic defects. Surprisingly, the Waorani of all ages had high rates of dental decay. Only 5 out of the 230 people checked by the dentist were found to be completely free of cavities. It was suggested that such exceptionally high cavity rates were due to the unusual fact that the Waorani, unlike most Amazonians, consumed their manioc drink unfermented, while it still had a high sugar content. Although no estimate of mortality rates was given, it appears that many adults died in violent conflicts. Like James Neel's (1970) report, the Waorani study attributed much of the excellent health of the Indians to the high quality of their diet, low population density, and relative isolation from outside diseases.

---

associated with relatively recent dietary changes related to food marketing, processing, and storage, such as salting, pickling, and refining, and to dramatic increases in consumption of fat and simple carbohydrates or refined sugars (Cohen 1987). Of course, foods eaten by self-supporting subsistence peoples are also free of the contaminants and additives that are introduced into industrially produced foods by the chemicals used in agriculture and in processing.

Perhaps the first scientific evidence that tribal peoples could be shown to be physically superior to "civilized" peoples appeared in an article published in 1894 in the *Journal of the Royal Anthropological Institute* by Wilberforce Smith, who compared the teeth of Sioux Indians with those of typical Londoners. Smith became interested in this problem while conducting a survey of the teeth of his fellow Englishmen, which he found to be disastrously decayed. He knew that the skulls of prehistoric European "savages" invariably contained healthier teeth than contemporary peoples and decided to find out if modern "savages" also had healthy teeth. Taking advantage of the appearance of Buffalo Bill's Wild West Show in London, he obtained permission to examine the teeth of ten Sioux men, roughly ages

15–50. He found that all had "massive admirably formed teeth, evenly ranged." They were well worn, but none were decayed, and no molars were missing. He concluded, "Their teeth alone proved them to have led the life of genuine savages" (1894:110). By comparison, the younger portion of the 300 Londoners whom he also examined had half as many usable pairs of opposed molars as the Sioux of the same age category, while Londoners ages 35–45 had some 80 percent fewer paired molars than the older Sioux.

When Smith (1894) presented his findings in a lecture before the Royal Anthropological Institute, he displayed a dental cast made from a member of his own family, which showed the terrible condition of a typical Londoner's teeth alongside the skull of an average "savage" showing beautifully preserved teeth. To test the possibility that the remarkable health of the Sioux's teeth was because they were exceptionally robust and healthy people, Smith did a comparison check of the teeth of twelve men of the regiment of Horse Guards from the Royal Household Cavalry, who would have been in superb physical condition. He found that the cavalrymen had teeth that were only a "trifling degree better preserved" than the average Londoner's.

Smith correctly concluded that the lack of dental decay and tooth loss observed in tribal peoples was due to increased tooth wear, which kept the teeth clean and polished. He attributed the increased wear to the consumption of less cooked and less refined food, to the absence of knives and forks, which meant that more chewing was required, and to the presence of grit or "dirt" in the food. It was later learned that the absence of refined carbohydrates also contributed to healthy tribal teeth. The reduced tooth wear of contemporary peoples who eat industrially processed foods is also likely related to the common problem of impacted molars, as Grover Krantz (1978) has observed. People eating coarse foods wear down not only the grinding surfaces of their teeth but also the sides of their teeth, which creates enough jaw space to accommodate the third molars when they erupt. When there is no significant wear, these "wisdom teeth" often must be extracted.

The association between traditional dietary patterns and healthy teeth was documented more systematically in a series of field studies conducted by American dentist Weston Price (1945) between 1931 and 1936. Price visited some of the most traditional peoples in Amazonia, East Africa, Australia, and the Pacific and found that tooth decay and periodontal disease were virtually absent among self-sufficient peoples but steadily increased as these same peoples adopted the food patterns of industrial societies.

In 1956, shortly after Price's dental research, T. L. Cleave, a doctor in the British Royal Navy, used medical data on tribal peoples to isolate a single feature in the diets of industrialized peoples that caused what he called the "saccharine disease," a wide-ranging complex of conditions including tooth decay, ulcers, appendicitis, obesity, diabetes, constipation, and varicose veins. Like both Smith and Price before him, Cleave (1974) was impressed by the fact that tribal peoples did not suffer from many of the common ailments of civilization. Thus, he attempted to find the special conditions that made tribal peoples healthier. His primary finding was that the traditional foods of tribal groups were consistently much higher in dietary fiber than the highly refined complex carbohydrates consumed by industrialized peoples. High-fiber diets speed the transit time of food through the digestive system, thereby reducing many common diseases of civilization. It took many years for his findings to be incorporated into popular nutritional wisdom in the industrial world, but now high fiber, along with low fat and low salt, is widely accepted as an important component of a healthy diet.

Clifford Behrens (1986) provides some insights into how traditional classification systems are related to the maintenance of a high level of nutrition in tribal diets. Behrens found that the Shipibo of the Peruvian Amazon grouped their most preferred foods into two main emic categories, which he called "not-wild and cooked" and "wild and cooked." The Shipibo placed garden products such as plantains, maize, and manioc, which are high in carbohydrates, in the first category, and fish and game, which are high in protein and fat, in the second. The Shipibo considered their diet adequate only when it contained a balance of foods drawn from both categories. They accurately identified garden foods as the source of the energy needed for daily activities, while they felt that fish and game were needed for long-term health and growth.

Tribal Life Expectancy and Quality of Life

Why is it difficult to reasonably judge the quality of life in domestic-scale, self-sufficient societies?

At a special symposium on the health of tribal peoples, held at the CIBA Foundation in London in 1976 and attended by more than two dozen specialists, it was concluded that self-sufficient tribal groups were generally healthy, and it was recognized that intervention by outsiders, even when well intended, could seriously undermine existing balances (CIBA 1977). However, Betsy Lozoff and Gary Brittenham (1977) found that some important tribal health "paradoxes" remained unanswered: (1) How is population growth regulated? (2) If foragers are well nourished, why are they physically small? and (3) If disease rates are low, why is tribal mortality high?

We still cannot fully answer these apparent paradoxes. Population regulation is a critical issue because maintaining a stationary population seems to be a key to relative balance between resources and quality of life. Population stability at constant, low-density levels also seems to be a general, but not invariable, characteristic of tribal groups. More recent interpretations suggest that fertility-limiting cultural mechanisms, such as prolonged lactation and postpartum sex taboos, were probably more important population regulators than raiding and infanticide, but the evidence is incomplete. High mortality due to raiding and infanticide would imply a reduced quality of life because it would lower average life expectancy. Yet, from a functionalist perspective, it might arguably increase life quality for the survivors by promoting stability between people and resources.

There are some troubling and probably unanswerable philosophical issues involved in the preceding paradoxes. Although tribal peoples in general are often smaller and slighter than Europeans and appear to have shorter life expectancies, how does one decide that a given stature or life expectancy should be an appropriate cross-cultural measure of well-being? Some evidence suggests that very low birth weights or relatively low infant weight gain or growth rates may be associated with higher infant mortality rates. Some researchers also argue that small stature may indicate poor nu-

trition, especially in densely populated tribal areas (Dennett and Connell 1988). However, taller and longer may not always be better, especially if taller or longer-lived people experience a reduced quality of life within their particular cultural and environmental setting.

Estimating the life expectancy of tribal populations is an inherently difficult task because there are few reliable data that unambiguously represent fully independent populations. Many widely cited demographic profiles of tribal peoples are actually inferences based on paleodemographic techniques of questionable validity. Life tables, such as those used by insurance companies to show the probability of someone surviving to a given age, have been drawn up for various tribal and prehistoric populations and generally show a significantly lower life expectancy for tribal peoples than for contemporary industrial populations (see Table 5.3). When using life tables, it is important to specify at what age life expectancy is based because life expectancy at birth may be skewed down by high infant mortality rates in tribal populations. The figures compiled by Fekri Hassan (1981) in Table 5.3 yield an estimated average life expectancy at age 15 for seven ethnographically known foraging groups, including three from Australia, of only 26.4 years. By

TABLE 5.3 *Estimated Life Expectancy of Prehistoric and Tribal Populations*

Population	Life Expectancy at Age 15
Upper Paleolithic	16.9
Catal Huyuk (Neolithic)	17.0
Neandertals	17.5
Natufians (Mesolithic)	17.5
Angamgssalik Eskimo*	19.2
Aborigines (Groote Eylandt)*	23.3
East Greenland Eskimo*	23.5
Birhor (foragers, India)*	24.0
England (fourteenth century)	25.8
Baker Lake Eskimo*	27.7
Aborigines (Tiwi)*	33.1
Aborigines (northern territory)*	34.0
White Americans (1986)†	61.3

SOURCE: Hassan (1981:118).
*Ethnographically described foragers; average life expectancy = 26.4 years.
†Data from Wright (1990:225).

comparison, the figure for white Americans in 1986 was 61.3 years at age 15; however, 26.4 years was higher than the figures estimated for several archaeological populations and was higher than in fourteenth-century England.

Although tribal life expectancy is lower than that of modern industrial populations, this should not be surprising because life expectancy has made dramatic increases only within the past two centuries. Tribal peoples compare favorably with many preindustrial groups. However, all demographic estimates for tribal peoples must be used cautiously. Only figures based on reliable census records can be accepted at face value.

There are significant sources of bias and uncertainty in demographic research on tribal populations, as noted in our previous discussion on estimating infanticide rates from sex ratios. Hypothetical life expectancy tables for tribal populations are sometimes generated from fixed age-specific mortality rates, which must be specified ahead of time. An inherent circularity here makes it illegitimate to read mortality rates from life tables, because the rates must be known before the table can be constructed. Researchers Jean-Pierre Bocquet-Appel and Claude Masset (1981) warn that attempts to reconstruct life tables based on estimated age of death in prehistoric skeletal populations can yield life expectancies that are systematically too low. Paleodemographic age estimates can only be valid if the burials are compared with a population that is already known to be identical in age structure. Furthermore, they caution that the common indicators of skeletal age, such as the age at which certain cranial sutures close, have changed over time.

tures, their collective view of the world as reflected in myth, religion, and linguistic classification differs in significant ways that may be related to cultural scale and the absence of writing. However, when viewed from a relativistic and culturally sensitive position, tribal peoples are no more irrational, ignorant, or childish than people anywhere.

Tribal peoples have tremendous stores of culturally transmitted knowledge about the world around them, and their religious beliefs are perpetuated because they work effectively and because their validity is reinforced by the experience of daily life. This position must be spelled out clearly because some anthropologists have suggested that developmentally, tribal peoples are children who do not use adult logic and have difficulty separating fantasy from reality. Others have argued that tribal religious practices such as shamanism are the product of psychopathology.

Formal schooling and institutionalized medicine clearly are not the only route to understanding and health. Not only are there inherent problems in data collection on these issues, but there are dangers in generalizing from individuals to groups and major problems in deciding what standard of comparison can be used. The evidence suggests that although infant mortality rates appear to be high and life expectancy low relative to those of urban industrial populations, tribal peoples are generally free of infectious disease and nutritional deficiencies and avoid many of the dental problems and degenerative diseases that are so common in other populations. The most conservative conclusion is that tribal peoples show no basic differences in their mental abilities, even though they lack writing. The average tribal person would appear to enjoy a healthy vigorous life, relatively free of disease.

SUMMARY

This chapter demonstrates the difficulties of making meaningful cross-cultural quality-of-life comparisons of mental ability and health. It should make anyone cautious of simple stereotypes about tribal peoples as "underdeveloped." Although tribal individuals have the same basic intellectual and perceptual abilities as people in larger-scale cul-

STUDY QUESTIONS

1. Explain the views that each of the following took on the nature of "primitive" mentality: Boas, Tylor, Frazer, Lévy-Bruhl, Lévi-Strauss, and Hallpike.

2. In what respects are popular American racial categories cultural constructions rather than biological realities?

3. Why are popular racial categories unscientific? What genetic processes make racial purity a misleading concept?

4. How do human descent groups based on selectively neutral traits compare with populations defined by environmentally selected genetic traits?

5. Explain the cultural context of *Malgri*.

6. Use the Wawilak myth to illustrate the effectiveness of symbols.

7. Why are cross-cultural tests of cognitive ability difficult to apply and interpret?

8. Critique the psychopathological explanation of shamanism.

9. What conditions of domestic-scale cultures contribute to health?

SUGGESTED READING

COHEN, MARK, AND GEORGE ARMELEGOS (eds.). 1984. *Paleopathology and the Origins of Agriculture*. Orlando, Fla.: Academic Press. A collection of essays on the health consequences of the transition to agriculture.

EATON, S. B. BOYD, MELVIN KONNER, AND MARJORIE SHOSTAK. 1988. *The Paleolithic Prescription*. New York: Harper & Row. An examination of the health aspects of forager dietary patterns that applies them to contemporary society.

HARNER, M. J. 1980. *The Way of the Shaman*. New York: Harper & Row. A "how-to" manual that can be used by anyone interested in experimenting with the shamanistic experience.

6

*Pacific Islanders:
The Ranked Chiefdoms*

The vast Pacific region, known as Oceania, was successfully explored and colonized by Austronesian-speaking voyagers, who spread out from their earlier footholds in the western Pacific, beginning about 3500 years ago. By 1000 BP (before the present), virtually every habitable Pacific island supported thriving societies. When Europeans began to arrive in significant numbers in the nineteenth century, they found the Pacific Islanders, except for those in New Guinea, organized into chiefdoms, or small kingdoms. Pacific cultures were perched on the "great divide" between tribes and states, displaying much of the social equality and equilibrium of domestic-scale cultures, yet maintaining a pervasive concern with rank. Pacific Islanders have simple forms of social stratification and are important examples of the way politicization divides people based on differing access to wealth and power. From a human perspective, pervasive social stratification is perhaps the most important aspect of political- and commercial-scale cultures.

Remote from the centers of power in the industrializing world and offering relatively few resources to attract outsiders, many Pacific islands have maintained much of their traditional cultural system. They also offer ideal material for examining the contrasts between tribes and states and for understanding the initial rise of political-scale cultures. Given the severe environmental constraints of small islands, Oceania also offers an important place to examine the relationships between population, culture, and resources.

OCEANIA: LIVING IN THE ISLAND WORLD

Searching for Paradise: From High Islands to Low Coral Atolls

How have people responded culturally to the unique physical challenges posed by the Pacific islands? How do physical differences between islands affect their suitability for human habitation? When and how did people reach the islands?

In the popular imagination, the reef-fringed, palm-shaded islands of the Pacific are paradises. In reality, many Pacific islands have no drinking water, no soil, and virtually no native plants or animals, and they may be subject to devastating typhoons. Furthermore, without a chart, they are difficult to find in the first place. Exploring and successfully colonizing the Pacific world was one of the greatest human adventures, and it is surely a tribute to the courage and ingenuity of generations of Austronesian-speaking peoples who accomplished this feat roughly a thousand years ago.

The Pacific Ocean covers roughly one-third of the earth's surface. Yet, focusing on the area from Hawaii south and excluding the Asian continental islands of Taiwan, Indonesia, the Philippines, and Australia, the remaining area, which is traditionally called Oceania, contains less than 500,000 square miles (mi^2) (1.3 million square kilometers [km^2]) of land (see the box entitled "Pacific Island Culture Areas"). If the islands of Melanesia, Hawaii, and New Zealand, which are mostly large, are also excluded, there remains a vast area of ocean containing some 10,000 islands comprising a mere 4500 square miles of land, an area less than half the size of the state of Vermont, and with an estimated population (in 1970) of 570,000 people. And these islands are scattered over an immense distance. For example, it is some 8000 ocean miles (12,872 km) from Palau in western Micronesia to Easter Island at the extreme of eastern Polynesia. Micronesia includes 2000 islands, with just 715 square miles (1852 km^2) of land and a native population of 180,000 people, scattered over an area of ocean the size of the forty-eight contiguous United States. Before the arrival of Europeans, the two largest cultural areas, Polynesia and Micronesia, which will be the focus of this chapter, together contained a population estimated at 700,000 people (Oliver 1989).

Many factors affect the habitability of islands. Generally, large, high, volcanic islands, such as those found in Melanesia and Polynesia, contain relatively more land resources than the small coral islands of Micronesia. High islands will support a larger human population and are likely to have several zones of natural vegetation, rich soils, and flowing freshwater. However, there may be significant environmental differences between the moist windward side of these islands and the dry leeward side because mountain slopes form a rain shadow. There is also a general decline in biological diversity with increasing distance from the Asian mainland and Australia. For example, only a few reptiles, rats, and bats colonized the oceanic islands; even on New Zealand, there were no native land mammals other than bats. The most remote islands had only a few species of seabirds. This meant that unless human colonists brought animal domesticates with them, animal protein could only be obtained from marine life. Similarly, few if any edible plants occurred naturally on the smaller islands, and a reliable source of carbohydrates in the form of domesticated plants had to be introduced.

The availability of marine resources is related to many details of the local environment, such as the extent of tidal flats where marine invertebrates can be collected. Generally, the larger islands and those nearer the continental areas are richer. Fishing is usually not as productive in the open ocean as it is along the reef and in the lagoons of coral atolls, but the extent of these areas can vary widely from island to island.

Perhaps the most critical limiting factors are related to climate and the absolute size of an island. The tiny coral islets might be no more than 6–8 feet (2–3 meters [m]) above sea level and lack flowing freshwater. But if they are at least 350 feet (107 m) in diameter, they might support an underground layer of freshwater, the Ghyben-Hertzberg lens, which forms when rainwater percolates through the porous coral and mixes only gradually with the denser seawater beneath. Many islets support a small freshwater or brackish swamp in the center, but they depend on rainfall that is regionally variable and erratic, so that in some places serious droughts can occur. The freshwater supply of small atolls may also be temporarily destroyed by typhoons that occur with greater frequency within certain zones and that can wash saltwater completely over low islets. Despite all these limitations, an islet as small as 0.25 square miles might sustain 200 people, given the appropriate technical skills, as long as they maintained contacts with neighboring groups who could be relied on for support.

Speculation on the origin of the Pacific Islanders began as soon as outsiders encountered them. But in the absence of solid linguistic, archaeological, and biological data, many fanciful and mutually exclusive theories were devised (Howard 1967). Pacific Islanders were variously thought to have come from North America, South America, Egypt, Israel, and India, as well as Southeast Asia. Many older theories implicitly deprecated the navigational

Pacific Island Culture Areas

Following the original distinctions drawn in 1832 by French geographer Dumont d'Urville (1790–1842), Oceania customarily is divided into three ethnogeographic regions: Melanesia, Polynesia, and Micronesia (see Figure 6.1). These divisions make sense geographically but are anthropologically less precise. Melanesia (meaning "black islands") includes New Guinea, New Britain, Bougainville, the Solomons, Vanuatu, New Caledonia, and the Fijis. Melanesia originally was distinguished from Polynesia on ethnocentric and racist grounds. The early European explorers were more comfortable with the Polynesians because they were lighter skinned and more hierarchically organized and were seen as attractive, friendly, and almost civilized (Thomas 1989). By contrast, the relatively dark-skinned Melanesians were associated with Africans and were viewed as savage, tribal, and hostile, and even as cannibals and headhunters. In reality, however, the boundaries between Melanesia, Micronesia, and Polynesia were not that sharp, either biologically or culturally, as we will see. Furthermore, the emphasis on Melanesian cannibalism is problematic, and even its very existence has been questioned because cannibalism is such a common negative stereotype (Arens 1979).

Melanesian islands are predominantly large, mountainous islands formed on the Indian continental plate of granites, andesite, and metamorphic rocks. They derive their rich and varied terrestrial ecosystems from their close proximity to the Southeast Asian mainland and Australia. The true oceanic islands, which make up most of Polynesia and Micronesia, are formed on the vast Pacific plate, a huge sheet of magma-fed basalt that, according to plate tectonics theory, is floating slowly toward the northwest and sliding under the Philippine and Indian plates, creating deep trenches. Oceanic islands are either the above-water tops of volcanoes or coral that was formed in the shallow waters on undersea volcanic slopes (see Figure 6.2). Polynesia (meaning "many islands") forms a vast triangle with the Hawaiian chain in the northern corner, New Zealand in the south, and Easter Island in the east. Except for New Zealand, which is situated on the Indian plate, Polynesia contains many high volcanic islands, most of which lie south of the equator. Micronesia (meaning "tiny islands") lies north of Melanesia and north of the equator. Micronesian islands occur primarily as islets on coral atolls formed from the reefs that fringed ancient, now submerged volcanoes.

abilities and overall cultural creativity of the Pacific Islanders. For example, British diffusionists G. Elliot Smith (1928) and W. J. Perry (1923) assumed that only Egyptians would have been skilled enough to navigate and colonize the Pacific. They inferred that the Egyptians even crossed the Pacific to found the great civilizations of the New World. In 1947, Norwegian adventurer Thor Heyerdahl drifted on a balsa-log raft westward with the winds and currents across the Pacific from South America

FIGURE 6.1 *Three Pacific island culture areas—Melanesia, Polynesia, and Micronesia—with the principal island groups and cultures discussed in the text.*

to prove his theory that Pacific Islanders were Native Americans. Later Heyerdahl (1952) suggested that the Pacific was peopled by three migrations: by Native Americans from the Pacific Northwest of North America drifting to Hawaii, by Peruvians drifting to Easter Island, and by Melanesians. In 1969, he crossed the Atlantic in an Egyptian-style reed boat to prove Egyptian influences in the Americas, thus indirectly supporting Smith and Perry but reversing the direction of diffusion to the Americas. Contrary to these theorists, however, the overwhelming evidence of physical anthropology, linguistics, and archaeology shows that the Pacific Islanders came from Southeast Asia and were sufficiently skilled as navigators to sail against the pre-

vailing winds and currents (see the box entitled "The Origin of the Pacific Islanders").

The basic cultural requirements for the successful colonization of the Pacific islands include the appropriate boat-building, sailing, and navigating skills to get to the islands in the first place; domesticated plants and gardening skills suited to often marginal conditions; and a varied inventory of fishing implements and techniques. It is now generally believed that these prerequisites originated with peoples speaking Austronesian languages and began to emerge in Southeast Asia by about 7000 BP. The Proto-Austronesian culture of that time, based on archaeology and linguistic reconstruction, presumably had a broad inventory of cultivated plants

FIGURE 6.2
Examples of island types.
(a) Rarotonga, a high,
reef-rimmed volcanic is-
land; (b) Uvea (Wallis
Islands), a small, high is-
land with fringing coral
reef; (c) Penrhyn, an
atoll. (SOURCE: Cumber-
land 1956.)

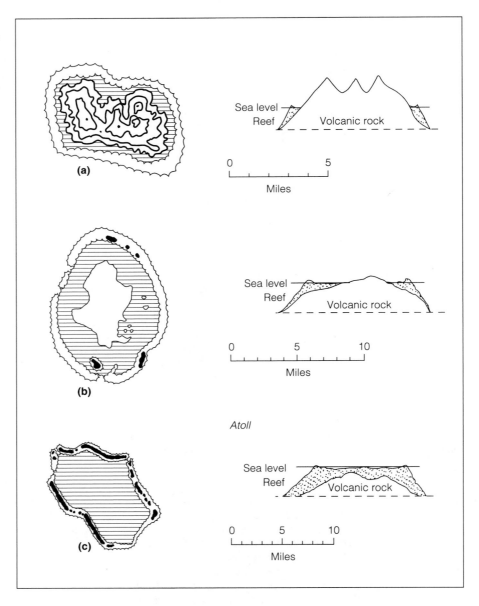

including taro, yams, banana, sugarcane, bread-fruit, coconut, sago, and rice. Just as important, the culture possessed the basic foundation for an effective maritime adaptation, including outrigger canoes and a variety of fishing techniques effective for overseas voyaging.

Contrary to the arguments of some that much of the Pacific was settled by Polynesians accidentally marooned after being lost and adrift at sea, it seems reasonable that this feat was accomplished by deliberate colonization expeditions that set out fully stocked with food and domesticated plants and animals. Detailed studies of the winds and currents using computer simulations suggest that drifting canoes would have been a most unlikely means of colonizing the Pacific (Levison, Ward, and Webb 1973). These expeditions likely were driven by population growth and political dynamics on the home islands, as well as the challenge and excitement of exploring unknown waters. Because all Polynesians and Micronesians and many Melanesians speak Austronesian languages and grow crops derived from Southeast Asia, all these peoples most certainly derived from that region, and not the New World or elsewhere. The undisputed pre-Columbian presence in Oceania of the sweet potato, which is a New World domesticate, has sometimes been used to support Heyerdahl's "American Indians in the Pacific" theories. However, this is but one plant in a long list of Southeast Asian domesticates. As Patrick Kirch (1985) points out, rather than being brought by rafting South Americans, sweet potatoes might just as easily have been brought back by returning Polynesian navigators, who could have reached the west coast of South America.

Glottochronology: Word Tracks Across the Pacific

How have linguists reconstructed the history of Austronesian migrations by analyzing word lists?

The general picture of the settlement of Oceania seems to conform well with linguistic reconstructions based on *glottochronology,* which suggests that most of the differentiation of Austronesian has occurred within the past 6000–7000 years (see Figure 6.4 on page 160). The Austronesian language family, or Malayo-Polynesian as it has also been called, is one of the most widely distributed language families in the world and includes some 900 languages scattered throughout the Pacific, from Madagascar to Indonesia, Malaysia, Taiwan, and the Philippines (Ruhlen 1987). Most classification systems show the Polynesian languages forming a cluster of closely related languages, which are presumed to have separated with Fijian from a common Proto-Central Pacific ancestor language about 3500 years ago. Most Micronesians are more closely related

linguistically to Melanesians than to Polynesians, but both Micronesians and Polynesians shared a common ancestral language in Proto-Eastern Oceanic about 4000 years ago. The Oceanic languages may have separated from their Austronesian ancestors in Southeast Asia about 5000 years ago.

As a method of linguistic reconstruction, glottochronology is based on a number of ultimately unverifiable assumptions. It provides relative dates that are useful additions to chronologies derived from biological data and archaeology, but they are not precise and should not be accepted without question. Glottochronology assumes that all languages lose words from a common core vocabulary at a constant rate historically documented for Indo-European languages (Gudschinsky 1956). Groups of related languages likely do change at a constant rate, but many cultural factors may influence this rate, and the specific Indo-European rate is not reliably applicable to all languages. The core vocabulary is a list of 100–200 words for cultural universals such as body parts and geographic features. The years since two languages separated from a common ancestor are calculated from the percentage of cognates identified in the core vocabulary. **Cognates** are words that are recognizably derived from a common source in a parent language, and thus their frequency is assumed to be a measure of their separation time. To cite a Polynesian example, Table 6.2 on page 160 lists the words for *deity, chief,* and *taboo* in Tikopian, a member of the Samoic branch of Nuclear Polynesian, and Hawaiian, an Eastern Polynesian language. The words in both languages obviously are similar enough to be considered cognates, implying a common ancestry, even though their speakers live more than 3000 miles apart.

Languages sharing more than 80 percent cognates are considered to be dialects of the same language and are assumed to be separated by no more than 500 years. Languages sharing 33–80 percent cognates suggest a separation of 500–2500 years

---

glottochronology A method of estimating the relative date at which related languages separated from a common ancestral language, by calculating the percentage of cognates shared between the related languages.

cognates Related words that are found in more than one language and that were derived from a common proto-language.

The Origin of the Pacific Islanders

The basic outlines of the prehistory of the Pacific islands and adjacent Island Southeast Asia are presented in Table 6.1. By about 5000 BP, Austronesian-speaking peoples began to expand toward the Pacific islands, first into Taiwan and the Philippines and then along coastal New Guinea. By 3000 BP, virtually all of Melanesia and much of Micronesia was occupied, and the Proto-Polynesians had established a firm foothold in Fiji, Tonga, and Samoa on the western edge of what would become Polynesia.

Some of the best archaeological evidence for the sequence of colonization in the Pacific is based on the discovery of a distinctive red, stamped, and incised pottery style, known as Lapita, and associated domesticated plants and fishing technology. Lapita peoples ultimately were derived from the Proto-Austronesians of Island Southeast Asia. But they appear to have developed their distinctive style in the New Britain area off of eastern New Guinea about 3600 years ago before spreading through the closely spaced chain of Melanesian islands to New Caledonia (Kirch 1985). The crossing of the 528 miles (850 km) of open ocean between Vanuatu and Fiji, which took place about 3250 BP, judging by the appearance of Lapita pottery in Fiji at that time, was a major achievement that set the stage for expansion into the rest of the inhabitable Pacific (see Figure 6.3). The 1000-mile (1600-km) crossing between Samoa and the Marquesas in central Polynesia, which took place approximately 2000 years ago, was a logical continuation of the earlier voyages of discovery. Even longer voyages from the Marquesas to Hawaii, Easter Island, and New Zealand followed shortly thereafter.

and membership in a common language family. In theory, relationships as remote as 10,000 years might be suggested on the basis of extremely low percentages of shared cognates. However, the identification of "true" cognates is plagued with difficulties, such as the problem of deciding whether cognates are similar due to common ancestry or because of borrowing from a common source. Also, languages do not always separate completely and may continue to share vocabulary even as they evolve in different directions.

Given the present interpretation of Pacific prehistory, Polynesia is a well-defined area with a common ancestry, language, culture, and physical type. Micronesia shows many cultural similarities to Polynesia but is physically and linguistically closer to Melanesia and Island Southeast Asia. Melanesia, with its Papuan and Proto-Oceanic foundation, is a more complex mix of language, culture, and physical type than Micronesia and Polynesia.

Islander Survival Skills: Outrigger Canoes and Navigation

What special navigation skills do Pacific Islanders use for long-distance voyaging? What problems are posed by the unusual design of outrigger canoes?

The outrigger canoe and very sophisticated knowledge of the sea and island ecosystems supported Pacific island societies. Seagoing Micronesian outriggers, which were routinely used to cross more than 300 miles (483 km) of open ocean, were only 25 feet (8 m) long, whereas the huge double-hulled Polynesian canoes used in overseas colonization

The human biological evidence is less clear, but genetic traits show consistent separations between Australian aborigines, Tasmanians, Papuan-speaking Melanesians, and all Austronesian-speaking peoples (Bellwood 1985). Using genetically based dental traits, Christy Turner (1989) has proposed that a second major population group emerged in the Sunda region about 30,000–17,000 years ago, which he calls "Sundadonts." By approximately 20,000 BP, Turner suggests, the Sundadonts had expanded northward into China, where they developed other unique dental traits and formed another population, which he called "Sinodonts." The distribution of these distinctive dental traits suggests that Sinodonts settled China, Siberia, and the Americas, whereas Sundadonts settled the Pacific islands. Polynesian peoples are relatively homogenous physically, which is to be expected if they spread rapidly from a single source. They differ as a group from the coastal Melanesian Austronesian speakers from whom they presumably derived. But they are not beyond the range of Melanesian variation, allowing for the "founder effect" that results when a migrating subset of a larger population takes only a portion of the genetic variation of the parent population. There are similarities in blood proteins between Native Americans and Pacific Islanders, as Heyerdahl observed, but these similarities are shared with other Asian populations and demonstrate only that both Native Americans and Pacific Islanders had common ancestors.

were nearly 100 feet (30 m) long and could easily accommodate supplies for an extended voyage. Canoes were designed to be extremely seaworthy and, unlike rafts, were highly maneuverable and could be propelled by both sail and paddles. The most widely distributed canoe type was the outrigger, which in Micronesia was usually constructed from a carved breadfruit-log hull with wooden planks lashed on the side. The outrigger was a wooden float suspended approximately half a hull length off the windward side of the canoe and counterbalanced by a platform suspended off the lee side (see Figure 6.5). The outrigger was oriented so that the float would be lifted by the wind on the sail. When the float dipped into the water, it pulled the canoe back into the wind. The great advantage of the outrigger was that it maximized speed and stability without a deep keel (to counterbalance the sail), which would impede passage over the reefs surrounding most Pacific islands.

The addition of an outrigger posed many design problems that traditional canoe builders solved in very sophisticated ways. The hull had to be asymmetrical in cross section, and its overall contours were shaped within very narrow tolerances to achieve a balance between seaworthiness, speed, and maneuverability (Gladwin 1970). Only a few specialists had the necessary skills to direct construction of such a complex craft. The bow and stern of the outrigger were reversible, and when a major change in direction was made, the sail was shifted from end to end to keep the float facing the wind.

The navigational techniques that allowed Polynesian explorers to maintain a steady course across vast distances in search of islands are still being

TABLE 6.1   *Prehistory of the Pacific Islands, 250,000 BP–AD 1522*

AD 1522	Magellan expedition crosses Pacific Ocean
Polynesian Expansion (AD 800–300; 2000–3600 BP)	
800	New Zealand settled
500	Sweet potato introduced from South America
400	Easter Island settled
300	Hawaii settled
2000 BP	Marquesas settled
2700	Melanesian colonies in Fiji
3000	Lapita pottery in New Caledonia
3200	Lapita pottery in Tonga
3250	Lapita pottery in Fiji
3000–3500	Proto-Nuclear Micronesian divergence begins from northern New Hebrides
3500	Proto-Polynesian divergence begins
3600	Lapita cultural complex, New Britain
Proto-Oceanic Expansion (3800–5000 BP)	
3800	Red pottery in Marianas, Micronesia
3500–5000	Cord-marked pottery, Philippines to Timor
4000–5000	Outrigger canoes enter Oceania
5000	Proto-Oceanic divergence begins maritime specialization
Proto-Austronesian and Domestication (6000–9000 BP)	
6000	Proto-Austronesian divergence begins
6500	Domestic pigs in highland New Guinea
7000	Cord-marked pottery in Taiwan; Proto-Austronesian culture; taro, yams, banana, sugarcane, breadfruit, coconut, sago, rice, fishing, outrigger canoes
9000	Earliest horticulture in New Guinea, yams and taro
***Homo Sapiens* Foragers (15,000–60,000 BP)**	
15,000	Niah Cave, Sarawak: edge-ground axes, adzes
17,000	Niah Cave: intentional burials
20,000	Low sea level facilitates island hopping
17,000–30,000	Sundadonts develop in Sundaland
26,000	Kosipe, New Guinea: stone tools
32,000	Niah Cave, Sarawak: bone points
40,000	Niah Cave, Sarawak: *Homo sapiens* skull
53,000	Low sea level facilitates island hopping, likely first Sahul colonization
60,000	Sundanoid foragers in Sundaland; ancestral Australians and Papuans
Protohumans	
250,000 BP–1.5 mya*	*Homo erectus* in Java; stone choppers, hand adzes, hand axes

SOURCES: Bellwood (1980), Kirch (1985), Oliver (1989), and Turner (1989).
*mya = million years ago.

practiced by a few skilled navigators on some of the most isolated Micronesian atolls. Thomas Gladwin's (1970) research on the atoll of Puluwat revealed the main features of the system. Gladwin found that Micronesian navigation was based on an elaborate body of formal knowledge, both empirical and mythical. A few titled specialists, known as master navigators, controlled the system and offered formal instruction to aspiring navigators. Out of the island population of 400 people, only 6 men were considered master navigators. Successful navigation depended on the ability to sail a steady course on a specific bearing while keeping a mental record of the distance traveled, for days or weeks at a time, at night, during storms, across changing currents, and in unfamiliar waters. The key to the high-status individuals. Canoes were treated with great care. They were stored in special canoe houses to prevent them from becoming waterlogged, and the lashings and caulking might be replaced every 2 years.

Long-distance voyages also depended on a reliable system of food storage. Whole coconuts were a ready, storable source of food and drinking water, but there were elaborate ways of processing other important staples such as breadfruit, pandanus palm fruits, and taros so that they could be stored indefinitely without canning or refrigeration (Schattenburg 1976). Micronesians had at least four different ways of preserving breadfruit, involving grating, pounding, soaking, fermenting, cooking, and sun drying. In one method, peeled slices of raw ripe breadfruit were soaked for 1½ days in the lagoon, fermented for 2 days on the ground, then squeezed and stirred with freshwater for 3 more days to convert them to dough. When the dough was shaped into slabs and sun-dried, it could be stored for up to 2 years before being reconstituted by soaking again in water (Murai, Pen, and Miller 1958).

Breadfruit is more nutritious than potatoes and is rich enough in calories and vitamins to supply virtually all daily food requirements when supplemented with fish and coconut. Because many of the cultivated plants in the Pacific are grown from cuttings, special techniques were developed for transporting them. Patricia Schattenburg (1976) reported that when the root balls of delicate young breadfruit trees were wrapped in rotted coconut husks, bound with dried leaves, and bundled in woven baskets, they were protected from saltwater.

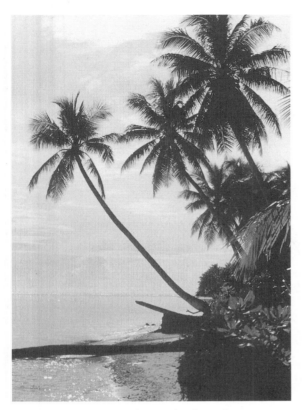

FIGURE 6.3   *Coconut palms on the shore of a Micronesian atoll.*

system was a star chart with thirty-two named bearing points based on the rising and setting points of specific stars (see Figure 6.6). For each route traveled, a navigator had to commit to memory a unique sequence of bearing stars.

The navigators on Puluwat routinely sailed between 26 islands using 110 different routes. To follow a given bearing, the navigators needed to know what stars would be observed en route, and they kept careful track of wave patterns and weather conditions. There was little margin for error on a long voyage because small atolls were only visible for 10 miles (16 km) at sea and so might easily be missed in passing. And even upon arrival, the navigator had to find narrow passes through treacherous reefs.

Canoes and navigation were a vital part of Pacific island culture. Navigators were greatly respected,

Fishing and Gardening: The Island Technological Base

What are the most important island crops, what do they contribute to the diet, and what makes them especially suited to the island environment? What is the gender division of subsistence labor? What special skills does fishing require?

Pacific island subsistence was similar to that of Amazonia in that it was based on two rather distinct systems: (1) fishing and gathering of marine animals to provide protein, and (2) gardening to

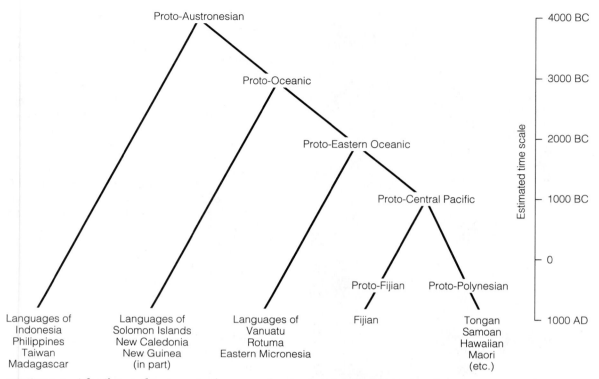

FIGURE 6.4   *A family tree of Austronesian languages showing time depths of separations for the Oceanic branches.* (SOURCE: *Kirch 1985:62.*)

TABLE 6.2   *Cognates Between Tikopian and Hawaiian Languages of Nuclear Polynesian*

Word	Tikopian (Samoic Outlier)	Hawaiian (Eastern Polynesian)
Deity	*Atua*	*Akua*
Chief	*Ariki*	*Ali'i*
Taboo	*Tapu*	*Kapu*

SOURCES: Firth ([1936] 1957), Malo (1951), and Ruhlen (1987).

produce the bulk of dietary calories. According to the usual gender division of labor, men did the fishing and heavy gardening work while women gathered marine animals and did the daily garden cultivating and harvesting. Three crop zones, which on small islands were often arranged in concentric zones according to altitude and proximity to the ocean, included orchard crops, dry crops, and wet crops. The orchard crops were the breadfruit trees and the relatively salt-tolerant coconuts

and pandanus palms that could grow near the beach (see Figure 6.7a). All of these trees provided food as well as raw materials for canoe building, house construction, and basketry. On the smaller islands, they were the only significant sources of wood and fiber. The subsistence importance of coconuts is indicated by the fact that Polynesians named seventeen different stages of nuts according to their edibility (Handy and Handy 1972). Micronesians specialized in producing a fermented drink from the sap tapped from the unopened flower stem.

The dry gardens produced sweet potatoes, yams, and bananas, but the extent of such gardens was severely limited by soil conditions and rainfall, especially on the smaller coral islands and atolls. On many of these islands, soil other than coral sand was virtually absent, and humus had to be created and maintained by a continuous process of mulching. Throughout much of the Pacific, the most im-

FIGURE 6.5
Micronesian outrigger.

portant food plants were the taros, members of the arum family (*Araceae*), known as aroids (see the box entitled "Taro" and Figure 6.7b).

The productivity of taro and its subsistence importance are indicated by data obtained by William Alkire (1965) on the Micronesian atoll of Lamotrek in the central Caroline Islands. In Lamotrek, approximately 200 people live on a 0.25-square mile (158-acre or 64-hectare) islet. Alkire estimated that taro supplied approximately three-fourths of the average 2 pounds (0.9 kg) of plant food consumed daily by adults on the island. An estimated 500,000 taro plants grew on the island, with some 15,000 per acre in the 58 acres of the island's swampy interior. Annual consumption was only about 20 percent of the total crop, but even if most of the plants were slow-growing swamp taro, the consumption rate still would have been well below potential production. However, if typhoons swept saltwater into the swamp and destroyed the crop, recovery would take at least 3 years.

Taro-based subsistence was a time-consuming female task on Lamotrek. During the half of the year when breadfruit was not being harvested, Lamotrek women worked over 2 hours a day in the taro swamp, cultivating and harvesting. Taro processing took nearly an additional 3 hours a day. Breadfruit harvesting and processing required about 3 hours a day in season.

Fishing was a primary male activity throughout the Pacific. Alkire (1965) found that on an average day, nearly one-fourth of the male population of

FIGURE 6.6   *Stick figure from the Marshall Islands, used to teach the fundamentals of the Micronesian star chart.*

FIGURE 6.7 *Primary Pacific island subsistence crops (a) Tree crops: (1) coconut palm, (2) breadfruit, (3) banana, and (4) pandanus palm. (b) Root crops: (1) yam, (2) sweet potato, and (3) taro. (SOURCE: Based on Oliver 1989:186, 191.)*

Lamotrek would be out fishing. Men typically spent over 5 hours fishing at a time and brought back 9 pounds (4 kg) of fish. Virtually every major fishing technique was used, including traps, nets, spears, and hook and line. Fish were also raised in fish farms—rock-lined pools in tidal shallows—where they were fed and allowed to reproduce.

Coral reefs are composed of rough limestone (calcium carbonate) built up from the skeletons of generations of tiny marine invertebrates. Coral

Taro

The arum family includes many familiar leafy tropical ornamentals, such as the philodendron. The edible aroids grow large heart-shaped ears and are sprouted from cuttings. They produce starchy corms and bulbous underground stems and are highly productive, but they require large amounts of relatively fresh water. The true taro, *Colocasia esculenta*, is sometimes grown in terraced, irrigated ponds on high islands, given the availability of abundant water. It can be planted at any time and is harvested within a year, but it does not store well, either in the ground or after harvest. Another important aroid, *Cyrtosperma*, the swamp taro, produces a more fibrous corm. It takes 3 years to reach full maturity, but it can be harvested over a longer period, allowing it to be stored in the ground, and it keeps for about 2 weeks after harvest. It is the preferred taro in much of Micronesia, where it is grown in the swampy center of small coral islands where the freshwater lens reaches the surface. Another aroid, *Alocasia macrorrhiza*, or giant taro (elephant ear), grows under drier conditions, but its corms require special processing to remove irritating crystals.

only grows under very narrow tolerances of temperature (73°–78°F [22.7°–25.5°C]), salinity, and sunlight, but when conditions are right, it can grow at ocean depths of 150 feet (46 m). Coral reef ecosystems cover less than 0.1 percent of the globe, but they produce some 10 percent of the world's fish and support many other traditionally important food animals, such as sea turtles, and edible marine invertebrates, such as shellfish. Estimates for sustained productivity of these rich coral reef zones range as high as 22 tons (20 metric tons) of fish per square kilometer of reef per year (Kenchington 1985). If 50 percent of this amount is edible and is counted as 20 percent protein, then 0.4 square miles (1 km²) of reef would produce 4400 pounds (2000 kg) of protein per year, which would supply 110 people with a minimum annual protein requirement of 1.8 ounces (50 grams) per day. As noted previously, different islands varied greatly in the extent of available reef zones. For example, Bikini Atoll in the Marshall Islands of Micronesia contained some 30 square miles (78 km²) of reef strung along a broken circle some 70 miles (113 km) around, while the Ulithi Atoll in the Carolines enclosed a lagoon of 183 square miles (474 km²). Protein was probably not a limiting factor for most Pacific islands.

The amount of specialized knowledge that successful fishing required was most impressive. Many important marine ecozones were exploited in different ways. Atolls, for example, included at least five broad marine zones (Knudson 1970): the lagoon in the center of the atoll, shallow waters, deep waters along reef edges and coral heads, intertidal reefs and flats, and the open ocean. Pacific Islanders themselves recognized many finer distinctions. The shallow waters, reef edges, and lagoons generally were the most intensively exploited zones, where nets, traps, and weirs could be used most effectively (see Figure 6.8). According to a study by **Don Rubinstein** (1978), the people of Fais, in the Carolines, named four broad marine zones and thirteen subzones ringing their 1-square-mile (2.6-km²) raised coral island. They located specific fishing areas by reference to some sixty submerged coral heads, which were individually named, and they identified eleven lines radiating from the island and aligned with named features on shore and at sea. Phil Lobel (1978) found that the Gilbertese Islanders in Kiribati have names for 254 fish species, 95 marine invertebrates, and 25 fish anatomical features.

Marine biologist Robert Johannes (1981) has documented the knowledge employed by native

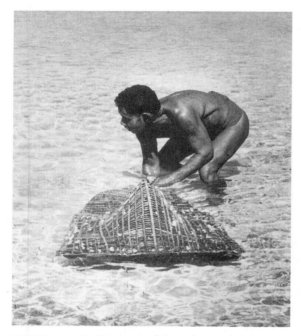

FIGURE 6.8   *In Micronesia, fish are frequently taken in traps.*

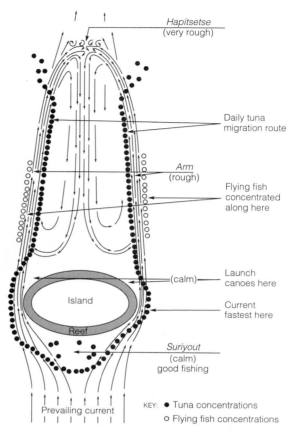

FIGURE 6.9   *Micronesians in Palau use their knowledge of ocean currents to locate fish.* (SOURCE: *Based on Johannes 1981, Figure 3.*)

fishermen on Palau (Belau) in Micronesia. A critical element in organizing Palauan fishing activities was keeping careful track of the seasons. For this purpose, the Palauans utilized a 12-month lunar calendar that allowed them to predict with considerable precision changes in wind, weather, and waves and the movements and breeding patterns of many pelagic fish, turtles, and seabirds. Palauans understood how ocean currents, when they were deflected for miles by islands and reefs, reacted, and they knew where specific fish would concentrate seasonally in relation to the eddies and calm places (see Figure 6.9).

Johannes shows how a profusion of fishing gear and techniques reflected an understanding of the specific feeding habits, life history, and anatomy of many different fish species. He points out that the curiously incurved shell fishhook, so widely used in the Pacific, works more effectively than the standard barbed steel hook, which Europeans assumed to be superior. The traditional shell hook is designed to slide to the corner of the fish's mouth after a light tug and then to rotate, penetrating and locking securely in the fish's jaw.

PACIFIC ISLAND SOCIETIES: LIVING WITH INHERITED RANK

According to Robert Carneiro (1981), chiefdoms are a critically important cultural type, representing multicommunity political units. In Carneiro's view, chiefdoms are the first step in supra-village political aggregation, "the first transcending of local autonomy in human history" (1981:37–38), which only occurred in the past 7500 years. This was the beginning of the politicization process that produced states and empires.

The Polynesian Chiefdoms: Elementary Aristocracies

How are Pacific chiefs different from Amazonian headmen? How do Pacific Islanders measure relative human worth? What is the cultural basis of islander ranking systems?

Irving Goldman (1970) undertook a systematic, controlled comparison of Polynesian societies because of his interest in the role of *aristocracy* in the development of civilization. He saw aristocracy as the basic theme of Polynesian societies; they represented the sort of elementary aristocracies that formed the developmental foundation of all of the world's great civilizations. In Goldman's view, the underlying principle of aristocracy is a belief in the "inherent superiority of a line of descent" (1970: xvi). Chiefdom societies were thus preeminently kinship societies because they used genealogical principles to determine personal rank, prestige, and political leadership far more systematically than any of the domestic-scale societies considered in previous chapters.

Drawing a distinction between leadership based on pragmatic, or utilitarian, principles—as was the case in aboriginal Australia, in Amazonia, and among the East African cattle peoples—and Pacific Islander leadership based on aristocracy, Goldman (1970) observed that utilitarian leadership lacks continuity because it is limited to the personal qualities of individuals and specific crisis situations. The aristocrat bases his position on genealogy and religious authority and does not need to prove himself; at the same time, he will be supported by a group of close but lower-ranked kinsmen, and he will be succeeded by his descendants.

Earlier, Marshall Sahlins (1963) drew a similar contrast between Melanesian "bigmen," who—like some Amazonian headmen—were self-made leaders who constantly had to verify their positions by their generosity and success in warfare, and Polynesian chiefs, who were born to office. Sahlins (1958) also noted that throughout Polynesia, the chief was the "agent" of societywide redistribution of goods; his generosity gave him prestige and di-

rect control over social processes. For Sahlins, the key to the system was the economic power of the chief at the center of a *redistribution* system in which he promoted the production of otherwise "surplus" food and goods (see the box entitled "Chiefdoms and the Politicization Process"). These resources were concentrated and then used to support communitywide rituals, public works for the common good, or the stratification system itself.

Aristocracies are based in both religion and history in a way that differs strikingly from domestic-scale tribal societies. Whereas Australian aborigines used totemism to create exclusive groups and to regulate territories, Pacific Islanders used religious sentiments to help expand the political community and to support the superiority of individual chiefs and their descent groups—that is, to create aristocracies. Australian aborigines derived certain degrees of political authority from their relationships to totemic ancestors. But it is significant that totemic ancestors were nonhuman, and when important men died, their souls were recycled and they were forgotten as individuals. In this respect, typical of domestic-scale societies, aboriginal society could be considered ahistorical. By contrast, aristocracies are historical in that they keep lengthy genealogical records of the names and acts of specific chiefs. Such genealogies are used to verify claims to rank and chiefly title and may be as historically accurate as chronologies based on archaeological dating and linguistic reconstruction. Goldman (1970), using 25 years as the average tenure of a chief, found that traditional dates for the original settlement of New Zealand, Easter Island, Mangareva, and the Marquesas were within 50–100 years of estimates based on archaeology and glottochronology.

According to Goldman's (1970) interpretation of Polynesian chiefdoms, they are best understood not in relation to political or economic processes as such. They are not simply results of the needs of a large or dense population for political administration to organize production; rather, they are

---

aristocracy   A political system in which a small, privileged elite rule.
redistribution   A form of exchange in which goods, such as foodstuffs, are concentrated and then distributed under the control of a central political authority.

Chiefdoms and the Politicization Process

Robert Carneiro (1981:45) defines the chiefdom as "an autonomous political unit comprising a number of villages or communities under the permanent control of a paramount chief." The great divide in human cultural development between a world totally controlled by domestically organized cultures and a world dominated by politically and commercially organized cultures occurred when the first villagers surrendered their political autonomy to chiefs from other villages. This created a second level of political authority, with villages aggregated under a paramount chief to form a chiefdom. Adding a third administrative level to form a state and a fourth to form an empire are logical steps in the growth process (see Figure 6.10). Archaeologists have used a number of criteria to identify chiefdoms, including monumental architecture, ceremonial centers, elaborate grave goods reflecting high social status, and several large settlements, as administrative centers, surrounded by small villages. The first two criteria suggest that the coordinated activity of people from beyond local villages would be required. Many of these criteria identify Polynesian chiefdoms.

It is not easy to explain why chiefdoms emerge in the first place, because the benefits of elite status are enjoyed by the chief while most people are burdened by reduced social status, higher taxes, warfare, and insecurity. The question thus becomes, Why would people put up with chiefdoms? The key to this politicization process is the concentration of social power in the hands of a political elite. Concentrated power disproportionately improves the chief's quality of life and genetic fitness while diminishing the fitness of others. Power also can be used coercively to threaten or otherwise manipulate cultural choices so that people are persuaded to lend their support to the chief. As William Durham (1991:211) notes, "cultural evolution is an intrinsically political process." The emergence and persistence of chiefdoms is an example of the imposition of cultural patterns by a power elite,

fundamentally a system of **social status,** a scale of human worth, that has economic and political consequences. Goldman saw this as a more "realistic" way to view Polynesian societies than through functionalist models, which consider the abstract goal of cohesion for a society as a whole, because status concerns directly influence individual actors. Goldman defined *status system* as:

the principles that define worth and more specifically honor, that establish the scales of personal and group value, that relate position or role to privileges and obligations, that allocate respect, and that codify respect behavior. (1970:7)

In this definition, status is equated with honor. Status systems are found in all societies; but, where age, sex, and personal characteristics are the only status criteria, as in most domestic-scale societies, relative equality and balance are likely to prevail. Emphasis on hereditary *rank* (social position in a status hierarchy) creates a different situation. Goldman finds the standard distinction between systems of **ascribed status** (inherited position) and **achieved status** (demonstrated ability), which corresponds to Sahlins' distinction between chiefs with ascribed status and bigmen with achieved status, to be inadequate in the Polynesian context.

rather than free choice by the population at large. Chiefdoms are produced by biased cultural transmission that actually works against the sapienization process for most households. Politicization is the first step in a maladaptive evolutionary process that rewards a powerful, self-interested minority for promoting cultural ideas that support runaway growth harmful to others.

Politicization requires growth. Power seekers must mobilize household labor, warriors, technology, trade, and religion in their growth projects. Politicization works because as growth occurs, political leaders become a mathematically smaller proportion of society and their power steadily increases. Elites are thus naturally rewarded for developing cultural ideas that remove the barriers to growth. Marshall Sahlins (1958) pointed out that the power of Polynesian chiefs increased simultaneously with economic productivity as measured by the size of the networks in which food was redistributed, the frequency of redistribution, and the number of specialists who were not directly involved in primary food production, and who were therefore supported by "surplus" production.

Population size is an important variable because size constrains decision-making processes. In a social group of 150 or fewer people, virtually everyone can participate in decisions; but in a society of 500 or more, public decision making is likely to be controlled by the adult men. A consensual village head might be able to informally coordinate up to 500 household heads within a local group of 2500 people, but a formal political elite is necessarily required to manage larger settlements. Five hundred is a crucial number because the limits of human memory and information-processing ability make it difficult for people—including chiefs—to keep track of more than that number of items in any domain (Kosse 1990).

Hereditary-ascribed systems usually are considered to be static, whereas achieved systems allow for individual mobility; Polynesian systems, however, are aggressive and expansive, not static and rigid. When a chief enlarges his community, he increases his status. Polynesian chiefs combine elements of both ascription and individual achievement, and they base their actions on sacred and formal principles, as well as secular and pragmatic ones.

In a formal sense, succession to chiefly office is genealogically ascriptive, according to ***primogeniture*** (priority by order of birth and rank of descent

social status A position that an individual occupies within a social system; defined by age, sex, kinship relationships, or other cultural criteria and involving specific behavioral expectations.

rank Social position in a status hierarchy.

ascribed status The social status that one is born into; includes sex, birth order, lineage, clan affiliation, and connection with elite ancestors.

achieved status Social position based on a person's demonstrated personal abilities apart from social status ascribed at birth.

primogeniture Preferential treatment to a couple's first-born offspring or oldest surviving child; may be a basis for establishing social rank.

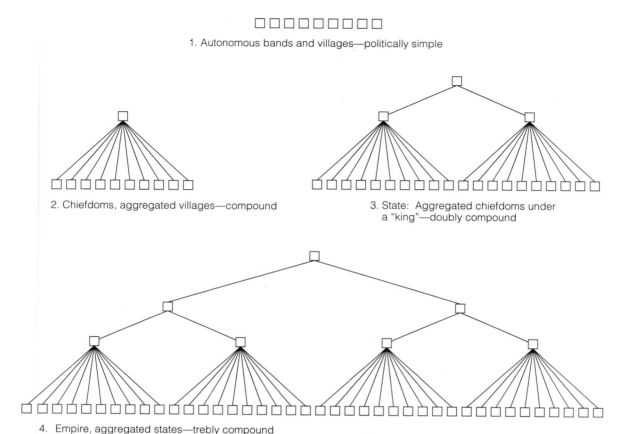

1. Autonomous bands and villages—politically simple

2. Chiefdoms, aggregated villages—compound

3. State: Aggregated chiefdoms under a "king"—doubly compound

4. Empire, aggregated states—trebly compound

FIGURE 6.10   *Levels of political complexity.* (*SOURCES: Carneiro 1981, Spencer 1967.*)

line), but considerable ambiguity remains in any particular case. The importance of seniority by age and generation permeates the entire social system. Anyone who is descended from a firstborn has a potential claim to chiefly rank, but descent through exclusively male lines also carries special distinction, and deeper genealogies are more worthy.

The religious basis of Pacific island status systems appeared most conspicuously in the related concepts of *mana* and *tabu* (taboo), or *tapu*. **Mana** has been variously defined as an impersonal supernatural force, or power, which could manifest itself in people, objects, and spirits. The Melanesian term *mana* was first noted by the missionary ethnographer R. H. Codrington in 1891. Cognate terms occur throughout the Pacific, and the *mana* concept has close parallels in many parts of the world. It is sometimes referred to as animatism to distinguish it from the more elementary belief in souls, or animism.

Mana was inherited with chiefly rank, and its presence was demonstrated in the chief's objective ability to control his followers. A chief with powerful *mana* could give goods to his subjects in exchange for their labor services, and he could influence nature as an agent of the gods. Thus, in a circular fashion, the hereditary elite demanded respect because they had *mana*, and the presence of *mana* was expressed in the respect that they received. The elite could possess various degrees of *mana*, while commoners might have none. The Polynesian term ***tabu***, usually translated as "forbidden actions," refers to a wide range of ritual avoidances that lower-ranked individuals must observe as an acknowledgment of the sanctity of elite status. Deference toward chiefs included such things as bowing, keeping one's head below the chiefs' head, using special "respect language," and making special offerings.

Chiefly prerogatives might also be marked by special forms of dress, badges, housing, and foods, which accrued to the chief by birth to the status; but perhaps more important were the claims that a chief could make in land, labor, and goods, as an expression of his personal power. Polynesian status inequality also appeared in honorific titles that were applied to outstanding warriors and to a variety of individuals, including priests and craftsmen, who displayed special skills. These individuals, especially if they were already elites with *mana*, were important challenges to chiefly authority.

Goldman (1970) distinguished three levels of Polynesian status systems: traditional, open, and stratified. The traditional system defines status primarily by genealogical criteria, and the chief assumes relatively little power. Open systems add military and political power as a more important criterion for chiefly status, thus generating intense competition, or status rivalry, and ultimately leading to stratified systems in which status and power are equally important and commoners become a landless class. The emergence of class is an important event because it is part of the political process leading to the formation of states and civilization.

The argument that status rivalry creates *social stratification* challenges both classical functionalist and cultural materialist explanations of Polynesian politicization. In the functionalist view, chiefly powers arise as a means of increasing economic productivity, thereby contributing to the overall adaptability of a society. Sahlins (1958), who argued this view, tried to show a direct correspondence between ecologically determined levels of productivity in Polynesia and levels of stratification. He found that larger islands tended to have more powerful chiefs, but as Goldman (1970) pointed out, there are some outstanding exceptions. The New Zealand Maori, for example, had the most abundant resources available to them, yet they displayed only traditional status systems; by contrast, the materially poor Mangareva were highly stratified.

Theoretical explanations for politicization have varied widely. Sahlins (1958) emphasized the caus-

ative role of surplus production, which in turn was largely a function of technoenvironmental variables, such that in Polynesia the islands with the richest natural resources would produce the strongest chiefdoms. In Carneiro's (1981) view, technological and ideological, or religious, factors played supporting, not causative roles in the development of chiefdoms. Similarly, he argues that status differences as such are aspects of chiefdoms, not causes. Carneiro emphasizes that a significant surplus will not be produced, regardless of technoenvironmental potential, unless there is either an economic or political incentive. In Polynesia, the political power of the chiefs could provide such incentive. Simple redistribution by a chief who gives away everything people donate to him may give him prestige, but his political power can increase only if he diverts goods to his political supporters. By this means, simple gifts to the chief may become first tribute and then taxation as requests become more coercive and the return to the community is restricted. The more "advanced" Polynesian chiefdoms, such as those in Tahiti and Hawaii, seem to have been based on tribute and taxation rather than community redistribution, because little of the extracted surplus returned to benefit the community, contrary to the Sahlins model of redistribution.

Carneiro (1981) derives chiefdom organization directly from warfare or threats of coercion, combined with environmental or social *circumscription* that prevented villages from escaping threats of political domination. He assumes that conflict arises from perceived shortages of land and resources as population densities increase in limited areas. If conquered or coerced villagers have nowhere else to go because their territory is

---

mana   An impersonal supernatural force thought to reside in particular people and objects. In the Pacific islands, *mana* is the basis of chiefly power.

tabu   Actions that are forbidden under the sanction of supernatural punishment. *Tabus* may be imposed by chiefs and are supported by chiefly *mana*.

social stratification   A ranking of social statuses such that the individuals of a society belong to different groups having differential access to resources, power, and privileges.

circumscription   Carneiro's explanation for the development of political centralization—that villagers may be forced to surrender their autonomy if they are unable to move away from authorities because of geographic barriers or neighboring societies.

circumscribed by geographic barriers or because neighboring areas are already occupied, they will have little choice but to pay tribute to a paramount chief. Such a scenario may well have been played out on tiny Tikopia (discussed in the next section), but real evidence for population pressure is equivocal. Furthermore, the small size of the island has limited the power of the chief. Goldman's theory of status rivalry, referred to previously, is closely in line with Carneiro's circumscription theory; both views emphasize the political outcome of conflict. In general, these theories seem to be going in the right direction. Sahlins' original hypothesis about stratification may also be correct—that is, the power of the chief clearly expanded with the size of population that he could control, and population size ultimately was limited by the availability of island resources. However, the specific relationships between these variables are very difficult to sort out.

To give a clearer picture of how the politicization process worked, we will examine two case studies: first, Tikopia as a traditional system, and second, Hawaii as a stratified system.

Tikopia: A Traditional Small Polynesian Chiefdom

How is Tikopian society organized? What is the role of the chief? How would an Australian aborigine view this society?

Tikopia is 3 square miles (4.6 km²) of land, a miniature high island dominated by the jagged rim of an extinct volcano surrounding a crater lake. It is occupied by one of the best-described traditional Polynesian cultures, thanks to the detailed monographs published by Raymond Firth (1957, 1967, 1975), the British functionalist student of Bronislaw Malinowski. Firth conducted his initial fieldwork in 1928–1929, when Tikopia was virtually self-sufficient, and returned for a restudy in 1952. Patrick Kirch and Douglas Yen (1982) carried out archaeological and ecological research in 1977–1978. Tikopia is considered a Polynesian outlier because it is situated well inside Melanesia, some 1200 miles (2000 km) west of Samoa and Tonga in western Polynesia and just 130 miles (210 km) east of the Melanesian Santa Cruz and Banks islands. In

1928, Tikopia was inhabited by 1200 "healthy and vigorous natives," and Firth considered them "almost untouched by the outside world" although European explorers had landed on the island in 1798. It was included in the British Protectorate of the Solomon Islands in 1896, and Christian missionaries were introduced in 1911. However, in 1928, there were no European residents, and the traditional chiefs clearly were in control.

Archaeological research revealed 3000 years of continuous occupation of Tikopia, presumably initiated by Austronesian-speaking peoples carrying Lapita-like pottery (Kirch and Yen 1982). In their excavations, Kirch and Yen recovered 35,000 bones representing 85 different types of animals, 2204 pounds of shells, and thousands of artifacts. The record was complete enough to provide a reasonably clear picture of the human impact on Tikopia's ecosystem. The first settlers found a pristine environment teeming with wildlife. The island was covered with rain forest, and the crater lake was then a saltwater bay or lagoon. During the early centuries of settlement, the wild protein resources were decimated. Harvests of fish, shellfish, and sea turtles rapidly declined in volume and diversity and increasingly were augmented by domestic pigs and chickens. At least one wild bird, the megapod, a chickenlike scrub fowl, was locally exterminated, whereas, according to local tradition, sea turtles apparently were protected by *tapu*.

Continuous slash-and-burn cultivation gradually led to severe deforestation that had the effect of enlarging the land base by some 40 percent at the expense of the reef zone, through infilling by eroded materials from the volcanic slopes. This greatly extended the gardening areas on the west end of the island but also cut off the lagoon, turning it into a lake, thus further reducing marine resources. Over the centuries, the inhabitants gradually abandoned shifting cultivation in favor of a system of permanent gardens and selectively planted domesticated forests. Tikopian arboriculture created a multistoried, multispecies forest-orchard of useful trees and shrubs that replaced virtually all of the natural forest on the island. It also stabilized the slopes and dunes and helped buffer the damaging effects of typhoons. At the same time, according to their own accounts, the Tikopians decided to eliminate pigs, thereby reducing demands on their gardens because pigs, although they contributed protein, competed directly for garden produce.

As severely restricted environments, small islands such as Tikopia should be excellent testing grounds for cultural ecological theory. However, it is difficult to discuss carrying capacity and balance with resources on Tikopia because the relationship between people and resources is not simple. Since 1929, the resident population has fluctuated between about 1000 and 1700. Population growth historically was regulated by numerous cultural means, including ritual sanctions, abortion, and infanticide, and by emigration. Firth reported that celibacy was required of younger brothers. Traditional history, verified by archaeology, records that bloody intergroup conflicts, exterminations, and expulsions of whole groups occurred a few centuries ago and were attributed to land conflicts. However, this cultural interpretation may have been a rationalization for what was actually a rivalry between competing chiefs. Furthermore, serious food shortages occurred after hurricanes hit the island in the 1950s. Direct and indirect human action has

improved the island's agricultural potential, but there has been no effort to intensify agricultural production through terracing or irrigation. The island continued to be virtually self-sufficient as recently as the mid-1970s.

The 1200 people living on Tikopia in 1928 were organized into two districts, or "sides," divided by the crater rim. Faena was on the lee side and Ravenga on the windward (see Figure 6.11). There were some twenty-five named villages concentrated in the lowlands near the western and southern shores. Districts and villages acted as individual units in ritual and economic activities, although they were crosscut by descent-based groups that formed the status hierarchy and organized land tenure.

Each village consisted of a row of named hereditary house sites with attached orchards or garden sites. Houses were accompanied by canoe sheds and ovens. The houses themselves contained the graves of their former owners aligned along the "sacred" inside half of the house, facing the beach. This made each house, in effect, a temple, and long-abandoned houses of important chiefs were marked by upright slabs of stone and were recognized

FIGURE 6.11
Map of Tikopia districts, villages, and temples. (SOURCES: Based on Firth [1936] 1957 and Kirch and Yen 1982.)

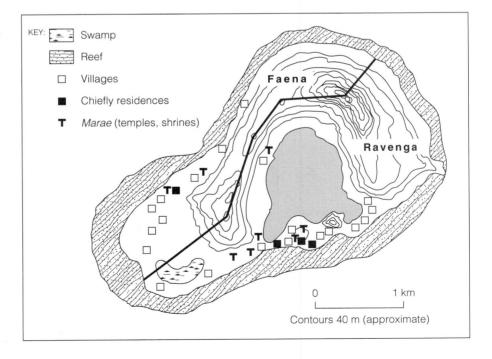

as *Marae*. They served as important temples and sites for major rituals. Land was so important that virtually every part of the island was under some form of ownership, which was inherited patrilineally. Boundaries between gardens were carefully demarcated, and every feature of the island was named. Even the lake and reef zones were under chiefly jurisdiction.

The status system, as described by Firth, was the key to understanding most claims of ownership and explained most personal interaction. Every person was assigned a position in the status hierarchy, which was organized into units at four distinct levels: household; *Paito*, or lineage; *Kainanga*, or clan; and the entire island community (see Figure 6.12).

At the highest level, the islandwide ritual community was presided over by a single chief, or *Ariki*, who controlled an elaborate series of rituals founded by the ancestral deity of the chief's descent group. These rituals, known as "the work of the gods," promoted the welfare of the entire island, ensuring productive gardening and fishing.

At the second level were four named descent groups, or *Kainanga*, which were ranked by order of ritual precedence and ranged in size from 89 to 443 people (see Figure 6.12). Firth called these groups clans, and they claimed patrilineal descent from founding tutelary deities (supernatural entities guarding specific descent groups) enshrined at specific clan "temple" sites. However, the clans were neither localized nor exogamous and only indirectly owned land of their constituent lineages and households. Membership recruitment was usually by patrifiliation, but it was also possible to marry in, as when a stranger would be adopted after marrying the chief's daughter. Each *Kainanga* had its own chief, named for his *Kainanga*, and partici-

FIGURE 6.12   *The ritual status hierarchy on Tikopia. (SOURCE: Based on Firth [1936] 1957.)*

pated as a unit in the islandwide "work of the gods." The *Kainanga* were linked in pairs for ritual food exchanges, and the chief of each *Kainanga* also had ritual responsibility for the fertility of one of four major food plants: taro, coconut, breadfruit, and yams.

At the third level, the *Kainanga* segmented into individual, named patrilineages called *Paito*, or houses. The primary property-holding unit, these groups averaged about forty persons each. There is no question about the cultural reality of these clan and lineage groups. Regardless of how the rules of rank or recruitment worked, Tikopian culture had names for these groups, and they had clearly defined functions. The highest ranked *Paito* (lineage) in a *Kainanga* (clan) supplied the *Ariki* (chief) for that *Kainanga*. Below the *Ariki Paito*, chiefly lineage, were high-ranking lineages, *Pure Paito*, that supplied ritual specialists, or priests, known as *Pure*. Lower-ranked *Paito* were *Fakaarofa Paito*, commoner lineages, whose relative order was irrelevant.

The lowest-level unit was the individual nuclear family household, although polygyny, especially among higher-ranked people, might extend the size of this unit. The husband was the ritual head of the family. The rank of the household was determined by his seniority within the lineage, the seniority of its lineage within the clan, and the ritual precedence of the clan. Relative rank within the *Ariki Paito*, chiefly lineages, was most critical. The households most closely related to the chief supplied the assistants, or *Maru*, who helped carry out his directives.

The authority of the chiefs was derived from their religious position as hereditary representatives of important ancestral deities who were responsible for the welfare of the land. Clan chiefs held titular control over all the lands owned by the members of their clan. Chiefs were sometimes called upon to settle territorial disputes and could impose *tabus* to restrict use of local resources under certain conditions. It was assumed that they worked for the community's benefit, and they seem to have been genuinely respected. They often owned more land than other individuals, but this only helped them fulfill their ritual responsibilities. Chiefs might claim ritual ownership of the freshwater springs near their villages, but they did not deny community access. Wealth in land was generally independent of rank, and even commoners could be richer than chiefs. Land ownership did not mean exclusive use; upon request, individuals were often allowed to plant or harvest resources from land they did not own in return for a token gift of food. There were no landless classes.

A visiting Australian aborigine would have been overwhelmed by the density and permanence of the population on Tikopia and by the degree to which people manipulated the environment for productive purposes. But the aborigine also would have understood many features of Tikopian culture. As in any domestic-scale society, kinship was certainly the most important organizing principle of domestic life on Tikopia, and households were largely self-provisioning units that worked cooperatively with kin-related households in the local settlement. Tikopian villages were similar in size to aboriginal bands, but the villages were circumscribed by their neighbors and were much less independent than the mobile bands. The belief that mythical ancestral beings continued to influence human affairs would have been familiar to the aborigine, but the sanctity of specific descent lines linked to the gods and the pervasive ranking of social units would have seemed strange. Even stranger to the aborigine would have been the islandwide authority carried by the Tikopian hereditary title *Ariki* and the extreme deferential behavior accorded the person of *Ariki* status. This calls to mind Firth's summary of the chief's politicized role on Tikopia, which has no parallel in domestic-scale societies:

the chief has been shown to be the most important single human factor in the economic life of the Tikopia. Not only does he play a part as a producer within his immediate household, but by initiative and example he gives direction to the productive work of the community; he is titular owner of the most valuable property of the members of his clan; he imposes far-reaching restrictions on production and consumption and in many important activities he acts as a focal point in the processes of exchange and distribution. ([1965:231] 1975)

Hawaii as a Protostate

How do the power of Hawaiian chiefs and the organization of Hawaiian society compare with those of Tikopia? What environmental factors are related to these differences? What is a political economy, and how does it contrast with a subsistence economy?

From the original settlement of Hawaii, perhaps as early as AD 300, the native Hawaiian population had grown to a conservatively estimated 200,000 people, organized into numerous complex chiefdoms, when Captain James Cook arrived in 1778. The Hawaiian Archipelago is extremely isolated from the rest of Polynesia, and indeed from everywhere else. Although there is considerable diversity because of differences in geological age, the major inhabited Hawaiian islands are high, volcanic islands and very large for Polynesia. Hawaii, the largest, contains 6500 square miles (10,458 km²) of land, more than all the rest of Micronesia and Polynesia combined, with the exception of New Zealand. The highest point on Hawaii is 13,800 feet (4206 m) above sea level. Such large, high islands trap considerable rainfall on their windward sides, which are often sharply eroded into steep, narrow valleys, and they support a wide variety of plant communities, from deserts to wet mountain forests with many endemic species. If, as Marshall Sahlins (1958) argued, rich environmental resources would favor the development of Polynesian social stratification, Hawaii should show some of the most developed examples, and indeed it does.

There are some limiting factors, however, as Patrick Kirch (1985) points out. For example, the reef zones are smaller than might be expected because of the relative youth of the larger islands; furthermore, much of the shoreline is inaccessible because of the steep cliffs. Rainfall and soil were critical variables for crops, yet they were very unevenly distributed. Only restricted windward valleys offered the alluvial soils, abundant rainfall, and flowing streams most favorable for the cultivation of Polynesian crops such as taro, yams, and bananas. Forest clearing increased erosion and sometimes caused floods that destroyed crops. Droughts, seismic waves, and volcanic eruptions were also significant environmental hazards.

In comparison with Tikopia, the most obvious difference in Hawaiian subsistence patterns was in the elaborate complexes of ditches and terraced and irrigated pond fields for taro cultivation, as well as the extensive area devoted to permanent dry-field cultivation. Kirch (1985) also emphasizes that the Hawaiians developed true aquaculture, in which fish were raised on a large scale in special fish ponds constructed on reef flats. The 449 fish ponds known to have existed prehistorically may have produced as much as 2 million pounds of fish annually.

The irrigation systems have the most interesting theoretical implications because many theorists have speculated that control of irrigation systems was the primary route to state formation for all the world's great civilizations. Hawaiian irrigation systems were well developed by Polynesian standards. As a significant form of **agricultural intensification,** they helped produce the surplus that supported the elites, but the construction of these systems seems not to have required either technical specialists or large labor forces. Archaeologist Timothy Earle (1978) examined twenty-nine traditional-style irrigation systems still used to grow taro in the Halelea district of Kaua'i, and he mapped eight others that were in use in 1850. Earle concluded that these systems grew in gradual stages and were small enough in scale to be independently managed by local peoples. The Hawaiian irrigation systems, however, were vulnerable to floods, drought, and warfare, and some form of regional assistance would have been needed as a backup.

Many features of the traditional religious system were abandoned by the Hawaiian rulers in 1819 following the shock of contact with Europeans. But native Hawaiians who were closely connected with the highest chiefs have written detailed eyewitness descriptions of the system at its peak (Ii 1983, Malo 1951). Hawaii represented a dramatic expansion of the basic Polynesian status hierarchy system operating on Tikopia. The most striking differences involved the elaboration of the *tabu* system, which sharply demarcated the person of the chief and the remarkable powers that chiefs, especially high chiefs, could exercise (see Figure 6.13). The *tabu* system was complex, and chiefs could possess or impose several different types of *tabu*, but they all were expressions of the chief's personal power.

The highest chiefs were so *tabu* that people had to prostrate themselves on the ground when the chief passed or even if only his personal possessions were carried by. Special retainers ran ahead

FIGURE 6.13 *Statue of Hawaiian chief Kamehameha, who united rival chiefdoms.*

carrying a special staff signaling the *tabu*, and they shouted a warning to people to prostrate themselves. Chiefs sometimes traveled at night to minimize the inconvenience that the *tabus* created. No one could allow his or her shadow to fall across the chief or any of his personal possessions, including his house. No one, other than his immediate retainers, was allowed to approach closer than 12 feet (4 m) to the chief's back. When the chief ate, everyone in his presence had to remain on their knees.

The paramount chiefs had life-and-death powers over their subjects, including lower-level chiefs. They could kill them or expel them from their land at will. They apparently sometimes did so, although not all chiefs were considered to be abusive and oppressive. Infractions of *tabus* were strictly enforced by burning, strangulation, or stoning. Sometimes, people who violated seemingly minor *tabus* were put to death. John Papa Ii (1983), who became a personal attendant to high chief Liholiho, de-

scribed a case in which three men were caught eating coconuts with women while a major ritual for the general welfare was being performed at the paramount chief's temple, or *luakini heiau* (see Figure 6.14). Because there was a general *tabu* against men and women eating together and against women eating coconuts, the three men were seized and sacrificed along with pigs on the altar before a row of images of the deities (Ii 1983). Human sacrifices of this sort apparently only took place at the temples of paramount chiefs and on special ritual occasions.

On Tikopia, it was understood that the deities might be angered if rituals were neglected or improperly performed and might even take a human life as a sacrifice (Firth [1940] 1967). But it would have been unthinkable for a chief or any of his priests to carry out such an act themselves. Clearly, the high chiefs of Hawaii enlarged upon an underlying Polynesian belief that chiefs were descended from the gods, and they assumed the role of gods themselves.

Malo (1951) reported that it was preferable for the highest-ranked chief to marry his full sister. The child of such a union was called a deity and possessed the most powerful *tabus*. Given the enormous powers that the high chiefs wielded and the terrifying punishments they could inflict, it follows that "the people held the chiefs in great dread and looked upon them as gods" (Malo 1951:61). It is possible that these accounts, written by missionary-trained Hawaiians, may overstress the oppressive practices of the chiefs, but many of these details are corroborated by the earliest European observers.

The ethnohistorical descriptions, written by Hawaiians in the nineteenth century, use language typically applied to state-organized societies to describe the Hawaiian system. Paramount chiefs are called kings; they have governments and royal courts, tax collectors and priests, temples and armies; and they fight wars to conquer territory. The only difference between Hawaiian states, or proto-states, and states in other parts of the world was that the Hawaiian states were relatively small and

agricultural intensification Changes in farming technology, such as shortened fallow periods, use of fertilizers, new crops, or irrigation, in order to produce more food per year in a given area, often at greater energy cost.

FIGURE 6.14
The Hawaiian luakini heiau, *or paramount chief's temple, where human sacrifices were performed.*

Annú tower

Images

Lele altar

Drum house

Image   Image

Waiea house

Oven house

Mana house

Entrance
Image   Image

110 feet

60 feet

lacked massive **monumental architecture,** urbanization, metal, and writing. Structurally, it is appropriate to call Hawaiian societies "states" because they clearly possessed at least two administrative tiers above the village level (see Figure 6.15). The paramount chief, who in some cases controlled an

FIGURE 6.15
*Hawaiian political hier-
archy. (SOURCE: Based
on Earle 1978.)*

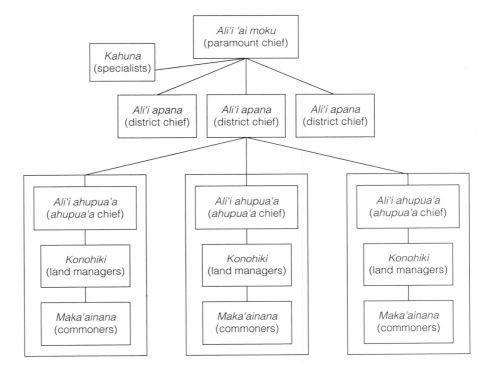

entire island, surrounded himself with an elaborate
court. David Malo (1951) listed more than a dozen
categories of **specialists** who were directly attached to the chief's personal household, including
political advisors, military experts, architects, as-
trologers, food handlers, robe masters, priests,
masseurs, keepers of his images and paraphernalia,
and servants to whisk away flies and stand over him
as he slept, in addition to miscellaneous "hangers-
on." It is unclear how many people this might have
involved in actuality, but this is an obvious expansion over the Tikopian chief's *Maru*.

Below the paramount chief and his immediate
court were numerous lower-ranked chiefs in charge
of smaller territorial divisions. There were at least
ten chiefly ranks distinguished below the highest
divine chief, based on diverse genealogical criteria,
and land was grouped into as many as six administrative segments, with household plots as the lowest segment. The lowest potentially self-sufficient
land unit was the *ahupua'a*, which was a long, narrow strip of land, running uphill from the coast and
thereby providing access to several environmental

zones. It was further subdivided into family-size
holdings, and the entire unit was supervised by a
lower-level chief and his assistants.

Land rights at the household level were controlled primarily not by local descent groups but by
the local administrator, the *Konohiki*, who acted on
behalf of the district chief and did not even belong
to a local descent group. Land ownership was ultimately vested in the paramount chief, and use
rights depended on payment of the annual taxes.
The *ahupua'a* was probably equivalent in population size to the clan on Tikopia, although the *ahupua'a* chief exercised much more power over his
subjects than did Tikopia's paramount chief.

---

monumental architecture Large-scale permanent
structures, such as temples, palaces, or tombs, that require large labor forces and central planning.
specialist An individual who provides goods and services to elites in hierarchically organized societies. Such a
specialist does not produce his or her own food but is
supported from the surplus that is politically extracted by
central authorities.

In the Hawaiian bureaucracy, there was no place even for independent local clan chiefs. Hawaiian priests had their own ranking system and were grouped into various specialist orders. The commoners, called *maka'ainana*, were the most numerous segment of the population and were not further subdivided by rank. They supported themselves through basic subsistence activities, they produced the "surplus" food and luxury objects that supported the elites, and they were on call to provide labor service. Below the commoners were the *kauwa* (sometimes called slaves), a despised category of hereditary outcasts. There were also special terms for vagrants, beggars, and the landless. In comparison, Tikopian commoners did not form a powerless class; Tikopia had no outcasts, beggars, or landless, and Tikopian chiefs remained relatively inconspicuous and unassuming.

The differences in wealth and power between the Hawaiian elites and the commoners were so extreme that it is appropriate to call them **social classes.** The most conspicuous class markers were the lavish and magnificent feathered short capes, long cloaks, leis, helmets, and whale-tooth necklaces, which only the elite could wear (see Figure 6.16). Chiefs were accompanied by bearers of 20-foot

(6-m) poles topped with brilliantly feathered banners as insignias of rank (Feher 1969). These intricately crafted articles were made from feathers removed from several specific birds of the honey eater (*Melphagidae*) and honeycreeper (*Drepanididae*) families, which were endemic to Hawaii. The iiwi, a bright red honeycreeper, was the primary source of tiny red plumes but was only 6 inches (15 cm) long and restricted to forested areas. Plumes were collected as part of the annual tax levy. The birds were live-trapped during the moult and released to protect the supply. Because as many as 10,000 birds might have been required to produce a single feathered cloak, it had major ostentatious value (Earle 1987).

The remaining key question is, How and why did the extreme Hawaiian status hierarchy develop? If, as Timothy Earle (1978) argued, the food requirements of an expanding population were met by agricultural intensification through irrigation and dry-field systems that did not require centralized bureaucratic management, perhaps the Hawaiian hierarchy developed because the chiefs redistributed resources from diverse environments, thus helping to integrate locally specialized economies for everyone's benefit. This interpretation is sug-

FIGURE 6.16
Hawaiian feather work.

gested by Elman Service's (1962) model of the adaptive advantages of chiefdoms as redistribution systems. However, Earle stressed that the local *ahupua'a* administrative units were designed to be self-sufficient because they crosscut diverse ecological zones and virtually eliminated the community need for centrally administered economic exchange. The so-called redistribution functions of the Hawaiian chiefdoms were designed to benefit the chiefs' elites, not the subsistence needs of the commoners.

Hawaii would appear to support Robert Carneiro's environmental circumscription theory because the islands themselves are geographically circumscribed, as are the narrow coastal valleys where the best agricultural zones were concentrated. However, as Earle (1978) noted, many observers argued that great untapped potential remained for agricultural development given existing technology and that there was little actual population pressure. In many districts, there is also no evidence that warfare was conducted between local communities, given the dispersed settlement pattern and lack of defensive positions, or that it led to victorious communities taking over conquered territories. Instead, Earle argued, Hawaiian warfare was conducted between rival chiefdoms for the purpose of expanding their own self-serving redistribution networks, or tribute systems. Thus, chiefdoms may not have been an adaptive response to population pressure in a circumscribed environment.

Earle (1978) attributed the expansion of the Hawaiian chiefdom to competition for political office, Goldman's (1970) "status rivalry," which, given a large enough population base, can result in the intentional development of a ***political economy*** dedicated to support the elite, alongside the ***subsistence economy,*** which continues to support the commoners. The political economy tends to promote its own expansion, whereas the subsistence economies of domestic-scale societies tend toward equilibrium. Two options seem to be open to a Polynesian population colonizing a new island: It could segment into many equal-sized units as it grows, or it could centralize by promoting a senior lineage to a higher management level (Flannery 1972b). Environmental conditions on Hawaii seem to have been especially suited for centralization because agricultural production was so easily expanded and thus readily supported expanding political economies. Chiefs used the "surplus" extracted from the commoners to maintain their control over potential political rivals by rewarding their loyalty with lavish gifts of expensive wealth objects such as feather cloaks. Capital investment by chiefs in expanded irrigation systems was a specific means to increase their political power by increasing their local labor population. Thus, in this case, population increase results from subsistence intensification, not the reverse, which is usually thought to occur in unstratified domestic-scale societies. Expansive warfare directed by chiefs was another means of increasing a chief's wealth and total political power. Warfare of this sort was a form of capital investment because it was an expensive business requiring equipment produced by specialists and the feeding of the commoner army on campaign.

As Earle (1978) stressed, chiefdoms are not simple developments out of domestic-scale autonomous village societies. Chiefdoms are not merely aggregated villages because villages lose their political and economic autonomy when they are subordinated to paramount chiefs in stratified chiefdoms such as Hawaii. Hawaiian commoners did not own their lands and had little control over their day-to-day lives. They became social isolates with truncated kinship systems. Peace is imposed on local communities, self-help networks collapse, and individual households must depend on centralized authority for emergency aid and defense. Kirch's (1985) summary of Hawaiian archaeology shows that the most expansive phase of Hawaiian politicization, which established the basic structure as described here, occurred relatively quickly between AD 1100 and 1650, after some 800 years in which the Hawaiians—organized as more traditional, smaller-scale Polynesian societies—gradually settled into the most favorable environments.

---

social class A group of people in a stratified society, such as elites and commoners, who share a similar level of access to resources, power, and privilege.

political economy A cultural pattern in which centralized political authority intervenes in the production and distribution of goods and services.

subsistence economy Production and distribution carried on at the local community level, primarily for local consumption.

SUMMARY

The Pacific islands presented formidable obstacles to successful human occupation because they were so widely scattered and were often very small and resource-poor. They were settled by skilled Austronesian-speaking farmers, sailors, and navigators who originated in Southeast Asia about 6000 years ago. The farthest reaches of Polynesia were settled during a period of approximately 1000 years ending by AD 800 with the settlement of New Zealand.

The societies of Polynesia and Micronesia represent a major contrast to the domestic-scale societies of Australia, Amazonia, and East Africa examined in earlier chapters. Pacific island societies were characterized by a great concern with rank, and they developed permanent political and economic structures above the level of local village communities. These island societies were chiefdoms that elevated certain high-ranking individuals to permanent leadership positions as chiefs. The example from the Polynesian island of Tikopia showed that chiefs in small chiefdoms coordinated ritual and economic activities between villages, but they had relatively little power and so there were no social classes. On larger islands, such as Hawaii, political struggles between chiefs led to the formation of powerful chiefdoms. These societies became divided by class into the elites, who extracted tribute from the commoners, who produced food and wealth objects. The highest-ranking chiefs claimed the supernatural power of deities and gained life-and-death control over lower-ranked people. Some of the Hawaiian chiefdoms were complex enough to be considered protostates, or small kingdoms.

STUDY QUESTIONS

1. Characterize and distinguish between each of the following cultural areas: Polynesia, Melanesia, and Micronesia.

2. Discuss the physical constraints limiting settlement on Pacific islands, characterizing the cultural response.

3. Discuss the role of status rivalry, irrigation, redistribution, environmental circumscription, and economic productivity in the development of Pacific island chiefdoms.

SUGGESTED READING

BELLWOOD, PETER S. 1987. *The Polynesians: Prehistory of an Island People.* London: Thames & Hudson. An authoritative archaeological overview of the original settlement of Polynesia and subsequent cultural developments.

FIRTH, RAYMOND. [1936] 1957. *We the Tikopia: A Sociological Study of Kinship in Primitive Polynesia,* 2nd ed. New York: Barnes & Noble. The basic ethnographic description of Tikopia, with an emphasis on social organization.

FIRTH, RAYMOND. [1940] 1967. "The Work of the Gods." In *Tikopia,* 2nd ed. London: Athlone Press. Describes in detail the system of ritual feasting on Tikopia.

FIRTH, RAYMOND. [1965] 1975. *Primitive Polynesian Economy.* Reprint. New York: Norton. An analysis of the subsistence economy and distribution system on Tikopia.

KIRCH, PATRICK VINTON. 1985. *Feathered Gods and Fishhooks: An Introduction to Hawaiian Archaeology and Prehistory.* Honolulu: University of Hawaii Press. A detailed prehistory of Hawaii.

7

Early States: The Near East and the Andes

Although many Pacific island chiefdoms crossed the "great divide" from the social equality of domestic-scale societies into rank- and class-based social systems, a major gulf separates these island cultures from the larger-scale states and empires to be considered in this chapter. Early states—politically centralized societies with at least two levels of authority above the local community—created monumental temples, pyramids, palaces, and cities that have been hailed as major achievements and attributes of civilization. However, the impressive monuments and museum-quality artworks produced by the early states clearly depended on pervasive social inequality, and these states were characterized by an inherent instability not found in domestic-scale cultures. The politicization mutation that produced city-states and conquest empires represented a major departure from the domestic-scale cultural patterns that had sustained humanity for so long. The rise of centralized state political power is perhaps the greatest anthropological mystery of all. Although no explanation is completely satisfactory, states clearly arose under unique circumstances that made it difficult for households and communities to escape the influence of elite power and that could support increases in cultural scale through intensified subsistence production.

Urban civilizations drastically modify ecosystems and place enormous demands on natural resources. They intensify the political and economic implications of the social hierarchy such that human dependency and servitude may be institutionalized. They concentrate despotic power in a few hands, often creating a split between the economically dependent urban center, with its culturally distinct Great Tradition, and the more autonomous and stable rural village culture, with its own more egalitarian Little Tradition.

The contrasts between domestic-scale tribal cultures and state civilizations are so extreme, and the comparative disadvantages of state civilizations for all but the elite minority are so obvious, that explaining how states originate and function as cultural systems continues to be a major theoretical challenge for anthropology. Understanding the full implications of urban civilization for the long-term future of humanity is also a critical issue. It is important to remember that urban civilization has existed for only 5000 years and could be considered a very shaky experiment when its short span and record of chronic collapse are compared with the 50,000-year record of domestic-scale foraging cultures in Australia. In this chapter, we will review the issues surrounding urban civilization within the

Carneiro

181

context of two major civilizations from different parts of the world: the Sumerians of Mesopotamia and the Inca of Peru.

The "early states" discussed in this chapter are "early" in that—in the case of the Sumerian city-states of Mesopotamia, which date to approximately 3000 BC—they are among the very earliest states anywhere in the world. Chronological priority in itself need not be especially significant, but treating a clearly "pristine" state—that is, one that arose independently of previously existing states—helps to isolate the distinctive features of state organization and to illuminate the process of its original development. The Andean states were also chronologically early and pristine, and they were fully functioning when Europeans conquered them in AD 1532.

ANCIENT CIVILIZATIONS AND THE TRIUMPH OF STATE POWER

Civilization is about social power. The cities, writings, monuments, and artwork that identify civilization give certain people massive and historically unprecedented power over others. The principal function of civilization is to organize overlapping social networks of ideological, political, economic, and military power in ways that differentially benefit privileged households (Mann 1986). For the first time in human history, civilization gives some households institutionalized coercive power to permanently control private property in ways that reduce the material opportunities of other households. This coercive use of social power would baffle tribal peoples because it overrides the sapienization process that equally provided for everyone's material needs in domestic-scale cultures. Simple chiefdoms, such as in Tikopia, introduced differential ranking between individuals, but rank was not used to deny anyone the right to satisfy material needs. Politicization was the cultural process that elites used to institutionalize social inequality in the state, but it is difficult to explain why people allow this to happen. Civilization is unlikely to develop directly out of domestic-scale cultures because tribal peoples self-consciously refuse to grant anyone permanent, coercive social power over other households. Tribal war leaders

and village heads are temporary and have no coercive authority; ideological power is open to everyone; and there are no cultural incentives for depriving anyone of life's necessities. In *The Eighth Day*, Richard Adams (1988) observes that like the earlier coevolutionary process of domestication, civilization differentiates society into two subsystems: (1) a dominant regulatory sector, in which an elite controls and directs, and (2) a working sector, in which goods and services are actually produced. This is dehumanizing because the subordinate people in the working sector are "domesticated" by the regulatory sector. From an evolutionary perspective, a higher level of cultural complexity is achieved, but subordinated workers are treated as objects; in effect, they become cattle, exchanging the freedom and equality of domestic-scale culture for uncertain material advantages.

The centralization of political power is the most important underlying feature of civilization because it is functionally connected with many other "civilized" traits; this, in turn, suggests that explanatory theories that focus on political power will be most productive. Before treating the issue of the origin of civilization, let us consider in more detail the traits that have figured prominently in definitions of civilization.

The shift to political-scale cultures requires an increase in cultural complexity, which is illustrated in a scale diagram constructed by archaeologist Kent Flannery (1972b). Flannery showed an approximate temporal sequence for the development of selected cultural institutions or traits distributed along a continuum from mobile foragers ("bands"), to domestic-scale villagers ("tribes"), to chiefdoms and then the state (see Figure 7.1). Similarly, Robert Carneiro and Stephen Tobias (1963) have demonstrated that a number of cultural traits indicative of the move toward state organization demonstrate scalability as cultural complexity increases, such that the presence in a given culture of a more state-like trait (for example, taxation) can be used to predict the presence of presumably earlier traits (for example, agriculture or temples). Figure 7.2 clearly shows the cumulative nature of politically significant traits for all the institutions that first appear with chiefdoms and then continue after states develop.

The Cultural Evolution of Civilizations

	Type of Society	Some Institutions, in Order of Appearance	Ethnographic Examples	Archaeological Examples
Political-scale	State		France England India United States	Classic Mesoamerica Sumer Shang China Imperial Rome
Political-scale	Chiefdom		Tonga Hawaii Kwakiutl Noontka Natchez	Gulf Coast Olmec of Mexico (1000 BC) Samarron of Near East (5300 BC) Mississippian of North America (AD 1200)
Domestic-scale	Tribe		New Guinea Highlanders Southwest Pueblos Sioux	Early formative of inland Mexico (1500–1000 BC) Prepottery Neolithic of Near East (8000–6000 BC)
Domestic-scale	Band		Kalahari Bushmen Australian Aborigines Eskimo Shoshone	Paleo-Indian and Early Archaic of United States and Mexico (10,000–6000 BC) Late Paleolithic of Near East (10,000 BC)

Institutions (in order of appearance): Local group autonomy, Egalitarian status, Ephemeral leadership, Ad hoc ritual, Reciprocal economy, Unranked descent groups, Pantribal sodalities, Calendric ritual, Ranked descent groups, Redistributive economy, Hereditary leadership, Elite endogamy, Full-time craft specialization, Stratification, Kingship, Codified law, Bureaucracy, Military draft, Taxation.

FIGURE 7.1 *Selected institutions appearing along the band–tribe–chiefdom–state continuum in ascending scale of sociopolitical complexity.* (SOURCE: *Based on Flannery 1972a:401, Figure 1.*)

Carneiro and Tobias (1963) sorted through a list of 354 potentially scalable traits and produced a short list of 50 traits that represented what they considered to be part of a "main sequence" in the development of cultural complexity. In Table 7.1, compare the organization of the Inca as a very complex state and the Hawaiian chiefdoms as a relatively simple state. The traits "social stratification" and "craft specialization" suggest a well-developed chiefdom, and "empires" and "two or more cities" would indicate a very large-scale state. The "three or more levels of territorial administration," which in Chapter 6 was proposed as the defining criterion for state organization, falls almost in the middle of the list and demonstrates the difficulty of drawing sharp lines to distinguish between large chiefdoms and small states. However, most of the traits in the upper two-thirds of this list clearly reflect the increasing use of political power.

City-States and Village-States: The Structures of Power

How is the state defined? What are the major types of ancient state organization?

Probably the most useful definitions of the state cite the presence of government institutions, or administrative hierarchies, often characterized as having a monopoly on the legitimate use of force. Thus, kings, courts, and judges, concentrated in an urban center and supported by temples, treasuries, writing systems, police forces, and armies, might be considered the essential features of states. Such

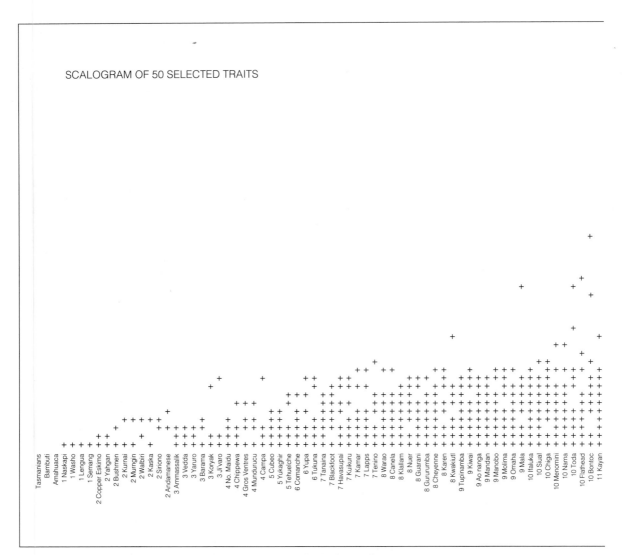

FIGURE 7.2   *Scalogram of fifty cultural traits and one hundred cultures showing increasing*
levels of complexity. Numbers total pluses in columns and rows. Note the comparison between
Hawaiians and the Inca. (SOURCE: Carneiro and Tobias 1963.)

formal institutions are uniquely important developments because, as C. R. Hallpike (1986) notes, they have explicit goals, such as the preservation of the social order, and they can legitimately be analyzed in functional terms. Perhaps most importantly, institutionalized state power historically has tended to enclose people within "social cages" (Mann 1986) and to make it difficult for them to escape from exploitative relationships. States operate within bounded territories and create fixed societies and ethnic groups where previously there were highly flexible, domestic-scale societies that allowed people to shift allegiances in ways that deprived would-be despots of power.

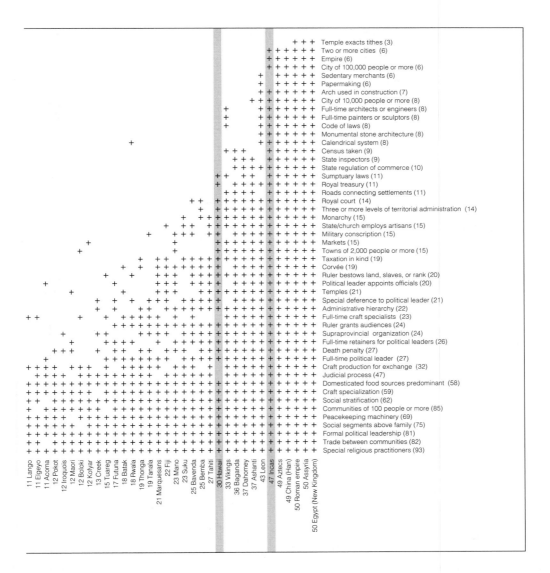

Anthropologist Charles Maisels (1990) distinguishes two broad types of ancient states, **city-states** and **village-states,** based on the different ways they organized social power. City-states, such as Ur in ancient Mesopotamia, were unusual social formations that apparently arose under unique conditions. They were small, relatively self-sufficient states with an urban core that drew subsistence from the immediately surrounding hinterland occupied by dependent, or client, groups. Private ownership of land by individual households was a key feature of city-states, fostering a particular kind of social stratification. Households that did not

---

city-states Political-scale cultures based on relatively self-sufficient city-states, drawing their primary support from their immediate surroundings.
village-states Political-scale cultures based on an urban administrative and ceremonial center, drawing their support from peasant villages scattered over a vast region.

TABLE 7.1 *Thirty Scalable Culture Traits Related to Civilization and State Organization**

+ Two or more cities
+ Empires
+ City of 10,000 people or more
+ Full-time architects or engineers
+ Full-time painters or sculptors
+ Code of laws
+ Monumental stone architecture
+ Calendrical system
+ Census taken
+ State inspectors
H+ Sumptuary laws
H+ Royal treasury
H+ Royal court
H+ Three or more levels of territorial administration
H+ Artisans employed by state/church
H+ Military conscription
H+ Towns of 2000 or more
H+ Taxation in kind
H+ Corvée
H+ Land, slaves, or rank bestowed by rulers
H+ Officials appointed by political leaders
H+ Temples
H+ Special deference to political leader
H+ Administrative hierarchy
 + Full-time craft specialists
H+ Full-time retainers for political leader
H+ Death penalty
H+ Full-time political leadership
H+ Craft specialization
H+ Social stratification

SOURCE: Data from Carneiro and Tobias (1963).
*+ = Inca culture; H = Hawaiian culture.

own land were forced to attach themselves as dependents to their more affluent neighbors or to exchange their labor for subsistence rations. The government was in the hands of privileged citizens. Thus, city-states produced a form of social inequality and an internal dynamic that ultimately led to capitalism and the global culture. Different city-states within a region could belong to the same interaction network, sharing a common language and religion, and would collectively constitute a single civilization.

Village-states, such as imperial China and Inca Peru, were loosely structured empires based on a royal capital city with a state bureaucracy that extracted tribute from essentially self-sufficient peasant villages scattered over a vast territory. Villagers held land communally such that everyone was ensured of their basic subsistence. Village-states resembled greatly extended chiefdoms in that they placed everyone in ranked lineages within a single giant genealogy, with a divine monarch at the top. People received supernatural rewards in exchange for their tribute. The imperial capitals contained the royal residence, temples, and a retinue of court followers but were not self-sustaining cities. Because village-states were so large, they were best integrated by a powerful collective ideology of common kinship and shared beliefs in the divine authority of the monarch.

Explaining State Origins: Natural Growth or Quest for Power?

How do anthropologists and other scholars explain the emergence of the state and ancient civilizations?

Historically, many scholars have explained the emergence of the state as a progressive, beneficial process that inevitably unfolded as human creativity increased or as human populations grew. However, there were actually only a few places in the world where states developed in apparent isolation from other states (see Figure 1.9), and there is no reason to suppose that innate creative genius is unevenly distributed. It is also not obvious what specific benefits people in successful domestic-scale cultures would have wanted states to provide. Another problem with the "benefits" explanation is that historically state power has most often been used to uphold an *inequitable* distribution of benefits. Furthermore, governments and civilizations are notoriously costly and prone to collapse, as will be discussed in Chapter 10. The ancient agrarian civilizations examined in this chapter and in Chapters 8–10 demonstrate that cultural development and population growth are neither natural nor inevitable; rather, they are the outcome of particular human actions shaped by particular cultural ideas. This means that many possible political organizations are culturally possible. Governments can be created and directed by democratic decision making to reflect the interests of the majority of their citizens. Such states would be expected to be relatively stable, peaceful, and prosperous, with risks and rewards equitably distributed. Utopian thinkers have designed such ideal states at least since the third century BC, when Plato wrote his *Republic*, but only a few modern states have attempted to institute such balanced systems.

To explain the rise of states, we need to know *who* successfully creates and transmits the cultural ideas that guide the politicization process, as well as *who* takes the risks and *who* enjoys the benefits. Perpetually growing societies will eventually require government bureaucracy and more productive technology. But viewed only in these terms, the explanation becomes circular, because political power and new technology also can be used to induce growth. Human agency is the crucial determining variable. For example, it is not at all clear that intensive irrigation systems arose naturally in response to steady population growth. It is just as reasonable to assume that power-seeking individuals persuaded other people to build irrigation systems that could then support a larger dependent population.

Temporary imbalances between population and resources, unpredictable environmental events, or intergroup conflict represent opportunities for individuals to increase their personal political power (Arnold 1993). Power seekers can use such crises to force people to accept otherwise undesirable technologies or potentially oppressive bureaucracies, thereby increasing their own decision-making power. The archaeological record shows that states often emerged quickly after chiefdoms appeared. This is understandable because chiefdoms generate the kind of conflict and crisis that political opportunists need to make growth a seemingly natural, self-generating process. Furthermore, the creation of a political bureaucracy to maintain a small state or kingdom is the only way a chief can expand his power.

Charles Spencer (1990:7) argues that a single ruler can only feasibly maintain direct personal control over a political domain accessible within half a day's travel from the center. In the absence of mechanized transport and bureaucracy, this sets a practical limit to the size of a chiefdom at approximately 965 square miles (2500 km²) and a few thousand people. Full-blown government bureaucracy, with administrative specialists capable of managing a minimal state of some 50,000 people within

a territory of 19,300 square miles (50,000 km²), could be expected to emerge quickly out of a growing, crisis-generating chiefdom. Minor organizational changes to delegate authority more gradually would be risky because in an unstable social environment, an ambitious subordinate might seize power. Over the past 5000 years, global population has increased dramatically even as the emergence of empires reduced the number of political units, demonstrating that political rulers steadily increased their power by overcoming the cultural and natural limits to political control and population growth (Carneiro 1978b, Taagepera 1978a, 1978b, 1997). (The limits to state power are discussed in Chapter 10.)

Julian Steward (1949) was a pioneer in the effort to place the development of civilization within a global scientific framework based on typologies and predictable causal sequences. Steward believed that civilizations in Peru, Mesoamerica, Mesopotamia, Egypt, and China all developed independently along similar ***multilinear evolutionary*** lines. He stressed the regularities in this process, noting that these early civilizations all developed in arid or semi-arid environments. In Steward's view, irrigation was clearly a key to the development process, because maximum agricultural production depended on irrigation, which, in turn, produced population growth, religiously based administrators, and social classes. According to Steward,

There is no question that maximum production in these areas of critical and minimal precipitation required irrigation, and that in proportion as irrigation works develop, population will increase until the limits of water are reached. Social or political controls become necessary to manage irrigation and other communal projects. As early societies were strongly religious, individuals with supernatural powers—lineage heads, shamans, or special priests— formed a theocratic ruling class. (1955:206)

The developmental sequence that Steward outlined for Mesopotamia overemphasized the role of technology and population growth, but it is still

---

multilinear evolution   Steward's theory that, given similar conditions, cultures can develop independently along similar lines. For example, he argued that irrigation agriculture led to state organization several times.

endorsed by prominent historians like William McNeil, who, in referring to Sumerian civilization, declares,

Farmers had to be able to produce a food surplus for civilization to get started. Only then could a substantial number of persons free themselves from the task of finding food and begin to spend their time doing other things. This, in turn, allowed specialized skills and new ideas to multiply until society as a whole became sufficiently complex, wealthy, and powerful to be called "civilized." (1987:31)

McNeil's explanation suggests that simple farmers, rather than power-seeking political elites, intentionally directed their activities toward the goal of eventually creating civilization. Increased farm-

ing productivity releases subsistence farmers, who then develop new technology, luxury goods, and monuments. However, continued population growth leads eventually to population pressure, interstate conflict, and empire building, with increased tribute, declines in productivity, and collapse of the system. This approach treats the whole process as too natural and inevitable and diverts attention from important political processes and complex interconnections.

Charles Redman (1978a, 1978b) has produced a more refined systems theory approach, which he applies specifically to Mesopotamia. Redman added the dimension of positive feedback loops that operate within a complex causal network to promote

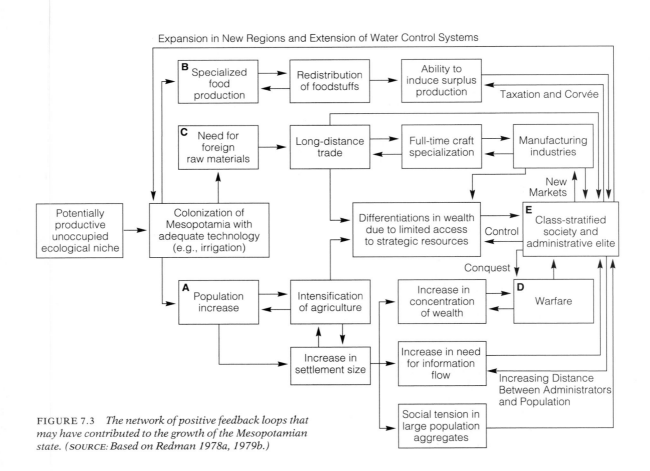

FIGURE 7.3   *The network of positive feedback loops that may have contributed to the growth of the Mesopotamian state. (SOURCE: Based on Redman 1978a, 1979b.)*

further growth (see Figure 7.3). In 5500 BC, the Mesopotamian plain was an empty ecological niche with great agricultural potential waiting to be tapped. Soon after the area was colonized by village farmers from the adjacent uplands, the following variables identified in Figure 7.3 acted as primary positive feedbacks:

A. Population increase

B. Food production by independent farmers

C. The need for imported raw materials

D. Warfare

E. Social stratification and bureaucratization

Items A–C led to craft specialization, unequal wealth distribution, and urbanization; items D and E resulted in the formation of regional empires.

These positive feedbacks, driven by individuals seeking politically based wealth and power, gradually transform the cultural system from farming villages to temple towns, city-states, and, ultimately, national empires.

Redman (1978a, 1978b) was aware that his explanation for the development of Mesopotamian civilization was simply an "interpretive theory" and a "plausible story," "logical but not objectively confirmed." The obvious unanswered question is why previously domestic-scale cultures would have permitted such runaway growth in the first place. Some specialists have argued that a major shift in the channel of the Euphrates River, which occurred during the Early Uruk period around 3300 BC, may have forced many independent villagers to move into the urban centers (Gibson 1976). It is possible that irrigation agriculture in this setting increased the scale of production in a way that favored large landholders and disadvantaged small farmers, much like the later impact of factory farming and the Green Revolution discussed in Chapters 12 and 13.

Clearly, there can be no single explanation for such a complex phenomenon as state organization. It will perhaps be most useful to move to specific case studies. The following sections will examine some of the archaeological evidence for the development of Mesopotamian civilization within the larger context of Near Eastern prehistory and environment, as well as a comparative view of Andean civilization.

The Mesopotamian World of Two Rivers: Heartland of Cities

What unique opportunities and challenges did the Mesopotamian environment offer the first settlers who occupied this region 10,000 years ago? What is the archaeological evidence for the emergence of the state?

Mesopotamia lies within the Fertile Crescent of the ancient Near East, which is famous as the center of the world's earliest sedentary villages, plant and animal domestication, and urban, literate civilizations (see Figure 7.4). The Fertile Crescent is a 1500-mile-long (2414 kilometers [km]) curve of territory stretching from the mouth of the Tigris-Euphrates at the head of the Persian Gulf, northwest through Iraq, Turkey, and Syria, and south along the Mediterranean Levant to the lower Nile Valley in Egypt. A unique combination of postglacial conditions favored the formation of large Neolithic farming villages in this area by about 8000 BP (see the box entitled "Neolithic Origins of Near Eastern States" and Table 7.2). The deep, riverborne silt, or alluvium, in the Mesopotamian lowlands was perfectly suited for irrigation and provided an ideal setting for the first civilizations.

The general region of Mesopotamia, where city-states developed by 5000 years ago, is a flat, 500-mile-long (805 km) alluvial plain, or basin, lying between the Zagros Mountains of Iran on the east and the Arabian plateau on the west (see Figure 7.6). For much of its length, the Mesopotamian plain is less than 200 miles (322 km) wide, and it is traversed by the parallel Tigris and Euphrates rivers. An arid region, it is best suited for pastoral nomadism except for the irrigation potential provided by the river systems. The Euphrates is less subject to flooding and tends to build natural levees, which elevate it above the level of the surrounding land, making it more amenable to irrigation than the Tigris (Adams 1981). The Euphrates is a meandering river that has constantly changed its channel such that ancient cities may stand in barren desert, miles from the modern riverbed.

Several hazards threaten subsistence activities in this region. Pastoralism is subject to great fluctuation in rainfall and periods of drought, along with the related possibility of overgrazing. Agriculture

FIGURE 7.4
Map of the Near East showing the Fertile Crescent, Mesopotamia, and major archaeological sites referred to in the text.

is dependent on irrigation, but crops can be destroyed by floods, and yields can be reduced by salination due to an elevation of salty water caused by overirrigation. Shifting river channels can unexpectedly dry up irrigation works. Charles Maisels (1990) points out that these unpredictable conditions could have forced some households to become dependent clients and landless laborers for more fortunate households that managed to accumulate surplus grain.

The early states that developed in Mesopotamia were primary states, or pristine states arising independently of other states; therefore, they offer a good place to test theories of state origin. In this section, we examine the research of archaeologist Gregory Alan Johnson (1973), whose work was part of a team effort to explore the origins of the state in Mesopotamia. In 1970–1971, Johnson surveyed the remains of ancient settlements in southwestern Iran on the eastern margin of the Mesopotamian lowlands that were occupied during the Uruk period (approximately 4000–3100 BC), when the shift from chiefdom to state organization took place.

Johnson wanted to learn if changes in settlement patterns reflected the political and economic changes associated with the emergence of the state. Based on his analysis of potsherds, Johnson was able to measure the size of sixty-seven ancient settlement sites and assign them to a relative chronology within four sequential stylistic phases spanning a 1000-year period beginning roughly in 4000 BC (see Table 7.4). His dates do not correspond precisely with the dates shown in Table 7.2 because there is considerable disagreement on the precise calibration of absolute dates in Near Eastern archaeology.

The switch from the earliest phase (Terminal Susa A, equivalent to the Ubaid on the Tigris-Euphrates) to Early Uruk was dramatic. At first there were relatively few villages, and they were clustered in relation to larger centers in a way that suggested chiefdom organization. During the Early Uruk, the population suddenly tripled in size, density increased, and the site of Susa became an "urban" center of 2400 people. This change in settlement pattern and population suggests that villages and small centers came under some form of centralized control.

Based on the assumption that each hectare of settlement area was occupied by 200 people, the total population of the region may have increased from 6000 people to 20,000 in the Early Uruk. The earlier 6000 people lived in sixteen villages under two small chiefdom centers. By Early Uruk times, there were forty-five villages under three small centers, with Susa as an overall center. Johnson inferred that Susa may have operated as a *central place* because villages were evenly spaced in a pattern that would support the most efficient communication with the center regarding the distribution of resources. The center contained workshops where craftsmen using pottery wheels produced large quantities of specialty ceramics for distribution to outlying villages. The villagers apparently produced their own food and a surplus to support nonfood-producing administrators and artisans.

During Early Uruk times, there was an increase in the use of identifying seals, or marks stamped in soft clay, to seal bundles, jars, and other containers. Clay seals would be broken when a container was opened, and their use suggests that officials in the centers were becoming more concerned with controlling the production and distribution of goods. Given the settlement pattern evidence of three administrative levels, it seems reasonable to treat Early Uruk as a small protostate.

By the Middle Uruk period, there was a further increase in settlement number, size, and total population (see Table 7.4) and an obvious elaboration of administrative functions. Monumental architecture appeared in the large centers in the form of large buildings, and residences were differentiated, suggesting an increase in bureaucracy, status differences, and wealth inequality. The presence of elite government administrators in outlying villages is suggested by the appearance of clay seals and small painted ceramic cones normally used to create lavish decorative mosaics on walls in the centers. Further evidence of exchange between centers and villages can be found in the appearance in the villages of pottery manufactured in the centers where the kilns and workshops were exclusively located.

The mobilization of significant village labor forces during the Middle Uruk is inferred from the most abundant form of pottery, a simple bowl with a distinctive beveled rim (see Figure 7.7). These bowls were apparently mold-made by specialists using assembly-line procedures. They were produced in three standardized sizes and may have been used to distribute barley rations to pay workers in service to the state (see Table 7.5 and the box entitled "The Mesopotamian Ration System"). Other evidence of elaborate administrative controls included the appearance of cylinder seals, which allowed identifying marks to be applied more efficiently by rolling instead of stamping, and the extensive use of counting devices known as *bullae*, which were marked with numerical notations and contained hollow clay balls, or tokens. Archaeologist Denise Schmandt-Besserat (1982) believes that these clay tokens represented specific quantities of goods that were collected as a tax to support centrally controlled rituals. Their use seems to be directly related to the development of writing systems in Mesopotamia, which is discussed later in the chapter. The presence of clay tokens in very early Neolithic times some 10,000 years ago suggests that chiefdomlike political authority may have very ancient roots in the Near East.

The archaeological record from the Susiana plain seems to refute both the irrigation and the conflict theories of state origin. Uruk irrigation systems were small and apparently did not require state administrators. Conflict, whether internal or external, did not arise until after the state was in place. Similarly, long-distance trade seems not to have been an important factor in state formation during Uruk times, although regional trade certainly occurred. Environmental circumscription due to population increase can also be discounted because similar densities were reached earlier in the same area without leading to state organization. Johnson (1973) concluded that the most critical factors may have been an increase in the demands for information processing on the relatively simple decision-making structures of the Susa chiefdoms, perhaps related to increasing interaction with adjacent pastoralists.

Johnson's emphasis on the administrative and distributive functions of the early Mesopotamian state correspond closely to Elman Service's (1975) view that the state evolved as a society-maintaining

---

central place A settlement that serves as the focus of a regional communication network.

Neolithic Origins of Near Eastern States

The Near East is a unique area where mobile foragers became settled village farmers through a long process by which they became increasingly dependent on the abundant wild ancestors of sheep, goats, cattle, wheat, and barley (Maisels 1990). The earliest traces of domestic plants are found in the Zagros Mountains, at sites such as Jarmo on the hilly flanks of the Fertile Crescent (Braidwood and Howe 1960), not in the rich alluvial soils of the Tigris-Euphrates floodplain where civilization later developed. Anthropologists still debate how and why the transition to settled farming life occurred, but it was certainly a gradual process with a revolutionary outcome, and not a sudden event.

Many earlier theorists focused on demographic and environmental factors as the underlying causes of domestication. Kent Flannery (1965, 1972a) argued that domestication and sedentary village life developed in the Near East as part of a "broad spectrum subsistence revolution" that took place in response to worldwide resource–population disequilibriums following the Ice Age. Broad-spectrum subsistence involves eating a wide range of food resources such as wild grains and small animals that might require significant labor costs to procure and process. In contrast to this view, Charles Maisels (1990) suggests that rather than being driven by shortages, people in the Near East settled down to take advantage of the uniquely abundant—and easily harvested and stored—wild grain resources. Sedentism then might have encouraged population growth because the incentives for family planning related to nomadism were abandoned. People turned to farming and raising stock as favorable foraging areas filled up and wild game became scarce.

The Neolithic process began some 12,000 years ago when the Near Eastern climate turned warm and humid, causing wild grains to proliferate. Settlement pattern data from the earliest Neolithic sites in the Levant show a continuing trend toward sedentism, cultivation, and herding because sites are larger and located in the best farming areas (see Table 7.2). Recognizably domesticated forms of wheat,

system. Robert Adams (1981) challenges these conclusions with data from his own site survey from the central Mesopotamian floodplain. He finds no evidence for central-place redistribution functions and argues that the ubiquitous beveled bowls may have been used in rituals, and not to distribute rations. Adams suggests that the earliest Mesopotamian urban sites were formed as cult centers augmented by political subordination and military coercion.

THE MESOPOTAMIAN CITY AS A WAY OF LIFE

Royal Tombs, Ziggurats, and Cylinder Seals

How was the ancient city-state organized? Who were the rulers of the Mesopotamian city-state? What institutional structures and do-

barley, and lentils are known to have existed in the Levant region by approximately 10,000 BP. Solomon Katz and Mary Voigt (1986) argue that people may have been motivated to farm in order to increase the supply of grain used to brew beer, but at this time there were no political authorities as yet to extract grain surpluses.

By 8000 BP, villages had become large and were increasingly dependent on domesticates, farming, and herding. A tantalizing glimpse of what these earliest Near Eastern Neolithic villages may have looked like is provided by the site of Çatal Hüyük in south-central Turkey (Mellaart 1967, Todd 1976). Çatal Hüyük was a compact 32-acre (13-hectare) site, perhaps the largest Neolithic village in the Near East (see Figure 7.5). There were specially decorated structures with likely religious functions, and craft production was well developed, but there is no evidence of full-time specialists or social stratification.

Archaeological and linguistic reconstructions suggest that Neolithic farmers spread agriculture and Indo-European languages across Europe from the Near East in a gradual 2000-year migration, beginning about 8500 BP (Renfrew 1989). Physical anthropologists Albert Ammerman and Luigi Cavalli-Sforza (1984) estimate that a rapid fiftyfold increase of population density occurred as farmers moved peacefully into Europe at a rate of 0.6 miles (1 km) a year, with new homesteads spreading out 11 miles (18 km) at random every 25-year generation. Grover Krantz (1988) proposes a similar model of Neolithic expansion.

Renfrew (1989) suggests that Afro-Asiatic languages such as Semitic (Egyptian, Arabic, and Hebrew), Cushitic, and Berber may have spread into Arabia and North Africa and that Dravidian-speaking peoples migrated into India, all as part of the same Neolithic wave of advance. Renfrew also speculates that Indo-European, Afro-Asiatic, and Dravidian languages all separated from a single superfamily called Nostratic, located in the Near East about 10,000 BP, at the beginning of the Neolithic.

mestic arrangements controlled labor and the flow of resources?

During the Early Dynastic (approximately 3000–2000 BC), Mesopotamian culture acquired the unmistakable marks of a well-developed, stratified, urban, state-organized system. Adams (1981) suggests that by the Early Dynastic, Mesopotamia had become the world's first predominantly urban society, with 70–80 percent of the population living in urban centers of 1000 people or more. The city of Uruk, for example, quadrupled in size between the Late Uruk and the Early Dynastic I, growing to perhaps 40,000 people or more. Because he found little evidence for subsistence intensification, Adams infers that dependent villagers must have worked under bureaucratic control to help support the nonfood-producing urban population.

TABLE 7.2   *Near Eastern Prehistory and Early History: Mesopotamia and the Levant, 18,000–600 BC**

2300–600 BC	1600–600	Kassite and Assyrian dynasties
	2000–1600	Isin-Larsa and Old Babylonian dynasties
	2100–2000	Third Dynasty, Ur (Sumerian)
	2300–2100	Akkadian dynasties
	2300–2100	Ur I and II (Sumerian)
Early Dynastic (2900–2300 BC)	2900–2300	Early Dynastic I (Sumerian); urbanized city-states, cuneiform writing well established
Uruk (4000–3100 BC) (Mesopotamia/Khuzistan)	4000–3100	Large centers with temple mounds; use of cylinder seals; earliest writing systems; probable state organization
Ubaid (5500–4000 BC) (Mesopotamian/Khuzistan Chalcolithic)	5500–4000	Probable chiefdom organization; painted ceramics; some articles of copper
Neolithic (8500–3700 BC) (Levant)	5000–3700	Neolithic 4 (developed): further population growth; ceramics, domestic pigs
	6000–5000	Neolithic 3 (developed): climate increasingly hot and dry; full dependence on mixed dry farming and herding in upland forest zones
	7600–6000	Neolithic 2 (archaic): farming and herding of domestic sheep and goats, supplemented by hunting and foraging; sites larger, steppe occupied; large, permanent egalitarian villages
	8500–7600	Neolithic 1 (archaic): simple farming and herding
Epipaleolithic (18,000–8500 BC) (Levant)	10,000–8500	Epipaleolithic 2 (Natufian): climate cool and wet; larger, semisedentary settlements; selective hunting; population increases; intensive use of wild grains, microlith sickles, ground-stone tools; possible simple cultivation and beginnings of animal domestication
	17,000	Persian Gulf dry land
	18,000–10,000	Epipaleolithic 1 (Kebaran): climate cool and dry; mobile foragers and hunters; microlithic tools
Upper Paleolithic		Upper Paleolithic: fully modern humans; mobile foragers

SOURCES: Moore (1983) and Voigt (1987).
*Absolute chronologies for Near Eastern archaeology vary widely in different sources and are frequently recalibrated; thus, they must always be used with caution.

The nature of early Mesopotamian society has been a subject of scholarly debate for many years. Karl Wittfogel (1957) considered Sumerian society to be an example of ***agromanagerial despotism,*** in which the economy was based on "hydraulic agriculture" involving "large-scale and government-managed works of irrigation and flood control" (1957:3). He thought that such systems required large-scale cooperation and a division of labor between managers and farmers. As Wittfogel explicitly declared,

Thus a number of farmers eager to conquer arid lowlands and plains are forced to invoke the organizational devices which—on the basis of premachine technology—offer the one chance of success: they must work in cooperation with their fellows and subordinate themselves to a directing authority. (1957:18)

The managers then gained absolute power over their populations and became tyrannical and despotic rulers who terrorized their subjects into absolute submission. The primary problem with this view, as noted in our earlier discussion of Hawaii, is that effective irrigation systems apparently did not require the kind of large-scale coordination Wittfogel envisioned. In the Near East, there are examples of local villagers managing their own re-

FIGURE 7.5
Çatal Hüyük, a very large early Neolithic pres-tate village in what is now south central Tur-key: (a) a reconstructed view of densely packed multistoried buildings in the village; (b) a reconstruction of a structure that is thought to have been a religious shrine.

(a)

(b)

gional irrigation systems in a basically egalitarian way (Adams 1982). Furthermore, as Johnson's (1973) research demonstrated, bureaucracies and city-states developed in the Near East before the large-scale, labor-intensive irrigation systems that probably did require centralized administration.

TABLE 7.3   *Settlement Size in the Epipaleolithic–Neolithic Levant, 18,000–3750 BC*

	Average Size	Maximum Size	Estimated Inhabitants
Neolithic 4	—	—	—
Neolithic 3	—	—	—
Neolithic 2	—	—	+ 2000
Neolithic 1	—	4 hectares	—
Epipaleolithic 2	<500 m²	2000 m²	—
Epipaleolithic 1	300 m²	—	30

SOURCE: Moore (1983).

Charles Maisels (1990) reconstructed Mesopo-tamian society, drawing inferences from the floor plans of excavated houses, inscriptions describing ancient property transfers, and clay tablets con-taining household inventories. Maisels suggests that Mesopotamian society was designed to serve elite patrilineal households whose large private landholdings were cultivated by their retinues of dependent laborers. The residential core of the urban centers contained large household com-pounds, each controlled by a senior household residing in a large central hall. Junior extended-family households and dependent nonkin lived in small, individual household apartments arranged along the side of the main hall and in detached

agromanagerial despotism   Wittfogel's explanation for the rise of the Mesopotamian state, arguing that the first rulers controlled irrigation and agriculture.

FIGURE 7.6　*Ancient settlement mounds in the Mesopotamian lowlands of southwest Iran,*
surveyed by archaeologist Gregory Allen Johnson.

TABLE 7.4　*Settlement Pattern Changes*
in Mesopotamia, 4000–3000 BC

	Terminal Susa A	Early Uruk	Middle Uruk	Late Uruk
Sites	18	49	52	—
Large centers	0	1	3	3
Small centers	2	3	4	1
Large villages	0	0	12	0
Villages	16	45	33	10
Area (hectares)	30	95	127	53
Population	6000	20,000	25,000	10,600
Density/km²	2	7	9	4
Village land, (hectare/ person)	—	0.49	—	—
Center land (hectare/ person)	—	2.12	—	—

SOURCE: Johnson (1973:97–98).

outbuildings. Dependents held reduced titles to land or were totally landless. Household archives show that these compounds were large economic enterprises managing people, land, grain, food, livestock, and craft products. The heads of these private "great-house" economic units formed the citizens of the Mesopotamian city-state. They also ran the temples and the city government.

Sumerologists agree that an institutionalized temple–city, or temple–palace, bureaucracy controlled the urban centers in early Mesopotamia. Each city belonged to a founding god drawn from the rich Sumerian pantheon and contained temples dedicated to it. The Sumerian word for temple, *ebitum*, meant "house," so the temple was the god's house, and the temple personnel existed as the god's caretakers. The visible focal point of major Sumerian cities was the *ziggurat* (an Akkadian word for "temple tower"), a stepped pyramid of clay bricks built as a shrine to the city's deity. This was monumental architecture at its finest.

The Ziggurat of Ur, the best-surviving example, was completed during the third Sumerian dynasty, around 2000 BC. The Ziggurat of Ur, which was excavated by Sir Leonard Woolley (1982) between 1922 and 1934, is one of the best preserved early ziggurats. The base platform was 200 feet by 150 feet (61 m by 46 m) and 50 feet (15 m) high. Two other levels were built on top of this, and they were topped by a small shrine to the moon god Nanna, so that the total height was at least 70 feet (21 m) (see Figure 7.8). Because the ziggurat was built on an elevated terrace, the whole structure must

FIGURE 7.7
Mass-produced, beveled-rim ceramic bowls from ancient Mesopotamia. Their presence suggests the existence of state organization because they were used to distribute rations to laborers.

TABLE 7.5   *Rations in Mesopotamia by Age and Sex*

	Se-ba (Barley) (*sila*/month)*	*I-ba* (Oil) (*sila*/year)	Sig-ba (Wool) (*ma-na*/ year)[†]
Men	60	4	4
Women	30	4	3
Children	—	1.5	1.5
Boys	20–30	—	—
Girls	20	—	—
Infants	10	—	—

SOURCES: Gelb (1965), Johnson (1973), Kramer (1963).
*Sila = 0.85 L, 705 g of barley.
[†]Ma-na = 500 g.

have been an imposing sight rising above the surrounding plain. The ziggurat was part of the *Temenos* (Greek for "sacred ground"), a sacred enclosure containing a major temple to Nanna, other shrines, storehouses, courtyards, and quarters for temple personnel. At this time, Ur was a walled city of some 321 acres (130 hectares) that might have contained 25,000 people, according to some estimates.

The spiritual head of the Sumerian temple bore the title *En*, and he or she resided in an elaborate complex within the *Temenos*, called the *Giparu*. The temple administrator was titled *Sanga*, and there were many other named temple or priestly offices. The temple claimed ownership of at least three named categories of land:

1. *Nigenna*, whose produce directly supported the temple

2. *Kurra*, used to support those who worked *nigenna* land

3. *Urulal*, lands that could be farmed by temple personnel for their own use, in exchange for a share of the produce

Thus, the temple administration, besides conducting major religious activities, managed the farmland, collected and stored grain, and paid out rations to laborers. This arrangement must have reflected the structure of elite private households. The temples also took in dependents, but they were public institutions, and their grain surpluses were probably available in times of shortage.

Secular rulers apparently rose to prominence as military leaders in conflicts with neighboring city-states. As kings (*lugal*), they founded dynasties, built palaces and temples, raised armies, maintained the city walls, and were buried in royal tombs. In 1927–1928, Woolley discovered some of the most spectacular art treasures of the ancient Near East in the royal tombs of Ur. A series of royal burials dating to the Early Dynastic period were unearthed in a cemetery just beyond the *Tenemos* wall (Woolley 1982). The burials contained a treasure trove of grave goods, including lyres decorated with golden bull heads (see Figure 7.9), gold and silver weapons, jewelry, and headdresses.

Most remarkable was the discovery that the royal personages were accompanied in death by an entourage of soldiers and retainers, in full regalia, as well as wagons and oxen. One tomb contained seventy-four additional people, including four male guards, four female musicians, and sixty-four women of the royal court in ceremonial dress. Woolley (1982) infers that many of the sacrificed attendants may have taken poison in a mass suicide ceremony as part of the royal funeral. Human sacrifice on this scale certainly attests to the strength of the religious system, as well as to the despotic

The Mesopotamian Ration System

The early Mesopotamian city-state was populated by a large number of full-time urban specialists, who included priests, scribes, overseers, and artisans. All these people were supported by monthly allotments of rations, which in Sumerian were called *Se-ba* (*Se* means "barley"; *ba* means "distribution"). According to I. J. Gelb's (1965) analysis of the textual evidence, standard rations included *Se-ba*, *I-ba* (oil), and *Sig-ba* (wool) and were distributed in standardized units according to a set formula specifying the amounts that people would receive by age and sex. For example, barley was distributed by the *sila*, a volume measurement equivalent to 0.85 liter (L). Men normally received 60 *sila*; women, 30; boys, 25; girls, 20; and infants, 10 (see Table 7.5). The rations were probably generous, and people no doubt bartered the surplus to fill other basic needs. According to figures used by Johnson (1973), 1 L of barley contained 829 grams (g), and 100 g of barley produced 350 calories (cal). The average adult ration of 45 *sila* would have provided 3698 calories per day. Barley was the most important subsistence staple, but it probably accounted for only 66 percent of people's average caloric consumption, the balance being supplied by animal products, fruits, and vegetables. Thus, people probably consumed directly only about half of their barley allotments. The oil ration was generally animal fat, although sometimes it might have been sesame oil, and it was used for consumption and in ritual anointings. Besides barley, oil, and wool distributions, there were also irregular distributions of wheat, bread, flour, and cloth. Standard rations were sometimes replaced with equivalent substitutes, such that 1 *sila* of oil could replace 2 *sila* of barley. On ritual occasions or to specific categories of people, there were also supplemental distributions of meat, dairy products, beer, wine, fish, dates, fruits, and vegetables.

power of the temple–palace complex. It makes the occasional human sacrifice associated with the Hawaiian temple cults seem almost trivial by comparison.

Henry Wright (1969) used a combination of archaeological evidence and inscribed tablets to reconstruct the complexities of the administrative bureaucracy of Early Dynastic Ur in about 2800 BC. He inferred that at that time, the city itself contained about 4000 people, while another 1800 lived in the immediate vicinity. He found direct archaeological evidence of ceramics, stone bowls, copper vessels, spinning, and cylinder seal cutting within the city. Inscribed tablets found in the city refer to bricklayers, carpenters, smiths, gardeners, cooks,

kitchen supervisors, maltsters, and physicians, all of whom are named as specialists. Tablets also attest to the distribution of bread and grain from the temple storehouse to various groups.

The most critical temple function was the management of agricultural production. Temple lands and lands held in large estates, perhaps as allotments from the temple, were all farmed at the lowest levels by small farmers who cultivated plots of 7–17 acres (3–7 hectares). A work foreman supervised a 99–123-acre (40–50-hectare) unit of land, worked by perhaps ten small-scale farmers. Several foremen, in turn, reported to an overseer. Another official supervised the harvest, and the temple administrator controlled the stored grain.

FIGURE 7.8
The central Ziggurat (temple tower) of Ur, built around 2000 BC.

FIGURE 7.9   *A lyre decorated with a golden bull's head from the royal tombs of Ur.*

Wright (1969) estimated that the planting, harvesting, and irrigation maintenance involved in the annual cultivation of the land that supported Ur could have been readily performed by the 2500-person work force that could have been mobilized. This centrally managed production system could have supplied an average adult barley ration for 1200 urban specialists and the 2500 farmers (see Table 7.5).

Economist Karl Polanyi (1977) has described the Mesopotamian economy as a nonmarket redistribution system, emphasizing the managerial role of temple and palace. The Mesopotamian administrative system, however, was clearly different from the relatively small-scale redistribution described for Tikopia (Chapter 6), where independent, basically self-provisioning village farmers contributed to a chief who returned their contributions in the form of religious feasts. It is possible that much of the managed agricultural production in Mesopotamia was carried out by landless, dependent laborers working for rations. At the same time, abundant evidence suggests that there were "free" peasants, as well as large landholders and merchants, who may have operated independently of the central administration.

Adams (1982) stresses that the textual accounts of land ownership and agricultural production may be describing a formal urban code that had only limited applicability in the countryside, where more egalitarian practices may have continued to operate. Modern villages in the region have resisted government efforts to regulate their land-use systems and have used tribal systems, which periodically reallocate land in ways that minimize risk and help ensure equal access to land of different quality. Royal dynasties and elite families came and went, but villagers may have formed closed-corporate communities that effectively insulated them from many forms of state intrusion.

Cuneiform Writing and the Literary Tradition

How did cuneiform writing develop? What was its function within Mesopotamian society?

As the administrative bureaucracy in the Mesopotamian city-states grew, the requirements for information storage increased dramatically. The earliest written inscriptions appeared about 3100 BC in a pictographic script found in the city of Uruk and involved economic control functions such as bookkeeping of receipts, expenses, and goods. By 2400 BC, Mesopotamian writing had become a well-developed cuneiform system (Nissen 1986). The word *cuneiform* (*cunei* means "nails") refers to the distinctive nail shape produced when a stylus with a triangular cross section is pressed into a soft clay tablet at an angle. The early pictographs represented the names of naturalistically portrayed objects, but this limited and cumbersome system was readily improved by simplifying the pictographs into abstract forms and giving some of them phonetic meanings (see Figure 7.10). The basic cuneiform system was used throughout the Near East by the Sumerians, Babylonians, Assyrians, and Persians over a 2000-year period.

A scribal school, the *edubba*, became institutionalized as a formal means to standardize the writing system and to produce the professional body of scribes needed to write and archive the great masses of clay tablets required for routine administration. Students memorized some 2000 different cuneiform signs by copying standard texts that often consisted of word lists. One such list contained a ranking of one hundred professions and

FIGURE 7.10   *Clay tablet inscribed in an early Mesopotamian writing system.*

titles. The writing system went through a rapid development over a period of about 150 years (Nissen 1986) and then became very stable. It was a medium for sacred temple literature, epic poetry, and royal decrees, but the bulk of the material concerned mundane administrative matters and domestic accounts. Numeration was based on a sexagesimal (60s) system with place values, but it also used a numeral for 10. There was no concept of zero, but complex mathematical calculations—such as multiplication, square roots, and area problems—were still accomplished.

Mesopotamian Religion in Service of the State

How did the Mesopotamian ideological system support the political economy?

In his analysis of Mesopotamian religion, Sumerologist Thorkild Jacobsen defined religion as the human experience of the numinous, or "confrontation with power not of this world" (1976:3). Because the numinous is unworldly, it cannot be directly described; thus, people must resort to religious metaphors that are shared within a culture—for example, by imagining the numinous as specific gods in specific form. In Mesopotamian religion, the numinous was seen as immanent, as an intrinsic part of nature. So, for example, the sun god *Utu* was the sun and the sun's numinous power, all at the same time. The gods thus represented the indwelling power of specific natural phenomena. Mesopotamian religion was highly ***polytheistic*** because there were a multitude of situations in which the numinous could be experienced. People could invoke numinous power by building temples and shrines as sacred dwellings for deities, by performing rituals, or by making images.

Jacobsen suggested that during the 4000-year span of Mesopotamian culture, three different metaphors of numinous power existed. The earliest and most persistent metaphor was of the intransitive power of specific nature deities. By the Early Dynastic, gods began to be called "rulers," just as human rulers began to take power in the emerging city-states. By the second millennium BC, during the Old Babylonian period, personal gods began to appear who were concerned with the security of individuals.

The earliest Mesopotamian deities, as revealed in a series of engravings and lyric poems preserved in clay tablets, were nature gods concerned with fertility. Initially, these deities were depicted in the form of the natural objects they represented, but over time they were gradually given more human form. Prominent among them were the gods associated with specific cities and expressing the power of economically important natural resources, such as *Enki* the water god, *Nanshe* the fish goddess, and *Dumuzi*, who was concerned with livestock and the date palm. The most important annual rituals, no doubt performed at the temple, involved a sacred wedding, in which nature deities as bride and groom perpetuated the return of fertility in the spring and mourned the decline and death of fertility in the fall. The temple deity and associated storehouse were direct embodiments of nature's fertility.

By the third millennium BC, deities were referred to as "Lords" or "Masters" and mirrored the actions of human rulers. People were now impressed by the awe-inspiring energy and majesty of the numinous, not simply their life-sustaining powers of fertility. The major city gods assumed new roles as spiritual estate managers, judges, and warriors. This sequence of development supports the general cultural materialist theoretical position that religion, as part of a culture's ***superstructure***, changes in response to changes in the sociopolitical ***structure***. G. E. Swanson (1960) provided further support for this view with a global cross-cultural sample showing a statistical association between the presence of high gods and hierarchical political structures.

The new Mesopotamian deities obviously reflected the rising importance of political rulers in the emerging city-states of the Early Dynastic. For example, Jacobsen (1976) showed that *Ningirsu*, god of life-giving spring thunderstorms and floods and titular deity of the city of Girsu, was head of a twenty-one-deity pantheon of gods who staffed his temple and supervised his estate. Counted as deities were a high constable, a steward, a chamberlain, two musicians, seven handmaidens, a councilor, a secretary, two generals, two herdsmen, a plowman, a fisherman, and a general manager of natural resources. These deities had their human counterparts who directed human laborers in service to *Ningirsu*. Whereas the original nature deities had no functions beyond their immanent qualities and could thus be considered "intransitive," the new ruler-gods could make demands on people, and their wills were transmitted through dreams and signs that had to be interpreted by diviners.

The entire Mesopotamian cosmos was hierarchically arranged, with deities holding titles and offices. There were seven primary gods, who determined the fate of other gods and humans, and some fifty "great gods," along with a vast multitude of lesser deities, who collectively met as a formal

---

polytheism   A religious system based on belief in many gods, or deities.

superstructure   The mental, ideological, or belief systems, as expressed in the religion, myths, and rituals of a culture. According to Harris' cultural materialist theory, superstructure is shaped by the structure.

structure   The social, economic, and political organization of a culture, which is shaped by the technological base, or infrastructure, according to Harris' cultural materialist theory.

assembly of gods. City deities such as *Ningirsu* served the higher-ranking deity *Enlil*, Lord of the Wind and primary executive god. The water god *Enki*, Lord of the Soil and Owner of the River, was credited not only with establishing the seasonal regime of the Tigris-Euphrates system but also with placing various deities in charge of a number of recognized occupational specialties such as farming, brickmaking, architecture, and weaving. *Enki* made *Utu*, the sun god and god of justice, responsible for boundary maintenance. Even the creation myths were brought in line with the realities of the political system. By the second millennium BC, the primary Mesopotamian creation epic, known as *Enuma Elish*, was a lengthy account of how the god *Marduk* became the permanent king of the universe and all the basic elements of the Mesopotamian cosmic politics were in place.

THE INCA EMPIRE IN THE LAND OF FOUR QUARTERS

Andean Environment and Prehistory

How did the Inca empire function as a state, pulling far-flung villages into a vast network based on kinship reciprocity? What unique environmental conditions shaped the development of Andean culture?

The Inca empire, which reached its peak between AD 1476 and 1532, was the last in a series of political-scale indigenous cultures that developed independently in the Andean region of South America beginning approximately 4000 years ago (see Table 7.6 and the box entitled "The Prehistory of Andean Civilization"). This last pre-Columbian empire extended over an area of some 380,000 square miles (mi²) (984,000 square kilometers [km²]), covering the Andean regions of modern Ecuador, Peru, Bolivia, and the northern Andes of Chile and Argentina (see Figure 7.12). Estimates of its population range from 6 million to 32 million people. The Inca empire was a village-state that rivaled the Roman empire in scale, yet it was maintained without wheeled vehicles, writing, or draft animals by the effective mobilization of a vast labor force, within the framework of an elaborate bureaucracy that

was ordered and sustained by a compelling religious system.

The dominant geographic feature of the Andean region is the Andean mountain chain. The Andes are the world's longest mountain range, stretching 5500 miles (8800 km) along the west coast of South America from Venezuela to southern Chile. They were formed by tectonic uplift during the past 2.5 million years, and volcanic activity and earthquakes continue to be frequent occurrences. Because the Andes run north and south, they form a barrier to global winds and currents, blocking westward-flowing moisture from the Atlantic and creating one of the world's driest deserts in the rain shadow along the coast of Peru and Chile. A series of narrow, short valleys descend from the Andes to the Pacific and offer significant irrigation potential not unlike that offered by the Mesopotamian floodplain. An additional advantage of the Andean region is that the cold, upwelling Peru current lifts rich nutrients toward the ocean surface from the deep offshore trench and thereby supports one of the world's richest marine fisheries. Unfortunately, during an unpredictable phenomenon called El Niño, the Peru current has been replaced by warmer water that disrupts the ecosystem, destroying marine life and causing rains and flooding.

The bulk of the Andean population occupied the altiplano, the high plateau, at elevations from 12,000 feet (3658 m) to over 16,000 feet (4877 m) (see Figure 7.13). Each time I visited the highlands after living in the Amazon lowlands, I was struck by the penetrating cold, and the thin air made me light-headed. One acclimatizes to such conditions, but the mountains are an inhospitable place for farmers because soils are thin, freezes can occur at any time, and droughts are frequent. The treeless vegetation, called *puna*, supports only the hardiest grazers such as the native camelids, the guanaco and vicuna. Domesticated camelids, llamas and alpacas were valued for their meat and wool, and as pack animals they were capable of carrying up to 100 pounds (45 kg). Dried llama dung was an important fuel on the treeless *altiplano*, and, as fertilizer, it helped keep thin mountain soils productive. Another important domesticate, the guinea pig, lived on kitchen scraps and was eaten. The potato was the primary highland subsistence crop because it was highly nutritious, tolerated frost, was readily stored,

TABLE 7.6   *Andean Prehistory, 32,000 BP–AD 1532*

AD 600–1532	AD 1476–1532	Inca empire
	AD 1000–1476	Chimu state on north coast
	AD 600–1000	Middle Horizon, Tiahuanaco, and Huari empires
1400–2200 BP	1400–2200	Mochica and Nazca regional coastal states
2200–2800 BP	2200–2800	Early Horizon; Chavin; metallurgy
2900–4000 BP	2900–3500	Initial Ceramic period, city-states or advanced chiefdoms; ceramics, irrigation, population growth
	3500–4000	Late (Cotton) Pre-Ceramic chiefdoms; maize, manioc
5000–6000 BP	5000	Sedentary coastal fishing villages; domestic-scale farming of cotton, gourds, beans, squash
	5800	Domesticated potatoes in highlands
	6000	Domestic camelids
6000–32,000 BP	6000–14,000	Mobile foragers and hunters
	14,000–32,000	Earliest settlement

SOURCES: Burger and van der Merwe (1990), Lanning (1967), and Wheeler (1984).

and could be grown at elevations of up to 14,000 feet (4267 m). Andean farmers developed some 3000 varieties of potatoes, selecting for differing tuber qualities and environmental tolerances (Brush, Carney, and Huaman 1981). Another important early highland domesticate was quinoa, which also grows well under the harsh conditions of the *altiplano* and produces a protein-rich, grainlike seed. Some 200 varieties of quinoa were developed.

Unlike ancient Mesopotamian civilization, Inca civilization was not based on city-states and private property. Inca cities were administrative centers, not autonomous city-states. They were populated by bureaucrats and their servants, whose existence depended on sustaining a power network that extended throughout the Andean region. The primary producers were highly self-sufficient village farmers and herders who lived in the countryside and worked communally managed land to meet the domestic needs of individual households. Why independent villagers would support the empire is a mystery, because the empire apparently gave them few material benefits. As in Mesopotamia, Andean civilization was an improbable development that depended on certain environmental and cultural circumstances. The Andean cultural tradition was in place 3000 years ago. The cyclical record of state growth and collapse suggests that domestic-scale agricultural village life, not the state, was the optimal human adaptation for the Andean world. Like

their predecessors, the Inca were able briefly to exploit a particular combination of distinctive Andean cultural principles and an agricultural system based on a unique mix of domesticated crops and animals that could thrive in the harsh conditions of the high Andes.

The immediate beginnings of the Inca dynasty can be traced to a small Quechua-speaking chiefdom in the region of Cuzco in approximately AD 1200. Quechua is a member of the Andean branch of Amerind languages, which also includes the languages of the foraging peoples of Patagonia and Tierra del Fuego (also see Mannheim 1991). The rapid expansion of the Inca empire, which began in 1438 under Pachacuti, is difficult to explain even though it is not totally unprecedented. The empire joined together preexisting regional states, chiefdoms, and domestic-scale communities into a centrally managed system. The ultimate ideological foundation of the empire was the religious belief in the supreme divinity of the Inca ruler, who was the sun god personified. The Inca's identity with the sun had a literal reality, given the vast energy resources at the ruler's disposal in the form of enormous quantities of foodstuffs stored in state warehouses scattered throughout the empire. The Inca state also supported large numbers of full-time craft specialists, part-time corvée laborers (laborers on public-works projects), and military personnel. Over a 60-year period, the state financed

The Prehistory of Andean Civilization

People were hunting mammals like the guanaco and vicuna in the high Andes by 7200 BP, and they domesticated llamas and alpacas by 6000 BP (Wheeler 1984) and potatoes by 5800 BP. But Andean civilization was a maritime development. The earliest coastal inhabitants foraged in a unique fog-belt vegetation zone until climate change forced them to live in fishing villages around 5000 BP. There, they cultivated cotton and gourds for fish nets and floats (Lanning 1967). The abundant marine resources supported relatively large, permanent settlements, with ranked social systems (Lanning 1967, Mosely 1975, Quilter and Stocker 1983). El Paraiso, a monumental complex of stone and mortar buildings that dates to 4000 BP, may have been an advanced chiefdom society comparable to Uruk-period Mesopotamian temple centers. This is remarkable for a society with no pottery and no cultivated crops other than cotton and gourds.

Irrigation farming developed in the coastal river valleys only after the arrival of pottery and new food crops, such as maize from Mesoamerica and manioc from Amazonia. A series of *El Niño* episodes—in which the Peruvian current is replaced by warmer water—may have disrupted the marine ecosystem, encouraging people to intensify their subsistence activity. Michael Mosely (1975) considers Andean subsistence intensification—the changes from foraging to fishing to farming—to be the result of population expansion. However, irrigation may have been promoted by the political elites because it provided a more easily controlled source of political power than production systems based on marine resources.

The basic elements of the Andean cultural tradition were firmly in place 3000 years ago. These included state-level political organization, intensive agriculture based on maize and potatoes, high-altitude llama pastoralism, monumental architecture, religious shrines, urban centers, and elaborate ceramics and textiles. Pre-Inca Andean peoples were masters at metallurgy, weaving, and ceramics. Andean peoples worked copper, gold, bronze, and silver, using a variety of tech-

innumerable monumental building projects, constructed and maintained a vast road network (Hyslop 1984), and developed large-scale agricultural projects. These impressive activities ultimately depended on maintaining the loyalty of villagers, who cared first and foremost about the day-to-day well-being of their domestic households.

Potatoes, Maize, and Gold: Foundations of the Empire

How did the Inca elite use wealth objects and stored food surpluses to manage their empire?

The material foundation of the Andean empire was in the hands of the self-sufficient villagers who operated a highly productive, intensive agricultural system based on communal land and complementary labor exchange. Without an effective subsistence sector, there would have been no part-time labor force to sustain the Inca elite. The community-level Andean agricultural system was a major achievement in which egalitarian villagers cooperated to increase agricultural production in an otherwise hostile environment by draining and ridging fields in low areas, terracing steep hillsides, and creating and maintaining irrigation canals.

niques, including lost-wax casting, to produce elaborate jewelry and simple implements (see Figure 7.11). Textiles, including tapestry and embroidery, were highly
developed and, along with jewelry, became important markers of status. The pre-
Inca Chimu state's urban center at Chanchan covered 6 square miles (16 km²) and
may have contained 50,000 people (Moseley and Day 1980, Moseley and Mackey
1973). The Chimu built vast irrigation works that were comparable to any of the
monumental constructions of the ancient Near East (Hadingham 1987).

By 2800 BP, a striking art style portraying snarling jaguars and birds of prey on
stone and pottery spread from Chavin, a temple site in the north-central highlands
to some thirty other temple centers on the coast and in the adjacent highlands.
The Chavin art style apparently represented a widespread belief system that provided a foundation for chiefdoms and kingdoms and that endured throughout the
Andean region in some form for 2000 years (Keatinge 1981). The original Chavin
temple was likely an important oracle shrine and a major site for long-distance
pilgrimages. The temple contained a hidden inner sanctum where the principal
deity was housed and public courtyards where other images were displayed. The
priests thus had privileged access to supernatural power, as was also apparently
the case in Mesopotamia. Richard Keatinge (1981) argues that Chavin-style pilgrimage centers, which were scattered in diverse environments, would have guaranteed safe passage and may have fostered regional trade networks between coast,
highlands, and Amazonia. Religion thus may have been an important integrating
mechanism and may have provided further ways for the developing political elite
to increase their power without using direct military force. The Inca were the last
in a series of Andean civilizations that followed Chavin networks, including the
Mochica, Nazca, and Chimu coastal kingdoms and the highland empires of Tiahuanaco and Huari.

FIGURE 7.11
*Inca bronze tools and
implements, which re-
veal that Andean peoples
were accomplished
metallurgists.*

FIGURE 7.12   (a) Map of the Andean region and the Inca empire with its division into four quarters: Chinchasuyu, Antisuyu, Condesuyu, and Collasuyu; (b) map of the same region with today's nation's territories. (SOURCE: Figure 7.12a based on Conrad and Demarest 1984.)

Community leaders managed a technically sophisticated sectoral fallow system in which each sector, or plot of land, was rotated through a 5–15-year production cycle of carefully selected annual crops and grazing fallow periods that maximized yield while maintaining long-term soil fertility. In successive years, specific crops were sequentially planted to take advantage of the particular qualities of a dozen or more distinct environmental zones that were available to the community. This system served everyone. Each household received enough land to sustain itself in exchange for participation in cooperative labor projects that collectively maintained the system (Hastorf 1993).

The highly successful village-level subsistence sector has been characterized as a vertical economy because households and villages exploited resources in different ecological zones at different elevations, rather than depending on trade or market exchanges. The extremely steep Andean topography often meant that several sharply different environments would be within a village's reach. Four major zones, in descending elevation order, produced grazing, potatoes, maize, or tropical crops (see Table 7.7).

Andean political centralization is not explained by population pressure or the adaptive advantages of exchange, specialization, or irrigation

FIGURE 7.13
View of the Inca city of Machu Pichu on the eastern edge of the Andes, showing elaborate agricultural terraces and stone architecture, which were the products of a complex bureaucratic state.

TABLE 7.7   *Productive Zones in the Andean Vertical Economy*

Zone	Altitude*	Subsistence Production
Puna—alpine	14,000+ feet (4267+ meters)	Grazing of llamas and alpacas on wet and frosty alpine pastures
Puna/Jalka—subalpine	11,000–14,000 feet (3353–4267 meters)	Potato cultivation in dry, frost-prone zones
Kichwa—temperate	7000–11,000 feet (2134–3353 meters)	Maize and beans
Tropical	Lowest	Tropical crops such as manioc, avocados, coca, and papayas

SOURCES: Brush (1976) and Murra (1972).
*Elevations of each zone vary from north to south in the Andes and are only approximate.

management because these were already effectively handled by relatively egalitarian local communities without coercive hereditary rulers. Archaeological evidence suggests that ambitious local leaders shrewdly manipulated the power vacuum left by the collapse of the Wari and Tiawanaku empires to increase their personal power, turning local intercommunity rivalries into aggressive conquest warfare. People were forced to move into large, fortified towns for defense, and they accepted increasingly centralized authority as the best of a bad bargain in a threatening world (Hastorf 1993).

Agricultural work was intensified when large, walled settlements had to be formed, but people resisted inequality. For example, during the century before the Inca conquerors arrived, all households in the fortified settlements of the Upper Mantaro valley had access to land and metal goods, and everyone farmed. Community leaders were distinguished only by their larger, wealthier households. For political centralization to emerge, preexisting Andean cultural principles, which fostered community balance, kinship reciprocity, and social equality, had to be subverted to first create and then perpetuate coercive power structures and elite privilege (Hastorf 1993).

The Inca state was a nonmarket political economy based on "supply on command" rather than the "supply and demand" of a market economy (La Lone 1982). The state economy was functionally divided into a staple economy and a wealth economy (D'Altroy and Earle 1985). The **staple economy** was concerned with the production and storage of potatoes and other primary foodstuffs to provision the army and the vast numbers of full-time state employees. Maize was an important crop used to brew *chicha* beer, which state officials provided to part-time laborers in ritual feasts in exchange for their labor (Murra 1960). The **wealth economy** involved the state-directed production of luxury goods such as gold and silver jewelry, featherwork, and fine textiles, which were status markers used to reward the ruling class. Gold symbolized the sun god and was a marker of the Inca nobility. Wealth objects also bought the loyalty of local village leaders turned Inca bureaucrats; these bureaucrats, backed by the coercive power of the Inca state and army, facilitated the extraction of the labor tax.

Under the Inca, specialized laborers in full-time service to the state were called *camayo* (*camayoc*), with an additional designation to specify their duty. For example, there were *llama camayo*, who herded llamas; *coca camayo*, who raised coca; *chacara camayo*, who farmed; and *pukara camayo*, who garrisoned frontier fortresses (Rowe 1982). The *mitima* (*mitmaq*) were members of ethnic groups who were relocated as colonists to work on large-scale agricultural projects. Commoner women might also become *acllas*, or "chosen women," who worked full-time to produce high-status textiles known as *kumpi*. *Acllas* might also be married to the *yanacona*, commoners who served the nobility. Nonspecialist commoners were called *suyu runa*, "people of the quarter," and were subject to periodic labor service, known as the *mita*.

Royal Lineages and Chosen Women

How was the Inca bureaucracy structured to meet the labor requirements of the state? How did kinship structure the elite class?

The Inca empire was known as *Tawantinsuyu*, or the land of four quarters. It was directed from the capital of Cuzco, at the center of the named quarters: *Antisuyu* covered the tropical lowlands; *Chinchasuyu*, the north coast and highlands; *Collasuyu*, present-day Bolivia; and *Condesuyu*, the south coast (see Figure 7.12a). Each quarter was directed by a member of the royal family and was subdivided into provinces, also ruled by the nobility. The eighty or so provinces were further subdivided into paired *suyus*, or moieties, which were ranked as upper and lower, and contained *ayllus*, or localized kin-based groups. Territorial units were defined in part by the individual *huacas*, or cult shrines, for which they were responsible, reminiscent of how Australian aboriginal estate groups, or clans, were responsible for Dreamtime sacred sites. In theory, productive lands were owned by the Inca state, temples, and local communities. Much land was centrally administered, but, as in Mesopotamia, the line between temple and state was not always clear, and newly elevated local elites administered many locally controlled estates. The empire was apparently not as monolithic as it might appear.

Much of the rural population was also organized as a labor force into a formalized hierarchy of

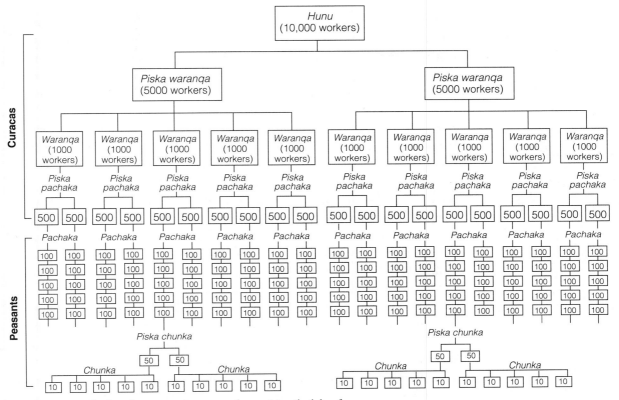

FIGURE 7.14   *The Inca bureaucratic system of organizing the labor force.*

workers in units that were subdivided alternately into units of two and five. The largest unit was the *hunu*, which contained approximately 10,000 workers. It was divided into two units of 5000 called *piska* (five) *waranqa*. Each *piska waranqa* contained five *waranqa* units of 1000 workers. The *waranqa*, in turn, were divided into two units of 500 called *piska pachaka*, which, in turn, contained five *pachaka* units of 100 workers (see Figure 7.14).

This bureaucratic system may have existed more in the mind of central administrators than in reality in the hinterland, but it did have some functional reality and is closely connected with the *quipu* recording system (see the box entitled "The *Quipu:* An Andean Information Storage System"). Decades after the Spanish conquest, local native leaders were still able to describe the system in de-

tail, and the Spaniards immediately recognized its utility as a census and control mechanism.

Superimposed on the hierarchy of territories and labor units was a hierarchy of offices and social classes and a variety of named occupational specialties and ethnic groups. Social status was defined by a dress code and associated privileges and duties. The Inca god-king was personally sacred in the same way as the Hawaiian rulers. He also married a full sister and was the head of the *Capac*

staple economy   The state-controlled production, storage, and distribution of subsistence staples, such as potatoes and maize in the Inca case, to support nonfood-producing specialist groups and to provide emergency aid.
wealth economy   The state-controlled production, storage, and distribution of wealth objects that support the status hierarchy.

The Quipu: An Andean Information Storage System

A social system as complex as the Inca empire required an effective system of information storage. Instead of writing, the Inca used a highly specialized information system based on bundles of knotted cord known as *quipus* (*quipu* means "knot" in Quechua), which closely paralleled the structure of the Incan bureaucracy as depicted in Figure 7.14. The *quipu* was a complex symbolic system of signs for recording statistical information by category of object. The signs were provided by a series of strings or cords, with multiple branches off the top and bottom of a central cord. Besides varying in position, individual pendant cords could vary in color, direction of twist, and ply. Even multicolored cords were used, such that hundreds of color combinations could be produced. Subsidiary cords could be attached at several places to create subcategories. Quantity was recorded using three different knot types and a decimal positional system employing a zero concept. *Quipus* were "written" to and "read" by a class of professionals known as *quipu camayo*, who must have resembled Mesopotamian scribes. The highly specialized knowledge involved in the use of the *quipus* has been described in detail by Marcia Ascher and Robert Ascher (1981).

The *quipu* is a good example of the many ways that cultures can be functionally integrated. The Aschers (1981) point out that *quipus* reflected many aspects of Inca aesthetics and other features of the culture that gave it a uniquely Inca ethos. For example, the Inca were concerned with spatial relationships, symmetry of pattern, portability of objects, methodical and repetitive design, and an overall conservatism, which can be seen in the Inca political system, architecture, ceramics, and textiles. On a much larger scale, the *ceque* system, which related *ayllu* social groups and *huaca* sacred places within a larger political whole, represented the same cultural reality.

A *quipu* might contain several thousand cords, but each cord occupied a specific place, oriented vertically along a horizontal axis. Like cloth, *quipus* were highly portable and based on spatial relationships. A *quipu* could be designed to represent different levels of the Inca bureaucracy and could record the quantities of goods such as various types of cloth, crops, and animals that were moved and stored, as well as the numbers of soldiers and workers of different types. It was an ideal device for keeping track of *mita* service and goods stockpiled in storehouses.

The Aschers (1981) emphasize the close parallels between Sumerian writing and the *quipu* and argue that *quipu* makers were, in fact, writing. The *quipu* could be read verbally, and the act of tying knots was tactilely and visually comparable to using a stylus in clay or a pencil on paper. Furthermore, both systems recorded information in the service of the state.

Ayllu, or Inca royal family, which consisted of a central patriline and nine ranked **cognatic lines,** or side branches. The members of the royal *ayllu* constituted the nobility, the highest social class, and were the most powerful officials in the bureaucracy. The Spaniards called them *Orejones,* or "big ears," because they were privileged to wear enormous gold earplugs and distinguished headgear. Their social status was finely ranked by genealogical distance from the Inca king.

According to the analysis of R. Tom Zuidema (1990), the marriage of the Inca king to his sister was a cultural statement that symbolically used kinship categories and marriage form to dramatize the hierarchical nature of Inca society. All those men within the royal *ayllu* in Cuzco who could claim descent from the Inca king belonged to *ayllus,* which were ranked in several ways. Descent was calculated back five generations to a mythical founding Inca king-ancestor, yielding a six-ranked generational system. The ruling Inca's direct line was considered to be a straight line, or *ceque,* and its members were most highly ranked, whereas those who belonged to a branch *ceque,* sister's-sons lines, were treated either as high-ranking "sons" with Inca mothers or as low-ranking "nephews" with non-Inca mothers. These categories may also be distinguished as "older" and "younger" sons, with older being superior. Men of the highest genealogical rank, and thus closest to the ruling Inca, were called lords and were associated with eagles; the most distant were called skunks and stinkers, thus emphatically spelling out their relative social worth, even though they were all superior to commoners.

Depending on the genealogical depth of their closest link to the royal *ceque,* these men might be actual grandsons, great-grandsons, and so on of the founding Inca ruler. Those called nephews were the children of the Inca's dozens of secondary non-Inca wives. Sons became administrators over the upper moiety of Cuzco, and nephews were placed in charge of Cuzco's lower moiety. Sons were associated with ruling lords, and younger sons or nephews were servants or priests and sometimes played ritual feminine roles.

Who the men of the royal *ayllu* were permitted to marry revealed their rank along a continuum from extreme endogamy to maximum exogamy, with marriage to the closest kin demonstrating the highest rank. The marriage of the king to his sister represented the highest degree of endogamy and was reserved for the highest-ranking person. Individuals ranking immediately below the Inca were permitted to marry half-sisters and parallel cousins. Third-ranking individuals could marry cross-cousins. Finally, people more than five generational ranks removed from the ruling Inca married non-kin, thereby reflecting maximum exogamy.

Zuidema (1990) shows that women of the royal *ayllu* were placed in six ranked *aclla* (chosen women), categories based on age grades that were associated metaphorically with an invidious ranking based on physical appearance. These age–beauty ranks apparently corresponded to the genealogically based male ranks, such that women of high-ranking genealogical standing relative to the ruling Inca were assigned to high-ranking *aclla* age grades. Those women who, because of their genealogical rank, were assigned to the most prestigious *aclla* group at approximately 20–24 years of age were considered "most beautiful" and remained in that category for life. They were never supposed to speak to men and performed ritual services in the most sacred shrines. Women of lower genealogical rank were selected for lower-ranked *aclla* age grades as they grew older, and they carried out lower-level ritual duties. For example, the three lowest *aclla* grades were joined at ages 35, 40, and 50, and these women wove textiles of increasingly lower quality and social worth. At age 35, an *aclla* could make very fine cloth for ritual use in the most important *huacas,* whereas women who became *acllas* at 50 years of age were commoners who made the most ordinary textiles such as belts and bags.

Below the nobility were *curacas,* officials who were in charge of decimal units down to the *pichaka* (100s) level. These Inca appointees held positions that became hereditary offices. Leaders of lower-level units were commoners. The highest non-*curaca* status was that of *yanacona,* who worked as retainers to the nobility. Raised as children in royal households, they were trained to become servants

---

cognatic line   A descent line that is traced to a common ancestor and that need not rely on exclusively male or female links.

and attendants in the palaces and temples. Sometimes they were rewarded with *Orejon* status.

The decimal-based hierarchy was well suited for labor mobilization, which was a primary and self-serving state function. For example, if a *hunu*-(10,000) level *curaca* needed to draft 1000 laborers, they could be readily assembled from the bottom up, if one man from the *chunka* (10) level was sent up the hierarchy. A typical labor assignment that was documented for four *waranqas* (4000 men) showed nearly half the men assigned to permanent assignments as *camayo* craft specialists, in the military service, and as *yanacona*. The other half served on rotating *mita* in the mines, on construction projects, and as soldiers and carriers (Julien 1982).

Inca Cosmology: The Universe Is Order and Sharing

How did Inca cosmology appropriate kin-based ideals to help villagers feel good about supporting the needs of the Inca rulers?

The Inca bureaucracy was based on traditional Andean cosmology and conceptions of spatial order and reciprocity, of which the Inca rulers were quick to make use. The concept of four quarters still organizes the space around rural Andean villages (Urton 1981). Conceptually, the quarters are derived from the great cross in the sky formed by the Milky Way as it shifts its position relative to earth between 6 PM and 6 AM. This sky cross defines a center and divides the night sky into quarters that people imagine projecting to the ground. Each village contains its own center, called *chawpi* in Quechua, and the individual quarters, or *suyus*, are usually grouped into upper and lower divisions. Imaginary lines, called *ceques*, radiate from the village center toward sacred points situated on the mountain skyline and along the way align with specific shrines or *huacas*.

Zuidema (1990) found that there were forty-two *ceques* in Cuzco, radiating as vectors or lines of sight toward the horizon as viewed from the main temple. There were 328 *huacas* located along the *ceque* lines. The *ceques* divided the province of Cuzco into territories, which were assigned to specific *ayllus*, *suyus*, and moieties. This system was integrated with a ritual calendar established by astronomical observations in which special rituals were performed sequentially at specific *huacas* on certain days of the year. The most important of these rituals concerned agricultural activities. The two most basic principles underlying the interaction among households within the village community and among households and nature and the Inca state were *ayni* (reciprocity) and *mita* (a turn or a share) (Earls and Silverblatt 1978). *Ayni* referred to the exchange of services between a variety of entities and was considered essential to the orderly operation of the cosmos. It applied to marriage exchanges, food and drink given for communal labor within the village, gifts of drink to the earth mother at harvest, and water cycling between earth and sky. Labor service to the state was also *ayni* and was rewarded by ritual *chicha* distributions. *Mita* added temporal order to *ayni*. *Mita* referred to crop rotation, calving seasons, human generations, and an individual's share in labor service to the state. *Ayni* and *mita* were thus ritually sanctioned as part of the natural order.

The divine right of the Inca to rule was supported by the Inca nobility's origin myth, which recounts how the first Incas conquered the indigenous inhabitants of the valley of Cuzco. This event is commemorated in the annual rituals that mark the first planting of maize and the harvest. These elaborate ritual events were presided over by the Inca ruler himself and by the nobility. Because no one in the empire could plant or harvest before these rituals were performed, they gave the Inca effective power over nature, in effect naturalizing their rule (Bauer 1996).

Figure 7.15 presents a native view of Andean cosmology based on a representation appearing in the temple of the sun in Cuzco, the imperial capital. To provide ideological support for a supreme ruler, the Inca elevated the creator deity, *Virakocha*, and the celestial sun god, *Inti*, to dominant positions above the pantheon of local mountain, earth, and lake deities that connected local communities with their territories. The cosmological model employs the Andean concept of *yanantin*, or balanced oppositions, and presents a parallel hierarchy of divinities, showing male and female aspects. It clearly

FIGURE 7.15
An Andean model of the place of people, culture, and the flow of energy in the cosmos, based on a plaque in the Inca temple in Cuzco. (SOURCE: Based on Earls and Silverblatt 1978.)

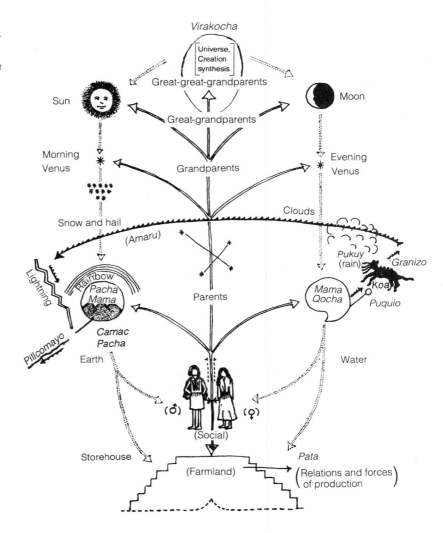

reflects the central elements of the state hierarchy, even to the detail of depicting *ayni* relationships and showing the state storehouse (*collqa*), terraced agricultural land, and a domestic couple as the foundation. This cosmological system shares some features with the Amazonian tribal cosmology (see Figure 3.16) discussed earlier, with which it is no doubt historically connected, but the Inca message is that giving labor to the state is part of the natural order.

Huanaco Pampa: An Inca City

How are the basic institutional structures of the Inca state represented in a typical administrative center?

All elements of Inca society are shown diagrammatically in the layout of Huanaco Pampa, a representative Inca city (see Figure 7.16). Huanaco Pampa was a planned city, built about AD 1475 as an administrative center. It covered 0.8 square

FIGURE 7.16
Layout of the Inca administrative city of Huanaco Pampa: a 0.8-square-mile (2-km²) planned city at 12,471 feet (3801 m), built around 1475; the Spanish took over in 1539. It had 4000 structures and 10,000–15,000 residents. (SOURCE: Based on Morris and Thompson 1985.)

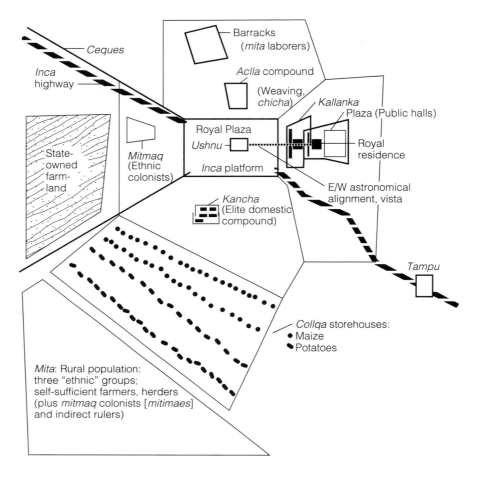

miles (2 km²) and was situated at an elevation of 12,471 feet (3801 m) in a prime potato-growing region. The city contained a special platform where the Inca ruler could lead public ceremonies, and a residence where he could be accommodated on royal visits. There were elite residences, barracks for rotating *mita* laborers, and great halls where they were entertained at ritual *chicha*-drinking feasts. The *aclla*, or chosen women, were securely sequestered within a walled compound (Morris and Thompson 1985). The city's primary function must have been warehousing great quantities of food, judging by the 30,065 cubic yards (yd³) (23,000 m³) of space in storehouses devoted to potatoes and 18,301 cubic yards (14,000 m³) for maize. The potato storehouses alone could have supplied more

than 50,000 workers a year with a pound (0.5 kg) of potatoes a day, which is more than the average daily consumption of potatoes by rural Andean peoples today (Orlove 1987). This calculation is based on a rough estimate of 36 pounds (16 kg) of potatoes per bushel and 33 bushels per cubic meter, less 25 percent for storage loss. If, as is likely, potatoes were stored in the form of freeze-dried *chuno*, then annual provisions for 100,000 people might have been stored in Huanaco Pampa. Additionally, the stored maize could have been used to brew vast quantities of *chicha* beer.

Some authorities consider food storage to be the most important functional advantage of state organization in the Andean region (D'Altroy and Earle 1985, Isbell 1978). The state storehouses could have served to average out environmentally determined fluctuations in food production, which occurred both seasonally and from year to year with *El Niño*–related events and unpredictable droughts and frosts. Large-scale storage might have raised the overall carrying capacity of the region. This food–energy averaging interpretation tends to support the redistributive social benefits theory of state origins, and many observers have described the Inca system as a great socialist welfare state. The Inca state could equally well be considered despotic and totalitarian because individual freedom was constrained by how wealth and power were distributed. The state moved whole communities at will and imposed a national language. The real advantage in expanding the scope of national control was that it increased the power of the privileged elite.

SUMMARY

The early state shows a systematic pattern of social inequality and concentration of power into relatively few hands. When modern scholars, who are themselves members of state systems, view these early states, they are impressed with the monumental architecture, great art, and massive technological achievements, and they minimize the social costs of such developments. Political-scale systems tend to expand to the limits, and sometimes beyond, what the natural environment can sustain because they reward individuals who manage to increase their personal power.

STUDY QUESTIONS

1. In what way is centralized political power a fundamental element of "civilization" as it is usually defined?

2. Discuss the role of irrigation, population, and political factors in the origin of the state, distinguishing between prime mover and multivariate theories. Refer to Mesopotamian case materials.

3. Discuss the explanations that have been proposed to account for the gradual process of plant and animal domestication in the Near East.

4. What archaeological evidence can be used to trace the earliest development of the state in Mesopotamia?

5. Describe the role of religion in the early Mesopotamian city-state. Make specific comparisons with religion in the Inca state.

6. What was the role of record keeping, and how was it carried out in ancient Mesopotamia and in the Inca empire?

7. Distinguish between wealth economy and staple economy, and show how each operated in the Inca empire.

SUGGESTED READING

ASCHER, MARCIA, AND ROBERT A. ASCHER. 1981. *Code of the Quipa: Study in Media, Mathematics, and Culture.* Ann Arbor: University of Michigan Press. Explains how the *quipu* was used to encode information.

EARLE, TIMOTHY K. 1987. "Specialization and the Production of Wealth: Hawaiian Chiefdoms and the Inka Empire." In *Specialization, Exchange, and Complex Societies*, edited by Elizabeth M. Brumfiel and Timothy K. Earle, pp. 64–75. Cambridge, Eng.: Cambridge University Press. Compares the political use of wealth in Hawaii and the Inca empire.

HADINGHAM, EVAN. 1987. *Lines to the Mountain Gods: Nazca and the Mysteries of Peru.* New York: Random House. Shows how Andean ideology and astronomical observations were related to the landscape.

KRAMER, SAMUEL NOAH. 1967. *Cradle of Civilization.* New York: Time-Life Books. A well-illustrated, popular description of Mesopotamian civilization by a respected scholar.

MORRIS, CRAIG, AND DONALD E. THOMPSON. 1985. *Huanaco Pampa: An Inca City and Its Hinterland.* London: Thames & Hudson. Uses archaeological analysis to describe an Inca city.

REDMAN, CHARLES L. 1978. *The Rise of Civilization: From Early Farmers to Urban Society in the Ancient Near East.* San Francisco: Freeman. Presents a complete overview of the origin of Mesopotamian civilization.

WOOLLEY, SIR LEONARD. 1982. *Ur "of the Chaldees."* London: Herbert Press. A detailed account of the royal tombs of Ur by the original discoverer.

8

The Chinese Great Tradition

In this chapter and Chapter 9, we will examine the great cultural traditions of China, India, and Islam. All are important area-study specializations that anthropology shares with history and geography. Because these cultures continue to shape the lives of well over half of the contemporary world's peoples, understanding them is essential to understanding world cultures. Traditional China is the largest imperial state to survive into the twentieth century on a preindustrial base. With a population that probably numbered 400 million people by 1850, China is a dramatic example of an empire based on moral authority and a superintensive agricultural system using human labor. Yet it was also the largest early literate civilization, with cities and a monetary economy continuously in place for more than 2000 years. Chinese villagers, as a tax-paying rural peasantry, provide a sharp contrast with the egalitarian, politically autonomous tribal villagers of Amazonia seen in Chapter 3.

THE CHINESE VILLAGE-STATE: MANDATE OF HEAVEN

In China, the politicization process produced a village-state civilization, which began with the Shang dynasty, perhaps as early as 2000 BC, and continued with only minor change up to 1949, when the People's Republic was established. As with Andean civilization, under the village-state mode of production, the persistence of Chinese civilization required self-sufficient villagers to support the royal capital and the ruling class with taxes, tribute, and labor. The villagers did so in the belief that the divine monarch would, in turn, keep the cosmos in order, thus ensuring the good life in the villages. Chinese cities were political and ceremonial centers where the elites and their retainers lived. They were sustained by the labor and surplus production extracted from the villages. The Chinese state was thought to function like an enormous village based on patrilineages, ancestor worship, and kinship-based reciprocity. Village life revolved around subsistence farming, the performance of rituals centered on nature deities and patrilineal ancestors, and the daily obligations of kinship and community. The ritual observances and sacrifices by the villagers were mirrored by similar rituals conducted in the royal capital for the benefit of the entire kingdom. Rulers were divinely appointed and held power as a "mandate from heaven" as long as they promoted village welfare and maintained order in the kingdom.

"Chinese" is not a single language, although there was a proto-Chinese common ancestor language. The predominant Chinese languages are all classified as Sino-Tibetan and are probably spoken by more than a billion people. Sino-Tibetan includes 8 modern Chinese languages and more than 200 other languages scattered throughout southern and eastern China, Tibet, the Himalayas, and Burma. (Japanese, Korean, and Mongolian are grouped in the Altaic language family, which also includes Turkish and Ainu [Ruhlen 1987].) The long use of a common writing system by speakers of related languages that are mutually unintelligible has led to the unfortunate use of the term *dialect* to refer to what are actually distinct languages. Chinese written characters are logographic—they refer to entire words and can retain their meaning with different pronunciation, in different languages. According to linguists, dialects must be mutually intelligible variations of a single language.

In China, the term *Han* is applied to all speakers of Chinese languages. Standard Chinese, or Mandarin, is spoken in northern China, and official Chinese is based on the Beijing dialect. All Sino-Tibetan languages are based on monosyllable words, and most are tonal—that is, the tone of a syllable constitutes a phonemic distinction, which makes a meaning difference in words.

The Nature of Early Chinese Civilization

What were the distinctive cultural features of Chinese civilization under the village-state mode of production? What was the material basis of Chinese civilization? What was the role of kinship? How did Chinese imperial cities differ from Mesopotamian city-states?

China is a vast subcontinental area of 3.6 million square miles (mi^2) (9.5 million square kilometers [km^2]), approximately the same size as the United States. In the south, China reaches into the tropics; in the north, it reaches the subarctic. Much of the eastern half of the country, including the Tibetan Plateau and the Xinjiang (Sinkiang) region, is mountainous, relatively barren, and inhospitable and will not be treated in this chapter. Eastern China is divided into a northern temperate zone and a southern subtropical zone, with a dividing line running midway between China's two great rivers, the Hwang Ho (Huang He), or Yellow River, in the north and the Ch'ang Chiang (Yangtze), or Long River, in the south (see Figure 8.1). The great Chinese agrarian civilizations developed on the rich alluvial soils along the lower reaches of these two rivers, primarily in the relatively flat plains and lake areas of the North China Plain at elevations below 650 feet (200 meters). The temperate Hwang Ho zone was the center of millet and wheat production, while the warmer and wetter Ch'ang Chiang tropical zone was the main rice-producing area. Collectively, these grains were the primary foods.

Marvin Harris (1988) characterizes traditional China as an agromanagerial state resembling the Inca state. The Chinese *peasantry* was subject to large-scale conscript labor service but, in theory, received emergency aid from the state in times of scarcity. The peasantry was also subject to the local elite, who extracted taxes and rents. A contrast can be drawn between this type of peasantry and European *feudalism*, in which serfs were granted hereditary rights to use land in exchange for payment of rent and military service to local lords. Chinese peasants were potentially subject to exploitation by both local elites and the central government, although the peasant was allowed relative freedom to relocate and upward mobility was possible.

Historian David Keightley (1990) finds that the institutionalization of *ancestor worship* by the Shang state had important consequences that helped set the future direction of Chinese civilization. With ancestor worship, the king was the central religious figure who served as his own priest, and the kingdom was in effect a *theocracy*. All lineage heads also worshiped their ancestors, and the whole kingdom was integrated as a single great

---

peasantry Village farmers who provide most of their own subsistence but who must pay taxes and are politically and often, to some extent, economically dependent on the central state government.

feudalism A political system in which village farmers occupy lands owned by local lords to whom they owe loyalty, rent, and service.

ancestor worship A religious system based on reverence for specific ancestors and sometimes involving shrines, rituals, and sacrifice.

theocracy State government based on religious authority or divine guidance. The Chinese emperor was the highest civil and religious leader.

FIGURE 8.1
*Map of the major rivers
and regions of China.*

politicoreligious family, leaving little room for conflicting loyalties. Ancestor worship, especially involving lavish mortuary gifts and human sacrifice, emphasized the permanence of the social hierarchy and kinship structure. There was no difference between the secular and the sacred, there was no ambiguity in the system, and everything was assumed to work as long as everyone followed their hierarchically structured kinship–ritual obligations.

Ancestor worship was thus a "strategic custom" that provided the foundation for the later elaboration of the concept of *hsiao*, or **filial piety.** In Mesopotamia, by contrast, there was a distinct priesthood, although temple and palace were not always in harmony, and the clan and lineage system was not institutionalized. Even though one can speak analytically of social classes in early China, the emic view of the social system was kinship-based, and the dominant value was family harmony. This certainly must have minimized the

potential for conflict that the grossly unequal flow of resources might otherwise have generated.

Wealth and power in the Chinese system derived from control of the labor force, as in Inca Peru. A vast conscript labor army was mobilized for the construction of the 1400-mile (2250 km) Great Wall along the northern boundary of China (see Figure 8.2) during the Ch'in dynasty (approximately 215 BC). Significantly, the major river valleys, as Keightley (1990) notes, run east and west and thus remain in broadly similar ecological zones, reducing the importance of trade and providing little incentive for the development of a merchant class. The Grand Canal, only one of many monumental water development projects, linked the Ch'ang Chiang in the south with the Hwang Ho in the north by AD 610, providing a major boost to trade.

Chinese cities contained temples and palaces and were walled like Mesopotamian cities, but there were important differences. Chinese cities

FIGURE 8.2   *The Great Wall of China, constructed along the northern frontier during the Ch'in dynasty, 215 BC.*

were intentionally designed to symbolize the emperor's central position in the universe. The city was a great square, aligned with the four cardinal directions, with the palace in the center, presumably aligned with the North Star on the earth's central axis. The world was literally thought to pivot about the emperor (Wheatley 1971, Wright 1977). In contrast to the Mesopotamian city-state, Chinese cities were not economically self-sufficient, but depended on their immediate hinterlands. They were not economic centers, but were designed to reproduce the political and ideological infrastructure.

The imperial system of Chinese government was an expansion of the earlier Shang system, and it remained in place with variations in detail until 1911, when the last emperor was removed from power. Historian Jack Dull (1990) distinguishes four stages in the development of Chinese government: patrimonial (1766–221 BC), meritocracy (221

BC–AD 220), aristocracy (220–906), and gentry (960–1911) (see Table 8.1). Over the centuries, the political structure varied with cycles of civil war and conquest, with fluctuations in the strength of the central government versus regional kingdoms, and with shifts in the importance of local families. Important changes also occurred in the system of recruitment to political office. The patrimonial stage will be described in the next section using the Shang example. The Chou dynasty, which overthrew the Shang, elaborated the concept of the mandate of heaven (*t'ien-ming*) as the formal legitimation of dynastic rule. Chou kings called themselves "The Son of Heaven" to emphasize that their rule was a mandate from heaven. This led to the related concept of the "bad last emperor" because a dynasty could end only when the mandate of heaven was withdrawn due to the emperor's misconduct.

The Ch'in rulers, who ushered in imperial rule in 221 BC, called themselves *Huang-ti*, literally "august god" usually translated as "emperor" because their kings were not considered to be gods. The imperial bureaucracy under the Ch'in was territorially structured and more elaborate than the familial organization of the Shang, presumably because the former patrimonial system could not deal with the increased scale of empire. The emperor had three officials and nine ministers who ran the central government. The hinterland was divided into forty-two commanderies (*chun*), subdivided into prefectures (*hsien*); each territorial unit had an imperially appointed administrator, an inspector, and a police chief. Imperial officials were "outsiders," prohibited from operating within their home territories to minimize opportunities for corruption. Regional governments developed their own large bureaucracies with many positions that, in theory, were filled by local individuals who were promoted on the basis of merit; thus, this entire period was characterized as a meritocracy. The constant struggle against corruption led to the creation of provinces as a higher-level political unit, whose officials could oversee the commanderies.

During the aristocracy period, recruitment to the bureaucracy was dominated by membership in

---

filial piety   *Hsiao*, the ritual obligation of children to respect their ancestors, and especially the duty of sons to care for shrines of their patrilineal ancestors.

TABLE 8.1 *Chinese Empires, 1766 BC–Present**

Modern China (AD 1912–)	1949–	People's Republic of China
	1912–1949	Republic of China
Gentry China (AD 960–1911)	1644–1911	Ch'ing dynasty: civil service exam abolished (1905); last Chinese monarchy
	1368–1644	Ming dynasty (Chinese rule)
	1272–1368	Yüan dynasty (Mongol rule)
	960–1279	Sung dynasty: civil service exam established; invention of movable type; Confucian-scholar officials
Aristocratic China (AD 220–906)	618–906	T'ang dynasty
	610	Great Canal built
	265–420	Tsin dynasty
Meritocratic China (221 BC–AD 220)		Han dynasty: paper invented (AD 105); Buddhism introduced (AD 65); Confucianism established as state orthodoxy (141–87 BC)
	202 BC–AD 220	
		Ch'in dynasty: imperial rule; hereditary rule abolished; written language standardized; Great Wall built
	221–206 BC	
Patrimonial China (1766–221 BC)		Chou dynasty: iron; cavalry; mandate of heaven established; written laws; era of Confucius (551–479), Mencius (371–289), Hzun Tzu (298–238); followed by Warring States (403–221)

SOURCES: Chang (1986) and Dull (1990).
*This is not an exhaustive list of all Chinese kingdoms and empires. Only the most prominent are included, corresponding to the major phases in political development. Precise dates used by different authorities do not always agree, and there are gaps in the sequence and in the historically overlapping empires.

a nine-level hereditary hierarchy of social status. Recruitment during the gentry period was based on the examination system, which became highly elaborated and allowed more social mobility than under the aristocracy. Prospective bureaucrats took highly competitive examinations in the Confucian classics. There were three exam levels: provincial, national, and imperial (palace). The system was potentially open to anyone who could gain admission to the government schools. Only 2–3 percent passed their preliminary exams and were permitted to take the palace exam; after passing the palace exam, the person was rewarded with entry to elite or gentry status and a position in the bureaucracy. The examination system, which was ultimately controlled by the emperor, reduced the potential conflicts between the aristocratic families and the government and gave more people an interest in maintaining the system.

High Shamanism: The Emergence of the Shang Dynasty

How did the earliest Chinese dynasty develop? How could shamanism, which is characteristic of domestic-scale cultures, be used to support the state?

The earliest Chinese states appeared by approximately 2000–1000 BC out of a Chinese co-tradition, or interaction sphere (see the box entitled "The Prehistoric Origins of Chinese Civilization"). Like Chavin in Peru and the Andean cultural tradition, the Chinese co-tradition contained elements that are still prominent features of Chinese culture and directly preceded the first Chinese urban civilizations (see Table 8.4). In the politicization process, towns became administrative and ritual centers, chiefs became kings who founded dynasties, simple writing systems were developed, and the production of crafts and specialized wealth objects was greatly expanded. This was the beginning of the period of initial Chinese civilization, which historians refer to as the Three Dynasties—the semimythical Hsia, the Shang, and Chou.

Shang (1766–1045 BC) is the earliest well-described civilization of early dynastic China, thanks to extensive excavations carried out since 1928 by Chinese archaeologists at An-yang, a major Shang center north of the Hwang Ho in Henan (Honan) province (see Figure 8.3). An-yang was a sprawling urban complex centered on a palace–temple complex of elaborate wooden buildings constructed on low platforms of stamped earth (see Figure 8.4). The center was surrounded by residential areas, cemeteries, and specialized workshops (Chang 1980). The graves of nobles and commoners were clearly distinguished by the quality and abundance of grave goods. In addition, rank was indicated by the better quality of the dentition in higher-status individuals. This suggests that social stratification, as defined by Morton Fried (1983), operated such that the nobility enjoyed better nutrition than commoners.

One of the most spectacular aspects of An-yang was the royal cemetery where eleven Shang kings and their consorts were buried. The royal tombs were wood-lined pits, up to 59 by 52 feet (18 by 16 m) at the top and 98 feet (30 m) deep, which were entered by four long excavated ramps oriented to the four compass directions. It is estimated that some 7000 working days may have been required in their construction (Chang 1986), but even more labor was invested in the treasure trove of bronze and jade grave goods.

Most royal tombs were looted over the centuries, but in 1976 an unlooted tomb belonging to Fu Hao, wife of a Shang king, was found to contain 440 bronzes, 590 jades, and many other bone, stone, ivory, and ceramic objects, along with 16 human sacrifices and 6 dogs. Similar to royal tombs at Ur, the An-yang royal burials and palace foundations were often accompanied by human and animal sacrifices. Whole chariots with horses still in harness were buried. One An-yang tomb contained 111 human skulls, and more than 600 people were sacrificed in the construction of a single Shang building (Chang 1980). Such large-scale sacrifices clearly foreshadowed the recently uncovered 7000-man life-size terra-cotta army buried with the first Ch'in emperor about 210 BC (see Figure 8.5).

Fried (1983) explicitly rejects the general interpretation accepted by many China specialists—that Shang civilization, as the earliest Chinese state, developed out of the Shang "tribe" as a result of warfare against neighboring tribes (see the box entitled "Tribe to State or State to Tribe?"). In Fried's view, there was never a discrete Shang tribe; rather, local domestic-scale village communities gradually became ranked and stratified as they grew. Tribes and *ethnic groups* were produced by states.

As Paul Wheatley (1971) pointed out, even though Chinese urban civilization emerged some 1500 years later than Sumerian city-states, urbanization in China apparently occurred independent of outside influences. There was no colonial expansion from Mesopotamia into China that might have led to the founding of urban centers, nor was there any obvious stimulus diffusion leading to the introduction of economic, religious, or political influences from Mesopotamia that might have indirectly stimulated cultural development. Stimulus diffusion could be said to occur if the *idea* for some cultural trait, rather than its direct transfer, inspires its development in another culture.

In K. C. Chang's (1983, 1986) view, the Chinese state emerged after political elites gained control of the religious system and used it to increase their political power, creating a self-reinforcing cycle of wealth and power that led to urban civilization. Such an interpretation shifts attention away from the Shang agricultural *infrastructure* and toward the political *structure* and ideological *superstructure*, emphasizing religion to an extent that might make a cultural materialist uneasy.

Chang calls the religious foundation of Chinese civilization high shamanism because it was a direct elaboration of the shamanistic communication with spirits that characterizes domestic-scale cultures. The official cosmologies of early dynastic China incorporated concepts of a stratified universe

---

ethnic group A dependent, culturally distinct population that forms part of a larger state or empire and that was formerly autonomous.

The Prehistoric Origins of Chinese Civilization

China is famous for the site of Zhoukoudian (Chou-k'ou-tien), west of Beijing (Peking), where fossils of the early hominid *Homo erectus*, dating to the Lower Paleolithic at approximately 1 million–200,000 BP (before the present), were discovered in the 1930s. *Homo erectus* began to look more like *Homo sapiens* beginning about 200,000 years ago (see Table 8.2), and fully modern peoples were clearly present by at least 25,000 BP. The pre-Neolithic of China is not well known, but this Late Pleistocene–Early Holocene period from about 15,000 to 7000 BP seems to mirror some of the general trends seen in other parts of the world, with foraging peoples steadily intensifying their subsistence activities. This trend is suggested, for example, by the appearance of microlithic tools—small, thin pieces of sharp stone, often a fragment of a long blade, which may be mounted on a shaft.

Wild rice and millet, which became the foundation of Chinese civilization, are spread through a wide zone from the Ganges region of India to southern China. Millet, which includes several grasses producing small round seeds, was being cultivated in the Hwang Ho river basin by 6000 BC, and rice in the lower Ch'ang Chiang region by 5000 BC, only a few centuries after their Neolithic counterparts in the Near East (see Table 8.3). Peter Bellwood (1985) speculates that domestication in East Asia may have followed a path similar to that of the Near East. The wild ancestral rices and millets may have expanded during favorable climatic conditions in the Early Holocene. The availability of very rich and predictable resources may have encouraged mobile foragers to sedentarize, which resulted in gradual population growth. Subtle climatic changes might have threatened the natural supply of the wild grains and encouraged people to turn to intentional

connected by a world tree, animal intermediaries, and transformations. The critical difference, however, was that unlike Amazonian or Australian shamanism, Chinese high shamanism involved highly exclusive communication with specific ancestors and deities who were sources of wisdom and supporters of the social hierarchy. Communication with the ancestors was by means of scapulimancy, which was conducted by full-time ritual specialists (see the box entitled "Early Chinese Scapulimancy").

K. C. Chang (1983, 1986) thus rejects many established theories of state formation that rely on economic determinants as prime movers. In his view, early Chinese kings did not gain their positions because they controlled irrigation systems, trade, or the means of production, as Marxist theorists would argue, or because certain social classes gained control over strategic subsistence resources, as Fried suggests. Chang notes that no significant change in Chinese agriculture preceded state formation. Bronze was an important technological innovation, but it was used to manufacture ritual paraphernalia, weapons, and chariots, which provided religious and military support for elite political power.

Shang Society

How was Shang society organized?

At the center of the Shang social hierarchy was the king, who was a member of the royal lineage (*wang* cultivation, selecting plants that produced larger, more numerous seeds that ripened at the same time and stuck together when harvested. T. T. Chang (1983) suggests that domestication may have occurred independently in China, at the limits of the natural range, where conditions would have been marginal and selection pressures most severe.

Early farming villages developed into seven regional cultures scattered throughout northern and southwestern China (Chang 1986). These apparently were domestic-scale, basically egalitarian cultures, with a wide range of domesticates, including millet, pigs, dogs, chickens, and water buffalo. People used stone sickles, mortars and pestles, and ceramics, including the three-legged pot, or *ting*, which later became such a prominent shape in bronze. The period from approximately 5000 to 4000 BC was characterized by steadily increasing cultural complexity, growing diversification, and emerging social ranking, as in the Mesopotamian and Andean regions. Status differences in burials appear in the Yang-shao culture in the lower Hwang Ho plain. K. C. Chang (1986) suggests that by 4000–2000 BC, a proto-Chinese interaction sphere had emerged. He infers that the expanding regional cultures had begun to influence one another such that a pan-Chinese culture could be distinguished on the basis of shared art styles, burial practices, and inferred common religious beliefs involving shamanism and ancestor worship. The best example of this period is the Lung-shan culture (3000–2000 BC), which showed the first bronze work, divination based on scapulimancy (divination using animal bones), elaborate burials, craft specialization, and large villages fortified with walls of stamped earth.

TABLE 8.2   *Paleolithic China, 1,000,000–10,000 BP*

13,000–10,000	Holocene begins; modern climate; foragers, microlithic tools
15,000	Sinodont population develops in China
20,000	Sundadont population expansion into China
50,000–12,000	Upper Paleolithic, *Homo sapiens*
200,000–50,000	Middle Paleolithic, early *Homo sapiens*
1,000,000–200,000	Lower Paleolithic, *Homo erectus* in the Zhoukoudian caves

SOURCE: Chang (1986).

tsu), within the ruling clan (*tsu*), a patrilineal descent group that was not strictly exogamous. In many ways, the Shang system shows striking parallels to the organization of the Inca royal *ayllus*, but the differences are obvious enough that no direct connections need be posited. K. C. Chang (1980) suggests that the Shang royal lineage was divided into ten ritual units named after the celestial signs naming the ten days of the week and structuring the ritual calendar. These units were

TABLE 8.3   *The Chinese Neolithic, 7000–3000 BC*

Yang-shao Culture (5000–3000 BC)	Postglacial climatic optimum; north greener, wetter, warmer; shifting settlement, cultivation; domesticates—millet, wheat, dogs, pigs, cattle, sheep, silk, hemp; painted pottery, domestic crafts; inferred clan and lineage organization; burials showing some status differences
Regional Neolithic Expansion (5000–4000 BC)	Increasing complexity, diversity, stratification; Yang-shao culture in Hwang Ho, with new cultures in the north and south
Regional Neolithic Cultures, Early Farming Villages (7000–5000 BC)	*North China, Hwang Ho:* four related cultures; semisubterranean round houses, sunken grain storage pits; stone sickles, stone mortars and pestles, microlith tools; domesticates—millet, pigs, dogs, chickens; deer hunted; stamped and marked pottery, *ting* tripod pots *South China, Ch'ang Chiang River:* three isolated cultures; domesticates—water caltrop (herbs), fox nut, lotus, arrowhead, water chestnut, rice, wild rice, bottle gourd, dog, pig, water buffalo

SOURCE: Chang (1986).

TABLE 8.4   *Chinese State Formation, 4000–1000 BC*

Early State, Urbanization, and Civilization (2000–1000 BC)	1400 1766–1045	Written records Late Shang dynasty: highly elaborate mortuary cults, "mortuary taxes"; hereditary rulers; earliest writing, bronze; in Zhengzhou (Chengchou), earliest urban center, rammed-earth construction, workshops, bronze foundry, distillery
Proto-Chinese Interaction Sphere (4000–2000 BC)		State threshold; regional interaction sphere; cultural exchange
	3000–2000	Lung-shan culture: permanent settlements; domesticates—rice, chickens; scapulimancy; burials distinguished by abundant wealth and elaborate ritual; ancestor cult; ceremonial crafts, ritual specialists, craft specialists; warfare, fortified villages, rammed-earth-walled towns; social stratification; copper objects, pottery wheel, earliest bronze implement (2500 BC), 139 signs on ceramics

SOURCE: Chang (1986).

arranged in two groups between which the kingship alternated according to specific rules of succession, with the alternate group serving as the king's councilors. The royal court contained the king's many wives or consorts, princes, and at least twenty categories of titled officials, such as priest, prime minister, and diviner. The court and its dependents must have been large, because individual kings are known to have had up to 64 wives and 120 diviners (Chang 1980).

The political power of Shang rulers is shown by the standing armies of up to 10,000 men that they commanded, and there are reports of some 30,000 war captives being taken in a single campaign. The

FIGURE 8.3
Map of Shang China,
1766–1045 BC.

army was organized into 100-man foot companies, with three companies to a regiment, and chariot companies of five chariots and 15 men, with five companies to a squadron. Troops were armed with bows, bronze halberds, knives, and shields. Rural towns were also organized as militia units and could supply thousands more troops if needed. Military force was an important means of expanding the state and maintaining internal order.

Law, in its formal sense (see the box entitled "The Law and the State"), supported the Shang social hierarchy, as in ancient Sumer, although no Shang law codes survive. Early historical texts referring to this period and fragmentary Shang records indicate that a well-developed court system must have existed. Subordinates were obligated to obey their rulers, and lawbreakers were harshly punished by various forms of shackling, mutilation, and execution. Rulers were obligated to not be too oppressive; if they failed, they faced supernatu-

ral punishments such as natural disasters or overthrow by a rival state.

The underlying religious basis of the Shang state was the assumption that the king was the exclusive channel, via his personal ancestors, to *Ti*, the high god, who was responsible for the welfare of the entire population and the fertility of nature. The king was a key node in a supernatural communication network. He called himself "I, The One Man" or "I, The Unique One," assuming absolute power as the parental authority over the whole land. By means of his diviners and through proper ritual, prayer, and sacrifice, the king could persuade his dead ancestors to appeal to the high god on behalf of the whole community.

The status and prestige of Shang royalty was further affirmed by the symbols of royalty: banners, battle axes, and bronze pots of particular size and shape, bearing specific decorations and inscriptions. Royal objects were often decorated with

FIGURE 8.4
Shang civilization, early dynastic China (1766–1045 BC). (a) Reconstruction of a wooden palace building; (b) structural model of the An-yang urban network during the Shang dynasty. (SOURCE: Chang 1980:130, Figure 38.)

(a)

(b)

KEY: N   Nobility
      C   Commoners
      I   Industrial workshops
      Ch   Chariot burials
      X   Inscribed oracle bones

stylized animals such as tigers, which reinforced the king's religious role, because animals also served as supernatural messengers in Shang mythology.

The Shang state, like the Inca empire, was divided into four quarters, oriented to the compass directions. Away from the capital, which was the political, economic, and ceremonial center, the hinterland population lived in walled towns (*yi*), ruled by lords. The king claimed formal title to all the

kingdom and was responsible for its welfare, but the lords personally managed it to maintain and increase the power of the royal lineage. New towns were centrally planned and built as a unit by ranked lords to whom the king granted a clan name, town land, a title, ancestor tablets, and appropriate ritual paraphernalia. The townspeople constituted the working class or peasantry (*ch'ung-jen*) and were organized into ranked patrilineages (*tsu*). Because

FIGURE 8.5   *A view of the life-sized ceramic troops buried as part of the royal tombs of the first emperor (Ch'in dynasty) over a unified China about 210 BC.*

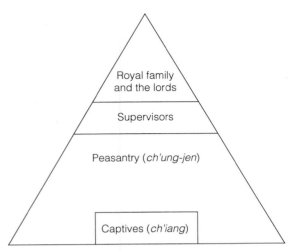

FIGURE 8.6   *Social hierarchy of the Shang state.* (SOURCE: *Chang 1980:231, Figure 60.*)

numerous pictographic lineage names depict various economic activities, lineages may have been occupationally specialized. War captives (*ch'iang*) were at the very bottom of the social pyramid (see Figure 8.6) and served as laborers; they also were probably the primary source of human sacrifices, because divination records list more than 7400 such victims (Chang 1980).

Modern Chinese scholars, following Marxist terminology, often refer to Shang as a slave society, whereas Western writers refer to a "free" peasantry. Probably only the war captives were slaves in a formal sense, but the bulk of the population enjoyed few of the benefits of their own labor. Even their semisubterranean housing symbolically separated them from the elite, who resided on stamped-earth platforms.

It is difficult to see what benefits, other than protection, the peasantry derived from the Shang state. Goods and services flowed to the center to support the army and the royal court, although some wealth returned as rewards to the lords ruling the towns. Writing was not concerned with recording economic transactions but dealt only with divination records and the identification of clans and lineages. There was no market system or trader class. Kinship obligations and religious duty were the primary foundations of the social structure, which basically resembled a political-scale Hawaiian chiefdom.

Confucianism and Liturgical Government

In what respects did the Confucian Great Tradition create a moral order that helped maintain a stable system of social inequality in imperial China?

Confucianism is a Western label for what the Chinese themselves referred to as *ju-chia,* "family of scholars." It is a scholarly tradition and moral order, based on the humanistic teachings of Confucius (K'ung-Fu-tzu, 551–479 BC). Confucianism was not a religion as such, but it became a virtual

Tribe to State
or
State to Tribe?

The notion that tribal organization was a necessary stage on the way to states and civilization is firmly entrenched in much of the anthropological literature and classical scholarship on China. However, this view obscures the egalitarian nature of domestic-scale cultures and the qualitative transformation that occurs when they become political-scale cultures. Many Chinese scholars were influenced by the theories of Karl Marx, Friedrich Engels, and Lewis Henry Morgan, all of whom identified some form of politically organized "tribe" as a precursor of the state. As these scholars defined it, the "tribe" is a loosely organized collection of villages or bands, united by common language and culture, under a centralized, noncoercive political leadership.

Morton Fried (1983) uses Chinese material to argue that prestate cultures did not form politically discrete "tribes"; rather, such bounded tribal organization results when autonomous local communities are intruded upon and consolidated by states for their own purposes. Prestate societies may indeed have shared common features of language and culture, as suggested by the proto-Chinese interaction sphere, but archaeologically defined cultures like the Lung-shan were not politically unified "tribes" under a central authority until ranked chiefdoms and states emerged. Thus, Fried would invert the sequence "tribe to state" to read "state to tribe." Discrete tribes are more easily exploited by states than the relatively amorphous and overlapping domestic-scale cultural systems that precede them.

Fried identifies an organizational sequence that runs from egalitarian (domestic-scale) cultures, to ranked cultures (chiefdoms), to stratified cultures, which may

state cult because it advocated filial piety and perpetuation of the ritual and political traditions of the Chou dynasty, which was at the core of Chinese civilization.

Confucianism taught that social order was based on virtue that came from ritual performance, beginning with household-level ancestor worship and moving up the hierarchy to the emperor. Confucius—whose teachings were preserved in the "Analects"—and other major teachers who followed, such as Mencius (Meng-tzu, 371–289 BC) and Hzun Tzu (298–238 BC), sought to promote practical ideals of good government, citizenship, and domestic life that would preserve a stable system of social inequality.

Confucianism was institutionalized by 124 BC with the creation of an imperial university focused on the five classics:

1. The *I Ching*, "Book of Change," is concerned with divination according to the principles of Confucian ethics and yin-yang complementary oppositions.

2. The *Shu Ching*, "Book of Documents," spells out the ideals of statecraft to be followed by the "Sage King" and all bureaucrats.

3. The *Shih Ching*, "Book of Songs," contains Confucian poetry.

4. The *Li Chi*, "Book of Rites," specifies the formal duties and rituals between social classes, kin, and husbands and wives.

5. The *Ch'un-ch'iu*, "Spring and Autumn Annals," deals with dynastic history (Wei-ming 1990).

Confucianism constituted the Chinese **Great Tradition**—elite culture, or high culture—because become states. The status differences in the Yang-shao burials suggest ranking and chiefdoms, whereas the larger mobilization of human labor implied by the monumental constructions and craft specialization of Lung-shan and the later Shang cultures suggest social stratification and either large chiefdoms or states. In the politicization process, individuals gain access to coercive political power by limiting the access of others to key subsistence resources. Fried (1983) sees the state arising because of the potentially disruptive contradictions between kinship-based sharing and the exclusion and exploitation of dependency relations created by social stratification. Fried argues that the state arises within individual communities, via stratification, and then produces tribes and ethnic groups:

The stratified local community that has gone into formal state organization . . . utilizes its less well-organized surroundings as a source of manpower and raw materials. In its expansion it creates tribes in the hinterland and ethnic groups within its own polity. (1983:480–481)

In this view, *ethnic groups* are understood to be formerly autonomous domestic-scale cultures that have been fully incorporated into the state yet still retain distinctive linguistic or cultural characteristics. State-created tribes are dependencies that retain more autonomy than ethnic groups because they are relatively remote from the centers of state power. These tribes may still be permitted to run some of their own village-level affairs, but they are nevertheless subject to various forms of state control. This interpretation accounts for the many linguistically distinct ethnic groups and "tribes" in China, as well as in the Andes and ancient Mesopotamia.

it was propagated by the literate elite and was directly involved with official ritual and the maintenance of the bureaucracy. Under Confucian ideals, which remained important until modern times, Chinese society was divided into a class system that was very similar to that of Shang times, but increased population resulted in extreme social inequality.

The Confucian Great Tradition represented the power of the state in the form of great palaces, temples, rituals, literature, and artworks, which collectively must have inspired feelings of awe and subordination in the commoners. This elite culture, together with the literate and institutionalized elements of Taoism and Buddhism, receives most attention from Western historians and students of comparative religion, art, and literature. However, commoners, who constituted 98 percent of the pop-

ulation, were only passive participants in the Great Tradition; they also maintained their own **Little Tradition,** or popular culture. (The Chinese Little Tradition will be examined in the section on village life.)

By the end of the Ch'ing dynasty, under the Manchu rulers (AD 1644–1911), some 700 people belonged to the emperor's clan at the top of the hierarchy (see Figures 8.7 and 8.8). Perhaps 40,000 more were part of the formal administrative bureaucracy. Beneath this group were four social

---

Great Tradition   The culture of the elite in a state-organized society with a written tradition that is not fully shared by nonliterate, village-level commoners.
Little Tradition   Ritual beliefs and practices followed by nonliterate commoners, especially rural villagers who are part of a larger state-level society.

Early Chinese Scapulimancy

The basic technique of divination by scapulimancy involves interpreting the pattern of cracks that develops in a heated piece of flat bone, such as a scapula or turtle plastron. In Shang China, scapulimancy was used to guide the conduct of official business in the royal court and was carried out by specialists at the request of the king (Chang 1980). A royal representative would submit an official yes or no question to the diviner—for example, asking whether a proposed military campaign would be successful. The diviner would then apply heat to a specially polished, grooved, and notched bone, usually a turtle plastron or water buffalo scapula. The preparation helped direct the cracking into a center-line crack with intersecting side cracks. The angle of the side cracks and other details were then interpreted by an official prognosticator, who came up with an answer to the question. Each piece of cracked bone was inscribed by an official archivist with signs and pictographic characters, recording the date, name of the inquirer, question, answer, and final outcome. These bones were then archived for future reference. Some 100,000 inscribed oracle bones have been recovered from An-yang, and they have provided detailed insights into the organization of Shang society.

The Law and the State

Law, if broadly defined as social control, is a universal (Hoebel 1968). However, significant differences exist between social control in domestic-scale societies—where basic equality and low population density reduce internal conflict to levels that kinship roles can easily manage—and that in political-scale societies. Political-scale societies face more difficulties. Anthropologist Leopold Pospisil (1972) identifies four attributes of law:

1. *Authority:* the ability to enforce a decision
2. *Intention:* the assumption that legal decisions will be applied universally
3. *Obligation:* specific rights and duties for different categories of people
4. *Sanction:* punishment for lawbreakers

These attributes can be recognized in the conflict-resolution mechanisms of some domestic-scale societies. Law as a formal concept, however, is most appropriately applied to larger-scale, ranked-and-stratified societies and especially to politically organized states, where it serves a critical social-control function. States have courts, judges, and formally codified laws, which may be written. The authority of a king comes from his executioners, the palace guard, and the standing army. Legal codes specify what a ruler can demand of his subordinate subjects and what the subjects can expect from their rulers.

FIGURE 8.7
*Map of Ch'ing China,
1900.*

FIGURE 8.8
*The structure of Ch'ing
society, 1900. Of the total
population, 7.7 percent
(30.8 million people)
was urban, and 92.3 per-
cent (369.2 million peo-
ple) was rural.*

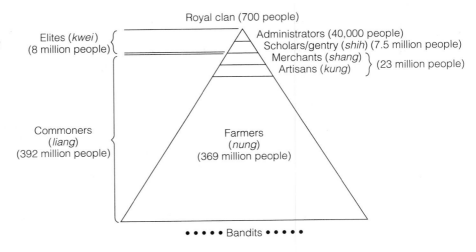

classes: (1) scholars (*shih*), (2) merchants (*shang*), (3) artisans (*kung*), and (4) farmers (*nung*). The 7.5 million or so scholar-bureaucrats were part of the privileged elite (*kwei*) gentry, who controlled local affairs and enjoyed many special privileges (Stover and Stover 1976).

The elite were set apart by special dress and their rigid adherence to Confucian ideals, linguistic forms, and ritual. In all, elites and their families may have totaled 8 million by 1900, perhaps less than 2 percent of the total population (Michael 1964, Wolf 1969). Some authorities distinguish between three elite subgroups: (1) the upper gentry, who were entitled to formal offices in the bureaucracy, (2) scholars who did not qualify for high office, and (3) nonscholars who derived elite status from independent economic or political power (Eastman 1988).

The bulk of the population, which may have grown to some 400 million by the mid-nineteenth century, constituted the commoners (*liang*), who were primarily farmers with very small landholdings. At the very bottom were outcasts, such as bandits and prostitutes.

Confucian concepts of formal ritual and etiquette, or *li*, regulated social conduct and helped people feel good about their social station. Leon Stover and Takeko Stover (1976) have characterized the Chinese system as **liturgical government,** or "culturalism," arguing that Confucianism created a form of moral nationalism that held the empire together in the absence of overt political or military force. According to the Stovers, the emperor occupied the ritual center of the world, where he held lavish state rituals and established a formal ritual calendar. The emperor lived a leisurely life of conspicuous consumption, defining and legitimating the cultural ideal for the elite. In this view, which was probably accurate only during certain historical periods, the emperor was a politically weak figurehead who supported himself from local tribute, the imperial monopoly on the Grand Canal connecting north and south China, the salt tax, and foreign trade. The emperor's primary political role was to award scholarly degrees and official appointments and to maintain overall peace and security.

The local nobility and elite had virtually full political and economic autonomy in the countryside. Because they earned only token salaries, they supported themselves by extracting taxes and rents from the peasantry. The provincial elite returned little material support to the center but acknowledged the superior status of the imperial court by following the centrally issued ritual calendar and by observing the *kowtow* (*k'ou-t'ou*), or ritual prostration. Whenever an official received a message from the emperor, the official was required to bow to his knees three times, rapping his forehead against the floor three times for each bow. This was a small cost to pay to support a high culture that quieted the peasantry with the sayings of Mencius and Confucius that "inequalities are in the nature of things" (Mencius) and that one should "seek no happiness that does not pertain to your lot in life" (Confucius) (Stover and Stover 1976:166, 170).

The Li Chi, "Book of Rites"

How did the Confucian classics codify in writing the visible cultural distinctions between ranks, offices, and social status in imperial China?

The Confucian classic, the *Li Chi*, was compiled during the Han dynasty in the first century BC by Confucian scholars. It specified details of dress, diet, ritual, and interaction between all ranks, offices, and kinship categories. The Inca state was no doubt guided by a similar cultural code; however, in the Inca case, the details were part of the oral tradition and were not compiled in a formal book. The *Li Chi* provides a remarkable inside view of the the cultural minutiae of the Chinese Great Tradition. For example, for state rituals during the first month of spring, the *Li Chi* specifies the alignment of stars; the day names to be used; the deities, animals, and musical notes, numbers, and tastes; the temple room in which sacrifices are to be offered by the emperor; the bells on the royal carriage; the type of horse drawing the carriage; the color of flags on the carriage; the color of the emperor's robes; and the type of jade ornaments on his cap. According to the *Li Chi*, the emperor is also supposed to eat mutton and wheat from vessels carved to represent sprouting plants, during the first month of spring (Legge 1967).

In excruciating detail, the *Li Chi* prescribes deference behavior between officials of different rank. For example:

All (officers) in attendance on the ruler let the sash hang down till their feet seemed to tread on the lower edge (of their skirt). Their chins projected like the eaves of a house, and their hands were clasped before them low down. Their eyes were directed downwards, and their ears were higher than their eyes. They saw (the ruler) from his girdle up to his collar. They listened to him with their ears turned to the left. (Legge 1967, vol. 2:17 [Bk. 11, sec. 3, pt. 1])

The respective contributions of individuals, families, officials, and the emperor to harmony are described as follows:

When the four limbs are all well proportioned, and the skin is smooth and full, the individual is in good condition. When there is generous affection between father and son, harmony between brothers, and happy union between husband and wife, the family is in good condition. When the great ministers are observant of the laws, the smaller ministers pure, officers and their duties kept in their regular relations and the ruler and his ministers are correctly helpful to one another, the state is in good condition. When the son of Heaven [the emperor] moves in his virtue as a chariot, with music as his driver, while all the princes conduct their mutual intercourse according to the rules of propriety [Li], the great officers maintain the order between them according to the laws, inferior officers complete one another by their good faith, and the common people guard one another with a spirit of harmony, all under the sky is in good condition. All this produces what we call (the state of) great mutual consideration (and harmony). (Legge 1967, vol. 1: 390–391 [Bk. 7, sec. 13])

When everyone does their duty, the living are fed, the dead are properly buried, and the ancestral spirits are taken care of.

Taoism and Buddhism

What other literate religious systems were part of the Chinese Great Tradition? How did these traditions relate to Confucianism?

Taoism and Buddhism are other important religious and philosophical systems that were part of the Chinese Great Tradition. Both had literate components and shared many elements with Confucianism, but they did not enjoy the official support the state gave Confucianism.

Most prominently, Taoism shares with Confucianism a concern with the *tao*, or "way," which could be identified with the "way of heaven" and all the cosmic forces, as well as with one's social and ritual duty. However, unlike Confucianism, which is strongly secular, Taoism is a mystical religious system that appealed to disaffected commoners and contained messianic elements that sometimes mobilized the peasantry to oppose the established political order. Taoism traces its origins to Lao-tzu (Lao-tze), a religious sage and contemporary of Confucius, who wrote the primary sacred text of Taoism, the *Tao-te Ching*. As a formal religious institution, Taoism has its saints and divinities, diverse sects and schools, and is represented in temples throughout China. There are full-time Taoist priests, who are celibate and live in monasteries. Taoist thought has been an important influence on both Confucianism and folk religion.

Buddhism reached China from India by AD 65, during the Han dynasty, and simply added another literate temple-monastic system and enriched the Chinese pantheon. It ultimately shaped the Taoist and Confucianist traditions and was absorbed into the folk religion, adding concepts of hell, sin, *karma*, and judgment.

DAILY LIFE IN VILLAGE CHINA

Farmers of Forty Centuries

How did preindustrial Chinese agriculture support dense populations and maintain soil fertility?

U.S. Department of Agriculture soil scientist and agriculture professor F. H. King (1911) visited China and Japan during the first decade of the twentieth century to learn how these "farmers of forty centuries" could support dense populations and still maintain soil fertility after so many years of permanent agriculture. King found that Chinese farmlands were being cultivated so intensively that they directly supported 1783 people, 212 cattle or oxen, and 399 pigs per 1 square mile (2.6 km²), nearly thirty times the comparable human density for the United States at that time. He attributed the success of Chinese agriculture to favorable climate

---

liturgical government   The use of ritually prescribed interpersonal relations and religious, moral authority as a primary means of social control in a state-level society.

and soils and choice of crops, along with labor-intensive multicropping, intertilling, and terracing and highly efficient use of water and organic fertilizer. He estimated that some 200,000 miles (321,800 km) of major canals supported rice cultivation. Soil fertility was maintained by composting, reclamation of canal mud, manuring, and extensive application of night soil, or human waste. Soil and subsoil were sometimes carried to the village to be mixed with compost and then returned to the field. King credited the Chinese with judiciously rotating legumes in their gardens to improve fertility, even though Western scientists failed to understand their nitrogen-fixing role until 1888. Most of all, King was impressed with the Chinese economy of resource use:

Almost every foot of land is made to contribute material for food, fuel or fabric. Everything which can be made edible serves as food for man or domestic animals. Whatever cannot be eaten or worn is used for fuel. The wastes of the body, of fuel and of fabric worn beyond other use are taken back to the field; before doing so they are housed against waste from weather, compounded with intelligence and forethought and patiently labored with through one, three or even six months, to bring them into the most efficient form to serve as manure for the soil or as feed for the crop. (1911:13)

Prerevolutionary China's 500 million people were supported by very small farms, usually of less than 5 acres (2 hectares), which were concentrated on just 8 percent of the land. As the Stovers (1976) noted, the Chinese agricultural strategy was to apply human labor intensively to the lands that would yield the greatest return per acre. They argued that, in a sense, Chinese agriculture was a capital-maintaining, labor-absorbing, intensive hand-gardening system, in which the real crop was human beings. People were produced in the smallest possible space at the lowest energy cost. A similar intensification process in Java has been called *agricultural involution* (Geertz 1963).

In parts of southwest China where the population is low, rice is grown by shifting cultivation in clearings in forested uplands. Rice seeds can also be broadcast onto plowed fields, but the highest yields are obtained when seedlings are grown in nurseries and transplanted by hand into specially prepared diked fields (see Figure 8.9). This is very intensive and highly skilled work. Carefully regulated irrigated flows of river water maintain a delicate ecosystem with the essential nutrients, fungi, and bacteria that produce maximum rice yields. Anthropologist Lucien Hanks (1972) pointed out that although transplanted rice brings the highest

FIGURE 8.9
Chinese wet-rice agriculture, a highly labor-intensive system that produces enormous per-acre yields on a sustainable basis.

TABLE 8.5   *The Productivity of Chinese Intensive Agriculture (kcal/kung/year), Luts'un, Kunming, 1940*

	Picuals	kg/year	kcal/kg	Total kcal
Rice, Hulled	3.8	192	3600	691,200
Broad Beans	2.6	130	3380	439,400
Green Beans	1.0	50	320	16,000

Total kcal produced: 1,146,600
Input: 20.3 days × 7.5 hours × 150 kcal = 22,837
Output–input ratio: 50.2 to 1

Comparison with U.S. Rice Production

	kg/Acre	kcal/Acre
U.S., 1975		
Hulled		
Rice	828	298,080
Luts'un, 1940		
Multicrop	5952	18,345,600

SOURCE: Fei and Chang (1945:70, Table 12).
NOTES: The caloric value of "waste" by-products such as bean stalks, rice hulls, and straw, which are used as animal feeds, are not included. 1 picual = 50.1 kg; 1 *kung* = 250 m² of land, 40 *kung* = 1 hectare, 16 *kung* = 1 acre; 1 *kung* of labor = 1 person day of labor, 7.5 hours; 1 hour of labor = 150 kcal expended.

returns, it requires large, precisely timed labor inputs for uprooting seedlings, replanting, and harvest and thus is impractical unless population is high and landholdings small. I have observed intensive rice replanting in the Philippines by wage laborers on vast commercial estates using chemical inputs, as well as by tribal Ifugao villagers on steep hillsides. The Philippine Ifugao fully appreciated the ecological complexity of their terraced paddy system. Given an appropriate labor force and small landholdings, villagers do not consider capital-intensive technological innovations such as mechanization to be an advantage. Thus, not surprisingly, virtually all of the seventy-seven farm implements described in traditional Chinese agricultural manuals published since AD 1313 were still in use in the mid-twentieth century (Perkins 1969).

The productivity of labor-intensive Chinese agriculture is remarkable. In 1940, researchers investigated a village of 611 people, which they called Luts'un, in central Yunnan province in south China (Fei and Chang 1945). They found that when multicropped, a standard 2688-square-foot (250-m²) unit of land (called a *kung*) produced 821 pounds (372 kilograms [kg]) of rice and beans per year, yielding approximately 1.147 million kilocalories (kcal) of food. This assumed good-quality land and an input of 152 hours of human labor (see Table 8.5). This is more than sixty times the per-acre productivity from industrially grown American rice in 1975, which required enormous inputs of chemical fertilizers, pesticides, and fossil fuels. The Chinese production system yielded a return of 50 kilocalories of food energy for each kilocalorie of human labor expended, whereas the American rice was grown at an energy deficit because of the energy cost of the fossil fuels expended.

The Stovers (1976) further observed that the Chinese subsistence system is effective because it makes limited use of draft animals or animal protein. The Chinese diet is typically vegetarian, with only 2–3 percent of the caloric intake derived from meat (Eastman 1988). Only chickens, ducks, and pigs, which are scavengers, are raised to be consumed. They can also be fed rice hulls and bean stalks, whereas large draft animals are costly to feed, especially if valuable cropland is devoted to

---

agricultural involution   Geertz's concept of a labor-intensive agricultural system that provides an incentive for population growth.

raising animal food. In some areas, fish ponds were also a significant source of food.

Immiseration, Overpopulation, and Exploitation

Does China represent a clear case of population growth outstripping food-producing capacity, as Malthus predicted?

With periodic wars and famines, the population of China fluctuated between 30 and 60 million people during most of the first millennium AD, jumping to 100 million by AD 1100, then moving steadily upward (see Figure 8.10). The most dramatic change was the fivefold increase that began after 1400, during the Ming dynasty, and approached 500 million by the end of the Ch'ing dynasty in 1911. By 1975, China's population reached 800 million, and, by 1990, it exceeded 1 billion. Several factors have been proposed to explain the Ming–Ch'ing increases, including a prolonged period of peace and stability; improvements in health, such as the development of smallpox vaccinations in the sixteenth century; the introduction of new food crops from the Americas; and a global warming trend that improved agricultural conditions (Eastman 1988).

Although population growth had fundamentally changed the scale of Chinese society by 1900, the culture remained basically the same, and many observers argued that the Chinese peasantry was undergoing a steady Malthusian *immiseration,* or impoverishment. The English demographer Thomas Malthus (1766–1834) theorized in his famous *Essay on the Principle of Population* ([1798] 1895) that populations naturally increased faster than their food supply and were limited by the misery that ensued when poverty set in. However, the Chinese case demonstrates that cultural factors significantly shaped how Malthusian pressures were felt. By 1900, China's population was ten times larger than during the 2000-year period between 1000 BC and AD 1000, when the basic cultural system of a stratified, agrarian state was established, with a ranked bureaucracy extracting taxes, rents, and labor from the peasantry.

Large-scale migration out of the lower Hwang Ho and Ch'ang Chiang floodplains, as well as further agricultural intensification during the Ch'ing dynasty, helped the standard of living keep up with population growth. Pioneer expansion into the forested and hilly autonomous tribal areas of south and central China, and into Taiwan and Manchuria, accounted for a significant portion of the population increase. Large-scale deforestation and erosion accompanied this expansion, resulting in drastic changes in the Chinese landscape. Farmers tended to cultivate smaller plots more intensively. Maize, potatoes, and sweet potatoes from the New World complemented existing crops and certainly increased productivity. The fragmentation of plots was accelerated by the Chinese practice of giving each son an equal division of the family land. There were also incentives for population growth. Patriliny and ancestor worship provided strong cultural reasons for having sons; indeed, Confucian ideals stressed the importance of maintaining the lineage. Furthermore, agricultural intensification depended on greater and greater inputs of human labor, as discussed previously.

It is difficult to demonstrate the extent to which conditions for the peasantry deteriorated significantly with population increase. Albert Feuerwerker (1990) argues that per-capita economic productivity peaked during the Sung dynasty (AD 1000) and that there was no significant change in the basic standard of living until after 1900, despite population increase. However, other researchers point to a steady reduction in the urban proportion of the population and the increasing fragmentation of land as evidence of overpopulation (Chao 1986). Kang Chao also argues that population growth prevented an early industrial revolution in China, even though China in AD 1000 was technologically more advanced than Europe, because there was no incentive to produce labor-saving machinery.

Lloyd Eastman (1988) suggests that immiseration was a myth because the lot of the peasantry had always been poor, although conditions reached a low during the political and economic upheavals of the 1930s and 1940s. However, the fact that the population continued to increase suggests that, contrary to Malthusian predictions, conditions did not become absolutely intolerable. Perhaps the most important factor underlying the pervasive impoverishment of the peasantry was the operation of a highly nonegalitarian market economy in which

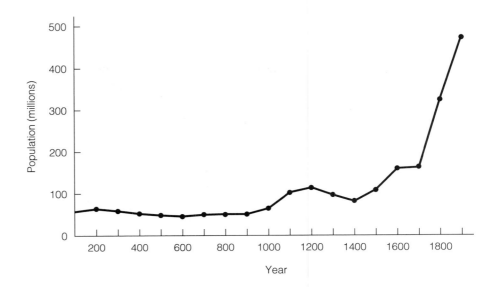

FIGURE 8.10
Chinese population growth, AD 100–1900. (SOURCE: Feuerwerker 1990.)

most of the population were subsistence farmers. The class structure in which a small elite controlled most of the best farmland kept the poorest classes at a permanent disadvantage. Peasants paid rent even to use "communally" owned clan land, and privately owned plots were often only tiny inheritances. Cash cropping to pay for land was risky and could undercut subsistence production.

The extent of social inequality at the household level in village China by 1940 is clearly shown in the data collected by Hsiao-Tung Fei and Chih-I Chang (1945), which revealed three social classes in the village of Luts'un. At the top was a landowning leisured class that managed its land to produce enough subsistence and cash crops to ensure a minimum standard of living for the least effort. Men in this group often refused to engage in any agricultural labor and spent their time relaxing and smoking. The "middle" class was composed of owner-tenants who had to rent additional land to farm in order to produce a slim subsistence margin. At the bottom was the landless class—those who had to survive by hiring out their labor and purchasing basic necessities. In Luts'un, 41 percent of the farmland was owned by 15 percent of the households, and 31 percent of the households were completely landless. Nearly half of these nonlandowning households were too poor to even rent land.

Energetics analysis (comparing annual input and output ratios, and energy flow patterns between a modest landowning household in Luts'un village and a landless household) dramatically illustrates the physical dimensions of this social stratification (Bodley 1981b). The sample households differed in size, with five individuals in the landholding family and only two in the landless household. The landowning household controlled only 27 *kung* (1.6 acres [0.65 hectares]), which placed it in the lower range of the landowning class, but it still enjoyed a comfortable standard of living. When the caloric value of rice was used as a cash equivalent, the landed household showed a potential per-capita food consumption five times that of the landless household. On a per-capita basis, it also consumed more than four times the goods and produced at more than twice the energy efficiency of the landless household. The wealthy household had enough savings to last it for 1 year and was able to support pigs with its garden waste. The poor household was able to purchase only enough rice to meet its minimal caloric requirements and had difficulty meeting its protein needs. There was

immiseration Malthusian impoverishment, a declining standard of living attributed to continuous population growth on a limited-resource base.

FIGURE 8.11
Chinese market towns grouped about higher-level central places as predicted by central-place theory. (a) Map view of towns and the road network; (b) a diagrammatic view on a hexagonal grid (numbers represent market days in 10-day weeks). (SOURCE: Skinner 1964.)

(a)

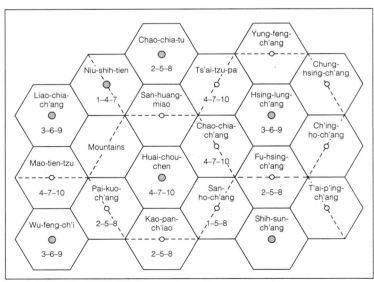

(b)

little left over for housing, clothing, fuel, or medical needs. Significantly, the poor household paid enough in rent and taxes to support two additional people, and this was actually more than was paid by the wealthy household. Inequality of this magnitude could not have existed in an unstratified tribal village.

It would seem appropriate to call the Chinese system exploitative, at least by late Ch'ing times, if *exploitation* is defined as the unjust or improper use of another person for someone else's benefit. In Marvin Harris' (1988) view, exploitation exists if the lower class is deprived of basic necessities relative to the upper class and if the upper class derives luxuries from the lower class yet refuses to redistribute its wealth. By this definition, exploitation was probably a frequent social problem in Chinese civilization. Confucian teaching explicitly condemned such abuse of the peasantry because it was not good government, and Buddhist and Taoist sages spoke against it. However, inequities of wealth and power were inherent features of the Chinese state. Whether the Chinese peasantry conceived of themselves as an oppressed social class in an emic sense is another matter. From a social scientist's etic perspective, social classes existed in China for at least 4000 years, but the powerful ideology of ancestor cults and Confucianism made such inequality seem part of the natural order of things. Furthermore, the examination system always held open the possibility of upward mobility.

The Chinese Village System

How were relatively self-sufficient villages interconnected in regional networks that formed the basic unit of Chinese folk society?

The daily life of the Chinese peasantry was centered on the highly self-sufficient village, which probably contained an average of 400–500 people, approximately the same number as in Australian "tribes" or the largest Amazonian village communities. Unlike these domestic-scale societies, which maintained essentially horizontal interaction links with structurally similar neighbors, however, Chinese villages were the lowest rural units in an organizational hierarchy ultimately linking them to the imperial center. This system of social, economic, ritual, and political ties linking the literate elites of the Great Tradition and the peasantry of the Little Tradition has been called the *folk-urban continuum* (Redfield 1941). Cultural elements of the Great Tradition are most prominent in the urban capitals and decline steadily as one moves toward smaller towns and villages, where the Little Tradition becomes strongest.

In China, G. William Skinner (1964) has used central-place theory (see Chapter 7) to show that villages group themselves around local centers, which he calls standard market towns, in order to most efficiently exchange their produce for the limited range of goods and services that they cannot produce themselves. Villagers were usually self-sufficient in food, but they purchased such items as lamp oil, candles, incense, needles, soap, and matches and occasionally made use of blacksmiths, coffin makers, medical practitioners, scribes, and ritual specialists.

Skinner (1964) found that an average of eighteen villages were arranged about a standard market town within an area of some 19 square miles (50 km²), such that the most distant village was only about 3 miles (5 km) from the center, although where population density was low, the most remote villagers might need to walk 5 miles (8 km) to town (see Figure 8.11). Markets were held in adjacent market towns according to a regular schedule, following the lunar calendar, that divides the month into three 10-day "weeks." A typical cycle meant that a market would be held in the same town every 5 days; thus, an itinerant peddler or specialist could visit a different market every day and thereby greatly increase his potential customers. This system made it possible to efficiently sustain a very large and dense rural population without a costly and fuel-intensive transportation technology such as developed in industrial Europe and North America.

Skinner (1964) argued that the villages using a standard market town constituted the basic unit of the Chinese Little Tradition, or folk society. These

***

exploitation Unjust use of someone to differentially benefit another, especially when one social class is deprived of basic necessities while the elites live in luxury.
folk-urban continuum Redfield's concept of a gradual distinction between the Little Tradition culture of rural commoners and the Great Tradition culture of the urban elites in a political-scale culture.

7000 or so people formed a relatively discrete social network that regularly interacted on market days and was united by ties of kinship and marriage. They thought of themselves as a group; shared details of dress, ritual, and dialect; and sometimes even used their own system of weights and measures. The market town was where the villagers paid their rents and taxes; it also contained religious shrines, and teahouses where the members of secret societies and mutual aid societies could meet. With its varied specialized functions, the market town often served as the power base of a single large lineage or clan, whose various members might be localized in villages within the market district.

An average of six standard market towns were grouped in hexagonal territories around an intermediate market town where the local gentry conducted much of their business (see Figure 8.11). Intermediate market towns were often enclosed by walls and contained a temple to an urban deity. They might serve an overlapping area of 135 square miles (350 km²) containing 50,000 people and were connected, in turn, with a central market town, where the lowest-level officials of the official bureaucracy were located. People maintaining connections between intermediate or central market towns likely were literate elites, whereas most peasants never left their local market districts.

In theory, Chinese social organization was based on the patrilineal *tsu*, usually translated as either "clan" or "lineage." These genealogically defined units were segmented, localized, property-holding groups, with a specific surname and clan temples or halls, where tablets dedicated to specific clan ancestors were kept. Villages or towns might be dominated by a single clan, with lineage segments occupying specific blocks. There might also be written genealogies of remarkable depth. For example, a village of 1100 people examined in Guangdong (Kwangtung) province in 1957 contained members of two clans. The dominant clan preserved ancestor tablets back forty-two generations to the founding of the village in AD 1091 (Freedman 1966).

There are conflicting interpretations of how Chinese descent groups were organized and how they functioned. Francis Hsu (1963) probably presented an incomplete picture when he described the "clan" as a large extended family, which forms a warm,

peaceful, mutually self-contained unit. Freedman (1966) called the same descent group a "lineage" and stressed that it was characterized by both internal conflict and harmony, similar to the Nuer system of segmentary opposition. Freedman speculates that Chinese lineages may have gained special importance as landholding groups when lineage members cooperated in the development of local irrigation systems for wet-rice agriculture or formed self-defense groups on the frontiers of pioneer settlement.

Village Cosmology and the Little Tradition

What were the basic features of village-level ideology and ritual in China? How did these beliefs and practices differ from the Confucian Great Tradition?

In their daily lives, the commoners directly perpetuated shamanistic cultural traditions that were rooted in the Neolithic past, underlying both the Great and Little Traditions. Commoners practiced a syncretistic folk religion that drew freely on elements from formal Confucianism, Taoism, and Buddhism. Part-time Taoist priests, who did not live in the monasteries, were often called on as ritual specialists to perform at marriages, funerals, and curing ceremonies. The most prominent cultural elements shared by elites and commoners included the basic family system, with its emphasis on patrilineal descent lines and the ancestor cult, and basic cosmological traditions. The lowest-level deity, who operated at the household level, was the stove, or kitchen, god, who symbolized the domestic unity of the family. The stove god represented the bureaucracy and could report directly to the god symbolizing the emperor in the supernatural bureaucracy (Wolf 1974).

Complementary opposition, a prominent element in Australian and Amazonian cosmologies, was also a basic feature of Chinese popular culture. Complementarity was represented in Chinese cosmology by the yin-yang concept, symbolized in Figure 8.12. Yin is female, passive, dark, and cool, and is associated with earth, winter, valleys, tigers, and the color orange. Yang is male, light, and hot, and is associated with heaven, summer, mountains, dragons, and the color blue. The yin-yang concept was formalized by the Great Tradition dur-

FIGURE 8.12
Yin-yang.

ing the early dynasties and combined with other philosophical features such as the concept of the five elements—metal, wood, water, fire, and earth—which were connected in a transformation cycle emphasizing balance, harmony, change, and continuity. According to five-element philosophy,

> Water produces Wood but overcomes Fire
>
> Fire produces Earth but overcomes Metal
>
> Metal produces Water but overcomes Wood
>
> Wood produces Fire but overcomes Earth
>
> Earth produces Metal but overcomes Water
> (Chai and Chai 1967:lxviii)

The five elements were correlated with colors, directions, musical notes, and periods of Chinese history to produce an elaborate, often occult, cosmology. Color symbolism has also been important in Chinese popular culture. White, considered the color of mourning, was associated with the west, and the east was blue-green. Red was auspicious and south, black was north, and yellow was associated with the emperor (Rawski 1987).

This popular belief system has sometimes been called a correlative cosmology because it provided a framework that helped elites and commoners alike structure their daily lives in proper alignment with the cosmic forces to guarantee prosperity. Concern for proper alignments was reflected in the layout of cities, temples, tombs, and houses; in the timing of ritual events; in the selection of mates; and in the seating of guests. Specialists in geomancy took cosmic forces into account when they studied the topographic details of a particular locality to select the most auspicious location for houses and graves. Correlative cosmology also influenced popular medicine, diet, and astrology.

Domestic Life and the Role of Women

How were Chinese families organized? What cultural factors seemed to subordinate Chinese women to men?

Given the patrilineal descent system, the ideal Chinese nuclear family would produce many sons who would bring their wives to live in their father's house, or at least to his village. This would increase the strength of the lineage and ensure its perpetuation. Wealthy families could also add new members by adoption. Maurice Freedman (1966) described two broad types of Chinese families by size. The ideal was a large family containing two or more married sons, often called a joint family. The small family was either a nuclear family with no married sons or a stem family with only a single married son. Joint families were likely to be relatively wealthy, and they could form large lineage segments, whereas small families were usually poor members of disappearing lineages. The male members of Chinese families, large or small, held joint property, which was usually divided equally.

Western observers often regard the position of women in Chinese society negatively. Sons were said to be preferred over daughters and women did not own lineage property. Furthermore, a child bride was dominated by her mother-in-law. Such domination, which reinforced the control of the extended family by the elders, was reflected in the common practice of adopting a girl into the family for the son to marry (A. Wolf 1968). Marriages were often arranged, and even though monogamy was the pattern, concubinage occurred, divorce was difficult, and widow remarriage was discouraged. Upon marriage, a woman was virtually absorbed into her husband's family. Marriage was so essential for women that if they died unmarried, their spirits could be married later in a pattern reminiscent of Nuer ghost marriage.

Footbinding produced small, stunted feet, leaving many women virtually crippled. This practice demonstrated a man's affluence because it meant that his wife did not do heavy domestic work. But footbinding was apparently not limited to the elite. It was thought to make women more attractive, but

The Meaning of Chinese Kinship Terms

Chinese kinship terminology is complex because of the great diversity of terms that can be employed, but careful linguistic analysis reveals an orderly system that reflects the organization of Chinese society. In his study of the kinship terms used in Guangdong province by male speakers of Toishan, a Cantonese dialect of south China, John McCoy (1970) listed sixty-nine different terms used in indirect reference to kin and some fifty-three terms used in direct address. Table 8.6 presents a simplified list of thirty-five selected terms drawn from this list, but representing only terms used by males for five generations of consanguineal kin, excluding affines. The Chinese terms appear in column 2 in phonemic linguistic notation. The terms can also be written using Chinese characters to represent each syllable. Column 1 describes the terms using the abbreviated primary kin terms introduced in Chapter 2 (two new abbreviations are O, which means "older," and Y, which means "younger").

The formal components of Chinese kin terms are coded in the right-hand columns and are diagrammed in Figure 8.13. *Componential analysis* is a formal way of exploring the meaning of kinship terms (see, for example, Goodenough 1965 and Lounsbury 1964). A kinship terminological system is a list of words applied to an individual's relatives. The meanings of different terms can be described according to a logical set of rules based on specific contrasts in meaning. In the Chinese kinship system, a mere five points of contrast, or components, are used to define the meaning of each kin term: descent, collaterality, generation, sex, and relative age. For example, the Chinese term *fu 4 thin 2*, "father," means a male, related lineally to ego through the male line, one generation above ego. An advantage of componential analysis is that terms can be described without reference to primary

---

it also supported the ideal of wifely virtue by making it more difficult for women to venture unattended from the home (Ebrey 1990).

This picture of female subordination is incomplete. Freedman (1979) points out that Chinese women bring a sizable endowment of domestic articles and personal wealth with them when they marry. A woman can also manage her husband's share of the family estate, and she owns her private earnings. Although new daughters-in-law may be treated harshly, they will become mothers-in-law in turn. As a wife, a woman has important responsibilities in domestic rituals, and her tablet will rest in her husband's ancestor hall (see the box entitled "The Meaning of Chinese Kinship Terms").

The House of Lim: Chinese Marriage, Family, and Kinship

What inherent tensions disrupt Chinese family life?

The intimate realities of a Chinese joint family and its stresses and strains as a common domestic unit are sensitively documented in a remarkable ethnography, *The House of Lim*, by Margery Wolf (1968), wife of anthropologist Arthur Wolf. The Wolfs lived for 2 years (1959–1960) with the Lim terms, such that underlying common elements, which were not intuitively obvious, may be revealed.

The genealogical distribution of the kin terms is diagrammed in Figure 8.14, which is keyed to the kin term numbers used in Table 8.6. Close inspection shows the importance of the male descent line and relative age, which is a very ancient pattern in Chinese culture. For example, FB's children (numbers 8, 9, 10, and 11) are terminologically distinguished from all other cousins because they could share surnames as members of ego's patrilineal descent group, the *tsu*, which existed during the Shang dynasty nearly 4000 years ago. Cross-cousins were not distinguished from parallel cousins, and no cousins were typically considered marriageable. Mates normally had different surnames and were unrelated, and probably even unacquainted.

Older or younger age relative to ego is distinguished for everyone in ego's generation and for male siblings of ego's male lineal kin in higher generations. Concern with relative age reflects the increased ceremonial responsibilities of older siblings in carrying out the duties of *hsiao*, filial piety, and the preferential treatment that they might receive in many areas, including inheritance.

Lineal relatives, who are ego's direct ancestors and descendants, are distinguished from all collateral relatives, who are off to the side. This distinction is important because it is lineal kin who must care for the elderly, play specific roles in mourning, and conduct ancestor rituals, all expressions of *hsiao*. Thus, an understanding of the meaning of Chinese kinship shows how important Chinese cultural patterns are enacted at the domestic level.

---

family (a pseudonym) while they studied daily life in a small farming village they called Peihotien (Hai-shan) on the Tamsui (Ta-han) River in northern Taiwan, 15 miles southwest of Taipei. The Lim family was part of a large patrilineage whose Hokkien-speaking ancestors has migrated to Taiwan from Fukien province in adjacent mainland south China about 1770.

The House of Lim was the wealthiest family in the village. The Lims had realized the Chinese ideal with their three-generation joint family of fourteen people living as a single domestic unit, under one roof, with one kitchen. The household occupied a walled compound enclosing a large rectangular brick house with a central courtyard. The Lim family jointly owned the house, 5 acres of farmland, a small cement-bag factory, and a dozen pigs. They worked together, sharing their common economic resources under the general management of the senior male of the Lim patrilineage, Lim Chieng-cua. The joint family contained two branches (see Figure 8.15):

1. Lim Chieng-cua, his wife, Chui-ieng, and their six unmarried children.

2. Lim A-bok, Lim Chieng-cua's deceased brother's son, with A-bok's wife, A-ki, their two unmarried children, his mother, Lim A-pou, and his younger unmarried brother.

TABLE 8.6   *A Componential Analysis of Chinese Kinship*

Description*	Chinese Term†	Components‡				
		D	R	G	S	A
1. F	*fu 4 thin 2*	M	L	+1	M	
2. FOB	*pak 2 fu 4/*	M	C	+1	M	O
3. FYB	*suk 2 fu 4/*	M	C	+1	M	Y
6. FZ	*ku 2 mu 5*	M	C	+1	F	
8. FBOS	*hong 3 hen 2*	M	C	0	M	O
9. FBYS	*hong 3 ?ai 4/*	M	C	0	M	Y
10. FBOD	*hong 3 tei 1*	M	C	0	F	O
11. FBYD	*hong 3 moi 1/*	M	C	0	F	Y
12. FZOS, MZOS, MBOS	*piau 1 hen 2*	C	0	M	O	
13. FZYS, MBYS, MZYS	*piau 1 ?ai 4/*	C	0	M	Y	
14. FZOD, MBOD, MZOD	*piau 1 tei 1*	C	0	F	O	
15. FZYD, MBYD, MZYD	*piau 1 moi 1*	C	0	F	Y	
16. FF	*tu 1 fu 4*	M	L	+2	M	
17. FM	*tu 1 mu f/*	M	L	+2	F	
18. FFOB	*pak 2 tu 1 fu 4*	M	C	+2	M	O
19. FFYB	*suk 2 tu 1 fu 4*	M	C	+2	M	Y
22. FFZ	*ku 2 tu 1 mu 5/*	M	C	+2	F	
24. M	*mu 5 thin 2*	F	L	+1	F	
25. MB	*khiu 5 fu 4*	F	C	+1	M	
27. MZ	*i 3 mu 5/*	F	C	+1	F	
38. MF	*ngoi 4 tu 1 fu 2*	F	L	+2	M	
39. MM	*ngoi 4 tu 1 mu 5*	F	L	+2	F	
40. MFOB	*ngoi 4 pak 2 tu 1 fu 2*	F	C	+2	M	O
41. MFYB	*ngoi 4 suk 2 tu 1 fu 2*	F	C	+2	M	Y
44. MFZ	*ngoi 4 ku 2 tu 1 mu 5/*	F	C	+2	F	
46. OB	*ka 2 hen 2*	M	C	0	M	O
47. YB	*pou 2 ?ai 4/*	M	C	0	M	Y
50. BS	*cit 4*	M	C	−1	M	
51. BD	*cit 4 nui 1*	M	C	−1	F	
52. OZ	*ka 2 tei 1*	F	C	0	F	O
53. YZ	*pou 2 moi 1/*	F	C	0	F	Y
56. ZS	*sang 2 tu 1*	F	C	−1	M	
57. ZD	*sang 2 nui 1*	F	C	−1	F	
58. S	*tu 1*	M	L	−1	M	
62. D	*nui 1*	F	L	−1	F	

SOURCE: Modified from McCoy (1970).

*The numbers in this column are keyed to kinship terms in Figure 8.14.

†Linguistic symbols: tones 1–5, respectively, high, mid, low, mid-falling, low-falling; / = high-rising; \ = low-falling; ? = glottal stop.

‡D = descent line: M = male line, through F, S, or B; F = female line, through M, D, or Z. R = relationship of alter to ego's line: L = lineal, same line; C = collateral, off to side. G = generation of alter in relation to ego: 0 = ego's generation; +1, +2 = first and second ascending generations; −1 = first descending generation. S = sex of alter: M = male; F = female. A = relative age of alter: O = older; Y = younger.

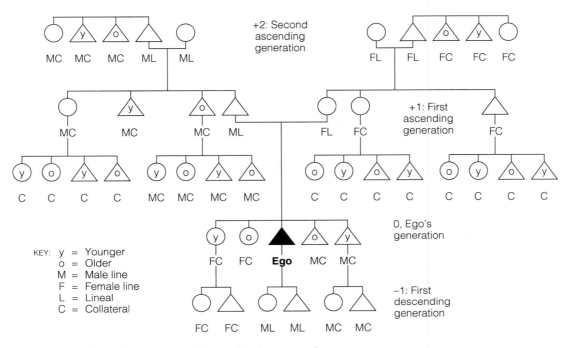

FIGURE 8.13   *Formal components of Chinese kinship terminology.*

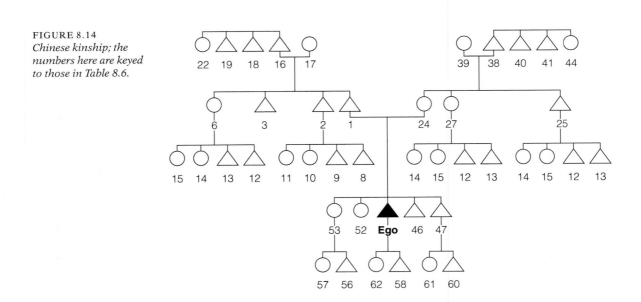

FIGURE 8.14
Chinese kinship; the numbers here are keyed to those in Table 8.6.

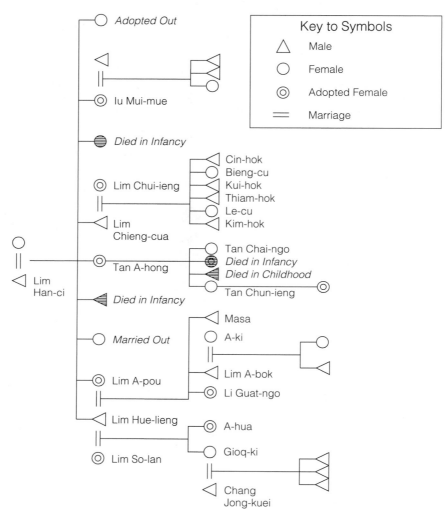

FIGURE 8.15
*The House of Lim family
diagram. (SOURCE:
M. Wolf 1968.)*

THE HOUSE OF LIM

Lim A-bok managed the farm while his mother took care of the pigs. The two wives, Lim Chui-ieng and A-ki, shared the cooking on a 5-day rotation. Everything seemed to run smoothly in the family, but beneath the surface there was considerable tension between the two branches of the family, between spouses, and between parents and children. Many interpersonal problems seemed related to the practice of adoptive and arranged marriages. The family head, Lim Chieng-cua, had refused to marry his foster sister and then agreed to a marriage with

Chui-ieng, arranged by her foster parents. Chui-ieng was not happy with her marriage, especially when her husband took on a mistress. She berated him and threatened to leave, and he violently assaulted her. One of the family's adopted daughters turned to prostitution after she was given to another family but remained unmarried.

Lim A-pou had been adopted into the family as an infant, but her foster brother took a second wife after marrying her. Lim A-pou was a little daughter-in-law (*sim-pua*), selected to later marry her foster brother. Her husband's new wife was a love match. *Sim-pua* marriages were not prestigious, but they were very practical because they saved expensive bride-wealth expenses. They accounted for nearly half the marriages in Peihotien, but this practice has now completely disappeared in Taiwan. The preference for sons over daughters is a strong incentive for giving away daughters in such adoptions. In China, where patrilineages are so important, sons are the best old-age insurance. Furthermore, giving away infant daughters saves the expense of raising a "useless" daughter, who would require a dowry. One woman bluntly told Margery Wolf,

Why should I want so many daughters? It is useless to raise your own daughters. I'd just have to give them away when they were grown, so when someone asked for them as infants I gave them away. Think of all the rice I saved. (1968:40)

The downside of such arrangements is that marrying someone with whom you have grown up does not make for a healthy marriage. Arthur Wolf's (1995) later analysis of the Chinese material seems to confirm Edward Westermark's theory in his *History of Human Marriage* (1922) that people who are raised together from infancy are likely to develop a sexual aversion to one another. Such aversion is especially likely in the Chinese case in which the couple actually called each other "brother" and "sister" before they married. Wolf found that Chinese marriages to adopted daughters showed lower fertility and higher adultery and divorce rates than other marriages.

The obvious insecurity of the women of the Lim household was reflected in frequent bickering between them, especially over work loads and the allocation of economic resources. Shortly after the Wolfs completed their fieldwork, the Lim family divided their property and set up a separate stove and kitchen for Lim A-bok and his branch of the family. The two households continued to live in the same house and worshiped at the Lim family altar in the guest hall where the ancestral tablet was kept, but they no longer formed a joint family.

domestic-scale Neolithic farming cultures that had developed in the great river valleys of China 2000 years earlier. Their foraging ancestors can be traced to at least 15,000 BP in the same region. Many of the distinctive features of Chinese civilization were in place by the time of the Shang dynasty, which began nearly 4000 years ago and continued with only minor modifications until the last emperor was overthrown in 1911. Chinese civilization provides an important perspective on the debate over state origins because, in this case, control of religion by the political elite seems to have played a critical role in both the origin and long-term continuity of the state system. Chinese emperors were not deities, but they ruled with the mandate of heaven, and the political order has been described as a liturgical government based on moral authority backed by military force. Ancestor worship and the associated concept of filial piety were key elements in this system, especially at the domestic level. The entire ideology was expressed in a complex correlative cosmology based on complementary oppositions such as yin-yang and symbolism drawn from the five elements, which were correlated with colors, music, compass directions, and calendrical rituals.

Chinese agriculture was a gardening system powered by human labor on small family farms, operating within a highly efficient village system that provided basic subsistence needs to a very large and dense rural population at a minimal energy cost. This labor-intensive system is a significant contrast to the industrial farming, fossil fuel system described for the United States in Chapter 12.

Chinese culture tended to encourage large families and population growth, but the intensely hierarchical system kept living standards extremely low for most of the population. Chinese domestic life was structured around the patrilineage and extended family, which were dominated by men. The importance of males, relative age, and the patrilineage is demonstrated by a componential analysis of Chinese kinship terms.

SUMMARY

The Chinese Great Tradition began to develop some 7000 years ago as a gradual transformation of the

STUDY QUESTIONS

1. Identify, define, or discuss the following Chinese ideological concepts: Confucianism, Taoism, five classics,

five elements, filial piety, *li*, mandate of heaven, august god, yin-yang, stove god, ancestor tablet, and *kowtow*.

2. Discuss the following political concepts within the Chinese context: meritocracy, patrimonial, aristocracy, and gentry.

3. Discuss the following aspects of subsistence intensification using Chinese examples: multicropping, intertillage, permanent agriculture, labor intensive, capital intensive, and population density.

4. How does the Chinese state fit within the various theories of the origin of the state?

5. Discuss problems with the concepts of exploitation, immiseration, and Malthusian overpopulation, using Chinese material.

6. Discuss the role of ancestor worship as a central integrating device in Chinese culture.

7. Show how the components of descent line, relative age, lineal and collateral, sex, and generation are significant in Chinese kinship terminological systems.

SUGGESTED READING

CHANG, KWANG-CHIH. 1986. *The Archaeology of Ancient China*, 4th ed. New Haven, Conn.: Yale University Press. An authoritative overview of Chinese prehistory.

ROPP, PAUL S. 1990. *Heritage of China: Contemporary Perspectives on Chinese Civilization*. Berkeley: University of California Press. An interdisciplinary collection of articles on China including such topics as Confucianism, the origin of Chinese civilization, and the development of government, economy, and family.

STOVER, LEON N., AND TAKEKO STOVER. 1976. *China: An Anthropological Perspective*. Pacific Palisades, Calif.: Goodyear. A wide-ranging analysis of Chinese culture.

WHEATLEY, PAUL. 1971. *The Pivot of the Four Quarters: A Preliminary Enquiry into the Origins and Character of the Ancient Chinese City*. Chicago: Aldine. Examines the physical organization of Chinese cities through time in relation to worldview and cosmology.

9

Great Traditions: Hinduism and Islam in South Asia

One-third of the contemporary world's people identify themselves as either Hindus or Muslims. These two Great Traditions arose independently more than 1000 years ago and are culturally distinct, but both are centered on formal religions with sacred texts. These religions provide charters for a hierarchically organized society and regulate the smallest details of daily life, including family structure, male–female relationships, and diet. Europeans, as members of the Christian Great Tradition, have been both fascinated and repulsed by Hindus and Muslims for centuries, but they have consistently misunderstood them. In this chapter, we focus on classical Hindu civilization, especially the relationship between religion and society, and show how the ancient culture is reflected in modern India. The South Asian culture area is emphasized because it is the homeland of the Hindu Great Tradition and because Muslims and Hindus have coexisted here for 800 years. This area is examined again in Chapter 13 in relation to contemporary issues of poverty and economic development.

THE SOUTH ASIAN CULTURE AREA

Languages and Geography of South Asia

How can the two great cultural traditions, Hinduism and Islam, that exist side by side in South Asia be distinguished? What are the major languages of South Asia, and how do they relate to Hinduism and Islam? What features of South Asian geography shape cultural development?

The South Asian culture area covers modern Pakistan, India, Nepal, Bhutan, Bangladesh, Burma, and Sri Lanka. It is a complex mix of languages and culture types, with more than 1 billion people occupying an area less than two-thirds the size of the United States. South Asia is centered on the Indian subcontinent and is predominantly a Hindu and Muslim region, with important Buddhist elements as well as many coexisting domestic-scale cultures.

Most South Asian languages belong to one of three major language groups: Indo-European,

FIGURE 9.1
Map of South Asian languages and geography.

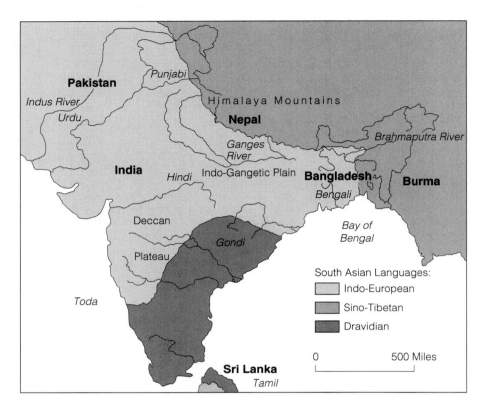

Dravidian, and Sino-Tibetan (see Figure 9.1). India alone recognizes fifteen official languages, including four of the twelve most populous languages in the world: English, Hindi, Urdu, and Bengali. Many other languages are spoken within the political boundaries of the country. The last three languages are members of the Indic branch of Indo-European, related to ancient Sanskrit, and are spoken by some 600 million people in the densely populated Indus Valley of Pakistan and the Gangetic Plain of India (see Figure 9.2). Dravidian languages are spoken in southeastern India and Sri Lanka. They are presumed to have preceded the Indo-European languages in India and are spoken by many tribal groups. Sino-Tibetan languages are spoken in the Himalayan region, in Burma, and by many tribal peoples in extreme eastern India and Bangladesh.

The cultural Great Tradition with which people identify may be associated with a particular language. There are perhaps 60 million Buddhists in

South Asia, primarily in India, Burma, and Sri Lanka, and some 200 million more in East Asia (see Figure 9.3a). Buddhists are most likely to be speakers of Dravidian or Sino-Tibetan languages. Furthermore, many Dravidian and Sino-Tibetan peoples are tribal peoples who do not identify with any Great Tradition. The largest cultural group in South Asia is composed of some 700 million Hindus centered in India, Bangladesh, and Nepal, who are primarily speakers of Indic languages. At its peak, the Hindu Great Tradition expanded into Southeast Asia as far as Java in what is now Indonesia (see Figure 9.3b). Approximately 300 million Muslims live in Pakistan, Bangladesh, and India. South Asian Muslims are predominantly speakers of Urdu and Bengali. There are more than 800 million Muslims worldwide, including some 170 million in Malaysia and Indonesia and more than 200 million in Africa and the Middle East (see Figure 9.3c). The Islamic Great Tradition, although originated by speakers of Arabic, a Semitic lan-

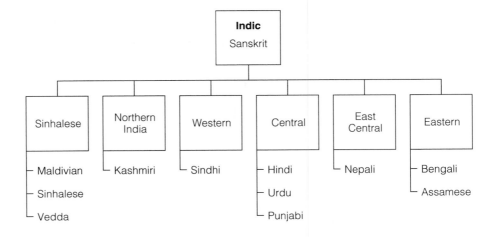

FIGURE 9.2
Indic languages (Indo-Iranian branch, Indo-European). (SOURCE: Ruhlen 1987.)

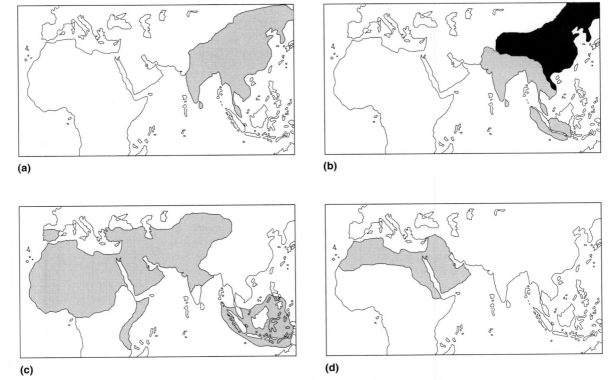

(a)

(b)

(c)

(d)

FIGURE 9.3   *Maps of Asian Great Traditions: (a) Buddhist, (b) Hindu (light screen) and Chinese (dark screen), (c) Islamic, and (d) speakers of Arabic.*

Early South Asian Prehistory

South Asia is not as well known archaeologically as the Near East, but cultural developments seem to have followed a similar pattern in both areas. The Lower Paleolithic is well represented by Acheulean hand axes and choppers found throughout India (see Table 9.1). The Middle Paleolithic flake tools and Upper Paleolithic blade tools are also well represented. Archaeologists working in South Asia refer to cultures based on microlithic tools, foraging, fishing, and nomadic herding as Mesolithic. This adaptation began during the Early Holocene, about 12,000–8000 BP, and continued in various parts of the subcontinent into the twentieth century. It is significant that this date for the earliest possible use of domestic animals corresponds to similar events in the Near East.

The South Asian Neolithic also goes through a pre-Ceramic phase of initial farming villages at about the same time as in the Near East (8000–5000 BC) and a full ceramic Neolithic (5000–3500 BC), which includes paint-decorated pottery. Because the earliest South Asian farming villages are known from the Indus region and the eastern edge of the Iranian plateau in Baluchistan, especially the site of Mehrgarh, it is inferred that developments here were perhaps part of the same process that occurred in the Near East, especially given the similarities in ecological setting.

guage, is now practiced by more Indic speakers in South Asia than Arabic speakers in the Middle East. Furthermore, because not all Arab speakers are Muslim, the common stereotype that equates Muslim with Arab is misleading (compare Figures 9.3c and 9.3d).

The South Asian subcontinent (see Figure 9.1) extends more than 2000 miles (3218 kilometers [km]) east to west and north to south, encompassing many sharply different environments. Because of this diverse expanse, cultures of very different scale have been able to interact with one another over the millennia while retaining their essential autonomy. South and central India lie within the tropics, while north India extends well into the temperate zones. Tropical rain forest is found along a narrow coastal strip of western India, Sri Lanka, and the hill tribe areas of Bangladesh, eastern India, and Burma. Much of southern India is an arid upland dominated by the Deccan Plateau, which is composed of vast tertiary basalt lava flows, perhaps formed when a giant meteor punched a hole in the earth's mantle. The Deccan region was not condu-

cive to intensive agriculture and sheltered many Dravidian-speaking tribal peoples.

India is separated from China and Central Asia by the Himalayan–Hindu Kush mountains, which form the southern boundary of the vast Tibetan Plateau and contain the world's highest mountains and the largest permanent snowfields outside the polar regions. The 1500-mile (2414-km) east–west trend of the massive Himalayan range creates an enormous rain shadow to the north and funnels tropical monsoonal rainfall from Southeast Asia onto the rich alluvial soils of the low Gangetic Plain, making it a highly productive agricultural zone. The Himalayas, which contain many peaks over 20,000 feet (6096 m) high, are the source of the Indus, the Ganges, and the Brahmaputra rivers, which annually carry tons of Himalayan alluvium to the Indo-Gangetic Plain. The Indus Valley, where Indian civilization began, lies on the opposite end of the Iranian plateau from Mesopotamia, which it ecologically resembles. The Indus Valley is an arid alluvial plain, bordered by mountains. The Indus, like the Euphrates, is a silt-laden, aggrading river,

TABLE 9.1 *History and Prehistory of South Asia, 1,000,000 BP–AD 1947*

British and Muslim India (1200–1947)	1818–1947	British colony
	1526–1761	Mogul empire
	1192–1526	Early Muslim period
Classic Hindu India (600 BC–AD 1200)	AD 320–550	Gupta empire
	350–100 BC	Mauryan empire: Asokan edicts; writing; cities; Arthasastra, Dharma Sastra, Code of Manu compiled
	540–468	Mahavira, founder of Jainism
	563–483	Buddha (Siddhartha Gautama), founder of Buddhism
	900–300	Upanishads compiled
Vedic India (1600–600 BC)	1000–600	Early Iron Age
	1000–800	Brahmanas compiled
	1500	Indo-Aryan chiefdoms in Bramavarta; Rig-Veda Samhita compiled
	1600	Intrusion of Indo-European peoples
Mature Indus Valley civilization (2500–1500 BC)	2500–1500	Harappan civilization; cities; writing; temples; trade
State formation (3500–2500 BC)	2800–2500	Early Indus Valley civilization: incipient urbanism; regional interaction sphere; walled sites; cattle as religious icons
	3500–2800	Chalcolithic: population expansion; increased use of copper
Neolithic India (8000–5000 BC)	5000–3500	Ceramic Neolithic: Mehrgarh painted pottery; copper beads; microlithic sickles; cotton
	8000–5000	Pre-Ceramic Neolithic: in Mehrgarh (Indus Valley), permanent settlements, mud-brick architecture; grain storage; domesticates—wheat, barley, dates, cattle, water buffalo, sheep, goats; burials; figurines; long-distance trade in turquoise
Mesolithic India (12,000 BP–8000)	12,000–8000	Hunters, fishers, nomadic herders; possible domesticated sheep and goats in Hindu Kush valleys; microlithic tools
Paleolithic India (1 million BP–17,000)	18,000–17,000	Upper Paleolithic: blade tools
	200,000–25,000	Middle Paleolithic: flake tools; mobile foragers
	1 million–200,000	Lower Paleolithic: quartzite Acheulean hand axes and choppers

SOURCE: Allchin and Allchin (1982) for prehistoric data.

ideally suited to floodplain agriculture yet frequently changing course.

Significant changes in the South Asian environment may have affected cultural development in ways that are still not understood. Changes in sea level and alluvial deposition on the floodplain have altered the area of prime agricultural lands. The Himalayas are still being pushed up by the northward-moving Indian continental plate colliding with the Eurasian plate, and this has happened rapidly enough to modify regional climate during the period of human occupation. Since the Lower Paleolithic, in some areas of India the climate has been both wetter and drier than at present (Allchin and Allchin 1982).

EARLY HINDU CIVILIZATION

Origin of the Hindu Kingdom

What basic patterns of Hindu civilization were present in the earliest Hindu kingdoms more than 2000 years ago? How did the early Hindu kingdom differ from the Mesopotamian city-state? What archaeologically distinguishable changes in settlement patterns trace the emergence of the Hindu kingdom?

The Indian subcontinent has a very long prehistoric background, beginning with the Lower Paleolithic. The South Asian Neolithic seems to have been an outgrowth of the Near Eastern Neolithic (see the

Harappan Civilization: The Earliest South Asian State

After 3500 BC, the agricultural potential of the Indus floodplain began to be realized, and the settled population began to increase. Between 2800 and 2500 BC, small, walled urban sites appeared, and highly uniform ceramic styles over a wide area, together with further evidence of long-distance trade, indicate that a socioeconomic interaction network had developed. Over the next several centuries (approximately 2500–1500 BC), Harappan civilization flourished throughout the Indus region. This was the earliest state-level culture in South Asia.

Harappa, at the upper end of the Indus floodplain, and Mohenjo-Daro, in the lower, were major urban centers, both built according to a similar plan. Mohenjo-Daro may have had a population of 35,000 people. It contained an elevated brick-walled citadel with a large ritual bath, grain storehouses, and probably a temple. Near the citadel was a separate, lower, and much larger grid cluster of brick buildings, which were residences and workshops. Houses had bathrooms complete with drains that emptied into what appeared to be a public sewer system. The diversity of house plans and the presence of single-room barracks suggest differences in social class or wealth, but no royal tombs have been found, and the Harappan elite remain anonymous.

The Harappans produced finely crafted utilitarian objects in bronze and copper, as well as jewelry and beads in gold, silver, and semiprecious stones. Because the floodplain lacked mineral resources, they maintained extensive trade contacts throughout India and as far as Central Asia and Mesopotamia. Standardized sets of weights and measures and numerous incised seals, resembling those from Mesopotamia but bearing unique Harappan markings, are further indications of the importance of trade (see Figure 9.4). The Harappan language is unknown, and its unique writing system has never been successfully deciphered, but there does not seem to have been a developed literary tradition. Terra-cotta figurines and

box entitled "Early South Asian Prehistory"), but Harappa, the earliest civilization in the Indus Valley, may have arisen independently (see the box entitled "Harappan Civilization: The Earliest South Asian State"). A clear break seems to have occurred between Harappa and the later Hindu civilization centered on the Gangetic Plain, which is attributed primarily to Indo-European-speaking Aryan pastoralists.

Hindu civilization has its roots in the religious hymns and verses preserved in the Vedas, especially the four Samhita Vedas compiled as oral texts be-

tween 1500 and 1000 BC. Pre-Aryan peoples, including members of the Harappan civilization, certainly contributed to what was, in effect, a second period of state formation, urbanization, and civilization in South Asia. The rise of early Hindu civilization between approximately 600 and 200 BC seems to have been primarily a political process that does not easily fit the Mesopotamian, Andean, or Chinese models of state origin examined previously. Hindu civilization developed after the Aryan invaders conquered the earlier domestic-scale residents of the Ganges region and incorporated them inscriptions of earth mothers, horned men, bulls, composite animals, and human-animals have been interpreted to be cult objects and forerunners of important Hindu deities such as Siva and Parvati. The Harappan civilization apparently collapsed completely around 1500 BC for reasons that are not well understood, as will be discussed in Chapter 10.

Sometime around 1600 BC, Indo-European-speaking peoples apparently moved from the Iranian plateau to the Indus plains. These were the Aryans, who were probably seminomadic pastoral people, speaking an early form of Sanskrit and organized in chiefdoms. These Aryans should *not* be confused with the imaginary north European "Aryan" superrace of Hitler's Nazi Germany and neo-Nazi racist political ideology. The Aryans of ancient Asia and the Neolithic settlers of Europe may well have had common ancestors in Southwest Asia some 8500 years ago and may belong to the Indo-European language family, but otherwise they were different peoples.

The Aryans portrayed in the Vedas were cattle herders and warriors who fought with the earlier, presumably Dravidian-speaking, peoples whom they encountered. Some historians believe that the Aryans may have contributed to the collapse of the Harappan civilization, but this is difficult to establish. The Aryans settled initially in the Punjab and between the Indus and Ganges rivers, the region that was identified in the Vedic texts as Brahmavarta, the Aryan heartland. They then expanded steadily eastward into the fertile Gangetic Plain, such that by 600 BC they effectively occupied the entire region and were becoming increasingly sedentary and stratified. Over the next four centuries, classical Indian civilization became fully established, with cities, writing, states, empires, and the Great Traditions of Hinduism and Buddhism that continue to shape Indian culture to the present day (see Table 9.1).

into larger-scale centralized polities, which then began to war against one another. Because the Ganges, as an incised river, was a difficult source of irrigation water, early Gangetic states were not hydraulic societies; that is, they were not directed by rulers who also controlled irrigation works. Furthermore, because significant increases in population density took place only after political centralization, neither population pressure nor environmental circumscription could have been important causes of state formation. However, because Hindu civilization incorporated some elements of Harappan civilization and may also have been indirectly stimulated by contacts with Mesopotamian and Persian civilizations, it should not be considered an example of strictly pristine state development.

In his investigation of the development of Indian civilization, archaeologist George Erdosy (1988) focused on urbanization in the central Ganges region, following the approach that Henry Wright (1969) and Gregory Alan Johnson (1973) used with early Mesopotamian civilization. Erdosy defines cities as "the containers of those institutions that

FIGURE 9.4   *An incised steatite Harappan seal with undeciphered script from Harappa.*

such that their appearance signals the arrival of state-level organization.

Erdosy (1988) surveyed settlement patterns at intervals covering the period from 1000 BC to AD 300, looking for changes in the size, distribution, and function of settlements that might serve as clues to changes in cultural complexity. During the first 400 years, up to 600 BC, only two types of settlements could be distinguished: (1) numerous small villages of perhaps 275 people and (2) a small center of 1600 people, which was in a position to control the flow of imported mineral resources. Even in the absence of clear archaeological evidence of rank, this two-level settlement hierarchy suggests that simple chiefdoms existed at this time on the Ganges Plain (see Figure 9.5a), but the institutions of social control must have been primarily religious and relatively unspecialized.

After 600 BC, an obvious change in political organization occurred, perhaps as high-ranking Aryans sought to enhance their control in the region. A functionally diversified, four-level settlement hierarchy emerged, clearly indicating the emergence of the state (see Figure 9.5b). The largest settlement within the study area became a small fortified city of perhaps 8000 people. It contained material evidence of formal administrative, economic, and religious functions, in the form of coins, beads, sculptures, and iron slag. After 350 BC, the Ganges

are required for the maintenance of increasingly complex and inegalitarian societies" (1988:5).

Domestic-scale societies did not need cities because small villages were self-regulating. Cities were places where the instruments of social control could themselves be developed and controlled,

FIGURE 9.5   *Settlement patterns, Ganges Plain: (a) chiefdoms (1000–600 BC) and (b) early states (600–350 BC).*

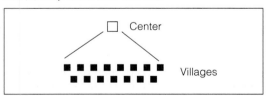

(a)   1 center = 1600
15 villages of 275 = 4125
5725 people

(b)   1 fortified city = 8000
1 town = 1920
2 centers of 1000 = 2000
17 villages of 240 = 4080
16,000 people

Valley settlement hierarchy, as archaeologically detected, successively revealed the presence of the kingdoms and empires of early classic Hindu civilization, which have also left their own historical record.

Kautilya's Hindu Kingdom: An Emic Political Model, 250 BC

How was state power organized in the Hindu kingdom? How did the organization of the Hindu kingdom compare with that of imperial China? What was the structure of Hindu social inequality?

The ideal organization of the early Hindu state is precisely detailed in Kautilya's Arthasastra, a written manual on ancient Indian statecraft. The Arthasastra is attributed to Kautilya, a minister in the Mauryan empire in 250 BC, but was probably written by several people in the early centuries AD. It is a composite treatise on political science for kings and aspiring kings, written with candor, cynicism, and insight. As a manual for public administrators, it resembles the Confucian classics, but instead of professional ethics and ritual, the Arthasastra advocates the use of coercive power backed by the army, the police, the courts, and covert state security agents. The Arthasastra may be taken as a portrayal of the ideal structure and function of a hypothetical Indian kingdom during the early centuries of classic Hindu civilization. As an emic view, composed by elite political professionals, it may not be an accurate picture of any specific kingdom, and the ideal rules may not have been followed. However, the general system as described is probably valid and provides a useful model for comparison with the organization of domestic-scale tribes and other state systems.

The Arthasastra offers insider views on the use of state power for the king's personal advantage. It is filled with practical advice on palace intrigue—complete with how-to examples of the use of spies, sex, poison, and deception for political assassination—and ways to test the loyalty of government officials. In the Arthasastra, religion was simply another self-conscious tool of statecraft. Kings were advised to use rituals and pilgrimages as excuses to raise revenue. It was even

ie Ashoka!

proposed that omens, such as spirits speaking in trees, be deliberately staged to stir up fear so that people would increase their religious donations.

The difference between political leaders in Indian kingdoms such as this and tribal leaders who might also use deception and treachery to personal advantage was simply that domestic-scale cultures limited political power. Tribal leaders did not have standing armies, police forces, and secret agents at their disposal. They could not personally control the availability of basic subsistence goods to thousands of households. Tribal peoples feared and avoided those who abused their limited powers and thereby denied them control. Peasant villagers living in a world of rival kingdoms were pawns for the ruling kings, who tried to keep the levy just below the point at which disaffected villagers would join an enemy kingdom.

In 500 BC, there were some eighteen large kingdoms in northern India centered on the Gangetic Plain (Erdosy 1988). According to the Arthasastra, an ideally organized kingdom would have been divided into four districts, each containing 800 villages dominated by a fortified city, with smaller cities, towns, and centers hierarchically arranged to facilitate administration and the flow of revenue. The government officials in two cities would have administrative responsibility for 400 villages each, officials in four towns would control 200 villages each, and some eighty local centers would each be responsible for very specific census taking, tax collecting, and police work in 10 villages within the district (see Figure 9.6). Such an arrangement closely corresponds to the archaeological record, and combining Erdosy's population estimates based on site size (160 persons/2.5 acres [1 hectare]) with the Arthasastra model, we can reconstruct the demographic parameters of a hypothetical Indian kingdom (see Table 9.2). These estimates suggest that a kingdom might have contained some 1.6 million people, with perhaps 143,000 people, 9 percent of the total population, living in cities of more than 2000 people.

A kingdom of 1.6 million people would have been much more amenable to management by direct political power than the 50–500 million people living in the vast Chinese empire. Traditional China and India make an interesting comparison because they were both preindustrial, agrarian civilizations,

FIGURE 9.6
Settlement hierarchy
within a Hindu kingdom,
250 BC. (SOURCE: Shama-
sastry 1960 [Arthasastra].)

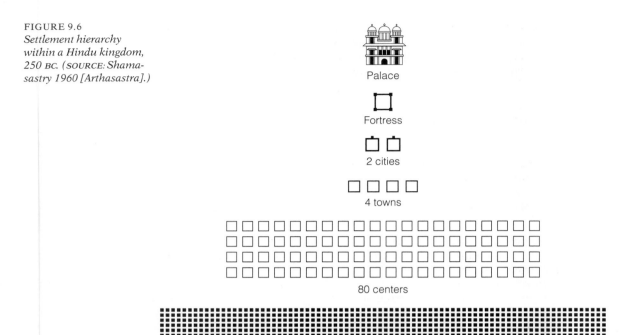

Palace

Fortress

2 cities

4 towns

80 centers

800 villages

TABLE 9.2   *Population of Model Hindu Kingdom, 350 BC*

Number per District	Population in Each*	Total
Fortified city (1)	20,000	20,000
Cities (2)	3,500	7,000
Towns (4)	2,000	8,000
Centers (80)	1,000	80,000
Villages (800)	350	280,000
Total district population		395,000
4 Districts	=	1,580,000	
Capital city	=	35,000	
Kingdom total	=	1,615,000	
Urban population (cities over 2000 people) = 143,000 (8.8%)		

SOURCES: Erdosy (1988) and Kautilya's Arthasastra (Shamasastry 1960).
*The Arthasastra states that villages ranged in size from 100 to 500 families. Erdosy estimates 3.5 persons per family and average villages of 240 people, assuming 160 people per hectare of archaeological site. Thus, villages of 350 people represent the lower range for the Arthasastra figures but are higher than predicted archaeologically.

yet there were significant cultural differences. As shown in Chapter 8, China relied primarily on ethical principles, ritual, moral authority, and patrilineal descent groups to maintain social order. Hindu India, in contrast, used the moral authority of religion to support an endogamous caste system and

TABLE 9.3   *Estimated Population of Social Groups Within Model Hindu Kingdom, 350 BC*

	Salaried Elite	State Workers	Farm Workers	Total
Capital	175	33,425	1,400	35,000
Fortresses	350	74,050	5,600	80,000
Cities	140	22,260	5,600	28,000
Towns	50	20,750	11,200	32,000
Centers	—	96,000	224,000	320,000
Villages	—	—	1,120,000	1,120,000
Total	715	246,485	1,367,800	1,615,000

NOTES: Salaried elites are palace officials and high-ranking government administrators receiving salaries of 1000 pana or more. State workers include all lower-level salaried officials, state-supported specialists, retainers, and merchants who pay taxes in cash. It is assumed that the capital and fortress cities each include the equivalent farm workers of four villages, and smaller settlements include the equivalent of two villages each. All figures include all family members.

relied on coercive political authority to a significant degree.

The most critical difference between India and China was probably total population size. There were no reliable census figures for ancient India, but the first British census of 1872 listed a population of only 238 million for all of India, while the population of China at that time exceeded 400 million. More importantly, empires during the classical period of Hindu civilization were relatively short-lived, and the most permanent political unit was the small kingdom, which formed a relatively autonomous cultural system. All eighteen kingdoms of the Gangetic Plain probably combined into an unstable empire of less than 30 million people.

The territory of an Indian kingdom was also relatively small. The total population of 1.6 million people, in theory, could have been supported by a minimum of 3991 square miles (10,336 km²) of cultivated land, if we accept Erdosy's rough calculations that Indians consumed the caloric equivalent of 508 pounds (230 kilograms [kg]) of grain per person per year and produced 795 pounds per 2.5 acres per year (360 kg/hectare/year), so that each person required 1.6 acres (.64 hectare) of cultivated land. However, the actual territory must have been much larger because the Arthasastra states that each village had a territory extending 1.2–2.5 miles (2–4 km) from the village. This extra land would have provided for pasture and forests and allowed for less intensive farming.

If village territories are assumed to have been hexagonal with sides averaging 1.7 miles (3 km), each territory would have contained approximately 8.9 square miles (23 km²), which would yield a total village territory of 28,417 square miles (73,600 km²). Farmers living in larger settlements might have utilized another 6287 square miles (16,284 km²). Such a kingdom thus might have contained a total territory of approximately 34,749 square miles (90,000 km²), 186 miles (300 km) on a side. In comparison, the 500 million people of the Chinese empire at its height were spread over a territory of 1865 miles (3000 km) on a side. It is not surprising that Chinese civilization came to rely so heavily on moral authority.

The approximate social composition of a hypothetical Hindu kingdom is shown in Table 9.3, which suggests that a surprisingly small elite maintained absolute power. Most of the population, probably about 85 percent, lived in farm households, which supplied basic subsistence for the other 15 percent. State-supported craft specialists did produce consumer goods for the villagers, but much of their production directly supported the state.

The Arthasastra gives a detailed picture of the revenue system and basic administrative structure of the Hindu kingdom. State-controlled wealth was concentrated in the capital and in district fortresses. An underground royal treasury vault contained gold, jewelry, coins, and precious textiles.

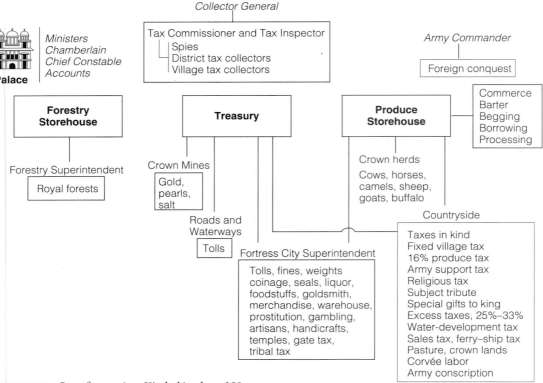

FIGURE 9.7   *State finance in a Hindu kingdom, 250 BC.*

Special storehouses held grain and other products, which were collected as taxes in kind or produced on crown land. Farmers paid an average grain tax of 16 percent, which was raised to 25–33 percent under emergency conditions. There were also village taxes, temple taxes, gate taxes, sales taxes, income taxes, tolls, fines, and excise taxes of various sorts. Some villagers submitted to corvée labor or military inscription in place of the grain tax.

Although there were no vast canal systems or irrigation works in ancient India, large armies were mobilized for frequent wars, and royal construction projects and defensive works required large labor forces. For example, Erdosy (1988) estimates that construction of the 49-foot- (15-m)-tall earthen ramparts stretching for 3.7 miles (6 km) around a fortified city would have engaged 20,000 workmen for 250 days.

The state regulated commercial activities, mining, forestry, herding, and craft production to extract the maximum feasible revenue (see Figure 9.7). Even prostitutes were licensed and paid a monthly income tax. The supply of marketable consumer goods was centrally controlled. Only the Brahmans, who formed the religious elite, and frontier villages and state-supported colonization projects were exempt from taxes. A collector general attached to the royal palace was responsible for all revenue collection received from district and village tax collectors. There was also a high-ranking tax commissioner and a tax inspector, who used covert means to monitor the flow of revenue. Detailed bookkeeping was carried out at all levels, and all government expenses were further monitored by the central accounts office.

Many diverse functions were carried out in the fortified city, especially if it was also the capital. As described in the Arthasastra, the city was divided into twelve major sections, where specific categories of people were expected to live and where specific activities and buildings were to be located (see Figure 9.8). Each of the four *varna*, or "colors," representing the four ranks of Vedic society— Brahman, Kshatriya, Vaisya, and Sudra—was assigned specific quarters within the city, grouped together with appropriately ranked economic activities. These social categories will be discussed in more detail in the later section dealing with caste.

The *varna* were the early form of the **caste** system. During this early period of Hindu civilization, they were already associated with endogamy, relative purity, and occupation. For example, the Sudra, in the lowest-ranked *varna*, were assigned to the city's west quarter, where leather working, an especially polluting activity, was carried out. The royal palace occupied one-ninth of the city and was to be located just north of city center, opening onto the sections occupied by Brahmans, jewelers, and the royal deity. Merchants and high-ranking specialist crafts were located in the east quarter together with government ministers and the Kshatriya.

Law in the Hindu Kingdom

How did the Hindu legal system both reflect and sustain the inequalities of the caste system? How does this legal system contrast with the Anglo-American legal system?

The legal system in the Hindu kingdom upheld the authority of the state and the *varna* social system, which gave ritual priority and economic advantage to the upper ranks. Furthermore, fines imposed by the court were a source of state revenue and enforced the tax system. Law was based on tradition, or customary law, and on *dharma*, or sacred religious law, which resembled *li* in the Chinese system. Both *dharma* and *li* referred to duty, morality, and proper conduct; however, where *li* emphasized duty to emperor, ancestors, and family, *dharma* laid out different moral requirements for each *varna* and for individuals at different stages of the life cycle. Furthermore, the Hindu king was clearly a political ruler.

All law in the Hindu kingdom was ultimately vested in the king, who was assisted by his political ministers and priestly authorities on *dharma*. According to the secular authors of the Arthasastra, the king's traditional law had legal priority over *dharma*, and the king was expected to use the state's power and physical punishment to "maintain both this world and the next" (Shamasastry 1960 [Bk. 3, chap. 1]).

Laws were explicitly designed to support the *varna* system and provided a quantified measure of the relative worth of each rank. For example, one could be fined for causing a Brahman to violate one of his food taboos, and a Sudra could be burned alive for committing adultery with a Brahman woman. Brahmans were generally immune from taxes, fines, and punishments. The fine for selling a Brahman child into slavery was four times as severe as when the victim was a Sudra. The sons of a Brahman woman were to inherit four shares of their Brahman father's estate, but only one share if their mother was a Sudra. Twenty-four different terms existed to describe the conditions of birth according to the *varna* of the parents. Stanley Tambiah (1985) demonstrates that the caste system itself was generated by the legal classification and rank ordering of all the logically possible types of marriage between people in different *varna* categories.

There was a broad three-level scale for fines in pana, the basic monetary unit, ranging from under 100 to 1000 pana. According to the government's salary scale, the highest officials were paid 24,000–48,000 pana a year, midrange officials earned 1000–12,000 pana, and the lowest retainers earned just 60 pana. Those unable to pay fines could substitute an equal number of lashes or body parts according to a scale of equivalent values. A thumb was worth 54 pana; a right hand, 400 pana; and both eyes, 800 pana.

Verbal abuse or insults were scaled according to whether they were true, false, or sarcastic. For example, calling a blind man "blind" was true abuse, but telling a blind man that he had beautiful eyes was false abuse. Generally, the fine was doubled if the victim was in a superior *varna* and halved if the victim was inferior (see Table 9.4). More precise rank distinctions could also be made if one's profession was insulted, with the severity of the fine increasing by three for each increase in the victim's relative rank and decreasing by two for lower-level ranks.

---

caste An endogamous, ranked, occupationally defined group, known as *jati* in India.

FIGURE 9.8
*Functional diversi-
fication within a for-
tified Hindu capital,
250 BC. (SOURCE:
Shamasastry 1960
[Arthasastra].)*

KEY: G = Guild residences
D = Guardian deities

TABLE 9.4   *Legal Fines for Verbal Abuse, Insult, and Assault in Relation to* Varna
in the Hindu Kingdom, 350 BC

Verbal Abuse	Victim's Rank		
	Equal	Superior	Inferior
Valid	12+	6	0.5
False	12+	12	3
Sarcasm	12+	24	6

Insultor	Victim's Rank			
	Brahman	Kshatriya	Vaisya	Sudra
Brahman	12	10	8	6
Kshatriya	15	12	10	8
Vaisya	18	15	12	10
Sudra	21	18	15	12

Assault	Below Navel*		Above Navel		Head	
	Inferior†	Superior†	Inferior	Superior	Inferior	Superior
Throwing mud	0.5	6	3	12	6	24
Spitting	3	12	6	24	12	48
Throwing feces	6	24	12	48	24	96

SOURCE: Shamasastry (1960 [Arthasastra]).
*Target.
†Rank.

The legal severity of physical assault was measured along a graduated scale of violence reminiscent of that described for Amazonia because both considered the objects used and the body areas struck. The Hindu scale added relative rank. Throwing mud on a low-ranking person's feet was a minor offense (0.5 pana), whereas throwing feces on a high-ranking person's face was a very serious offense (96 pana). The most serious cases involved extreme differences in rank. Although striking with a hand or leg was normally a moderate offense, the Arthasastra declared "that limb of a Shudra with which he strikes a Brahmin shall be cut off" (Shamasastry 1960 [Bk. 3, chap. 19]).

To convince people of the "omniscient power of the state," the Arthasastra advocated routine use of undercover agents, entrapment, arrest on suspicion, torture to elicit confessions, severe punishment, and public display of criminals. Workers who failed to produce on time or who fled their workshops were fined. Theft of a minor commodity from a home or shop was punished with public humiliation, but theft of an object of one-fourth the value from the government could bring banishment. Taking any government property worth more than 8 pana, spreading rumors, letting out prisoners, or using government documents without authorization could mean death. Insulting the king was punished by cutting out the offender's tongue. The most severe punishment, burning alive, was reserved for those spreading disorder in the countryside.

HINDU IDEOLOGY, SOCIETY, AND CULTURE

Caste and Orthodox Hinduism: The Brahman View of Dharma

What are the basic principles of caste organization? How does caste contrast with clan? How does caste relate to marriage? What is the significance of food in Hindu culture?

Hindu civilization is most widely known for its caste system with its emphasis on hierarchy and on ritual **purity** and pollution, which continues to be a major fact of life in India. The caste system assumed its basic form in the Hindu kingdoms during the last centuries BC, as described in the preceding section. The term *caste* is an English version of the Spanish and Portuguese word *casta*, meaning "race," "breed," or "family." The corresponding Indian term is *jati*, "birth" or "breed," which emphasizes that caste membership is assigned by birth;

each caste is ideally an endogamous group. At its most general level, caste has been defined as a society "made up of birth-ascribed groups which are hierarchically ordered and culturally distinct. The hierarchy entails differential evaluation, rewards, and association" (Berreman 1979:73).

By this definition, caste could also describe race relations in the United States in the 1950s (Berreman 1960) and the positions of blacksmiths in East Africa. French anthropologist Louis Dumont (1970) took a more intellectualist approach, describing Indian caste as an ideological system of categories based on (1) hierarchically ordered social groups, (2) detailed rules of separation, and (3) a division of labor. The four *varna*—Brahman, Kshatriya, Vaisya, and Sudra—can be considered the most general castes, but castes are continuously segmented into many localized subcastes, which form finely ranked regional systems. The members of subcastes claim descent from a common founder and identify an original group specialty—such as herding, farming, blacksmithing, or weaving—even though it may not always be practiced.

Claude Lévi-Strauss (1966) offered an interesting structuralist comparison of caste and totemic clan as logically opposite systems. He pointed out that because castes are defined by permanent and hereditary occupational differences, they are like natural, biological species and can be distinguished by the goods that they produce. People thus exchange "naturally different" manufactured products and services between castes, but because castes are endogamous, they do not exchange women. By contrast, exogamous totemic clans are based on the cultural myth that women are "naturally" different "species," who are therefore exchanged between social groups that are otherwise functionally the same. Clans lack an economic division of labor but nevertheless create a cultural basis for interdependence. Lévi-Strauss condensed his comparison in this superficially enigmatic statement: "Castes naturalize a true culture falsely, totemic groups culturalize a false nature truly" (1966:127).

Caste organization and related concepts of ritual purity have a significant bearing on aspects of Hindu marriage and family life. Caste endogamy,

---

purity Ritually superior status; a category in logical opposition to impurity.

The Purusha *Myth: A Mythic Charter for Varna and Caste*

"But in order to protect this universe, He, the most resplendent one, assigned separate (duties and) occupations to those who sprang from his mouth, arms, thighs, and feet.

To Brahmans he assigned teaching and studying (the Veda), sacrificing for their own benefit and for others, giving and accepting (of alms).

The Kshatriya he commanded to protect the people, to bestow gifts, to offer sacrifices, to study (the Veda), and to abstain from attaching himself to sensual pleasures.

The Vaisya to tend cattle, to bestow gifts, to offer sacrifices, to study (the Veda), to trade, to lend money, and to cultivate land.

One occupation only the lord prescribed to the Sudra, to serve meekly even these (other) three castes."

SOURCE: Buhler (1886 [Manu 1:87–91]).

the requirement that one marry within the caste, helps define caste boundaries, but subcastes are often further subdivided into exogamous lineages and clans. Marriage between different subcastes is often characterized by **hypergamy,** in which low-rank women marry equal- or higher-ranked men. This practice may severely limit choices for women in high-ranked subcastes, whereas down-marrying men (**hypogamy**) are unlikely to experience difficulty.

Marriage is one of the most important Hindu rituals. It involves great expenditure by the bride's family and extreme concern for ritual purity and status. Normally, all marriages are arranged by the families of the prospective bride and groom. Chastity is a ritual requirement, especially for the highest castes, and is related to infant marriage, prohibition on divorce and widow remarriage, and the practice of *sati,* or widow self-immolation, in which a "virtuous woman" throws herself on her husband's funeral pyre to be transformed into a goddess. Many of these practices are followed only by the strictest Brahman subcastes, which adhere to the severest requirements for ritual purity. It must also be stressed that marriages did not always conform to the expected patterns, but when they didn't, a loss of ritual status could occur.

Dumont (1970) maintained that the three basic aspects of caste—hierarchy, separation, and division of labor—can all be reduced to the single principle of the opposition of pure and impure.

The pure are defined as superior, and impure castes are impure because of their association with impure occupational specialties. **Impurity** for Hindus means a loss of status and is caused by association with "polluting" organic products and biological events such as birth, puberty, menses, and death. In tribal societies, such events may put individuals temporarily at supernatural risk, but Hindu ideology permanently associates particular social groups with impure biological events or organic products. The Hindu system is a logical reversal of the practice common in chiefdoms in which the chief is considered to be endowed with sacred power (*mana*), which makes him dangerously *tabu* to lower-ranked individuals, but in India it is lower-ranked individuals who endanger higher ranks.

The mythical charter for caste is found in the *purusha* myth, an account of creation contained in the Dharma Shastra of Manu (Buhler 1886, Burnell and Hopkins 1884; see also the box entitled "The *Purusha* Myth"). According to this account, Lord Brahma, the creator god, "for the prosperity of the worlds" created the four *varna*—Brahman, Kshatriya, Vaisya, and Sudra—from his mouth, arms, thigh, and feet, respectively (Buhler 1886 [Manu 1: 31]). Separate duties were assigned by the creator to each *varna.* The Brahmans (see Figure 9.9) were the "Lords of Creation" and the perpetual incarnation of *dharma* (sacred law). They were the priests, teachers, sacrificers, and receivers of gifts, who, because of their "superiority and eminence of birth,"

FIGURE 9.9
A high-caste Brahman priest studying a sacred text.

were entitled to "whatever exists in the universe" (Buhler 1886 [Manu 1:88–100]). The Kshatriya were to be protectors of the people and took political roles as rulers and warriors. The Vaisya were responsible for cattle herding, farming, and trade. The Sudra were to serve the top three *varna*, "without grudging." Similarly, only the top three were allowed to participate in a series of initiation rites that allowed them to be considered "twice-born," and only the twice-born could request the Brahman priests to perform sacrifices.

There are thousands of castes throughout modern India, and many different ways of grouping and ranking them. It is common, particularly in census-taking, to group them by *varna* ranks, but caste clusters, castes, and subcastes may be distinguished. Caste membership may be defined in a very general way by occupational specialty and by endogamy, but food rules are also very important. Certain caste groups are distinguished by strict vegetarianism, avoidance of domestic pork and fowl, abstinence from alcohol, or the eating of pork or beef. At the village level, caste membership is also defined by the commensal hierarchy, according to which castes give or accept specific categories of food or water from each other or smoke together (Mayer 1970). Accepting food implies either ritual equality or inferiority on the part of the receiving caste; thus, Brahmans may typically give food to all other castes but accept it only from other Brahman-level castes. The commensal hierarchy is displayed at any social gathering, such as a wedding, where feasting occurs. Food restrictions are applied to food preparation and serving and to eating arrangements, as well as to who can enter a kitchen. The most common foods cooked in water, such as rice, are highly restricted, whereas rich foods cooked in clarified butter (*ghee*) and served on special occasions may be shared more widely between different castes.

The most extreme form of pollution could be transmitted by mere physical contact. This kind of impurity applied to the lowest caste, whom Westerners called untouchables, because any contact with such persons required some form of ritual

---

hypergamy   Marriage to someone of higher rank. For example, Hindu women may marry men of a higher subcaste.
hypogamy   Marriage to someone of lower rank.
impurity   Low ritual status attributed to association or contact with polluting biological events or products.

purification such as sprinkling with water. In India, untouchables are sometimes called Harijans, or "God's children," or "exterior castes." They are exterior because they are often excluded from many public activities due to their ritual disabilities. Untouchability was officially declared illegal by the Indian constitution of 1949 and by Pakistan's constitution of 1953, but it continues to be an important social phenomenon.

Village-Level Caste and Exploitation

How does the caste system structure daily life in India? In what respects can caste be considered exploitive?

From 1954 to 1956, anthropologist Adrian Mayer (1970) studied caste relations in the village of Ramkheri in the Malwa district of Madhya Pradesh in central India. Ramkheri was a relatively large village with 912 people belonging to twenty-seven different castes. The castes were grouped by mutual consent into five groups and eleven ranks, with the Brahmans at the top and five untouchable castes at the bottom. Groups of castes at a similar rank tended to be localized in distinct quarters of the village. An interdependent division of labor, called the *jajmani system*, operated between the castes, with certain castes, such as barber, carpenter, blacksmith, potter, tanner-shoemaker, and sweeper, providing communitywide services. For example, the sweeper caste was responsible for cleaning latrines and disposing of dead animals—highly polluting functions that benefited everyone. In exchange for their services, caste members received foodstuffs according to a regular schedule. Some caste members, such as farmers and tailors who sold their products in town, were paid in cash for their goods by their fellow villagers.

All castes could draw water from the village well except the Harijan, who used their own wells and even washed their clothes and bathed at a separate place in the stream. The Harijan were expected to avoid the village temple and stood in the background during community meetings.

In the case of Ramkheri, the caste system had obvious implications for social stratification. Mayer (1970) found that the high-caste individuals owned more and tended to be more prosperous than low-caste people. However, wealth differences were not extreme and were partly attributed to expectations about relative occupational abilities. The economic advantages enjoyed by the upper castes were to some extent offset by the mutual advantages provided by the caste division of labor, and people appeared to accept their traditional occupations as a religious duty. Basic Hindu beliefs in *karma* and reincarnation support such acceptance by implying that one's *karma* (deeds or action) in life reflects previous existences and shapes one's future lives. The next life might be more pleasant.

Researchers in other areas described more extreme wealth inequities between castes. For example, Gerald Berreman (1979), who worked in the Himalayan foothills of Uttar Pradesh in 1957–1958, found that the Rajput and Brahmans enjoyed what M. N. Srinivas (1959) called "decisive dominance" in the region. At the district level, Brahmans and Rajput castes were not only the most numerous but also the most powerful groups politically and economically. The artisan castes were a small minority, effectively dependent on and exploited by the higher castes. Jonathan Parry (1979), who worked in the Kangra district of Himachal Pradesh in 1966–1968, also found that the highest castes received the best education, owned the most land, and held the best jobs.

The conspicuous inequality inherent in the caste system has led Western observers to focus on its economic component and to see caste as an exaggerated form of social stratification and rank, perhaps designed by the Brahmans for their own benefit. Dumont (1970) acknowledged that there is an important material dimension to caste but suggested that exclusive emphasis on this aspect is ethnocentric and obscures the native view in which caste forms a rational intellectual system. Dumont argued that it is most useful to examine caste as a "state of mind." He did not claim that mental facts cause the caste system—rather, they make it intelligible.

British anthropologist J. H. Hutton, in his classic study of caste (1963), identified the functionalist advantages of caste at several levels. He argued that it provides individuals with employment, a pattern for living, and personal security. The individual castes also function as self-reproducing corporate groups. They provide for themselves many services that the state might otherwise be required to supply. Hutton further argued that the caste system contributes to Indian national stability by creating a "plural society" capable of absorbing diverse groups into a single cohesive whole. Hutton was also critical of the inequities of caste—especially the disadvantages that women suffered under it—but as a functionalist, he cautiously concluded that it is too central to Hindu culture for reform-minded government administrators to attack directly.

The Hindu caste system is an extreme form of institutionalized inequality, which, as Berreman (1979) argued, arose in the process of state building by the Aryan invaders of India. Many castes are historically known to have been distinct tribal groups that were absorbed into expanding Hindu kingdoms. In the process, the hierarchical ranking of kin within tribal societies was replaced by the hierarchical ranking of castes within the state system, which was actually an incipient form of social stratification. The new ranking system helped to secure the advantageous position of the political elites by making the former tribal groups dependent and divided against themselves.

Regardless of how it may be described in intellectualist or functionalist terms, or how it may be understood emically, the caste system is a form of oppression and exploitation that benefits certain elite groups at the expense of other groups. Ultimately, it is political power that perpetuates the system. As Berreman observed,

Poverty and oppression, whether rationalized by criteria of race, ethnicity, caste, or class, are endured not because people agree on their legitimacy, but because they are enforced by those who benefit from them. (1979:221)

Hindu Aesthetics: Divine Image and the Religious Power of Art

What emotional compensation does Hindu religion provide for the inequities of caste? How do Hindu views of pleasure compare with Christian views? What is the cultural significance of "seeing" for Hindus?

The caste system, with all its inequities, is closely identified with and supported by the Hindu religion. However, beyond the belief in spiritual reincarnation, Hinduism also provides important emotional compensations for those wishing to escape the very real material inequities of caste. As monotheists, Christians have great difficulty understanding the Hindu religion because, from a Christian viewpoint, it is based on the worship of "idols." Furthermore, the prominence of erotic themes in Hindu religious art blurs the Western distinction between the sacred and the profane, thus making Hinduism appear very profane. Closer inspection of Hinduism shows that it contains an aesthetic system that makes culturally distinctive assumptions about art, worship, and the relationship between secular and sacred. Hinduism uses religious art as a powerful tool for helping individuals at all levels of the social hierarchy to experience a feeling of contact with an ultimate, eternal reality that transcends their daily mortal concerns. Christianity may accomplish the same objectives through different means.

Two key Hindu concepts, *rasa* and *darsan*, draw attention to some of the most important contrasts between Western and Hindu notions of religion and art. Richard Anderson (1990) notes that early Hindu philosophers felt that art was an important enough component of Hinduism to be considered a "fifth veda" on a par with the principal sacred texts, but open to everyone, regardless of their *varna* level. Art in the Hindu context refers, first, to drama, poetry, music, and dance, all of which emphasize a temporal dimension, and, second, to painting, sculpture, and architecture, which are relatively static. According to classical Hindu scholars, art is supposed to be an unconscious vehicle for moral improvement and pleasure, which are assumed to be mutually reinforcing.

Rasa refers to the emotional pleasure that the experience of art can provide. Anderson (1990) shows that Hindu art is thought to be pleasurable because it helps people attain the most important goals of the Hindu good life: righteousness, spirituality, prosperity, and pleasure. It is this linking of pleasure with religion that offends some Christians, who at the same time would readily acknowledge that doing "good" should make one feel good. The Hindu concept of good merges the "sacred" goals of righteousness and spirituality with the "profane" goals of material prosperity and sensual pleasure. Thus, for Hindus, there is no contradiction in erotic religious art. The religious use of sensuality is even more obvious in Tantrism, which is a Hindu and

Buddhist sect that uses food and ritualized sex as a form of religious meditation.

Rasa refers to the fleeting peak experience that art can inspire, as distinguished from religious meditation, which also has an important role in Hinduism. In a more mundane sense, *rasa* also refers to culinary flavor, spice, or relish. Scholarly definitions of *rasa* identify eight universal human emotions—happiness, pride, laughter, sorrow, anger, disgust, fear, and wonder—which may be experienced as *rasa*. Some Hindu authorities add tranquility as a ninth *rasa* emotion. Thus, religious art uses culturally specific symbols to manipulate emotion to help people feel good. As Anderson explains, art in the service of religion

can sweep us away, transporting our spirits from the tedious cares and anxieties that besiege our daily lives. . . . It provides a means whereby we can transcend the sensory world around us and escape to a state of superior pleasure, practical betterment, and, ultimately, spiritual bliss. (1990: 171–172)

Although Hinduism assumes the existence of one ultimate divine reality, it encourages great diversity in how this reality is culturally expressed and approached. Christianity, in contrast, is a very exclusive religion and recognizes relatively few images of divinity, such as the Father, Son, Holy Ghost, and the Virgin Mary.

Darsan refers to religious "seeing." For Hindus, viewing an image of the divine is in itself a form of worship or devotion (Eck 1985). It is expressed in pilgrimages to sacred places, in the special reverence for Hindu holy persons, and in the attention given to religious art, sculpture, temples, and shrines. Religious seeing, as Diana Eck (1985) points out, is a two-way process. The Hindu deity must "give" its image, and the observer must receive it. Hindu polytheism is expressed in a vast variety of religious images, which may be called icons when they take on a definite form—for example, as a representational painting or sculpture (see the box entitled "Siva Iconography"). Often Hindu icons combine animal and human shapes with multiple arms, heads, or eyes to indicate different aspects of the deity. They are aniconic images when they are nonrepresentational, "formless" shapes, such as colored stones or a flame. Hindu religious images are not empty idols to Hindus;

they are simply different forms or manifestations of the divine. Divine images are divine, and they focus the mind on the divine. Hindu devotion is expressed through the offering of humble gestures, flowers, food, and water or other special gifts, chants, and hymns to the divine images (see Figure 9.10).

Controversy over the Sacred Cow

How could we argue that treating Indian cows as sacred is a rational cultural practice?

Cattle sacrifice, which was central to the ritual system, was a monopoly of the Brahman priests during the Vedic period in India. As Hinduism and the caste system developed, cattle were treated as deities and became an important feature of the ritual purity complex. The five products of the cow—fresh milk, sour milk, butter, urine, and dung—were important purifying agents, whereas the consumption of a cow's flesh and leather working were polluting. According to the Dharma Sastra, cows were not to be disturbed or injured. The Arthasastra was blunt: "Whoever hurts or causes another to hurt, or steals or causes another to steal, a cow, should be slain" (Shamasastry 1960 [Bk. 2, chap. 29]). Under the influence of the *ahimsa* doctrine of nonviolence toward people and all animals, promoted by the Jains and Buddhists since the sixth century BC, this reverence for cows was carried to the point that special templelike homes were maintained to care for aged and abandoned cattle. The sacred status of the cow was increased by the arrival of the beef-eating Muslims and the British because cow reverence became a conspicuous marker of Hindu culture.

The Indian Sacred Cow Complex has been the center of a theoretical debate between anthropologists, economists, and geographers over whether Indians keep too many cows for primarily religious reasons. Anthropologist Marvin Harris (1965, 1966) initiated the controversy by arguing that practical economic choices by poor farmers were more important determinants of cattle practices in India than strictly religious considerations.

Harris (1965, 1966) was responding to numerous assessments by Indian public officials and development experts that Indians wastefully maintained vast numbers of useless cows because of ir-

Siva Iconography

Siva, or Shiva, the "Auspicious One," is one of the most prominent Hindu deities and illustrates the complexity of Hindu polytheism and iconography. Siva incorporates many universal complementary oppositions and ambiguities. He is a creator and a destroyer, a sensuous ascetic, benevolent and vengeful. He may be portrayed with multiple faces, three eyes, and four arms and sometimes as both male and female. He is often portrayed as a dancing figure in a ring of fire. Diana Eck provides a concise exegesis of this image:

The flaming circle in which he dances is the circle of creation and destruction called samsara *(the earthly round of birth and death) or* maya *(the illusory world). The Lord who dances in the circle of this changing world holds in two of his hands the drum of creation and the fire of destruction. He displays his strength by crushing the bewildered demon underfoot. Simultaneously, he shows his mercy by raising his palm to the worshiper in the "fear-not" gesture and, with another hand, by pointing to his upraised foot, where the worshiper may take refuge. It is a wild dance, for the coils of his ascetic's hair are flying in both directions, and yet the facial countenance of the Lord is utterly peaceful and his limbs in complete balance. Around one arm twines the* naga, *the ancient serpent which he has incorporated into his sphere of power and wears now as an ornament. In his hair sits the mermaid River Ganga, who landed first on Siva's hair when she fell from heaven to earth. Such an image as the dancing Siva engages the eye and extends one's vision of the nature of this god, using simple, subtle, and commonly understood gestures and emblems.* (1985:41)

rational religious beliefs. Much of the criticism was over the poor quality of many of the animals and the quantity of fodder that they consumed. Harris challenged this interpretation, arguing that it was based on irrelevant market-economy cash accounting. He emphasized that the relationship between people and cows in India was more likely to be symbiotic. Cattle subsist on the byproducts of the grain production system, which they in turn help sustain. He suggested that ecological pressures encouraged the maintenance of seemingly unproductive cattle, as well as the ideology of *ahimsa*, which supports the practice.

Harris (1965, 1966) maintained that the most important contribution of Indian cattle was their support of the grain-based subsistence system as draft animals and through the production of dung for fuel and fertilizer. Bullocks pulling plows and carts help produce and transport the grain that supplies 80 percent of the calories people consume. For most peasant families, tractors would be prohibitively expensive to purchase and operate, and a pair of bullocks is an absolute necessity. There appears to be an actual shortage of traction animals during periods of intense plowing activity, which is determined by the annual cycle of monsoon rains. Furthermore, Harris argued, up to half of the cow dung may be used as a domestic cooking fuel, while the remainder serves as fertilizer. Considering the volume of energy involved in a country as densely populated as India, this resource would be very costly to replace with commercially produced fossil fuels. Harris concluded that

it should be obvious that without major technical and environmental innovations or drastic population cuts, India could not tolerate a large beef-producing industry. This suggests that insofar as the beef-eating taboo helps discourage growth of beef-producing industries, it is part of an ecological adjustment which maximizes rather than minimizes the calorie and protein output of the productive process. (1966:57)

The Cattle Complex of India strikingly contrasts with the pattern in East Africa; these contrasts

FIGURE 9.10   *A richly costumed spirit dancer preparing to leap into a mound of white-hot coals to demonstrate the purity of his devotion to a particular Hindu deity.*

are related to major differences in subsistence patterns. Indian cattle are managed primarily to produce male traction animals, yet the direct production of animal protein remains an important secondary outcome. At 413 pounds (187 kg) of milk a year, average milk production of Indian cattle is less than half that of East African cattle (1606 lb [728 kg]) and 8 percent of an intensively managed U.S. dairy cow (5000 lb [2265 kg]). However, even this relatively low production rate represents a significant contribution to the animal-protein intake of the Indian population. It is also important to remember that beef is consumed in India by Muslims, Christians, and members of the untouchable castes who can afford it, and cattle are an important source of leather, which is produced by the despised castes.

Critics such as Alan Heston (1971), Frederick Simoons (1979), and Stanley Freed and Ruth Freed (1981) charged that Harris unduly minimized the role of religious ideology and the possibility that too many cows may be uneconomic. Most economists think that a cow surplus exists at the national level. For example, Heston (1971) looked at the well-being of the larger society in monetary terms. He argued that under different herd-management practices, a smaller number of female animals, if better cared for, could produce the same number of traction animals and more milk because well-fed animals are more efficient. Harris (1965, 1966) agreed that cattle can be environmentally destructive and are part of the problem of increased human pressure on resources. But he still argued that poorly fed, relatively inefficient cattle can nevertheless be advantageous to individual poor farmers.

The problem with the approach of those who attack the apparent economic irrationality of Hindu religion, as Harris (1971a) pointed out, is that it ignores the inequities of the caste system and the difficult situation of the poorest Indian farmers, who would be unable to maintain well-fed animals. Indian cattle are malnourished during the dry season, but when their services as draft animals are most required, they rebound when grazing improves with the monsoons. Like their East African counterparts, they tolerate drought conditions better than larger breeds, and they rebound more quickly. Free-ranging cattle feed themselves at public expense and no doubt, in some cases, at the expense of wealthy farmers and landlords; thus, they may play a role in wealth redistribution where great economic inequality exists.

The origin of the Sacred Cow Complex has also been part of the debate. Harris (1966) proposed that it may have begun in the Ganges Valley by 1000 BC when population pressure resulted in decreased farm size and made cattle more valuable as draft animals. The religious taboo on killing cattle thus came about so that people would not be tempted to slaughter them for food and thereby threaten their agricultural system. Simoons (1979) argued that the ban on killing cattle may have been proposed by the early Hindu kingdoms in order to secure a surplus for the expanding urban centers, thus benefiting the elite rather than the peasants. This is in agreement with Harris' view that the prohibition on cattle killing was part of an "imperial cult" that supported the elite and is not incompatible with the view that the ban also benefited the peasants.

At the village level, evidence supports rational herd-management practices by farmers as well as decision making based on religious principles (Freed and Freed 1981). People do say that they protect cows as an act of worship, and there is no reason to doubt their sincerity. At the same time, as Harris observes (1988), from an etic point of view, Indians selectively starve unwanted calves, while emicly they claim that all calves must be protected.

On balance, the controversy has drawn attention to the economic value of seemingly useless cows, but it also demonstrates the difficulty of positively determining why people do what they do. Contrary to what some observers have assumed, the sacred cow case does affirm the importance of religious belief. For example, as Simoons (1979) pointed out, many low-caste groups have stopped eating beef in order to avoid the ritual stigma of pollution and thereby enhance their social standing. The relationships between belief and actions are complex, and the best analysis would take a holistic ethnographic approach as recommended by the Freeds (1981). A full understanding of India's sacred cow must take into account both materialist and ideological factors. Assigning priority to one over the other may be useful as a research strategy, but it should not preclude a comprehensive understanding.

WOMEN IN SOUTH ASIA

South Asian women, whether under Hindu or Islamic Great Traditions, are clearly at a cultural disadvantage in comparison with men. This disadvantage is based on myth and religious ideology recorded in sacred texts and is expressed in ritual and physical separation between men and women, whereby men take leadership roles and enjoy relatively greater freedom outside the family. In this section, we will review the cultural-historical background of Islam to facilitate comparison with the Hindu Great Tradition. Then we will consider the position of women under both cultural traditions.

The Islamic Great Tradition

When and where did Islam arise? How did it reach South Asia? In what respect does Islam offer a major alternative to Hinduism?

Striking parallels exist between the rise of Islam as an expansive state system and the development of Hindu civilization. Both cases are examples of secondary state formation from a pastoral tribal base in response to the influence of preexisting states. In both cases, a complex interethnic conquest state was integrated by means of a literate Great Tradition ideological system. It is remarkable that both traditions came to coexist in India even though the two systems were incompatible on fundamental issues of belief.

In contrast to Hinduism, the details of the founding of Islam are well known. Islam is a revealed religion, transmitted in Arabic directly by Allah to his messenger, the Prophet Muhammad (AD 570–632). God's message is recorded as sacred scripture in the *Qur'an* (Koran) and is augmented by the *hadith*, or traditions surrounding the Prophet. Islam, which in Arabic means "surrender," refers to the need of the Muslim (believer) to surrender to the will of Allah, the one God. The fundamental articles of faith are encompassed by the Five Pillars of Islam:

1. Recitation of the Shahadah, confession of faith: "There is no God but Allah and Muhammad is his Prophet"
2. The performance of five daily prayers
3. The giving of alms (*zakkat*)
4. Observance of the fast of Ramadan
5. Pilgrimage to Mecca (the *hajj*)

Muhammad was a member of the Quraysh, a sedentarized north Arabian Bedouin tribe that controlled the Red Sea trade from Mecca, which was already an important ritual center. Muhammad's religious visions began in about 610; by the time of his death in 632, he had succeeded in uniting all the Bedouin tribes of Arabia into a religious state based on the new faith. The pre-Islamic Bedouin tribes were relatively egalitarian, patrilineal segmentary systems, led by popularly supported "chiefs" or *shaykhs* (sheiks), who led raids, settled disputes, and enjoyed some prestige but were still considered "first among equals." An essential element in this tribe-to-state transformation was the replacement of tribal and kinship loyalties with membership in the Umma, the Islamic community, which created a united front by suppressing the blood feud that had characterized intertribal relations throughout Arabia (Lewis 1960).

The Umma was a nascent religious state, united by common belief and military opposition to unbelieving outsiders as expressed in the *jihad*, or holy war. Under Islam, the Prophet Muhammad was accepted as the divinely appointed head of state. However, Muhammad did not specify how his successor, the caliph, was to be selected. Conflict over the succession resulted in a sectarian split between the Sunnites, who believed they were following the *Sunna* (the Prophet's sayings) in selecting the caliph, and the Shi'ites, who favored keeping the imam (foremost of the community) in the Prophet's closest line of descent and recognized their own line of imams. The caliph or imam, as the leader of the Islamic state and chief defender of the faith, was expected to lead prayers at the Friday service in the mosque. He was also responsible for settling disputes, collecting taxes, and organizing the *jihad* against unbelievers.

After the death of Muhammad, a period of rapid military expansion began that brought the Mesopotamian region—much of Persia, Egypt, and North Africa—under Islamic control by 700. Next, Muslims entered Spain and began to raid northern India. Conquest was a major source of state revenue, whether directly as battlefield booty or as tribute or tax in agricultural production. During the expansion of Islam, unbelievers with literate sacred scriptures—such as Jews, Christians, and, by extension, Hindus—were granted protection as peoples of the book as long as they acknowledged Islamic political authority and paid their taxes. Small Islamic kingdoms, or sultanates, were established in India by 1200, and from 1526 to 1761, the Islamic Mogul empire ruled over most of the Indian subcontinent. Although the Mogul rulers generally tolerated Hindu practices, there were many areas of conflict between the two Great Traditions, as illustrated by the modern partitioning of British India into Muslim Pakistan and Hindu India in 1947 (see Figure 9.11).

The Islamic state was based on the *shari'a*, which, like *tao* in Chinese, means "path" or "road."

FIGURE 9.11   *A Pakistani mosque, a striking reminder that the Islamic Mogul empire ruled over much of South Asia from 1526 to 1761.*

Like the Hindu concept of *dharma*, *shari'a* is God's law as outlined in the Koran and the *Sunna* or the *hadith* accepted by the Shi'ites (Levy 1962). Islamic law is a detailed prescription for all areas of life, specifying whether individual acts are required, forbidden, recommended, disapproved, or permitted. Islam, like Hinduism, constitutes a complete social system and has had a profound influence over preexisting cultural practices whenever Islamic states have been established.

Women in Islamic Society

Although in Islamic society women are considered to be legally and morally inferior to men, in what respects does this interpretation need to be qualified?

Any discussion of Islamic social practices must begin with a careful disclaimer acknowledging the great diversity of practices in specific countries and regions, at different historical times, between urban and village settings, and between different social classes. Furthermore, the Koran itself is interpreted in many different ways. However, certain principles do stand out. According to fundamentalist Islamic interpretations, women are generally viewed as morally and legally inferior to men. They are to be protected by their husbands and close male kin and are to stay out of public life. In several respects, in comparison with men, Muslim women are at a legal disadvantage by many interpretations of Islamic law. Daughters inherit less than sons. Women are permitted only one spouse at a time, whereas men may have up to four wives as long as they can provide for them and treat them fairly. Muslim women are expected to marry only other Muslims, whereas men may marry unbelieving peoples of the book. It is more difficult for a woman to obtain a divorce. Furthermore, modesty and male honor often require female seclusion (discussed in detail in the following section).

Many observers stress that Koranic law actually represented an improvement in the position of women over the common practice of pre-Islamic times. Women's rights in marriage, divorce, inheritance, and property ownership are specified in ways that no doubt increased their security.

A modern expression of Islamic gender roles is a common tendency toward gender segregation in education and employment. Labor migration by men for extended periods, leaving wives to maintain the household, is a common pattern. Women are less likely to work outside the home than men, and when they are employed as professionals, women tend to work with other women as teachers or doctors. Both high-status and low-status positions in the complementary occupational pairs—such as doctor–nurse, principal–teacher, executive–secretary, which are commonly seen as male–female sets in Western industrial countries—are more likely to be filled by men in Islamic countries (Papanek 1982).

When they address Western audiences, and especially Western feminists, Muslim female social scientists often stress that many of the cultural patterns that Western women take as evidence of Islamic oppression of women are misunderstood in ways that perpetuate the view that Muslim women are passive and ignorant, if not inferior. For example, Leila Ahmed (1982) argues that Westerners usually describe the harem entirely in male terms, as an institution for confining and controlling women to provide men with secure sexual access to multiple wives. The harem system does segregate women from men; Islamic women themselves, however, recognize that such segregation need not be oppressive in itself. Ahmed notes that the word *harem* is derived from the Arabic word *haram*, meaning "forbidden." She suggests that it is women who forbid males to enter exclusively female space. The harem is a gathering place for women where they can freely discuss and ridicule men and the world of men. It is also a place where a feminist critique of Islamic society can take place. Many Western women, isolated in nuclear families, do not enjoy such freedom. Thus, although Islamic women are in many ways discriminated against by their societies, seeing specific Islamic social institutions in entirely negative terms can be misleading. According to Ahmed,

to believe that segregated societies are by definition more oppressive to women, or that women secluded from the company of men are women deprived, is only to allow ourselves to be servilely obedient to the constructs of men, Western or Middle Eastern. (1982:531)

It must be remembered, however, that the harem is part of a larger Islamic society, which is controlled primarily by men.

Female Seclusion: The Purdah System

What cultural understandings support the common South Asian practice of secluding women? What functional explanations do anthropologists offer?

The practice of *purdah*, the veiling and seclusion of women, is a conspicuous South Asian cultural pattern, shared by Hindus and Muslims alike, and is related to the institutionalization of gender inequality shared by both cultures. *Purdah* means "curtain" or "veil" and refers to the physical separation of the living spaces used by men and women, as well as the actual veiling of a woman's face and body. This is a South Asian variation of the harem of the Arab Islamic world. The concept of *purdah* is also commonly extended to refer to types of avoidance or deference behavior practiced by women, including not looking at or speaking to certain people. Adherence to *purdah* restrictions is related to specific factors such as employment, education, social class, politics, and religion. Some Muslim sects have abolished or intensified seclusion by decree. Western observers often denounce *purdah* as another example of male oppression, but, like the harem, it plays an important functional role in the culture and is supported by many of the women who practice it.

In the strictest form of *purdah*, a woman must remain completely within the confines of her home throughout her adult life. Within a large house, there may be women's rooms and entrances that outside men cannot use, and special screens and partitions may be set up to hide women from view. In some cases, seclusion of women extends to otherwise public buildings and public transportation. Although there is considerable variation in the degree to which veiling is practiced, in extreme form, a Muslim woman in *purdah* can leave the seclusion of her home only when wearing the *burqa*, a full-length garment covering head and body (see Figure 9.12).

Hanna Papanek (1982) considers *purdah* to be based on two interconnected principles in South Asian culture, which she calls *separate worlds* and *symbolic shelter*. The principle of separate worlds is expressed in a sharp division of labor and workplace and in the corresponding economic interdependence between men and women. The principle of symbolic shelter is founded in the belief that women are especially vulnerable in a hostile outside world and therefore must be kept sheltered at home. The outside danger from which women need protection is the threat of uncontrolled sexual and aggressive impulses. The underlying assumption seems to be that people need close external supervision to control themselves; thus, *purdah* restrictions physically remove women from possible harm. Papanek suggests that Hindus and Muslims may view the dangers to women somewhat differently, with Hindu women seen as potential temptresses and Muslim women seen as potential victims, but either way they need to be protected. The dependency of women and supremacy of men are as deeply rooted in Hindu culture as they are

FIGURE 9.12   *An Indian Muslim woman wearing* burqa.

in Islam. In certain details, the Hindu version of *purdah* has been influenced by Islamic traditions, but the principles of symbolic sanctuary existed prior to Islam in India. For example, Manu, in the Dharma Sastra, declared the following laws for women:

No act is to be done according to (her) own will by a young girl, a young woman, or even by an old woman, though in (their own) houses. In her childhood (a girl) should be under the will of her father; in (her) youth, of (her) husband; her husband being dead, of (her) sons; a woman should never enjoy her own will. She must never wish separation of herself from her father, husband, or sons, for by separation from them a woman would make both families contemptible. She must always be cheerful and clever in household

The Ramayana: A Hindu Mythic Charter of Feminine Virtue

The Ramayana is one of the most popular Hindu myths, dating to 300 BC, during the early classic period of Hindu civilization. This epic romance is a part of the cultural identity of all Hindus. It is frequently recited in dramatic performances and is required reading in Indian schools. It presents a compelling role model of the ideal Hindu wife.

Briefly stated, the Ramayana (the Romance of Rama) tells the story of Rama, an incarnation of Vishnu, who weds the beautiful Sita, the heroine, after passing a heroic test. However, he is cheated out of his place as heir to his father's throne and banished to a 14-year exile in the forest. Out of devotion to her husband, Sita follows her husband into exile, even though he urges her to stay behind. Later, Sita is treacherously abducted by an evil king who wants to marry her, but she rejects his advances and is imprisoned. Meanwhile, her husband, Rama, recruits an army and rescues her, but he suspects that Sita was unfaithful to him during her imprisonment and forces her to pass an ordeal by fire to prove her loyalty before accepting her back. Rama takes his rightful place on the throne of his kingdom with Sita as queen. When his subjects gossip that Sita really was unfaithful after all, Rama sends her away again to the forest, where she raises his twin sons. When Sita sends his grown sons back to him, he invites her to return but insists that she again prove her virtue. She has, of course, been completely faithful and totally devoted to him throughout her ordeal, but this time she accepts his rejection and asks the earth to swallow her up. This is a fitting gesture because in the myth she was born from the earth.

---

business, with the furniture well cleaned, and with not a free hand in expenditure. But him to whom her father gives her, or (her) brother with the father's consent, she must obey alive, and dead must not disregard. (Burnell and Hopkins 1884:130–131)

Papanek (1982) stresses another important dimension of symbolic shelter: Women are "status demonstrators" for their husbands. The Muslim concept of *izzat*, family "honor" or "pride," extends to the modesty and virtue of a man's wife, sister, and daughter. Of course, the reverse is not the case; that is, a woman's status is not determined by the virtue of her husband, brother, or father. This is the famous double standard that also has a long history in Western civilization. The observance of *purdah* is an expression of modesty, social solidarity, and family respectability. The importance of feminine virtue is emphatically demonstrated by the ideal of Sita, the heroine of the Ramayana, one of the best-known Hindu myths (see the box entitled "The Ramayana").

Anthropologist Manisha Roy (1975), a Bengali woman, has carefully documented how the experience of growing up in the Hindu extended family creates culturally conditioned expectations for women that are often unfulfilled. The popular Hindu myths, which stress the ideals of romantic love and self-sacrificing devotion to the husband, conflict with the realities of arranged Hindu marriages and generate psychological frustration for women. A woman's husband often turns out to be an emotionally remote protector who is close to his wife only when he relates to her as mother of his children. Upper-class, urban Bengali women are able to find some compensation for the frustrations in their domestic lives by developing a long-term relationship as a devoted disciple of a guru outside the extended family, but this is only possible after their children are grown.

There are significant differences between the way Muslim and Hindu women in South Asia practice *purdah*. For example, Muslim women are secluded from all outside men, whereas Hindu women are secluded from all male affines, especially from their husband's kinsmen (Papanek 1982, Vatuk 1982). The Hindu pattern has been described in detail by Doranne Jacobson (1982), based on her research in the Bhopal region of central India. In this area, a Hindu woman remains fully veiled before virtually all male affines in her husband's joint family. She must also be partially veiled before many of the senior women in her husband's joint family. However, when she visits her natal village, she is virtually free of *purdah* restrictions.

Before examining the possible functions of *purdah*, it is important to consider the emic view. Women who practice *purdah* often attribute their adherence to feelings of shame, shyness, or embarrassment, and they relate it to parallel concerns for honor and respect. Their enculturation, especially through internalization of the heroic role models provided by mythic figures such as Sita, makes it an internal response that does not require outside sanctions. As Jacobson reports, "Most secluded women, too, pride themselves on their strict observance of purdah" (1982:96–97). This emic view supports the symbolic sanctuary interpretation, but women also recognize that *purdah* can be a marker of elite status because only economically well-off households could afford to observe it fully.

Many functions of *purdah* have been proposed, and it seems clear that it does not represent a simple conspiracy of males to oppress women. *Purdah* also restricts men and imposes responsibilities on them. It creates dependency between men and women because a woman who cannot leave her home must rely on her husband, children, or servants to perform outside errands, such as shopping. A man, in turn, might not do domestic chores such as cooking and cleaning. It has been suggested that Hindus might use *purdah* to reduce the danger of female ritual pollution and to safeguard the purity of caste endogamy (Yalman 1963). The most direct function of *purdah* is that it helps sustain the integrity of the patrilineal extended or joint family, which is the most viable minimal social unit in stratified state societies based on plow agriculture (Boserup 1970, Jacobson 1982). This system requires careful control of small parcels of land and support from neighboring families and seems to work best with unambiguous lines of authority, a strict division of labor, and a maximum of domestic tranquility.

Purdah imposes social distance between men and women and intensifies their respective role differences. *Purdah* also minimizes the possibility for potentially disruptive incidents of adultery, both within and outside the extended family, and supports the common pattern of arranged marriages. Unmarried girls who are secluded in their homes are unlikely to find lovers to marry who might undermine established community alliance networks. In Muslim societies, marriage may be arranged between patrilateral parallel cousins (a man marries FBD), which helps to concentrate lineage resources and furthers a woman's seclusion by making even her affines relatively close kin.

In Jacobson's view, *purdah* has played a vital cultural role:

However inimical such a system may be to the ideals of Westerners, urban-educated South Asians, or even to the preferences of a certain number of veiled women themselves, there can be no doubt that arrangements of this kind have allowed hundreds of millions of people to live—and sometimes even to prosper—over the course of several centuries in various corners of the earth. It should also be acknowledged that for many fortunate women, sequestered life in bustling and affectionate family units has provided security and satisfaction. Only as alternative family structures become economically feasible or necessary are male-dominated societies undergoing alteration in the direction of allowing females to assert their individuality in any but limited circumstances. (1982:84–85)

Bride Burning: Dowry Deaths in Modern Hindu India

What is the cultural context for the criminal practice of bride burning to collect dowry in contemporary India?

In recent decades, Indian newspapers have increasingly reported on new brides who were burned to death in unexplained grease fires in their kitchens.

It is generally understood that in these cases, the bride has been murdered by her husband after he has extorted as much dowry as possible from her family. The murderer is then free to seek more dowry "gifts" from a new bride.

In their analysis of this problem, anthropologists Linda Stone and Caroline James (1995) estimate that 2000 or more dowry deaths occur every year in India. Stone and James suggest that some of the cause of this violence against women is found both in traditional Hindu culture and in recent changes related to commercial-scale culture. Hindu culture provides many incentives for a woman's family to arrange marriage for their daughters and to give large dowries. In traditional India, it was not acceptable for a woman to be unmarried, even if widowed, as the traditional custom of *sati* demonstrated. Divorce is seen as dishonoring the family. Furthermore, with the cultural ideal of hypergamy, a Hindu bride and her parents are considered to be gifts from social inferiors. This places them in a subservient position relative to the groom's family, making them vulnerable to harassment and demands for higher dowry payments. Dowry payments reflect the reduced economic value of women in cultures in which plow agriculture, which is a male domain, is the dominant economic activity. Dowry payments are also associated with private land ownership and wage labor in agrarian civilizations. Bride-wealth is more common in domestic-scale cultures, such as in East Africa, where women are valued for both their subsistence and their reproductive roles.

The emergence of a consumption-based middle class in modern India has inflated dowry payments. Traditionally, the Hindu dowry involved household articles that were produced directly by the bride's family. Modern dowry payments may include large amounts of cash and expensive consumer goods such as televisions and refrigerators that are beyond the financial means of many middle-class Indians. It is significant that bride burning is primarily an urban, middle-class phenomenon. Frustrated consumer aspirations are a powerful motivation for these murders.

"Sita," who survived an attempted bride burning, told Caroline James that she brought a lavish dowry of $8000 along with 500 saris, jewelry, a television, a freezer, furniture, and kitchenware, but this was not enough to please her husband's family.

Sita overheard her mother-in-law telling her husband, "Leave this woman and we will get another one; at least the other party will give us more and better dowry than what these people have given us. What her parents have given us is nothing. Moreover, this girl is ugly, and she is dark" (Stone and James 1995:128). Sita woke up one night to find that her husband had doused her with kerosene, but she escaped when he couldn't find a match.

Stone and James (1995) note that in traditional Hindu India, women were not likely to be subjected to such violence because female fertility was highly valued as the means of perpetuating the patrilineage. A woman's ability to produce sons gave her significant domestic power and security. It is probably not a coincidence that bride burnings have emerged just as fertility rates in India have begun to decline, especially in urban areas, where children are more likely to be an economic burden. The vulnerability of women is further increased in the modern urban setting because, relative to men, they can contribute little to household income in the wage economy. The status of women is higher in domestic-scale cultures than in traditional agrarian civilizations, especially when the commercial culture transforms domestic economies.

SUMMARY

The Hindu civilization of South Asia is a literate Great Tradition with significant cultural continuity over the past 3000 years. The earliest South Asian Neolithic cultures were probably participants in the domestication process that occurred throughout Southwest Asia during the Early Holocene period. The Harappan civilization of the Indus Valley was the earliest South Asian state and probably had some connections with Mesopotamia. Hindu civilization arose in the Ganges region after the collapse of the Harappan civilization. Hindu culture apparently drew on some Harappan cultural elements but was primarily derived from the Indo-European-speaking Aryans who invaded South Asia from the west about 1600 BC.

The early Hindu kingdoms were a by-product of the Aryan conquest and the incorporation of the preexisting domestic-scale cultures of the subcontinent. Classical Hindu kingdoms, as described in the Arthasastra, were organized around a complex government bureaucracy based on secular political power backed by a formal legal system with fines and physical punishments for offenders. It also relied on a religious system that divided society into four ranked groups, or *varna*. The dominant structure of Hindu society up to the present time is the caste system, which assigns everyone to a ritually ranked endogamous occupational group. This generates great social inequality, but it is justified and supported by Hindu religious beliefs that emphasize religious duty, the hope of reincarnation at a higher level, and the opportunity for people at all social levels to enjoy transcendental contact with the divine. Hindu religious beliefs also provide ritual protection for cows, which are an important source of fuel, food, and traction power for poor people who might otherwise have great difficulty supporting themselves.

Women are placed in inferior positions relative to men by both the Islamic and Hindu Great Traditions. These cultures rigidly separate men's and women's worlds in a way that supports the continuity of male-dominated extended families. Men occupy dominant roles in both their own families and the larger society. Women gain greater power as they grow older, and they benefit in certain ways from culturally prescribed separation. But women in modern India have been increasingly the targets of violence. Bride burning is related to the demand for high dowries and the difficulty women have contributing financially in a male-dominated wage economy.

STUDY QUESTIONS

1. Discuss the cultural significance of the following South Asian language groups: Indo-European, Dravidian, Sino-Tibetan, Hindi, Bengali, and Urdu.

2. Describe the basic social structure of the early Hindu kingdom. How did early Hindu kingdoms use direct political power to maintain and extend the state?

3. Compare and contrast the organization of the state in China and Hindu India.

4. How did the Hindu legal system reflect the inequalities of Hindu society?

5. Describe the basic structural features of the Hindu caste system, distinguishing it from class and clan.

6. In what way was ritual purity a central feature of Hindu culture?

7. Distinguish between *varna, jati,* Brahman, Kshatriya, Vaisya, and Sudra. Discuss the economic correlates of caste, and weigh the arguments that it served positive social functions or was exploitive.

8. In what ways does the Hindu Sacred Cow Complex have positive adaptive functions? What are the arguments for the religious explanations of the Sacred Cow Complex?

9. Describe the position of women according to fundamentalist Islamic principles.

10. Distinguish between the Islamic and Hindu cultural context of *purdah,* referring to the principles of separate worlds and symbolic shelter. What are the functionalist explanations of *purdah?*

11. Contrast the basic features of Islam and Hinduism, placing each system in its appropriate cultural-historical context.

12. Discuss how bride burning is related to modern Indian economics and the status of women.

SUGGESTED READING

ALLCHIN, BRIDGET, AND F. RAYMOND ALLCHIN. 1982. *The Rise of Civilization in India and Pakistan.* Cambridge, Eng.: Cambridge University Press. An archaeological overview of South Asian prehistory and the early development of Harappan and Hindu civilization.

BASHAM, A. L. 1954. *The Wonder That Was India: A Survey of the Culture of the Indian Sub-Continent Before the Coming of the Muslims.* London: Sidgwick & Jackson. A widely respected basic textbook on South Asian history and culture.

ECK, DIANA L. 1985. *Darsan: Seeing the Divine Image in India.* Chambersburg, Penn.: Anima Books. An in-depth treatment of the visual aspects of Hindu religion.

PAPANEK, HANNA, AND GAIL MINAULT (EDS.). 1982. *Separate Worlds: Studies of Purdah in South Asia.* Delhi: Chanakya Publications. An interdisciplinary collection of papers on the seclusion of women in South Asia.

TYLER, STEPHEN A. 1986. *India: An Anthropological Perspective.* Prospect Heights, Ill.: Waveland Press. An anthropological overview of many aspects of Indian culture with an emphasis on linguistic and cognitive categories.

IO

The Breakdown of States

A recurrent issue in Chapters 6–9 was how to explain the increases in social complexity that culminated in social stratification, state political organization, and Great Tradition civilizations. The origin of the state has been a central research problem in anthropology for many years; but much less attention has been devoted to the equally important issue of the continuity of states and the reasons for their frequent collapse. In this chapter, we consider the breakdown of states, which also forces us to reconsider theories of cultural development and the nature of the state itself. History has shown that states are unstable entities, prone to collapse from internal conflict and external invasion. Considering the multiple, interconnected potential threats to which states are vulnerable, it is remarkable that they ever arose in the first place. The failure of deterministic origin theories to satisfactorily account for all cases suggests that state formation is not an entirely predictable process. Similarly, the frequent collapse of states helps demonstrate that evolutionary progress is neither irreversible nor inevitable, despite persistent popular beliefs in "progress."

THE VIABILITY OF THE STATE

The Concept of Collapse

What cultural changes occur when states break down? What happens to people?

Our primary concern here is understanding the process by which states and empires decompose into smaller political units. This kind of system collapse must be distinguished from the fall of particular dynasties and their replacement by other sets of rulers. Changing dynasties is a major topic for historians but will not be treated here, except when the change represents a major cultural discontinuity. The focus of this discussion is the fate of ancient, precapitalist systems, because additional dynamics influence states in the modern world system; these new factors will be explored in Chapters 11–15.

In dealing with dynamic cultural and biological systems, defining when an entity ceases to exist and when it has changed into a different system is always a problem. As cultural ecologist Roy Rappaport observed (1977b), processual continuity—the continuation of culturally established processes of government despite a change in dynastic leadership—is the most useful criterion. But some ambiguity will always remain, and arbitrary judgments must be made about whether a particular culture, state, or civilization has been extinguished. The issue in this chapter is those conspicuous cases in which governments collapse and cities are abandoned. We will also consider a related but distinct issue: the less common problem of the total disappearance of particular Great Traditions.

Like any cultural system, a civilization is composed of the individuals or societies that perpetuate it, as well as the technologies, organizational patterns, and ideological systems that maintain it. States can break down while the population continues to transmit significant elements of the culture. The total disappearance of a people with their language and culture is an unlikely event, except when modern states have exterminated tribal peoples and cultures as a policy of national expansion (see Chapter 14).

It is important to ask, What changes when states collapse? The fall of states is not just an inconsequential change of political regimes; it also carries important human and environmental costs. State systems are based on social inequality and exploitation, but they do provide vital social services for very large populations. The government elite has a clear vested interest in maintaining a large, productive population because people are the main source of state revenue and the troops used to extract booty from other states, to extend the boundaries of the state, or to defend the state against aggressors. People under state control may resent paying taxes, but, like it or not, their personal security depends on government institutions, like the police, the law, the courts, and the army. The state provides famine relief and promotes capital-intensive agricultural development. The state also develops and maintains the communications system and public services required for commerce and foreign trade. Living standards may be drastically reduced during periods of extreme political instability, as trade and marketing networks break down, and many people may be killed when social control mechanisms disappear or foreigners take over. Collapsing states may deplete valuable nonrenewable resources and leave behind seriously degraded ecosystems.

The Vulnerability of Inequality and Political Hierarchy

In what ways are states more vulnerable to system collapse than domestic-scale cultures?

Although no culture can claim perfect functional integration, focusing on the issue of collapse makes it clear that states are significantly more precarious than domestic-scale cultures. States are more complex systems with more pieces and more things to go wrong. However, this is not just a quantitative matter. Tribes cannot break down because there is no tribal political structure to collapse. Villages and bands undergo continuous reorganization and can be dissolved at any time with no particular impact on the larger society and culture. By contrast, large regional states break down into local kingdoms or city-states, which, in turn, may further split into chiefdoms or autonomous villages and bands.

States are especially vulnerable to collapse because they contain social classes based on major inequities in wealth and power. States create special-interest groups and give them a reason to risk bringing the whole system down in order to improve their own position. A limitation on the number of political offices generates perpetual rivalries. Inequalities of wealth and power may be the most critical defining feature of states and the single most important cause of their breakdown. The creation of wealth requires revenue, but revenue extraction by taxation is a doubly risky state function. State authorities will seek as much revenue as possible, but if they demand too much, the peasantry may rebel. Too high a rate of revenue extraction also forces people to intensify their subsistence activities, which will increase the pressure on natural ecosystems.

Unequal concentrations of wealth—whether in the form of luxury goods, stored food, or labor-intensive construction projects—appear to be functional prerequisites for state organization; their presence, however, also causes dangerous instability. Warehoused food is required to support non-food-producing specialists and to sustain dense populations that might be threatened by fluctuations in production. Luxury goods are necessary status markers and rewards for political service. Storehouses are prime targets for looters from both within and without a particular state, and their defense requires expensive walls and standing armies. The unequal distribution of luxury goods also makes police forces and court systems necessary.

Creating and defending state wealth was a primary reason for costly military campaigns against neighboring states. The maintenance of a full-time officer corps, palace guards, and frontier garrisons were permanent military expenses, and specific campaigns in which large numbers of peasant soldiers were mobilized could be extremely costly. Military expenditures may have been the largest category in many state budgets and created constant pressure for potentially destabilizing increases in revenue extraction.

In comparison with a cultural universe occupied exclusively by domestic-scale tribal cultures, states introduced a qualitatively different cultural dynamic into any regional system. Whereas chronic feuding was endemic in tribal systems, territorial conquest was a permanent characteristic of states. Tribal raids and blood feuds did not require permanent leaders or a standing professional army and thus were not incentives for increased production. However, the appearance of states in a nonstate area stimulated trade and raiding by tribal groups against the state. This sometimes pushed tribes into political developments leading to wealth inequality and tribal instability.

STATE SYSTEMS THAT FAILED

In the following sections, we will examine possible causes of political collapse and the relationship between collapse and the continuity of particular civilizations or Great Traditions. Examples are drawn from the cultures that were discussed in previous chapters, which were focused on state origin and the basic cultural features of states. In Mesopotamia, foreign invasion definitively terminated 3500 years of cyclical state building and collapse. Mesopotamian civilization disappeared a few centuries later. Harappan urban civilization collapsed after approximately 1000 years but contributed significantly to later cultural developments in India. Andean civilization was characterized by perhaps 4500 years of processual continuity, punctuated by

frequent collapse of individual states and empires, until it was halted by foreign invasion. In the Andes, however, there is major cultural continuity after nearly 500 years, even though the political economy has been totally transformed. China, which is not examined in this chapter, also demonstrated nearly 4000 years of processual continuity, even though individual states and dynasties repeatedly collapsed. In China, the foreign invaders were absorbed by the Great Tradition, which persisted despite political change. These cases show the complexity of the issue of political collapse and the fate of civilizations. Cultural continuity clearly is stronger than political structure.

Mesopotamia: The End of a Great Tradition

What inherent cultural and environmental problems did Mesopotamian civilization deal with effectively for 3500 years? Why did this civilization finally end?

If state organization began in Mesopotamia with the Uruk period in 4000 BC and if, as Norman Yoffee (1988a) suggests, the Persian conquest of Babylonia in 539 BC marked the end of the distinctively Mesopotamian political system, then the Mesopotamian political system based on the state lasted for approximately 3500 years. Yoffee dates the final termination of Mesopotamian civilization some 500 years later, in AD 75, when the last cuneiform document is known to have been written. After that time, no recognizable Mesopotamian language, economy, or belief system persisted, although certain specific cultural connections can still be traced in succeeding civilizations. This raises the question of whether Mesopotamian culture or civilization can be considered an entity. Yoffee defines Mesopotamian civilization as

that fragile, but reproducible, set of cultural boundaries that encompass a variety of peoples, political and social systems, and geographies marked as Mesopotamian and that, importantly, include the idea of a political center. (1988a:44)

Mesopotamian civilization clearly was a complex, multiethnic system, incorporating peoples speaking different languages, practicing different subsistence activities, and worshiping different gods. The written tradition and related religious beliefs gave the civilization great continuity. The Mesopotamian political system was based on a network of city-states, which at various times were combined into regional states or empires. There were constant power struggles between the rulers of different cities, and cities were abandoned or relocated after military defeats or changes in the course of major rivers. Dynasties were replaced following foreign invasions or internal conflicts.

The Sumerian King List shows how unstable the political situation was in Mesopotamia. The list is an official written record of the sequence of individual kings, together with their capital cities, who were entitled to rule over the Mesopotamian empire. The list begins in approximately 2900 BC in the Early Dynastic and continues through the last Sumerian dynasty in approximately 2000 BC. The list creates the fiction of perfect continuity, with a single ruler always in control of the entire region; thus, it cannot be accepted as literal history. The time span attributed to individual dynasties is purely metaphorical, and the list is an incomplete emic view, idealized for political purposes. Nevertheless, it provides a glimpse of the kind of upheavals that must have characterized the Mesopotamian scene.

The list names 146 rulers in twenty-six dynasties over the 900-year period (see Table 10.1). This suggests an average of just 6 years per king and 35 years per dynasty, and the dynastic turnover is invariably attributed to military defeat. Some authors

TABLE 10.1   *Sequence of Dynasties Recorded in the Sumerian King List, 2900–2000 BC*

City	Source	Rulers	Cause of Loss	Putative Duration (years)
Eridu	Heaven	2	City abandoned	64,800
Badtibira	Transfer	3	City abandoned	108,000
Larak	Transfer	1	City abandoned	28,800
Sippar	Transfer	1	City abandoned	21,000
Shuruppak	Transfer	1	Flood	18,600
Kish	Heaven	23	Battle	24,510
Eanna	Conquest	1	Transfer	324
Erech	Transfer	12	Battle	2,310
Ur	Conquest	4	Battle	177
Awan	Conquest	3	Battle	356
Kish	Conquest	8	Battle	3,195
Hamazi	Conquest	1	Battle	360
Erech	Conquest	3	Battle	187
Ur	Conquest	4	Battle	116
Adab	Conquest	1	Battle	90
Mari	Conquest	6	Battle	136
Kish	Conquest	1	Battle	100
Akshak	Conquest	6	Battle	99
Kish	Conquest	7	Battle	491
Erech	Conquest	1	Battle	25
Agade	Conquest	11	Battle	197
Erech	Conquest	5	Gutian invasion	30
Gutians	Conquest	21	Battle	91
Erech	Conquest	1	Battle	7
Ur	Conquest	5	Battle	108
Isin	Conquest	14	—	203

SOURCE: Kramer (1963).
NOTE: This is the "official record," the given length of particular dynasties.

(Jacobsen and Adams 1958) have pointed out that overirrigation under state management may have played a role in the abandonment of southern Mesopotamian cities and the collapse of the third Ur dynasty, which effectively marked the end of the Sumerian period. The argument is that so much irrigation water was used that it inadvertently elevated the water table, causing subsurface saltwater to contaminate the soil and inhibit the growth of crops. Evidence for salt damage is found in the records of declining crop yields, increased seed requirements reflecting poor germination rates, and specific references in ancient texts to salt-damaged fields. Documents show that barley yields declined by nearly two-thirds over 700 years, while wheat, which is more salt-intolerant, was virtually abandoned as a crop even though it had previously been as important as barley. Identifying such an ecological factor as a sole cause of collapse would be misleading because underlying political factors caused the mismanagement of the irrigation system and created the demand for increased production.

Foreign invaders, or "barbarians," such as Amorites, Kassites, and Gutians, have sometimes been credited with bringing down Mesopotamian states. However, as Yoffee (1988a) observes, Mesopotamian civilization incorporated different ethnic groups that actually contributed to its persistence. It was only when the Persian invaders from a still larger empire conquered Mesopotamia that the established political system, and later the entire civilization, was brought down. Previous breakdowns did not prevent the city-states from being regrouped into regional states.

Thus, in the Mesopotamian case, we see a cultural tradition that maintained itself for a very long time despite chronic political instability. In the end, Mesopotamian civilization was superseded by a more powerful regional civilization, within what had become a western Asian world system based on extensive tributary empires. Mesopotamian civilization apparently was so weakened when it lost its central position within the local world system that it was unable to recover from a routine dynastic collapse. This outcome could be considered an example of Elman Service's (1960) law of evolutionary potential, but we are leaving out the specific historical details. The world system concept will be discussed in more detail in Chapter 11.

Harappa: Deurbanization and Cultural Continuity

What are the arguments against the foreign invasion, natural disaster, and resource depletion explanations for the collapse of 1000-year-old Harappan civilization?

By 1500 BC, the cities associated with the Harappan civilization in the Indus Valley had been abandoned, perhaps 1000 years after their founding. Without the cities, the state also disappeared, along with the writing system. The best-known cities of Harappa and Mohenjo-Daro (see Figure 10.1) apparently were rebuilt several times during that period, but the civilization ultimately succumbed to a process that has been called deurbanization (Gosh 1982). As A. Gosh describes it, deurbanization is the reverse of the urbanization process and implies a breakdown of political authority at the top. The population of cities dwindles; fewer full-time specialists, craftsmen, and administrators are needed; and long-distance trade in luxury goods ceases. Judging by the steady decline in the quality of housing, which is archaeologically documented, the city of Harappa seems to have turned into a slum before it was completely abandoned (Possehl 1977).

The cause of the demise of the Harappan civilization has been a long-standing mystery because there is no documentary account of the event. However, three different explanations have been posed: (1) destruction by foreign invasion, (2) natural destruction by Indus floods, or (3) exhaustion of the resource base through overuse. The foreign invasion theory typically cites the Aryans as the principal villains and the skeletons piled in the streets of Mohenjo-Daro as evidence of conquest and massacre. However, on close inspection, this interpretation seems weak. The Aryans did have a warrior tradition, but as noted previously, their arrival cannot be correlated precisely with the fall of Harappan civilization. Furthermore, no hard evidence supports an invasion at either Harappa or Mohenjo-Daro.

The famous massacre is probably a myth, according to archaeologist George Dales (1964), who directed excavations at Mohenjo-Daro in the 1960s. The thirty-five skeletons were found in six different groups, and the deaths may not have occurred at

FIGURE 10.1
Mohenjo-Daro, one of the two urban centers of the Indus Valley civilization, which collapsed about 1500 BC.

the same time; this suggests that most were probably intentional burials. Two bodies may have inadvertently been buried on top of a much older street, which may have fed the "bodies in the street" myth. There is no evidence of weapons or destruction to fortifications to indicate an assault ever took place, nor is there evidence that the "victims" died of traumatic injury, according to Kenneth Kennedy (1982), who reexamined all the remains. Dales argues that bandits might have killed some people who remained in the city after it was abandoned for other reasons.

Perhaps the most dramatic single-cause explanation of Harappan collapse is the theory developed by Dales (1965, 1966, 1982; Dales and Raikes 1968) and his associate hydrologist Robert Raikes (1964, 1965): A series of great floods caused the cities to be abandoned. This theory, which Raikes (1964) admitted is pure speculation, suggests that Harappan civilization was destroyed not by the normal fluctuation in the Indus seasonal flood regime but by catastrophic tectonic uplift and associated earthquakes and flooding. Uplift below Mohenjo-Daro caused perhaps several gigantic earth dams to block the flow of the Indus, flooding out the settlements immediately upstream and

then drowning them in a sea of mud. Earthquakes throughout the region would have destroyed other settlements and disrupted trade. Repeated attempts to rebuild or move the major cities ultimately failed. Dales summarized this natural disaster view as follows:

Flooding was the principal enemy of the Mohenjodarians, and of all the Harappan period inhabitants of the lower Indus Valley. Bands of raiders from the nearby Baluchistan hills could well have taken advantage of the chaotic conditions following the floods, but they were apparently not the cause of such conditions. (1965:14)

The Dales–Raikes flood theory has been rigorously attacked by other researchers. H. T. Lambrick (1967) found insufficient geophysical evidence that an earth dam over 100 feet (30 meters [m]) high and more than 30 miles (48 kilometers [km]) long had formed across the Indus. He also argued that the sediment deposits in the Harappan cities could be accounted for in other ways. Gregory Possehl (1967) also challenged the physical evidence for the dam and further argued that even if Mohenjo-Daro was so destroyed, that would be an insufficient explanation for the destruction of the entire civilization. Flooding was, after all, a normal problem along the Indus, and Possehl agreed that Mohenjo-Daro itself may have been repeatedly flooded out and rebuilt. Instead of flooding, Possehl favored the ecological argument that the Harappan civilization collapsed because of resource depletion.

Possehl cited conjectural evidence assembled by Walter Fairservis (1967) to suggest the level of resource demand posed by a city the size of Mohenjo-Daro. Based on data from contemporary Indus Valley villagers, Fairservis estimated that Mohenjo-Daro may have contained 41,250 people. The total population would have required at least 22,715 acres (9200 hectares) to supply 384 pounds (174 kilograms [kg]) of grain per person per year. The necessary bullocks for plowing (one bullock plows 8 acres [3 hectares]) would require a herd of 8755 cattle and another 3097 acres (1254 hectares) just to grow 25 percent of the fodder. Vast additional grazing lands would be required, but deforestation to supply building materials and fuel must have degraded much of the surrounding territory.

Dales and Raikes (1968) defended their "natural disaster approach" and rejected Possehl and Fairservis' "pre-conceived socio-economic model" by pointing out that there was no evidence for resource depletion or "wearing out of the landscape," especially because the soil was seasonally renewed by Indus flooding.

Disregarding the specific causes of the breakdown of the urban phase of Harappan civilization, it is likely that it was largely expressed as a steady economic decline over a period of perhaps 200–300 years, with a reduction in the production of luxury goods (Rao 1982). Because, as some have suggested (Miller 1985), Harappa may have been less socially stratified than other ancient civilizations, the deurbanization transition may have been relatively smooth, with considerable cultural continuity. A recognized post-Harappan archaeological culture suggests that the Harappan peasantry maintained much of the earlier culture and folk tradition and that significant cultural elements must have been reflected in the second urbanization that took place in the Ganges by 600 BC, culminating in the Hindu Great Tradition (Allchin 1982).

Like Mesopotamia, the Harappan case might also be considered an example of the local discontinuity of progress. However, the lengthy temporal gap between the fall of Harappa and the rise of classical Hindu civilization makes it difficult to argue that Harappa was outcompeted by a more "progressive" civilization. India provides numerous other examples of the rise and fall of states. After Harappa, over the centuries between 500 BC and AD 1970, sixty-two large regional states have successively arisen and collapsed in India (see Figure 10.2).

Andean Civilizations: Fragile Empire, Robust Culture

What internal cultural factors explain the rapid collapse of the Inca empire during the Spanish conquest?

The Inca empire is as famous for the manner in which it collapsed as it is for its great size and wealth. The vast 380,000-square-mile (mi^2) (984,200-square-kilometer [km^2]) empire, which may have encompassed 32 million people, was brought under foreign control within less than 5 years. Much of its wealth was subsequently extracted to benefit the even larger Spanish empire, whose capital was more than 5000 miles (8045 km) away. Even more remarkable was the fact that only 180 men made up the conquering Spanish army. The Inca empire was, in fact, a very fragile political superstructure that had grown rapidly following the long-established tradition of Andean civilization. The basic nature of Andean civilization, and the way political power developed and the empire expanded, helps explain the relative fragility of these complex systems, as well as their underlying cultural continuity. The following analysis is based largely on the work of Geoffrey Conrad and Arthur Demarest (1984).

According to Conrad and Demarest, the most critical factor underlying the dynamics of the Inca state was an ideological emphasis on ancestor cults. By AD 1000, ancestor worship as practiced by the kingdoms along the Peruvian coast began to assume forms that would set the stage for Inca expansion. A key cultural pattern related to the ancestor cult, one that the Inca shared with the north coast Chimu state, has been called split inheritance by Conrad (1981). Both the Chimu and Inca kings were worshiped as divinities after they died; even in death, they continued to hold title to the vast

KEY: • *Time of Apogee of Power*

1. Haryankas	10. Kusanas	19. Early Kalacuris	28. Paramaras
2. Saisunagas	11. Ksaharatas	20. Pusyabhutis	29. Candellas
3. Nandas	12. Kardamakas	21. Calukyas of Vatapi	30. Colas
4. Mauryas	13. Vakatakas	22. Greater Pallavas	31. Kalacuris
5. Sungas	14. Guptas	23. "Varmans" of Kanyakubja	32. Calukyas of Kalyani
6. Northern Sakas	15. Pallavas	24. Karkotas	33. Caulukyas (Solankis)
7. Indo-Parthians	16. Southern Hunas	25. Rastrakutas	34. Gahadavalas
8. Mahameghavahanas	17. Maukharis	26. Patas	35. Cahamanas
9. Satavahana	18. Later Guptas	27. Gurjara-Pratiharas	36. Ghurids

37. Mamluks	46. Gajapatis	54. Sivaji
38. Yadavas	47. Sharqis	55. Nizam-ul-Mulk
39. Khaljis	48. Lodis	(Hyderabad)
40. Tughlugs	49. Tuluvas	56. Peshwa
41. Saiyyids	(Vijayanagara)	57. British
42. Sangamas	50. Moguls	58. Sindhia (Gwali)
43. (Vijayanagara)	51. Surs	59. Bhonsle (Nagpu)
Bahmanis	52. Adil Shahis	60. Mysore
44. Ahmad Shahis	(Bijapur)	61. Republic of India
45. Khaljis (of Malwa)	53. Qutb Shahis	62. Pakistan
	(Golkonda)	

FIGURE 10.2 *Major powers of the Indian subcontinent, 500 BC–AD 1970. (SOURCE: Schwartzberg 1977.)*

wealth that they had accumulated during their reigns. The office of kingship was inherited by the deceased ruler's principal son, but his other heirs were made trustees of the royal mummy and the deceased's treasury.

The practice of ancestor worship is very ancient in the Andean tradition, as indicated by the great attention devoted to funerary textiles and ceramics and by the fabulous treasure of gold and silver objects recently discovered in 2000-year-old unlooted Mochica royal burials (Alva 1990). The royal burials found in the Chimu city of Chanchan from the late empire period, immediately preceding the Inca, were contained within royal palaces, which were converted into royal temple-tombs upon the ruler's death. Ten such temple-tomb palaces have been identified in Chanchan, and the royal mummy apparently was publicly displayed during repeated funeral ceremonies. This royal mummy cult also included human sacrifices and is reminiscent of funerary patterns described earlier for Mesopotamia and Shang China. As in those cases, the Andean cult

also must have functioned to reinforce the legitimacy of the rulers. More importantly for empire building, however, the added feature of split inheritance forced the newly installed ruler to engage in military conquest to build the personal wealth that would become the basis for his own ancestor cult. Thus, an ideological pattern provided a clear motive for state expansion in the Andean area.

The Inca system of ancestor worship is well described in the ethnohistoric material recorded immediately after the Spanish conquest. It reveals the same functional connections between kinship, land, and political power that characterized Chinese ancestor worship. In the Inca case, as described by Conrad and Demarest (1984), the mummified bodies of the dead became sacred objects, or *mallquis*, and specialist diviners, known as *mallquip-villac*, communicated with the ancestors through these mummies (see Figure 10.3). The concept of *huaca*, shrine or sacred object, links the related concepts of *mallquis* (mummy), *ayllu* (descent group), and the kinship term *vilca* (great-grandfa-

FIGURE 10.3 *Richly decorated skull from the pre-Inca Nazca culture, used by a cult of the dead, a prominent feature of Andean civilization.*

ther or great-grandson, which also means ancestor). All these terms were used interchangeably. Furthermore, there are specific associations between specific ancestors and specific shrines. As in China, the well-being of the descent group was thought to depend on the proper ritual respect being accorded the *huaca* and mummy. In pre-Inca times, individual *ayllu* groups cared for their own mummies and *huacas*. Women wove special textiles for funeral rituals, and *ayllu* members cultivated specific plots to support the relatively small-scale ceremonies that were part of *ayllu*-level ancestor worship.

Conrad and Demarest (1984) argue that the earliest Inca rulers consciously manipulated the ideological system to increase their power. They subdivided the preexisting and generalized creator/ sky deity into at least four different manifestations, to make room for an imperial ancestor deity as the progenitor of the Inca dynasty. Because Andean religious beliefs were so interconnected and widespread, the divine–royalty concept was easily accepted. Whenever the members of an *ayllu* conducted their own ancestor worship, they were, in a sense, also worshiping the divine ruler of the empire.

The Inca system of split inheritance was a simple elaboration of the established practice of ancestor worship and may have arisen to facilitate orderly succession to kingship. The earliest Inca rulers were probably war leaders, and factionalism was a chronic problem because there was no formal rule of succession. Split inheritance provided a major ritual function and guaranteed material support for the political faction that did not inherit political power. The Inca royal mummy cult was a conspicuous feature of the state religion and, as such, was certainly not a lowly consolation prize. The mummies were identified with the manifestation of the solar or sky deity who founded the Inca dynasty, and thus were key legitimizing symbols of the state. They also were identified with specific natural forces and therefore could ensure the welfare of the general population.

When the Spaniards arrived, the mummies of at least five earlier rulers in the Inca dynasty, dating back as far as Viracocha Inca, who died in 1438, were being maintained in the Coricancha, the main temple in the capital city of Cuzco (see Figure 10.4). Each mummy was treated as lavishly as it had been in life. It was attended by its descendants, who served it as retainers and formed a corporate descent group, known as *panaqa*. *Panaqa* members were the Orejones, the Inca hereditary elite, who occupied the highest offices in the Inca bureaucracy. The *panaqa* was a special type of *ayllu*, a royal court focused on the deceased ruler who was treated as a *huaca*. The members of the *panaqa* paraded the mummy for important ceremonies, sacrificed food and drink to it, and managed its property.

The Inca system of split inheritance promoted imperial expansion because a ruler's personal wealth was derived from the production of his personal landholdings and the *mita* labor service that he could call up from his domain. The king needed to control land because labor service had to be

FIGURE 10.4
Reconstructed view of the Coricancha, the main temple and center of the state religion in the Inca capital of Cuzco. (SOURCE: Conrad and Demarest 1984.)

rewarded with food and drink as discussed in Chapter 7. All his personal royal estate remained with the *panaqa* of each ruler and significantly reduced the resources available both for the state as a whole and for succeeding rulers. Therefore, the newly installed king was obligated to expand the total territory of the empire to finance the government and build his own wealth in food surpluses and subjects to support his *panaqa*.

Although the underlying incentive for empire building was imposed on new rulers by split inheritance, successful conquest effected wide benefits. Conrad and Demarest (1984) point out that subsistence security improved for the population as a whole because new lands were available for agriculture and because state food stores could be stocked with staples from the new provinces. The hereditary elite Orejones derived additional wealth and power from war booty and must have formed a powerful interest group in support of further conquest. Individual citizens could also rise in the ranks as outstanding warriors and be rewarded with wealth and status as well as supernatural benefits.

In late pre-Inca times, the southern Andean highlands were divided into warring petty states or chiefdoms, which were the political units remaining after the fragmentation of the earlier Tiahuanaco empire. Apparently, the institutionalization of split inheritance and the royal mummy cult, which began under the rule of Pachakuti Inca in 1438, gave the Inca rulers a decisive advantage in their struggles with their neighbors. However, Conrad and Demarest (1984) argue that continuous expansion quickly proved unsustainable. Within less than a century, the empire reached its maximum extent (see Figure 7.12). Beyond the limits of the familiar Andean environment, the Inca armies floundered at the edges of the Amazon rain forest, while further extension north or south along the Andean chain was hampered by communication difficulties. Administrative costs soared. The well-endowed *panaqa*, in effect, became rival kingdoms led by their mummy kings and were a constant challenge to the authority of the living Inca ruler. There were also problems with rebellious ethnic groups that were forcibly incorporated into the empire.

Even with no more frontiers open to easy conquest, the practice of split inheritance continued to push the elite to increase production. But now this meant confiscating prime land from the citizenry, increasing the labor tax to support the mummy cult, and mounting large-scale and costly agricultural development projects on marginal lands subject to chronic crop failures. A further response to increasing economic pressures was the use of *yanacona* retainers and the *mitima* colonists as full-time agricultural laborers in service to the state and the nobility. Contrary to long-established Andean tradition, these changes made the rulers less obligated to maintain their reciprocal ties with the peasantry, and they undermined village self-sufficiency.

The final crisis began when the death of the Inca ruler Huayna Capac in 1525 resulted in controversy over the succession between two of his sons: Huascar, who assumed the throne in Cuzco, and Atahuallpa, who controlled the army. By this time, the economic deterioration of the empire had become so serious that Huascar attempted to abolish the royal mummy cult in an effort to stabilize the situation. However, this move threatened the position of the *panaqa* elite, and they joined with Atahuallpa in a civil war against Huascar. Atahuallpa won but was treacherously taken captive by the Spanish in 1532 before he could consolidate his victory.

Historians can cite many reasons for the remarkable success of the Spaniards, but above all else, they simply had lucky timing. They were veterans with steel swords, metal armor, guns, and horses, who were at first thought to be supernatural beings. The Inca population was being seriously disrupted by epidemic European diseases that reached Peru in 1524, 8 years ahead of the Spaniards (Dobyns and Doughty 1976). However, despite these material and psychological advantages, the empire would not have fallen so easily if internal contradictions had not prepared the way. In the Inca case, split inheritance and a special form of ancestor worship seems to have caused a frenzied period of self-destructive expansion that drove the empire to collapse within less than 100 years. Huascar's reforms might have worked, but it was already too late. The empire was hopelessly divided against itself and simply fell apart. The Spanish forces were met by a peasantry that no longer had any vested interest in supporting the Inca mummies, the Inca elite, or the living emperor.

The Spaniards succeeded in destroying the last of the royal mummies by 1559, and although a fragmented Inca government remained in the hinterland until 1572, Inca civilization was effectively destroyed when the Spaniards occupied Cuzco in 1533. The Andean cultural tradition—including subsistence practices, social organization, material culture, and beliefs—continued with little significant change at the village level. The Spanish conquerors replaced the Inca elite and turned the Inca labor tax into a harshly exploitative system that further impoverished the countryside. The Andean peasantry kept their language and culture, but they were forcibly incorporated into the emerging world system dominated by Europeans. The Spanish treatment of Atahuallpa was symbolic of the transformation. He was taken captive and held for ransom. To gain his release, he amassed a treasure of more than 13,000 pounds (5889 kilograms [kg]) of gold and 26,000 pounds (11,778 kg) of silver—three times the treasure that Cortez took from Mexico—but he was killed and the treasure went to Spain (Dobyns and Doughty 1976).

THE LIMITS OF PROGRESS

Explaining Collapse

What evolutionary and functionalist explanations have anthropologists offered to explain the collapse of civilizations?

The collapse of civilizations has been viewed from several different perspectives, as Norman Yoffee (1988b) has outlined. German philosopher-historian Oswald Spengler thought that civilizations, like organisms, inevitably went through regular life cycles in which they either slipped into a permanent state of stagnant "decline" or died completely. British historian Arnold Toynbee thought that civilizations arose in response to environmental challenges and declined as their creative spirit waned. Unfortunately, both approaches were highly subjective, personal interpretations and were not readily testable. Anthropologist Julian Steward (1955) identified "cyclical conquests" and "dark ages" as predictable final stages in the development of civilizations. In each case, he argued that collapse occurred when continued population growth and increased taxation reduced per-capita production rates, depressing living standards and raising mortality rates for the peasantry to the point of rebellion.

Elman Service has proposed that the rise and fall of states and civilizations is simply an example

TABLE 10.2   *Hierarchical Adaptive Structures in Cultural Systems*

Hierarchical Level	Function	Examples	Qualities
Highest	General purpose	Deities	Eternal principles, value-laden
Higher	Relations between lower-order regulators	Legal codes, economic systems, traditions, ritual	Rules, general directives, arbitrary
Lowest	Special purpose, specific behavior	Subsistence practices, domestic routines	Rapid response, reversible, sensitive

SOURCE: Rappaport (1977a).

of the law of evolutionary potential, which states: "The more specialized and adapted a form in a given evolutionary stage, the smaller is its potential for passing to the next stage" (1960:97). This means that a given state can become so overinvested in a particular Great Tradition pattern that it is unable to convert to a new pattern that might offer important adaptive advantages. The corollary principle of *local discontinuity of progress* suggests that cultural "advances" are likely to occur in cultures that did not participate in earlier "advances" and are thus able to bypass their formerly more "progressive" but now overspecialized neighbors. These generalizations can be historically verified after the fact, but they do not identify the precise causes of collapse.

Roy Rappaport (1977a) offered a formal systems theory analysis of the adaptive structures operating in cultural systems to identify some of the inherently "maladaptive" aspects of political-scale cultures. Rappaport defined ***adaptation*** as the process by which cultures maintain equilibrium despite both short- and long-term environmental fluctuation. Equilibrium in this case refers especially to the well-being of human organisms, human population stability, and the maintenance of supporting ecosystems.

The adaptive structures of a culture can be arranged in hierarchical levels according to the amount of information and decision making they regulate (see Table 10.2). Lowest-level regulators, such as individual farmers managing their domestic subsistence gardens, are responsible for very specific environmental details of soil and rainfall. They can respond quickly and precisely to changing conditions in their immediate environment. Higher-level regulators, such as a villagewide ritual,

might control the individual farmer's production decisions but would be less responsive to conditions in his specific garden. Higher-level regulators, such as remote rulers in a capital city, would also influence the farmer's actions but would be even more arbitrary and less responsive. Highest-level regulators, such as deities, would represent virtually eternal, and thus unresponsive, value-laden principles that would guide behavior at all lower levels.

Maladaptations are any factors within a culture's adaptive structures that impede the culture's ability to adjust to changes in its environment. Higher-level system regulators can function only if they selectively exclude very specific information; therefore, they are likely to misunderstand the conditions at the lowest levels. What Rappaport called hierarchical anomalies, which undermine balancing functions, tend to increase as levels are added to the hierarchy. Higher levels are likely to either underreact or overreact, thereby disturbing the finely tuned responses of lower-order regulators to environmental changes. An equally serious structural problem created by states is what Rappaport calls usurpation, or escalation, in which particular subsystems gain effective power over the larger system. According to Rappaport, this is maladaptive:

Thus, for the narrowly defined short-run interests of some individuals to prevail over the long-run requirements of the societies and ecosystems of which they are parts is, it seems to me, maladaptive per se. (1977b:83)

Diminishing Returns and Breakdown

How can cost–benefit analysis offer an overall explanation for the collapse of civilizations?

FIGURE 10.5
The principle of diminishing returns.

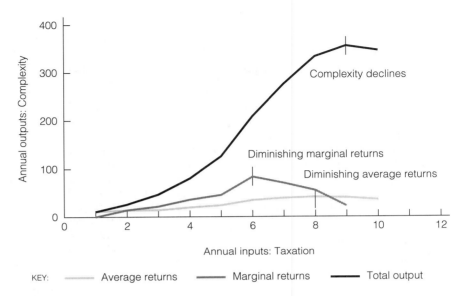

The Mesopotamian and Harappan examples raise questions about the explanatory value of both environmental factors and foreign invasion as sole causes of the breakdown of states. Joseph Tainter (1988) explicitly rejects both explanations and instead proposes the use of cost–benefit analysis to pinpoint the inherent weaknesses of states. This approach resembles Rappaport's (1977a) "system maladaptation" approach, but Tainter treats states as general "problem-solving organizations" and does not focus on environmental equilibrium as such. Tainter stresses that it would be surprising if environmental problems were the primary cause of state collapse because, according to some theories of state origin, states arise to help alleviate resource deficiencies. The case for the collapse of food production systems as a cause of political breakdown is especially hard to make because cause and effect is difficult to establish from archaeological evidence. Furthermore, complex state-supported production systems would almost certainly be abandoned in the event of political breakdown.

Tainter (1988) argues that environmental imbalance is only one example of a more general problem of ***diminishing returns,*** which affects virtually all state functions and most human endeavors. Technological or organizational changes that increase or maintain cultural complexity will eventu-

ally experience diminishing returns, and "collapse" will occur when the cost of maintaining cultural complexity becomes prohibitively expensive.

Diminishing returns apply to three conceptually distinct outputs, or products: ***marginal returns,*** average returns, and total output. Each output behaves somewhat differently, but marginal returns are most sensitive to the prognosis for the system. When marginal returns decline, more and more effort must be expended for less and less of whatever is being produced, whether it be food or cultural complexity. A decline in marginal returns means that average returns are also likely to decline soon. Even though total output might continue to increase for a time, it, too, will experience a decline. Figure 10.5 shows diminishing returns on a scale of cultural complexity in relation to increases in tax revenues for a hypothetical state. This example

---

adaptation   The long-term cultural process of maintaining a balance between population levels and natural resources within a given environment.
diminishing returns   The situation in which output values will decline as effort is increased in any production system.
marginal returns   The increase in the total output produced by the additional input; in subsistence production, the additional amount above what was produced the previous year, resulting from the increased effort.

arbitrarily assumes that average returns in complexity would increase for each added unit of revenue up to 8 units and would then decline steadily. Such a decline would be due to rising inefficiency and corruption, as the bureaucracy became more cumbersome. In this case, marginal returns begin to decline when revenue inputs reach 6, but total complexity declines only when inputs reach 9. Thus, an inattentive ruler interested in rapid state building might be tempted to raise taxes too high by disregarding the warning sign of diminishing marginal returns.

Agricultural Intensification

What are the costs and benefits of intensifying agricultural production?

The primary problem for the ruler of a state is how to increase the production of food staples, which can be taxed to finance growth in the nonfood-producing sector of the population. There are two immediate ways to increase agricultural productivity: (1) by increasing the number of peasant farmers and/or (2) by increasing the amount of land farmed. Either approach, however, will ultimately require technological changes because of diminishing returns on labor. Danish agricultural economist Ester Boserup (1965) has argued that intensification of food production typically follows a predictable sequence of diminishing returns, involving shortened fallow periods, increased effort per unit of land, and technological change. People must work harder for a smaller return for their effort in order to increase the total production per unit of land.

The typical agricultural intensification sequence would begin with a shifting-cultivation production system, such as the Amazonian example presented in Chapter 3. This is a *forest fallow system* because a plot must be allowed to return to forest before it can be recultivated, in order to maintain soil quality. Productivity per unit of labor input with shifting cultivation is relatively high, but the output per unit of land is very low when the forest is counted as part of the production system. The forest fallow system can, in theory, remain stable if no additional demands arise from population increase or political pressure to extract a surplus. When increases are required, this can be accomplished by shortening the fallow period and thereby putting more land into production at a given time. The problem with this is that secondary forest is brushy and requires more work to clear than primary forest, thus increasing the labor input. As the fallow period is shortened further, hoes will be needed to dig out the weeds and composting may be required to maintain soil fertility. When the fallow period is reduced to 1 year, a plow and draft animals will be needed to turn over the grass sod, which has replaced the forest.

The data presented in Table 10.3 and shown graphically in Figure 10.6 are largely conjectural, but they make more concrete the abstract principle of diminishing returns in agricultural intensification. Because documenting the intensification process for a single culture through time would be difficult, these figures were generated using an Amazonian shifting-cultivation system and a Chinese irrigated rice-growing village to define extreme points along a straight-line continuum. The intermediate values were simply extrapolated. Calculations of this sort are imprecise because the underlying data are estimates subject to sampling error and because the different systems themselves may not be strictly comparable. For example, not all the potential production of a shifting-cultivation system is ever harvested, and a garden plot may continue to be productive to some degree as it goes through the fallow process. Also, different estimates would generate different curves. Nevertheless, the figures demonstrate the magnitude of difference between land-extensive systems, which make little demand on labor, and highly intensive systems, which require a very large labor force.

These figures also help explain why extensive systems are more likely to be found with domestic-scale egalitarian cultures. It could certainly be argued that people would not willingly move to the more intensive system, which clearly increases work loads, unless they were pushed by population growth or political pressure. Political factors, such as taxation, are probably the most important determinants of agricultural intensification because, when a ruler extracts a steadily increasing "surplus" from a peasantry with a fixed land base, the only way for the peasants to reduce their rising labor costs is to raise a larger family and divide the work load. Thus, the population will tend to grow, but it

TABLE 10.3   *Diminishing Returns in Agricultural Intensification*

Subsistence Type*	Input/Hectare (in thousands of kcal)	Average Return (in kcal)	Total Output (in millions of kcal)	Marginal Return (in millions of kcal)
Forest fallow	24	72	1.7	—
Bush fallow	250	68	17.0	15.3
Short fallow	475	62	29.0	12.0
Annual crop	700	56	39.0	10.0
Multicrop	912	50	45.8	6.8

*Forest fallow system is based on estimates for Amazonian shifting cultivation of manioc (30,000 lbs [13,590 kg] of manioc/acre/year for 1606 hours/year), 25-year fallow. Multicrop system is based on the Chinese village of Luts'un (see Chapter 8). Data for the intermediate systems are based on extrapolations from the Amazonian and Chinese data. Bush fallow assumes hoe cultivation on an 8-year rotation. Short fallow assumes plow cultivation on a 2-year rotation.

FIGURE 10.6
Diminishing returns in agricultural intensification.

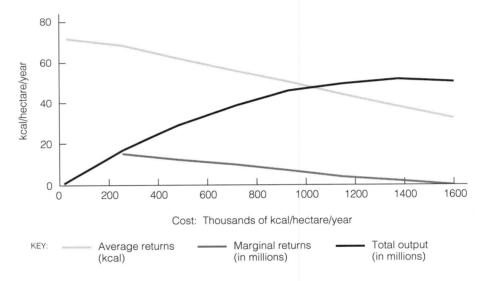

KEY: .... Average returns (kcal)   ▬▬ Marginal returns (in millions)   ▬▬▬ Total output (in millions)

is important to note that the underlying cause is the *political policy* of the state, not the inherent tendency of population to rise. In previous chapters, it was argued that diminishing returns in subsistence might provide a cultural incentive for limiting family size in tribal cultures where individual households are free to set their own production goals.

State Institutional Functions and Costs

What special problems arise as states grow? What institutional structures are needed to

solve these problems? How do states meet these new costs? What inherent factors cause bureaucracy to proliferate?

As a state system develops, a series of new problems arise, each of which offers further areas in which costs rise and returns diminish. The state has institutional responses to the special problems it creates, but each response requires further increases in the number of nonfood-producing specialists

forest fallow system   Using regrowth of the forest to restore soil fertility.

FIGURE 10.7
*State functions and
costs.*

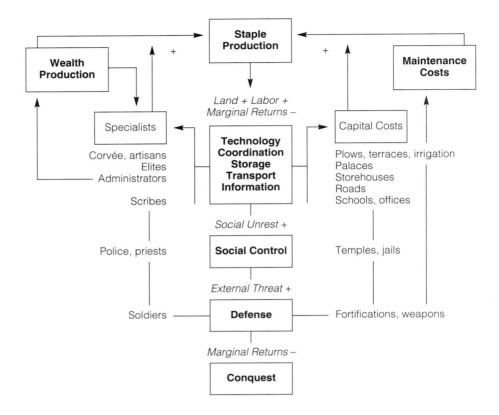

and includes additional capital costs and maintenance costs. The states' institutional responses themselves generate new problems that call for new institutional solutions, in a continually expanding positive-feedback system with steadily diminishing returns.

Figure 10.7 illustrates some of these complex interconnections. The key functions that the state must support if it is to survive are staple production, wealth production, maintenance costs, technology, coordination, storage, transport, information, social control, defense, and conquest. The specialists carrying out specific functions—corvée laborers, artisans, and so on—are shown on the left in the figure, opposite the functions they serve. The physical constructions, or capital costs—palaces, irrigation systems, storehouses, and so on—are shown on the right. State functions, institutional responses, and new problems are arranged in the

diagram along a vertical axis in a general developmental sequence from top to bottom.

The most critical state function, increasing staple-food production, is met at first through taxation, which forces the peasantry to put more land into production, shortens fallow periods, and encourages larger families. However, increased pressure on land and labor generates the problem of marginal returns as the soil is depleted and cultivation becomes more difficult. The state must then finance a series of technological changes in order to apply more and more labor to each unit of land. Full-time artisans are needed to manufacture new tools such as metal hoes and then plows. Eventually, large drafts of corvée labor must be mobilized to build terraces and irrigation canals. These developments themselves require increased production of food staples and more administrative elites to coordinate their activities and to collect and store

TABLE 10.4   *State Finance in the Early Dynastic City-State of Ur, Mesopotamia*

Capital Construction*	Total Cost (5 years)	Annual Cost
Irrigation canals	1,544,825	308,965
Storehouses	500,000	100,000
Palace	965,515	193,103
Ziggurat	2,395,310	479,062
City wall	500,000	100,000
Total construction costs	5,905,650	1,181,130

1,181,130	Total annual construction costs
+ 253,500	500 workmen × 507 kg of grain per year
+1,102,000	5800 citizens × 380 kg of grain per year × 50% famine reduction
2,536,630	Subtotal 1
+ 380,495	Subtotal 1 × seed grain (15%)
2,917,125	Subtotal 2
+ 729,281	Subtotal 2 × storage loss (25%)
3,646,406	Total annual cost

$$\text{Annual production} = \text{hectares} \times \frac{\text{kg of grain}}{\text{hectare}}$$

$$2,400,000 = 6000 \text{ hectares} \times \frac{400 \text{ kg of grain}}{\text{hectare}}$$

Revenue = annual production × tax rate (25%)
600,000 = 2,400,000 × .25

SOURCES: Data for capital construction costs from Erdosy (1988) and Wheatley (1971). Estimates for storage, seed, population, and grain production from Wright (1969) and Adams (1981).
*Capital construction costs are expressed in kilograms of grain required to supply a workman's official barley ratio of 60 *sila*/month, 507 kg/year (see Chapter 7).

the revenue. Palaces, storehouses, roads, and offices also must be constructed and maintained. But the increased taxes and social inequality will generate social unrest, calling for social control functions provided by priests and police, temples and jails. A successful state with large storehouses and wealthy palaces will tempt neighboring states to invade; therefore, soldiers, weapons, and fortifications will be needed for defense functions. Eventually, as marginal returns decline in all areas, territorial expansion and looting through conquest will become an attractive means of perpetuating the system.

Table 10.4 gives some indication of the relative cost of state functions. Like previous estimates, these figures are largely conjectural, but they illustrate some of the constraints with which ancient

rulers had to contend. This example shows the possible costs of capital construction in an early Mesopotamian city-state such as Ur. The values represent kilograms of barley, which was the basic ration used to pay laborers. With a combined population of perhaps only 5800 people, the small city of Ur and its support communities would have needed to draft large numbers of temporary laborers from outside to complete these projects within a short time. If the canals, storehouses, palace, ziggurat, and city walls were all built within 5 years as Table 10.4 assumes, more than 11,000 construction workers would have been needed each year. Shortening construction time would have been difficult.

Given potential grain production in the 14,815 cultivated acres (6000 hectares) surrounding Ur and a tax rate of 25 percent, grain stores would

FIGURE 10.8
*Growth of population
and bureaucracy.*

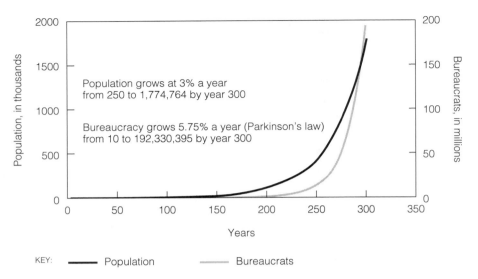

Population grows at 3% a year
from 250 to 1,774,764 by year 300

Bureaucracy grows 5.75% a year (Parkinson's law)
from 10 to 192,330,395 by year 300

KEY: ━━━ Population   ━━━ Bureaucrats

have to accumulate for 6 years to finance each year of construction. In the meantime, losses in storage would take an increasing toll. It would take the state 2 years simply to accumulate enough surplus grain to supply half the annual subsistence needs of its regular citizens in the case of a crop failure.

Because the capital costs of state functions are relatively high, they would probably only be taken on as they became absolutely necessary. Construction projects would probably be carried out in the order listed, with technological improvements in agricultural production coming first. Large-scale temple construction and expensive royal tombs would probably be later elaborations designed to reduce social unrest by lending greater religious legitimacy to the state apparatus.

Any increases in nonfood-producing elites or other government specialists would add to the state's financial burden. However, as C. Northcote Parkinson (1957) showed, bureaucracy exhibits an inherent tendency to expand, even as total output declines. According to Parkinson's law, administrative staffs will expand at a predictable rate of 5.75 percent a year, regardless of the actual work produced. This is because overworked officials prefer to add at least two subordinates rather than divide their work with a potential rival. At the same time, the added officials increase the work load because they slow the flow of information. The potential

growth rate of bureaucracy thus vastly outstrips population growth and helps explain the diminishing returns that occur with increases in cultural complexity.

Figure 10.8 illustrates the significance of Parkinson's law by demonstrating that in 300 years a staff of 10 theoretically would expand to more than 192 million people. At the same time, the base population would expand from 250 to under 1.8 million people if it grew at 3 percent a year, which is a very high but possible rate. Such an outcome would, of course, be impossible because if the bureaucracy actually did increase at 5.75 percent a year, the system would collapse long before the demand for bureaucrats exceeded the total population. Tax revenues to support the nonfood-producing administrators could not be sustained by the dwindling farm labor force. In this case, collapse could occur without environmental deterioration.

SUMMARY

State breakdown, like the rise of states, is an overdetermined phenomenon. That is, it can be caused by many different, often interconnected, factors, such that identifying the most important causes is often difficult. Because the state is a form of political organization, it could be argued that the best explanations for its demise will be political. However, as the examples demonstrate, specific environmental problems, ideological factors, and foreign invasion can all amplify the political weaknesses inherent in state organization. The best explanations in any particular case require detailed historical information. The most critical weakness of states is their vulnerability to diminishing returns in many important state functions.

STUDY QUESTIONS

1. What does state breakdown mean? How can it be identified? Use specific examples.

2. How can state organization be considered maladaptive from a systems theory perspective? Include the following concepts in your discussion: adaptive equilibrium, adaptive structures, maladaptation, system regulators, hierarchical anomalies, and usurpation.

3. Relate the principle of diminishing returns and Parkinson's law to the problem of state breakdown. Include the following concepts in your discussion: cost–benefit analysis, diminishing marginal returns, average returns, and total output.

4. Explain how diminishing returns operate in agricultural productions.

5. Critically discuss each of the following explanations for the demise of Harappan civilization: foreign invasion, floods, and resource depletion.

6. Why was the Spanish conquest of the Inca empire so easy?

7. Explain the law of evolutionary potential and the principle of local discontinuity of progress. Apply them to specific case material.

SUGGESTED READING

LOWE, JOHN W. 1985. *The Dynamics of Apocalypse: A Systems Simulation of the Classic Maya Collapse*. Albuquerque: University of New Mexico Press. One of several interpretations of the Maya case.

PARKINSON, C. NORTHCOTE. 1957. *Parkinson's Law and Other Studies in Administration*. Boston: Houghton Mifflin. The classic study of why bureaucracy tends to expand and become unworkable.

TAINTER, JOSEPH A. 1988. *The Collapse of Complex Societies*. Cambridge, Eng.: Cambridge University Press. A nice review of explanations for collapse that includes many case studies and treats the Romans, Maya, and Chaco Couzon in detail.

YOFFEE, NORMAN, AND GEORGE L. COWGILL (EDS.). 1988. *The Collapse of Ancient States and Civilizations*. Tucson: University of Arizona Press. A collection of case studies by specialists covering Mesopotamia, the Maya, Teotihuacan, the Romans, and Han China.

II

Europe and the Commercial World

In this chapter and Chapters 12–15, we look at cultural developments in the modern world as it has been shaped by commercially driven increases in the speed and volume of production and distribution associated with modern technology and by related changes in the organization of social power. A gradual expansion of mercantile activities beginning in western Europe in the fifteenth century led to a wave of European colonial expansionism. By 1780, mechanization of textile production was underway in England. Within a century, coal-burning factories and railroads, telecommunications, and giant corporations appeared in western Europe and North America. Almost overnight, commercial interests became the primary influence on political systems, as well as on the daily life and well-being of people throughout the world. In this commercialization process, world population increased nearly sixfold, from some 800 million people in 1750 to 5.8 billion by 1997, while per capita rates of resource consumption soared to unprecedented levels in the industrial centers. A few people became fabulously wealthy, a comfortably well-off middle class emerged, and millions of people sank into poverty. All societies and cultures are now interconnected within a single economically stratified global system of nation-states dominated by

giant corporations, and dependent on the flow of finance capital. These dramatic cultural changes present a major challenge for anthropologists and other social scientists seeking to understand how and why they occurred and to evaluate their human impact. Technological changes, especially the adoption of mechanized mass production and the use of fossil fuels, were crucial factors in this transformation, but the human agents that directed these technologies and the underlying cultural changes were even more fundamental causes of this remarkable process. After examining the dominant features of this remarkable cultural transformation, this chapter presents ethnohistoric data on European cosmology, feudalism, peasant farming systems, specific mercantile capitalists, and the London poor in order to trace the development of commercialization.

CULTURE-SCALE PERSPECTIVES ON THE CONTEMPORARY WORLD

This chapter examines specific human-directed cultural changes that increased the scale of European societies and produced a commercially organized world system. I argue that these changes were neither natural nor inevitable. This view contrasts sharply with popular explanations for the "inevitability" of cultural development as due to (1) *natural* population growth, (2) *natural* technological progress, and (3) *natural* economic progress. Given the relative stability of human population under domestically organized cultures and its sudden expansion under politically organized cultures, population growth likely is a culturally mediated process, not a natural constant. Furthermore, technology and economic organization clearly are cultural, not natural, phenomena.

In a recent book on the global economy, Lester Thurow (1996) used the geological principles of plate tectonics to explain how economic forces shape the world. And in 1998, economists called the unexpected collapse of Asian financial markets a "contagion," suggesting that it had no human causes. These views may correspond to common beliefs in the irresistible force of economics, but they ignore human agency. A major assumption in this book is that economic growth is not a "natural" process. Rather, the growth is the result of many individual decision makers seeking greater economic power in particular places.

Those who now design and direct commercial technology also maintain that technological change is natural. For example, Bill Gates (1996:11) insists:

No one gets to vote on whether technology is going to change our lives. No one can stop productive change in the long run because the market inexorably embraces it. . . . I believe that because progress will come no matter what, we need to make the best of it—not try to forestall it.

Individual decision makers use specific cultural institutions and cultural processes to promote or limit growth, and they guide cultural development in particular directions. In previous chapters, we saw that political rulers used population growth, technology, and economic organization to increase the scale of society, and thereby to enlarge their own social power. The disadvantage of this kind of directed culture change is that decion makers cannot know what the consequences will be or how many will suffer or benefit. Gates (1996:10, 313) speaks optimistically of the revolutionary, even "seismic" effects of computer technology, assuring us that computers will change every aspect of our lives. But he acknowledges some unanswered, and

troublesome, questions when he asks: "What will happen to our jobs? . . . Will the gulf between the haves and the have-nots widen irreparably?" These are serious questions, because commercially directed technological change plunged millions into poverty even as it elevated a few to great wealth and power.

The contemporary world is fundamentally different from everything that preceded it because it is dominated by *commercialization*, a new, untested cultural process that now supersedes both politicization and sapienization. *Politicization*, the process that produces and maintains centralized political power, has become a secondary cultural process in the commercial culture, maintaining the conditions of economic growth in support of the commercialization process. The world's dominant national and international institutions primarily are concerned with promoting perpetual growth in the commercial production, exchange, and consumption of goods and services.

This overwhelming focus on the accumulation and concentration of wealth, as an end in itself, is an extremely unusual cultural development. Neither wealth nor poverty exists in domestic-scale cultures, where production occurs at the household level to meet the needs that households define. There is no cultural incentive for a household to accumulate more than any other or to produce beyond immediate needs. In ancient Mesopotamia, the Andes, imperial China, and Hindu India, wealth was used to maintain the politicization process— wealth accumulation was not an end in itself. In ancient civilizations, surplus production was extracted from the peasants to finance temples, irrigation works, and fortifications. Wealth maintained the infrastructure of state power, and wealth objects verified political rank, rewarded loyalty, and were buried in royal tombs and in mummy cults.

We know that domestic-scale cultures were successful because they were the world's only form of human culture for at least 50,000 years. We can assume that these cultures worked effectively so that they did not need to be changed. A mere 6000 years ago, a unique series of events in particular environments overwhelmed the constraints on the politicization process in domestic-scale cultures. This allowed political-scale cultures to emerge in a few places, but these ancient kingdoms and chiefdoms went through frequent cycles of growth and collapse and did not threaten the viability of domestic-scale cultures beyond their frontiers. The infrequent rise and regular collapse of ancient states and empires suggest that they were not the most reliable human adaptations. Commercial-scale culture is only 200 years old, but it has already transformed and destabilized the world in unusual ways. Its cultural superiority remains to be demonstrated.

Human Needs and Culture Scale

How effectively do domestic-, political-, and commercial-scale cultures satisfy basic human needs? How does social inequality differ in political- and commercial-scale cultures?

By definition, domestic-scale cultures were the only ones to focus exclusively on satisfying basic human needs. Every household had access to the subsistence resources it needed and controlled its own production and consumption. Every household was, in effect, guaranteed what Paul Radin has called the "irreducible minimum," an inalienable right to "adequate food, shelter and clothing" (1971: 106). Under political-scale cultures, the politicization process took some decision-making power and control away from households and communities; however, human labor power continued to be important, and labor still was required to fulfill the needs of most people. Enormous differences in social power, wealth, and status separated the social classes in ancient civilizations. The lower classes were certainly exploited, but relatively few people, usually outsiders, were enslaved and sacrificed. Most people were able to maintain viable households.

In the commercialization process, everything that people need for their well-being has been converted into a commodity to be sold for profit. State power is used to encourage people to become wage laborers—producing, purchasing, and consuming commodities rather than pursuing noncommercial subsistence activities. The inherent problem with this system is that millions of people no longer have access to basic subsistence resources and cannot earn a sufficient wage to purchase a decent living. Thus, millions are unable to provide for such basic needs as food, shelter, clean water, and pure air. Infant mortality rates soar, and malnutrition is

now common. This kind of poverty makes the commercial-scale culture seem inhumane relative to both political- and domestic-scale culture.

Energy, Adaptation, and the Evolution of Culture

What is the adaptive significance of energy use by cultures of different scale?

Many older anthropological concepts of cultural evolution that considered civilization an inevitable achievement were based on inadequate concepts of adaptive success. For example, in 1949, Leslie White proposed that culture evolved "as the amount of energy harnessed per capita per year increased" (1949:368–369) and that a more highly evolved culture would be better adapted. White's energy theory reflected the general optimism of his day that technology would remove all limits to continuous growth and economic progress. A more cautious observer later pointed out that within 200 years, a mere 5 percent annual increase in world energy production would produce a "Sun Day" in which waste heat would equal solar radiation and burn up the planet (Luten 1974). Obviously, increased energy consumption by itself is not the best measure of successful cultural adaptation.

In White's materialist view, foragers were "underdeveloped" because they were restricted to human energy, whereas farming made additional sources of energy available that permitted states to "arise." However, not all village farmers developed states, and the archaeological record demonstrates the adaptive success of low-energy foragers and independent villagers. Although White was aware that domestic-scale cultures enjoyed important long-run advantages, his interpretation overemphasized the importance of purely technological innovation and ignored the advantages of moderate use of renewable energy sources.

Marshall Sahlins (1972) argued that monumental, state-funded construction projects became possible because political controls were used to increase the scale of society and concentrate "surplus" energy. He suggested that per-capita energy use in preindustrial states was not significantly higher than in tribes. This is confirmed by Earl Cook's (1971) estimate of the daily per-capita con-

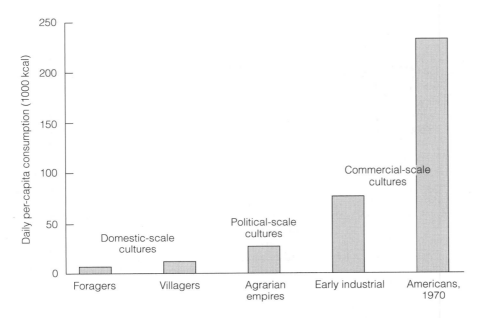

FIGURE 11.1   *Daily consumption of energy per capita by culture-scale level. (SOURCE: Based on Cook 1971:136.)*

sumption of all forms of energy (food, fuels, wind, water, and electricity) by culture scale. Cook suggested that domestic-scale cultures used 5000–12,000 kilocalories (kcal), while the most technically advanced preindustrial states barely doubled this amount to 26,000 kilocalories per person per day. In contrast, the magnitude of energy use by commercial-scale cultures is qualitatively unique. By drawing heavily on fossil fuels, Americans in 1970 consumed 230,000 kilocalories per person per day (see Figure 11.1). This was more than eight times the amount used in preindustrial states and can be attributed primarily to commercialization.

Continuing his emphasis on the technological determinants of evolutionary "progress," White (1949) applauded the use of coal and oil as the ***fuel revolution*** that led to industrialization. White suggested that the discovery of nuclear energy would bring another great evolutionary advance. What was missing in White's concept of progress was a time perspective that included the depletion of energy sources and the full environmental cost of accelerated energy use. Historically, both political- and domestic-scale cultures relied primarily on so-

lar energy. This was highly adaptive because it contributed to stability and set some limits on total growth. Since White wrote, it has become embarrassingly obvious that increasing energy use can be extremely maladaptive, especially when the primary energy base is not renewable and when it is expended at rates that exceed the biosphere's ability to recycle the waste by-products.

THE NATURE OF CAPITALISM

Systems of Production and Exchange

What are the significant cross-cultural differences in modes of production?

The modern capitalist economy is radically different from all previous systems of production and exchange; the distinctive features of capitalism created the global political economy. The concept of *political economy* emphasizes the fact that

---

fuel revolution   The large-scale adoption of fossil fuels such as coal and oil.

economics cannot be separated from politics. This shifts attention from the technological and ecological foundations of economic activity to a consideration of cultural factors such as political organization and ideology, which ultimately determine the ways in which humans exploit the earth. Capitalist economic organization uses social inequality to promote wealth accumulation and political expansionism on a scale unequaled in human history (see Figure 11.2).

The concept of an economy existing apart from the rest of society began as a uniquely European cultural construction. All societies have cultural systems of production and distribution, but only Europeans came to believe that human well-being

FIGURE 11.2   *The New York Stock Exchange, one of the central institutions of the capitalist market economy, which drives the commercial-scale culture.*

depended on having a *growing* economy. What Europeans call the *economy* is embedded within everyday household activities in domestic-scale societies. For comparative purposes, Eric R. Wolf (1982) distinguishes three different systems of production and distribution: kin-ordered, tributary, and capitalist.

Kin-ordered production characterizes the domestic-scale cultures treated in Chapters 2–5. In these systems, kinship constitutes the culturally defined social categories around which productive activities are organized. Relationships between individuals established by marriage or family connections, real or fictive, determine the form of food-producing and -sharing groups. In all systems that are ordered exclusively by kinship, production is primarily for direct consumption, or ***use value,*** rather than for ***exchange value.*** From a Marxist perspective, political power in kin-based systems is derived from the age hierarchy and male control over women, which, in theory, could give older men greater control over the organization of labor. Significant inequalities and conflict can arise in a kin-based political economy when intensive agriculture or herding increases the importance of land and labor.

Kin-based groups fluctuate in size as a result of random demographic processes, and conflict may lead to fissioning, but domestic-scale cultures tend to resist overall changes in the basic mode of production. However, as we have seen, under certain conditions, descent groups may become ranked, and the heads of politically more powerful branches may become the basis for chiefdom organization. Wolf's (1982) emphasis on mode of production clarifies the distinction between relatively small-scale chiefdoms such as Tikopia, where production is ordered by kinship, and larger-scale systems such as Hawaii, where social classes appear to be based on tribute payments.

With ***tributary production,*** which characterized the civilizations examined in Chapters 6–10, the peasantry remained in control of their basic resources and produced their own food, while the state supported itself by extracting the surplus as tribute. Title to land was often claimed by the state, but it was political power and ideology that compelled the peasantry to turn over surplus production to the state. The structure of surplus extraction was maintained by placing primary producers in subordinate status positions relative to the non-food-producing elites. Much of the accumulated wealth went into maintaining status differences by means of the conspicuous display of luxury goods or the construction of awe-inspiring temples and funerary ritual. Bureaucratically organized tribute extraction often existed alongside long-distance, market-oriented exchange systems managed by merchants or traders. Developed market systems helped the state acquire exotic luxury goods, but a fully commercialized distribution system would have undermined the status structure that supported the tribute system and would, in theory, have transformed it into a *capitalist production* mode.

The Uniqueness of Capitalism

What are the key distinguishing features of capitalism as understood by economists?

Capitalism is a commercial system of production and exchange that treats land, labor, technology, money, raw materials, and goods and services as commodities to be bought and sold for a profit. The emergence of a monetary market for labor is a key distinguishing feature of capitalism as a system of production and distribution, because wage labor reduced the self-sufficiency of the household far more decisively than did tribute systems. Radical political economist Karl Marx (1818–1883) argued that the labor market emerged historically when capitalists separated the peasantry from their land and other resources that constituted their means of production, thus compelling the peasantry to sell their labor to secure basic subsistence. Laborers came to constitute a social class characterized by their separation from the means of production. Land and tools became *capital,* which only a few owned, and basic products became *commodities* to be marketed. As a social class, capitalists, or the owners of capital, made a profit by appropriating surplus production above the costs of labor and capital. In this mode of production, the capitalist seeks to accumulate a surplus to increase profit. The surplus can be increased by depressing the wage of the laborers and by raising the level of technology. The interest of capitalists to increase their profits by keeping the labor wage low is opposed to

the interest of laborers to increase their own share of the products of their labor. Individual capitalists also compete with one another to increase their profits. This incentive to increase profits, as well as the contradiction of interests between social classes, accelerates the inherent tendency of states to promote technological development and territorial expansion.

The contrast between the market-capitalism conception of economy and the ancient tributary economy can be demonstrated by a modern textbook critique of the economic theory of Greek philosopher Aristotle (384–322 BC). According to economists Robert Ekelund and Robert Hebert (1983), the Greek concept of economy was unprogressive because ancient economies were socially *embedded.*

Aristotle advocated a production and exchange system that, in theory, was remarkably reminiscent of the "original affluent society" of foragers as described by Marshall Sahlins (1968). Aristotle felt that human wants were limited and that economic scarcity was not a problem. This ideal was probably not actually realized in the Greek city-state, but it represents a view that is in direct opposition to the modern definition of a

---

kin-ordered production A mode of production organized at the domestic or kinship level and producing primarily for domestic use rather than exchange.

use value The value of goods produced for domestic consumption, usually within a kin-ordered mode of production.

exchange value The value of goods when used as commodities.

tributary production A mode of production in which products are extracted as surplus from a self-supporting peasantry and used to support the state.

capitalist production A mode of production in which a few people control the means of production and purchase the labor of those who could not otherwise support themselves.

capital Marx's term for land and tools as the means of production; also refers generally to accumulated wealth used for productive purposes.

commodities Basic goods that are produced for their exchange value in a market economy to generate profit to be accumulated as capital.

embedded economy An economy that can only be observed and understood within the context of the social, political, and religious systems of the culture.

disembodied economy, which assumes limited means and unlimited wants. Aristotle's ideal city-state assumed a small community based on reciprocal exchange, self-sufficiency, and justice. In this system, individuals were not supposed to make a profit at their neighbors' expense because this would lead to inequality that would threaten community solidarity. Aristotle accepted money as a medium of exchange but argued that too much market trade would undermine the good life, and he considered wealth accumulation to be contrary to natural law.

Ekelund and Hebert (1983) are quick to point out the "apparent wrongheadedness" (p. 17) of Aristotle's economic theory, observing that it "is not economics as we know it" (p. 15) because it lacks an institutional economic framework and makes erroneous assumptions about human behavior. After all, as followers of Adam Smith, we now know that people are "naturally" self-seeking, individualistic, and acquisitive.

Economists Robert Heilbroner and Lester Thurow (1987) point out that earlier noncapitalist societies did not institutionalize private property and had no organized markets for land, labor, and money. Production and trade were directed by political rulers, and people became wealthy because of their political power. Furthermore, people lacked the concept of economic freedom and were bound to their occupations. In contrast, "the capitalist employee has the legal right to work or not work as he or she chooses" (Heilbroner and Thurow 1987:12–14), as well as the right to buy up farmland and turn it into a shopping center. Presumably, this allows one to find the most profitable arrangement.

Heilbroner and Thurow (1987) consider capitalism to be "utterly alien" and a "volcanic disruption" in comparison to the "tradition and command" systems that preceded it. In their view, there were no "factors of production" in precapitalist societies, because "labor, land, and capital were not commodities for sale." Instead, these factors

are the creations of a process of historic change, a change that divorced labor from social life, that created real estate out of ancestral land, and that made treasure into capital. Capitalism is the outcome of a revolutionary change—a change in laws, attitudes, and social relationships as deep and far-reaching as any in history. (1987:15–16)

Inequality and Instability in the Capitalist World System

What destabilizing features and contradictions are characteristic of the contemporary global culture? What ideological beliefs help people deal with the problems of global culture?

Modern social science theorist Immanuel Wallerstein helped found an important new interdisciplinary approach to world culture with his 1974 publication of the first volume of *The Modern World System.* Wallerstein observed that the emergence of capitalism in sixteenth-century Europe led to a uniquely organized global world economy by the early twentieth century. In his view, capitalism succeeded as a social system because it proved to be a more effective means of appropriating surplus production than the earlier tributary empires. Empires that used coercion to extract surplus were expensive to maintain and very fragile. Earlier noncapitalist states were, in effect, "homeostatic systems," in that they tended to rise and fall within certain limits set by their unstable political organization. In comparison with tribal cultures, the early states and empires functioned at a much higher density and total size, but they were still limited in absolute scale.

In the capitalist *world system,* expansion to the limits of the globe becomes theoretically possible because the system can function without a centralized state political authority. Individual states are needed only to maintain internal order and to encourage the international market economy. The key to the success of capitalism was that the market economy provided incentives for technological improvements that increased productivity, while a world division of labor allowed costs and benefits to be unequally apportioned.

In an argument anticipated in André Gunder Frank's (1967) model of the modern world divided into a developed *core* of wealthy capitalist nations and a *periphery* of dependent underdeveloped nations, Wallerstein (1974) proposed that the emerging capitalist world system was a multilayered economic hierarchy divided into a European core, a southern European semiperiphery, and an eastern European and New World periphery. Each zone was defined by distinctive geography, political organization, economic production, and its form of labor control, but the zones were all linked to the center by **unequal exchanges** that contributed to **capital accumulation** in the core. The exploited lower classes were concentrated in the periphery and semiperiphery, where they were coerced to work as slaves and serfs for European managers. Conditions were somewhat less coercive for the tenant farmers in the semiperiphery. In the core, laborers worked for wages, and small farmers worked their own land, while merchants and industrialists profited enormously from their privileged positions as the ultimate beneficiaries of the unequal exchange.

It is important to note the distinctions between *world* and *globe* in this context. The world system initially did not encompass the globe; it began in Europe and expanded outward. Wallerstein (1974) distinguished four distinct historical phases in the development of the world system. It originated in an economic crisis that undermined European feudalism by 1450 and encouraged capital accumulation at the expense of the peasantry. The system was spurred on by the gold and silver extracted as booty from the New World and was consolidated as a system between 1640 and 1815. The Industrial Revolution, utilizing coal as a new energy base, facilitated further expansion that transformed the world system into a global system between 1815 and 1917. Since 1917, the system has consolidated further.

Wallerstein (1990) lists six destabilizing realities that characterize the modern world system:

1. A hierarchical division of labor
2. Periodic expansion and incorporation
3. Continuous accumulation
4. Continuous progress
5. Polarization of individuals and groups
6. The impossibility of perpetual growth

These characteristics imply critical contradictions in the system and have generated particular ideologies that tend to obscure the realities and help keep the system functioning.

According to Wallerstein (1990), the global division of labor integrates the world into a single production system based on exploitation and inequalities that paradoxically are supported by ideologies that stress universal values of peace and world order. Racist ideologies are also used to justify the disadvantaged position of peripheral groups, with economic rewards apportioned differentially according to the intrinsic merit and ability of different groups.

Since 1450, the world system has gone through cycles of expansion marked by the steady incorporation of external cultural groups into the periphery. This trend has been supported by the ideology calling for all peoples to be assimilated into a universal Western culture, on the assumption that other cultures were simply incapable of "advance."

Continuous capital accumulation is made easier when workers are persuaded by an ideology that extolls the virtues of hard work and competitiveness to overcome inequality (see Figure 11.3). German social scientist Max Weber (1864–1920) was the first to point out that extreme Calvinist forms of Protestantism encouraged capital accumulation, in his famous book *The Protestant Ethic and the Spirit of Capitalism* ([1904–1905] 1930). According to Weber, German Calvinists believed that continuous hard work and self-denial were the best way to demonstrate that one was predestined for salvation. Such a belief was a religious endorsement for precisely the behavior that the capitalist economy needed.

---

disembodied economy   The concept of an economy as something that can be understood apart from the rest of society and culture, especially with a capitalist mode of production.
world system   An international hierarchy of diverse societies and cultures integrated into a single economic system based on unequal exchange that allows wealth to accumulate in the core.
core   The wealthy industrial countries at the center of the world system where the recipients of unequal exchange reside.
periphery   Capital-poor areas that supply raw materials and labor to the core; this area was integrated into the early capitalist world system through conquest and coercion.
unequal exchange   Market-based exchanges in which one party is consistently able to accumulate a disproportionate share of the profit or wealth.
capital accumulation   Expanding wealth and the means of production that can be devoted to further production.

FIGURE 11.3
A cotton mill in Lancashire, England, 1900. Factory workers in the industrial core of the global system worked long hours, but they were encouraged by their religious faith that hard work was the key to salvation and by their belief in continuous economic growth.

Wallerstein (1990) observes that the capitalist quest for continuous progress and change contains a contradiction because it implies that even the political system should be changed. This can be countered by extreme nationalist ideologies emphasizing patriotism, which, if pushed too far, lead to destructive wars.

According to Wallerstein (1990), capitalism tends to polarize people by steadily widening the gap between rich and poor. However, such a reality is destabilizing and is therefore vigorously denied based on the world system's "central myth of the rising standard of living." Wallerstein argues that elites in the core countries use "math tricks" to persuade peripheral peoples that wealth inequality is decreasing. Such myths ignore population increase, work loads, and environmental impacts, which might show a declining standard of living. Core elites also exhort the periphery to greater "development" efforts, while implying that failure to achieve development must be due to racial or cultural inferiority.

The most serious contradiction of the capitalist world system is its failure to acknowledge that the system as constituted cannot expand forever. The existence of K-waves or of 54-year "long-wave" cycles of commercial growth and decline is becoming widely recognized (Goldstein 1988, Kondratieff 1984, Stoken 1993), and other economic cycles have been identified (see Chapter 12). However, it is not clear what such cycles will mean for globally integrated cultures because they have such a short history.

Elites clearly have further concentrated their social power by moving beyond the constraints of nationally based political economies and creating transnational commercial empires based on capitalist market exchanges. This shift to transnational commercial empires has enormous significance for humanity, yet it has received remarkably little attention from anthropologists. Commercially organized, globally integrated cultures are important because (1) they are reducing cultural diversity at an unprecedented scale (Bodley 1999), (2) they have increased the number of poor, and (3) they may be ultimately limited by the integrity of the biosphere itself or by the human ability to tolerate mass impoverishment.

THE EUROPEAN ORIGINS OF CAPITALISM

Western Cosmology and the Industrial Revelation

What are the distinctive features of European commercial cultures? How do these features contrast with domestic-scale cultures and ancient agrarian civilizations?

Marshall Sahlins (1996) points out that Judeo-Christian cosmology is apparently unique among cultural traditions because it attributes the evil in the world to a human act of free will, as recounted in the Book of Genesis. Western cosmology assumes that because of their original sin in the Garden of Eden, humans are inherently evil, and human misery is the natural punishment for this evil human nature. This gloomy cosmology derives from religious beliefs, but the underlying assumptions about human nature and economic scarcity seem to have permeated Western scientific and secular thought.

The European Enlightenment, which made riches a desirable goal, represented a change in thought that kept the underlying belief in original sin and human inadequacy intact. Material progress was assumed to be natural, although this view overlooked the contradiction that progress also increased human needs, leaving people perpetually unsatisfied. Commerce, industrial technology, and the science of economics are all seemingly designed to help people *reduce*, but never *overcome*, the inevitable scarcity that insatiable human nature implies. What Sahlins calls the *industrial revelation* is the sad realization that "in the world's richest societies, the subjective experience of lack increases in proportion to the objective output of wealth" (Sahlins 1996:401). In effect, economic growth must impoverish.

In the Western cosmology, people are driven by natural law to seek pleasure and avoid pain. Society

itself is thought to be the product of selfish individuals seeking self-satisfaction, just as the "laws" of market supply and demand, or "free trade," will give us the best distribution of economic goods. As we have seen in previous chapters, this view of human existence is strikingly different from the belief of tribal peoples that life is good and that they can provide for all of their material and emotional needs through their own efforts. Liberated and empowered by their culture, tribal peoples maximize individual freedom and personal autonomy and do not view society as a coercive force. By contrast, Western philosophers from Bishop Augustine to Thomas Hobbes, as well as many modern sociologists and anthropologists, consider society to be a coercive power structure. This view equates society with government and treats it as a natural response to a selfish, and thus dangerous, human nature. Sahlins even argues that the "invisible hand" theorized by Adam Smith (discussed later in the chapter) and the functionalism of anthropology and sociology can be derived from the understanding of Divine Providence found in medieval cosmology, in which whatever happens is God's, or society's, plan and will result in collective good. This natural law of the Enlightenment philosophers provided the foundation for economics, natural science, political science, and national constitutions.

The notion of a spiritual soul existing apart from the physical body is virtually a human universal, but only Westerners see body and soul in conflict. Medieval philosophers extended the mind/body dualism to humans and nature. They situated humans midway between animals and gods in a hierarchical "chain of being," giving humans the mortal bodies of animals and godlike intellects. Judeo-Christian notions that humans exist apart *from*, and with dominion *over*, nature prepared the way for capitalism by making it easy to objectify nature—that is, to treat natural objects as commodities. Such dualism and universal commodification is quite alien to virtually all other cultures, where even the concept of nature as distinct from the supernatural does not exist. The outcome of this Western cosmology of evil humanity, natural scarcity, insatiable wants, human separation from nature, and presumably perfect markets based on free trade, is that people are persuaded to believe that their culture evolved *naturally* to meet our human needs, not that it was designed by particular people to meet their particular needs.

Commercialization Under the Feudal Monarchs

What were the relative proportions and absolute numbers of people living at different socioeconomic levels in feudal England? How and why did commercialization change the scale of English society and distribution of social power? Who benefited from growth?

The roots of the commercialization process were present in the rudimentary markets, trade structures, monetary systems, and craft specialization found in most ancient agrarian civilizatons, but political rulers jealously regulated commercial activities to safeguard their personal power. It was in Europe in the centuries after the collapse of the Roman empire that merchants and commerce gradually became the dominant forces in cultural development. How this vast cultural change came about is an intriguing anthropological problem, because under the politicization process virtually all resources were officially controlled by church and state, a rigid social hierarchy became entrenched, and an apparent ceiling on economic growth was reached. The hereditary rulers were ambivalent about the rising commercial elite; they sought both to restrict their activities and to form alliances with them, establishing a pattern that still continues. The crucial point is that merchants gradually became the driving force of cultural development.

The Domesday Survey of England, conducted in 1086 for William the Conqueror shortly after the Norman Conquest, provides an excellent baseline for measuring the astounding cultural transformations eventually brought about by commercialization. Designed for tax purposes, the great Domesday Book enumerated every manor in the country and all the plows, land, and cattle, and ranked all adult males by social category. The survey dramatically reveals a remarkable concentration of social power and shows the limits of power under preindustrial technology with little commercial activity. More than 90 percent of the perhaps 2 million inhabitants were farm laborers living on the manors and dependent villages scattered over the country-

side. A hierarchy of centrally placed market towns existed, but the peasantry produced most of their own food and manufactured domestic consumer goods by working part-time as independent millers, iron smiths, potters, and weavers in the household, village, or manor. Only 12,000 people lived in London, the largest city. Overseas trade and much of the industrial activity centered on supplying luxury goods to the hereditary nobility, who probably numbered fewer than 40,000 people, counting men, women, and children—about 2 percent of the population. Political power and land ownership remained in the hands of the king and nobles. Forty percent of the land was controlled by thirty-two great landlords under Royal Charter, and much of the other productive land was held in manors under other subtenants. All landlords served as the king's representatives.

The bulk of the English population were serfs, who held use rights to small subsistence parcels in return for working two to three days per week for the lord of the manor and who provided various additional services, taxes, and payments. These small holdings were worked cooperatively under the open-fields system, which allowed the serfs to retain enough of the advantages of domestic-scale life to make serfdom bearable (see the box entitled "The Open-Fields System"). Almost 10 percent of the population were chattel slaves. Except for the nobles and a few wealthy burghers (townsmen) and clergy, most people had little control over the conditions that influenced their daily lives. Over the next 300 years, the bulk of the peasantry experienced steadily declining living standards, but conditions improved for the few landlords and merchants who gained access to the growing international market in wool. The English population increased threefold to some 6 million, with perhaps 15 percent living in the expanding urban centers (Miller and Hatcher 1995:396).

The manorial system had obvious limits, because a feudal land baron could effectively control only so many manors, but money was an inherently expandable form of wealth. Economic growth during this period is demonstrated by the dramatic forty-four-fold increase in the supply of royal coinage in circulation in medieval England—from £25,000 in 1086 to £1,100,000 by 1320. Under constant promotion by the emerging merchant class,

The Open-Fields System

For landlords, industrialists, and merchants to gain the labor and raw materials necessary to increase their wealth, they had to force the self-sufficient European peasantry out of the *open-fields system* of land use that had sustained them for millennia. Egalitarian peasant communities that relied on cooperative plow agriculture used the open-fields system primarily to meet their subsistence needs, not to produce marketable surpluses (Orwin and Orwin 1967, Seebohm 1905). This system helped individual farmers minimize the risk of crop failure in an unpredictable natural environment, where politics were uncertain and access to markets was limited (McCloskey 1976, Townsend 1993). It was easier for farmers to plow cooperatively, especially when not every farmer owned plows and full draft teams.

The open-fields system produced a patchwork of individually held strips of land, each roughly an acre in area and representing one day's work for a single plow team. Each farmer held use rights from his landlord to a *virgate*, a collection of perhaps 30 acres of land scattered in strips throughout the manor (see Figure 11.4). This would be sufficient to allow him to cultivate half to meet the annual subsistence needs of his household, and keep half fallow to maintain soil fertility. A farmer's holdings were in scattered strips because this distribution made plowing most equitable and ensured that each farmer would have land of equal quality and distance from the village. The patchwork effect resulted because fields were plowed in blocks of *furlongs* (parallel plow strips), and the contour of the land determined the direction of plowing. As long as the cultivated area remained unfenced, it was open for common grazing after harvest. Every household also had access to common pastures, meadows, and woodlands beyond the cultivated fields for hunting, grazing, and gathering wood and materials.

The essentially tribal open-field system predated the Romans and operated in various forms throughout medieval Europe, but it was incompatible with the demands of large-scale commercial agriculture. By the fifteenth century, English landlords began to find feudal tenure and the open-field system ill-suited to the new opportunities presented by the emerging urban and international markets. Landowners increasingly fenced their holdings in order to raise great herds of sheep to supply the growing urban market for wool. In the process, self-sufficient tenants and smallholders were driven off the land. A second wave of enclosures in the eighteenth century was prompted by the adoption of new crops and more intensive production systems.

money steadily replaced barter exchange, greatly facilitated government finance, and made trade much more profitable. However, the serfs could barely participate in this kind of economic activity, because they did not control sufficient productive land. Small farmers were being forced below a

FIGURE 11.4   *The open-field system of the village of Hitchin in 1816. (SOURCE: Seebohm 1905.)*

comfortable subsistence level at the same time that money to pay taxes and buy essentials was becoming critical for survival. Under the existing social structure, modest technological improvements barely increased total agricultural production and brought few benefits to the peasants. Land that could have generated adequate subsistence was devoted to the production of wool for export, and was held in vast hunting preserves, horse pastures, and forests as a private luxury. By the fourteenth century, the social system was in crisis. Then disastrous famines and a series of plagues known as the

Black Death reduced the population almost to the Domesday level.

Growth in medieval England clearly produced great wealth (see the box entitled "Richard Fitzalan"). However, the *proportion* of the wealthholders at the top of the feudal hierarchy probably did not increase as economic growth occurred. Rather, the scale of society and the total amount of extractable wealth increased, making those at the top more powerful. Most of the newly wealthy merchants were probably already members of the upper class, whose numbers may have increased by 80,000 in

Richard Fitzalan: Medieval England's Richest Lord

The level of wealth and luxury that this emerging commercial system could support at the top of the social pyramid is illustrated by an enterprising fourteenth-century nobleman, Richard Fitzalan, the earl of Arundel and Surrey, then the richest private person in England. When he died in 1376, Richard had amassed capital of £72,245 in cash, property, and credits (Given-Wilson 1991)—three times the sum *in circulation* in 1086. Fitzalan owned multiple residences, vast estates, and 25,000 sheep. His fortune came from the sale of wool, metals, and livestock; from overseas investments; from loans to the king and other nobles; and from political favors. He was a capitalist who used his money to make money.

Let us put Fitzalan's wealth and this early phase of commercialization in perspective. Consider that at the beginning of the politicization process in southern England in 3000 BC, the most powerful Neolithic chiefdom might have been able to mobilize the 1200 people a year to build a megalithic monument. By contrast, even as a private citizen, Fitzalan could support more than twice that number from his annual income, and more than ten times more from accumulated capital. His annual landed income alone was sufficient to support 2857 manor servants at the high grain prices of that time. And his total capital would have allowed him to hire 15,451 annual laborers.

Fitzalan's Arundel Castle.

this era. Before the Black Death struck in 1349, there were 3.6 million more impoverished peasants than at the time of the Norman Conquest. In the absence of culture change to produce a more equitable power structure, the growth in scale associated with commercialization left more people in England poor than wealthy.

The Financial Revolution and the Power of Money

What conceptual changes in the way money was used made capitalism possible? When and where did these changes occur?

Mass-production industrial technology did not have a major influence until the 1800s, but the basic institutional structures of capitalism, including joint stock corporations, securities trading, and investment banking, were firmly in place in Europe prior to 1700. Less savory cultural features such as monopoly, bribery, and market manipulation were also commonplace. In medieval Europe before the emergence of capitalism, commercial activities were strictly regulated by church and state in ways that discouraged the accumulation of money by private individuals. Prices were often fixed at what was considered to be a "just price." Moneylenders and the wealthy were looked down on, and there were sumptuary laws restricting luxury and gambling, as well as laws against usury (charging exorbitant interest rates). Profit-generating practices such as monopolies and reselling at a higher price were forbidden as "offenses against public trade." Money itself existed only as a relatively fixed supply of coins, and there were no banks. As merchants steadily increased interregional trade, and rulers began to wage longer and more expensive military campaigns, they began to adopt more flexible ways of conceptualizing and handling money. Money is symbolic as well as "real." It exists both as numbers recorded in accounts and in the form of circulating coin and currency. And money can exist in the imagination. Credit (from the Latin *credere,* "to believe") is based on belief in return payment and makes it possible to multiply and manipulate money in truly amazing ways. The concept of credit was a simple extension of the concept of contract, based on the distinction between possessions in hand and possessions one was due to receive. When credit, interest charges, banking, and paper money and securities all became culturally acceptable, a *financial revolution* occurred that made capitalism possible. This cultural transformation was as significant as the Neolithic revolution.

The Amsterdam Exchange Bank, founded in 1609, was perhaps the first major bank, and it was followed shortly by the Amsterdam Stock Exchange. The first bank notes, the forerunners of modern paper money and checks, were issued by the Bank of Stockholm in 1661. Paper bills of exchange and bank notes greatly facilitated international trade, government and commercial finance, and capital investment. Economic growth quickly accelerated when enterprising bankers discovered they could lend out more money than they actually held in deposit. *Finance capital* is at the heart of capitalism, and money as a cultural symbol makes infinite economic growth seem deceptively possible.

The financial revolution suddenly gave the wealthy a powerful means of influencing the course of cultural development to their own advantage. The popular wisdom that money is power is correct, but successful financiers did not need to be personally wealthy. Credit, and the newly created financial institutions allowed them to magnify their own power by using other people's money. Capitalism didn't just happen. Economic historians attribute the emergence of capitalism to rising consumer demand, but market demand came from people who could use money, not from the mass of the European population struggling to maintain themselves. The "demand" was for palaces, mansions, luxury goods, and military power to satisfy the aristocracy and to support their dependent servants, artisans, soldiers, and courtiers. The wealthy also demanded profitable new investments. These were the financial demands that created exciting opportunities for the most powerful merchants and financiers, who came to manage enormous accumulations of capital. A few prominent families such as the Fuggers in Augsburg (1367–1641), the Medici in Florence (1434–1737), and the Rothschilds in Frankfurt (1770–) were the principal financial architects of European capitalism (see the box entitled "Fuggers and Rothschilds"). These families, together with the owners and directors of

The most successful early European capitalists accumulated great fortunes by forming family-owned business enterprises based on kinship and strategic marriage alliances. These corporate lineages became commercial dynasties that paralleled and were often intertwined with political dynasties (Ehrenberg 1928, Flynn 1941).

The German Catholic Fugger family created what became the richest and most influential business of the time. The Fugger enterprise began as a simple family-owned cotton and textile business in Augsburg, Bavaria, in 1367. The business expanded into the overseas spice trade, and eventually grew into a distinctly modern, diversified mining, trading, and banking business with branches and property throughout Europe. By the third generation in 1485, four Fugger brothers operated the company offices in Rome and Florence in Italy, in Innsbruck in Austria, and at their Augsburg headquarters. The Fuggers cultivated the patronage of the most powerful civil and religious rulers of the time and profitably financed wars and political intrigues, buying elections and offices, and loaning money to create profitable supporters. After 1500, the Fugger company gained monopolistic control over copper and silver mines and smelters in Austria and Hungary, which were then Europe's principal source for these metals. Benefiting from Spain's conquests in the New World, they developed mining interests in Peru and became involved in the African slave trade. By 1546, their fortune had grown to more than 5 million guilders. If converted to wheat at prevailing prices, this would have been sufficient to support 521,477 persons for a year—a thirtyfold increase in social power over Richard Fitzalan's record in 1376. The Fuggers' lucrative monopoly and behind-the-scenes manipulations of church and state generated labor unrest, peasant revolts, protests from other merchants; eventually led to nationalization of their mining interests; and contributed to the Protestant Reformation.

Much like the Fuggers, the Rothschild family rose from humble beginnings, in the Jewish ghetto in Frankfurt in 1744, to create an international banking dynasty operated by brothers from offices in Frankfurt, London, Paris, Vienna, and Naples by the 1820s. The family married carefully to increase their power, sometimes practicing cross-cousin marriage to keep their growing power and influence intact. Like the Fuggers, they maintained alliances with the most powerful political figures of the time and were able to control an enormous flow of finance capital in the most profitable way. By the end of the tumultuous nineteenth century, the Rothschilds had accumulated the world's largest private fortune. Their descendants are now billionaire financiers.

SOLOMON ROTHSCHILD, HEAD OF THE VIENNA HOUSE.

ANSELM MAYER ROTHSCHILD, HEAD OF THE PARENT HOUSE AT FRANKFORT, 1812-55.

CHARLES ROTHSCHILD, HEAD OF THE OLD HOUSE AT NAPLES.

a handful of banks and trading companies, such as the Bank of Amsterdam, the Bank of England, the British East India Company, and the Dutch East India Company, were the driving forces behind the accumulation, exchange, and marketing of money that began to increase the scale of culture and transform the world long before the Industrial Revolution.

European Marriage and Family

How did preindustrial European economic conditions and social class influence marriage patterns and family structure?

The system of kinship and marriage in medieval Europe was severely constrained by economic inequality. While European civilization was still predominantly agrarian, people needed access to individual landholdings before they could marry and establish a new household. Given the manorial system, land was in extremely short supply, and even a peasant's right to rent tiny parcels was a crucial inheritance to be safeguarded. Land rights were normally transmitted by inheritance to men, whereas women received a dowry of movable property or money upon marriage. This meant that men might not be able to marry until they were over 25. It also meant that many men and women could never marry, and they instead joined the religious monasteries as celibate monks or nuns.

British social anthropologist Jack Goody (1976: 14–25) pointed out that European marriage was characterized by class endogamy, in which the bride's dowry and the groom's inheritance had to be a good "match" for a marriage to take place, because inheritance and dowry served as rough measures of social standing. This meant that parents usually arranged marriages for their children within their own class, but at the same time people tried to marry up. Dowry thus helped the upper class keep their wealth intact. Dowry also made monogamy the preferred European form of marriage, because of the impossibility of sorting out multiple dowries within a single household. The European emphasis on female premarital chastity, chaperons, and arranged marriage may also be related to the importance of preventing lower-class men from marrying higher-class women and

thereby diluting the family estate (Stone 1997: 229–234).

Most European households were based on the small nuclear family, with peasant households averaging only 4.5 persons. On the manors, there were many single-person households, which would be unthinkable in the tribal world. There were no corporate descent groups, because impoverished peasants had too few resources to form a meaningful corporate estate. In this respect, European peasants were far poorer than people in most tribal societies, where everyone had access to an abundance of physical, social, and spiritual resources. In contrast to the peasants, the few upper-class Europeans often maintained large extended families and large households with many family members and domestic servants. As an extreme example, the French king, Louis XIV (reigned 1643–1715), maintained a household of 500 personal attendants. Family and kin were important to the aristocracy because they had vast corporate estates and wealth to pass on to the next generation. The English dukes, marquesses, earls, viscounts, and barons needed extensive genealogies to keep track of their complex kinship networks. and inherited titles.

GROWTH AND POVERTY UNDER EARLY BRITISH INDUSTRIAL CAPITALISM

The Industrial Revolution and the Culture of Consumption

What cultural processes drove industrialization? How have the core countries in the commercial-scale culture managed to maintain consumption levels at otherwise unsustainable levels? How did the rise of the commercial culture transform nineteenth-century Europe?

The most outstanding physical transformations accompanying the modern world system were dramatic increases in population and resource consumption, which began in England between 1760 and 1830. Immediately prior to the Industrial Revolution, world population growth was relatively slow, with a doubling time of approximately 250 years. However, with industrialization well established, the European population doubled in just 80 years after 1850, while the European population of the United States, Canada, Australia, and Argentina tripled between 1851 and 1900, thanks in part to large-scale immigration. Between 1851 and 1900, some 35 million people left Europe (Woodruff 1966).

This growth in population was accompanied by a shift in consumption patterns that marked a radical break with the relative stability of prior political-scale cultures. Capitalist economic growth requires continuous per-capita increases in consumption, which would inevitably deplete resources, at least in the core countries. For example, by 1850, England was unable to satisfy its needs for grain, wood, fibers, and hides from within its immediate borders (Woodruff 1966). Newly industrializing countries initially secured more resources by expanding trade networks and colonial territories to draw resources from throughout the world. Equally important was the switch in energy resources from the renewable, solar-driven fuels, such as wood, wind, and water, and a reliance on traction animals and human labor, which had characterized ancient civilizations, to the use of nonrenewable fossil fuels, such as coal, to power industrial machines. Many earlier civilizations utilized a complex division of labor, assembly-line mass-production techniques, and a wide variety of simple machines; however, their reliance on renewable energy sources was compatible with relatively stable consumption patterns.

Coal fueled the factories, ships, and trains of western Europe and North America in the nineteenth century and prepared the way for the age of oil. In the short run, use of fossil fuels allowed the industrial, capitalist world system to consume global resources at unsustainable levels, subsidizing otherwise impossible growth. Industrial civilization is unique in human history as a culture of consumption (Bodley 1996). In such a culture, economy, society, and belief systems are geared to "nonsustainable levels of resource consumption, and to continual, ever-higher elevation of those levels on a per-capita basis" (Bodley 1996:65). Biologically, this is overconsumption, as ecologist Howard Odum explained:

In the industrial system with man living off a fuel, he manages all his affairs with industrial machinery, all parts of which are metabolically consumers. . . . This system of man has consumption in excess of production. The products of respiration—carbon dioxide, metabolic water, and mineralized inorganic wastes—are discharged in rates in excess of their incorporation into organic matter by photosynthesis. If the industrialized urban system were enclosed in a chamber with only the air above it at the time, it would quickly exhaust its oxygen, be stifled with waste, and destroy itself since it does not have the recycling pattern of the agrarian system. (1971:17)

This biological imbalance in its urban centers and the pressure to increase consumption force the industrial civilization to be a world and global system because it would have difficulty sustaining itself in any other way.

The label *Industrial Revolution* that historians apply to this great cultural transformation overemphasizes the role of technological factors; but, as with the Neolithic, more than technology changed. It was not simply the inventive genius of a particular people that caused the Industrial Revolution. It was cultural changes in social organization and ideological systems that called forth technological innovation.

British historian T. S. Ashton (1969) argued that organizational and technological changes, rather than population growth, accelerated production during the Industrial Revolution in England. Increased production was initiated by organizational changes that brought more land into production and facilitated the adoption of technological changes, such as new crops and cropping systems. Like Adam Smith, Ashton argued that social inequality, perhaps even "injustice," was the key that encouraged the accumulation of capital that funded the technological innovations of the Industrial Revolution:

It is generally recognized that more saving takes place in communities in which the distribution of wealth is uneven than in those in which it approaches more closely to modern conceptions of what is just. (1969:7)

Technological innovations are not chance discoveries. They involve repeated trial and error and are often based on combinations of previous inventions. This is a panhuman process, but it is accelerated by specific cultural conditions. Invention was especially encouraged by specialization and the complex division of labor that emerged with the first states, but the unprecedented pressures for perpetual growth in the emerging capitalist world system set in motion the positive feedback between technical innovation and capital accumulation that became the Industrial Revolution.

Historians identify the enclosure movement as an important organizational change leading to the Industrial Revolution. In Europe during the seventeenth and eighteenth centuries, the shift from village self-sufficiency to market-oriented agriculture was accompanied by the transformation of open communal pastures and woodlands into numerous enclosed, privately controlled plots dedicated to the production of wool, meat, and hides.

Many historians urge us not to dwell on the fate of the formerly self-sufficient villagers who were forced off the land and impoverished by the enclosure process, which was supported by government decree. These peoples were surely being victimized by industrial progress. But according to the ideology of capitalism, we should focus on "the constructive activities that were being carried on inside the fences" (Ashton 1969:20). The historical interpretation of this dispossession process is that it was used to increase agricultural productivity while reducing the rural population, in order to raise the national standard of living. Those who were pushed off the land were considered to be "free to devote themselves to other activities," which meant they could either become vagrants or accept poorly paid jobs in the newly appearing industrial factories in the cities.

The enclosure movement was only the beginning of a series of vast cultural disruptions that ultimately spread throughout the globe as the capitalist world system began its expansion. In the following section, we examine the second phase of this expansion process, using the production, distribution, and consumption of sugar as a specific case study.

Sugar Eaters and the World System

Who benefited and who paid the costs of the global sugar trade?

As anthropologist Sydney Mintz (1985) details in his book *Sweetness and Power*, refined sugar, or sucrose, played a major role in the rise of the modern world system, contributing to the accumulation of capital and helping the English lower class adjust to their changed life conditions. During the Industrial Revolution, sugar was transformed from a rare European luxury before 1750 to a household necessity by 1850. In this process, the English subsistence system changed from its traditional reliance on a local, inexpensively produced complex carbohydrate, primarily wheat, to a system in which an imported, energy-intensive simple carbohydrate, sucrose, became a virtual staple for the lower and middle classes. England became a nation of sugar eaters, not because people naturally liked sweet things but because of the cultural forces associated with expansive capitalist development.

Sugarcane is a tropical plant that was probably domesticated in Melanesia by 8000 BC for its sweet sap. By 400 BC, it was being grown in India, where the earliest processed sugar is known to have been prepared by at least AD 500. Muslims spread sugarcane growing and sugar processing throughout the Mediterranean region by AD 1000. In medieval Europe, sugar was treated as a spice and had many medicinal uses but was too scarce to be available to any but the most wealthy. In medieval England, sugar was used in the royal court to prepare edible decorative works of art, which served as symbols of power and status. Such objects were a special expression of power because they could be conspicuously consumed as a valuable on a ritual occasion. By 1500, sugar decorations were an important part of ritual feasts throughout the upper classes, and within 200 years, such use had become common even among the middle classes as sugar became more readily available.

During the early phase of capitalist development in England, from approximately 1650 to 1750, sugar was the single most important product imported from its colonies. Produced by slave labor on plantations in the British West Indies, sugar supported a major trade triangle that contributed to the accumulation of profits in the capitalist core. Shipments of manufactured goods, such as cloth, tools, and iron shackles, moved from England to Africa; slaves were carried from Africa to the West

FIGURE 11.5
The sugar trade triangle.

Indies; and sugar was shipped from the West Indies to England, where it was further refined (Figure 11.5). Thus, sugar helped generate direct profits while providing a market for manufactured goods. In the process, millions of African slaves were forced to work 12-hour days, often while supplying their own provisions. After slavery was abolished in the British colonies in the 1830s, perhaps 50 million Asians, primarily from India, were carried to sugar-producing areas as contract laborers during the nineteenth century.

Perhaps as important as sugar's role in the trade triangle was the nutrition and comfort it gave to the English working class who supplied the human energy for the Industrial Revolution. This support role for sugar developed gradually as the plantation system expanded to make sugar more available and as sugar proved to be an ideal complement to the tropical "drug foods" such as tea, coffee, and chocolate, which began to reach England in the seventeenth century. These are all bitter, calorie-free, stimulating drinks that are sweetened and calorie-fortified by the addition of sugar. Tea had been imported from China by an English trading monopoly beginning in 1660, but it became the most popular English drink after tea plantations

were established in British India by 1840. In combination with sugar from the British West Indies, tea from British India became cheaper than beer as a stimulating and nourishing drink for the English working class.

As Mintz (1985) explains, sugar consumption by the English working poor grew in stages. It was used first with tea and then in rich puddings, which by the nineteenth century became a dessert course to end a meal. Sugar was combined with wheat flour in sweetened baked goods; by the end of the century, bread and jam became a meal, especially in households in which both parents were employed. At the national level, per-capita sugar consumption tripled from approximately 30 pounds (14 kilograms [kg]) per year in 1800 to approximately 90 pounds (41 kg) per year by 1900. By the 1970s, per-capita consumption seems to have peaked at about 115 pounds (52 kg). As a proportion of total caloric consumption, sugar rose from 2 to 14 percent over the course of the nineteenth century (Mintz 1985). Such an increase was possible because the price of sugar in England decreased by 50 percent between 1840 and 1870 (Mintz 1985). Sugar became a relatively cheap source of calories and tended to supplement and replace more expensive grains, fruits, vegetables, meat, and dairy products.

The per-capita consumption figures mask the important role that sugar played in the diet of the working poor because actual rates varied by class and by age and sex within households. By 1850, sugar consumption by the English working class exceeded that of the upper class. Increased sugar intake was accompanied by a decline in bread consumption, from which some historians infer that more meat must have been eaten and nutrition improved. However, Mintz (1985) argues that in most lower-class households, the working man ate the meat while his wife and children were left with the sugar as empty calories and were thereby systematically malnourished. This was justified by the householders because the husband had to remain in top physical condition to be an effective worker. This nutritional inequality, however, must have elevated infant mortality rates.

Sugar was especially important in the capitalist transformation of the world system because its capacity to stimulate perpetually increasing consumer demand neatly supported the endless-growth ideals of capitalism in opposition to the equilibrium theories of mercantilist economists. Sugar became the first great consumer product. It was a substance of which people never seemed to get enough, and it proved that basic human needs could be culturally redefined and expanded as an instrument of national policy. Precapitalist economic theory held that most wage laborers were "target workers" who worked only long enough to satisfy their fixed needs. Alcohol consumption was potentially elastic, but alcoholics made poor workers. Sugar, on the other hand, made for contented workers and was especially attractive at first because its use was a marker of high social status. However, in the long run, it was the factory system itself, with its physically demanding work schedule, that helped increase sugar consumption by raising both demand and supply.

Mintz (1985) argues that England was converted into a nation of sugar eaters, at least in part, because such a change served the interests of individuals who were in a position to exercise political power. Many of the early West Indian sugarcane planters were themselves members of Parliament; along with the investors who supported them and those in slaving, shipping, refining, and marketing, who benefited from sugar, they formed a significant interest group that influenced government policy. It is not surprising that sugar was issued to the inmates of English poorhouses or that a half-pint of rum made from West Indian molasses became an official daily ration of the British Navy in 1731 (an amount that was soon raised to a pint a day). The British government gained revenues from the sugar trade and indirectly subsidized the Caribbean planters by helping keep prices high. By the 1850s, the government shifted in favor of a free-trade policy to reduce the price of sugar and thereby increase the supply, thus making it more widely available.

The Invisible Hand and the Problem of Poverty

How did Adam Smith think the market would work to benefit society? How were the poor actually affected by the economic transformation of England? What was the government's response?

Adam Smith (1723–1790), Scottish philosopher, political economist, and founding father of capitalism, presented an insightful and remarkably frank, emic view of how the early capitalist market economy was theoretically expected to work. In his famous book *Wealth of Nations* (1776), Smith identified labor specialization and private ownership of land, together with the related emergence of landlords, manufacturers, laborers, rent, and profit, as the fundamental elements of a market, or "commercial," economy. In this system, landlords received their share of production as rent and advanced part to laborers as wages for their maintenance. Labor specialization in manufacturing required that manufacturers accumulate stock or capital, but it permitted dramatic increases in production. Wealth inequality helped make the system work.

Smith (1776) felt that most laborers "naturally" needed masters to maintain them between harvests and to carry out productive tasks. The relative poverty of laborers gave manufacturers and landlords a strategic advantage in any disputes over wages. Even though they were ultimately dependent on their laborers, most manufacturers and landlords, with their larger stockpiles of wealth, could last more than one year if the laborers stopped working in order to enforce a demand for increased wages. Smith estimated that most laborers would not have enough stores to hold out more than one week without their wages.

Smith argued that as long as government did not intervene unduly, economic competition caused by people's natural desire for self-improvement would maintain orderly economic growth, as if by an *invisible hand.* Smith advocated that workers receive the lowest wage "which is consistent with common humanity" (1776:103). This minimum wage would be determined by the short-run maintenance needs of individual workers combined with approximately double that amount to provide enough for workers to reproduce. Smith did not quantify this amount precisely, but he assumed that a worker would support a wife and four children, only two of which would reach adulthood. According to Smith, a direct feedback operated between increasing demand for labor during times of economic growth and an increase in the labor supply, because wages would necessarily go up, which would mean that the poor could better support their children so that more would grow up to become workers. If there were too many workers, wages would go down, and the ensuing poverty would increase infant mortality, thereby reducing the number of workers and sending wages back up.

Smith thought that improved wages would increase production, because it would give workers hope and make them work harder. Thus, continuous growth seemed to be the most desirable condition, as Smith explained:

It is in the progressive state, while the society is advancing to the further acquisition . . . that the condition of the labouring poor, of the great body of the people, seems to be the happiest and the most comfortable. It is hard in the stationary, and miserable in the declining state. The progressive state is in reality the cheerful and the hearty state to all the different orders of the society. The stationary is dull; the declining, melancholy. (1776:123)

As the industrial era began, despite Smith's optimistic view of the invisible hand, England's lower class was desperately squeezed between declining agrarian living standards in the countryside and abysmally low wages in the towns and cities. The growing money economy had already made poverty such a serious social problem that long before Smith's time, severe compulsion was required to force people to find employment, even at wages that would not provide adequate subsistence. Family life disintegrated when households could not support children and elders, and the state was forced to deal with the problem. The first poor laws, in 1531–1536, called for compulsory almsgiving and made willful unemployment a crime punishable by forced labor, mutilation, and death. Later creative variations called for whipping, burning, branding, slavery, hard labor in chains, and *then* death for repeat offenders. Reforms in 1601 called for placing paupers, such as widows and those physically unable to work, in poorhouses, while the children of the poor were to be apprenticed to masters in workhouses. But welfare subsidies intended to bring the working poor up to a subsistence level only encouraged employers to offer substandard wages.

By the 1830s, conditions among the working class in England had deteriorated so badly that the government took further measures in an effort to minimize the damage. Officially, 1.4 million people, nearly 10 percent of the population, were receiving relief under the poor laws. But this was an incomplete reckoning of poverty, and the assistance provided was woefully inadequate. A massive report presented to Parliament in 1842 by Edwin Chadwick (1965) showed unequivocally that the poor were being forced to live in crowded and unsanitary conditions that contributed to contagious disease, high mortality, high fertility, and reduced life expectancy. For example, in Liverpool in 1840, health conditions were poor for everyone, but Chadwick found that laborers died at an average age of 15, whereas upper-class people died at 35. More people were dying from poverty than in England's many wars. Chadwick viewed this costly and unnecessary loss of life as a public health problem and advocated better sewage drainage and administrative changes. But many others called for drastic social reforms. The working poor understood

---

invisible hand   The capitalist belief that market forces, operating through supply and demand, will lead to continuous economic growth and benefit everyone.

that their basic problem was inadequate and irregular wages and the loss of control over their subsistence resources brought about by unbalanced industrialization. The Luddites who destroyed the textile machines in 1811–1816 and the farm workers who rioted against the new threshing machines in the 1830s were not opposed to technological progress as such; they simply did not want to surrender their economic autonomy (Noble 1993).

The London Poor

What were the relative proportions and absolute numbers of people living at different socioeconomic levels in London in the second half of the nineteenth century? What were conditions like at the bottom?

By the 1840s, immigration and internal growth had swelled the population of metropolitan London to more than 2 million people, but employment opportunities remained inadequate. The human degradation that accompanied London's rapid industrial development was most vividly portrayed by novelist Charles Dickens ([1852–53] 1953), journalist Henry Mayhew ([1861–62] 1968), and shipping magnate turned sociologist Charles Booth (1892–1903). Mayhew's pioneer ethnographic work was explicitly anthropological. Mayhew viewed the existence of such poverty in the midst of wealthy London as a "national disgrace." He was incensed that the British public knew more about distant tribes than they knew about the poorest Londoners, who were not even counted in the national census. He wanted "to give the rich a more intimate knowledge of the sufferings, and frequent heroism under those sufferings, of the poor." Mayhew spent years observing life on the streets of London and collecting life stories and personal accounts of hundreds of street folk, which he carefully recorded in their own words.

Most of Mayhew's ethnographic work was devoted to London's working poor, who comprised a ragged assortment of some 50,000 self-employed street vendors, refuse collectors, performers, artisans, vermin exterminators, and manual laborers. The street vendors, or costermongers, survived by selling everything from fresh produce and flowers to old books, dog collars, live birds, second-hand clothes, and old glassware. Mayhew found the cos-

termongers to be hard-working and honest, and he admired their resourcefulness. Children sold things on the street as soon as they could walk and talk; most children went unschooled and might be informally married by age 14. Costermongers had minimal economic reserves, but those who were fortunate and extremely careful with their meager funds might have precariously comfortable lives. Others lived in squalor and struggled to survive.

Because of their economic marginality, many costermongers were too poor to buy the carts, donkeys, and miscellaneous equipment needed for their work. Their low and erratic income made them easy prey for those immediately higher in the economic hierarchy. Annual rent for a simple handcart was more than twice the cart's value. At those rates, enterprising capitalists turned a modest investment in handcarts into a profitable business. One man amassed an economic empire of 150 handcarts, which he rented to the costermongers at exorbitant weekly rates for a tidy return. Hard-pressed costermongers were also an easy target for unscrupulous moneylenders and pawnshop owners. Interest rates were so outrageous that costermongers were forced to pay £65 to borrow £25 during the year to buy their stock. Costermongers lived in specific neighborhoods and supported each other, even holding raffles to raise money for those in most distress. In good times, the average annual income of costermongers could provide a minimum living, but if a few days of bad weather depressed sales, thousands would face starvation. The lives of many of the street people were unbelievably bleak (see the box entitled "Mud-Larks, Bone-Grubbers, and a Coster Lad's Story").

At the end of the nineteenth century, England's political leaders still lacked a clear picture of the scale of the country's social problems (see the box entitled "Marx and Engels: *The Communist Manifesto*"). London's population had now grown to 5 million people, and radical reformers claimed that 25 percent were impoverished. Successful London businessman Charles Booth thought this figure was an exaggeration, and in 1886, following Mayhew's lead, he set out to systematically count London's poor. Funding his own research, he picked the northeast quarter of the city, where nearly a million people lived, and spent the next 17 years methodically mapping income levels, occupations, and

Mud-Larks, Bone-Grubbers, and a Coster Lad's Story

Mayhew thought that the most degraded workers in London were the collectors who wandered the streets searching for marketable refuse, such as cigar butts, bits of metal, rags, rope, bone, lumps of coal, and dog feces. Three pounds of bone fragments was worth a penny, and a good bone-grubber (see Figure 11.6) could gather 6 pence (half a shilling) worth in a day—only a third of the 10 shillings that a costermonger might earn per day. Apples sold at six for a penny, and a 4-pound loaf of bread cost 4 pence. Fortunate bone-grubbers would spend 2 pence of their meager earnings on the most wretched lodging and have 4 pence left to spend on a little sugar, coffee, and a quarter loaf of bread. Mayhew interviewed other unusual collectors including old-wood gatherers, dredgers, sewer hunters, and mud-larks. He thought the condition of the latter was the most deplorable—they were reduced to scavenging trash from the river mud at low tide. He described them as follows:

Among the mud-larks may be seen many old women, and it is indeed pitiable to behold them, especially during the winter, bent nearly double with age and infirmity, paddling and groping among the wet mud for small pieces of coal, chips of wood, or any sort of refuse washed up by the tide. These women always have with them an old basket or an old tin kettle, in which they put whatever they chance to find. It usually takes them a whole tide to fill this receptacle, but when filled, it is as much as the feeble old creatures are able to carry home. (Mayhew [1861–62] 1968, vol. 2:155)

Mayhew ([1861–62] 1968, vol. 1:39) recorded the following life history from a 16-year-old coster lad. This illustrates the physical and emotional stress that misfortune caused economically marginalized families in nineteenth-century London:

"Father I've heard tell died when I was three and brother only a year old. It was worse luck for us! . . . Mother used to be up and out very early washing in families—anything for a living. She was a good mother to us. We was left at home with the key of the room and some bread and butter for dinner. Afore she got into work—and it was a goodish long time—we was shocking hard up, and she pawned nigh everything. Sometimes, when we hadn't no grub at all, the other lads, perhaps, would give us some bread and butter, but often our stomachs used to ache with the hunger, and we would cry when we was werry far gone. She used to be at work from six in the morning till ten o'clock at night, which was a long time for a child's belly to hold out again, and when it was dark we would go and lie down on the bed and try and sleep until she came home with the food. I was eight year old then.

"A man as know'd mother, said to her, 'Your boy's got nothing to do, let him come along with me and yarn a few ha'pence,' and so I became a coster. He gave me 4d. [pence] a morning and my breakfast."

THE BONE-GRUBBER.

[From a Daguerreotype by BEARD.*]*

FIGURE 11.6   *The London bone grubber.*

housing conditions—street by street, house by house, even room by room. To precisely identify the truly poor, he sorted his data along different dimensions using an eight-level scale, ranked A to H and color coded, black to yellow, by living standard. At the bottom of the scale in Class A, coded black, were semicriminals, loafers, and occasional laborers, with minimal family life. On a Class A street, Booth found 200 households, containing probably 1000 people, living in forty four-story houses in a 2-acre (4.8 hectares) section of London near the British Museum. Entire families were crowded into single 8- by 8-foot, vermin-infested rooms. Fifty people shared a single outside toilet and water tap, drawing from a cistern. Most of these people found occasional work as market porters and costermongers, or they were unemployed. The "very poor" in Class B were characterized by "casual labour, hand-to-mouth existence, [and] chronic want." The "poor" in Classes C and D could find seasonal, or poorly paid work, which was "barely sufficient for

decent independent life." Members of all "poor" classes lived in crowded housing with two or more persons per room and were at or below a poverty level of 21 shillings of weekly income. Working-class people in Classes E and F were regularly employed and "fairly" paid, and Booth considered them to be "comfortable." At the upper end, Class G, "well-to-do" families had one or two servants. In Class H were "wealthy" families, which kept three or more servants and lived in houses valued at £100 pounds or more. In his final analysis, Booth discovered that more than 30 percent of London's population were poor by his own definition (see Table 11.1 and Figure 11.7). The radical reformers actually had underestimated the problem. The 1.2 million poor living in London in 1890 exceeded the entire population of the city in 1801, suggesting that a century of growth had produced an unusual sort of progress. The 18,000 wealthy constituted the top 0.5 percent of London society.

London's poverty in the 1890s was related to social conditions in the countryside. Rural land ownership had become so concentrated that an official inquiry was held in 1875, and for the first time the government published the names and holdings of all major landowners in a "New Domesday Book" (Bateman 1883). There were some 24 million people in England and Wales in 1875, in 4.8 million households; but fewer than 14,000 large landowners, who represented only 0.28 percent of all households, held nearly 75 percent of the land. This land tenure system distinctly resembled the Norman system of the original Domesday Survey. Ninety-five percent of households held less than 0.5 percent of all individually owned land. The smallholders represented 15 percent of the population, but their properties averaged less than a quarter acre each, certainly not enough to sustain a farm family.

The British Empire

What was the extent of British domination of the world's land and people at the height of their empire? How was this empire structured?

By 1878, a political hierarchy in the global system was clearly established. More than half the world's land area was claimed by just four giant states and their related territories: Britain, Russia, China, and

Marx and Engels: The Communist Manifesto

Social revolutionaries Karl Marx (1818–1883) and Friedrich Engels (1820–1895) were both living in London and directly experienced the wretched social conditions described by Mayhew. Engels' book *The Condition of the Working-Class in England: From Personal Observation and Authentic Sources* (1845) was written to inspire a social revolution. Marx and Engels coauthored their famous *Communist Manifesto* in London in 1848. They conceptualized the human problems of commercialization as a class struggle between "two great hostile camps"—the bourgeoisie (capitalists) and the proletariat (workers). Their solution called for "the forcible overthrow of all existing social conditions," declaring in the famous last lines of the Manifesto:

Let the ruling classes tremble at a Communistic revolution. The proletarians have nothing to lose but their chains. They have a world to win. WORKING MEN OF ALL COUNTRIES UNITE!

More specifically, Marx and Engels advocated worker control of government; the abolition of private property; government control of production, communication, and transportation; free education; and the elimination of social classes. They understood that culture change was not a natural process, but they were overly optimistic about the possibility of eliminating social classes. Consequently, they did not solve the problem of how to more equitably distribute social power in very large-scale social systems. However, they clearly understood the importance of political economy, and they recognized the human problems of the commercialization process. Marxist political ideology has certainly shaped the course of modern history, but simply placing commerce under state control does not solve all problems of scale and power, as the experience of the Soviet Union demonstrated.

TABLE 11.1   *Living Standards and Social Class in London, 1890*

Living Standard	Class	Income	Housing	Number	Percentage
Poor	A (lowest)	Occasional	Very crowded	37,610	0.89
Poor	B (very poor)	Casual	Very crowded	316,834	7.53
Poor	C–D (poor)	Ill-paid	Crowded	938,293	22.29
Comfortable	E–F (working class)	Fairly paid	—	2,166,503	51.47
Well-to-do	G (middle class)	—	—	732,124	17.39
Wealthy	H (upper class)	—	—	17,806	0.42
Totals				4,209,170	100.00

SOURCE: Booth (1892–1903).

FIGURE 11.7
The London social hierarchy, 1890. (SOURCE: Booth 1892–1903.)

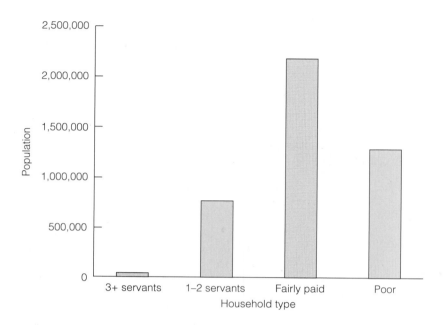

the United States. Together with seven other colonial countries, these major states held claims over two-thirds of the world (Clark 1936). Most of Africa was still under the control of traditional kingdoms, chiefdoms, and tribal systems. Minor independent modern states had emerged in Latin America, but vast areas were still occupied by autonomous tribal groups.

Beginning in the 1880s, the major colonial powers scrambled to extend their political control over Africa and the Pacific, and by 1913 more than three-fourths of the world's land area was controlled by just thirteen countries.

Throughout the modern colonial period from 1800 to 1945, a single power, Great Britain, remained dominant. At its height in the 1930s, the British empire spanned the globe, encompassing roughly one-fourth of the world's land area and population (see Figure 11.8). The empire included the United Kingdom; British India; the relatively independent Dominions of Canada, Newfoundland, and New Zealand; the Commonwealth of Australia; the Union of South Africa; and the various crown colonies, dependencies, and protectorates—a total territory of more than 12 million square miles (mi²) (31.3 million square kilometers [km²]) and 500 million people. The British empire was pri-

marily a loose federation held together by diverse political connections and the common British origin and English language of the ruling elites in each political unit.

In most of the colonies, a very small minority of European colonists enjoyed a privileged status over the majority native population, who were held in a structurally inferior position. Coercive military power was used to establish and maintain administrative control, but the common objective was the capitalist development of productive resources, growing markets, and the expansion of trade, not the extraction of tribute as in ancient empires. Some 35 percent of the empire was controlled at least indirectly by London, but local colonial governments often enjoyed considerable autonomy. Depending on its size, a given colony might be governed by a governor general, governor, lieutenant governor, administrator, high commissioner, or commissioner. Some colonies elected their own parliaments, and their legislation was subject only to rare vetos by the crown. This promoted the uncontrolled frontier, where the government allowed colonists to deal with tribal peoples in their own way, as will be described in Chapter 14.

Even before the modern era of decolonization began, Grover Clark (1936) carefully examined the

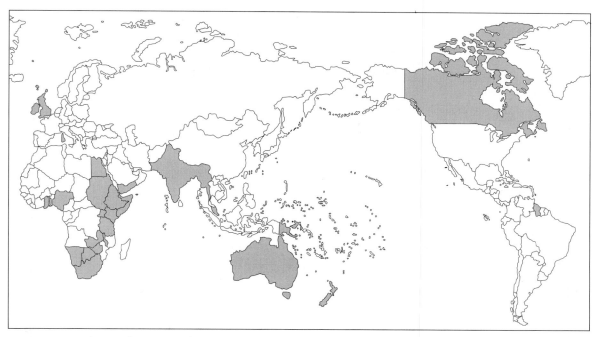

FIGURE 11.8   *The British empire in the 1930s.*

economic balance sheets of imperialism and concluded that by the 1930s, colonial expansion no
longer yielded an economic gain for colonizing
countries. Prior to 1800, while colonial territories
still were readily available, imperialism proved
profitable for both governments and private business interests. Between 1800 and 1880, costs began
to increase, and governments had to subsidize the
colonial enterprise; but private profits remained
high. After 1880, colonial expansion became costly
because of rebellions by colonized peoples and because rivalries between competing colonial powers
forced them to maintain large armies and navies;
this contributed to World War I.

Clark (1936) also challenged the standard defense of imperialism—that it provided an outlet for
excess population and was necessary to ensure the
flow of resources to the imperial centers. The territories conquered in the Western Hemisphere by the
Spanish, Portuguese, French, and British during
the first round of expansion before 1800 became
important outlets for colonizing European populations, as did South Africa, Australia, and New Zea-

land. However, Clark showed that only 2.6 percent
of European immigration since 1880 had been to
the tropical colonies. Clark also showed that modern trade depends more on communication links
than on political control. Trade monopolies are difficult to maintain, and most colonies and their major colonizing powers were not dependent on one
another for markets.

THE NEW FREE-MARKET
GLOBAL ORDER

Colonialism was a clumsy system of capitalist economic competition organized by nation-states; it
has now been totally superseded by a decentralized
global market. Commercialization's triumph over
the politicization process has produced a world
dominated by transnational corporations and financial elites with no national loyalties. The global
market economy is free in that it is subject to less
and less control by any national government or

international political institutions. Centrally planned economies, such as the former Soviet Union, have all but disappeared. International trade agreements, such as the GATT (General Agreement on Tariffs and Trade) and NAFTA (North American Free Trade Agreement), have greatly reduced national barriers to commerce such that commodities and finance capital now flow easily across borders. The world's 5.6 billion people are being combined in a single commercial network, which is ultimately dependent on computerized financial transactions taking place in a few organized markets in the richest countries (see Figure 11.9). Unfortunately, the human risks and rewards are not equitably distributed in this new world order.

Since 1944, when the Bretton Woods Conference established a single global monetary system based on the American dollar, the World Bank, and the International Monetary Fund (IMF), *financialization* has emerged as a new global cultural process controlling commercialization (Phillips 1994). Financialization refers to the flow of money, or finance capital, rather than the production and distribution of physical goods and services. The flow of finance capital is now more important in commerce than the flow of goods and services. As much as 90 percent of the world's commercial transactions may now involve stocks, bonds, and commodity futures, rather than actual goods (Barnet and Cavanagh 1994). The rapid proliferation of consumer credit, such as through credit cards, also reflects the increasing importance of the financialization process. This process rapidly shifts wealth to financial elites, who already control large sums of finance capital, because they can realize handsome returns from very large financial exchanges with small profit margins.

The International Monetary Fund was designed to integrate the monetary policies of member nations to facilitate international trade and promote economic growth. The most crucial monetary policies influenced by the IMF are the exchange values of national currencies and the credit standings of governments. In 1998, there were 182 member nations in the IMF. Each nation had a representative on the IMF Board of Governors, but voting rights reflected the relative monetary contribution of each nation to the IMF's reserve funds. Nine nations (the USA, Germany, Japan, France, the United Kingdom, Saudi Arabia, Italy, Canada, and Russia) collectively controlled more than half of the IMF's voting power and were thus able to play a dominant role in shaping the global financial system. The most powerful member, the United States, controlled 18 percent of the votes, and the Group of Seven (the USA, Germany, Japan, France, the UK, Italy, and Canada) controlled 45 percent of the votes. These seven countries represented the world's largest national economies and were strategically situated to shape international monetary policy in the interests of the world's corporate and individual investors.

In a sense, the prime beneficiaries of the global flow of finance capital are the approximately 6 million high-net-worth individuals (HNWI), primarily European and American multimillionaires with investable assets of more than a million dollars (Gemini Consulting 1998). In 1997, these private financial elites collectively controlled $17.4 trillion, an amount representing more than 50 percent of the world's gross domestic product, yet they constituted a mere 0.1 percent of the world's population. Their assets were growing at more than 5 percent a year. Their investment decisions were shaping the world and profoundly influencing the lives of billions of people.

British sociologist Leslie Sklair (1991) presents a new view of the emerging global order in which the primary agents are all transnational (see Table 11.2). This means that most of the world's people have little ability to influence the decisions that shape their daily lives. The transnational corporations that dominate the economic sphere of the global system have become enormously powerful. For example, in 1993, General Motors, the world's largest corporation, owned 312 other companies and employed 750,000 people in thirty-six countries. Its sales of $133 billion exceeded the gross domestic products of all but eighteen of the world's wealthiest countries. The world's fifteen largest banks held $5.7 trillion in assets in 1992, a sum that exceeded the gross national product (GNP) of every country in the world and represented approximately one-fourth the global GNP. The transnational capitalist class controls national and international political institutions in ways that benefit their financial interests. This fabulously wealthy financial elite accumulates wealth by in-

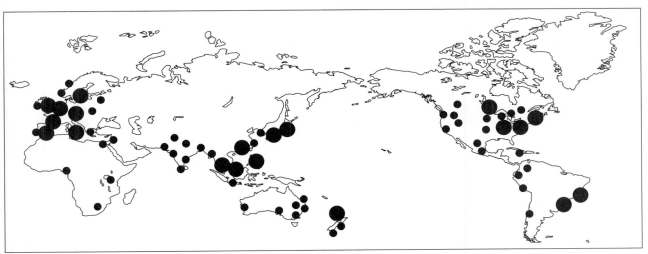

KEY: ● (small dot) = 1 exchange
      ⬤ (large dot) = 2 or more exchanges

FIGURE 11.9   *Securities and futures exchanges in the global market, 1990.*

TABLE 11.2   *Transnational Agents in the Global System*

Spheres	Primary Agents	Transnational Practices (TNP)
Economic	Transnational corporations (TNCs)	Commodities production and marketing services Job creation and destruction
Political	Transnational capitalist class	Political support for marketing and international trade
Cultural-ideological	Transnational mass media and advertising	Consumerism

SOURCE: Based on Sklair (1991).

vesting their finance capital, rather than profiting directly from the output of factories or from their salaries. In 1993, the cumulative personal wealth of the 101 richest individuals in the world totaled $451 billion and represented more than 2 percent of the global GNP (Rogers 1993).

The new global elite use their wealth to maintain a dominant influence in the world, or **cultural hegemony,** which maintains consumerism as a primary cultural ideal. Commercial advertisers shape people's beliefs and the smallest details of their behavior through the mass media. For example, Coca-Cola—arguably the world's most successful brand—markets its soft drinks to 20 percent of the world's people. In 1992–1993, it had sales of more than $13 billion. Coca-Cola spent $392 million in the United States to persuade people to drink an average of 37 gallons of Coke products per capita per year, producing sales of $4.3 billion (Huey 1993). It is not surprising that in 1998, Warren Buffett, a principal Coca-Cola shareholder and corporate director, was

financialization   A cultural process involving the flow of finance capital, money, and securities, rather than the actual production and distribution of goods and services.
cultural hegemony   Dominant influence by elites over the cultural symbols and beliefs that influence human behavior.

perhaps the third-richest individual in the world, with a personal net worth estimated at $33 billion.

When the postcolonial era of national economic growth slowed in the 1980s, political economists promoted "New Growth Theory" favoring an even more *globally integrated* economy based on small and weak governments, minimal regulation of commerce, and removal of all trade barriers (Beach and Davis 1998; Johnson, Holmes, and Kirkpatrick 1998:4). This new commercially organized world economic order is directed by a loose network of economic planners who occupy key positions in newly created international economic institutions, such as the International Monetary Fund, the World Bank, and the World Trade Organization, and on the boards of the world's largest corporations. The promotion of economic growth is the single objective of this new global-scale power elite, but the planners are often divided over key policy approaches and conflicting interests.

SUMMARY

Capitalism is a commercial system of production and exchange that treats land, labor, technology, money, raw materials, and goods and services as commodities to be bought and sold for a profit. This cultural system is totally unique and has transformed the world. The wealthy elite who most benefit from the capitalist market economy have used industrial production based on fossil fuel energy sources, colonialism, and unequal exchange to integrate the diverse societies and cultures of the world into a single global economic system. An ideology of continuous economic expansion and high rates of consumption are central features of this system that are derived from more fundamental European beliefs in natural scarcity, insatiable wants, and a dualism between mind and body, humans and nature.

During the early stages of commercialization in medieval England, the number of poor actually increased. Capitalism required a financial revolution that made money the dominant means of organizing social power. The most successful mercantile capitalists used kinship and marriage to organize their far-flung business enterprises and transmit their growing commercial estates from generation to generation. Early economic theorists such as Adam Smith assumed that capitalist development directed by self-seeking entrepreneurs would ultimately benefit everyone. However, ethnographic data collected in nineteenth-century London showed that unrestrained economic growth produced enormous poverty and serious public health problems.

The global process of sugar production and consumption illustrated the early expansion of the global system. Commercially driven colonial empires, exemplified by the British empire at its peak, controlled much of the world during the first half of the nineteenth century. Since the breakdown of the colonial system after World War II, many supranational political and economic institutions, such as the United Nations and the World Bank, have assumed formal leadership of the global system. But the policies of these institutions are influenced by powerful nations and by giant multinational corporations that benefit from the global structure of inequality. A new cultural process, financialization, controlled by the wealthiest individuals and financial institutions, is emerging as the dominant force in the world.

The next chapter will examine the United States as an example of one of the most dominant national cultures in the present global system. Chapter 13 will explore the problem of poverty in the countries that are "peripheral" to the wealthy industrial core.

STUDY QUESTIONS

1. Define the following concepts: embedded economy, kin-ordered production, culture of consumption, mode of production, capitalist production, tributary production.

2. Distinguish between a market and nonmarket economy.

3. Define a capitalist political economy, and explain how it differs from the economic systems of ancient states.

4. Describe the modern world system as defined by Immanuel Wallerstein, referring to core, periphery, semi-periphery, labor control, division of labor, unequal exchange, and accumulation.

5. What are the principal ideological features of the capitalist world system? Draw illustrations from Adam Smith and modern economists, and discuss the contradictory realities listed by Wallerstein.

6. Discuss the specific changes in cultural organization that accompanied the Industrial Revolution in England. Refer to the role of technology, population, capital accumulation, inequality, and the enclosure movement.

7. What is the evidence for the argument that more people were impoverished than enriched by the cultural transformations that swept England between 1086 and 1890?

8. How were European economic conditions from 1086 to 1890 reflected in household organization and in kinship and marriage patterns?

9. What features of European cosmology and ideology supported capitalism?

10. Explain how dietary change (sugar and tea) in England was related to the Industrial Revolution and the expanding world system.

11. Describe the political and economic structure of modern colonialism in contrast to the empires of the past. Make specific comparisons between the Inca empire in the Andean world and the British empire in the modern world.

SUGGESTED READING

CROSBY, ALFRED W. 1986. *Biological Imperialism: The Biological Expansion of Europe, 900–1900.* Cambridge, Eng.: Cambridge University Press. Discussion by a historian of the biological consequences of European colonialism on ecosystems and people throughout the world.

DUMONT, LOUIS. 1977. *From Mandeville to Marx: The Genesis and Triumph of Economic Ideology.* Chicago and London: University of Chicago Press. Documentation by a French anthropologist of how the economy came to be treated as an independent reality within the global culture.

EKELUND, ROBERT B., JR., AND ROBERT F. HEBERT. 1983. *A History of Economic Theory and Method,* 2nd ed. New York: McGraw-Hill. A modern emic view of the capitalist economy that serves as a good comparison with Adam Smith.

SMITH, ADAM. 1776. *An Inquiry into the Nature and Causes of the Wealth of Nations,* vol. 1. London: Strahan and Cadell. The classic formulation of the key features of the early capitalist economy.

WALLERSTEIN, IMMANUEL. 1974. *The Modern World-System: Capitalist Agriculture and the Origins of the European World-Economy in the Sixteenth Century.* New York: Academic Press. The pioneer statement of world system theory.

WOLF, ERIC R. 1982. *Europe and the People Without History.* Berkeley: University of California Press. An anthropological treatment of European expansion since 1400, focusing on the political economy and showing how the capitalist system incorporated tributary and kin-based systems.

12

The American Capitalist State

Thanks to the enormous success of both its ideological and material culture, the United States is often a model for the rest of the world and is certainly an appropriate anthropological subject. For many, the United States represents the ideals of freedom, democracy, equality, and material abundance. Its size and economic power give it enormous influence; this means that even such seemingly trivial matters as the American food preference for beef can have a profound impact on peoples in distant parts of the globe. Furthermore, its economic success makes the United States a critical source of stress in the global ecosystem. In the 1980s, Americans made up less than 5 percent of the world's population but consumed more than 25 percent of the world's commercial energy.

Attempting to understand a country as large and complex as the United States is a formidable task, one that has engaged anthropologists and other social scientists for a long time. Studying America is a significant shift from anthropology's earlier role in support of colonialism. It means that American anthropologists must ask basic questions about their own culture and its place in the world. This chapter focuses on aspects of American culture that offer the strongest contrasts with domestic-scale cultures and the tribute-based civilizations discussed in Chapters 7–10. In the first section, we examine the unique cosmological and ideological features of American culture, highlighting Americans' beliefs about their political system and the proper relationship between business, government, and households. A contrast will be drawn between the American emphasis on individualism and the Chinese emphasis on kinship and family, based on the perspective of a Chinese-American anthropologist. This section also examines the historical context behind America's most sacred texts—the Declaration of Independence and the Constitution. Next, we focus specifically on the commercialization process by examining the organizational and technological changes behind the evolution of business enterprise and the rise of the giant corporation in nineteenth-century America. Ethnohistorical case studies of a Pennsylvania textile mill village, twentieth-century factory farming, and the cattle industry will illustrate the impact of commercialization on various aspects of American culture. Finally, we draw on a variety of American ethnographic materials to evaluate the human risks and rewards of the growth process itself.

AMERICAN CULTURAL IDEALS VERSUS REALITY

An American Profile

How does the United States compare in size and ethnic diversity to other major industrial countries? In addition to interviews and direct observation, what rich sources of data can an anthropologist utilize to study American culture?

With a total territory of 3.6 million square miles (mi²) (9.3 million square kilometers [km²]), the United States is the world's fourth largest nation by land area, after Russia, Canada, and China. By 1997, when the United States had grown to approximately 267 million people, America ranked as the third largest national population in the world, after China and India. America is large enough to support great cultural diversity and is truly a complex culture. There are eight American cities with more than 1 million people each.

The United States contains many subcultures representing diverse nationalities, speaking distinct languages, and practicing different religions. Roughly 75 percent of the population is of European ancestry, some 12 percent is of African, 8 percent of Hispanic, and about 2 percent of Asian. Native Americans constitute only about 0.5 percent of the total population. Over 50 percent of the population are members of Christian churches, but there are important Jewish, Muslim, and Buddhist minorities. In many respects, the most significant cultural distinction in the country is by class, or level of wealth and power.

As an object of anthropological investigation, the United States is unique among all the cultures examined so far in the great wealth of information available. Federal, state, and local governments have continuously generated vast volumes of statistical material covering all aspects of American life. Newspapers, films, and books abound and constitute a cultural record of unprecedented detail. The challenge for cultural anthropologists is to sift and sort through the existing data to reach useful conclusions about this complex culture. The analysis that follows draws on statistical data from national, county, and city levels in order to offer a more precise and ethnographically realistic picture for comparison with domestic-scale cultures.

Utopian Capitalism: An American Cosmology

What do Americans believe about how their culture is designed? What roles do equality, the economy, and economic growth play in shaping American culture? How does the belief system differ from the cosmologies of smaller-scale, domestically and politically organized cultures?

Looking beyond the obvious cultural diversity of America, it is possible to identify a common cosmology that characterizes what most Americans believe about their culture. Americans may be political liberals or conservatives, Catholics or Protestants or Jewish. But a consistent cosmology cross-cuts these differences and reveals a dominant worldview that is remarkably different from the worldviews found in both domestically organized cultures and the politically organized agrarian civilizations we examined in earlier chapters. The most striking contrast is that in American culture, the economy is supreme, and all things are considered to be commodities to be regulated by the free market. There are three sectors to this economy: (1) business enterprises (the primary employers of labor and capital and the producers of products); (2) government (which taxes, spends, issues, and borrows money); and (3) individual households (which supply labor, own money, invest, and consume products).

The emphasis that Americans place on economic growth, and their belief that the world is defined by material scarcity, reflects the broader European cosmology discussed in Chapter 11. But this worldview is combined with the contradictory belief that production and consumption must forever expand. This conceptualization of the world is cross-culturally unusual, and it leaves isolated households remarkably vulnerable to autonomous economic forces that are assumed to be beyond the control of individuals. Most Americans believe in the supernatural, but specific religious beliefs are overshadowed by the overarching European belief that the economy is a physical thing that must grow to ensure everyone's well-being. Business corporations have an important place in the American cosmology, but there are no corporate kinship groups, and the isolated nuclear family replaces the extended family that is so prominent in noncommercial cultures. In comparison with Australian aboriginal and Amazonian cultures, the position of nature in the American cosmology is remarkable. Americans view nature as a part of *the environment*, which is separate from and often in conflict with humanity and *the economy*.

The autonomous market produces the culture as a whole, and as the driving force behind the economy, it has the same hallowed status. Like the economy, the market is conceived of as an entity quite apart from any physical marketplace, and a free market is assumed to work to benefit humans and society at large as Adam Smith imagined. Although many Americans realize that particular markets may be dominated by giant corporations or controlled by government regulations, the market is equated with *consumer demand* and is thus thought to represent what people want as expressed by what they choose to buy. Americans assume that markets are natural, and they make them the mysterious arbiters of societal well-being that call into being such diverse products as wholesome food, cars, cigarettes, and land mines.

Americans believe that their cultural universe is both unique and superior, because it is thought to maximize personal liberty and economic freedom. This is America's great strength. In this system of utopian capitalism, prosperity will be assured as long as individuals are free to buy and sell and to create and produce goods for the "free market." The self-serving actions of free people will produce continuous economic growth and material progress, which will ultimately benefit everyone. The only threats to this system are government interference with the free market, restrictions of individual liberty and private property rights, and reductions in individual incentive for economic activity through rewarding undeserving people with unearned material benefits. This grand view of the structure of American society and the functioning of the "free enterprise" system was clearly described by Dwight Eisenhower, who served as president from 1952 to 1960, during a period of especially rapid economic growth:

The economy of the American people has served this nation faithfully and well. . . . It has afforded not only material comfort, but the resources to provide a challenging life of the mind and of the spirit. . . . Our economy has grown strong because our people have made jobs for each other and have not relied on the government to try to do it for them. Our economy is the result of millions of decisions we all make every day about producing, earning, saving, investing and spending. Both our individual prosperity, and our nation's prosperity, rest directly on the decisions all of us are making. (Wall Street 20th Century 1960:7)

In line with this emphasis on liberty and freedom is the belief that there is no hereditary aristocracy in America and that social class is unimportant, because everyone can rise to any economic level by their own intelligence, hard work, and creative energy. Public education makes prosperity available to everyone who truly wants to succeed. In this respect, wealth is an indirect measure of an individual's personal worth, and poverty indicates personal failure or irresponsibility. American society and culture are thought to reflect the interests of a broad middle class, whose members direct the economy and democratically elect the government. The economy itself is believed to be created and directed by the independent action of individual decision makers who make rational economic choices, freely choosing to buy or not buy commercial products that appear on the market. The ultimate measure of well-being in American culture is the rate of economic growth—this is the single concern that unites political conservatives, liberals, and radicals. Only growth will create employment opportunities and make it possible for everyone to raise their standard of living.

In her analysis of American culture, anthropologist Margaret Mead (1942) attributed rapid urbanization and material progress to the American national character, which she argued was produced by child-rearing practices. Mead sidestepped issues of power and social class by declaring that in America, people were "more nearly equal than they had ever been before" (1942:204). In her view, social class was really a ladder that people moved up. The primary elements of the American character that Mead identified were a stake in conformity, a drive for success, and a belief in progress. These ideological features were associated with the upward mobility and general optimism of the period from 1945 to 1975, but they do not correspond to the experience of most Americans in the more recent, post-industrial era.

Americans conceptually divide their society into two broad sectors: (1) the public sector, composed of the government, and (2) the private sector, composed of individuals and business corporations. The government is expected to provide military defense, public education, and highways, and to enforce contracts and protect private property; the government also promotes economic growth by following optimum monetary, tax, and spending policies. Business corporations provide jobs, products, and profits that benefit everyone, and they are owned by everyone in a "people's capitalism." Individuals are employees and consumers. The entire system functions properly as long as government does not become too large and does not interfere with the freedom of business, and as long as individuals take full responsibility for their lives. Americans generally believe themselves to be free of racial, ethnic, or religious prejudices, assuming that distinctions between people of all nationalities will tend to disappear in the American "melting pot."

Cosmologies are cultural constructions that may not accurately reflect the practical realities in particular societies. The existence of factional disagreements in America over the proper balance of power between business and government suggests that the harmony implied in America's basic cosmology may not always exist. American beliefs about wealth and power are ambiguous, because wealth is highly desired but the wealthy are both envied and distrusted. America is believed to be a democracy in which everyone has an equal vote, but wealth inequality obviously gives some people more economic power than others, and this can become political power. The degree to which American cosmology matches historical and ethnographic reality will be explored in the following sections.

America from a Chinese Perspective

What are the implications of the cultural contrast between the American emphasis on individualism and self-reliance and the Chinese emphasis on kinship and dependency?

American culture has also been analyzed by a Chinese anthropologist, Francis Hsu, who grew up in China and has lived for many years in the United States. Hsu is a psychological anthropologist and, like Mead, is interested in socialization, values, and personality. Hsu's deep familiarity with both Chinese and American culture allows him to make very insightful comparisons between the two cultures and provides an effective balance to the materialist bias of many American anthropologists.

Hsu (1972, 1981) argues that many of the key differences in economic life and class structure between Chinese and American culture can be attributed to what he considers to be the American core value of individual self-reliance versus the Chinese pattern of family dependence and filial piety. The exaggerated emphasis that Americans place on self-reliance is represented by the ideal of the rugged individualist and a corresponding fear of dependence. For example, American children are socialized to value privacy, independence, and self-expression, and American parents are not supposed to interfere in the domestic lives of their adult children.

The Chinese emphasis on kinship and continuity of patrilineage highlights the virtues of dependency. Chinese children are socialized within families that include at least three generations and in-laws. They are cared for by a variety of elders. There is little individual privacy within a Chinese household, but individuals are always surrounded by many people who can be called on for physical and emotional support. There is little cultural incentive for an individual to pursue perpetual economic profit. An individual's primary responsibility is to parents and extended family, not self. Indeed, it is a source of pride for an aging Chinese parent to be taken care of by a child. By contrast, in the United States, one is expected to make it alone, and accepting economic aid from one's children might even be considered embarrassing.

Realistically, humans do depend on other people for many of their needs, and according to Hsu, culturally denying such dependence can generate psychological problems. Hsu maintains that the American ideal of self-reliance is likely to create emotional insecurity, which helps explain other seemingly contradictory American characteristics, such as racial and religious intolerance coexisting with an expressed belief in equality. Hsu suggests that personal insecurity drives Americans to accumulate material wealth to compensate and to demonstrate their self-worth. This not only makes Americans enormously competitive and intolerant of others but also serves the imperatives of a growth-centered capitalist economy. In contrast, the Chinese plow their earnings into family ceremonies, such as funerals, birthdays, and ancestor shrines, confident that they will be taken care of by their descendants.

The realities of American life pose some problems for Hsu's theory of self-reliance as a core value. The poorest classes in the United States likely survive by sharing with kin. Furthermore, the existence of economically based kinship groups among the American elite suggests that extended family dependency relations can be compatible with capitalist accumulation.

The role that Hsu ascribes to the American value of self-reliance fits well with the view that commercialization and profit making are the dominant cultural processes in commercial-scale cultures. Chinese civilization was created by a politicization process that does not require perpetual economic expansion. In support of this interpretation, Hsu observes that the small wealthy class in preindustrial China was composed of government bureaucrats, not merchants, and modern China has been very slow to industrialize. He also notes that most large Chinese cities are political capitals, whereas most large U.S. cities are commercial centers. American acquisitiveness generated economic growth and a relatively large middle class. This is not to argue that American values in themselves shaped the rest of American culture, but it suggests that values and personality are functionally connected to other economic and social variables.

A Mythic Framework: Founders and Sacred Texts

To what extent do the Constitution and the Declaration of Independence represent the basic design of American culture and present realities? What different interests were represented by the Founding Fathers, and what were their different visions for America?

America's cosmology is supported by a mythic history and by the functional equivalent of sacred texts, in the form of the Declaration of Independence, the Constitution, and the written commentary in the Federalist Papers, all produced by the "Founding Fathers." The fifty-six men who signed the Declaration of Independence appealed directly to natural law with their lofty affirmation:

We hold these Truths to be self-evident, that all Men are created equal, that they are endowed by their Creator with certain unalienable Rights, that among these are Life, Liberty, and the Pursuit of Happiness.

The Constitution, the legal framework for the federal government of the United States, was drafted in 1787 in the name of "We, the People." The purpose of the new government was to "establish Justice, insure domestic Tranquility, provide for the common defence, promote the general Welfare, and secure the Blessings of Liberty to ourselves and our Posterity."

Constitutional historian Forrest McDonald (1958, 1979, 1985) points out that many popular beliefs about America's founding are contradicted by the historical record. The sentiments of the patriots of 1776 could have produced a loose federation of small-scale agrarian nations with high levels of local autonomy and individual freedom. There was no popular consensus that economic growth through the development of manufacturing and finance capital was a desirable goal or that a strong federal government was needed to protect business enterprise. On the contrary, many, including Thomas Jefferson, third U.S. president and author of the Declaration of Independence, and James Madison, fourth president and often called the Father of the Constitution, feared that unregulated commercial growth and subsequent wealth inequality would undermine democracy. Those favoring a strong federal government did so for several reasons. Alexander Hamilton, first secretary of the treasury, wanted a strong banking and tariff system to promote industrialization, and a powerful navy to protect international commerce.

The Founding Fathers were idealistic statesmen, but the Constitution was not approved by popular vote. Historians have concluded that perhaps only 160,000 people, about 5 percent of the population, selected the delegates who attended the constitutional conventions in the various states, which in turn ratified the Constitution. Only free adult males could vote, and some states required them to be property holders or to have certain levels of wealth. Historian Charles Beard (1913) maintained that the Constitution was an economic document, drafted and promoted by a small, consolidated group interested in protecting their personal, national-, and even international-level economic interests. McDonald disagrees, contending that economic interests were too cross-cutting or pluralistic for a single economic group to dominate the process. The fifty-five men who drafted the Constitution were large landholders, merchants, and professionals, not poor farmers (see the box entitled "Robert Morris"). More than half held government securities, nineteen were slaveowners, and ten held bank shares. Although their personal economic interests often conflicted, they were all relatively wealthy men with significant economic power, and the document they produced did favor economic growth.

The Founding Fathers made a clear distinction between worthy, property-holding citizens and the propertyless. Propertyless people were considered to be too dependent to be informed citizens, and thus were assumed to be unfit to hold office or to vote. The Founders feared that popular democracy might lead to social disorder if an "overbearing majority" gained power and sought wealth redistribution. As a result, the Senate was designed as a "natural aristocracy" to balance the potential excesses of the more broadly representative House of Representatives. In the view of some historians, the social ideology of the federalists who assumed power in 1787 was not radically different from the elitist beliefs of the older European landed and wealthy aristocracy. Only the inherited titles were absent in America. However, the Constitution is an evolving, dynamic charter, and it produced an intricately balanced political system that can represent the democratic wishes of all the people.

The Evolution of Business, 1790–1890

Why did the scale of American business dramatically increase after 1790? Who made these *decisions? What was the role of technology? How did the organization of business change? How did these changes transform the entire culture?*

America was swiftly transformed, within the space of 40 years, from a rural agrarian nation in 1850 to an urban industrial nation by 1890, as a result of a rapidly unfolding series of institutional changes designed to increase the scale of business enterprise (see Table 12.1). Businessmen themselves created these new institutions, but they were supported by specific government policies and public expenditures. The decisions of a relative handful of prominent owner-investors, corporate board members, and their hired upper-level business managers created the modern, large-scale business enterprises that totally changed the lives of millions of people and now dominate the world. The speed and scope of this change was totally unprecedented in the history of cultural development.

In 1790, perhaps fewer than 2000 people (approximately the top 0.5 percent of households) were wealthy enough to dominate the fledgling commercial economy and significantly influence political decisions and major cultural developments. America's leaders chose maximum growth, by combining Jefferson's vision of agrarian expansion with Hamilton's commercial industrialization approach. This was the best way for the wealthiest to expand their wealth, but it also opened new opportunities for European immigrants who were denied all hope of improving their living standards by hereditary aristocracies in their homelands.

The most revolutionary changes were caused by the new technologies, especially the railroads, that businessmen used to expand the pace and scale of commerce. After 1787, America's new political economy especially favored increased commercial activity. Population growth was accelerating, and markets were expanding. Over the next century, the nation's territory was tripled by a policy of military conquest that reduced the population of Native Americans by 95 percent. The U.S. Navy protected American shipping. Furthermore, concentrated wealth produced eager investors, and the rural poor and impoverished European immigrants offered a steady labor force. Under these conditions, new technology to speed the flow of goods

Robert Morris: Prince of Merchants, Patriot Financier

A brief ethnographic sketch of the personal business interests of Robert Morris (1734–1806), considered the most prominent and powerful merchant and financier of the time, illustrates the extent of individual commercial power in preindustrial America and demonstrates how closely commercial power was linked with political power. This case study strongly suggests that commercial elites created America's political structure. Robert Morris was a politically active Philadelphia merchant, signer of the Declaration of Independence, and member of the Continental Congress, who handled the financial aspects of the Revolutionary War and the Continental Congress, helped draft the Constitution, and served on the Pennsylvania legislature and in the U.S. Senate. He was variously described by his contemporaries as a prince of merchants, patriot financier, and great man. He is still revered as a Founding Father, and his personal power certainly helped determine the course of cultural development in America.

Morris's economic interests were remarkably diverse and included manufacturing, shipping, and banking and finance; speculation in commodities, currency, land, and government securities; and trade with England, France, the West Indies, and India (Beard 1913, McDonald 1958, Ver Steeg 1954). Morris personally financed strategic troop movements during the Revolution, organized and was the largest shareholder in the original Bank of North America in Philadelphia, and organized and financed the first American trade expeditions to China. The key to his profit-making was *arbitrage*, buying low in one market and selling high in another market. He also secured handsome commissions from brokering large government transactions, such as when he helped the French provision their

suddenly became enormously attractive. The commercial revolutions in transportation, communication, and fossil fuel energy accelerated production and distribution. Modern business corporations emerged when mass production was combined with mass marketing within single large-scale enterprises.

As noted previously, railroads were the key to the scale increases in commerce. Demand from national and international investors for railroad securities contributed to the rise of powerful New York investment banks and brokerage houses. As railroads became complex systems, operational problems were solved when their top managers created a hierarchy of middle managers and lower-level supervisors. This required all the features of a modern business corporation including organizational charts, formal titles, job descriptions, lines of authority, regular reports, performance evaluations, and new accounting procedures. By the 1850s, the largest railroads were already being consolidated into the first giant holding companies—corporations that owned other corporations—by a few superwealthy stock speculators seeking to limit competition. American railroads soon became the largest business enterprises in the world. For example, in the 1890s, the Pennsylvania Railroad employed 110,000 workers, nearly three times the size of the United States military, and it took in more than a third of the revenue of the federal government.

Historian Alfred Chandler (1977) argued that mass-production technology developed as a "natural" response by investors, owners, and managers

American military expeditionary forces during the Revolution. He was an important member of nine major business partnerships and maintained numerous short-term partnerships, including business connections with at least five other delegates to the 1787 Constitutional Convention. For a time he owned millions of acres of undeveloped western land that was still controlled by Native Americans, and he brokered land purchases for European investors. He attempted to gain a monopoly over the tobacco trade with Europe, and he quickly bought up speculative property in Washington, D.C., as soon as the site was selected for the new national capital.

Politically, Morris was closely aligned with Alexander Hamilton and other prominent federalists who favored a strong federal government. He was a firm believer in free trade, maintaining that commerce should be "free as air to place it in the most advantageous state to mankind." Like Adam Smith, Morris praised the invisible hand, and he could imagine no conflict between his public and private life. Speaking of American entrepreneurs in general, he said: "Their own interest and the publick good goes hand in hand and they need no other prompter or tutor" (Ver Steeg 1954:38). However, he felt that only entrepreneurs themselves could be arbiters of the public good, and only they could define the proper balance of power between public and private. Morris's commercial vision certainly shaped America at a crucial moment in its history, but reckless speculation drove him into personal bankruptcy, and he was sent to debtors' prison in 1798, where he remained for three and a half years.

TABLE 12.1   *American Commercial Evolution, 1790–Present*

Date	Development	Characteristics
1790–1850	Traditional business firms	Generalized mercantile partnership Single-unit enterprises
1850–1900	Transportation, communication, and fuel revolutions	Multiunit enterprises Executive hierarchies Railroad empires
1850–1890	The Production and Distribution Revolution	High-Volume throughput Vertically integrated production Emergence of wholesalers and mass market retailers
1880–1917	Modern industrial corporations	Vertical integration of mass production and mass marketing Multidivision, multinational enterprises Oligopolies, and Monopolies
1960–present	Conglomerates	Corporate mergers in unrelated industries

SOURCE: Based on Chandler (1977).

to the potential to increase speed and volume and thus reduce unit costs, rather than out of demands by consumers for cheaper products. Mass production worked because changes in organization and technology speeded up the flow of materials through the factory. The inability of existing marketers to sell the increased volume of products forced mass producers to become their own marketers by integrating production and marketing within the same enterprise. The first advertising agencies appeared in the 1850s, and by the 1880s, advertising was being used to market mass-produced consumer goods such as cigarettes and breakfast cereals.

Business enterprise crossed a crucial threshold with scale increases and the emergence of a managerial hierarchy. Owners became separated from managers, and business managers themselves became a professional class in which specialized skills were more important than kinship or personal relationships. The business corporation itself effectively became an immortal living organism, with a physical existence and permanence that was never possible with partnerships and family enterprises. These enormously powerful business institutions were now in the hands of salaried professionals, who answered to their boards of directors, which represented the largest investors.

By the 1880s, giant, vertically integrated, multifunctional, multiunit, and often multinational business enterprises, controlled by a managerial class of corporate executives, dominated the American economy. These corporate giants created oligopolies, which allowed commercial bureaucrats to coordinate production and distribution decisions, effectively replacing the invisible hand of the market (Chandler 1977). The objective was to increase the volume, speed, and efficiency of commercial transactions, in order to reduce costs and generate a higher return on investments or to reduce competition by controlling markets. Large-scale business enterprises succeeded because they brought many formerly competing enterprises within a single organizational structure, thereby internalizing their diverse production, buying, and selling decisions within a single management hierarchy. Administrative coordination was the key. These institutional changes increased productivity and profits, because top managers could allocate resources more efficiently than could the managers of smaller firms competing in a decentralized marketplace with imperfect supply-and-demand information.

The Founding Fathers on the Business of Politics

How was democracy organized in America? Historically, what were the ideological orientations of the major political parties, and what interests did they represent? What is the evidence that commercial interests dominated the political system as originally constructed?

Constitutional historian Forrest McDonald has argued that the very genius of the American system was that voters were fragmented into diverse interest groups, while power itself remained dynamic and ill-defined. Arguing for the existence of an invisible hand in American politics that, like Adam Smith's free market, would turn private vice into public virtue, McDonald declared that the political system

could only be activated through deals and deceit, through bargains and bribery, through logrolling and lobbying and trickery and trading, the tactics that go with man's baser attributes, most notably his greed and his love of power. And yet, in the broad range and on the average, these private tactics and motivations could operate effectively only when they were compatible with the public good, for they were braked by the massive inertia of society as a whole. (McDonald 1979:316)

America is too large and too unequal to be a pure democracy. Instead, it is a representative democracy with officeholders elected by political subdivisions. American politics is largely a struggle between diverse commercial interest groups competing against one another to obtain favorable government policies. The competition is played out through national-level political parties. The Founding Fathers explicitly understood many of the economic conflicts inherent in a large-scale, commercially organized culture. The Constitution set the ground rules for an ongoing political struggle but could not resolve the underlying social conflicts because it ignored the reality of social class.

Madison enumerated "a landed interest, a manufacturing interest, a mercantile interest, a moneyed interest, and many lesser interests," but not a *household* interest, as necessary features of civilized nations. Madison foresaw that it would necessarily be the business of government to protect property and legislate a balance between these unavoidably conflicting commercial interests through the operation of factions and party politics. Setting the tone for the next two centuries, Hamilton defined the primary objective of politics and government as the promotion of commerce and effectively rejected the possibility that there could be any significant class divisions in American society that would not be solved by economic growth. Anticipating the emergence of export-dependent agriculture, he argued that there was no conflict between mercantile and agrarian interests, because increased trade would benefit both (Federalist Papers No. 12). He rejected political representation by social class as "visionary." He believed that artisans and laborers would prefer to give their votes to merchants as their "natural representatives," patrons, and friends, who would have more "influence and weight" in deliberative assemblies.

Madison knew that elected legislators would not be totally impartial, but he felt that pluralism, the great diversity of interests, would prevent the abuse of political power. Hamilton thought that the poorest tenants and wealthiest landlords were "perfectly united" on the issue of keeping taxes low, and thus there was no class conflict between them. He assumed that the poorest and wealthiest would have an equal chance of being elected, because voters would simply elect whomever they were most confident with. However, Hamilton correctly expected government to be composed of landholders, merchants, and lawyers (Federalist Papers No. 35).

A simply binary political party system developed during the nineteenth century out of the original contrast between Jefferson's and Hamilton's visions for America. Jefferson's ideal of an agrarian nation became identified with slavery, western expansion, property rights, farmers, and labor, and evolved in stages into the modern Democratic party. Hamilton's Federalists promoted wage labor over slavery and favored industrialization, a national banking system, and large-scale capitalism; by 1854, they had evolved into the modern Republican party.

Rockdale: An American Industrial Village, 1825–1865

How did the development of privately owned textile factories shape the quality of life in rural villages during the early Industrial Revolution?

Anthropologist Anthony F. C. Wallace (1978) produced a remarkable historical ethnography of the small textile-producing community of Rockdale in southeastern Pennsylvania during the four decades from 1825 to 1865 (see Figure 12.1). He spent 8 years poring over public records, newspapers, biographies, letters, and memorabilia to construct a richly detailed picture of the people of Rockdale. His study illuminates the difficult human problems that the new machine technology and the factory system produced as it developed under early American industrial capitalism.

In the 1820s, capitalist manufacturers intent on establishing new textile mills began buying up small, abandoned flour, paper, and lumber mills in the Rockdale district, southwest of Philadelphia. Their enterprises benefed from the federal government's policy of placing high tariffs on imported goods, rather than taxes, to encourage American manufacturing and to raise revenue. By 1850, there were 2000 people living in 351 households, in seven small hamlets along Chester Creek. Each hamlet was centered on a water-powered cotton mill, which provided the primary employment. Three local families, referred to by Wallace as "Lords of the Valley," owned most of the land and mills in Rockdale and determined the overall pattern of life.

Altogether, some twelve families of manufacturers, merchants, and gentlemen farmers sat at the top of the social hierarchy, forming a tightly integrated economic class. They lived in comfortable, well-appointed, hilltop stone mansions. The men agreed on their probusiness politics; traveled regularly to Boston, New York, Washington, and nearby Philadelphia; and vacationed with their families at beach resorts. The wives and daughters of Rockdale's elite formed a close-knit sisterhood that included elites in neighboring communities. These women were well educated, well read, intellectually active, and musically and artistically accomplished. They had the leisure time to correspond and visit each other frequently, and write diaries and poetry.

FIGURE 12.1
*Synthetic reconstruction
of a typical Rockdale mill
hamlet about 1850.*

Beneath this elite group was a "middle class" assortment of 150 professionals, teachers, ministers, and artisans; and beneath them were 162 mill worker families, who lived very modestly. Workers lived in inexpensive tenements at the bottom of the hill near the mill (see Figure 12.1). The low residential position of workers also reflected their low social, intellectual, and emotional standing as a depressed class in the minds of upper-class people. For example, Sophie Du Pont, a member of the nearby Du Pont industrialist family and member of Rockdale high society, expressed amazement in her diary that working-class women could be emotionally distressed by sick children. People in that "class of life" were not expected to be particularly sensitive.

The economic distance between top and bottom in the hierarchy was enormous. The minimum capital cost of a mill and its machinery was approximately $12,000–35,000, which was far beyond the means of all but the wealthy. A typical mill worker family could earn about $250 a year and might bring in another $175 from boarders, for a total of $425. Basic household subsistence expenditures for food, fuel, and rent were $300, leaving $125 for clothing and all other expenses. This meant that

with a stringent savings program, within a few years a healthy family might accumulate the $200 needed to move west and buy a small farm. Most of the mill workers hoped their jobs would be temporary. Many of them were recent immigrants from England and Ireland, where workers were clearly not as well off.

Relations between owners and workers were generally satisfactory; however, there remained an intrinsic conflict of interest, which eventually led to an open clash. The four owners determined everyone's quality of life, because they could hire and fire workers at will, set wages and hours, buy new machines that displaced workers, and determine health and safety conditions. Profits were always more important than the security and well-being of worker households. Owners hired workers as a specified number of "hands" supplied by household units. Many children, including some younger than 10, routinely worked in the factories, although they were probably better off than children in comparable British mills. The Rockdale owners considered mistreatment to be poor personnel management, as mill owner John Crozier testified in 1837: "When factories were first established in this vicinity, severe whipping was often practiced, but it was found not to be the best mode of management, and has been, in a great degree, abandoned" (Wallace 1978:180).

The 14-hour workday ran by the bell from 5 AM to 7 PM, with breaks for breakfast and dinner. The 6-day work week thus ran 72 hours. The mills were hot and poorly ventilated, and the air was thick with cotton fiber dust that gave workers chronic coughs. The work was so exhausting that young children sometimes fell asleep on the job. It was publicly acknowledged that factory conditions were mentally, morally, and physically unhealthy for children and less than ideal for adults. However, rather than calling for fundamental changes in the way factories were operated, religious reformers wanted the workers to improve themselves by attending Sunday School and becoming more responsible parents. The owners knew that working children did not have time for regular schooling, and many workers were illiterate. In principle, the Rockdale mill owners supported legislation that would shorten working hours and prohibit hiring workers younger than 12. But they refused to institute such social reforms, arguing that their mills would be economically uncompetitive unless all states had such laws. They blamed widows and lazy fathers and the absence of public assistance for child labor, not low wages. They recommended night school for working children. However, there were many female-headed households with small children in Rockdale, and many families were too poor to put their children in school. Obviously, the mills did not create a healthy social environment, but Crozier defended the economic necessity of child labor with impeccable functionalist logic: "The work of children cannot be shortened, without also abridging that of adults, as the labor of one is connected with that of the other, being part of a system, which, if broken in upon, destroys a connecting link in the chain of operations" (Wallace 1978:328).

For their part, Rockdale textile workers organized a labor union in 1836 and walked off their jobs in 1836 and again in 1842, demanding shorter hours and better pay. When the organizers were fired, strikers retaliated by destroying property. Later, some were fined and jailed. The commercial elite quickly aligned themselves with the religious establishment to denounce labor unions as anti-

Christian, un-American, and immoral. Social reform became a Christian enterprise, but it did not threaten the established capitalist order.

The Rise of Factory Farming

What are the important differences between industrialized, commercial farming and shifting cultivation, such as is practiced in Amazonia? How is fossil fuel an energy subsidy for factory farming?

The industrialization of farming and the general commercialization of the food system, which was well underway in Europe and America by the mid-twentieth century, must rank as a cultural transformation as significant as the domestication of plants and animals during the Neolithic. This great change is a continuation of the broad trend toward subsistence intensification that has accompanied each increase in the scale of human culture—more food is produced at greater energy cost and ecosystem degradation. This characterization may seem counterintuitive, but the true costs of industrialization have been masked by the cultural accounting system that emphasizes human labor and monetary cost. In an industrial culture such as the United States, farms are operated like factories. Often the emphasis is on a single crop that is mass-produced at the lowest possible monetary cost for the maximum cash return. Economic imperatives compel the farmer to use labor-saving machinery to reduce costs and to employ chemical pesticides and fertilizers to increase production.

When viewed from a cultural ecological perspective, this **factory farming** raises troubling questions for the long-term viability of industrial civilization. As ecologist Howard Odum (1971) observed, the factory farm replaces self-maintaining biological processes, which are fueled by renewable solar energy, with urban-based cultural processes that require vast **energy subsidies** in the form of nonrenewable fossil fuels. Factory farming

---

factory farming Commercial agriculture based on fossil fuel energy subsidies, mechanization, pesticides, chemical fertilizers, and large-scale monocropping.
energy subsidy The use of fossil fuels to increase food production above the rate that could be sustained through use of renewable energy sources.

simplifies natural ecosystems, making them less stable while extracting a larger energy share for human consumption. An obvious problem with this system is that it also rapidly depletes fossil fuels and soils and thus cannot be sustained indefinitely.

Because it requires relatively few farm laborers and produces very high per-acre yields, factory farming appears deceptively productive. In 1970, when viewed at the national level, each kilocalorie of American farm labor returned 210 kilocalories (kcal) of food—four times the yield of intensive Chinese rice farming as discussed in Chapter 8. However, when the full energy costs of production were calculated—including fuel, electricity, fertilizer, and farm machinery—2 kilocalories of energy were expended to produce 1 kilocalorie of food energy (Steinhart and Steinhart 1974).

Such **deficit production** is only possible when subsidized by vast inputs of solar energy stored in nonrenewable fossil fuels. Furthermore, when food production costs are calculated to include the costs of industrial processing and marketing, which necessarily precede domestic consumption in a highly urbanized society, then a minimum of 8–12 kilocalories were expended in the production of 1 kilocalorie of food (see Table 12.2). Even this figure underestimates the actual energy costs of the American food production system because it does not include all transport costs, especially the use of private automobiles in trips to the grocery store, or the costs of advertising commercialized food products and disposing of the trash by-products. A more realistic total would probably approach 20 kilocalories expended for each 1 consumed.

TABLE 12.2   *Energy Use in the U.S. Food System (in 10^{12} kcal), 1940 and 1970*

	1940	1970
Farm production*	124.5	526.1
Food processing†	285.8	841.9
Distribution‡	275.2	804.0
Totals	685.5	2172.0

SOURCE: Steinhart and Steinhart (1974).

*Farm production includes fuel, electricity, fertilizer, and irrigation and the costs of producing agricultural steel, farm machinery, and tractors.

†Processing includes production, machinery, packaging, transport fuel, and trucks and trailers.

‡Distribution includes commercial and domestic refrigeration and cooking.

U.S. farm production was not fully industrialized until fossil fuel–powered farm machinery and agricultural chemicals became widely used after 1940. The social corollary of these technological changes was a decline in the rural population. The number of individual farms actually declined, but those that remained became much larger than before.

Wheat for Topsoil: Erosion and Plenty in Whitman County

What were the social and environmental consequences of the industrialization of wheat farming in Washington State?

FIGURE 12.2   *Active soil erosion on a cultivated wheat field in Whitman County, Washington. Note the soil slumping on the steep hillside in the background.*

FIGURE 12.3
*Palouse farm inputs,
1910–1987.*

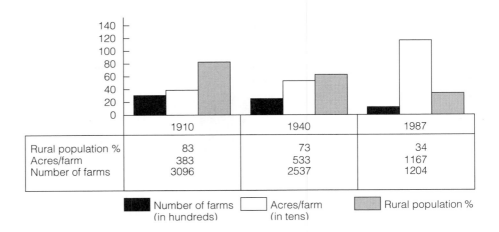

	1910	1940	1987
Rural population %	83	73	34
Acres/farm	383	533	1167
Number of farms	3096	2537	1204

■ Number of farms (in hundreds)   ☐ Acres/farm (in tens)   ▨ Rural population %

The impact of farm industrialization at the local level can be illustrated using Census Bureau statistics for Whitman County in eastern Washington. Whitman County is the heart of the Palouse region, an area of steep, dunelike hills composed of deep loess soils, which were deposited by the wind 100,000 years ago (see Figure 12.2). Climate and soil conditions in the Palouse are ideally suited for dry farming and help make Whitman County one of the world's leading wheat-producing regions. **Monocrop farming** of wheat was well underway in the Palouse by the 1880s.

According to Census Bureau figures, 27,000 people lived in rural Whitman County in 1910. Approximately 75 percent of the cash value of farm production was in grain. There were some 3000 farms, averaging 383 acres (155 hectares) (see Figure 12.3). The primary farm production inputs were human labor and horses. Because much of the feed for the 38,000 horses and mules was grown locally, the county enjoyed a high degree of energy self-sufficiency.

By 1987, the switch to industrialization in Palouse farming was strikingly apparent in Census Bureau data that showed a drastic reduction in human labor inputs, the virtual disappearance of horses, and an enormous increase in fossil fuels and chemical fertilizers (see Figure 12.4). Yields of wheat per acre suddenly doubled and tripled. Between 1910 and 1940, approximately 30 bushels were produced per acre, but by 1987, yields averaged 69 bushels and sometimes reached 100. Such

increases resulted from the use of newly developed "miracle grains," genetically engineered to take maximum advantage of agricultural chemicals and machinery. This energy-intensive production system became known as the **Green Revolution** and was widely exported to the developing world in the 1970s and 1980s.

The social and environmental consequences of the technological changes in Palouse wheat farming were equally striking. As the demand for labor declined, by 1987 the total rural population had shrunk to less than half of what it had been in 1910. More significantly, the number of farms declined even more steeply, while total farm acreage remained approximately the same. This meant that individual farms tripled in size. Land became concentrated in fewer and fewer hands, such that 15 percent of the farms came to control 46 percent of the land (see Figure 12.5).

The most ominous change was the steady loss of soil due to erosion caused by deep cultivation of

---

deficit production   The situation in which more calories are expended in food production than are produced for human food.
monocrop farming   Growing one plant species, sometimes only a single variety, often in very large continuous stands.
Green Revolution   Dramatic increases in agricultural production from genetically engineered hybrid grains that produce high yields in return for high inputs of chemical fertilizers and pesticides.

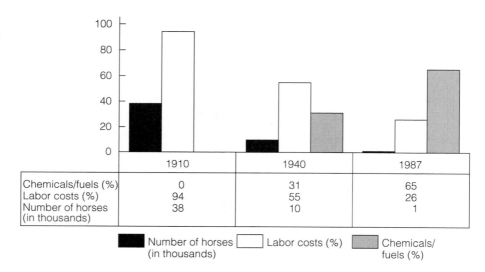

FIGURE 12.4
*Palouse farming trends,
1910–1987.*

	1910	1940	1987
Chemicals/fuels (%)	0	31	65
Labor costs (%)	94	55	26
Number of horses (in thousands)	38	10	1

FIGURE 12.5
*Palouse farmland
inequality, 1987.*

	Small: 1–999 acres	Medium: 1000–1999	Large: 2000+ acres
Farms (%)	57	28	15
Farmland (%)	20	34	46

steep slopes with heavy machinery. The U.S. Department of Agriculture (USDA) began an annual program to monitor the problem in 1939. In 1978, the USDA issued a report documenting the total loss of topsoil from 10 percent of the land and estimating that annual soil losses averaged 14 tons (13 metric tons) of soil per acre. This means that each metric ton of wheat produced costs 13.5 metric tons of topsoil. This kind of factory farming is truly mining the soil and cannot continue indefinitely.

Why would any culture institutionalize such a short-sighted technological system? This is a cultural problem that can best be understood by considering the dominant cultural role played by the capitalist market economy in the United States. The logic of competitive commercial production aimed primarily at generating a cash profit forces U.S. producers to steadily accelerate output in order to gain economies of scale. Accelerated output is facilitated by technological innovation and by the concentration of economic control by a wealthy few.

The concentration of economic power leads, in turn, to social inequality and many other long-term costs.

The American Cattle Complex: Good to Sell

How does the way that cattle are produced and processed reflect the demands of a capitalist market economy? How does the American Cattle Complex compare with the role of cattle in East Africa and Hindu India?

One can easily make the case that a Cattle Complex exists in America just as in East Africa. But the contrasts between the two cattle systems highlight the role of the market economy in shaping commercial-scale industrial cultures. Cattle are significant in American culture not only because they are "good to eat" but more importantly, as Marvin Harris (1985) emphasizes, because cattle are "good to sell."

In 1987, cattle accounted for one-third of the value of all farm products sold in the United States and at the same time supplied one-third of the calories Americans consumed, two-thirds of their protein, and one-half of their fat. There were 102 million cattle in the country, less than half a cow per person. Approximately 40 percent of this national herd was slaughtered to provide meat, while some 10 percent produced milk. In comparison, East African cattle peoples need 4 animals per person to supply an approximately equal proportion of their subsistence.

Extreme specialization and inequality are striking features of the subsistence role of cattle in American culture. Remarkably few specialists are involved in producing and marketing the bulk of the nation's cattle products. Focusing on beef cattle, for example, the National Cattlemen's Association estimated that in 1988, 45 percent of America's cattle were owned by only 6.7 percent of the producers (Pietraszek 1990). An estimated 71 percent of the 10 million cattle fattened at feedlots passed through just 1.4 percent of the nation's commercial feedlots, which were often vertically integrated with livestock wholesaling and meatpacking enterprises (Pietraszek 1990). The four largest meat packers, just 4 percent of the total, processed nearly 70 percent of all the cattle slaughtered, while three

wholesalers sold nearly 90 percent of all the meat sold in the country (see Table 12.3). This degree of control, by so few, over all aspects of such a major element of subsistence is a remarkable cultural arrangement that certainly has *no* parallel in any domestic-scale cultures or ancient civilizations.

Inequality and concentration of this magnitude are driven by the economic logic of production in a highly industrialized market economy. The production of market cattle is a costly process that can only succeed if producers take advantage of economies of scale.

Market forces shape how cattle are handled, categorized, graded, slaughtered, and butchered and how the meat is named, packed, and distributed. In the domestic-scale cultures of East Africa, cows are highly personalized, and slaughtering is a public and ritual act. The meat is distributed according to kinship relationships and is consumed immediately. In the United States, market cattle and meat are depersonalized commodities, the production of which is left entirely to specialists; few people have more than a vague idea of how their meat gets to them.

The production process is designed to move the animal to full slaughter weight as quickly as possible—usually within 24 months, although milk-fed calves may be slaughtered as veal at under 3 months. Calves may receive appetite stimulants and ear-implanted hormones to speed their growth. They are weaned at 6–9 months, either to be returned to the range as "stockers" to grow further or to be vaccinated and sold to feedlots as "feeders" to be "finished" for slaughter. At the feedlot, cattle receive more vaccinations and growth-hormone implants and are fattened on a weight-gain diet of grain, molasses, beef fat, and plant protein supplements, laced with antibiotics, vitamins, and growth steroids (Thomas 1986).

The entire production process is highly regulated by federal and state laws. Live cattle are sorted by federal inspectors into classes by sex condition—steer, bullock, bull, cow, and heifer—and into grades—prime, choice, select, standard, commercial, utility, cutter, and canner. Regulations specify every detail of the slaughtering process, even prescribing the rate (in head per hour) at which inspectors can examine specific parts of animals. Such detailed regulation and classification are

TABLE 12.3   *Economic Concentration in the Cattle Industry, 1988*

45% of cattle owned by 6.7% of producers
71% of cattle fed by 1.4% of feedlots
69% of cattle slaughtered by four largest packers
89% of wholesale beef sold by three largest packers
30% of wholesale beef sold by one packer*
35%–40% of retail sales of beef by twenty largest retailers

SOURCES: *National Provisioner* (1990a, 1990b) and Pietraszek (1990).
*Estimate for 1990 (*Spokesman Review* 1991).

necessary to ensure quality standards when animals move rapidly through a complex chain of buyers and sellers, each seeking to maximize monetary return.

Economies of scale are a major factor in slaughtering. Larger plants, using highly specialized technology, were able to increase the hourly kill-and-butcher rate from 100 head per hour during the 1970s to 300–350 head per hour in the 1980s, thereby reducing the unit price of processing by 25 percent (Pietraszek 1990). Faster butcher rates required a multitude of mechanized tools such as dehorners, dehiders, carcass splitters, brisket opener saws, bone saws, and primal cut saws. Further meat-processing operations use mechanical trimmers, dicers, massagers, tumblers, grinders, collagen films, patty machines, and vacuum stuffers. Meat cutting is a highly intensive, technical occupation in which the demand for increased efficiency produces a high rate of injuries in the workers.

Virtually every part of the animal finds some use. A beef carcass is split and quartered and then quickly reduced to six to ten primal and sub-primal cuts for wholesale. Numerous other edible by-products include gelatin, marshmallows, and canned meat. Inedible by-products include leather, buttons, and soap from beef tallow, as well as pet foods and animal feeds. A wide range of pharmaceuticals such as insulin, estrogen, and thyroid extract are also derived from cattle.

Anthropologist Marvin Harris (1985) argues that cultural preferences for specific meats are largely determined by utilitarian, ecological, and economic factors. He attributes the American preference for beef to the forced removal of bison and Native Americans from the Great Plains in the 1870s and their replacement by cattle. The ranchers were, in turn, displaced by grain farmers, and

cattle had to be grazed on the arid lands and in the logged-over forests further west. The real boom for beef, according to Harris, came after World War II when large numbers of American women began to work outside the home and fast-food dining on hamburgers suddenly opened a vast new market for beef. The key to the success of hamburger, which legally must be all beef, is that it can contain added beef fat, up to 30 percent. The added fat helps bind the meat when it is cooked. Thus, hamburger can be ground from relatively tough, range-fed steers, combined with the abundant fat trimmed from feedlot-fattened beef, which otherwise supply tender, marbled, and very expensive cuts of meat.

The Cultural Construction of Consumption

How can it be argued that U.S. consumption patterns are shaped by symbolic cultural categories rather than by utilitarian necessity? In what respect is economic scarcity a cultural construction?

Marshall Sahlins objected to Harris's utilitarian explanation for the American emphasis on beef, pointing out that economic **utilitarianism** is an American cultural bias shared by economists, producers, and consumers, as well as many anthropologists. Americans assume that the choices they make about production and consumption are entirely rational and logical and naturally economical. Sahlins stressed that the physical and biological limits of human social existence leave considerable space for cultural variation, and thus a wide variety of "rational" cultural systems can be constructed. In this view, production becomes a

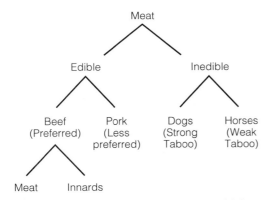

FIGURE 12.6 *The cultural structure of meat edibility in the United States. (SOURCE: Based on Sahlins 1976b.)*

"cultural intention," and there must be a "cultural account of production" before it can become fully intelligible. Sahlins argued that in American culture, because of its long cultural association with virility and strength, beef, and especially steak, has a central place in the diet. Pork takes second place, as a less preferred meat, while eating dogs or horses is virtually taboo.

Sahlins (1976b) showed that in their culturally defined levels of edibility, cattle, pigs, horses, and dogs form a structural metaphor on cannibalism that makes a statement about rank in U.S. society. Using symbolic analysis, Sahlins observed that in American culture, cattle and pigs form a structured set in opposition to horses and dogs (see Figure 12.6). Cattle and pigs are treated as unnamed objects and are eaten, whereas dogs and horses are named subjects and are not eaten. Dogs and horses are seen as more "human"—both are talked to and petted, and dogs may live in the house and be buried upon death. Eating dogs would be like eating kin and implies cannibalism. Horses are more like servants, and eating them is only slightly less taboo. Pork is less preferred than beef, in part because pigs scavenge human food and are thus closer to people than cattle, such that eating pigs would be slightly cannibalistic.

A further cultural code of edibility is imposed on beef itself. Meat is culturally distinguished as the most edible part of the animal, in opposition to "innards" such as heart, tongue, and liver, which, like pork, imply cannibalism. Cuts of beef are subdivided into dozens of named categories and products, each priced according to its culturally defined desirability, such that eating a given cut reinforces one's social rank. Sahlins (1976b) stressed that pricing and desirability are not obviously related to supply and nutritional quality, because liver is highly nutritious and relatively scarce yet is much cheaper than steak, which is more abundant per animal.

The use of cultural products to encode social differences among categories of people resembles the use of animal species as totems to distinguish cultural groups in domestic-scale cultures. However, in market-based industrial cultures, the differential exchange and consumption of culturally distinguished products creates a culture in which ever-expanding consumption becomes a cultural imperative and goes far beyond the egalitarian categories that tribals use.

Anthropologists Marshall Sahlins and Jules Henry both considered consumption patterns and their institutionalized supports to be the decisive point of contrast between tribal cultures and contemporary industrial cultures. In his wide-ranging critique of American culture, Henry (1963) stressed that Americans assume that wants are infinitely expandable, whereas tribal peoples assume fixed wants and produce only what is wanted. Tribal peoples culturally dampen wants and enjoy a complementarity between production and needs, whereas Americans deliberately create a disequilibrium by increasing needs above the level that can ever be satisfied. Sahlins made the same point in his famous statement on foragers as "the original affluent society," in which he observed that foragers easily satisfy their wants by desiring little, whereas for Americans,

scarcity is the peculiar obsession of a business economy, the calculable condition of all who participate in it. The market makes freely available a dazzling array of products, all these "good things" within a man's reach—but never his grasp, for one never has enough to buy everything. To exist in a market economy is to live out a double tragedy, beginning in inadequacy and ending in deprivation. All economic

utilitarianism The use of economic profit, direct material advantage, or physical welfare, such as food and shelter, as an explanation for cultural practices.

activity starts from a position of shortage . . . one's resources are insufficient to the possible uses and satisfactions. (1968:86)

Scarcity or poverty is thus not strictly a technological problem, and it is not inherent in nature; it is a cultural creation that is most elaborated by commercial-scale, industrial cultures. According to Henry (1963), the dependence of American culture on the deliberate creation of needs for goods and services constitutes a "psychic revolution" with far-reaching impacts on human thought and behavior.

GROWTH, SCALE, AND POWER IN AMERICA

Growth is such a dominant element in American culture that it is important to closely examine its relationship to increases in culture scale and changes in the distribution of social power. This section uses broad ethnohistorical data for the country as a whole since 1776, as well as more detailed ethnography from New York City and the Palouse region of eastern Washington, to examine the social realities of 200 years of growth in the world's most successful commercial culture.

Growth in America: Wealth and Opportunity, 1776–1997

How did growth in America affect the distribution of social power, considering specifically income, wealth, and economic power?

After his 9-month visit in 1831–1832, French political scientist Alexis de Tocqueville (1835–1840) described America as an egalitarian democracy, with a large middle class and few very rich or very poor. In his view, abundant resources, technological innovation, and hard work created equal economic opportunity in America. More recent observers point to the increasing numbers of wealthy as evidence of the benefits of American economic freedom, supporting the hope that economic growth makes it possible for everyone to become wealthy (Gilder 1981). However, three independent lines of evidence—probate estate records, census data, and tax assessments—suggest that for much of American history, social and economic reality seldom

matched the widespread belief that growth made America a land of equal opportunity.

To estimate the distribution of wealth and income in the thirteen colonies immediately prior to the American Revolution of 1776, historian Alice Hanson Jones (1977, 1980) used detailed probate inventories of movable property and real estate in personal estates for 1773–1775, supplemented with tax lists, newspaper accounts, records of deeds and land grants, and church and town records of baptisms, marriages, and burials. Her findings suggest that the distribution of monetary income in 1776 was as top-heavy as in 1994, when the top 5 percent of households received 20 percent of national household income, the middle 20 percent received 15 percent, and the bottom 20 percent received only 4 percent.

Remarkably, Lee Soltow's (1989) analysis of the distribution of property ownership recorded in the United States Census for 1798, 1850, 1860, and 1870 shows that political independence and a century of economic growth had no significant impact on the distribution of wealth in America. Soltow found extensive inequality in America throughout the nineteenth century. Perhaps half of American households owned no land. Soltow found such a strong correlation between wealth concentration and support for the Constitution that he concluded that it would not have been ratified by a popular vote because the poor saw no advantages in a strong federal government.

Other historians have used tax assessment data to examine the distribution of wealth in New York City during the nineteenth century when especially rapid urban growth occurred (Jaher 1972, 1982; Pessen 1971, 1973). Pessen documented very rapid wealth concentration during the first half of the century. In 1845, the top 1 percent held half of all wealth in property, and the top 4 percent owned an incredible 81 percent, including shares in New York's emerging corporate businesses (primarily banks and insurance companies). During this time, New York City's wealth grew faster than its population. Per capita wealth actually quadrupled, but the rich got much richer.

Careful analysis of the family connections of the economic elite showed conclusively that nineteenth-century New York was not a city of equal opportunity, because one needed inherited social status and wealth to prosper. Jaher found that the nineteenth-century New York economic elite proved to be closely integrated by kinship and marriage connections and were even forming marriage alliances with the European aristocracy. In 1898, 42 percent of New York's 1368 millionaires were related by blood or marriage (Jaher 1982: 255). Ninety-five percent of New York's wealthiest individuals were born into already wealthy families; only 2 percent started out poor. The wealthy proved to be very secure, with most holding their wealth intact during their lifetimes and successfully passing it on to the next generation, even through severe economic downturns.

Even though wealth was heavily concentrated at the very top of the social hierarchy in nineteenth-century America, there was still significant upward mobility in comparison with the virtually frozen hierarchy in Europe. Low-income American households were able to move up the economic ladder, but much of their increase was a function of aging within the domestic cycle and very gradual accumulation of small savings. Soltow (1975:53) estimated that in 1870, 43 percent of adult males were poor, because they held total estates worth less than $100. By 1870, perhaps 52 percent of Americans were middle class, in the sense that they held at least $100 in property. Fewer than 10 percent were wealthy.

According to contemporary observers, in the 1850s accumulated wealth of $60,000, which would have generated an annual income of $3,000, was sufficient to provide the good life: "a comfortable house—servants, a good table—wine—a horse—books—'country quarters,'—a plentiful wardrobe—the ability to exercise hospitality" (cited in Pessen 1971:997). Only the top 0.5 percent of the urban population were in this category. If mid-nineteenth-century wealth accumulations of a mere $60,000 made one quite comfortable, it is understandable that $150,000 was considered to be a very substantial fortune, yet Soltow (1975:112) estimated that there were already 41 American millionaires in 1860, 545 in 1870, and, as we have seen, 1368 in New York City alone by 1898.

By 1890, small farms were being rapidly replaced by giant farms, and small businesses by giant corporations. With the closing of the frontier and the rise of manufacturing, about half the population had become urban, and most people needed income-producing jobs to survive. There were perhaps 25 million new poor who were unable to produce enough income to comfortably meet basic needs. During the twentieth century, further growth produced even more poverty. By the government's official definition of poverty (a three-person family earning less than $12,516), there were 36 million poor in 1996, nearly ten times the entire 1790 population. If households that are not earning enough to comfortably buy a house are also considered poor, but not impoverished, then the number of poor in America doubled to more than 50 million between 1890 and 1993. The trend toward poverty increasing with growth can be seen at the regional level, as ethnographic data from the Palouse region of eastern Washington shows (see the box entitled "Property, Growth, and Power in the Palouse, 1890–1997").

Economic Elites and Urban Poverty, New York City, 1863–1914

How did growth affect rich and poor in New York City during the nineteenth and early twentieth centuries? What were the relative proportions and absolute numbers of rich and poor at this time? How did they differ in social power and quality of life? How did government respond to the social stresses produced by growth?

All of the social stresses generated by rapid growth occurred in New York City during the nineteenth century, making this city an ideal place to examine scale and power issues. A remarkable geography of power had emerged in New York City by 1845, with city government, party politics, corporate finance, and massive private wealth situated side by side (see the box entitled "Machine Politics in New York City, 1845–1873"). On the lower end of Manhattan Island stood City Hall, immediately flanked on the East River side by Tammany Hall and on the Hudson River side by the residence of John Jacob Astor, then richest man in the country. The New York Stock Exchange was located half a mile to the south in the Wall Street financial district. By 1890, New York had become, after London, the largest and the wealthiest city in the world. Home of the Statue of

Property, Growth, and Power in the Palouse, 1890–1997

I examined the well-being of households in different-sized communities in the Palouse region of eastern Washington State to test whether wealth-producing growth, and the resulting increases in population and economic value, produced more poor households. I also wondered if there would be local-level evidence that growth was directed by the people who most benefited from increases in community scale.

Rather than relying on census data on income, intrusive survey questionnaires, or official definitions of poverty, I used publicly available property assessments to measure the well-being of Palouse households. I inferred that households owning property assessed at less than $10,000 would be too poor to easily meet their basic needs. Households owning $10,000 or more but less than $75,000 in property could maintain themselves comfortably but would have difficulty saving. Households with $75,000 or more in property would be able to save, invest, and steadily increase their economic level.

By carefully sorting through computerized data from the county assessors, I found that individuals owned nearly $10 billion worth of urban property in the Palouse. This was sufficient to put every household comfortably above the maintenance level, but instead the top 20 percent of owner-residents actually owned nearly 70 percent of all individually owned property. Many of the wealthiest property owners did not even live in the Palouse. Incredibly, the top three owners held more property than all 10,200 people who lived in the twenty smallest towns.

Most significantly, community scale proved to be the best predictor of household well-being. More households were better off in small urban places with fewer than 2500 people. The average value of property ownership increased with community scale, but the wealthiest households gained disproportionately, and there was an enormous increase in the absolute number of poor households in larger towns. There were proportionately more maintenance-level households and more home ownership in the smallest villages. There were few poor villagers, and they were better off than the poor in larger places. The communities that grew the least showed the least wealth concentration and had the most democratic city governments. Property elites who generated wealth from the higher property values that accompanied urban growth needed progrowth municipal policies to expand city boundaries and change zoning restrictions. Not surprisingly, the communities that had grown the most proved to be places where big property owners were the most represented in the municipal government.

These findings suggest that in this case, wealth-promoting government policies were designed by the wealthy to serve the needs of the wealthy. Growth appeared to work against the interests of a significant number of households because elevated property values priced low-income households out of the housing market.

Machine Politics in New York City, 1845–1873

The scale of the American political apparatus at the state and national levels, and in the very largest cities, was such that individuals, as individuals, could have no significant influence. An organized political bureaucracy was required to select candidates and rally electoral support for them. The party system stood between individuals and the government and is often described as *machine politics*. For example, in New York City in 1845, the 68,000 potential voters out of the city's 400,000 people were effectively controlled by a Democratic party apparatus run by 2400 people. The party bureaucracy was organized on three levels, with a 51-man General Committee at the top and seventeen ward committees, each responsible for two to eight election districts of 500 voters (Gronowicz 1998). There were also dozens of party-affiliated associations that fostered an active social life for people at all levels of New York society.

The political machine in New York was called Tammany Hall, after the building where the General Committee met, which was owned by the Tammany Society, a

politically oriented social club originally formed to assist immigrants. The Tammany machines selected candidates and brought out the votes for some ninety-one elected or appointed offices, from state governor and U.S. senators and representatives to police commissioner and street inspector. From 1868 to 1873, the political machine was completely controlled by William "Boss" Tweed, who previously had held a series of public offices in the U.S. Congress, the New York State Senate, and the City of New York. He gained control of the city treasury and used false accounting to systematically steal millions of dollars.

Boss Tweed and Tammany Hall became synonymous with bribery, corruption, and political patronage. But the Democratic party in New York cross-cut all social classes and reached out to small artisans and laborers, especially Irish Catholic immigrants. Because of its support for slavery, however, the party became outrageously racist toward the city's African Americans. Party politics in New York certainly helped working people adjust to the uncertainties of urban life, but it also helped the city's most powerful commercial interests expand their financial empires.

Liberty, it was the primary port of entry for immigrants. It handled more than half of all U.S. international trade and provided headquarters for America's largest corporations. With 2.5 million people, New York was the nation's largest urban center, with the greatest ethnic and religious diversity. Perhaps most importantly from our perspective, it also had the most powerful economic elites and the worst urban slums in the country.

In 1890, New York's economic elites probably consisted of fewer than 2500 very wealthy individuals, representing no more than 0.5 percent of the city's households. The elite were a diverse lot, representing Anglo-American Protestants, German Christians, and German Jews. Many elites were members of aristocratic merchant and landholding families, while others were newly rich bankers, corporate entrepreneurs, and professionals. Members of these distinct elite groups sometimes had conflicting political and economic interests and belonged to different social, professional, and commercial associations. But they also were integrated by kinship and marriage ties, and all benefited from the tremendous economic growth that was occurring, especially in railroads, banking, oil, and manufacturing.

The wealthiest of the city's 200 or so most prominent citizens was John D. Rockefeller (1839–1937), who was personally worth perhaps $200 million in the 1890s. J. P. Morgan (1837–1913) probably ranked second, with an estate valued at $77.6 million in 1913. It is important to distinguish the personal wealth of these superwealthy from their actual social, political, and economic power, which was represented by the total assets of the corporations they controlled and the foundations they endowed.

Hearings held in Washington, D.C., in 1912–1913, by the House Subcommittee on Banking and Currency, the Pujo Committee, provided a rare glimpse of the financial power of J. P. Morgan. Summaries of this material by Supreme Court Justice Louis Brandeis (1914) showed that as an investment banker operating through J. P. Morgan & Co., Morgan stood at the top of a complex web of commercial relationships. Through the directors of companies in which he held controlling interests, Morgan exerted direct and indirect influence over 34 large banks and trust companies, 10 insurance companies, 32 transportation systems, 12 public utilities, and 135 other corporations, with combined assets of $45 billion. His power was such that he virtually dominated all sectors of the national economy.

Morgan had effectively gained control over other people's money, such that he could assemble vast transfers of capital between "his" corporations and extract hefty commissions in the process. Decisions that he and his associates made influenced employment conditions and the well-being of millions of low-paid working people throughout the country. Morgan's economic focus was national and international. He had little interest in or influence over New York's domestic issues, although he was president of a prominent New York social club. As a principal owner of Manhattan's elevated railway line, Morgan unsuccessfully resisted the city's plans to build a publicly financed subway system. New York's elites were so divided on public policy that it was difficult for even one of the most powerful economic elites to impose his will everywhere.

Immigration caused the population of metropolitan New York to more than double between 1850 and 1880, and again between 1880 and 1910, providing a rental bonanza for slum landlords. There was enormous pressure on housing, and the large landowners responded by replacing single-family houses built on narrow lots with tenements housing three or more families, which would yield higher rents but at a much reduced quality of life for the residents. The costs and benefits in this development process were clear. The New York housing market was a free-market paradise, with no pesky building codes requiring fire escapes and the like to interfere with developers' natural desire to maximize profits. The result was shoddy, even dangerous construction and unhealthy, overpriced housing for most of the city's people, who were overwhelmingly poor. Social reformers condemned crowded living conditions as conducive to immorality among the poor. It took a series of cholera outbreaks, centered in the tenements, to enable reform-minded physicians to persuade the city to establish a Metropolitan Board of Health in 1866. The government was forced to grudgingly acknowledge that inferior housing was a public health problem.

Journalist photographer Jacob Riis (1904) vividly portrayed conditions in New York's crowded tenements in *How the Other Half Lives*. Riis suc-

FIGURE 12.7
Model of a representative block in Ward 10, in Manhattan's Lower East Side, 1900.

ceeded in arousing public indignation that spurred the government to action. Investigators for the New York State Tenement House Commission found in 1900 that 2.3 million people, approximately 70 percent of the population of metropolitan New York, lived in crowded, unsanitary tenements (DeForest and Veiller 1903). The average floor space in these small apartments approximated 4.7 square meters per person. This figure almost precisely matched the 4.6 square meters (10 by 10 feet) of floor space that Charles Booth (1892–1903) had used to identify the residences of the London poor. Remarkably, this was about half the floor space enjoyed by a typical Ashaninka household. Furthermore, it was much less than the 6–10 square meters of floor space per person that seems to represent a cross-cultural constant for all precommercial cultures (Brown 1987, Naroll 1962).

In Ward 10, the Jewish quarter, a forty-five-block area on Manhattan's Lower East Side, 76,000 people were living in three- to seven-story tenements, with as many as 200 people to a house (see Figure 12.7). Buildings were dark and poorly ventilated, and many had only a single outside water tap and pit toilet for all families. Sometimes hallway water-closet toilets were situated on each floor to be shared by two to four families. There were no baths or showers. Not surprisingly, over one 5-year period, there were thirty-two cases of tuberculosis and thirteen cases of diphtheria in one sample block jammed with 2781 people, and 660 families requested public assistance.

These wretched living conditions made turn-of-the-century New York a center of labor unrest and union and socialist activism that eventually resulted in small increases in wages and acceptance of the 8-hour workday. Building codes were also gradually modified. The elites were often divided on what policies the city should pursue, which made it possible for working-class people to influence events with their votes. Some elites favored a form of municipal socialism in which tax dollars and private investment would improve the commercial prospects of the city by developing better public transit systems, public education, public health and housing, municipal government, and cultural institutions (Hammack 1982:56). The largest economic elites were reluctant to support reforms because they were suspicious of government involvement in the "free market," did not want their taxes to increase, and had much broader economic interests than in the city itself. Others blamed the city's problems on socialists, anarchists, immorality, and ethnic and religious diversity.

Corporate Power, Social Class, and Family in America

How has the growth of corporate power and economic globalization transformed American life? How is economic power distributed in America? Is there an American ruling class?

Giant commercial corporations now dominate American life. Corporations are given the same rights as individuals, but unlike individuals and sole-proprietorship businesses, corporations can live forever and grow ever more powerful. Corporations also are not limited to particular places, and they can project their commercial power throughout the world. Furthermore, corporate structure and limited liability makes it difficult to hold corporations responsible for the total costs of their activities, even when they are criminal.

The scale of giant corporations can be illustrated by Philip Morris, the fourteenth-largest industrial corporation in the world in 1991 and seventh-largest in the United States. Philip Morris sold a staggering $50 billion worth of products in 1993, an amount far exceeding the national budgets of many countries. As a huge conglomerate, Philip Morris contained some 222 operating companies, subsidiaries, units, and divisions in the United States, and forty-two countries. From top to bottom, there were at least four major organizational levels, such that the corporation, with its 210,000 employees worldwide, was structurally as complex as a political state. Philip Morris produced hundreds of food items. The company has had an enormous impact on American life through its employment practices, its choice of plant locations, and the health effects of the products it markets. Recent estimates suggest that wealth production by large corporations annually costs American workers, customers, communities, and the nation at large as much as $2.6 trillion to pay for monopoly pricing and corporate crime and for such "externalities" as workplace accidents and illnesses, dangerous products, and pollution. This figure does not include the higher taxes that provide corporate welfare in the form of government subsidies to big businesses (Estes 1996).

Thomas R. Dye (1983) and a team of graduate students at Florida State University painstakingly compiled and sorted biographical data on elites and concluded that 5778 individuals controlled America's giant corporations, the federal government, the news media, and the primary cultural institutions in the early 1980s. Some of these people are elected officials, but many are completely unknown outside the networks of power. Similarly, a very small number of owners and managers exercise real power over American business. My investigation of Securities and Exchange Commission filings in 1994 revealed that a mere ten people helped direct thirty-seven American companies whose combined assets of $2 trillion represented

nearly 10 percent of all corporate assets in the country. One individual directed five companies with $549 billion in total assets, or 2.5 percent of the national total. In 1995, a mere 600 people directed America's fifty largest companies, accounting for 16 percent of the country's business revenues and exceeding the combined revenues of all noncorporate businesses and nonprofit organizations. This change in the scale of business enterprise transforms commercial life in small American communities, making participation in markets difficult for many small-business owners. Concentrated wealth of this magnitude gives enormous freedom to a privileged few to produce and direct the economic processes that shape our future.

Anthropologist Marvin Harris (1981) attributes increased crime and family breakdowns to the rise of *oligopoly* in American business and the related shift from industrial production to services and information. These economic processes accelerated in the United States during the 1980s and 1990s, as changes in tax laws, deregulation of financial institutions, and the removal of global trade barriers prompted giant corporations to increase their financial power through leveraged buyouts and downsizing. This vast transformation, which has been called *deindustrialization* (Bluestone and Harrison 1982), parallels the social disruptions caused by the Industrial Revolution. Millions of American workers are losing their manufacturing jobs and are being forced to take low-paying, in-person service jobs. At the same time, as the economy grows, financial markets soar, and the privileged few—wealthy investors, corporate executives, and Robert Reich's (1992) symbolic analysts—prosper. Historian Christopher Lasch (1995) points out that upper-middle-class professionals may use "assortive mating"—marrying another well-paid professional—to double their income and join the financial elites. Meanwhile, downsized production workers and service workers can gamble on the lottery.

Giant corporations, because of their size, can eliminate competition and control markets to such an extent that locally owned businesses may have difficulty surviving. Large corporations also derive a significant proportion of their profits from buying and selling smaller corporations, rather than directly from production, and this reduces their long-term commitment to consumers, employees, or the local communities where their factories are located.

The increasing financial power of giant corporations is associated with a loss of power and control in local communities. Anthropologist James Toth (1992), who conducted ethnographic research on a small Pennsylvania town, found that the deindustrialization process reduced economic decision making by local businesspeople. Small businesses, local manufacturing plants, and independent contractors were being replaced by subsidiary electronics firms, shopping malls, banks, and realty agencies controlled by conglomerates headquartered in other cities, other states, and even other countries. This process drained financial capital from the local community.

Anthropologist Katherine Newman (1988, 1993) estimates that 10.6 million Americans lost their jobs to corporate downsizing between 1981 and 1992. To assess the impact of this process, she gathered life histories and conducted intensive interviews with hundreds of Americans, including members of sixty families in a suburban New Jersey community. Newman found that many middle-class people who were experiencing declining living standards felt that the American Dream of continuous economic progress was passing them by. They accepted this as evidence of personal failure, rather than attributing it to larger economic forces. Anthropologist June Nash (1989, 1994) found the same passive acceptance of economic misfortune among the 5000 workers in Massachusetts who were laid off when General Electric moved their plant to Canada in 1986. Displaced workers may find lower-paying jobs, but they are often forced to sell their homes, and their households experience the stress of downward mobility.

The vast changes in American business have directly impacted family life. Few married women worked outside of the home in the 1890s, but since 1965 the declining value of wages has forced many women to seek employment in an effort to maintain a constant standard of living (see Figure 12.8). Economic stresses are reflected in higher divorce rates and an increase in single-parent households. Furthermore, careful, large-scale statistical studies have demonstrated a direct relationship between income level and stability and mortality (Gregorio

FIGURE 12.8   *Stereotyped view of a typical American family in the 1950s. By the 1970s, women were increasingly drawn into the work force to help pay for new consumer goods, yet they were also expected to be housewives.*

et al. 1997). Differences in social class mean that in contemporary America, just as in nineteenth-century London and New York, well-paid professionals and managers live longer than laborers. Government reports have consistently shown that poor children are unlikely to see doctors or be vaccinated, and poor adults are more likely to be in poor health, to lack health insurance, and to die from chronic diseases (National Center for Health Statistics 1998). Medical researcher Richard G. Wilkinson (1996, 1997) argues that a high level of social inequality raises mortality at lower social levels, because inequality reduces social cohesion and

oligopoly   Concentrated economic power when a market is dominated by only a few producers—like a monopoly, which is controlled by a single producer.

deindustrialization   The replacement of factory employment with service sector employment in formerly industrial countries as production jobs are moved to low-wage countries.

Vice Presidential Nominee Nelson Rockefeller on Private Economic Power in America, 1974

During his confirmation hearings for the office of vice president, many interviewers questioned whether Nelson Rockefeller would have a conflict of interest, given his family's vast financial interests. In response, he explained that his family did not act as a centralized power structure. He described the "family office" as follows:

Well, I would define it as the 56th and 55th and 54th floors of 30 Rockefeller Plaza where there is a collection of individuals which include offices for my four brothers, my three brothers and myself, space for children and cousins, nieces, nephews, and then men and women who undertake certain functions, including the following: Investment of funds, advice to individuals, legal advice, accounting, tax advice, library service and research service, public relations advice in connection with somebody who is going to get married and they want to make a statement, or some other personal problem and want to put out a statement.

We do not operate as a corporation. We do not have activities where we sit down in a board meeting and decide will we make this investment, will we go into this market, will we do this, which is the normal activity of a corporate structure, and therefore I think that it is somewhat misleading to think that there is some very powerful central organization here that has many active connections all over that are coordinated, that are planned, that are administered, that are operated as a single unit with a tremendous central purpose.

It is a loosely knit conglomerate of family and individuals who try to be decent citizens and who have been very fortunate in living in this society and benefiting from the society and who would like to contribute to the society itself. (U.S. Congress 1974:94)

In an exchange with Congressman Paul S. Sarabanes, Rockefeller discussed his understanding of the relationship between private economic power and the American political system. Sarbanes asked Rockefeller if he thought his grandfather would have broken up Standard Oil if he had been president of the country and of Standard. Rockefeller thought it was an unfair question but replied:

increases stress. This connection between social cohesion, stress, and health is strongly supported by a 30-year longitudinal study of health in Roseto, Pennsylvania, an Italian American village of 1500 people, from approximately 1960 to 1990 (Wolf and Bruhn 1993). The Roseto villagers were the descendants of immigrants who came to Pennsylvania in the 1880s. Researchers found that, as long as their family and clan structure remained strong, the villagers were almost completely free from heart attacks. The incidence of heart attacks increased sharply when they began to lose social cohesion in the mid-1960s, even though other risk factors did not significantly change.

Americans are reluctant to talk about social class, but researchers such as Ferdinand Lundberg (1937, 1968), C. Wright Mills (1956), and G. William Domhoff (1967, 1983) have concluded that a very small upper class, perhaps the top 0.5 percent of the country, enjoys a disproportionate share of the benefits of the American economy and have a disproportionate influence over events. Indeed, in 1998, the $727 billion in combined wealth held by the 400 richest Americans was more than sixty times the wealth held by all the colonists in 1774, on the eve of the American Revolution (Jones 1978: Table 3.1). Many of the wealthiest Americans know one another and may interact socially, but they no

The great strength of the democratic system, it is the people's government—the people's government protects the people from interests, whether they are Standard Oil, whatever it is, or private fortunes, by law. And this is what this great Congress does, and that is why we are, as a nation, protected, from the power that may get out of hand in any segment of our economy or life of our country, because you pass laws to prevent it.

Mr. Sarbanes "Well, we are now beginning to get at what I think is a very fundamental philosophical question here."

Mr. Rockefeller "I think you are right."

Mr. Sarbanes "And that is that we have as a fundamental principle in this country that public power will be available to check and restrain and limit and control private economic wealth and power."

Mr. Rockefeller "Exactly."

Mr. Sarbanes "As a consequence, we permit an economic system that allows private individuals to accumulate significant economic wealth and power."

Mr. Rockefeller "That is right."

Mr. Sarbanes "On the assumption that the public power will be available to check it."

Mr. Rockefeller "That is correct."

Mr. Sarbanes "And of course, the basic question that your nomination raises is the melding together, especially if you were to succeed to the Presidency of the United States, of great public power and probably the most significant concentration of private economic power in the Nation."

Mr. Rockefeller "Well, I have got to now go back to what I was trying to explain before in an earlier conversation, which is that private economic power in the United States, as we have thought of it as the dominating factor, if you leave out some of these theories, which frankly I think are totally unrelated to reality, the power, the economic power of the United States is in the savings banks, the insurance companies, the pension funds." (U.S. Congress 1974:132)

---

longer form a cohesive, self-conscious social class. They share a common interest in perpetuating economic growth but may disagree on details of political policy.

The Rockefeller Dynasty

The remarkable Rockefeller family illustrates the extent to which wealth can be amassed in a commercial culture, be transmitted across four generations, and be used to exert enormous cultural, political, and commercial influence in the United States and in the world. The patriarch of the family, John D. Rockefeller (1839–1937), founded the Standard Oil Company in 1870 and gained monopolistic control over the American petroleum industry. The government dissolved the Standard Oil trust in 1911, but John D. Sr. had already become fabulously wealthy. In 1913, he established the Rockefeller Foundation with an endowment of $100 million "to promote the well-being of mankind throughout the world." Through the foundation and other charitable organizations, the family promoted worldwide public health, Christian missions, technical research, and public education (including anthropology) on an unprecedented scale. By the 1930s, John D. Sr. had controlling interests over a vast financial empire consisting of

FIGURE 12.9a
(a) The Rockefeller family estate at Pocantico, 1964. (SOURCE: Estate diagram from Pyle 1964.) (b) Numbers 1–6 in 12.9b correspond to households shown on the map in 12.9a. Numbers 7–9 live in adjacent areas.

Rockefeller Pocantico Estate, 1964

Estate boundaries
Fenced compound
1-6 Residences

0   800   1600   2400

Scale in feet

6

Playhouse

4

Guest House

Greenhouse
Coach House

5

Pocantico Hills
Staff Residence

3

2

1

Governor's Lodge

Barns

stockholdings and directorships in some 287 companies, with assets estimated at over $20 billion at that time (Colby and Dennett 1995, Collier and Horowitz 1976, Rochester 1936:56).

The Rockefeller family's personal estate has been wisely stewarded by the family and has grown significantly over the years. In 1998, *Fortune* magazine estimated the family's combined wealth at $8 billion (Gorham, Kafka, and Neelakantan 1998). The Rockefeller Foundaton was the nation's tenth-largest foundation with assets of $2.7 billion, and the Rockefeller Brothers Fund was worth $409 million (*The Foundation Directory*, 1998:xi). The family's interests were long centered in Chase Manhattan Bank, the International Basic Economy Corporation, and the Rockefeller Center in New York. But their interests remain dispersed in a complex web of national and international financial holdings and properties that included mines in Chile and oil and supermarkets throughout Latin America. John D. Sr. and John D. Jr. maintained residences in Manhattan, New Jersey, Maine, and Florida, and Nelson owned huge ranches in Venezuela and Brazil. But most members of the family

lived on the 3600-acre Pocantico estate, 25 miles north of downtown Manhattan (see Figures 12.9 and 12.10). This vast estate was carefully consolidated in various family trust funds, many of them managed through a family corporation, Rockefeller Family and Associates, headquartered in Rockefeller Center. Rockefeller family members were influential in building the World Trade Center and donated the property for the United Nations building. The Rockefellers also have been leaders in nature conservation and the arts, and their public policy interests have been fostered through support for conferences and organizations such as the Council on Foreign Relations.

The Rockefellers generally did not hold political offices, although Nelson served as governor of New York from 1958 to 1970, and as vice president of the United States from 1974 to 1977 (see the box entitled "Vice Presidential Nominee Nelson Rockefeller"). Nelson's brother Winthrop served as governor of Arkansas from 1967 to 1971 and as lieutenant governor in 1998. John D. IV was a U.S. senator and governor of West Virginia. Many close associates of the family, including Henry Kissinger,

FIGURE 12.9b

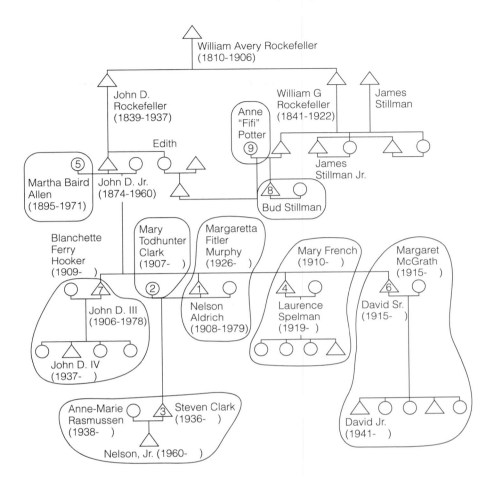

Walt Rostow, and Dean Rusk, served in high-level appointments in the federal government.

SUMMARY

America is unquestionably the dominant economic and political-military power in the global system and is viewed by its own citizens as an ideal cultural model for the entire world. However, certain aspects of the culture raise important questions about its effectiveness in providing for the health and well-being, social cohesion, and stability for all of its citizens. The American cultural ideal of individualism contrasts sharply with the Chinese emphasis on kinship, which is more representative of political-scale cultures. Individualism can make life less secure for Americans.

Economic growth is a crucial feature of America's cosmology. Economic growth can make it more difficult for any culture to maintain a balance with natural resources and ecosystems. Ethnohistoric examples from the nation's founding through the nineteenth century reveal the contradictions between the concentrated social power produced by growth in economic and social scale and the American emphasis on democracy, economic freedom, and equal opportunity. The key cultural transformation, which provided the real foundation of

FIGURE 12.10
The Rockefeller dynasty.

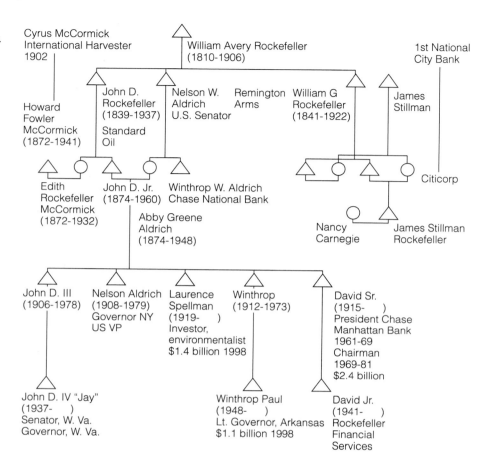

American culture, was in the evolution of business into ever-large-scale organizational forms that were capable of taking full commercial advantage of industrial technology.

The ethnographic example of the industrial village of Rockdale, Pennsylvania, from 1825 to 1865 illustrates the social inequality that sustained America's commercial development. The ethnographic examples of factory farming and cattle raising show how the commercialization and industrialization of food production and consumption transformed the organization of American life. Inequality in the distribution of economic power is perhaps the greatest threat to social cohesion and cultural continuity in America. Inequality in the United States involves differential access to status

and prestige, productive resources, income, and economic and political power generally. The existence of this kind of inequality is an objective contradiction in a country that enjoys formal democracy and a high degree of personal freedom. American culture demonstrates that the human problem of social inequality, which seems to be an intrinsic feature of states, is not necessarily solved by capitalist market economies and continuous economic expansion. It is important to understand the cultural significance of inequality in America and the way in which production and consumption is carried out, because at a global level the wealthiest industrial nations occupy the top of an international hierarchy of nations in which most of humanity is desperately impoverished.

STUDY QUESTIONS

1. Discuss the cultural ecological features of factory farming in comparison with less intensive subsistence systems. Refer to monocrop, Green Revolution, energy input–output ratios, energy subsidy, social consequences, stability, and ecosystem degradation.

2. How is economic and social power distributed in the United States?

3. In what sense is it legitimate to speak of a Cattle Complex in the United States? Make specific comparisons between the role of cattle in the United States and their role in an East African cattle culture. Briefly describe the pathway that American cattle follow as commodities from production to consumption.

4. Using the American beef industry as an example, show how market forces influence specific production and processing practices and promote inequality and social conflict.

5. Discuss how the realities of American society reflect American cosmology.

6. Use the Rockdale case study to illustrate the human impact of industrial development and wage labor.

7. What economic interests did the Founding Fathers represent? Were these interests reflected in the American Constitution?

8. To what extent is it reasonable to speak of social class in America? What are the correlates of social class?

9. Use New York City in 1890 to illustrate the urban problems of particular forms of growth.

10. To what extent is American growth from 1790 to the present related to the distribution of social power?

11. Describe Harris' utilitarian explanation for the importance of beef in American subsistence, in contrast with Sahlins' cultural interpretation. Describe how the edibility of meat can be used to encode differences in social class.

12. Describe how scarcity and consumption are culturally constructed in America. In what sense does Henry refer to advertising as a distinct cultural institution?

SUGGESTED READING

DeVita, Philip R., and James D. Armstrong. 1993. *Distant Mirrors: America as a Foreign Culture.* Belmont, Calif.: Wadsworth. Interpretations of American culture and descriptions of their experiences as outsiders by fourteen foreign scholars, primarily anthropologists.

Domhoff, G. William. 1983. *Who Rules America Now? A View for the '80s.* Englewood Cliffs, N.J.: Prentice-Hall. An updated version of Domhoff's 1967 book about the domination of the American political economy by the upper class.

Harris, Marvin. 1981. *America Now: The Anthropology of a Changing Culture.* New York: Simon & Schuster. A wide-ranging analysis of American culture by a prominent cultural materialist anthropologist.

Hsu, Francis L. K. 1981. *Americans and Chinese: Passage to Difference.* Honolulu: The University Press of Hawaii. A comparative analysis of American and Chinese culture by a Chinese psychological anthropologist.

Spradley, James P., and Michael A. Rynkiewich. 1975. *The Nacirema: Readings on American Culture.* Boston: Little, Brown. A collection of ethnographically based studies of diverse aspects of American culture.

13

The Impoverished World

During the decades following World War II, the disparity in material welfare between the wealthy industrial nations and the rest of the world steadily widened, as did the gap between rich and poor within individual countries. Even as decolonization and technological progress proceeded, increasing millions of people throughout the world came to live in absolute poverty. By 1980, an estimated 730 million people (excluding China) were living on diets considered inadequate by international standards and had extremely limited access to material resources. By the late 1980s, dramatic increases in poverty were occurring throughout the world. Real living standards plunged while public spending for social services declined as many countries found themselves deeply in debt to First World lenders.

Development, as it has been practiced throughout most of the twentieth century, has systematically undermined the self-maintenance abilities of domestic-scale peasant communities, leaving them highly vulnerable to outside exploitation. The primary ideological justification for externally planned development was that it would ultimately raise rural living standards, but the outcome of decades of development suggests that a fundamental reassessment of the entire issue is required. The barriers to progress are more likely to lie beyond, rather than within, local communities.

This chapter begins with a close look at the human realities of impoverishment using case material from Brazil and Bangladesh, where communities have been impoverished by technologically based development programs that leave grossly unequal power structures in place. Next, we examine the international development establishment since 1945, focusing on the United Nations and related agencies and the United States. We examine the complex structure of development at the global level, considering the flow of resources, costs, and benefits, and show why development often works against the interests of domestic-scale communities. Next, we discuss diverse anthropological perspectives on development, peasantries, and poverty. Finally, we present a famous anthropological experiment in community development in the Andes to show that even when local power structures are altered, development that undermines the unique strengths of domestic-scale culture may still leave rural communities impoverished.

DAILY REALITY IN THE IMPOVERISHED WORLD

National-level statistics show that for job-dependent people, low wages and underemployment produce malnutrition, high infant mortality, and wretched living conditions on a vast scale. However, the impersonal statistics diminish the human reality. A close look at real people, households, and communities gives a more complete view of the impoverishment produced by commercial-scale culture. The harshest reality is that when the commercialization and financialization processes dominate the sapienization process, children may be deprived of food, their most urgent human need. By contrast, domestic-scale cultures placed human needs first and guaranteed food security to everyone.

Infant Mortality in Brazil

What is it like to be poor in an impoverished country? How do landless sugar plantation workers deal with the effects of chronic malnutrition resulting from poor wages and underemployment?

During the 1980s, anthropologist Nancy Scheper-Hughes (1992) conducted extensive research on women living in a northeast Brazilian squatter town, which she called Bom Jesus. The growth of giant sugar plantations in this region since the 1950s had pushed subsistence farmers off their lands, forcing them to survive on inadequate wages. During the 1980s, men who worked in the sugarcane fields were paid the legal minimum of $10 a week, while women received $5. At the same time, a family of four required $40 a week to meet their minimum food needs, because even the most basic foods, such as beans, could no longer be grown locally. As a result, sugar workers and their families have had to adapt to a situation of chronic malnutrition. Babies are dying, just as Adam Smith (1776) had predicted, but unfortunately wages are not improving because Brazil's poor have little political or economic power.

The impoverished sugarcane workers are surviving on an average of 1500 calories a day, virtually concentration camp rations. Regional statistics show that 80 percent of the population, some 30 million people, constitute an impoverished underclass. Surprisingly, Scheper-Hughes (1992) found that people were actually able to survive under these conditions, even though two-thirds of their children were clinically undernourished and one-fourth were nutritionally dwarfed by their starvation diets. Women experienced high rates of miscarriage, and many of their babies were born underweight. Most disturbing was Scheper-Hughes' discovery that in 1987, infants in the community of Bom Jesus were dying at the rate of 211 per 1000. This is higher than any other national-level infant mortality rate in the world. The reality of this human cost of social inequality is partially buried in the regional statistic showing an aggregate infant mortality rate for northeast Brazil of 116 per 1000. This is still a very high rate, but even this figure is obscured by Brazil's national-level statistic of just 57 infant deaths per 1000 in 1993. The same obfuscation occurs with statistics that use per capita GNP (gross national product) as the primary measure of economic growth and prosperity. Indeed, Brazil has experienced an economic miracle. In 1971, its total GNP was just $421 per capita; by 1993, it had reached $2930 per capita. Brazil is now considered an upper-middle-income nation, but many Brazilians are desperately impoverished by unbalanced development.

Low wages put Brazilian working families in a terrible dilemma. Anthropologists Daniel Gross and Barbara Underwood (1971) investigated sisal plantation workers in the same region. They found that sisal workers, like sugarcane workers, were forced to buy the cheapest high-calorie food and systematically starve their children to give their working men enough food energy to keep them in the fields.

Protein-calorie deficiency diseases, such as kwashiorkor and marasmus, cause a wasting away of body tissues and have dramatic effects on children (Trowell 1954). Malnutrition is also known to damage the developing brain during early infancy (Montagu 1972), and it can inhibit a child's intellectual ability by making the child less active. Fortunately, new research suggests that some of these effects are reversible if malnutrition is prevented (Brown and Pollitt 1996).

Real detective work is required to measure the actual human cost of poverty. Scheper-Hughes visited the local cemetery and obtained the handwritten birth and death records from the registry books in Bom Jesus to learn how many babies were dying. She also collected full reproductive histories from 100 women and found that an average older (post-menopausal) woman had seen 4.7 of her children die. During the worst conditions, the infant mortality rate in Bom Jesus soared to 493 per 1000 in 1 year.

The women of Bom Jesus certainly understood the general nature of their impoverishment. As one woman declared, "Our children die because we are poor and hungry" (Scheper-Hughes 1992:313). However, similar to laid-off factory workers in the United States, the poor of Bom Jesus blamed themselves. They treated their own poor health as a problem of "nerves," which could be treated with tranquilizers and vitamins purchased at the pharmacy. Scheper-Hughes is emphatic about the real causes of sickness and death in Bom Jesus:

I do not want to quibble over words, but what I have been seeing on the Alto de Cruzeiro [the slum in Bom Jesus] for two and a half decades is more than "malnutrition," and it is politically as well as economically caused, although in the absence of overt political strife or war. Adults, it is true, might be described as "chronically undernourished," in a weakened and debilitated state, prone to infections and opportunistic diseases. But it is overt hunger and starvation that one sees in babies and small children, the victims of a "famine" that is endemic, relentless, and political-economic in origin. (1992:146)

The global financialization process itself has intensified the human costs of impoverishment. The Brazilian government borrowed heavily to finance economic growth and cut expenditures on public health in 1985 to help make its loan payments.

Land and Food in Impoverished Bangladesh

How did a once-prosperous region with rich agricultural land become one of the world's poorest nations, despite economic growth and technological development? How is this poverty reflected in national statistics?

The following pair of quotes encapsulate the way impoverishment was experienced by many south Asian villages and identify the commercial processes involved:

Between 1933 and 1960 the village became poorer, and was polarized into two groups of households, one owning insufficient land to support an average household, and another owning a sufficient or excessive amount of it. (Van Schendel 1981:82)

Thus, international systems of production and finance are changing the ways that the rich and poor [of Bangladesh] eat and lead their lives. (Lindenbaum 1987:436)

Bangladesh, formerly East Pakistan (1947–1971), is a primarily Muslim nation centered on the Ganges–Brahmaputra delta region known as East Bengal, in the northeast corner of the Indian subcontinent at the head of the Bay of Bengal. In 1990, the World Bank listed Bangladesh as one of the world's poorest nations, fifth from the bottom with a per-capita GNP of $170 (World Bank 1988–1995). In line with its status as an impoverished nation, average life expectancy in Bangladesh stood at 51 years, and infant mortality at 118 per 1000 live births; and 57 percent of its population, or 62 million people, were considered impoverished (World Bank 1988–1995). By FAO (Food and Agricultural Organization of the United Nations) caloric standards (2122 calories/day), 85 percent of the population had an inadequate diet. Nutritional deficiencies related to poverty were reflected in the low birth weights (under 5.5 lb [2.5 kilograms, kg]) of 39 percent of Bangladeshi babies due to a high rate of maternal malnutrition. Roughly 90 percent of the population were rural, and nearly half of all rural households were landless. Some two-thirds of the population were either unemployed or underemployed (Jansen 1986).

Given such precarious economic conditions, it is not surprising that several hundred thousand people died in famines in Bangladesh in 1974. These conditions existed even though Bangladesh experienced an average annual growth in GNP of 0.4 percent during 1965–1988, and from 1982 to 1988 received $13.8 billion in Official Development Aid (ODA). From 1985 to 1988, Bangladesh received 4.6 million tons (4.2 million metric tons) of food aid, much of it from the United States. The

Bangladesh experience suggests that economic growth and development assistance may not reduce poverty when the structure of social inequality remains unchanged.

Under the Muslim rulers of the Mogul empire (sixteenth to eighteenth centuries), East Bengal supported a prosperous cotton industry. The peasantry collectively controlled the land and remained economically self-sufficient, although they had to pay taxes to the zamindars, the title of local elites who were the appointed agents of the Muslim state. Shortly after the British completed their conquest of the region in 1765, they legally recognized the zamindar tax collectors as the rural landowners. Turning the zamindars into landlords, as well as tax collectors, amplified village-level inequalities. However, by giving the zamindars more power, it also made it easier for the new British rulers to maintain political stability and ensured a steady flow of taxes. The British also suppressed the indigenous cotton industry and converted the peasantry into agricultural laborers for the production of jute as an export crop to supply British-owned mills in Calcutta and England.

Thus, preexisting social structures created by state authority laid the foundation for the profound impoverishment of Bangladesh in the twentieth century. Despite various changes in the central government and apparent reforms in land laws, the rural elites have tenaciously maintained their grip over the best agricultural land in Bangladesh. Their favored social standing, which ultimately was supported by the state, permitted them to benefit at the expense of their less-favored fellow villagers when agricultural development programs became important during the 1970s. Thus, Bangladesh demonstrates that the incorporation of a regional state into the global system can increase internal inequality and reduce the quality of life for much of the population (see Figure 13.1).

The impoverishment process in Bangladesh is well documented at the village level in some two dozen modern ethnographic studies (for example, see Hartmann and Boyce 1983, Jansen 1986, Van Schendel 1981). A representative case is Goborgari, a single village described by the Dutch researcher Willem Van Schendel (1981).

Goborgari is a Bengali-speaking, mixed Hindu and Muslim village situated on a level alluvial plain

FIGURE 13.1   *Bangladeshi village. Bangladesh was the fifth-poorest nation in the world in 1990 according to the World Bank. Millions of impoverished people, such as these villagers, live in the flood-prone Ganges–Brahmaputra delta.*

north of the Ganges and west of the Brahmaputra River in northern Bangladesh. Goborgari was primarily settled by immigrants during the nineteenth and early twentieth centuries. A government survey showed that in 1933 Goborgari was a small village of nineteen relatively egalitarian and self-sufficient farming households. There were no landless households and few large landholders, and the average acreage per household stood at approximately 4.3 acres (1.7 hectares), which was adequate for basic needs. The situation had changed dramatically by 1977. The population had increased from 30 people to 392. Total acreage increased, and cultivation was greatly intensified with irrigation and with double,

TABLE 13.1   *Change in a Developing Bangladeshi Village,*
Goborgari, 1933 and 1977

	1933	1977
Population	30	392
Households	19	75
Average household size	1.5	5.2
Total land owned (acres)	83	122
Total land controlled (acres)	—	136
Total land cultivated (acres)	—	148
Total plows and teams	—	31.5
Average acres/household	4.3	1.5
Average fragments/household	—	6.5
Households landless (%)	0	32
Households without control of land (%)	—	16
Households own <2 acres (%)	—	70.6
Land owned by richest 10% of households (%)	10	46
Households own full plow (%)	—	34.7
1977 Villagewide Rice Production-Consumption		
Rice production/person/day		0.8 kg
Rice production/person/day (HYV rice)		1.3 kg
Nutritional requirement/person/day		0.7 kg
Basic needs requirement/person/day		1.75 kg
Acreage to produce basic needs/household		2.1 acres
Households not self-sufficient in rice		60%

SOURCE: Van Schendel (1981).

even triple, cropping, but most people were impoverished (see Table 13.1).

It might appear that natural population increase was the primary cause of impoverishment in Goborgari, but a closer look shows that this was not the case. Much of the growth of Goborgari since 1933 was because landless villagers moved in from other areas. More importantly, even with a tenfold population increase, subsistence resources still would have been marginally adequate if land were equitably distributed. If Goborgari had been organized as an egalitarian, domestic-scale culture, land resources and the risks of food production would have been shared equally. The primary crop in Goborgari by 1977 was the newly introduced Green Revolution **high-yield variety** (HYV) of rice, which increased production by a third. The problem with the new HYV rice, which was promoted by government extension agents, was that it required access to land and high levels of water and chemicals. Despite these technological improvements, the village was still relatively impoverished in comparison with earlier conditions. Average

household acreage dropped to 1.5 acres (0.6 hectare), which was insufficient to meet basic household needs. Thirty-three percent of households were suddenly landless, and the richest 10 percent of households owned 46 percent of the land. A full 70 percent of households were at or below the 2-acre line, which was the minimal acreage needed to produce what villagers considered to be a "moderately contented living" derived from full-time farming.

Van Schendel (1981) arrives at this poverty-line figure based on a minimal basic needs requirement of 3.86 pounds (1.75 kg) of rice per person per day. The latter figure is set at two and one-half times the daily nutritional requirement of 1.6 pounds (0.7 kg), in order to allow for a marketable "surplus" for the purchase of other food items and basic material needs.

The land situation was more complex than the facts of legal ownership suggest because land quality and productivity varied and land fragmentation made cultivation difficult. An average household might own 1.5 acres (0.6 hectare) in six and one-half separate pieces. A significant amount of land was also either mortgaged or sharecropped under an arrangement in which the sharecropper could keep half of the production. Holding a mortgage or rights to sharecrop a given piece of land gave a degree of control over "unowned" land and made it considerably more difficult to assess the actual degree of poverty and inequality in the village. Virtually as critical as control over land was ownership of a plow and team of draft animals, yet only 33 percent of households owned a full team. A farmer who did not own a team could not sharecrop, and hiring a team to plow one's own land meant reduced yields and increased expenses. To a limited extent, sharecropping gave the poorest villagers a chance to make up their deficiencies; nevertheless, 60 percent of all households were not self-sufficient in rice. They could not produce enough rice to meet their minimal nutritional requirements and were even farther from producing a marketable surplus to help meet their physical needs for moderately contented living by local standards.

Because agricultural self-sufficiency was out of reach of two-thirds of the villagers, they were forced to supplement their incomes with seasonal part-time labor, with petty—and sometimes illegal—business operations, and with whatever irregular and poorly paid service employment they could find. Under these conditions, most villagers faced continual economic emergencies and scarcity, and serious poverty and inequality appeared to be steadily increasing.

When he attempted to estimate the actual economic status of Goborgari households, Van Schendel found that cash values were inadequate to cover all of the significant economic exchanges that took place in the village and the varying requirements of individual households. Instead, Van Schendel used a 4-point scale based on the villagers' own estimates of monthly household maintenance requirements and standard of living. Villagers implicitly recognized at least four standards of living within the village, which Van Schendel labeled A (substandard), B (low), C (moderate), and D (comfortable) (see Table 13.2), according to a household's ability to produce sufficient rice for its total annual needs. The poorest 20 percent of households (category A) often went hungry and could not afford respectable clothing. The top 16 percent of households (category D) enjoyed an annual surplus that would allow them to maintain their modest comforts and simple luxuries for more than 3 months beyond a given agricultural year. Households in the two middle categories existed on a very narrow margin. The villagers themselves explicitly named only three wealth categories within the village, based on rice production, and two additional categories of "rich" landowners in neighboring villages.

The economic position of the village as a whole could be affected by war, famine, and fluctuations in the price of cash crops. Upward or downward mobility of individual households was determined by a variety of specific factors. Where the margin of economic viability is narrow, illness, a single poor crop, an expensive wedding or funeral, a robbery, or litigation could all push a household into extreme poverty.

The local rural elite were wealthy landowners who could live relatively comfortably, even though in comparison with the national-level urban elite they did not appear wealthy. The rural elite were heavily dependent on the labor of sharecroppers who worked their land, and they made significant profit from lending money to the chronically indebted peasantry at exorbitant rates. The rural elite thus had a vested interest in maintaining the long-established peasant landholding system, which was defined by a large, high-density agrarian population, living under very marginal conditions. The system's basic features—especially landless laborers, sharecroppers, mortgages, and high rates of indebtedness—severely inhibit upward mobility.

Bangladesh and the Green Revolution

Why didn't the Green Revolution significantly reduce poverty in Bangladesh?

As discussed in Chapter 12, the Green Revolution refers to the use of institutionalized agricultural research, large-scale capital resources, and energy-intensive technology to increase per-acre food productivity in the developing world. This approach to agricultural development began in 1943 when the Rockefeller Foundation funded a special project in cooperation with the Mexican government to

---

high-yield variety   High-yield plant varieties developed by selective breeding as part of the Green Revolution.

TABLE 13.2   *Household Economic Categories in Goborgari, 1977*

Category*	Households		Population	
	(no.)	(%)	(no.)	(%)
A: Substandard	15	20	74	19
B: Low	32	43	147	38
C: Moderate	16	21	90	23
D: Comfortable	12	16	81	20

SOURCE: Van Schendel (1981).

Etic categories distinguished by Van Schendel: (A) Substandard: virtually landless, tattered clothing, hungry; income insufficient for year. (B) Low: plow, less than 2 acres, basic annual food and clothing. (C) Moderate: more than 2 acres, 1–3 month's surplus. (D) Comfortable: metal-roofed house, tube well, expensive clothes, bicycle, wristwatches, as status symbols; surplus of 3 months or more. *Native economic categories within Goborgari:* (1) *Chhotolok:* laborers, cannot produce rice. (2) *Moidhom:* sharecroppers, must also buy rice. (3) *Dewani:* eat rice they produce; wealthy landowners in other villages. (4) *Mashari:* wealthy, owners of 10–25 acres. (5) *Adhoni:* very wealthy, owners of more than 25 acres.

improve the yield of grain crops by selective breeding. By the early 1960s, the program had successfully produced a dwarf hybrid wheat capable of tripling yields. In 1966, the Mexican research center became an international agricultural research institute known as CIMMYT (International Center for the Improvement of Wheat and Maize). By 1977, after an intensively funded international campaign, Mexican dwarf HYV (high-yield-variety) wheat was being grown on half of the wheatland throughout the developing world and was replacing many indigenously produced varieties and other crops (CGIAR 1980). CIMMYT became a model for a dozen other similar centers, which are now spread throughout the developing world under the sponsorship of CGIAR (Consultative Group on International Agricultural Research).

The HYV grains are often presented as the primary factors behind the large per-acre yields of the Green Revolution; however, these production increases are won at a cost. The local domesticates that the new plants replace were produced by many generations of local people to fit local environmental conditions and the requirements of small-scale, self-sufficient production techniques. The new plants can be called high-response varieties (HRVs), to emphasize that they depend on expensive inputs (Palmer 1972). The "miracle grains" are extremely demanding plants. They only produce high yields under optimum conditions. They require a specific amount of water and large quantities of chemical fertilizer. They are also vulnerable to disease and pests because they are a genetic monocrop; thus, successful production also requires generous applications of chemical pesticides. They are often dwarf forms because a short stock is needed to support the heavy head of grain, but this leaves the plants more vulnerable to flooding and means that they cannot be grown in many otherwise favorable areas. The special requirements of the new varieties mean that only the largest farmers with the best land and the best connections with the government can take advantage of the new technology and can afford the risk of occasional crop failure (Lappe, Collins, and Fowler 1979).

Joining the Green Revolution means that small farmers are linked to a complex global political economy in which the seeds they plant, the tools they use, and the most critical factors affecting their security, such as land, marketing, wages, and credits, are all removed from effective village control. Ultimately, the fate of "developing" rural villagers is determined by the heads of governments, banks, corporations, foundations, and other international development agencies, all operating through many interconnected bureaucracies. Under the Green Revolution, village-level agricultural production is connected to global-level institutions, by way of national-level institutions, through a series of unequal exchanges, or inputs and outputs, in which power is concentrated at the top at each level and costs and benefits are unevenly distributed.

Figure 13.2 illustrates the three levels—global, national, and village—at which the Green Revolution is organized and lists some of the exchanges between levels. Although the public purpose of this kind of agricultural development is "to help poor peasants feed themselves," at the global level it can be seen that important political and economic ben-

efits accrue to the elites of the donor nations. Many elites at the national level also derive important benefits in the form of food surpluses, land, profits, cheap labor, bribes, and votes. National elites, including government officials at all levels in the bureaucracy and the wealthy in private enterprises (who are often also in government), control the technological and financial inputs, as well as the natural resources of land and water, that make

FIGURE 13.2
*Input–output structure
of the Green Revolution.*

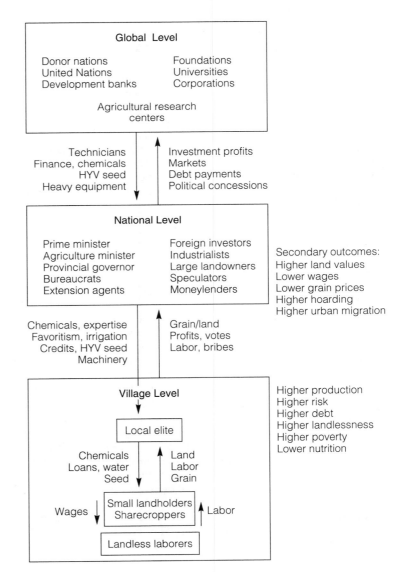

the HYVs produce. In exchange, the developing countries have accepted an increasing burden of debt to international donors and often find that they must submit to specific conditions in order to keep up their payments. Thus, a form of international debt peonage has become part of the development process. Ironically, at the village level, the local elite repeat the unequal exchanges of higher levels, such that the majority of the rural population becomes impoverished, not nourished and empowered, by the Green Revolution.

Impoverishment was one of the unintended secondary outcomes that accompanied increased production as the Green Revolution reached the village level (see Figure 13.2). This occurred as part of an interconnected process in which the new technology was linked to increased debt and landlessness and reduced nutrition in the villages. Nutrition declined because the monocrop HYVs replaced other food crops, while declining incomes made it more difficult for no-longer self-sufficient villagers to buy food. At the national level, land values increased along with grain hoarding by speculators, while grain prices fell. Many rural people forfeited their small landholdings when they were unable to pay off their debts. Increased mechanization reduced the demand for farm labor, and wages fell, driving many people to seek low-paying jobs in the cities. Elites at every level benefited from all of this while the total level of poverty increased (Lappe, Collins, and Fowler 1979).

Green Revolution impoverishment is well illustrated in Bangladesh. The local elite used their political connections to gain control of the tube wells required for irrigating the HYV crops. They also "cultivated" the government extension agents with bribes to make sure that the seeds, expertise, chemicals, and machinery came to them first. The elite dominated village agricultural cooperatives and effectively controlled whatever technological inputs reached the lower-class small landholders and sharecroppers. Skillful manipulation of their political and economic advantages helped the local elite to systematically appropriate the land of less fortunate fellow villagers, while extracting their labor and grain. The landless laborers at the bottom of the village hierarchy had only their labor to exchange for inadequate wages.

Wheat has steadily displaced rice and other crops as a primary food staple in Bangladesh because HYV wheat proved more suitable in Bangladesh than HYV rice. This crop change, however, has also had unexpected cultural consequences (Lindenbaum 1987). The traditional Bangladeshi diet consists of rice, lentils, fish, and vegetables. As inexpensive HYV wheat has become widely available, it has become the dominant food. The poor, who can afford little else, must abandon their preferred foods and eat wheat three meals a day even though this means a decline in the caloric and nutritional quality of their diet. Culturally, rice remains the most important food and is considered the essential element of a meal, whereas wheat is treated as a foreign snack food and is understandably associated with disease by villagers.

Some development experts have argued that the expansion of wheat production in Bangladesh benefits women because many women, who were formerly employed as rice hullers but were displaced by machines, may now find employment harvesting and threshing wheat. However, this work is taken only by the poorest women because it violates *purdah* restrictions, is very heavy and difficult work, and must take place during the hottest time of year.

THE FAILED PROMISE OF GROWTH, 1950–2000

During the last half of the twentieth century, the previous era of colonialism was replaced by a new era of international development. New international agencies, many of them formed in the aftermath of World War II, together with governments, philanthropic foundations, and private agencies, jointly engaged in a massive effort to improve public health and increase economic productivity. The assumption was that such development would raise living standards and reduce poverty throughout the world, but the reality was that the number of poor actually increased. Development failed to achieve its stated goals because poverty was treated primarily as a technical problem, rather than a cultural problem of scale and power.

TABLE 13.3   *UN Development Issues and Strategies, 1950–1999*

Decade	Issues	Strategies
1950–1959	Disease Poverty Ignorance	Public health programs Public education Technology transfer Promotion of economic growth
1960–1969	Population Urban growth Income inequality	Integrated economic and social growth
1970–1979	Social equity Global disparity Human environment	Unified economic-social-political approach
1980–1989	Foreign debt Energy cost Economic downturn	Human development Popular participation Grassroots development Appropriate technology International development cooperation
1990–1999	Poverty	Labor-intensive development Human-capital improvement

SOURCES: United Nations (1952, 1963, 1975) and World Bank (1988, 1989, 1990, 1991).

The United Nations and Development Decades

How have the United Nations and the World Bank historically diagnosed the problem of global poverty? What solutions were proposed?

The United Nations (UN) is the most prominent international organization concerned with global development issues. The UN Charter, which was formally adopted in 1945 by fifty-one nations, specifies that the promotion of "social progress and better standards of living" and "economic and social advancement of all peoples" are among the principal aims of the United Nations. Over the years since its founding, the United Nations has focused on a changing series of development issues and has proposed a variety of development strategies (see Table 13.3). To formulate and implement its development effort, the United Nations has also constructed an elaborate institutional framework of specialized agencies, councils, commissions, funds, and programs, each chartered by formal resolutions.

By the end of World War II, it was obvious to world leaders that much of the world was seriously impoverished. Vast numbers of people in many countries were living under conditions that were intolerable from a humanitarian perspective. Furthermore, because impoverished peoples made poor producers and consumers in the global economy and were potential sources of political instability, it was in their "enlightened self-interest" for wealthy industrialized countries to attempt to alleviate world poverty. War-caused impoverishment could be solved by reconstruction, but most authorities assumed that global poverty was caused by a vicious cycle of disease, ignorance, and poverty and would be eliminated by the transfer of industrial technology and education from rich to poor countries. In 1948, the United Nations began the international campaign to improve the human condition by issuing the Universal Declaration of Human Rights, which stated, "Everyone has the right to a standard of living adequate for the health and well-being of himself and of his family, including food, clothing, housing and medical care" (United Nations 1952:22).

As its first major development initiative, in 1949 the United Nations began its Expanded Program of Technical Assistance for Economic Development of Under-Developed Countries. In 1950, the United

TABLE 13.4   *Social Conditions in North America, Asia, Africa, and Latin America, 1947–1949*

	North America	Asia	Africa	Latin America
Birth rate/1000	25	42.5	42.5	40
Death rate/1000	10	30	27.5	17
Natural increase	15	12.5	15	23
Infant mortality/1000 births*	31.8	88	177	119.9
Life expectancy at birth†	68.7	27	33	39

SOURCE: United Nations (1952).

*National averages in the Asian countries Ceylon, Federation of Malaya, and Singapore; in the African country Sierra Leone; and in the Latin American countries Chile, Mexico, and Venezuela.

†National averages in the North American country United States (whites), in the Asian country India (1921–1931), in the African country Mauritius, and in the Latin American country Peru (Lima, 1933–1935).

Nations placed fifty technical experts in sixteen countries and expended $20 million on projects, while a UN affiliate, the International Bank for Reconstruction and Development (IBRD), or the World Bank, loaned $279 million to governments for large-scale development projects. This action showed that global poverty was considered to be a problem that would respond to increased technical proficiency and economic expansion.

Because, according to the UN Charter, the Economic and Social Council (ECOSOC) was expected to "help solve international problems in the economic, social, humanitarian and cultural fields," the General Assembly in 1949 asked it to prepare a general report on the world social situation. The council report, which was issued in 1952, emphasized standard of living and was based on existing data drawn from official government sources. Researchers examined basic demography, health, food, housing, education, and labor and found that conditions were shockingly "inadequate" for more than half of the world's people. The council compiled data showing dramatically higher fertility, crude mortality, and infant mortality rates and much lower life expectancy rates for populations in Asia, Africa, and Latin America, in comparison with North America. For example, infant mortality in some African countries was more than five times the North American rate, and life expectancy throughout much of the world was half that of North Americans (see Table 13.4).

The council report offered no absolute definition of *underdevelopment* or *poverty*. But it did provide figures showing that two-thirds of the world's population had only 17 doctors per 100,000 people and earned only $41 per person per year, whereas the "developed" 20 percent of the world earned $461 per person and had 106 doctors per 100,000 people (see Table 13.5). Such inequality had obvious implications for public health.

During the 1950s, UN experts treated the economic and social aspects of development as separate issues, and they focused on improving specific target indicators at national levels, especially in the area of public health. Initial efforts focused on relatively easily combated mass diseases such as

TABLE 13.5   *Average Social Conditions in Developed Versus Underdeveloped Countries, 1947–1949*

	Developed	Underdeveloped
Percentage of world population	20	66
Annual/person income (U.S. $)	461	41
Food supply (daily calories/person)	3040	2150
Physicians/100,000 people	106	17
Life expectancy at birth	63	30

SOURCE: United Nations (1952).

malaria, yaws, hookworm, tuberculosis, and gastrointestinal diseases, which accounted for much of the elevated mortality in the world and which responded readily to the insecticide DDT and to penicillin. Nutritional diseases, such as beriberi (vitamin B deficiency) and kwashiorkor (protein deficiency), were considered to be more intractable because they were caused by "ignorance and poverty" rather than microbes. For many development planners, disease was the most basic problem. As the council report explained,

A community burdened with ill-health is an impoverished community. There is a vicious circle: disease—underproduction—poverty—poor health services—more disease, which is manifest in those underdeveloped countries where the majority of a people are afflicted with gross diseases which rob them of vitality and initiative and which create social lethargy. . . . The control of disease . . . is a precondition of economic and social development. The advance of any community depends on the extent to which it reduces the burden of ill health which squanders human resources, wastes food in nourishing bacteria and parasites, produces social lethargy, and prevents people and countries from developing their full capacities. (United Nations 1952:22, 36)

This emphasis on technical progress steadily accelerated in the 1950s. By 1960, after a decade of major development effort and steady improvement in highly visible areas of public health and formal education, several ominous global trends had become inescapably obvious. In its 1963 Report on the World Situation, the UN Economic and Social Council observed that global population increased by 19 percent during the 1950s. Such a dramatic increase was partly due to a rapid decline in death rates. At a global level, the crude death rate dropped from an estimated 26 per 1000 in 1937 to 18 by 1960, while fertility rates remained approximately constant. A demographic change of this magnitude was absolutely unprecedented in human history and gave rise to the term *population explosion*. In specific countries, the figures were truly remarkable. For example, in Ceylon (Sri Lanka), overall mortality dropped from 25 to 10.1 per 1000 people, and infant mortality from 183 to 69 per 1000 live births. The global impact of these changes was much higher than most demographers had at first expected and led to a doubling in world population between 1950 and 1990.

Ironically, the world population increase experienced by 1960, in the absence of changes in wealth distribution, meant that the absolute number of impoverished people actually increased, even though the proportion of impoverished may have declined as a percentage of total population in certain countries. The UN report also observed that the gap between developed and less developed countries had widened in regard to consumption of material goods and per-capita national income, while inequality within individual developing countries increased. The UN report was emphatic on this point:

In many less developed countries, growth in national income appears to have been shared disproportionately by the minority already well-to-do, while in richer countries certain disadvantaged minorities have continued to lag behind the majorities in growth of income. (1963:2)

Even before the official report detailing the failures of previous development efforts was released, UN planners called for "integrated development" and initiated a 10-year plan designating the 1960s as the UN Development Decade. The Development Decade Resolution, adopted unanimously by the UN General Assembly in 1961, specified that each developing country should achieve a target annual growth rate of 5 percent in national income by 1969.

During the 1970s, a "unified" or "holistic approach" was recommended by development planners to solve the inequality problems recognized a decade earlier. A Second UN Development Decade was proclaimed in 1971, calling on poor countries to increase their annual growth rates of gross national product (GNP) per person by 3.5 percent, their annual agricultural output by 4 percent, and their manufacturing output by 8 percent.

Midway through the Second Development Decade, the original goal of a better standard of living for all peoples was still far out of reach. A new UN report found that development had not achieved "any significant narrowing of disparities in income or levels of living" (United Nations 1975:1), either within individual countries or between different countries at the global level. National development was helping to create wealthy national elites even as the absolute number of severely impoverished people continued to grow. Frustrated UN planners were forced to conclude that "policies geared to national or macro-growth objectives do not of themselves give rise to a more equitable distribution of income" (United Nations 1975:13).

During the 1970s, people became more aware that the existence of the global market economy made conditions in the developing world different from conditions existing in Europe during the Industrial Revolution. This implied that technological changes by themselves would not achieve development. In 1974, the United Nations even recommended the creation of a "New International Economic Order" based on more equitable trade relations between nations. During the 1980s, however, the rise in energy costs, the burden of development debts, and the related problems of inflation and economic recession dampened hopes for a new economic order.

Although the implications of expanding impoverishment were still not fully understood, new development issues continued to emerge. By the mid-1970s, the obvious failure of many projects at the local level made it desirable to refer to the need for "popular participation" in development. This meant some degree of decentralization and in-

volvement of local target populations in planning. A further issue emerging at this time was the environment, because many large-scale development projects were degrading the "human environment," simplifying ecosystems, lowering the quality of soil and water, and generating pollution.

As the Third UN Development Decade came to an end in 1990, the World Bank estimated that more than 1 billion people were living in absolute poverty, with annual incomes of less than $370 per person (see Figure 13.3) (World Bank 1990).

The wealth disparity between nations after four decades of concerted development effort is dramatically illustrated by the World Bank's international rank order of nations by annual per-capita GNP based on 1988 data. The wealthiest nation, Switzerland, showed a per-capita GNP of $27,500, which was 275 times greater than that of the poorest nation, Mozambique, with $100 per capita. These dollar GNP figures cannot be directly compared with the figures presented in Table 13.5 for 1947–1949 because of inflation. GNP figures also do not consider wealth distribution within a country and can disguise great inequities.

FIGURE 13.3
El Salvadoran peasant family. At the end of the Third UN Development Decade in 1990, there were more than 1 billion people living in absolute poverty. In 1988 the World Bank considered El Salvador to be a lower-middle-economy country based on GNP per capita.

The World Bank's 1995 ranking, based on 1993 population estimates, shows that only 24 nations, with just under 15 percent of the world's population, were high-income nations with per-capita GNPs of over $12,600, whereas 45 nations, more than a third of the 132 nations listed, were considered low income with GNPs under $660. Low income correlated with poor scores on many indicators of social well-being. For example, the average infant mortality rate in low-income countries was 64 per 1000, eight times the rate of high-income countries. Fifteen African countries showed infant mortality rates of over 100 per 1000 live births (see Figure 13.4). The 42 poorest nations included some 3 billion people, approximately 55 percent of the world's population in 1993.

In 1988, near the end of the Third UN Development Decade, there were more impoverished people in the world than ever before. Although global averages showed some improvements, the UN goal of an adequate standard of living for everyone clearly had not been realized. Obviously, poverty is not a problem of technological "underdevelopment" or "ignorance"; it is an amplification of the inherent inequities in the social hierarchies of political-scale cultures. These inequities are intensified by the operation of the global market economy. If eliminating poverty were the sole objective of technologically focused development programs, an impartial observer in 1988 might have concluded that the wrong course was being followed. But by then, development efforts had come to serve many other interests.

Utopian Futurists and the Growth of Global Poverty, 1965–2000

What kind of economic future did influential development planners and futurists predict for the world by the year 2000? What actually happened? Why did their judgments fail? What are the problems with applying a single measure of living standard to measure global poverty?

The culture of economic development had its roots in the recommendations of various economic specialists and planners who produced influential books during this period predicting a utopian future in a fully commercialized world. But these uto-pian visions were flawed by a narrow view of human cultural history and by a focus on national-level measures of economic activity. To better understand what went wrong, it will be helpful to examine the thinking behind international development efforts and to compare the reality of global poverty with the predictions.

In 1967, Hudson Institute futurists Herman Kahn and Anthony Wiener published their predictions for a "surprise free" world in the year 2000, assuming a continuation of what they called the *multifold trend* of technological progress and economic growth. Their multifold trend is the commercialization process. They traced it back to the eleventh and twelfth centuries—precisely where we began in Chapter 11 with our examination of the rise of money and markets in medieval Europe. Kahn and Wiener were convinced that unrestricted economic growth was benefiting the world. They optimistically expected that for at least the next 30 years, every nation would follow the *natural* progression of development stages from takeoff, through maturity, to the high mass consumption outlined so elegantly in M.I.T. economist Walt Rostow's influential 1960 book *The Stages of Economic Growth*. Rostow conceived of economic *takeoff* as a watershed event in which the "forces making for economic progress . . . [would] come to dominate the society" and overcome the "old blocks and resistances to steady growth" (1960:7). As advisor to presidents Kennedy and Johnson, Rostow's utopian vision of unlimited growth supported the thinking and interests of America's top intellectual, political, and economic leaders. In reality, of course, many of these people were the "forces making for economic progress" that ultimately directed the global flow of finance capital.

In line with Rostow's view, the Hudson Institute futurists expected world population to double and the global economy to increase more than fivefold by the year 2000. They ranked nations by per-capita gross national product and predicted that 25 percent of the world's population would bask in the luxury of "post-industrial" societies by the end of the century, controlling 85 percent of the world's wealth, while the rest of the world steadily grew to maturity and mass consumption. Kahn and Wiener expected growth to dramatically improve economic conditions in the less developed nations,

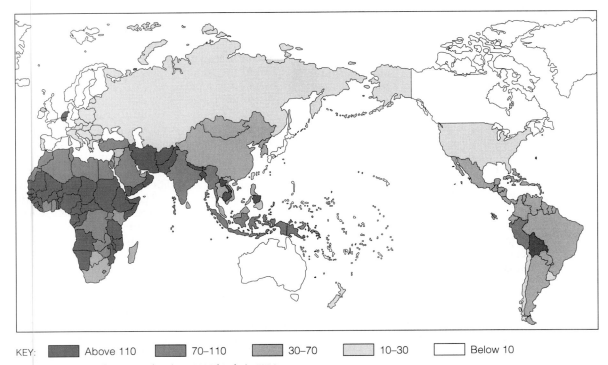

KEY: Above 110   70–110   30–70   10–30   Below 10

FIGURE 13.4 *Infant mortality (per 1000 births), 1988.*

although the absolute gap between rich and poor would increase.

By 1997, 30 years later, population growth turned out to be very close to the Hudson Institute's predictions, and economic growth was only slightly lower than expected. But, most significantly, poverty was much more prevalent and wealth far more concentrated than they expected. A serious short-coming of the futurists' predictions was that they focused on **gross national product (GNP)** or **gross domestic product (GDP)** rather than real people. These aggregate measures of the flow of money, goods, and services make no distinctions between rich and poor or between different kinds of goods and services. Economic growth by itself need not reduce poverty. Thus, capital-intensive industries may generate tremendous economic growth, meas-ured as increased cash flow, but produce few new jobs. The arms race was also a big boost for gross national product even as it diverted support away from public health and education.

To assess the human effects of economic devel-opment more meaningfully, it is necessary to view the problem differently by moving beyond national-level measures and considering how people use their income. What is needed is a single cross-national, before-and-after measure of standard of living applied to all the world's people. Such a mea-sure can be approximated using the World Bank's estimates of percentage share of **national income** in individual countries by quintile (World Bank 1995:Table 30). This measure can be converted to a per-capita income figure for each percentage group. People can then be sorted by income level into three broad levels of economic well-being: growth, maintenance, or poor. This assumes (1) that *growth*-level income is sufficient to permit sav-ing and investment, (2) that a *maintenance*-level in-come meets all basic needs, and (3) that people with a *poor*-level income must borrow to meet basic needs. It must be emphasized that for cultures that are not dominated by the commercialization process, monetary income is a meaningless measure of living standard. Obviously, too, cultural definitions of basic needs and monetary requirements will change as development occurs. However, because economic planners now treat capital and labor as part of a single pool in a one-world economy, it seems reasonable to insist that a single monetary measure of economic prosperity be uniformly applied to everyone in the world. Presumably, development agencies hope to achieve such cultural homogeneity for all of humanity.

The following analysis arbitrarily treats per-capita annual incomes of less than $2500 as poor-level, incomes of $2500–12,499 as maintenance-level, and incomes over $12,500 as growth-level. These figures place the standard-of-living thresholds higher for the crucial maintenance level than is implied by the World Bank's 1995 classification of national economies by per-capita GNP, which places *low* income at below $700, *middle* at $700–12,000, and *high* at $12,000+. The World Bank would, in effect, minimize the number of poor in the world, whereas my figures more realistically reflect the living-standard levels prevailing in the developed nations that most benefit from global economic growth. My figures expand the concept of poverty by attempting to include all those who must borrow to meet basic needs and are unable to own land or their own homes, together with the World Bank's "absolute poor," within a single "poor" category. This analysis also shows more poverty because sorting income figures by quintiles within each country more accurately reflects the extremes of wealth and poverty in particular countries than does a single national-level per-capita GNP figure. Using these consistent categories, and adjusting for inflation, it is possible to ask whether economic globalization since 1965 produced more wealth than poverty in the world.

The new totals for 1997 show more than 4 billion (70 percent) poor people, 1.23 billion (25 percent) maintenance-level people, and 300 million (5 percent) growth-level people (see Figures 13.5–13.7). The figures show a decline in the proportion who were poor by this new standard, but their actual numbers increased much more dramatically than the World Bank's categories suggest. By 1997, there were 260 million new individuals with growth-level incomes worldwide, but this increase

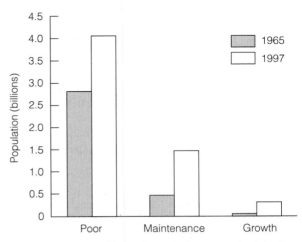

FIGURE 13.5   *World population by living standard, 1965 and 1997. (SOURCES:* Information Please Almanac Atlas and Yearbook 1967 *1966, United Nations 1968a, 1968b: Table 7B,* World Almanac and Book of Facts 1998, World Bank 1995.)

was more than overshadowed by a new cohort of 1.25 billion poor. The wealthiest 5 percent of the world's population enjoyed 40 percent of global income. The 25 percent of maintenance-level people in the global "middle class" also had more than their share with 40 percent of the wealth, whereas the 70 percent of the world who were poor were left with less than 20 percent of global income. Clearly, if we accept this global standard of economic well-being, growth since 1965 impoverished more people than it enriched.

The Roots of Poverty: Overpopulation or Development?

What is the argument that poverty is produced primarily by inequality, not overpopulation, and that it is intensified by development itself?

---

gross national product (GNP)   The total output of a country's goods and services, by monetary value; includes profits from foreign activities.
gross domestic product (GDP)   The total output of goods and services produced within a country, by monetary value.
national income   All wages, salaries, and profits received by the members of a country, calculated by subtracting various indirect taxes from NNP (net national product).

FIGURE 13.6
World population and income, 1965. (SOURCES:
Information Please Almanac Atlas and Yearbook 1967 *1966, United Nations 1968a, 1968b: Table 7B.)*

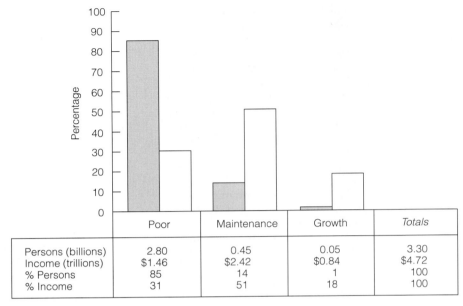

	Poor	Maintenance	Growth	*Totals*
Persons (billions)	2.80	0.45	0.05	3.30
Income (trillions)	$1.46	$2.42	$0.84	$4.72
% Persons	85	14	1	100
% Income	31	51	18	100

KEY: Persons   Income

FIGURE 13.7
World population and income, 1997. (SOURCES:
World Almanac and Book of Facts 1998, World Bank 1995.)

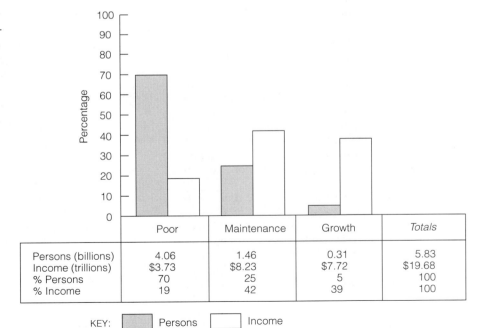

	Poor	Maintenance	Growth	*Totals*
Persons (billions)	4.06	1.46	0.31	5.83
Income (trillions)	$3.73	$8.23	$7.72	$19.68
% Persons	70	25	5	100
% Income	19	42	39	100

KEY: Persons   Income

Especially since the 1960s, when the population explosion began to be recognized as a global problem, overpopulation has often been identified as the primary cause of impoverishment in the developing world. It has been easy to attribute hunger and malnutrition to "too many people" and "too little food," as biologist Paul Ehrlich did in his influential book, *The Population Bomb* (1968). However, a close examination of the evidence shows that impoverishment is not that simple. People die in famines because food is scarce, but food is scarce because people lack *entitlement* to food—that is, either they are unable to produce food directly, they are landless, or they are unable to purchase food (Sen 1981). Thousands died in famines in Bangladesh in 1943 and 1974 because they did not have the social power to give them access to food.

Defense strategist Thomas Homer-Dixon (1991) makes a population pressure argument similar to Ehrlich's, warning that population growth is linked to environmental stress and "environmentally induced economic decline" that causes poverty, social upheaval, and conflict. He states this explicitly:

As developing societies produce less wealth because of environmental problems, their citizens will probably become increasingly discontented by the widening gap between their actual level of economic achievement and the level they feel they deserve. (1991:109)

Homer-Dixon warns that the desperate poor might then attempt to impose "distributive justice," which would only lead to authoritative, abusive regimes. What Homer-Dixon fails to consider is that the growth of global capitalism and the global financialization process itself produce environmental stress and shift the costs to poor countries, regions, and communities.

Anthropologists who have examined the population stress argument in specific regions have consistently found that the distribution of land-ownership, and related political factors, was the crucial cause of both poverty and environmental deterioration—not population density. For example, William Durham (1979) conducted an in-depth ethnohistorical and ethnographic analysis of the dynamics of population and land scarcity in Honduras and El Salvador in 1892–1974. He found that the expansion of commercial agriculture by large landholders on the most productive lands forced the peasantry into marginal lands. Increasingly, anthropologists treat these issues as problems of *political ecology*, rather than population pressure (Durham 1995).

Susan George (1992) observes that between 1982 and 1990, rich countries in the Northern Hemisphere transferred $927 billion in economic assistance, charity, loans, and private investment capital to poor debtor nations in the Southern Hemisphere to finance poor countries' economic growth. The investor nations received $1.345 trillion in return, for a modest profit of $418 billion. The developing nations used the money for massive projects such as dams, highways, power plants, manufacturing facilities, and vast agricultural programs. Much of this money came directly back to the rich nations that supplied some of the heavy equipment and material. These projects often contributed directly to environmental stress, and because they favored the interests of the wealthy, they also contributed to the further impoverishment of millions. Many poor people were pushed off their small landholdings by wealthy developers and were forced onto marginal lands on steep slopes, and forested regions, where further environmental damage is taking place.

The impoverishing dynamics of this financially driven process were intensified, beginning in the 1980s, by the **structural adjustments** that were imposed by the World Bank and the International Monetary Fund (IMF) to help poor debtor nations repay their international loans. Structural adjustments involve currency devaluations, reduced social support programs, and increased pressure to produce for export, which further stress the poor and the environment.

The United States, AID, and the Development Industry

What role does the United States play in the international development arena? To what extent is development assistance a self-serving activity?

The formal structures through which technical assistance and development finance reach the

---

structural adjustments Austerity measures designed to increase foreign exchange through increased exports.

FIGURE 13.8
The structure of international technical assistance.

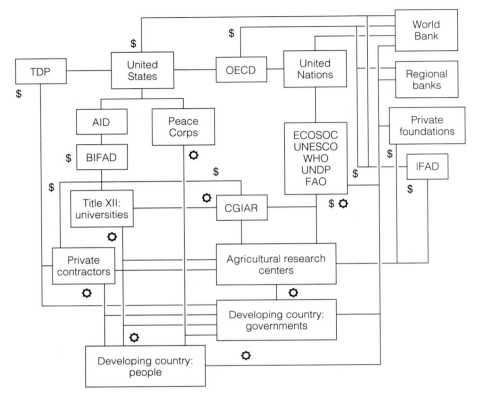

KEY: ⚙ Technical assistance $ Financial assistance

developing world consist of many complex bureaucracies linked in a ponderous network. Priorities are set by relatively few key organizations at the top that make decisions that affect the smallest details of life for millions of people living in remote villages throughout the impoverished world. Development decisions pass through so many hands before actually being implemented that the entire enterprise is extremely costly and often proves counterproductive. The development establishment itself is a classic example of the maladaptive process described by Roy Rappaport (1977a, 1977b), in which high-level regulators take over lower-level functions (see Chapter 10). Understanding how this can happen requires some knowledge of aid categories, specific organizations, their functions, and interconnections.

The United Nations and related agencies offer what is called ***multilateral development assis-*** ***tance*** because it is financed by many nations and thus must offer assistance without political considerations or special trade preconditions. All development assistance given by individual countries is called ***official development assistance (ODA).*** It must either be a gift or grant or be loaned at less than commercial rates. The largest aid category was bilateral assistance, or ODA supplied directly from one country to another. ***Bilateral development assistance*** can, and often does, have political and trade conditions attached and thus can serve the interests of the donor. A donor country might give only to "friendly" countries and then require them to spend their aid money on goods and services provided by the donor.

Figure 13.8 presents a simplified view of the network through which technical assistance is channeled from the United States and the Organization for Economic Cooperation and Development (OECD) countries to developing nations as bilateral aid and through the major multilateral aid organizations. This figure emphasizes agricultural technology. The acronyms appearing in Figure 13.8 are identified in the box entitled "International Assistance Agencies."

Global poverty has been consistently treated as a technological problem, partly because professional elites who are far removed from the daily realities of poverty formulate and finance development policies. Development is much more than a humanitarian concern; it has become a thoroughly institutionalized and highly complex industry with important political and economic functions for the wealthy donors that may be unrelated to the needs of the poor.

The assistance policies of the United States deserve a closer look because they play such a major role in the development process. U.S. development policies and programs were formally initiated by Point Four in President Truman's 1949 inaugural address, in which he declared, "We must embark on a bold new program for making the benefits of our scientific advance and industrial progress available for the improvement and growth of underdeveloped areas."

This was at the beginning of the Cold War, and the objective of Point Four development assistance was to use U.S. technology to advance U.S. interests in the world as part of Truman's policy of Soviet "containment." The U.S. development effort received a major boost in 1961 under President Kennedy when the Agency for International Development (AID), the Peace Corps, and the Alliance for Progress were all launched (see Figure 13.9). In the same year, Kennedy urged the UN General Assembly to create the UN Development Decade program. Between 1962 and 1969, a staggering $33.5 billion worth of food commodities and economic assistance flowed directly to developing countries and through development banks and the Peace Corps (U.S. Department of Commerce 1990).

Significant changes were brought about in U.S. policies by the 1975 Freedom from Hunger Title XII amendments to the Foreign Assistance Act of 1961, further reinforcing the narrow view that world hunger was primarily a technological problem. The Title XII amendments directed AID to recruit U.S. universities to apply "science to solving food and nutrition problems of the developing countries" (U.S. Code 1982, Title 22, Section 2220a). The assumption of this legislation was that because agricultural research, especially by the land-grant universities, had successfully increased farm productivity in the United States, this was the best way to deal with hunger in the impoverished world. The potential costs in energy, resources, and social inequality of implementing American-style factory farming in the developing world were disregarded.

U.S. development policy shifted again in the 1980s under the Reagan administration. Although continuous economic growth and technological advance remained the primary development objectives, "free market forces" and the "private sector" were now considered "the principal engines of sustainable development" (United States AID 1985:iv). AID's new development objectives were, in some cases perhaps realistically, less than the goals set by the United Nations for the Third Development Decade. For example, the United Nations wanted infant mortality rates to be 50 per 1000 live births or below by the year 2000, but AID set below 75 as the target. Privatization called for the increased commercialization of agricultural systems while emphasizing biotechnology. Seed and fertilizer companies were to become "extension agents," and many poor farmers were encouraged to produce export crops instead of locally consumed subsistence crops. The problem with applying this approach to the impoverished world is that market forces select for large-scale enterprises and inequality. In the United States, as shown in Chapter 12, this process makes small farms "uneconomical" and forces much of the rural population into the cities. Furthermore, many poor peasants simply lack the financial resources to take the expensive risks that producing for the international export market requires. Critics also charge that some aid

---

multilateral development assistance Aid that is donated by several countries and channeled through a single international agency such that it can be free of political favoritism.
official development assistance (ODA) Aid given by a government for development purposes, including both direct gifts and low-rate loans.
bilateral development assistance Aid that is given directly from one country to another and that may be given under conditions that favor the donor.

International Assistance Agencies

AID   Agency for International Development: Founded in 1961 to administer the U.S. government's foreign economic assistance program.

BIFAD   Board for International Food and Agricultural Development: Founded in 1977 to promote U.S. land-grant university involvement in AID agricultural development activities under the provisions of the Title XII amendment to the Foreign Assistance Act.

CGIAR   Consultative Group on International Agricultural Research: Formed in 1971 to coordinate and sponsor international agricultural research centers in various countries; a major promoter of the Green Revolution.

ECOSOC   Economic and Social Council: An official body of the UN organization with primary responsibility for coordinating development activities in the United Nations and related agencies.

FAO   Food and Agricultural Organization of the United Nations: The UN special agency formed in 1945 to promote food production; directs the Freedom from Hunger campaign.

IFAD   International Fund for Agricultural Development: Founded in 1976 to assist the poorest countries make technological improvements in food production.

OECD   Organization for European Economic Cooperation and Development: Formed in 1961 and composed primarily of wealthy industrial nations, its member countries provide official development assistance (ODA) to developing countries, either individually (bilateral assistance) or on a multilateral basis.*

TDP   Trade and Development Program: Created in 1980 to help U.S. technicians conduct feasibility studies for development projects in middle-income developing countries that might not otherwise qualify for technical assistance; serves to promote the export of U.S. technology.

UNDP   UN Development Programme: Established in 1966 to coordinate all development activities of the United Nations and related agencies.

UNESCO   UN Educational, Scientific and Cultural Organization: A UN special agency, established in 1946, that promotes international welfare.

WHO   World Health Organization: A UN special agency, established in 1948, that promotes public health in developing countries.

*Multilateral development agencies provide support that has been pooled from many sources. OECD members in 1990 were Australia, Austria, Belgium, Canada, Denmark, Finland, France, West Germany, Greece, Iceland, Ireland, Italy, Japan, Luxembourg, Netherlands, New Zealand, Norway, Portugal, Spain, Sweden, Switzerland, Turkey, United Kingdom, United States, and Yugoslavia.

FIGURE 13.9   *Peace Corps volunteers inspecting a rural water system in the Bolivian Andes. The Peace Corps, initiated by President Kennedy in 1961, has played an important role in America's development aid program.*

programs may be an obstacle to democratic development because they support unpopular governments and thereby delay necessary land reform while devaluing the products of local farmers (Lappe, Collins, and Kinley 1981; Lappe, Schurman, and Danaher 1987).

ALTERNATIVE DEVELOPMENT STRATEGIES

The dominant development strategy pursued by the most powerful international agencies calls for high-energy industrial technology and rapid growth in the total output of goods and services as measured by GNP per capita. It is recognized that, just as in the early centers of capitalist development in Europe and North America, poverty and inequality may actually increase as economic growth occurs, but many assume that everyone will eventually benefit as long as growth remains strong. Many agencies acknowledge that the world's poorest groups may need some special assistance and perhaps even low-cost, environmentally sensitive "appropriate technology," but this does not negate the importance of perpetual economic growth.

The only major alternative to the perpetual growth approach to development is wealth redistribution emphasizing social justice. In effect, this is a development process that would return priority to the sapienization goals championed by domestic-scale cultures. Ideally, the satisfaction of basic human needs with maximum social equality would be the objective of this kind of development. This alternative is inherently difficult because it offers no immediate benefits to the wealthy and powerful; however, it has been tried in a few cases with some success, as the following examples show.

Wealth Redistribution as Development in India

How did radical political reforms in the Indian state of Kerala actually improve the quality of life for the poor?

The state of Kerala in southwest India represents an unusual attempt at development directed by the poor to meet their needs. This was a social transformation process organized by poor farmers, workers, and tenants, who engaged in decades of political struggle to transform a cultural system that was dominated by inequities of caste and grossly concentrated wealth and power. This struggle for social justice, as analyzed by Richard Franke and Barbara Chasin (1989), has important implications for development theory. When Franke and Chasin assessed Kerala's economy in 1989, it had not grown significantly, as measured by per-capita GNP, and unemployment remained high. But the people's basic needs were being more effectively satisfied than in many countries where more economic growth had occurred.

According to Franke and Chasin (1989), protests against caste injustices opened the way for a broad range of social reforms. The Kerala variant of the

Hindu caste system required some of the most extreme and degrading forms of ritual separation in India. Lower-caste people were kept in perpetual servitude to higher-caste people while being denied access to marketplaces, temples, schools, and public roads. In a series of peaceful mass protests against these indignities during the 1920s and 1930s, low-caste people and their political supporters in the Indian Communist party used open violations of the taboos to win political reforms that eventually eased caste restrictions. "Eat-ins" were held in which higher-caste political organizers ate with untouchables in their homes, thus publicly violating the Hindu concepts of purity and pollution that sustained caste differences. Anticaste movements eventually combined with labor movements and peasant unions, and together they succeeded in forcing the government to adopt wide-ranging political reforms that restructured society, redistributing wealth and power. These reform movements were conducted without resorting to armed violence, even though protesters were often murdered and imprisoned.

Before land reform was implemented in 1969, Kerala's agricultural land, the basic source of wealth and subsistence in the state, was controlled primarily by an upper class of Brahman landlords, who constituted about 2 percent of the population. The Brahmans owned both the irrigated rice fields and the plots where poor farmers built their house compounds and maintained small food-producing gardens. The landlords leased their land to a class of superior tenants, who often subleased to inferior tenants, who, if possible, hired untouchables to do the actual farmwork. Poor farmers were often perpetually in debt yet were forced to pay 50–94 percent of their gross harvest to landlords or face eviction. The land reform process turned former tenants into landowners while compensating the former landlords. Limits were also set on the size of landholdings.

Specific food distribution programs, some underway since early in the twentieth century, have included school lunch programs, free daily meal programs for infants and their mothers, and a system of ration shops selling basic foodstuffs to the poorest households at controlled prices. These programs appear to have had a significant effect. Regional food surveys in Kerala in the 1980s suggested that people were getting approximately 2300 kilocalories per day. This was above the national average of 2126 kilocalories and much more than the 1500 kilocalories that the impoverished sugarcane workers in northeast Brazil were receiving, as discussed earlier. Childhood growth studies show that Kerala's young children are doing slightly better than the average for India, even though percapita income is actually lower in Kerala.

Political reformers in Kerala regarded adequate housing, clean water, sanitation, and vaccinations as public health issues and campaigned for government programs to make these basic needs available to everyone. These goals have not been fully achieved, but the government has been successful in making health services, including doctors, primary health care centers, and hospitals, more available in Kerala than in other parts of India. The clearest measure of the overall success of this wealth redistribution effort can be seen in Kerala's figures for adult literacy (78 percent), life expectancy (68 years), and infant mortality (27 per 1000 live births), which were significantly better than the Indian 1986 average of 43 percent, 57 years, and 86 per 1000, respectively. Kerala's infant mortality rate of 27 was a spectacular achievement in comparison with the rate of 211 that Scheper-Hughes (1992) found in Bom Jesus in the Brazilian northeast in 1987. Improvements in infant mortality, life expectancy, and education, together with government pension programs, have reduced the incentive to raise large families, particularly for poor farmers. When these social gains were combined with government-supported family-planning programs and general improvements in the status of women, birth rates declined significantly in comparison with the rest of India.

Conventional development programs emphasize economic opportunities for men and often adversely affect the economic contribution of women in the household. This is certainly the case in India and is a factor in the recent increase in bride burnings, as discussed in Chapter 9. Thus, it is significant that the health status of women in Kerala is better than elsewhere in India. This improvement in the status of women is due in part to effective social support programs and has occurred despite high rates of female unemployment.

Kerala is a historically unique case, but it suggests that informed underclass groups can organize themselves and use democratic political processes to overcome the disadvantages imposed by the inequities of wealth and power. This kind of redistribution occurred in the absence of economic growth. In this post–Cold War world, it is also important to recognize that in many impoverished countries, leftist or socialist political organizations may be able to contribute positively to development, where externally financed and directed programs may have failed to meet the needs of the most impoverished classes.

Development Anthropology and Peasants

What unique perspectives have anthropologists applied to development problems? In what ways do peasants maximize their subsistence security and social support networks?

Cultural anthropologists enthusiastically supported post–World War II international development efforts by turning their attention to rural peasantries and the urban poor. Many researchers shifted their focus from the functional equilibrium of domestic-scale cultures to the realities of poverty, the process of cultural change, and the "obstacles" to modernization or development progress. This research shift corresponded to changes within anthropology itself. Since 1950, many anthropologists have found full-time employment in development. In 1968, roughly three-quarters of the new PhDs in American anthropology still took academic positions. But by 1982, when there were few new academic positions, only 28 percent found teaching positions, and many of the others took positions as development anthropologists (Weaver 1985). For example, in 1980, there were fifty anthropologists doing development work as full-time employees of AID. This was probably greater than the total number that ever worked as colonial anthropologists for the British empire. In the 1980s, many more American anthropologists conducted temporary contract work through universities or private firms (Hoben 1982). One such firm, the Institute for Development Anthropology, held contracts with AID and the FAO for over $5.8 million in 1987 and had conducted projects in forty-eight countries. "Development" is clearly what many contemporary anthropologists do, often within an academic framework.

The anthropological approach to development and poverty has gone through significant changes since the 1950s. Initially, some prominent an-thropologists uncritically accepted the established view that poverty was caused by ignorance and disease—in effect blaming the poor, or their culture, for poverty while ignoring the inequalities of economic and political power that sustained poverty. For example, Margaret Mead (1961) argued that people everywhere would be modernized and enriched simply by exposure to "obviously better" ways of life. Thus, culture change involved "seeing a light and following it freely" (Mead 1961:19–20). Such a "poverty is ignorance" view did not at first acknowledge that "development" might require outside coercion and might generate legitimate resistance from its intended beneficiaries. Mead's narrow view of cultural development made it easy for planners to overlook the ways in which domestic-scale cultures were already designed to satisfy basic human needs.

Anthropologists Conrad Arensberg and Arthur Niehoff (1964) presented a similar tone of technological arrogance. They emphasized the superiority of industrial technology and compared change agents to "brain surgeons" who were introducing "new ideas, which constitute the medicine of social change" (1964:6). This inherently ethnocentric view of change implicitly denigrated traditional cultures for their backwardness while endorsing bureaucratically planned, technologically based development projects that ignored the views of the target population. Such an approach directly supported the official position of the international development establishment of the time and certainly had widespread popular support. But in the 1960s, few Americans questioned the wisdom of high-energy factory farming or worried about the social or environmental impacts of giant hydroelectric projects.

Many anthropologists have long been aware of the complex ethical issues they face when working for development agencies (Manners 1956). Applied or development anthropologists now subscribe to formal codes of ethical conduct, but many difficult judgments must still be made. Development contractors necessarily have a dual, sometimes irreconcilable, responsibility to their employers and to the people who will be affected by development projects. They must consider the political agenda of funding agencies and the differential costs and benefits at all levels. Predicting all consequences of development changes is not possible, and even the most well-intended programs can still increase poverty and inequality.

Because target populations, the assumed beneficiaries of development programs, often have little power, it is vital that their views be taken into account. When domestic-scale cultures control their own resources and are able to support relatively self-maintaining communities, they often resist development programs designed to integrate them into large-scale national systems. This can create a dilemma for anthropologists who disavow the use of force in development projects. Some early development writers attributed resistance to ethnocentrism on the part of the target people, suggesting that they mistakenly believed their own culture to be superior (Arensberg and Niehoff 1964). Other social engineers even recommended that change agents try to make people feel inadequate so they would desire change (Goodenough 1963). Development anthropologists, however, have increasingly recognized that resistance to change is often justified.

As development efforts were first beginning, some anthropologists correctly identified critical features of peasant culture that acted as apparent obstacles to the kind of development progress envisioned by government planners. However, these researchers also emphasized the rationality and practicality of peasant culture. For example, Robert Redfield (1947) used his "folk society" concept as an ideal type, to draw a contrast between the *peasantry* and members of urban societies. Redfield's folk society was defined by cultural features that also characterize domestic-scale tribal societies, such as small population, homogeneity, high social solidarity, simple division of labor, and economic self-sufficiency. In Redfield's view, peasants were members of former tribal societies that had been incorporated by states. State intervention, however, caused significant cultural changes in the folk society, including inequality, loss of autonomy, and impoverishment.

Focusing on political economy, Eric Wolf (1955, 1957) defined peasants as subsistence agriculturalists who control their own land but do not produce primarily for the market to make a profit. Wolf suggested that a common characteristic of peasants in Latin America and Island Southeast Asia is their organization as *closed corporate communities* in defense against conquest and exploitation by outsiders backed by state authority. Closed corporate communities either own land communally or regularly redistribute ownership of individual plots to ensure equal access for all members. To protect their lands, peasants also try to exclude outsiders and discourage members from becoming too involved with the larger national society. Peasant communities are corporations in that they seek to be self-perpetuating and self-sufficient (see Figure 13.10). They promote internal security by means of *wealth-leveling devices* such as expensive rituals and feasting that tend to reduce economic inequality, while inhibiting economic growth and capital accumulation by consuming potential surplus within the community.

FIGURE 13.10 *Women are making corn tortillas during a fiesta in San Pedro Chenalhó, Chiapas, Mexico. Corn, a symbol of fertility and regeneration, is the primary food eaten and circulated in fiestas. Many domestic-scale subsistence agriculturalists engage in rituals and feasting that promote cohesiveness.*

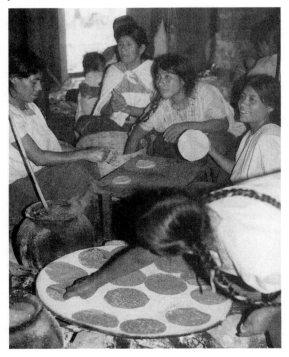

When cultural features of the closed corporate community are practiced by peasants, they are a defense against state exploitation. These same features may also be found in domestic-scale tribal societies, where they inhibit the concentration of internal political and economic power that leads to the state in the first place. Given this self-defense emphasis, peasants often prefer to grow their own locally adapted crops for their proven hardiness, and they emphasize domestic food crops over market crops. They are also likely to reject exotic and expensive agricultural technologies to avoid debt and loss of independence. Peasants maximize subsistence security, and they value social support networks and strategic reserves over risk taking. Such cultural objectives may be conservative, but they are not ignorant or irrational.

George Foster (1965, 1969) identified the "image of limited good" as the key cognitive orientation in peasant societies. **Limited good** refers to the assumption that "all desired things in life . . . exist in finite and unexpandable quantities" (Foster 1969: 83). This view was a direct expression of a stable, egalitarian, predominantly nonmarket economy and meant that a wealthy peasant was gaining his wealth at the expense of his less fortunate neighbors. The contrasting principle of **unlimited good** assumes that "with each passing generation people on average will have more of the good things of life." Unlimited good reflects a capitalist market economy and is compatible with poverty and inequality. Unfortunately, many development planners mistakenly concluded from the limited good concept that peasants were poor because they believed in equality, not because they were oppressed and exploited. (See the box entitled "The Culture of Poverty" for a closer look at this controversy.)

Andean Development: The Vicos Experiment

How did development anthropologists intervene directly in an Andean community to empower the local peasantry? What was the result of this effort?

The Cornell Peru Project conducted at the hacienda of Vicos in the Peruvian Andes from 1952 to 1963 is one of the best-known development anthropology projects (Dobyns, Doughty, and Lasswell 1971). This was a unique, long-term development effort, planned and directed by anthropologists as a **participant intervention** experiment in cultural change designed to empower the peasantry. Using research funds provided by the Carnegie Corporation of New York, the project codirectors, American anthropologist Allan Holmberg, then of Cornell University, and Peruvian anthropologist Mario Vazquez, rented the traditional colonial-style hacienda of Vicos where some 2000 peasants lived as virtual serfs on a 60-square-mile (mi^2) (155-square-kilometer [km^2]) estate. The anthropologists then used their position as managers of the hacienda to gradually turn political power back to the peasants and help them regain control over their ancestral land. This was a novel approach to development and was widely considered a success; however, as an externally imposed solution, the project did not enhance the potential of domestic-scale Andean cultures.

The **hacienda** system in the Peruvian Andes in 1952 was a continuation of colonial social structures created by the Spaniards following their conquest of the Inca empire in the sixteenth century. The original Spanish conquerors created great landed estates for themselves out of the best lands. These estates, or *encomiendas*, like European manors, included rights to extract labor and produce

---

peasantry Village farmers who provide most of their own subsistence but who must pay taxes and are politically and often, to some extent, economically dependent on the central state government.

closed corporate community Communally organized peasants who exclude outsiders and limit the acquisition of wealth and power by their members.

wealth-leveling device Any cultural means, such as ritual feasting, used to redistribute wealth within a community and thereby reduce inequality.

limited good A belief often found in peasant communities that total wealth is limited and that anyone who acquires too much is taking away from others. This is a justification for wealth leveling.

unlimited good The belief in continuous economic growth often used to justify wealth inequality.

participant intervention A form of culture change in which those in control become members of the system they seek to change.

hacienda A Latin American agricultural estate with dependent laborers that produced for local rather than global markets and was designed to maintain the social status and lifestyle of the *hacendado* landowner.

The Culture of Poverty

Anthropologist Oscar Lewis studied Latin American urban poor in Mexico, Puerto Rico, and New York and described some seventy specific features of the *culture of poverty*. Lewis (1959, 1966a, 1966b) found the poor to be relatively unorganized, yet "disengaged" from and suspicious of the political and economic institutions of urban society, even though they lived within cities. The poor lived in crowded slums (see Figure 13.11), were chronically unemployed and short of food and cash, and were forced to make small, expensive purchases and to borrow at exorbitant rates. Marriages were often not legalized and easily dissolved. Poor families were unstable, and often matricentered, and children quickly assumed adult roles. Lewis found that as individuals, the poor tended to be fatalistic, with feelings of inferiority and dependency. They were present-oriented, were unwilling to defer gratification, and had little sense of history or their place in society.

Lewis argued that these behavior patterns formed a culture of poverty that served "adaptive functions" in response to economic deprivation. He thought that poverty traits defined a self-perpetuating subculture, which he attempted to describe in positive terms. The culture of poverty, however, proved controversial because many poverty traits were negative stereotypes about the poor, which attributed poverty to ignorance. Lewis himself often acknowledged the negative aspects of poverty traits and even referred to them as pathologies. He also attributed the culture of poverty to specific conditions in the political economy, especially a capitalist economy with high unemployment, inadequate government assistance, an absence of supportive descent groups, and a dominant class that

from the natives who were already residents on the land. After Peru became independent from Spain, the descendants of the conquerors retained their dominant position in Andean society, and many of the *encomienda* estates remained in place as vast haciendas and plantations.

The Andean haciendas were agricultural estates with a dominant landowner and a dependent labor force that produced primarily for subsistence and local markets (Miller 1967, Mintz and Wolf 1957). In the twentieth century, haciendas were often administered by absentee owners who intentionally kept the resident natives impoverished so that many would be forced to provide cheap labor. The hacienda was divided sharply into two classes that were each further stratified. Power was concentrated at the top with the *hacendado*, the Spanish owner, and his hired administrators. The *hacendado*, or *patron*, used his landholding to enhance his personal wealth and status and was supported in his power by regional and national political authorities and church officials.

Hacienda laborers, or *peones* (Quechua-speaking indigenous peoples), were granted small subsistence holdings, often on marginal lands, and were allowed to graze their livestock on the estate. As rent, the *peones* were obligated to work 3 days a week for the hacienda, for which they received a token wage. They were also required to provide the hacienda free service and the labor of their animals on demand. The *peones* were treated as ignorant children by the *patron* and his managers. As serfs, they were expected to show exaggerated, hat-in-hand respect for those in charge. Uncooperative *peones* were subject to imprisonment and fines, although formerly they might have been beaten. Hacienda officials created support by dispensing small favors and sometimes acted as godparents to speprizes wealth and attributes economic achievement to personal effort. Lewis argued that the culture of poverty was not just a response to deprivation, because not all impoverished groups shared these traits. Furthermore, he considered poverty culture to be an inadequate solution to poverty conditions. Lewis also suggested that poverty culture was self-perpetuating through socialization and might actually prove more difficult to eradicate than poverty itself. Thus, the culture of poverty concept gave support to those who would blame the poor for their poverty.

Critics found serious deficiencies with the culture of poverty concept. Charles Valentine (1968, 1969, 1971) objected to Lewis' use of the culture concept because Lewis relied on autobiographical oral histories of a few individual poor families. It is difficult to determine what, if any, actual subculture they represented. These families displayed numerous idiosyncrasies incompatible with the culture of poverty model. The poor neighborhoods of which they were part were also more organized than might be expected; however, larger organizational patterns do not stand out when analysis remains at the family level. The individuals in the sample families were often more "engaged" with the world around them than the model of passivity and ignorance suggests. Valentine argued that regardless of the distinctive traits the poor may share, poverty does not constitute a self-perpetuating subculture, because poverty traits are a response to conditions imposed by dominant classes and institutions. Lewis certainly would have agreed with the last part of this interpretation.

cific native families. Ritual co-parenthood, the institution of *compradazgo*, established an informal alliance between families of different social ranks.

When the Vicos participant intervention experiment began, the anthropologist-*patrons* immediately began to move the *peones* into administrative positions in the hacienda, replacing the former managers. Next they abolished free service and began to pay decent wages to their new native employees. Profits from agricultural production were returned to the community in the form of agricultural improvements and schooling. A formal group of community leaders was organized to participate directly in the planning of the entire project, and weekly meetings were held with all workers to discuss problems. In 1957, the project leaders petitioned the government for a decree of expropriation that would allow the natives to obtain full ownership of the hacienda. This action aroused the ire of the local elite, who accused the project of being a Communist plot, but after 5 years of persistent effort and the intervention of the U.S. ambassador and supportive officials within the Peruvian government, the Vicos hacienda was sold to its former serfs in 1962 (see Figure 13.12). The Cornell Peru Project terminated the next year. Holmberg attributed the apparent success of his experiment to its approach to political power:

The element of power proved to be the key that permitted the Cornell Peru Project to open the door to change; the devolution of power to the people of Vicos proved to be the mechanism that made the new system viable. (1971:62)

The emphasis on changing the local power structure in Vicos was certainly innovative in development anthropology; in retrospect, however, it is difficult to precisely evaluate the long-term impact of the project. Surveys conducted up to 1964

FIGURE 13.11
The slums of Bombay, an extreme example of urban poverty conditions. Whatever cultural patterns the world's urban poor may share, they are a response to conditions imposed by dominant classes and institutions.

showed measurable improvements in nutrition, education, and some indicators of material prosperity (Dobyns, Doughty, and Lasswell 1971). Nevertheless, the project and the economic opportunities it presented were designed to favor the "most progressive" community members, and it is possible that a new elite was created. More cash wealth was flowing into the community, and agricultural production had apparently increased, but it is unclear how the new wealth was being distributed or how long the community could remain competitive in the national economy.

The community did make some critical trade-offs in its "modernization." Responding to the program's directives, they formed an agricultural cooperative organized along capitalist lines as a profit-making agricultural corporation. This move carried significant risks because it weakened or replaced many pre-Inca subsistence practices, and this may explain why researchers found that by 1963, household heads showed a substantial increase in several clinical measures of anxiety (Alers 1971). To buy the land, the new Vicos corporation assumed a substantial long-term debt with the government for half of the total purchase price. Many

FIGURE 13.12   *Vicos farmers sorting their harvest of traditional potatoes grown for local consumption. The Cornell Peru Project was an applied anthropology experiment designed to turn control of the Andean hacienda of Vicos over to its former serfs.*

Vicos families also assumed large individual debts with the Peruvian government's agricultural bank to pay for the expensive new agricultural inputs required for profitable market production.

Even the new production technology involved additional trade-offs, but the project planners treated the development process as "enlightenment," virtually disregarding the centuries of accumulated agricultural knowledge already present in Vicos and the genetic value of local crop varieties. Stephen Brush and his associates (Brush, Carney, and Huaman 1981) have shown that high-yield hybrid potatoes produced by agricultural scientists have many disadvantages for Andean communities. The new potatoes are grown as a monocrop that requires exotic debt-producing inputs, and the crop must be sold on the national government-controlled market. By contrast, local communities control all the skills and other "inputs" required to produce and distribute native potatoes. Oxen and footplows are locally produced and maintained. Unlike tractors, they require no imported fuel and are highly reliable. There are more than 2000 varieties of traditional potatoes, each developed for special qualities of taste, storability, and hardiness under specific local conditions. These potatoes, greatly preferred by Andean people, are readily bartered and sold in the local markets.

Anthropologist Paul Doughty (forthcoming), who first visited Vicos in 1960, revisited in 1997 and provides an overview of the project's achievements and problems. He found that the trend toward material prosperity was continuing; however, in 1996, the people of Vicos formally disbanded their agricultural cooperative and replaced community land ownership with individual private ownership.

The Vicos project closely resembled Peru's later agrarian reform program of 1969, which also expropriated haciendas and promoted commercial agriculture. However, it is significant that although many Andean communities were eager to gain control over their lands under the new land reform program, they stubbornly and sometimes violently refused to form cooperatives and resisted agricultural "modernization." Diane Hopkins (1985) suggests that this refusal to cooperate with the government program was not because the peasants were ignorant and backward. They simply did not want the government to become their new *patron*,

and they rationally preferred their own forms of agricultural production.

At the local level, the Andean system is based on barter of food products between communities, exchanges of labor based on *ayni* (simple reciprocity), and household ownership of widely dispersed plots. This form of land ownership is a distinctively domestic-scale cultural pattern and assumes relative equality and self-sufficiency while it minimizes risk and makes effective use of local resources. In the Andean setting, small, intensively utilized plots, though disparaged by agricultural economists as **minifundia,** can be highly productive. The national agrarian reform plan calls for the peasants to be integrated into the national economy by means of agricultural cooperatives in debt to the government and dependent on the market economy. The advantage for the government of such an arrangement is that it gives it greater control over the peasantry and provides inexpensive food to support urban industrialization. This kind of rural development might make some farmers wealthy, but it brings substantial risks and means that local control systems will be effectively lost.

SUMMARY

Since the 1950s, poverty has been conceptualized as a development or modernization problem. Development planners assumed that people were poor because they were underdeveloped, and they were underdeveloped because they were technologically backward and culturally conservative. Hoping to reduce poverty, the developed countries optimistically financed the transfer of agricultural technologies, dam and highway construction, and other large-scale developments designed to promote economic growth throughout the world. Unfortunately, these efforts have not significantly reduced poverty.

Initially, anthropologists enthusiastically endorsed this development model and worked in small communities to identify the cultural barriers to economic progress. It became apparent, however, that traditional cultures were not the primary cause of

---

minifundia   Tiny landholdings of the Latin American peasantry.

poverty. National and international efforts to raise GNP in many cases actually further impoverished local communities by promoting debt and dependency and intensified internal inequalities that reduced access to basic resources. Anthropological data also show that many cultural traits, which development planners may consider to be causes of poverty, are rational coping mechanisms to conditions of extreme deprivation. Similarly, overpopulation cannot be a sole cause of poverty. Although population growth has certainly intensified poverty, the relationship is complex. Poverty and the development process itself have both fostered population growth.

The concept of culture scale offers a different perspective on the problem of poverty, suggesting that poverty is not entirely a technological problem to be cured by evolutionary progress. The evidence presented in previous chapters showed that poverty was essentially absent in autonomous domestic-scale cultures but was created by the inequality inherent in the social stratification of political-scale cultures. Poverty was further intensified by the process of colonialism and the global system of stratification that emerged with commercialization. To be effective, development efforts designed to reduce poverty must deal with the inequalities of wealth and power that exist at all levels of the global system.

STUDY QUESTIONS

1. How did UN experts conceptualize the problem of global poverty in 1950? What specific indicators of underdevelopment did they refer to? What was the vicious cycle? What solutions did they call for?

2. In what sense can it be said that poverty has increased since 1950? Refer to poverty indicators, absolute numbers of impoverished people, and GNP rankings between nations.

3. Describe the official charter and the institutional basis for the UN's approach to development, referring to the following: UN Charter, Universal Declaration of Human Rights, technical assistance, integrated development, Development Decades, Economic and Social Council, World Bank, FAO, UN Development Programme.

4. Define the following development-related concepts: official development assistance, multilateral assistance, bilateral assistance, and gross national product.

5. Describe how the issues and strategies of the UN's approach to development have changed in the decades since 1950.

6. Define underdevelopment and poverty, discussing the conceptual and cultural problems that limit the usefulness of your definitions.

7. In what sense can development itself be considered an industry?

8. Describe the major categories of U.S. foreign assistance and the institutional pathways that it follows to reach impoverished villagers in the developing world. Refer to multilateral aid, bilateral aid, military aid, development aid, food aid, and the economic support fund. What evidence is there that factors other than humanitarian concerns influence foreign aid?

9. Explain how the following concepts reflect changing priorities in official U.S. approaches to development: Point Four, Freedom from Hunger, privatization, free market, biotechnology.

10. How does U.S. food aid benefit U.S. interests?

11. Discuss how colonialism, social structure, population growth, and technological advance were related to poverty in Bangladesh at both national and village levels.

12. Describe village social structure in Bangladesh emphasizing access to land, labor, technology, food, and cash income in relation to standard of living.

13. What ethical decisions do development anthropologists confront? Refer to conflicting responsibilities and the problem of resistance.

14. Discuss cultural obstacles to development programs, referring to folk society, closed corporate community, and limited good.

15. What was the culture of poverty, according to Lewis? Why was this concept so controversial, and how was it related to public policy issues? What conceptual and methodological problems have been identified?

16. Define the following related to Latin American and Andean peasantries: *encomienda, hacendado, patron, peones, compradazgo,* hacienda, plantation, *minifundia, ayni.*

17. Describe the social structure of the Vicos hacienda when the Cornell Peru Project began in 1952. Explain how the participant intervention experiment was conducted and discuss the results.

18. Why did some Andean communities refuse to participate fully in Peru's agrarian reform program? Identify specific points of conflict, referring to production technologies, cooperatives, *ayni*, risk, debt, market economy, subsistence economy, barter exchange, and land ownership.

SUGGESTED READING

HARTMANN, BETSY, AND JAMES K. BOYCE. 1983. *A Quiet Violence: View from a Bangladesh Village*. San Francisco: Institute for Food and Development Policy. A detailed case study of development in Bangladesh, which expands on the coverage provided in this chapter.

LAPPE, FRANCES MOORE, JOSEPH COLLINS, AND CARRY FOWLER. 1978. *Food First: Beyond the Myth of Scarcity*. New York: Ballantine Books. Along with the following two books, provides the essence of Lappe's critique of development policy and emphasizes the importance of food self-sufficiency.

LAPPE, FRANCES MOORE, JOSEPH COLLINS, AND DAVID KINLEY. 1981. *Aid as Obstacle: Twenty Questions About Our Foreign Aid and the Hungry*. San Francisco: Institute for Food and Development Policy.

LAPPE, FRANCES MOORE, RACHEL SCHURMAN, AND KEVIN DANAHER. 1987. *Betraying the National Interest*. New York: Grove Press.

I4

Indigenous Peoples

Indigenous peoples are members of domestic-scale cultures who are engaged in a contemporary struggle for autonomy and survival in a world dominated by national governments and international markets. Previous chapters detailed the cultural background of these peoples as they existed under independent conditions (Chapters 2–5). In this chapter, we examine the conceptual, philosophical, and political issues involved in defining the place of domestic-scale cultures within the global system. First, we discuss the complexities of devising a non-ethnocentric concept of indigenous peoples. Next, we review the genocide and ethnocide that they suffered along the frontiers of national expansion. Finally, we examine the great humanitarian policy debate carried on by anthropologists, missionaries, and government officials since the 1830s over how states should relate to tribal peoples and their cultures.

To maintain maximum cultural context, we discuss these complex issues using extended case studies drawn from Australia (see Chapter 2) and Amazonia (see Chapter 3). The background of the International Labour Organization's controversial Conventions 107 and 169 and the promising new United Nations Universal Declaration on Rights of Indigenous Peoples are examined in detail because these are the most important modern international conventions on indigenous peoples.

INDIGENOUS PEOPLES AND THE GLOBAL CULTURE

The Politics of Labels: Defining Indigenous Peoples

What different understandings of indigenous peoples are implied by the various labels that are applied to them?

The labels that one employs in any discussion of "indigenous peoples" are a critical matter because use of any specific label implies a particular understanding of what indigenous people are like and how they should be treated. Choice of labels may also be an expression of political domination or superiority. For example, use of such labels as "Stone Age tribe" implies that an indigenous group is an anachronism, perhaps lost or at least in the wrong time and place. A "Stone Age tribe" may also be seen as especially weak, childlike, helpless, and naive. In the interests of cross-cultural understanding, anthropologists generally prefer to use the self-selected terms that specific cultural groups apply to themselves.

As threatened domestic-scale cultures became politically involved in self-defense movements early in the 1970s, many native leaders gradually adopted the term *indigenous* as a self-designation to use in pressing their claims in international forums such as the United Nations. Within the political arena, *indigenous* refers to the original inhabitants of a region and is posed in opposition to the colonists, usurpers, and intruders who came later in search of new resources to exploit. As a political category, indigenous people includes members of peasant groups and ethnic communities who have been absorbed by states but who still strongly identify with their cultural heritage and claim special rights to territory and resources on that basis.

Many other terms that anthropologists and others have applied to indigenous peoples have carried a variety of meanings and connotations, such that these terms must all be approached with care, giving attention to context, connotation, and the intended audience. Table 14.1 sorts out fourteen such terms in English according to the degree to which they emphasize ethnolinguistic distinctiveness, specific cultural features of the political economy, priority of settlement in a territory, and oppression, as well as whether the terms are applied by the people themselves or may be used pejoratively. Many of these terms are ambiguous, and the meaning may vary dramatically depending on who is using them.

In reference to most areas of the world, indigenous is an appropriate label for international discourse. However, if priority of residence in a territory is considered the most critical aspect of the concept of indigenous peoples, then the term *indigenous* must be applied cautiously in specific areas because indigenous peoples have sometimes displaced or absorbed other, more indigenous inhabitants. Archaeological evidence would be needed to sort out the details of settlement priority in some areas of Africa and South America. In general, however, the priority of indigenous groups relative to modern invaders connected with modern states and global culture is obvious.

Unfortunately, the term *indigenous* does not identify the specific cultural characteristics that underlie the political struggle of indigenous peoples (see Table 14.1). *Indigenous* does not distinguish between people living in domestic-scale cultures or in political-scale chiefdoms or who were incorporated as peasants into states and empires. However, it is adherence to such traits of domestic-scale cultures as community-level resource management, high levels of local self-sufficiency, and relative social equality that makes indigenous peoples so distinctive. It is also these traits that generate conflict with larger-scale cultures that seek to extinguish local control systems and create dependency in order to extract resources. Indigenous peoples are likely to resist any external pressures for change that undermine their autonomy, yet their small size and lack of political organization make them especially vulnerable to outside intervention and give them special claims before the international community. The term *indigenous* is often preferable to similar terms such as *native*, which in some settings carries negative connotations because of its use by colonial powers. In other areas, *native* may be a self-designation used interchangeably with *indigenous*. Indigenous, now a self-appellation, has no negative connotations for the people who use it. This usage, which is rapidly becoming internationally accepted, calls attention to both cultural uniqueness and the political oppression, or at least the disadvantage, that indigenous peoples must often endure from the larger-scale cultures surrounding them.

Colonizing peoples also used generic labels such as *Indian* or *aborigine* in much the same way as the term *native*, to refer to original inhabitants. Indigenous peoples themselves also used these terms, but in this case, a negative connotation is not implied. The disadvantage of *Indian* and *aborigine* is that they are regional terms and lack specific cultural content.

Historically, anthropologists have used the terms *savage, primitive, uncivilized,* and *preliterate* to call attention to cultural differences. These terms have sometimes enjoyed a certain scientific respectability, but they have not successfully avoided the popular negative connotation of backwardness. Some writers used *primitive* in the sense of primary or

---

indigenous   Peoples who are the original inhabitants of a territory and who seek to maintain political control over their resources and their domestic-scale cultural heritage.

TABLE 14.1   *Labels for Indigenous Peoples and Domestic-Scale Cultures*

	Ethnolinguistic Distinctiveness	Politicoeconomic Distinctiveness	Original Inhabitants	Self-Appellation	Oppressed	Pejorative
Indigenous	+/−	+/−	+	+	+	−
Indian	+	+	+	+/−	+	+/−
Native	+	+/−	+	+/−	−	+/−
Aborigine	+	+	+	+/−	−	+/−
Stone Age	+	+	+	−	−	+
Savage	+	+	+	−	−	+
Uncivilized	+	+	+/−	−	−	+
Preliterate	+	+	+/−	−	−	+
Tribal	+	+	+/−	+/−	−	+/−
Domestic-Scale	+	+	+/−	−	−	−
Ethnic Minority	+	−	−	+/−	+	−
Primitive	+	+	+/−	−	−	+/−
Folk	+	+	+/−	−	−	−
Fourth World	+	+	+	+/−	+	−

NOTE: + means the characteristic is implied by the label; − means the characteristic is not implied; +/− means the characteristic is sometimes implied, sometimes not.

original and emphasized positive cultural features (Bodley 1975, 1976, Diamond 1968), but the term has now been abandoned.

Tribes, Nations, and the Fourth World

In what respects can indigenous peoples be considered nations?

Tribal is sometimes used synonymously with *indigenous* and is an acceptable self-designation in many areas of the world. In this chapter, *tribal* will refer to indigenous groups that maintain significant degrees of independence. However, the term is usually avoided in Africa because in modern political circles, *tribal* may be used pejoratively to imply backwardness and ethnic division. Many anthropologists also reject the term on technical grounds, because tribes, as political divisions, were created by colonial administrators. Furthermore, as was shown in earlier chapters, domestic-scale cultures were not organized into discrete polities under centralized leadership. *Tribe* is also used to refer to a stage in cultural evolution, and missionaries often use the term to mean "ethnic group."

The problem of terminology also applies to labels given to specific cultural groups. Ethnic group names that find their way into the anthropological and popular literature may be pejorative labels applied by neighbors who despise the group in question. For example, the term *Eskimo* is an outsider term applied to people who call themselves "Inuit." Other names, like tribes, may be artificial creations of colonial governments.

Indigenous people self-identify as members of domestic-scale cultures and consider themselves to be the original inhabitants of the territories they occupy. Perhaps 200 million or more indigenous peoples are scattered throughout the world, often in remote areas containing valuable natural resources (see Figure 14.1). They are aware of the advantages of their cultural heritage in comparison with life in the larger-scale systems surrounding them.

Because indigenous people claim a territorial base and a history of independence, they resemble politically organized states and sometimes call themselves "nations." Geographer Bernard Nietschmann (1988) adopted the term **nations** in place of *tribes* to refer to indigenous people, pointing out that nations have a common territory, language, and culture, in contrast to modern states that are often composed of diverse ethnic groups. Further emphasizing the dimension of political struggle, Nietschmann also refered to indigenous people as the Fourth World to distinguish them from the developing states of the Third World. The First and

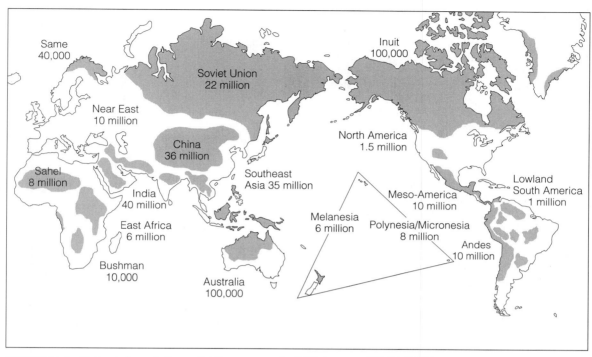

FIGURE 14.1   *Estimated populations of indigenous people, 1980. (SOURCE: IWGIA 1987.)*

Second Worlds represent the old Cold War division into Western, capitalist countries and Eastern, Communist countries. Many Third World states were created out of former colonies with little regard for the integrity of the Fourth World nations, which they incorporated and turned into internal colonies as their territories were thrown open for development.

Policy Alternatives:
Realists Versus Idealists

What different philosophies underly the various policy approaches that governments have applied to members of domestic-scale cultures?

Over the past 500 years, the fate of indigenous peoples has been determined by government policy. Indigenous peoples have flourished when they have remained autonomous, beyond the reach of state power, and they have had great difficulty maintain-

ing their cultural integrity and physical well-being when state power has been used against them. The extreme power differential between domestic-scale and commercial-scale cultures gives state governments an obvious advantage whenever direct confrontations have occurred. When indigenous peoples have prevailed, it is because of the moral force of their arguments at times when governments have been sensitive to human rights concerns. However, as the discussion in the following sections demonstrates, humanistic policies have not always been sufficient to protect the integrity of domestic-scale cultures.

The enormous human suffering caused by the commercially driven expansion of European civilization generated humanitarian concern almost immediately, but this concern was tempered by an acceptance of the reality of state power. One of the earliest and most outspoken advocates of humane

---

nation   A people with a common language, culture, and territory and who claim a common identity.

treatment of indigenous people was Bartolome de Las Casas, a Catholic priest who accompanied the Spanish conquistadores to the New World in 1502. He participated in the conquest, attempting to convert the indigenes to Christianity, but became convinced by experience that the Spanish system of colonialism was unjust. He freed the indigenous serfs on his *encomienda* and began a lifelong campaign against the exploitation and mistreatment of the indigenes. Las Casas composed a series of works condemning the worst abuses of colonialism, especially the *encomienda* system. In public debates with leading Spanish intellectuals, he championed the basic humanity of indigenous peoples, successfully challenging the concept that non-Christian indigenes were subhumans who could be mistreated with impunity. Las Casas gained royal support in Madrid for his views, but the reforms he proposed were never effectively implemented in the New World (Dussel 1975).

Even if the policies that Las Casas proposed had been implemented, it is unlikely that the integrity of domestic-scale cultures would have been secured because his policies did not question the legitimacy of the conquest itself. A fundamental philosophical difference between **realist** and **idealist** approaches separates even the most humanistic state policies toward indigenous peoples. Policies, such as those advocated by Las Casas, that are based on realist philosophy seek to moderate the negative consequences of conquest but do not challenge the authority of the state to use its power to reduce the political and economic autonomy of nonstate, domestic-scale cultures. Thus, from the Spanish conquest to the present, realist humanitarian policies would permit the intrusion of state power and commercial interests into indigenous territories for the extraction of indigenous labor and resources; for mining, lumbering, and ranching; and for the construction of dams, highways, and other projects.

State policies based on the opposing idealist philosophy set limits on state power and recognize the local political authority and territorial sovereignty of domestic-scale cultures. Such an approach has been the de facto practice beyond the frontiers of state power and during the earliest phases of conquest, but historically, states have dominated domestic-scale cultures in the long run. In recent decades, indigenous peoples have been able to ne-

gotiate greater autonomy, and there are indications at the international level that idealist policies are gaining support. This is the **self-determination** demanded by contemporary indigenous political leaders. Such devolution of power is a promising alternative, even for local communities that have been incorporated by Great Tradition civilizations for a long time and by capitalist nations within the global culture. Self-determination may be the best way for communities to meet the basic human needs of domestic-scale societies.

COLONIALISM AND DOMESTIC-SCALE CULTURES

Since the beginning of European colonial expansion, authorities on international law maintained that indigenous peoples held legitimate group rights to political sovereignty and territory that could be taken from them only by treaty or military conquest. Tribal groups were considered to be autonomous sovereign nations. Of course, tribal nations were often militarily weaker than the colonial powers that invaded their territories and were often easily defeated in war, but the important, internationally acknowledged legal point was that a formal written document had to define the relationship between the invading power and the tribal nation. Such a document would specify the details of landownership and the degree of independence that the indigenous group might enjoy. This left room for the legal abuses of ethnocide, genocide, and ecocide that accompanied colonialism and sparked the great debate over humanitarian policy. At the same time, failure to sign treaties, as was the case in Australia, deferred the question of specific rights and provided a basis for modern negotiations. Former agreements may also be renegotiated in reference to the higher international standards of conduct toward indigenous peoples that have steadily evolved along with the emergence of the global system.

Ethnocide, Genocide, and Ecocide

What have been the negative consequences of the expansion of the global culture into territories controlled by domestic-scale cultures?

During the first, preindustrial phase of capitalist expansion, which was underway by 1450, several European powers, such as Spain, Portugal, England, and France, gained political domination over large areas in North and South America, the Caribbean, and the islands of the eastern Atlantic. This was the beginning of a colonial process of conquest and incorporation that continued into the twentieth century.

Historian Alfred Crosby (1986) notes that the Guanches, the original inhabitants of the Canary Islands in the Atlantic 200 miles (322 kilometers [km]) off the northwest coast of Africa, were perhaps the first domestic-scale culture to be conquered by the advancing Europeans. The Guanches, who numbered some 80,000, appear to have been egalitarian village farmers with no metal tools. They resisted successive waves of French, Portuguese, and Spanish invaders from 1402 until the Spaniards gained full control of the islands in 1496.

The Guanches who survived the conquest were dispossessed, exiled, and enslaved. Their culture was destroyed, and by 1540, the Guanche had virtually disappeared as a people. The Spaniards stripped the forests and sold the timber and other resources of the Canaries. They replaced the native flora and fauna with European species and established sugarcane plantations based on slave labor. Deforestation initiated flooding and erosion and then caused the local climate to become arid. All of the negative impacts of colonial expansion—*ethnocide, genocide,* and *ecocide*—were underway in the Canaries when Christopher Columbus passed through in 1492 on his first crossing of the Atlantic.

In 1800, at the beginning of the Industrial Revolution, preindustrial states still existed in China, Japan, and Africa, and traditional kingdoms and chiefdoms in India, the Middle East, and the Pacific still retained considerable autonomy. The great Western colonial powers had made claims over 55 percent of the world's land area but exercised effective control over only 33 percent of the world (Clark 1936). Approximately half the world was still controlled by relatively autonomous and largely self-sufficient domestic-scale tribal cultures, containing perhaps 200 million people, roughly 20 percent of the global population (see Figure 14.2). Over the next 150 years, virtually all tribal territory was conquered by colonizing industrial states, and perhaps 50 million tribal peoples died. This process created

the modern world system, but at an enormous cost in the ethnocide, genocide, and ecocide suffered by the peoples and territories forcibly incorporated by the new system.

Incorporation, in this context, means that natural resources and/or human labor begin to flow into the world system from formerly "external" areas. From the viewpoint of the peoples and cultures being incorporated, incorporation sets in motion a process of demographic disruption and destroys political and economic autonomy. Demographic disruption first appears as drastic depopulation when people are enslaved and killed by invaders and when they die from newly introduced diseases to which they have little immunity. Mortality is increased when culturally established support networks are interrupted and food systems disturbed. Epidemic diseases that make everyone sick at once can be devastating in a domestic-scale culture.

Much of the increased mortality occurred as a direct result of violence perpetrated against tribal peoples during their conquest by outsiders. In rare cases, governments followed a policy of deliberate genocide in an effort to totally exterminate a tribal population, and many governments organized military campaigns against tribal groups. The largest tribal loss of life probably resulted from the actions of individual colonists who sought to profit from tribal territories before governments established formal political control. On the *uncontrolled frontier,* colonial governments, as a matter of policy, allowed their citizens to systematically kill and exploit tribal peoples (Bodley 1990) (see Figure 14.3). Where tribal peoples were not needed as a source of labor, they were classified as "nonhuman" savages and were killed with impunity to remove them from the land.

---

realist A policy position that maintains that indigenous peoples must surrender their political and economic autonomy and be integrated into dominant state societies.

idealist A policy position that advocates cultural autonomy for indigenous peoples as a basic human right.

self-determination The right of any people to freely determine its own cultural, political, and economic future.

ethnocide The forced destruction of a cultural system.

genocide The extermination of a human population.

ecocide The degradation of an ecosystem.

uncontrolled frontier A tribal territory that is invaded by colonists from a state-organized society but where the government chooses not to regulate the actions of the colonists.

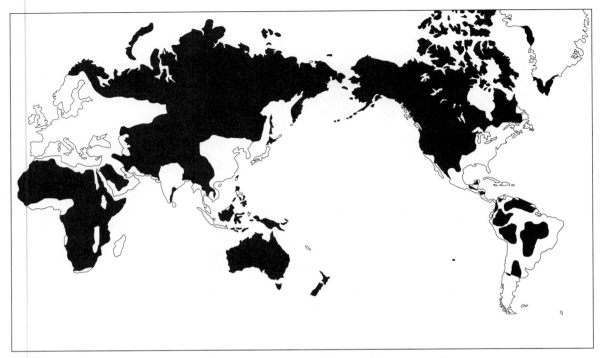

FIGURE 14.2   *Autonomous tribal peoples, approximately 200 million people (20 percent of the global population), 1800.*

Increased mortality is a special threat to the survival of tribal cultures that rely on fertility-limiting cultural practices to maintain their small, low-density, low-growth populations. Many of these groups simply disappeared when the frontier overtook them, and only their territories remained to be incorporated.

The loss of political autonomy by tribal peoples occurs when state governments gain enough power over a tribal territory to prevent tribal groups from acting in their own defense to expel outsiders. This can occur following military conquest, or it can be accomplished by formal treaty signing or some less formal process by which government control is extended over a formerly autonomous tribal area. In most cases, the relative difference in power between tribal cultures and states is so extreme that the state can impose control over a tribal territory virtually at will, although it can be a costly and time-consuming process.

State political control usually is symbolized by the appointment of political authorities and the introduction of a police force. State functions such as taxation, military recruitment, and census taking usually follow, along with the imposition of a legal system, courts, and jails. Administrative issues to be dealt with by colonial officials concerned specifying the differential rights of the native population and the colonizing population to land and other natural resources. Special regulations defined the conditions under which natives would be employed and how native culture could be expressed.

The loss of economic autonomy is fostered by political conquest because tribal groups must maintain control over their subsistence resources in order to remain self-sufficient. Drastic depopulation can reduce the economic viability of a tribal group, but competition with colonists over resources, especially when the tribal land base is reduced by government decree, is often the decisive

FIGURE 14.3   *Contemporary engraving of an attack against Australian aborigines. The uncontrolled frontier phase of capitalist expansion often involved direct physical violence against indigenous peoples.*

factor. Any factors that undermined the traditional subsistence base would push tribal peoples toward participation in the market economy, whether as wage laborers or ***cash croppers.***

There was also a desire to secure some of the manufactured goods, such as metal tools and factory clothing, produced by the world system's industrial centers. However, the "pull" forces in themselves were insufficient to compel tribal peoples into large-scale participation in the market economy without a strong "push." Whenever the subsistence economy remained strong, tribal peoples were often poorly motivated target workers, and colonial administrators resorted to legal mea-

sures such as special taxes and planting laws to force reluctant tribal groups into the market economy. Once initiated, involvement in the market economy can become self-reinforcing because wage labor leaves little time for subsistence activities and cash cropping can degrade the local ecosystem and reduce its potential for subsistence production.

The cost of industrial expansion was minimized or ignored by the economists and politicians who championed growth and "differential benefits," but anthropologists who conducted fieldwork on the colonial frontiers observed the devastation firsthand and often attempted to minimize it.

The Humanitarian Response

How did British humanitarians attempt to soften the harsh impact of colonialism without challenging the basic system?

Throughout their expanding colonial empire, the British used military force against resisting indigenous peoples, but they consistently drew up formal treaties to legalize the transfer of political authority and tribal lands to Europeans. British policy in Australia was a striking exception because the presence of the aborigines as mobile foragers was never legally acknowledged and no treaties were signed. The abuses of British colonialism, which flourished under such legalism, inspired a dedicated group of British humanitarians led by Thomas Fowell Buxton, who formed the Anti-Slavery Society in 1823 and successfully campaigned for a ban on slavery throughout the empire by 1833.

In 1835, Buxton, like Las Casas, turned his attention to the larger humanitarian issue of the negative impact of colonialism on tribal peoples. Buxton, as a member of Parliament, persuaded the House of Commons to appoint a Select Committee to formulate official policies to protect the rights of tribal peoples and to ensure their just treatment. The committee conducted an extensive survey of the impact of European civilization on tribal groups throughout the empire and issued a massive report concluding that European colonialism was "a source of many calamities to uncivilized nations"

cash cropping   The raising of crops for market sale rather than domestic consumption.

(an excerpt appears in Bodley 1988:63–69). The report elaborated:

Too often, their territory has been usurped; their property seized; their numbers diminished; their character debased; the spread of civilization impeded. European vices and diseases introduced among them (House of Commons 1837:5)

The committee recommended specific corrective measures that it hoped would bring justice to tribal peoples without hindering the growth of British colonies. The most important measure acknowledged the inherent conflict between invading settlers and indigenous peoples and recommended that colonial governors in consultation with the queen and Parliament, and not local legislatures, should safeguard the rights of indigenous peoples. The committee also called for curbs on alcohol, strict controls on contract labor to prevent debt slavery, and a prohibition on the acquisition of tribal lands by settlers, arguing that there was enough empty land to satisfy the needs of settlers. Legal dispossession of tribal peoples could still take place, but it required an act of Parliament; in such cases, dispossessed natives were to be protected and educated by missionaries who would be supported by the revenues the crown received from the sale of tribal lands. Thus, under the most liberally envisioned form of British justice at the time, the rights of natives were narrowly defined and remained secondary to the economic needs of the colonizers. This policy approach could be characterized as realist because it advocated no major changes in the existing political relationship between a dominant state power and a subordinate indigenous people. However, even these enlightened policies were seldom effectively enforced.

After the Select Committee issued its report, the committee's work was continued by the Aborigines Protection Society (APS), an advocacy group formed by committee members under the direction of Thomas Hodgkin in 1836 to "promote the advancement of Uncivilized Tribes." The APS was a model humanitarian organization that played a decisive role throughout the nineteenth century in keeping government attention focused on the painful human cost of colonialism for tribal peoples and lobbying for protective policies. Through its network of branch societies and corresponding members, the APS was able to closely monitor the condition of native peoples throughout the empire and directly petition government officials to take humanitarian action.

Proimperialist humanitarian concern for the welfare of indigenous peoples did not envision the persistence of independent domestic-scale cultures and tended to discourage any cultural diversity. The APS remained a firm supporter of British imperialism, but even this limited application of the principle of human rights to indigenous people was an important development in the ideological system of the emerging global system.

Early international conventions containing humanitarian provisions designed to protect indigenous peoples were sometimes outrageously ethnocentric. For example, when the major imperialist powers met in Berlin in 1884–1885 to facilitate the colonial partitioning of Africa, they described their action as a "civilizing crusade" and pledged to support all efforts "to educate the natives and to teach them to understand and appreciate the benefits of civilization" (General Act of the 1884–1885 Berlin Africa Conference). Europeans took control to protect their political and economic interests, justifying their action as an effort to end the illegal slave trade (see Figure 14.4). By 1892, the Brussels Act effectively mandated ethnocide as part of the "uplift," or civilization, process by declaring that the colonizing powers should civilize tribal peoples and "bring about the extinction of barbarous customs."

In 1907, the APS tried to persuade the international Hague Peace Conference to ban wars of extermination and punitive military raids against relatively defenseless tribal groups. This would have been a logical extension of the rules of war covered in the various Geneva Conventions, which began in 1864 with the establishment of the International Red Cross. Unfortunately, the APS proposal was not placed on the agenda because the British prime minister objected.

Toward the end of World War I, the APS had another opportunity to promote the rights of indigenous peoples during international discussions on the fate of Germany's former colonies. These territories were scattered throughout Africa and the Pacific and contained some 30 million indigenous people, many still living independently. The APS recognized that, ideally, this would be the time to

FIGURE 14.4 *Sir William E. Maxwell (seated on right), governor of the British Gold Coast colony, and a contingent of native police, 1895. The photo represents the political and military power used by Europeans to carry out the "civilizing crusade" formalized by the Berlin Africa Conference of 1884–1885.*

grant full political sovereignty to existing tribal nations and grant self-determination to detribalized groups. However, the APS rejected tribal independence because it would have threatened the colonial system, even though it was obvious that "protection and uplift" policies had not prevented massive depopulation of tribal areas. These policy debates, which ultimately determined the fate of countless tribal groups, were permeated with paternalistic, racist, and demeaning language. Tribal peoples were variously referred to as backward races, subject races, and child races. Under the mandate system, established by the League of Nations Covenant in 1919 to administer former German colonies, tribal peoples were called "peoples not yet able to stand by themselves under the

strenuous conditions of the modern world." They were to be administered according to the principle that "the well-being and development of such peoples form a sacred trust of civilization" (League Covenant, Article 22).

Applied Anthropology and Tribal Peoples

How did applied anthropologists work in support of colonial policies?

As the British colonial system matured and increasing numbers of tribal peoples were brought under formal administrative control, the value of anthropological knowledge became obvious to colonial authorities, and many anthropologists went to work for the empire. In many respects, anthropology, as an academic discipline and as a profession, was a product of colonial expansion. It was no accident that major anthropological associations were formed in Great Britain, the United States, and France during the nineteenth century and that their publications, such as the *American Anthropologist* and the *Journal of the Royal Anthropological Institute of Great Britain and Ireland*, were filled with ethnographic notes gleaned from native peoples on the colonial frontiers by administrators, missionaries, military men, and ethnologists.

The practical utility of anthropological knowledge for imperialist countries was recognized quickly. For example, Colonel A. H. Lane-Fox Pitt-Rivers, in his opening address to the anthropology section of the British Association for the Advancement of Science in 1871, declared,

Nor is it unimportant to remember that Anthropology has its practical and humanitarian aspect, and that, as our race is more often brought in contact with savages than any other, a knowledge of their habits and modes of thought may be of the utmost value to us in utilizing their labour, as well as in checking those inhuman practices from which they have but too often suffered at our hands. (1872:170–171)

From the 1870s through the 1930s, as the colonial empires reached their height, two themes were frequently discussed at the meetings of anthropological associations: (1) how to salvage the ethnographic data that were being destroyed by colonial expansion and (2) how to increase the practical value of anthropology for the empire. Lane-Fox Pitt-Rivers (1882) coined the term *applied anthropology* and declared, "no subject is more capable of being turned to useful account than the scientific study of mankind" (1882:507). By the turn of the century, British anthropologists had become enthusiastic imperialists. In 1901, C. H. Read, president of the Anthropological Institute, specifically emphasized the utility of anthropology for "private enterprise" such as the great trading and colonization companies, observing,

We should . . . be in a position to give the officers of such companies valuable information for the conduct of their affairs with natives, and thus be of distinct value to commercial enterprise. (1901:15)

Anthropologists of the Anthropological Institute and the Folklore Society addressed a formal memorandum to the Colonial Secretary in London, proposing the creation of a special commission, including anthropologists, to study native culture in areas of South Africa where colonial development was creating serious tensions between colonists and native peoples. The memorandum blamed native unrest on misunderstanding of native culture and argued that besides its obvious scientific value, anthropological knowledge would facilitate colonial administration because

1. *It will enable the Government to ascertain what customs may be recognized, and what customs must be forbidden or modified, and how to effect this object with the least disturbance to tribal conditions and native prejudices.*

2. *It will save time and ensure certainty in the administration of justice, and obviate many difficulties in other departments of government.*

3. *It will afford the Government authoritative materials for legislation adjusting the arrangements for native labour in the mines, and generally dealing with the relations between the natives and European settlers.* (Anthropological Institute 1903:70–74)

After many more petitions and endorsements by various scientific committees, colonial administrations finally began to hire government anthropologists and recommended anthropological training for administrators. In a short period of time in the 1920s and 1930s, applied anthropology became institutionalized in the British empire. In 1921, A. R. Radcliffe-Brown was appointed to an anthropology professorship in South Africa where he became a popular lecturer on the "native problem." Radcliffe-Brown stressed that understanding the "laws" of cultural development would give administrators "control over the social forces." More specifically, in 1923 he argued that knowing

the functions of native institutions . . . can afford great help to the missionary or the public servant who is engaged in dealing with the practical problems of the adjustment of the native civilization to the new conditions that have resulted from our occupation of the country. (Radcliffe-Brown 1958:32)

Applied anthropologists did not expect to be too directly involved in policymaking, for that was to be left to administrators. Applied anthropologists avoided value judgments about colonialism while hoping that anthropological knowledge would be used to minimize the damage that imperialist expansion was causing to native peoples. Aside from standard functionalist analysis, the major object of research for applied anthropologists was *acculturation,* or culture change; both of these were ethically neutral concepts that masked the harsh political realities of imperialism. According to a formal definition proposed by American anthropologists Robert Redfield, Ralph Linton, and Melville Herskovits, acculturation is the culture change that occurs when groups with different culture enter into "continuous firsthand contact, with subsequent changes in the original cultural pattern of either or both groups" (Redfield, Linton, and Herskovits 1936).

Acculturation studies inventoried highly visible changes such as the adoption by tribal peoples of European clothing, crops, implements, language, and Christianity and the corresponding abandonment of traditional cultural features. The loss of political and economic autonomy was not usually examined as acculturation. In reality, firsthand contact meant conquest and dispossession of native peoples by colonial soldiers and settlers. Acculturation was forced culture change and was primarily an unequal process in which tribal peoples were subordinated and exploited. However, applied anthropologists in the service of the empire could hardly be expected to draw attention to the negative side of imperialism.

The real native problem that perplexed colonial administrators was how to keep the natives from resorting to armed resistance while settlers were depriving them of their lands and how to turn them into docile taxpayers and willing and effective laborers on their former lands. Culture change was supposed to be slow to avoid detribalization, which would make control more difficult and could lead to depopulation and labor shortages.

The primary recommendation from applied anthropologists was for administrators to use *indirect rule* to maintain political control. This meant using local native chiefs to serve as government agents and intermediaries and creating them when they did not already exist. *Direct rule* by European officers was culturally insensitive and prohibitively expensive.

Bronislaw Malinowski, a prominent British functionalist, was emphatic on the advantages of indirect, or dependent, rule:

In fact, if we define dependent rule as the control of Natives through the medium of their own organization, it is clear that only dependent rule can succeed. For the government of any race consists rather in implanting in them ideas of right, of law and order, and making them obey such ideas. (1929:23)

The Native Problem in Kenya

How did a handful of Europeans administer their East African colony in a way that forced the indigenous peoples into a grossly inequitable situation?

Kenya colony in East Africa illustrates the political domination and economic exploitation that occurred as European powers forced much of Africa into the capitalist global system in the late nineteenth and early twentieth centuries. As discussed in Chapter 4, Nilotic-speaking cattle peoples and Bantu farmers effectively adapted their domestic-scale cultures to the distinctive ecosystems of East Africa some 2000 years ago. Around AD 800, the expanding Islamic empire reached the East African coast and established small centers that became important conduits for the slave and ivory trade. There was no Arab settlement in the interior, and the indigenous peoples retained their economic and political autonomy despite the disruption of the slave trade. The Maasai dominated the best pasturelands, centered in the Rift Valley, and raided their neighbors for cattle.

By the 1870s, European explorers ventured into the East African interior in increasing numbers. In 1886, Germany declared a protectorate over part of what is now Tanzania, taking advantage of a series

---

acculturation   The concept used by colonial applied anthropologists to describe the changes in tribal culture that accompanied European conquest but that minimized the role of coercion and the loss of tribal autonomy.
indirect rule   The situation in which European colonial administrators appointed local natives to serve as mediating officials, or chiefs, to help them control local communities.
direct rule   The use of European colonial administrators to control a native community at the local level.

of treaties arranged between African "chiefs" and German colonists. In the same year, Britain and Germany agreed to divide the entire East African region between themselves. Officially, the justification for British intrusion was to help end the slave trade and improve the condition of the Africans, in line with the rules established by the Berlin Africa Conference of 1884–1885 (see Figure 14.5).

In 1896, the British government created the East Africa Protectorate and established fortified outposts and used punitive expeditions, frequently pitting Maasai allies against their Bantu neighbors, to impose a *Pax Britannica*. The administrative arrangements that followed gave the European minority complete political power over more than 2 million disenfranchised Africans who were expected to serve as units of labor and pay their taxes while learning the "benefits of civilization." The

FIGURE 14.5   *Cecil Rhodes, prime minister of Britain's Cape Colony in southern Africa, astride the African continent. This 1892 political cartoon symbolizes the arrogance of European colonialism.*

THE RHODES COLOSSUS

STRIDING FROM CAPE TOWN TO CAIRO.

process of using political and economic force to create a dependent underclass of laborers resembles the enclosure movement that prepared the way for industrial capitalism in England (see Chapter 11).

The consolidation of political and economic control over the protectorate was a complex process that the British administration carried out in stages as specific legislation was drafted. The cool and fertile highlands were declared uninhabited and opened for European settlement, even though they were the center of Maasai territory. In 1924, areas of European settlement were given a separate administrative system, while "native" provinces and districts were placed under a chief native commissioner, senior provincial commissioners, and district commissioners—all Europeans. Village "chiefs" were appointed by the administration and treated like government employees with very limited authority. A simple system of native courts was given limited authority to maintain order at the local level. From the start, the political structure was designed to favor European interests at the expense of Africans. In 1920, the protectorate became the Crown Colony of Kenya. The colony's legislative council was dominated by twenty officially appointed European administrators. The interests of indigenous Africans were represented by two European appointees among twenty unofficial council members.

In 1911, there were only 3175 Europeans in the East Africa protectorate, which also contained an indigenous African population that was estimated at 2.5–4 million. The number of Europeans increased fourfold, to 12,529 by 1926, but even after the European population reached 30,524 in 1948, it still constituted barely 0.05 percent of the total population (Buell 1928, Hailey 1950).

Europeans were drawn to the protectorate by promises of low taxes and abundant resources, cheap land, and cheap African labor, all waiting to be exploited. Lumber, grain, livestock, rubber, copra, and gold were soon flowing to world markets, along with the hides, horns, and ivory of big game animals that were being slaughtered in great numbers by European hunters. By 1908, the value of exported East African natural resources exceeded 400,000 pounds sterling annually (Great Britain Board of Trade 1909) (see Figure 14.6). Nearly

FIGURE 14.6
The East Africa protec-
torate in the world sys-
tem, 1894–1908.
(SOURCE: Great Britain
Board of Trade 1909.)

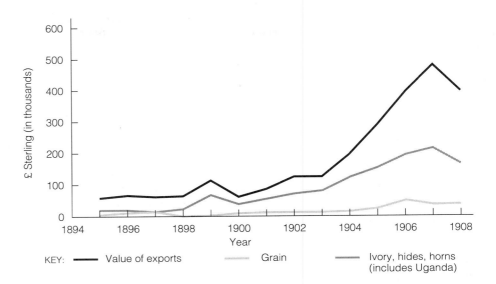

KEY: ——— Value of exports   Grain   Ivory, hides, horns
                                                    (includes Uganda)

one-fourth of these resources were destined for the United Kingdom, and two-thirds went to the world's major industrial powers: the United Kingdom, the United States, France, and Germany (Great Britain Board of Trade 1909) (see Figure 14.7).

The British administration gained control over African land simply by enacting the necessary legislation. The only concern was that the appearance of justice and legality be maintained so that humanitarians in London would not protest in Parliament. The Crown Lands Ordinance of 1902 merely specified that the government could not sell land that the Africans were actually occupying, but it provided that "unoccupied" lands could be "leased" to colonists in lots of 1000 acres (405 hectares) for 99 years. The Crown Lands Ordinance of 1915 left no doubt about who would control the land by declaring that all African lands were "crown lands" and could be alienated by the government. This policy permitted a tiny European elite to systematically acquire the best agricultural lands while dispossessing the indigenous owners.

More than 40,000 Maasai were forced to give up more than half of their territory under the terms of a treaty in 1904, by which they agreed to move into northern and southern reserves, abandoning the central Rift Valley to a handful of European set-

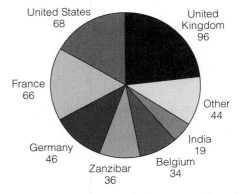

FIGURE 14.7   *Destination and value, in pounds sterling (in thousands), of exports from the East Africa protectorate, 1908. (SOURCE: Great Britain Board of Trade 1909.)*

tlers. The Maasai reserves were supposed to last "so long as the Maasai as a race shall exist" (Buell 1928: 312). However, in 1911, the northern reserve turned out to be good farmland, and by 1913, the protesting Maasai were consolidated on the much poorer southern reserve.

Harvard political scientist Raymond Buell examined the Maasai case and concluded that the government's action was legally unjustified, but he suggested that the Maasai themselves were partly responsible for the loss of their land because their culture was unsuitable. In exaggerated and ethnocentric terms that showed a complete misunderstanding of Maasai culture, Buell described them as

aimless and wandering pastoralists, owning economically worthless but continually increasing cattle. Their military organization was a constant menace to other natives, while their warrior villages were a corrupting influence inside of the tribe. (1928:315–316)

Between 1907 and 1912, a series of native reserves were proposed on "crown land" for African use in order to officially open land for European settlement. However, colonists objected that such reserves might be self-sustaining, and Africans would not need to work for Europeans in order to support themselves. Government commissions recommended that reserves be drawn up to suit the needs of only the immediate African population with the expectation that population growth would soon force people to seek wage labor. In 1919, Governor Northey justified such a policy with an appeal to the ideology of capitalist economics:

No one wants to take away any land that natives occupy or are using productively, but we can say, in these days of productivity and development, and world-wide shortage of food and raw materials, that Crown lands not made productive, may, by law, be made so as required. (Buell 1928:319)

This emphasis on productive use was somewhat misplaced, in view of the fact that in 1922, Europeans were cultivating only 6 percent of the land that they had appropriated. The inequities in the land system were obvious. Some 9000 Europeans were occupying 3.8 million acres (1.5 million hectares), with 422 acres (171 hectares) of prime land per capita. By 1926, twenty-three native reserves were actually established, and 2.5 million Africans were crowded into 29.9 million acres (12.1 million hectares), leaving them with only 12 often very poor acres (5 hectares) per capita.

Africans who wished to develop their land along European lines faced significant difficulties. They could not legally purchase land outside the reserves or individually own land within the reserves. The colonists encouraged dispossessed Africans to remain on their former lands as squatters, because African squatters were legally required to work 6 months per year for the landowners.

Hut and poll taxes were designed to provide revenue to help fund the administration and to force the Africans to find wage labor on European farms. The total African contribution to the state's revenue in direct taxes was twenty-five times the European contribution between 1900 and 1925 (Ross 1927). Africans also paid indirect taxes in the form of 10 percent custom duties that were added to the price of cloth, beads, and other trade goods. Because the total value of cash-crop farming on the native reserves covered barely two-thirds of the African tax, Africans were compelled to seek outside employment. Professional labor recruiters toured the reserves and paid local chiefs for rounding up workers. These efforts met with success because the number of employed Africans rose from 12,000 in 1912 to over 185,000 in 1927—approximately 14 African laborers for every man, woman, and child in the European population.

The attitude of Europeans toward African labor is illustrated by the British Masters and Servants Ordinances of 1906, which made it a crime punishable by a fine of a month's wages and up to a month in prison for a "servant" to be late to work, to be absent without permission, or to insult or disobey an employer. Six months' imprisonment was the punishment for quitting. In 1915, all African males over 16 were required to register with the government, be fingerprinted, and carry identity papers. This procedure helped, but desertion remained enough of a problem because of low wages and poor working conditions that in 1925 the government approved a proposal to establish special detention camps for labor offenders.

British colonial policies were unusually harsh in Kenya because European settlement was a primary objective, unlike in British colonies in West Africa, where the climate was considered unsuitable for European settlement. Indirect rule was also more easily practiced in West Africa, where traditional kingdoms were more common. In Kenya, indigenous peoples found it difficult to follow traditional cultural patterns in the absence of political and economic autonomy, and they were legally excluded from effective participation in the capitalist economy introduced by their British conquerors. The obvious inequities of the situation ultimately led to the Mau Mau armed rebellion of 1952–1959 and political reforms culminating in Kenya's independence from colonial rule in 1963.

THE AUSTRALIAN ABORIGINAL POLICY DEBATE

The experience of Australian aborigines further demonstrates how the political fate of tribal groups often is determined by government policies, which, in turn, are shaped by the demands of varied special-interest groups exercising political power. In Australia, as in East Africa, anthropologists have often played a role in shaping and supporting government policies toward indigenous peoples.

Genocidal Protection and Uplift

What policies led Australian aborigines to the brink of extinction?

The European invasion of Australia began in 1788 with the founding of Port Jackson, now Sydney, as a penal colony. Because the aborigines were not settled farming peoples and had no chiefs, colonial administrators declared Australia to be an "empty wasteland" and dispensed with treaty signing. The aborigines were granted no legal existence and no official claim to their land. As elsewhere, genocide and ethnocide followed the Australian frontiers of European settlement. Except where aborigines were useful as labor, they were systematically eliminated by poison, disease, and shooting as if they were wild animals. Tasmania's aboriginal population was reduced from 5000 to 111 within 30 years. In western Victoria, 4000 aborigines were reduced to 213 within 40 years, and 10 years later no one remained who could reliably describe the culture (Corris 1968). Witnesses before the Select Committee in the 1830s reported "many deeds of murder and violence" committed by settlers on the Australian frontier. This situation persisted well into the twentieth century. According to A. G. Price, in the Northern Territory in 1901, "It was notorious, that the blackfellows were shot down like crows and that no notice was taken" (1950:107–108).

Appeals by the APS led to the establishment of aboriginal reserves and protectors of natives in Australia by 1850. These actions did not prevent the wholesale extinction of aborigines in many areas of Australia, but they did demonstrate that such injustice was officially disapproved. Aboriginal reserves at this time were not considered to be aboriginal lands where aborigines could live independently; instead, they served a dual protection and "uplift" role. Reserves were to contain mission schools and farms where aborigines would learn civilized skills.

The fact, which no one disputed, was that aborigines were facing extinction as a result of frontier violence and dispossession. By contrast, from 1788 to 1880, the European population increased to 3 million. And by 1920, there were 5 million Europeans and barely 60,000 aborigines, a mere 20 percent of the widely accepted estimate of 300,000 for the pre-European population. All authorities anticipated a continuing decline in the aboriginal population, and many predicted their total extinction. Everyone agreed that the European invasion was responsible, but the government still followed the inadequate "protection and uplift" approach devised by the House of Commons Select Committee and the Aborigines Protection Society in the 1830s.

By 1880, the sparsely settled Northern Territory, which contained 17 percent of Australia's land area, had become the last great frontier. There were fewer than 700 Europeans throughout the territory's 500,000 square miles (mi[2]) (1.3 million square kilometers [km[2]]) stretching from the desert center of Australia to the tropical north coast. This vast, seemingly inhospitable region was the ancestral homeland of unknown thousands of aborigines still living independently. European Australians saw the territory as a great pastoral frontier, and there was still no national policy permitting the aborigines to defend themselves, their resources, and their culture against the final invasion that was just beginning.

The government encouraged immigration into the territory to promote economic development, fully aware that the aborigines would be victimized. To minimize the damage, humanitarians like Sydney's Archdeacon Lefroy (1912) recommended federal control of all aborigines by a permanent Native Commission and urged the formation of reserves on which aborigines could be preserved and "uplifted" by becoming cattle ranchers. A committee of the Australasian Association for the Advancement of Science, which included pioneer Central Australian ethnographers Baldwin Spencer and Francis Gillen, drafted a resolution to the government that incorporated Lefroy's proposals. The committee emphasized that aborigines were "a valuable labor asset" in the pastoral economy as a justification for a preservation policy. There was no attempt to protect aboriginal culture, except in museums, or to defend aboriginal political autonomy; instead, the emphasis was on "the well-being and preservation of the native race," presumably as units of labor (ANZAAS 1914). However, even these modest ameliorative proposals were ineffective.

By 1920, there were some 4000 Europeans and 600,000 cattle in the Northern Territory, steadily advancing against an aboriginal population estimated at 17,000 who faced a grim future. A mere 30,000 square miles (77,770 km²), barely 6 percent of the territory, had been designated for aboriginal reserves, even though the aborigines were still the majority population, outnumbering Europeans more than four to one. The reserves contained cattle stations and missions where the aborigines were to be "civilized," just as the Aborigines Protection Society envisioned in the nineteenth century.

Reserves, Assimilation, and Land Rights

How were the original aboriginal reserves structured to favor assimilation? What aspects of aboriginal culture provided the key to aboriginal land rights?

As the situation for aborigines in the Northern Territory became increasingly desperate, anthropologist Frederic Wood Jones (1928) issued a stinging condemnation of the established policy of limited protectionism and uplift. In an emotional presidential address to the anthropology section of the Australasian Association for the Advancement of Science in 1926, Wood Jones declared that "civilizing" the aborigine, whether on missions or cattle stations, meant extermination. Using missionary reports, he showed that the aborigines in the best condition were those most remote from civilization. Missionized aborigines were unhealthy and ill-housed and continued to die. Arguing that the missions were a form of humanitarian euthanasia that had failed in every sense, Wood Jones concluded, "I fail to see any sort of justification for a belief that salvation for the Australian native can ever lie in this direction" (1928:504).

Wood Jones was just as critical of the government effort to provide welfare to the aborigines on the fringes of civilization. He suggested that it was a form of conscience money that served to hide the fact that aboriginals were being dispossessed. He also challenged the belief that the aborigine could

be converted to a "coolie" population to provide cheap labor for the pastoral stations. He pointed out that although individuals might become successful station hands, they did not reproduce to replace themselves. There seemed to be no substitute for the traditional independent life.

He further argued that the existing reserves were "fictions and frauds" because they existed only on paper and were revoked whenever outside economic interests demanded entry: "There are no real reserves in Australia where the aborigine is free to live, what everyone is agreed on calling, a life uncontaminated by the white man" (1928:513).

A "real reserve" in Wood Jones' terms would be one that allowed the continuation of tribal "culture and traditions." Melbourne anthropologist Donald Thomson (1938) proposed making Arnhem Land, in the far north of the Northern Territory, just such a reserve after he conducted a government-commissioned field investigation there in 1935–1937. Some 1500 aborigines were still living independently in Arnhem Land, and when five Japanese fishermen and a policeman were killed on the reserve, the government hoped Thomson could help settle the matter peacefully. Thomson was trained in functionalist applied anthropology by Radcliffe-Brown at Sydney, but he was also a close associate of Wood Jones. Thomson's sympathies were clearly with the aborigines. He concluded that the killings were self-defense, and he recommended that Arnhem Land be made an absolutely inviolable reserve, with missionaries and ranchers excluded, in order to allow the aborigines freedom to maintain their nomadic settlement pattern, culture, and social structure (see Figure 14.8). This was perhaps the first time that an idealist policy approach was seriously proposed for Australia.

This approach was soundly rejected by Sydney anthropologist A. P. Elkin, who represented the vested interests of the government and missionary organizations. Elkin was an influential and outspoken advocate of "justice" for aborigines. But he also wanted to secure a place for both anthropology and missions in the business of smoothing what he considered to be the inevitable **assimilation** of aborigines from their independent tribal life into a settled existence within civilized Australian society. Trained by Radcliffe-Brown and Malinowski in functionalist applied anthropology, Elkin became a

FIGURE 14.8
Big Bill Neidjie and his son Jonathan Yarra-marna at a sacred site on their clan land in Kakadu National Park, Northern Territory, Australia. The park was created in 1979 as part of an agreement permitting uranium mining on ab-original land in Arnhem Land.

leading expert on aboriginal culture. However, he also accepted Radcliffe-Brown's ominous dictum that "the Australian Aborigines, even if not doomed to extinction as a race, seem at any rate doomed to have their cultures destroyed" (1934:3).

As an anthropologist, Elkin clearly understood the centrality of totemism in aboriginal culture. But he considered it an obsolete and ignorant belief that was to be replaced by "a religious and philosophical outlook which will enable them [the aborigines] to see that their own spiritual life and the future of natural species is not bound up with the integrity of particular spots on the earth's surface" (1934:7). Oblivious to his own ethnocentrism and convinced that the culture was doomed, Elkin went on to suggest, "Wise teaching on religion and in the rudiments of science should do much to enable the natives to pass through the difficult transition period for which we are responsible" (1934:7).

The irony of this is that the aborigines were right on this very critical issue. Totemism was not a matter of tribal ignorance over which the aborigines needed to be educated. The spiritual life of aborigines and the future of their natural resources are inextricably linked to the ultimate integrity of their sacred sites, but it was nearly 40 years before government policy grudgingly came to acknowledge this point with the Northern Territory Land Rights Act of 1971. Accepting the validity of the totemic system would have meant also acknowledging the legitimacy of the aboriginal claim to full control over their land, resources, and political and economic independence.

Rather than advocating aboriginal rights, Elkin called for a "positive policy" for aborigines, based on close collaboration between church and state to promote "education as well as law, order, harmony, and pacification." Elkin was a religious man, ordained in 1915 as an Anglican priest, and was in charge of a parish until 1937. Combining his religious role with his training as an applied anthropologist, he advised missionaries to "build on the religious life of the natives, modifying it where necessary, and seeking its fulfillment along Christian lines" (Elkin 1933:6).

Elkin opposed any aboriginal claim to the land that would stand in the way of outside development

assimilation Ethnocide without genocide; the loss of distinctive cultural traits as a population surrenders its autonomy and is absorbed into a dominant society and culture.

interests. In his view, keeping whites off the reserves "of course, cannot be done once gold or valuable land be found in them." Elkin's policy approach was probably related to his position in the Sydney anthropology department, which he began to chair in 1934. The department developed an applied program under Radcliffe-Brown's earlier direction and with Rockefeller Foundation grants. The Sydney program was designed to support the government's colonial development policies, and Elkin emphatically disassociated his department from any support for aboriginal autonomy:

It should be stated quite clearly and definitely that anthropologists connected with the Department in the University of Sydney have no desire to preserve any of the aboriginal tribes of Australia or of the islands in their pristine condition as "museum specimens" for the purpose of investigation; this charge is too often made against anthropologists. . . for change is coming, and anthropologists, like all good members of a "higher" and trustee race, are concerned with the task of raising primitive races in the cultural scale. (1934:3)

Twenty years later, Elkin's assimilation approach was still the government's solution to the "aboriginal problem." In 1952, Paul Hasluck, minister for territories, publicly attacked "a few" unnamed anthropologists whose "mystical" belief in "changeless primitive culture" had led them to advocate strict inviolability of aboriginal reserves. Hasluck declared contemptuously, "My view is that no society can live in such an isolated dreamland as that" (Hasluck 1953:156).

Of course, the real issue was not the existence of culture change, but the political independence of tribal peoples and whether outsiders should be allowed to dictate the kind of changes that occur on tribal land. Hasluck inadvertently admitted that the government had no intention of respecting the boundaries of tribal reservations when he rhetorically asked, "Do we expect that they can remain static even if protected by imaginary lines, drawn around reserves, when a new and active society and culture are brought into their country?" (1953:157).

Hasluck knew that the reserves were a sham, that the government would not permit tribal autonomy, yet he shamelessly argued that good social science culture change theory had led him to such a conclusion. The ethnocentric policy that Hasluck

promoted was uncompromising assimilationist, which he described in the following terms:

A policy of assimilation means, to my mind, that we expect that, in the course of time, all persons of aboriginal blood or mixed-blood in Australia will live in the same manner as white Australians do, that they will have full citizenship, and that they will, of their own desire, participate in all the activities of the Australian community. (1953:163)

The government continued this rigid policy of rejecting aboriginal self-determination and land rights into the 1970s when politically active aboriginal organizations began to publicly demand legal ownership of traditional lands. The protest began in 1971 when the government rejected aboriginal claims of ownership to the Arnhem Land Reserve. The aboriginal landowners wanted to protect their sacred sites by preventing a multinational mining company from strip mining bauxite inside the reserve. By 1973, the protest began to take on international dimensions, and the government appointed an Aboriginal Land Rights Commission to find a solution. The result was the Aboriginal Land Rights (Northern Territory) Act of 1976, which provided a legal mechanism for aboriginal communities to gain title to their traditional lands. This was a major victory for aborigines, although the act provided only limited protection from outside development and was later weakened by amendments. The real significance of the act was that it meant that the government was finally acknowledging the legitimacy of aboriginal culture and the right of aborigines to maintain themselves as independent communities.

DECOLONIZATION AND HUMAN RIGHTS

The decolonization era, which began with the founding of the United Nations in 1945, was also the beginning of a gradual shift away from the paternalistic and ethnocentric bias of even the most humanitarian of colonial policies toward indigenous peoples. The United Nations and affiliated organizations such as the International Labour Organisation (ILO) provided an international framework within which the concept of human rights was steadily expanded to include indigenous peoples as cultural groups and to legitimize their struggle for self-determination. The extension of fundamental human rights to indigenous peoples has been a slow and difficult process requiring decisive participation by indigenous peoples themselves.

The United Nations and Indigenous Peoples

What does the UN Charter say about indigenous peoples? What other UN resolutions and declarations support indigenous peoples?

The UN Charter provided an opening for indigenous rights, but it still contained ethnocentric thinking. Article 1 of the charter proclaimed support for "the principle of equal rights and self-determination of peoples," but it did not define *peoples*. The only provisions in the charter specifically applicable to indigenous peoples were in Chapters XI–XIII describing the international trusteeship system. The "Declaration Regarding Non-Self-Governing Territories" in Article 73 ethnocentrically speaks of "territories whose peoples have not yet attained a full measure of self-government." This language was obviously ethnocentric when applied to Pacific Islanders with functioning chiefdoms, but it was equally patronizing to call domestic-scale cultures "nonself-governing" when they clearly managed their own internal affairs without formal government. Many "nonself-governing territories" were already under the League of Nations mandate system, and the framers of the UN Charter borrowed from the League of Nations Covenant when they referred to a "sacred trust" to promote "the well-being of the inhabitants of these territories." There are demeaning references to "stages of advancement" and "constructive measures of development," which were direct carryovers from the "protection and uplift" civilizing policies of the colonial era.

From the perspective of indigenous peoples, the early institutionalization of international development under the UN system represented a direct continuation of the old colonialism under new leadership. Fortunately, additional international covenants helped expand the concept of human rights, providing a framework on which indigenous political leaders could build. For example, Article 22 of the 1948 UN Declaration of Human Rights states that everyone is entitled to the realization of the "cultural rights indispensable for his dignity and the free development of his personality." This was amplified by the International Covenant of Human Rights, adopted by the UN General Assembly in 1966:

> In those states in which ethnic, religious or linguistic minorities exist, persons belonging to such minorities shall not be denied the right, in community with the other members of their group, to enjoy their own culture, to profess and practice their own religion or to use their own language.

This is a significant statement because it refers specifically to the human rights of cultural groups as group rights, whereas most earlier international declarations have referred to individual human rights.

ILO Convention 107

What were the strengths and weaknesses of the first major attempt to set international policy standards for the humane treatment of indigenous peoples?

The first attempt to write an international convention devoted entirely to the relationship between indigenous peoples and governments was undertaken by the ILO in 1946 in cooperation with the United Nations, UNESCO, FAO, and WHO. Anthropologists were directly involved in this historic 11-year effort, which culminated in 1957 when the General Conference of the ILO adopted "Convention (No. 107) concerning the protection and integration of indigenous and other tribal and semi-tribal populations in independent countries" (United Nations 1959).

ILO Convention 107, a curiously ambiguous document that attempted to raise a new standard for the rights of indigenous peoples, fell short of its goal because it failed to incorporate the viewpoint of indigenous peoples themselves. Convention 107 made a strong statement in support of the human rights of tribal individuals while endorsing government programs that directly undermined tribal cultures. The key contradiction is found in Article 7:

International Labor Org. = ILO

These populations shall be allowed to retain their own customs and institutions where these are not incompatible with the national legal system or the objectives of integration programmes.

This convention merits careful study because the issues that it defined are still being debated. This section details the background to the writing of Convention 107 to show how ethnocentric misunderstanding of domestic-scale cultures can undermine even the most well-intended humanitarian efforts.

The ILO was created at the end of World War I as a League of Nations affiliate concerned with international labor conditions and standard of living. It became a UN affiliate, and by 1980, its membership included 144 countries. The ILO's original interest in indigenous peoples was restricted to labor problems in colonial territories. In 1946, the ILO expanded its concerns to include general issues of economic development and indigenous peoples, and it established a Committee of Experts on Indigenous Labor.

The general approach to "the problem of Indigenous populations" expressed at the committee's first meeting in 1951 indicated that indigenous peoples would be treated ethnocentrically as impoverished and underdeveloped people in need of development. This narrow interpretation closely followed the UN Economic and Social Council view of global poverty and underdevelopment, which launched the United Nations' development campaign at precisely the same moment (see Chapter 13). According to the ILO experts, indigenous people were disadvantaged because they were backward and ignorant. Their legal "rights" were being denied because they were not able to participate fully in development progress. The solution was formal education, economic development, new forms of political organization, and special legislation.

The ILO experts identified ***integration*** of indigenous peoples into the national society as the best policy objective. Integration would help tribal peoples "progress" and raise their "cultural level" so that they could overcome their social and economic "inferiority," but integration left little room for the existence of independent domestic-scale cultures. The committee noted that tribal culture might al-ready seem "attractive" and that change might disturb prior ecological balances, but they concluded that "the scientist must accept the fact that social change is inevitable as a result of the general economic and social development of the community" (ILR 1951:64).

At the same time, the committee expressed confidence that applied social science could overcome any problems. However, recognizing the potential for damage, efforts were to be made to set "standards that would prevent the indigenous groups from being overwhelmed" by change. Governments were to create special vocational training programs to provide

the aboriginals with proper opportunity to develop fully their occupational abilities, so as to improve their conditions of life, to obtain the greatest benefit to the national economy and to assist in their assimilation into the cultural life of the nation. (ILR 1951:65)

It was argued that vocational training could be used to improve the existing subsistence economy of a tribal group in order to raise their living standard, but it could also be used to modify the culture more directly (see Figure 14.9). The report specifically recommended that in some cases, "an attempt should be made to change the direction of the traditional activities of the group" (ILR 1951:65). It was suggested that special extension agents could deliver "oral advice" to tribal peoples on such matters as agricultural methods, handicrafts, and "good habits of living" (ILR 1951:66).

A second ILO Committee of Experts was convened in 1954 to discuss how to protect and integrate forest-dwelling indigenous groups such as Amazonians. This fifteen-member committee was also flawed by ethnocentric preconceptions, even though it was chaired by New Zealand anthropologist Ernest Beaglehole and included two other prominent anthropologists, Horace Miner, an American, and Darcy Ribeiro, a Brazilian. The committee's agenda was limited to helping forest-dwelling "populations" adapt to forced development change. The committee acknowledged that the expansion of "technologically advanced societies" into formerly isolated tribal refuges was disturbing ecological balances and cultural patterns, breaking up tribal communities, marginalizing tribal individuals, and leaving them easy prey to

FIGURE 14.9   *An Ashaninka shaman processing sheets of raw rubber for sale at a mission station in the Peruvian Amazon. This vocational activity operated within an extremely exploitative system of labor that was not effectively addressed by the ILO.*

economic exploitation. However, instead of condemning the invasion of tribal lands, the experts blamed the victims by declaring that tribal groups were "marginalized" because "they have failed to identify themselves with the values of technologically advanced societies" (ILR 1954:422).

By accepting the state's right to invade tribal areas in the interest of economic development, the Committee of Experts was placed in an ambiguous and contradictory position, and this contradiction was incorporated into ILO Convention 107. The experts endorsed a tribal right to self-fulfillment, to retention of traditional lands, and to free movement across national boundaries. However, the committee refused to condemn the greatest threat

to these noble objectives—the state's right to "integrate" tribal peoples on its own terms.

The Committee of Experts described all tribal groups as occupying various stages on their way toward "inevitable" integration with national society. Totally independent tribes represented the first stage of integration. When the integration process was inadequately directed, Stage 2 was characterized by violence, disease, disorder, ecological disruption, and other direct assaults on tribal culture. Stage 3 involved collapse of the tribal system and social disintegration, followed by marginalization of former tribal individuals in Stage 4. The experts argued optimistically that these negative outcomes could be avoided by more carefully planned integration programs, backed by special protective legislation. They envisioned a limited "cultural autonomy" for tribal peoples, who would be integrated into a pluralistic national society, where economic development would mutually benefit all groups. Successfully integrated tribal groups would "identify themselves with the values of technologically advanced societies." This positive outcome mirrored the "benefits of civilization" approach advocated by the nineteenth-century humanitarians and was equally prone to failure.

Like the anthropologists who identified the obstacles to economic progress in peasant cultures, the ILO experts recognized that successfully adapted indigenous groups might resist imposed integration. The committee found that "isolated" tribal peoples were healthy and self-sufficient, yet this was called "an undesirable state of segregation" (ILR 1954: 424) because it perpetuated tribal culture, thereby blocking successful integration. Committee chair Ernest Beaglehole (1954) was explicit on the value of applied anthropology in implementing culture change programs:

The anthropologist, through his detailed knowledge of indigenous life, can note the areas of resistance, blockage and susceptibility to change, so that local patterns will be circumvented or utilised in order to reduce friction and resistance. (1954:432)

integration   The absorption of a formerly autonomous people into a dominant state society, with the possible retention of ethnic identity.

Because force was not supposed to be employed in helping tribal groups realize their "inexorable destiny," the central problem for planners was "how to produce a shift from the satisfactions that indigenous forest dwellers find in their own societies to the satisfactions normally found in modern society" (Beaglehole 1954:424).

The experts proposed a four-point program for a combined "protection-integration" action plan:

1. *The safeguarding, preservation and development of the indigenous forest-dwelling population's economic base*

2. *The raising of its standard of living*

3. *The development of medical and health action with the object of maintaining at least the same health conditions as existed before contact with the invading society*

4. *The development of fundamental education* (Beaglehole 1954:425)

This program may have sounded promising, but it supported external conquest and invasion and was founded on outrageously ethnocentric assumptions. In a series of resolutions, the committee declared that tribal peoples were socially and economically "impoverished," their subsistence was "inadequate," and they were unhygienic. They needed outside technical experts to teach the "best agricultural, stock-rearing, forestry and handicraft techniques." They needed to be taught how to work efficiently, maintain subsistence reserves, and prevent waste and resource depletion and "irrational" deforestation. They needed to be instructed how to ensure the equitable distribution of water resources. And they needed to grow more crop varieties and increase their economic independence.

Ironically, undisturbed tribal peoples were doing just fine in all of these areas before outside intrusion; "integration" created the very conditions of impoverishment that it intended to prevent. This negative view of tribal culture likely resulted, in part, because the first session of the Committee of Experts was primarily concerned with the most depressed and exploited Andean peasantry and tended to generalize their unhappy condition to *all* tribal peoples while attributing its cause to the indigenous culture rather than the national political and economic structures that encouraged oppression.

The committee's final resolutions were contradictory because, although they advocated respect for tribal culture "as a legitimate way of life," they also accepted the self-fulfilling prophecy that tribal peoples were "doomed to change." Committee members were divided over whether change should be rapid or slow, but they agreed that development would be imposed. As Horace Miner explained, "The realist recognizes the inevitability of increasing encroachment of civilization on the remaining outposts of preliterate culture" (1955:441).

The drafting of ILO Convention 107 presented anthropologists with a golden opportunity to create a blueprint for the independence of domestic-scale cultures, but the momentum of global economic development was too strong. Convention 107 failed to support indigenous rights because it made the economic goals of commercial-scale state cultures the primary objective.

Indigenous Organizations and ILO Convention 169

How successful were indigenous organizations in influencing the rewriting of ILO Convention 107?

In the 1960s and 1970s, indigenous peoples throughout the world began to form political organizations to press their demands for full control over their traditional lands and communities. Indigenous organizations emerged at local, national, and international levels. In Amazonia, the Shuar of Ecuador were among the first to organize when they formed a federation in 1964 to unite communities that were fragmented by land invasions. Similar groups exist in other Amazon countries, including Peru. At the international level, the World Council of Indigenous Peoples (WCIP) was formed in 1975, with delegates drawn from indigenous organizations from throughout the world. The WCIP was one of the only indigenous organizations to have NGO (nongovernmental organization) status with the United Nations. This allowed it to play a consultative role in deliberations before the Economic and Social Council and UN affiliates such as the ILO. The primary objective of the WCIP was "to ensure political, economic, and social justice to indigenous peoples."

At the Fourth Assembly of the WCIP, which was held in Panama in 1984, some 300 indigenous people from twenty-three countries drew up a Declaration of Principles of Indigenous Rights. This declaration clearly lists the international standards that should define their position relative to state governments and international institutions. Three of the most critical principles are the following:

Principle 1. All indigenous peoples have the right of self-determination. By virtue of this right they may freely determine their political status and freely pursue their economic, social, religious and cultural development.

Principle 9. Indigenous peoples shall have exclusive rights to their traditional lands and its resources; where the lands and resources of the indigenous peoples have been taken away without their free and informed consent such lands and resources shall be returned.

Principle 12. No action or course of conduct may be undertaken which, directly or indirectly, may result in the destruction of land, air, water, sea ice, wildlife, habitat or natural resources without the free and informed consent of the indigenous peoples affected.

Indigenous organizations are supported by various religious, environmentalist, and human rights groups in many countries. International organizations such as Cultural Survival, IWGIA (the International Work Group for Indigenous Affairs), and Survival International, which are directed by anthropologists, have played important support roles for indigenous organizations by raising funds and by helping them establish national and international contacts where their views can be expressed.

A new possibility for raising the international standard on the rights of indigenous peoples arose in 1985 when the ILO decided to revise its 1957 Convention 107 on the protection and integration of indigenous peoples. Even though Convention 107 was ratified by only twenty-six states, it remained the principal international convention on indigenous rights. The ILO hoped to remove the integrationist tone of the old convention, while keeping the basic document intact. Indigenous groups and their supporters wanted a revised convention to be a strong statement in support of indigenous rights to self-determination and urged removal of the old convention's ethnocentric emphasis on integration and development and its ambiguity concerning indigenous land rights.

A new Committee of Experts took up the question in Geneva at formal meetings in 1986, 1988, and 1989. This time, indigenous people were permitted at least token representation, but the final wording and approval of the revision rested with the hundred or so experts who represented employers, governments, and workers, and not with indigenous people. The WCIP, the IWGIA, and Survival International were allowed to speak as NGOs, but they could exercise only indirect influence. The proceedings were also attended by official and unofficial indigenous observers representing various native groups from North and South America, India, and Australia, but they remained on the sidelines (Gray 1987).

As discussion proceeded, two familiar arguments emerged, and the specific terms used and precise definitions became critical matters. Experts representing the ILO, employers, and some governments urged realism and proposed that indigenous peoples be granted the right to participation and consultation in the process of integration and development. Indigenous people assumed that participation and consultation still meant integration, and they insisted on self-determination, with indigenous consent and control over government policies that might affect them. They wanted the power to veto undesirable development programs and refused to be seen as passive participants in programs already designed by others. The realists also wanted to retain the original language of Convention 107 that referred to "populations," thereby avoiding references to specific cultural characteristics that defined *peoples* as groups. Recognizing that cultural uniqueness was the most fundamental issue, indigenous people insisted that the term *people* should replace *population* in a new convention.

The indigenous representatives objected to the old convention's derogatory references to "stages" of development and integration. They also wanted to greatly expand references to "land" to refer to "territories of the earth" to emphasize their claims to land, water, ice, and air. Indigenous people considered themselves to be "custodians" of inalienable resources, not *owners* in the market economy sense. When the final deliberations appeared to be supporting the old integrationist approach, the

Australian aboriginal delegation withdrew in protest. Delivering an impassioned speech, aboriginal representative Geoff Clarke declared,

We define our rights in terms of self-determination. We are not looking to dismember your States and you know it. But we do insist on the right to control our territories, our resources, the organisation of our societies, our own decision-making institutions, and the maintenance of our own cultures and ways of life. . . . Do you think that we are unaware of the actual meaning of words like consultation, participation and collaboration? Would you be satisfied with "consultation" as a guarantee for your rights? Unless governments are obligated to obtain our consent, we remain vulnerable to legislative and executive whims that inevitably will result in further dispossession and social disintegration of our peoples. The victims are always the first to know how the system operates. (IWGIA Yearbook 1988, 1989:184)

A final revision was approved by the ILO in 1989 as Convention 169. It did eliminate most of the ethnocentric language, but the contradictory emphasis on integration remained. The term *people* was introduced but was avowed to have no legal significance. Over the objections of indigenous leaders, governments retained responsibility for development and policymaking, with indigenous peoples relegated to "participation" and "cooperation." There were references to respect for indigenous culture and recognition of land rights, but the qualifications and escape clauses were so numerous that in many respects, less real protection was provided than in the original covenant. Not surprisingly, the new convention has been widely rejected by indigenous peoples (Gray 1990).

The Universal Declaration on Rights of Indigenous Peoples

How does the Universal Declaration provide a solid basis for the coexistence of domestic-scale cultures within the global system?

Indigenous political organizations have presented their viewpoints on indigenous rights before a variety of UN human rights forums, beginning in 1977 when more than fifty indigenous leaders were invited to attend the International Conference on Discrimination Against Indigenous Populations in the Americas, organized in Geneva by the special UN Committee on Human Rights. Similar conferences followed, and in 1982 a special Working Group on Indigenous Peoples (WGIP) was established by the UN Sub-Commission on the Prevention of Discrimination and Protection of Minorities, of the UN ECOSOC Commission on Human Rights. The WGIP was directed to draft a Universal Declaration of Indigenous Rights for final adoption by the UN General Assembly in 1992. In this case, there was direct involvement of many indigenous groups in the proceedings and in the drafting of the declaration. In contrast to the ILO Convention, the real concerns of indigenous peoples with guaranteeing self-determination and preventing genocide, ethnocide, and ecocide were specifically addressed. The first revised draft, issued in 1988, listed thirty rights of indigenous peoples, including:

3. *The (collective) right to exist as distinct peoples and to be protected against genocide.*

5. *The individual and collective right to protection against ethnocide. This protection shall include, in particular, prevention of any act which has the aim or effect of depriving them of their ethnic characteristics or cultural identity, of any form of forced assimilation or integration, of imposition of foreign life-styles and of any propaganda derogating their dignity and diversity.*

12. *The right of collective and individual ownership, possession and use of the lands or resources which they have traditionally occupied or used. The lands can only be taken away from them with their free and informed consent as witnessed by a treaty or agreement.*

16. *The right to protection of their environment and in particular against any action or course of conduct which may result in the destruction, deterioration or pollution of their traditional habitat, land, air, water, sea, ice, wildlife or other resources without free and informed consent of the indigenous peoples affected.*

23. *The (collective) right to autonomy in matters relating to their own internal and local affairs, including education, information, culture, religion, health, housing, social welfare, traditional and other economic activities, land and resources administration and the environment.* (IWGIA Yearbook 1989, 1990:151–158)

These rights represent a significant departure from the ethnocentric uplift and limited protectionism of the colonial era. They also represent a clear repudiation of the forced-integration policies that were called "inevitable" by the realists during the modern era of economic development. These new indigenous rights, if they are recognized by the international community, will provide a firm basis for the coexistence of domestic-scale cultures within the global system. However, as the draft declaration declares in Article 29, "These rights constitute the minimum standards for the survival and the well-being of the indigenous peoples of the world."

The following case study from Amazonia shows how indigenous groups are continuing to be dispossessed by national development and integration programs that ignore these most basic of human rights.

NATIONAL INTEGRATION IN AMAZONIA

Because ILO Convention 107 was written with the welfare of indigenous Amazonians specifically in mind and because most Amazonian countries signed the convention, it is especially relevant to examine the effects of national integration programs that have been carried out in Amazonia and to consider policy alternatives.

Historically, the European invasion of Amazonia nearly annihilated the indigenous populations. In 1500, when Amazonia was first claimed by Europeans, there may have been as many as 6.8 million native residents (Denevan 1976), but by 1970, the population had declined by nearly 90 percent to less than 1 million. ILO committee member Darcy Ribeiro (1957) reported that in Brazil, more than one-third of the indigenous groups known in 1900 were extinct by 1957, the year Convention 107 was adopted. In 1968, the Brazilian government revealed that officials of its Indian Protection Service had conspired with wealthy landowners to remove indigenous people from their lands using machine guns, dynamite, poison, and disease. Thousands must have died in an extermination process that rivaled the worst abuses of the early colonial period. Native dispossession and deaths were accel-

erated when construction of the transamazon highway system began in 1970, followed by large-scale colonization, agricultural development, mining, and hydroelectric projects (Davis 1977).

The Ashaninka Versus Global Development

How have the Ashaninka been affected as their national territory has been opened for development? How have they responded?

The Ashaninka (Campa) of eastern Peru, who were introduced in Chapters 1 and 3, provide a useful case study of the integration process in Amazonia. In the 1960s, some 21,000 Ashaninka were still the principal occupants of their vast homeland in the forested eastern foothills of the Andes in central Peru. They were highly self-sufficient and only minimally involved with the market economy. Their first contacts with Europeans occurred in the 1500s, and over the next two centuries, Franciscan missionaries gradually established outposts throughout the region and imposed their own culture change program. However, the Ashaninka resented Franciscan disapproval of polygyny and other restrictions on their freedom. They destroyed the missions in 1742 and enjoyed complete independence for more than 100 years, demonstrating that the integration process was reversible, not inevitable.

The situation began to change in the 1870s when the Republic of Peru turned to Amazonia as a frontier of national expansion. Ashaninka territory was critical to government planning because it controlled the river pathways to the Amazon, but explorers and missionaries entering the area were frequently met with a rain of Ashaninka arrows. Military force and gift giving eventually overcame most Ashaninka resistance and cleared the way for colonists. A regional economic boom began after the Pichis Trail was successfully opened in 1891 as a mule road through the Ashaninka homeland to a navigable point on the Pichis River, and a huge tract of Ashaninka land was deeded to an English company for a coffee plantation. This development activity caused many Ashaninka to experience all the negative aspects of the uncontrolled frontier and led to further hostilities. In 1913–1914, frustrated Ashaninka warriors armed themselves with guns and attacked missions and outposts in the Pichis Valley, killing 150 settlers before they, in turn, were defeated by troops.

After these events, the government took little interest in the region until the 1960s. Scattered groups of fully independent Ashaninka dominated the remote areas, while the more accessible riverine zones were only lightly settled by outsiders who established missions, small cattle ranches, and farms, following successive economic waves of rubber and lumber extraction. The Ashaninka still maintained a viable culture after more than 400 years of colonial intrusion. But their future was increasingly threatened by a shift in government policy that began in 1960 with the Plan Peruvia, which selected some 45,000 square miles (116,550 km²) in Amazonia, including most of the Ashaninka area, for long-term economic development. A special unit (ONERN) was established, with U.S. AID funds, to evaluate the natural resources in the zone and to formulate a detailed development proposal. Military engineer units, supported by U.S. military-assistance programs, began constructing a network of "penetration" highways that would provide the primary infrastructure for the project.

In 1965, Peruvian president Fernando Belaunde-Terry (1965) announced a definitive economic "conquest" of Amazonia. Ignoring the native population, he characterized the region as underpopulated and underexploited and promised that developing Amazonia would solve the overpopulation, poverty, food shortages, and land scarcity of the Andean and coastal zones. Indeed, Peru's population had tripled since 1900 and exceeded 10 million by 1965. However, the real issue was inequality, not population growth, because the Inca empire had supported an even larger population without invading Amazonia. The government's development program was simply an accelerated eastward extension of the national market economy, which had already generated Andean poverty and was now impoverishing the Native Amazonians. The new, multimillion-dollar program was eventually cofinanced by U.S. AID, the UN Development Programme, the World Bank, and the Inter-American Development Bank, contributing to a vast increase in Peru's external public debt, from $856 million in 1970 to $12.4 bil-

lion in 1988. This debt arrangement helped make Peru a poor client state and made the fate of the Amazonians and the forest ecosystem ultimately dependent on management decisions made at the global level.

My own investigations in the region between 1965 and 1969 (Bodley 1970, 1972b) showed that when Belaunde-Terry's project began, some 2500 Ashaninka still remained fully self-sufficient, whereas many others were drawn into exploitive **debt bondage** with **patrons** who offered cheap merchandise in exchange for labor (see Figure 14.10). Many Ashaninka had already joined Protestant mission communities and were establishing a marginal and precarious niche in the expanding regional market economy. These new mission communities did not control an adequate land base and were quickly depleting local subsistence resources, increasing their dependence on purchased goods. This placed the Ashaninka at an enormous disadvantage in economic competition with the wealthier and more sophisticated colonists who were invading their lands.

The Ashaninka were largely ignored by development planners. For example, air-photo planning maps had "empty wasteland" printed over plainly visible Ashaninka garden plots. In the Tambo-Pajonal planning unit, a 5500-square-mile (14,245-km²) roadless area occupied by 4000 Ashaninka, plans called for 560 miles (901 km) of roads and the introduction of 145,000 settlers (ONERN 1968). There were legal provisions for granting limited land titles to the Ashaninka in accord with the general principles of Convention 107 but no provision for those who preferred not to be integrated into the national economy.

Because these events coincided with the widely publicized Brazilian massacres, many anthropologists began making public statements on indigenous rights at this time. The 39th Americanist Congress, assembled in Lima, Peru, in 1970, issued "recommendations" condemning ethnocide and calling threatened Amazonian communities "oppressed peoples" in need of "national liberation." In 1971, Stefano Varese, a Peruvian anthropologist who had also worked with the Ashaninka, joined with Ribeiro and nine other anthropologists to draft the Declaration of Barbados (Bodley 1990). They stated that native lands were being treated as

FIGURE 14.10
A newly recruited Ashaninka labor crew being interviewed by the author in 1969.

internal colonies, and they called on governments, the missions, anthropologists, and especially the indigenous peoples themselves to work for liberation. Varese (1972), optimistic that Peru's new approach to agrarian reform would reduce the exploitation and dependency of forest peoples, proposed that special government teams encourage native groups to mobilize politically in their own defense. Precisely what form "liberation" would take was unclear.

The Cultural Autonomy Alternative

What policy approach would give indigenous groups like the Ashaninka maximum self-determination while allowing them the option of maintaining their way of life?

In 1972, I proposed that the government demarcate the entire interfluvial upland zone as inviolable "Ashaninka Land" (see Figure 14.11). Development by outsiders would have been permanently prohibited in this vast 29,000-square-mile (75,110-km²) territory, which encompassed most of the traditional Ashaninka homeland (Bodley 1972b). This was realistic given the ONERN studies showing that most of this area was unsuitable for commercial agriculture, contained no important mineral resources, and was best maintained as a protected watershed. In lowland areas where integration was already underway, I recommended that very large reserves be established on the best agricultural soils to give market-oriented Ashaninka a competitive advantage. Later I called this approach the ***cultural autonomy*** alternative because it would allow domestic-scale cultures the opportunity to maintain their independence; it specified three key points:

1. *National governments and international organizations must recognize and support tribal rights to their traditional land, cultural autonomy, and full local sovereignty.*

2. *The responsibility for initiating outside contacts must rest with the tribal people themselves: outside influences may not have free access to tribal areas.*

---

debt bondage   An exploitive economic relationship that is managed to keep individuals in virtually perpetual indebtedness.
patron   A Spanish term for someone who extends credits or goods to a client who is kept in a debt relationship.
internal colony   A territory within a state containing an indigenous population that is denied the right of self-determination.
cultural autonomy   Self-determination by a cultural group.

KEY:

▨ Proposed Ashaninka land	—— Highways	▢ Proposed reserves
▤ ONERN study zones	- - - Proposed highways	• Towns, settlements

FIGURE 14.11   (a) Ashaninka territory in 1850 before the most recent wave of colonization and development by outsiders; (b) the Ashaninka land cultural autonomy alternative proposed in 1970, shown in relation to new colonization and economic development zones.

3. *Industrial states must not compete with tribal societies for their resources.* (Bodley 1975:169)

Granting this degree of autonomy to the Ashaninka would have forced drastic modifications in the government's programs, but the institutional momentum for large-scale development was so strong that my proposal was ignored. However, some aspects of cultural autonomy were coincidentally incorporated in the Manu Park, a 5800-square-mile (15,022-km^2) environmental sanctuary established in the southern Peruvian Amazon in 1973. Independent tribal groups already living within the park were allowed to remain undisturbed as long as they did not exploit park resources for commercial purposes (d'Ans 1972, 1981).

The cultural autonomy alternative was initially rejected by some anthropologists who argued that it was based on an idealized concept of traditional cultures and would prevent the necessary political mobilization and economic development of indigenous peoples (Aaby 1977, Varese 1972). Of course, cultural autonomy must ultimately be supported by governments, but it can be implemented by indigenous peoples themselves. It is a strategy for allowing indigenous groups to chart their own course, not a strategy that nonindigenous experts can use to impose their own concept of development on target groups. What matters is whether indigenous peoples are allowed to control their own resources and cultural destiny. The anticultural autonomy arguments repeated the earlier Australian debate over aboriginal policy. Some missionaries firmly opposed native autonomy in Amazonia, arguing that it was "unrealistic" and "romantic" and would artificially deny indigenous people the benefits of Christianity (Wise, Loos, and Davis 1977). Like Elkin, they maintained that missionary intervention would help the natives overcome maladaptive culture traits such as infanticide and shamanism and that Christianity would provide "spiritual help in facing the difficult life of the 20th century" (1977:521).

In 1974, anthropologist Richard Chase Smith (1977) proposed a development plan that would have allowed significant autonomy for the Yanesha (Amuesha), western neighbors of the Ashaninka, while protecting the vulnerable rain forest environ-

ment. Smith recommended creation of a 1200-square-mile (3108-km^2) zone, divided into three blocks to include contiguous communal reserves, deeded to specific Yanesha communities to protect natural resources for their exclusive use; tribal territory for all Yanesha as a cultural group; and a national park as an environmental preserve.

Smith's plan was initially approved by the Peruvian Ministry of Agriculture but was tabled by 1980 when the government actually began to implement its own project to bring 150,000 agricultural colonists into the Pichis–Palcazu Valleys and create a city of 20,000 people. No territory was deeded to the 12,000 resident Ashaninka and Yanesha for them to control as cultural groups, and less than half the fifty-one scattered indigenous communities were given discrete village titles. This left the original inhabitants either landless or with fragmented blocks of land that were inadequate for traditional subsistence activities or long-term commercial agriculture (Swenson and Narby 1986). Protests by a coalition of native organizations, religious and human rights groups, and anthropologists (*Amazonia Indigena* 1981) brought only token reforms represented by village land titles, community development advisors, and agricultural credits that fostered debt.

The World Bank, which provided $46 million for the Pichis Valley Project and cosponsored many similar projects that deprived indigenous groups of their resources and autonomy, responded to critics by issuing a position paper arguing that with "interim safeguards" it was possible to promote large development projects and still defend tribal people (Goodland 1982). The bank's report advocated support for "cultural autonomy . . . until the tribe adapts sufficiently." Thus, they seemed to reject genuine cultural autonomy as a permanent policy.

Anthropologists Sally Swenson and Jeremy Narby, who investigated conditions in the Pichis Valley in the mid-1980s, observed that development policies at international, national, and regional levels need to be changed if indigenous groups like the Ashaninka are to benefit from development. They urged that indigenous political organizations be allowed to participate directly in planning affecting them, and declared,

*A more appropriate approach would discourage coloniza-
tion and place priority on the participation in development
by current inhabitants; recognize native rights to, and title
land sufficient for, subsistence and commercial production;
and recognize the rationality of current native land use, incorporating native knowledge of the rainforest environment
into development.* (Swenson and Narby 1986:24)

This course was taken in the Upper Ucayali region of Ashaninka territory beginning in 1987,
when the Indigenous Organisation of the Atalaya
Region (OIRA) was founded. The group soon
brought together more than a hundred Ashaninka
communities, joining a larger regional indigenous
organization, the Inter-Ethnic Association for the
Development of the Peruvian Rainforest (AIDE-
SEP), formed in 1980. These organizations were
part of the worldwide political mobilization of
indigenous peoples, and they provided an effective basis for the Ashaninka to implement their
own cultural autonomy alternative. In 1988, with
the help of AIDESEP, the Atalaya Ashaninka de-
nounced the debt-bondage exploitation practiced
by the colonizing *patrons* before a special multi-
agency government commission. Next, with the
help of IWGIA and funds from the Danish government development agency (DANIDA), they succeeded in implementing the community land title
provisions of the 1978 Peruvian Law of Native
Communities. They demarcated their own territories to reflect their subsistence requirements, creating contiguous territories to block out *patrons*
(Gray n.d., Hvalkof and Gray 1990). By 1993, 113
Ashaninka communities in the region had secure
land titles. Many of the colonists had withdrawn
after being compensated for their holdings. The Ashaninka were proudly reasserting their culture. An
Ashaninka man, dressed in *cushma* and face paint,
told IWGIA's Andrew Gray how he felt about their
new autonomy:

*We have no problems with colonists. There are no patrons
or "colonos." Just Ashaninka. We wanted titles for our lands
and to work in the fields, harvest yuca [manioc], sow rice,
pineapple. That is why we need land. In the future I want to
live quietly. We in our community want to live in peace,
drinking our masato [manioc beer]. We hunt animals
throughout our land. We have a school now too. We think
that our organization OIRA helps us and we are very
pleased.* (Gray n.d.:24)

SUMMARY

Since the policy debate began over how states
should deal with tribal peoples, only two basic positions have been argued. A fundamental philosophical conflict exists between the realists, who
advocate policies to help indigenous people adjust
to the "inevitable" changes brought by colonialism
or postcolonial national integration and economic
development, and the idealists, who oppose the
state-sponsored invasion of indigenous territories
by colonists or externally imposed development
projects. This philosophical split has obvious political implications for indigenous peoples. If the
realists set national and international policies, indigenous peoples are likely to disappear as distinct
cultural groups, whereas the idealist position will
foster indigenous self-determination that will make
cultural survival possible.

The initial involvement of anthropology in the
colonial enterprise was in the context of British
colonialism. The specific process of colonial development in East Africa paralleled the conquest,
exploitation, and marginalization of Native Americans in the New World, under both colonial powers
and independent countries such as the United
States.

The global world system approach forces us
to consider the possibility that virtually all the
domestic-scale cultures that anthropologists have
described ethnographically have been shaped by
the existence of capitalist, commercial-scale cultural systems. Our discussion of these cultures in
Chapters 2–5 largely ignored this possibility by
treating domestic-scale cultures as if they existed
only within tribal worlds. However, more complex
cultures clearly have varied impacts on smaller-
scale cultures. In Chapters 6–10, we pointed out
that ancient kingdoms and empires often absorbed
tribal cultures or forced them to organize into
states in their own defense. In the modern era,
industrial civilization has exerted an enormous
economic and political influence in drawing
domestic-scale cultures into the emerging global
system.

Throughout the nineteenth and the first half
of the twentieth century, the realist policy approach
of adjustment and integration clearly dominated.
However, since World War II, a more evolved inter-

national concept of human rights, fostered by the UN system, has for the first time created conditions under which indigenous peoples themselves could develop their own formal political organizations and promote their own idealist perspective. This has given them the opportunity to directly shape international standards for the interaction between domestic-scale cultures and the larger state- and global-level forces surrounding them.

STUDY QUESTIONS

1. Distinguish between the realist and the idealist positions on policy toward indigenous peoples. Refer to specific examples, organizations, individuals, policies, or international conventions.

2. Define *indigenous people*. Differentiate between *indigenous people* and *indigenous population*. What are the limitations of the term *indigenous?* In what sense is *indigenous people* a political concept?

3. Why are the terms *tribal* and *primitive* sometimes avoided by anthropologists?

4. What features of domestic-scale cultures can be identified with indigenous peoples?

5. In what sense can indigenous peoples be referred to as *nations?* What is the Fourth World?

6. Describe the philosophical position and the policy recommendations of the Select Committee and the Aborigines Protection Society. How were they actually applied?

7. In what way did colonial policy toward Australian aborigines depart from standard British practice? How do you account for this?

8. Describe the different policies advocated by Wood Jones, Thomson, and Elkin in Australia. How did they defend their views?

9. In what way could the League of Nations mandate system, the UN Charter, and ILO Convention 107 be said to endorse ethnocentric policies that might be used to undermine the human rights of indigenous peoples?

10. What UN declarations or covenants provide a basis for the human rights of indigenous peoples?

11. Distinguish between the human rights of individuals and those of groups.

12. What were the assumptions of the anthropologists involved in drafting ILO Convention 107? How were they expressed in the convention?

13. Describe how Peru's economic development policies affected the Ashaninka and their neighbors. What alternative policies were proposed?

14. What is meant by "internal colonialism"? Use examples from Australia and Peru.

15. Using the East Africa Protectorate and Kenya as an example, explain how political and economic power was used by colonial administrations to create structural inequalities and unequal accumulation.

16. What are the most important human rights that indigenous peoples themselves define as the minimum conditions for their survival?

SUGGESTED READING

BODLEY, JOHN H. 1988. *Tribal Peoples and Development Issues: A Global Overview*. Mountain View, Calif.: Mayfield. An edited collection of materials including case studies, policy positions, assessments, and recommendations on indigenous peoples and development issues throughout the world from the nineteenth century to the present.

BODLEY, JOHN H. 1999. *Victims of Progress*, 4th ed. Mountain View, Calif.: Mayfield. Examines the official policies and underlying motives that have shaped the interaction between indigenous peoples and members of commercial-scale culture, since the early nineteenth century; includes many case studies drawn from throughout the world.

DAVIS, SHELTON H. 1977. *Victims of the Miracle: Development and the Indians of Brazil*. Cambridge, Eng.: Cambridge University Press. A critical analysis of the Brazilian government's development policies in the Amazon region and their impact on the native peoples.

15

Beyond 2000: The Future in the Global Greenhouse

As Bronislaw Malinowski (1944) pointed out long ago, culture is a mixed blessing because, in providing for basic human needs, it creates new, culturally derived needs and new problems for people to solve. Culture is both problem and solution, and the problems increase as culture scale increases. For example, farming as a means of subsistence intensification helped feed more people in a smaller area, but it also made it more difficult to maintain population stability and social equality. The problems generated by political- and domestic-scale cultures often were highly localized and occurred so imperceptibly that cultural adjustments were readily found and the tendency was toward equilibrium. The emergence of commercial culture, however, has completely changed the problem of human adaptation. The rate of culture change has become so rapid, and its scale so vast, that it is becoming increasingly difficult to respond effectively to new problems.

Today the world is threatened simultaneously by social and political conflict, impoverishment, resource depletion, and environmental deterioration on a level few would have anticipated at the beginning of the twentieth century. These problems exist at the global, national, and local level and are so serious that the future of humanity and the biosphere itself is at risk for the first time in human existence. It would not be too dramatic to say that a global crisis exists. Major cultural adjustments will be required to see us through the twenty-first century.

The commercialization process that created the global culture has totally transformed and homogenized the planet in an astonishingly short time. Many of the most pervasive items of daily life, such as computers, televisions, jet aircraft, nuclear power, and mass-produced organic compounds, have come into worldwide use only since 1950. The scale and quality of fossil fuel–based industrial production and the unprecedented increases in global population and consumption over the past 200 years are depleting resources and altering the biosphere in ways that threaten the future viability of the global culture itself (see Figure 15.1).

Previous cultural processes—whether the sapienization that generated language and domestic-scale culture, settled village life, and farming and herding, or the politicization process that created social stratification, cities, and states—did not have such a sudden destabilizing effect. Domestic-scale cultures manipulated natural ecosystems to satisfy basic nutritional needs, but the changes that they induced occurred over millennia, and the tendency

FIGURE 15.1
Steam rising from a nuclear power plant cooling tower in New Jersey. This image dramatically symbolizes the sudden transformation of the planet brought about by the commercialization process.

was toward equilibrium of population and resource consumption. Political-scale cultures promoted population growth and intensive food production to support political structures and social inequality. The environmental alterations produced by traditional states and empires were often drastic, but they occurred over centuries and were regional, not global, in their effects. The rise and fall of particular empires were common and relatively insignificant events in the broad sweep of culture, but the breakdown of commercial-scale culture would be devastating.

Commercial culture, driven by its consumption-based market economy, dominates the world's political- and domestic-scale cultures with its perpetually expanding quest for new resources and markets. This cultural domination is itself a problem because it leads to cultural homogeneity, which can reduce human adaptive potential. A multicultural world is not only a more diverse and interesting place but also a way to develop and test alternative cultural solutions to common problems. Since 1950, vast resources have been dedicated to national defense, international development, and environmental protection, but many of these problems have only become more severe. Much of this

problem-solving effort has been directed by specialists who offered purely technical solutions for what they assumed were isolated technical problems. The example of world poverty, examined in Chapter 13, suggests that the problems of commercial culture are actually cultural, not technical, problems. They are related to the most fundamental aspects of commercial culture and are thus best approached by a generalist anthropological perspective that takes cultural scale and diversity into account.

In this chapter, we assess the outlook for the world's peoples and cultures beyond the year 2000 by focusing on three major issues: (1) the potential for serious resource shortfalls, (2) environmental deterioration such as through global warming and deforestation, and (3) ways in which a sustainable world might be designed.

LIMITS TO GROWTH IN A FINITE WORLD

The Success of the Commercial Culture

In what respects may the achievements of commercial culture be illusory?

One of the most widely held ideological features of commercial culture is the deceptive belief that evolutionary progress has given people greater control over nature while increasing human security and adaptability. For example, anthropologist Yehudi Cohen (1974) treated hunting-gathering, cultivation, and industrialism as technological stages on the road toward "freedom from environmental limitations." Cohen argued that progress meant a more secure food supply, suggesting with a seemingly trivial example that the ability to produce and market frozen strawberries represented "perhaps one of man's greatest achievements."

When viewed from a culture scale, rather than a strictly technological perspective, frozen berries illuminate some of the critical problems of commercial culture because commercialized berries primarily exist to make a profit for the stockholders of large food corporations, not to increase human food security. Nonrenewable fossil fuels are expended in berry production, refrigerated transport, and storage. Even more significantly, when Cohen wrote, many of America's supermarket strawberries were being produced by giant U.S. agribusinesses using Mexican land and labor in an exploitative international system that perpetuated poverty and inequality while damaging the environment (Feder 1978, Lappe, Collins, and Fowler 1979). Arguing that this is culturally "adaptive," either locally or globally, would be difficult.

The adaptive success of commercial culture is sometimes defined by its "natural" ability to expand in population and territory at the expense of less "advanced" cultures. This has even been offered as an indirect explanation for the genocidal destruction of the members of domestic-scale cultures. For example, in 1915, Paul Popenoe assured the members of the 19th International Congress of Americanists that Native Americans were a "weak stock" that was being "killed off by natural selection." In 1960, anthropologist David Kaplan formulated a law of cultural dominance to explain the spread of industrial civilization: "That cultural system which more effectively exploits the energy resources of a given environment will tend to spread in that environment at the expense of less effective systems" (1960:75).

This "law" was offered as an ethically neutral scientific generalization, but it implied that ethnocide was inevitable and did not adequately define "effectiveness" of energy exploitation. Significantly, Kaplan acknowledged that in certain especially marginal environments, such as deserts and the arctic, domestic-scale cultures could indeed be considered adaptive successes, even in an environment that might temporarily be invaded by outsiders. In the same volume where Kaplan wrote, Marshall Sahlins and Elman Service agreed and commented in reference to peoples like the mobile foraging Inuit (Eskimo):

Nor are those cultures that we might consider higher in general evolutionary standing necessarily more perfectly adapted to their environments than lower. Many great civilizations have fallen in the last 2,000 years, even in the midst of material plenty, while the Eskimos tenaciously maintained themselves in an incomparably more difficult habitat. The race is not to the swift, nor the battle to the strong. (1960:26–27)

Writing somewhat later, anthropologists Richard Lee and Irven DeVore, who in 1966 organized the first major international conference on foraging peoples, expressed concern over the "unstable ecological conditions" created by industrial civilization and were even more emphatic about the adaptive achievements of mobile foragers, declaring that they were "the most successful and persistent adaptation man has ever achieved" (Lee and DeVore 1968).

Reproductive success may be a very poor measure of human adaptive success because beyond a certain point the growth of any population must cease. There were ten times as many people in the world in 1990 as in 1650, but the world in 1990 was measurably less secure. Humans are consumers ultimately dependent on the energy produced by green plants through photosynthesis, which is powered by a fixed quantity of solar energy. Biologist Isaac Asimov (1971) estimated that the planet could support a maximum of 2 million million tons of consumer biomass. Any expansion in the human population must inevitably displace other species. The commercial culture with its 1990 population of 5 billion people makes far different demands on the biosphere than the 0.5 billion people in the political- and domestic-scale cultures that existed in 1650. In 1986, it was estimated that humans were already appropriating some 40 percent of the food energy produced by green plants (Brown and Postel 1987, Vitousek et al. 1986). The pinnacle of cultural evolutionary achievement, if narrowly defined by short-term human reproductive success, would be reached when all natural "competitors" were eliminated and every gram of living material was available for human consumption. Asimov projected that in theory, this could occur by 2436.

The sudden planetary dominance of the commercial culture has initiated a dramatic decline in biodiversity that may equal in magnitude the mass extinctions of the geological past, including the disappearance of the dinosaurs at the end of the Cretaceous and the loss of marine animals at the end of the Permian (Wilson 1989, Wilson and Peter 1988). Foraging peoples may have contributed to the more recent extinctions of some of the megafauna, such as the woolly mammoth, at the end of the Ice Age (see Chapter 2), but natural changes in climate and vegetation likely were primarily responsible for those losses (Webster 1981). Since 1800, habitat destruction, or ecocide, caused by the expansion of commercial ranching, farming, and logging has been destroying species at a catastrophic rate. The developing world may have lost half of its forests since 1900. The bulk of current extinctions can be attributed to destruction of the tropical rain forest, where more than half of the world's species are found. In the 1980s, the tropical forests were being removed at the rate of 1–2.6 percent per year (Grainger 1980, Wilson 1989). At that rate, Edward Wilson estimated that 4000–6000 species were disappearing every year—more than 10,000 times faster than would be expected "naturally."

Much of the world's present wealth of species was produced over the past 200 million years. Extinction is an irreversible process. Loss of biological diversity is maladaptive for humans because it makes the biosphere less able to support human life. It also involves an economic loss because it is often more costly to replace natural goods and services with their cultural counterparts. Species are now disappearing before they are even scientifically described and their possible uses identified. Unfortunately, the extensive biological knowledge accumulated by domestic-scale cultures for many otherwise "unknown" species is also disappearing as genocide and ethnocide continue.

Commercial Culture and Resource Depletion

How much has the commercial culture elevated resource consumption rates over previous levels? What is the possibility that key resources will be exhausted?

Because the commercial culture is most distinguished by its elevated rates of resource consumption, the question of resource balance is critical for any assessment of the future of commercial culture. In theory, culture growth, like the growth of any organism, must be limited by the essential material that is in shortest supply, as predicted in 1840 by German chemist Justus von Liebig's law of the minimum. Identifying any single, irreplaceable natural resource required by the commercial culture, however, would be difficult, although petroleum would be a likely candidate. Resource depletion by itself is an inadequate predictor of cultural viability because resources are culturally defined and major economic and social instabilities are produced by more comprehensive changes in ecosystems or climate, as will be examined later.

From the very beginning of the industrial era, a number of scholars, including economist Adam Smith (1776), demographer Thomas Malthus ([1798] 1895), and pioneer conservationist George Marsh (1864), warned that the earth would not support endless economic progress. In 1873, scientists from the American Association for the Advancement of Science even petitioned the U.S. Congress to legislate conservation measures. However, the colonial expropriation of the resources controlled by political- and domestic-scale cultures postponed the inevitable shortages and fostered an ideology of unlimited growth.

The global issue of resource depletion was not even seriously addressed at the international level until 1949 when the United Nations convened 700 scientists from fifty nations to assess the resource demands of global economic development. At that time, H. L. Keenleyside, Canadian deputy minister of mines and resources, reported that between 1900 and 1949, more world mineral resources had been consumed than at any time in the past. He thought that the mineral situation was not yet critical but warned that

it is clear that the combination of an increasing population and rising standards of living will place a strain on our metal resources which will almost certainly in the end prove beyond the capacity of man and nature to supply. . . . [Unless] there is a fundamental change in the economic fabric of human society we will ultimately be faced with the exhaustion of many of our mineral resources. (1950:38)

Since the 1940s, American planners and resource scientists have kept a careful eye on the supply of strategically significant resources. This was prudent, given America's disproportionate consumption levels, as was demonstrated as early as 1952 in a study commissioned by President Truman, which amplified the Keenleyside report. Truman's commission estimated that between 1914 and 1950, Americans by themselves had consumed more of the world's fuels and minerals than the combined total of *all* previous consumption.

Given the inequities built into the global system, resource shortages likely will not be shared equally by peoples in different regions. Most U.S. assessments of resource limitations have been remarkably optimistic. For example, a major study to predict "America's Needs and Resources" up to 1960, commissioned by the Twentieth Century Fund in 1947, acknowledged that domestic mineral resources would eventually be exhausted but assumed that free access to foreign resources would support an "expanding American economy" for many decades (Dewhurst 1947). Another study in 1963 concluded that, given continued imports and substitution of synthetics for natural materials, no critical shortages would prevent Americans from tripling their consumption of natural resources by the year 2000 (Landsberg 1964). However, a 1975 report, "Mineral Resources and the Environment," issued by the National Academy of Sciences, was much more pessimistic and called on the government to establish a national policy of resource conservation, recycling, and reduced energy consumption. The report ominously declared, "Man faces the prospect of a series of shocks of varying severity as shortages occur in one material after another, with the first real shortages perhaps only a matter of a few years away" (National Research Council 1975:26).

Theoretically, solar-based cultures can last perhaps 5 billion years, when the sun is predicted to burn out, but a fossil fuel–dependent commercial-scale culture is mining a limited energy source that is rapidly being depleted. There are no absolute figures on the total supply of fossil fuels, but a study commissioned by President Jimmy Carter in 1977 to guide government planning up to the year 2000 estimated that at 1976 production rates, oil would be depleted within 77 years, natural gas in 170 years, and coal in 212 years (Barney 1980, vol. 2). Any such estimates are purely hypothetical and are based on assumptions about population levels, consumption rates, production technologies, use efficiencies, prices, and politics; nevertheless, the magnitude of the supply problem is inescapable and has been acknowledged by geologists for many years. Petroleum expert M. King Hubert (1969) estimated that even with the most optimistic estimates, oil production would peak about the year 2000 and would essentially stop by the end of that century. Remarkably, 80 percent of the total production would occur within a brief 64-year period (see Figure 15.2).

Curiously, the commercial economy is designed to thrive on resource depletion while theoretically denying its existence. According to an influential text, *The Economics of Natural Resource Availability*, by resource economists Harold Barnett and Chandler Morse (1963), there can be no limits on economic growth because market forces and technological advance will inevitably create new resources. Barnett and Morse argued that industrial progress makes nature "subservient to man." They emphatically declared, "The notion of an absolute limit to natural resource availability is untenable when the definition of resources changes drastically and unpredictably over time" (Barnett and Morse 1963:7).

Such an economic ideology, when uninhibited by political controls, allows resources to be systematically depleted. Historically, different types of trees, whales, and fossil fuels have been exploited as long as prices and production costs made it

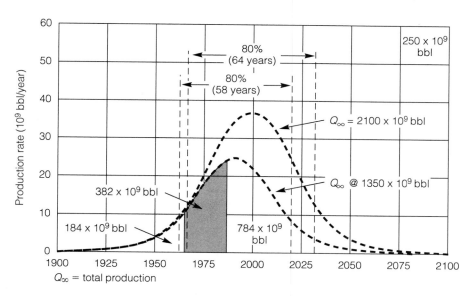

FIGURE 15.2
A chart of the complete cycles of world crude-oil production. Petroleum is perhaps commercial culture's most vital nonrenewable resource, yet its total availability is strictly limited. (SOURCE: *Hubert 1969:196.*)

profitable. Orthodox market theory suggests that a given resource will be replaced by a cheaper substitute the moment that it becomes too scarce or expensive to harvest. This makes economic sense, but it can lead to extinction.

Limits to Growth and the Global Environment

What is the argument that we will need to limit or redirect economic growth to prevent an ultimate collapse of the global system?

The Club of Rome study, *The Limits to Growth* (Meadows et al. 1972), published in 1972, was the first comprehensive predictive model of the global system to incorporate the interaction of cultural and biological components and to look relatively far into the future. The Club of Rome is unusual among futurist groups because it is an informal international organization formed in 1968 under the sponsorship of an Italian industrialist to study the global system and the "predicament of mankind." The *Limits to Growth* study was produced by a seventeen-member international team of experts who worked with a sophisticated "world model" computer program developed by Jay Forrester of the Massachusetts Institute of Technology. The model took a systems approach and considered the

positive and negative feedbacks between population, agriculture, industry, natural resources, and pollution. The objective was to see how long the global system could function if the exponential growth trends already observed in the world economy and population from 1900 to 1970 were to continue indefinitely.

The Club of Rome study consistently predicted a system collapse before 2100 because of the seemingly inescapable limits to growth (see Figure 15.3). Even when the researchers doubled world resources and assumed that pollution could be controlled and population stabilized, the global system still collapsed. In the "standard run" of the world model, industrial production peaks sometime after the year 2000, due to dwindling resources. Population continues to increase until death rates rise due to pollution, declining food output, and reduced medical services. The only way to prevent overshoot and breakdown was to stabilize both population and economic growth.

Technological optimists charged that the *Limits to Growth* study was either too simple or too complex, and there were accusations that it was simply a demonstration of the preconceived "doomsday" assumptions of the model's designers (Cole 1973). Twenty years later, the original authors of *Limits to Growth* published a new study reaffirming their earlier findings (Meadows, Meadows, and Randers

FIGURE 15.3
Graph of potential system collapse. According to this famous computer projection from the 1972 Limits to Growth *study, if historical trends in population and economic growth continued with no change, the global commercial culture would collapse well before 2100. (*SOURCE: *Meadows et al. 1972: 124.)*

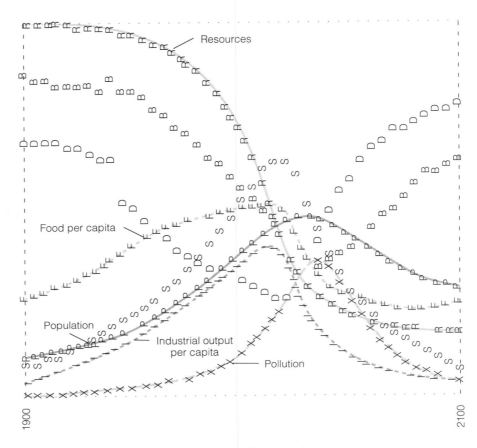

KEY: B = Crude birth rate (births per 1000 people per year)
D = Crude death rate (deaths per 1000 people per year)
S = Service per person (dollar equivalent per person per year)

1992). They stressed that their concern was sustainability, not fixing a doomsday date, and argued that resource consumption and pollution had already exceeded sustainable rates in many countries.

The 1977 Carter Commission *Global 2000* study referred to earlier was an independent and more conservative reexamination of the near future for the global system, carried out with a larger budget and the cooperation of thirteen U.S. government agencies. The *Global 2000* researchers assumed fewer negative feedbacks and limited their projections to the year 2000, but they still found that population would continue to increase and that there could be serious water shortages, deforestation, desertification, deterioration of agricultural lands, and massive extinctions, together with more poverty and political tension. The commissioners concluded,

The most knowledgeable professional analysts in the executive branch of the U.S. Government have reported to the President that, if public policies around the world continue unchanged through the end of the century, a number of serious world problems will become worse, not better . . . the world in 2000 will be more crowded, more polluted, less stable ecologically, and more vulnerable to disruption. . . . Serious stresses involving population, resources, and environment are clearly visible ahead . . . the world's people will be poorer. (Barney 1977, vol. 1:xvi, 1)

OVERSHOOT AND BIOSPHERE ALTERATION

Human-induced changes in global climate, which many experts conclude are now underway, are an ominous indication that critical natural thresholds may already have been crossed. During the 1980s, a sequence of environmental events occurred that made it difficult for even the most optimistic planners to deny the possibility that the commercial culture would need to make major adjustments to ensure its long-term survival. In 1982, German scientists announced that acid rain caused by industrial pollution was destroying European forests. In 1985, British scientists reported a thinning in the ozone layer over Antarctica, which was attributed to release of chlorofluorocarbons (CFCs) used in refrigerants and as propellants in spray cans. In 1986, world population passed the 5-billion mark; the Soviet nuclear reactor at Chernobyl exploded, spewing radiation worldwide; and an article in the British science journal *Nature* reported measurable evidence that global warming was taking place due to elevated levels of carbon dioxide (CO_2), the greenhouse effect (Jones, Wigley, and Wright 1986). Negative feedbacks of the sort predicted by the *Limits to Growth* model may well be taking place.

The Rising Tide: Global Environmental Change

What is the evidence that human activities are already altering global climate? What are the possible consequences of rising sea levels?

Global warming is probably the single most dramatic and far-reaching environmental impact of industrial development. The natural cycles of the past 2 million years would suggest that the world is more than halfway through an interglacial period and should be cooling, but instead it appears that the world has actually warmed by 1°F (0.5°C) on the average over the past 100 years (Edgerton 1991, Schneider 1989). The greenhouse effect, which has been recognized as a theoretical possibility since the nineteenth century, assumes that increased atmospheric CO_2 gas from the burning of fossil fuels would heat the earth like the glass of a greenhouse by trapping solar heat near the earth's surface. Pre-

cise measurements show an increase of nearly 8 percent in atmospheric CO_2 between 1958 and 1984 (Landsberg 1989). Scientists estimate that CO_2 has increased by 25 percent since the beginning of the Industrial Revolution, while CO_2 gas bubbles trapped in Antarctic ice show relative stability over the previous 10,000 years (Graedel and Crutzen 1989).

Carbon is stored in natural "sinks," or reservoirs, either as organic matter, especially in forest biomass, or in coal and oil, or in the ocean. In the natural carbon cycle, CO_2 is taken up by plants during photosynthesis. It is also stored chemically in the ocean. Carbon is released back into the atmosphere as CO_2 by respiration, decomposition, and other chemical and biological processes. Large-scale human burning of fossil fuels and forests imbalances the cycle by withdrawing carbon from storage faster than it can be reabsorbed by the forests and oceans (see Figure 15.4).

In the 1980s, CO_2 was considered to be responsible for more than half of the predicted global warming, while other less common but more active greenhouse gases such as methane, CFCs, and nitrous oxide contributed the remainder. Although methane is produced naturally as swamp gas and by termites, significant quantities are also produced by fermentation in rice paddies and in the digestive tracts of domestic cattle (Cicerone 1989). CFCs are a commercial product that chemists synthesized in the 1920s. Their ability to destroy the ozone that screens the earth from ultraviolet radiation has been suspected since 1974 (Rowland 1989).

It is impossible to predict with absolute confidence how much warming will occur; however, the Intergovernmental Panel on Climate Change (IPCC), established in 1988 by the World Meteorological Organization and the UN Environment Program, calculated that if no preventive action is taken, the global mean temperature could rise by 5.4°F (3°C) over the next century (IPCC 1991). There are substantial uncertainties with these projections because, like earlier global models, they depend on many variables that interact in complex ways. Skeptics argue that climate models rely too heavily on aggregate data and suggest that increased cloud cover and dust in the air may have a cooling effect that will balance any warming.

FIGURE 15.4
Forest burning. Tropical deforestation reduces biodiversity and releases stored carbon into the atmosphere where, in the form of carbon dioxide gas, it can contribute to global warming by increasing the greenhouse effect.

Predicting the temperature-moderating effect of the oceans also is difficult. However, the consensus is that some degree of warming is very likely to occur within a range of 3.6°–9°F (2°–5°C), depending on the *rate* of climate change and the human response.

The possible impact of global warming is also conjectural, but sea-level rise and regional changes in rainfall and vegetation would be virtually certain. Some experts believe that sea level has already been rising at the rate of 0.04–0.08 inches (1–2 millimeters) per year over the past century, and that rate is expected to increase (Edgerton 1991). The IPCC projected a rise in sea level of 2 feet (60 centimeters [cm]) over the next century, within a range of 1–3 feet (30–100 cm) (see Figure 15.5). Critical variables include thermal expansion of the oceans and the speed at which the vast ice fields stored in Greenland and Antarctica might melt. Rapid warming could produce a 3-foot (1-m) rise in sea level by 2050 (Edgerton 1991), while a breakup of the West Antarctic ice sheet could by itself cause a rise of 5–7.5 yards (5–7 m) (Kellogg 1989). Large uncertainties remain because the models are based on global averages; with increased precipitation, ice could accumulate in Antarctica and certain alpine glaciers while it retreated elsewhere.

Sea-level rise is an especially dramatic threat because many of the world's largest cities, densest populations, and richest agricultural zones are located in low-lying coastal areas. Very low island groups and atolls would be quickly overwhelmed. Flooding would cause great economic loss everywhere. It has been estimated that a 3-foot (1-m) rise in sea level would displace 50 million people worldwide. Bangladesh would be especially vulnerable because most of its population is concentrated in a vast delta region that is already subject to chronic storm-surge flooding (Jacobson 1989). Shifts in regional climates would disrupt agriculture worldwide, causing political and economic stress and population dislocation, but the precise impacts would be variable. Rapid environmental change would probably accelerate species extinctions because plants and animals would have difficulty moving to suitable environments quickly enough, especially when migration routes were blocked by developed areas.

FIGURE 15.5
*Global sea-level rise,
1985–2100, for policy
scenario A (no limitation
of greenhouse gases).
(SOURCE: IPCC 1991.)*

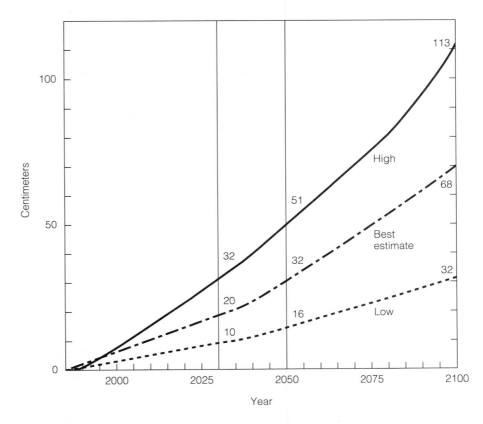

Food Production and
the Malthusian Dilemma

*Is there evidence that the earth's ability to pro-
duce food has already been stressed?*

Many researchers and policy planners have examined food production as a key variable limiting
global population, but this is not a simple matter.
Theoretically, treating global limits as a subsistence
carrying-capacity issue should be possible, but carrying capacity can only be defined for a specific
cultural system and technology in a given environment. This is difficult to do even for domestic-scale
cultures, where food is produced directly to satisfy
human needs, because neither environment nor
technology are constants, as the long history of subsistence intensification demonstrates. In the global
system, food production is only indirectly concerned with human nutritional requirements; it is
primarily directed by political and economic objec-

tives. Indeed, when food and the means to produce
it are controlled by governments, multinational
corporations, and market economies, the connection between food production and carrying capacity must be approached with caution. Hungry
people and empty granaries in a given country do
not necessarily mean that environmentally defined
production limits have been exceeded. Similarly,
steadily increasing grain output at the global level
may not mean that technology has defeated nature.
Diminishing returns and environmental deterioration are real and can be described at both local and
global levels.

In 1798, English economist and demographer
Thomas Malthus (1766–1834) correctly observed
that human population has the biological capacity
to grow faster than food production, but he did not
realize that domestic-scale cultures can maintain a
relative balance between food and population
without suffering chronic hunger. Ignoring the

culturally determined demographic imbalances and inequities that were generating hunger in the newly emerging global system, Malthus mistakenly concluded that misery worked "naturally" as the primary check on population growth. He supported his findings with historical data demonstrating that famine and hunger elevated mortality in states and empires. But he did not realize that he was also observing the action of cultural variables acting together with natural limits.

The Malthusian argument conveniently provided nineteenth-century policymakers with a justification for keeping public welfare low because it implied that only a certain level of human suffering would prevent overpopulation. This aspect of Malthusian theory has since been widely discredited, especially by demographic transition theorists. During the early post–World War II decades of economic development, some technological optimists argued that Malthus was also wrong about the ultimate limits of food production. However, granted that poverty and misery are cultural, not natural, checks on population, Malthus was indeed correct about the general relationship between food and population, even if it is difficult to define. Because of diminishing returns and the limits of water, soil, and energy, there are practical limits to subsistence intensification in any given region and at a global level. However, determining what the actual limits are is complicated by the intervention of governments, markets, and the fossil fuel subsidy in the food production process.

Any estimates of a maximum sustainable global population must consider not only physical limits but also cultural variables such as political and economic organization, as well as technology. In 1905, when world population stood at 1.5 billion, Harvard geologist Nathaniel Shaler (1841–1906) warned that world food production could not support a threefold increase to 4.5 billion people. That was probably a realistic estimate for the early twentieth-century world in which agricultural production was not fossil fuel–based and remained largely self-sustaining. This was still the situation at midcentury, when world population reached 2.5 billion, and only marginal or highly erodible lands remained undeveloped (Brown and Postel 1987). Given that poverty-inducing colonial inequities were perpetuated in the decolonized world, mas-

sive Malthusian crises were probably delayed by the introduction of the expensive technological inputs that began with the post–World War II campaign for economic development. During the technological optimism of the 1950s, there were projections that world population might reach 30 billion by 2075, but geochemist Harrison Brown (1956) calculated that such a population would literally eat up the world, even if it could feed directly on rock and seawater.

At a global level, food production has kept pace and even exceeded population growth since 1950, judging by world grain production figures (see Table 15.1). Per-capita grain production actually increased by one-third between 1950 and 1992, and total production and yield per hectare more than doubled, seemingly disproving Malthus on the general relationship between food and population. Because grain directly provides about half of the world's food and feeds much of the world's livestock, such figures suggest significant improvement in world living standards. However, because grain is distributed as a commodity and is used to political and economic advantage, global production averages mask the realities of world hunger and inequality, which were examined in Chapter 13. Remarkably, just five privately held corporations controlled the marketing and transport of most of the world's grain (Morgan 1979, Sewell 1992). Furthermore, a few countries hold decisive control over world oil production, which ultimately fuels agricultural intensification.

The rate of increase in grain per capita has been declining, just as Malthus might have predicted. After 1950, world grain production grew fairly steadily to a peak in the late 1970s and early 1980s but now seems to be in decline (Brown 1994). Total grain production fell in 1987 and 1988 (Brown 1989). Per-capita production in Africa has actually fallen steadily to 27 percent below its 1967 peak (Brown 1989), and some authorities believe that local population growth is outstripping food production in many areas of Asia, the Middle East, and Latin America (Keyfitz 1989). Short-term production shortfalls can be compensated for by tapping stored grain or by diverting grain from cattle feed directly to human consumption. However, any redistribution of this sort would be mediated by the global grain market and the political economy, and in 1989, only the United States, Canada, western Europe, Australia, and New Zealand were net grain exporters. Any long-term declines in the world food balance will compel the commercial culture to institute profound adjustments.

Numerous lines of evidence suggest that food production is already badly overextended in many countries, under prevailing cultural conditions. Food scientist Georg Borgstrom (1965) pointed out that developed countries were supplementing their agricultural production by drawing extensively on marine fisheries and market-based international trade. Borgstrom used the concept of ghost acres to refer to land that a given country would need to put into production to produce an amount of animal protein equal to its net food imports and fishery production. Ghost acres allow a country to subsidize what might otherwise be unsustainable economic growth by shifting production costs to the oceans or the farmlands of other countries. Obvious examples are Middle East desert countries that trade oil for food, but richly endowed agricultural countries such as the United States also take advantage of favorable trade conditions to import large amounts of food from poorer countries. In the 1960s, Borgstrom estimated that Japan's ghost acres were six times greater than its agricultural acreage. Since then, innovations in the fishing industry—such as the use by Japan, Taiwan, and South Korea of miles-long monofilament drift nets that sweep all the fish from vast areas of ocean—have extended ghost acreage to clearly unsustainable levels.

The concept of ghost acres also applies to Peruvian fish meal that is exported to the United States for use as chicken food, to native-grown oilseed cakes fed to European cattle, and to beef that is raised in former Amazonian rain forests and shipped to the United States. These seemingly irrational economic exchanges occur because they generate profit in a market system that does not count all production costs.

The danger of reliance on ghost acres is that global finance—including investment capital, tax subsidies, special loans, and grants—has produced a capital-intensive factory-fishing system, which is displacing small-scale, subsistence-level fisheries and harvesting fish faster than they can be replenished. Ecologist Carl Safina (1995) has shown that

between 1970 and 1990, the world's factory-fishing fleet actually doubled, and the world's major fisheries reached their production peaks between 1973 and 1989 and are now declining, in some dramatic cases by more than 50 percent. Some of the richest fisheries, such as the famous Grand Banks off Newfoundland, have been closed, yet the market price of fish has been buffered by shifts to other fisheries and the artificial subsidies to the industry.

Diminishing returns to inputs in fisheries and agriculture seem to be an inescapable law of nature (see Chapter 10). The rapid early increase in food production after 1950 can be largely attributed to a 22 percent increase in world cropland, as previously undeveloped marginal lands were plowed and irrigated. These lands had been undeveloped because they would not support intensive use or because the cost of their development was previously considered too high. Further production increases required large amounts of fossil fuel energy and chemical fertilizer. Between 1950 and 1986, irrigated land increased nearly threefold, world fertilizer use increased ninefold, and energy use in agriculture increased nearly sevenfold (see Table 15.1). Much of this increase in agricultural effort was a result of the intervention of the global institutions of development examined in Chapter 13.

TABLE 15.1   *World Population and Agriculture, 1950 and 1986*

	1950	1986
Population (in billions)	2.5	5.0
Cropland (in millions of hectares)	590	715
Irrigated cropland (in millions of hectares)	94	271
Fertilizer use (in millions of metric tons)	14	131
Fertilizer/person (kg)	5	26
Energy use (in millions of barrels of oil equivalent)	276	1903
Grain production (in millions of metric tons)	624	1661
Grain/person (in millions of metric tons of grain/billion people)	249.6	332.2
Barrels of oil/tons of grain produced	0.44	1.14

SOURCES: Brown (1987) and Brown and Postel (1987).

As diminishing returns theory would predict, increased yields have required steadily larger inputs of energy and fertilizer. In 1950, a ton of grain required 0.44 barrel of oil to produce, but in 1986, the same ton cost 1.14 barrels. Declining yields in relation to fertilizer inputs, despite the widespread use of high-yield-variety hybrids, suggest that many crops may be reaching the limits of photosynthetic efficiency, beyond which no further gains can be achieved regardless of the input (Brown 1989).

Such intensive production systems cannot be sustained for long because energy and fertilizer will inevitably become more costly. Elevated production is also mining highly erodible soils and withdrawing irrigation waters from underground aquifers at greater than replacement rates (Brown 1987, Brown and Postel 1987). Many marginal areas that were pushed too quickly into production have since been abandoned due to desertification, waterlogging, salination, and erosion. It now appears that world grain acreage has been declining since its peak in 1981 (Brown 1989). Acknowledging the problem of land degradation, the United States in 1986 initiated a federally legislated 5-year program, the Food Security Act of 1985, designed to convert the most erodible 12 percent of America's total cropland into permanent grass and woodland.

Technological Optimism

Are there reasonable limits to technological advances in food production?

Taking a more optimistic approach, some experts suggest that world food production might still support up to 10 billion people, given full application of environmentally "appropriate" technology. Economist Pierre Crosson and soils and climate specialist Norman Rosenberg, both of Resources for the Future, are skeptical of "apocalyptic scenarios," suggesting that damage to marginal soils may be overestimated. They point to the Green Revolution grain-yield achievements of the 1965–1985 period and a continued slowing of the annual growth rate of world population as cause for optimism. Advocating more high-tech progress, they call for "a steady stream of new agricultural technologies that can only come from the CGIAR system [see Chapter 13] and national research institutions in both the developed and the developing countries" (Crosson and Rosenberg 1989:132).

Many agricultural scientists hope that accelerated application of biotechnology will lead to new nitrogen-fixing plant varieties that will require less fertilizer or to plants that will tolerate salt and drought (see Figure 15.6). Such genetically engineered plants might thrive in the warming global

FIGURE 15.6
The Biosphere 2 complex in Oracle, Arizona, where people seek to design completely self-contained ecosystems. This complex represents the extremes of human intervention in and direction of natural systems.

greenhouse, and some climatologists point out that increased atmospheric CO_2 may even make plants grow 5 percent faster (Kellogg 1989). Furthermore, lasers and mechanical improvements might increase irrigation efficiency, and new cropping techniques might reduce pesticide requirements.

Lester Brown (1989) warns that biotechnology is unlikely to yield further dramatic production increases, and many genetic "improvements" may be accompanied by trade-offs that will actually lower yields. Robert Chandler, founding director of the International Rice Research Institute, CGIAR's oldest research center, is also cautious about the long-term potential for continued yield expansion. Chandler was a leading architect of the Green Revolution in Asia, and in 1988 he was awarded the Kraft General Foods Foundation's prestigious "World Food Prize" in recognition of his contribution to improving the world's food supply. In a 1989 address to the Smithsonian Institution–sponsored colloquium, Global Perspectives on Food, Agriculture, and Rural Development, Chandler (1990) predicted that Indian rice production might keep pace with population for another 20 years, given a 50 percent increase in irrigated acreage and a quadrupled application of fertilizer. He found the longer-term prospects for Asia as a whole "not at all bright," especially since the Rice Institute discovered that yields declined when rice was grown continuously on the same land for 20 years, even with the best management practices. Finding it "extremely unlikely" that Asian rice yields would ever be increased to more than double then current levels, Chandler cautioned,

It must be realized that the greatest gains in varietal improvement have already been made. There are limits not only to the amount of arable land and to fresh water supplies for irrigation but to the genetic improvement of plants. It is impossible at this stage to predict what advances in potential yield will come from genetic engineering and from other areas of biotechnology. . . . We should remember that we cannot increase average world precipitation or the quantity of solar radiation, the two most important factors limiting crop production. (1990:174)

TOWARD A SUSTAINABLE WORLD

Most global planners agree that significant cultural changes will be required if the global system is to remain intact through the end of the twenty-first century. In 1987, the report of the Brundtland Commission on environmental deterioration officially advocated sustainable development as a solution to global poverty and environmental deterioration (WCED 1987). Sustainability is now a widely endorsed planning goal, as shown by frequent use of the expression "sustainable agriculture" and the oxymoron "sustainable economic growth." Institutionalized planning, however, still sets relatively short-term goals, often focused on single technologically defined issues such as global warming or food production. More fundamental problems, such as the need for a redistribution of political and economic power to create a more balanced and equitable world, are not being adequately addressed.

If progress is now equated with sustainability, the obvious failure of utopian capitalism to produce a demonstrably sustainable cultural system after 500 years of continuous growth suggests that increased scale and the more concentrated social power that growth produces may themselves be the primary obstacles to progress. Phrasing the sustainability problem in these terms opens the door to very exciting possibilities, because growth, scale, and power are cultural constructions that can be changed. People can gain control over the cultural processes that produce instability. This final section discusses how social and economic scale relate to the distribution of power, examines the problems inherent in commercialization, and considers what cultural changes can produce sustainable development.

The Power of Growth

How does social and economic scale relate to the distribution of power? What is natural and what is cultural about scale effects?

In previous chapters, it was argued that power-seeking elites used growth to increase their power. This strategy works in regard to political power because as the scale of society increases, proportionately fewer elites will be in control, and consequently both their proportionate and their absolute power will increase. In a democracy, growth necessarily depreciates the value of an individual voter's vote, and in a representative democracy, each elected official must speak for ever larger numbers of constituents. For example, by 1990, America's population was more than sixty times larger than in 1790, which meant that each political leader had more power over more people. In 1790, there were 138 U.S. senators and representatives in Congress, each speaking for, on average, 28,000 people; by 1998, there were 535, each speaking for 500,000. These scale processes can produce feelings of powerlessness and voter apathy, even in the best-run democracies.

Economic power also displays important scale effects. Sociologists Bruce Mayhew and Paul Schollaert (1980a, 1980b) have demonstrated mathematically that an economic elite will almost invariably be a proportionately smaller, and thus more powerful, minority, as either the scale of society or the scale of wealth increases. The empirical evidence for this effect can be readily shown by comparing (1) the average household wealth equivalent of approximately $1000 in annual subsistence in a representative domestic-scale society of 500 people, (2) the wealthiest Roman worth $145 million in a political empire of 50 million people, and (3) the wealthiest American worth $50 billion in a commercially organized global society of 5 billion people.

Elites interested in increasing their power clearly have a powerful "natural" incentive to promote growth. However, this purely mathematical effect operates only in societies, such as under utopian capitalism, in which few if any cultural limitations are placed on the distribution of wealth. In the absence of cultural controls, increasing wealth inequality is a function of scale; as Mayhew and Schollaert (1980a:8) note, "by chance alone, an increase in population size creates an increasing concentration of wealth, ultimately pressing the system toward maximum possible inequality." Therefore, the most powerful also have an incentive to maintain control over the political system that sets the rules governing the distribution of power.

This suggests that it is not wise to give a powerful minority a free hand in running the world, because we can expect their primary interest to be producing, protecting, and concentrating more wealth and power, not promoting the general welfare and ensuring cultural sustainability. Of course, it would be perfectly natural for anyone to behave in this selfish way if given the chance, because power seeking is human nature. But what this means is that great wealth and power are too dangerous to be entrusted to a few people, unless they can be held accountable for their self-serving mistakes in judgment. Designing sustainable cultures will require restoring accountability and control functions to the domestic level of society.

Risks and Rewards in a Commercial Culture

What dynamic market processes create unique opportunities for investors in commercial economies? What unusual new risks do these processes also create?

When commerce becomes the most critical cultural influence on human welfare, households must deal with a new set of risks and opportunities for rewards. These risks and rewards are also inequitably distributed within society and are experienced differently by people at different income and wealth levels, at different life cycle stages, and even by sex. The primary risks faced by households in domestic-scale cultures are seasonal cycles and unpredictable variations in natural phenomena, such as weather, that threaten everyone's subsistence. By contrast, commerce can amplify or dampen natural cycles and random variations and can shift the risks and rewards to different social groups. Commerce has dynamics of its own that are not always related to natural cycles, as economist Paul Samuelson summarized in his introductory text:

Business conditions never stand still. Prosperity is followed by a panic or a crash. National income, employment, and production fall. Prices and profits decline, and men are thrown out of work. Eventually the bottom is reached, and revival begins. The recovery may be slow or fast. It may be incomplete, or it may be so strong as to lead to a new boom. The new prosperity may represent a long, sustained plateau of brisk demand, plentiful jobs, buoyant prices, and increasing living standards. Or it may represent a quick, inflationary flaring up of prices and speculation, to be followed by another disastrous slump. (1964:250–251)

These fluctuations in volume of production, consumption, and commercial activity are characteristic of money economies, and they can affect particular industries or entire market economies at regional, national, and even global levels. They are sometimes called the *business cycle*, but this implies a degree of predictability that may not be justified, because commerce has become so large and complex so quickly that historical experience may be an unreliable guide to the future. What is certain is that large fluctuations in commerce can have extreme human impacts. American economists have long recognized 20-year cyclical patterns in building construction and capital investment. Longer cycles, or great waves, of commercial activity lasting 50 years or more have also been described (Goldstein 1988). Employment, money supply, income, interest rates, investment, and saving rates vary according to cycle phase. Expansion and contraction in industrial investment, rather than agricultural cycles, have now become the dominant commercial risk in much of the world. Business cycles and associated market fluctuations also are a major source of economic opportunities that wealthy investors can manipulate to produce even larger fortunes. Investors who buy low and sell high can create enormous profits from very small percentage gains on large-scale transactions. This speculative arbitrage can itself create chaotic swings in the market and is a very different process from long-term investment in the production of goods and services that benefits society at large. All of this economic volatility would be more manageable in smaller-scale, culturally regulated markets in which many small enterprises operated. The scale at which business enterprise is organized, rather than commerce itself, is perhaps the most important threat to sustainability. Many observers argue that giant corporations are now more powerful than governments and have become *the* dominant forces shaping the global culture (Estes 1996, Grossman and Adams 1993, 1996, Korten 1996, Mander 1996).

Toward a Multiscale Cultural World

What specific steps could be taken to create sustainable cultures?

We can create sustainable cultures. But this will require the construction of a world system composed of many independent regional cultures, each working to establish a humane balance between the cultural processes that sustain households and those that sustain communities, polities, and commercial activities. Domestically organized indigenous

cultures could thrive in such a multiscale world while national polities also remained secure. The Basques of northern Spain have already shown that sustainable cultural systems can be designed that effectively integrate industrial technologies and commercialization within an existing nation-state (see the box entitled "The Mondragón Cooperatives").

Designing sustainable cultures will require a *localization* process to diffuse social power by limiting growth and reducing the scale of both government and business enterprise. Localization built on existing local and regional governments would make democratic decision making by all adults a reality. It would also make it easier for workers to act as business owner-managers and for business profits to benefit local communities. Diffusing social power would allow local communities to regulate growth and scale by giving priority to the maintenance and reproduction of healthy households. The optimum balance between political and economic power could then be democratically established by each cultural community.

To make these changes, people in each region of the world need to be free to manage culture scale and social power in ways that are most sustainable in their particular cultural and natural settings. Truly sustainable development should demand nothing less, but this is precisely the opposite of the wealth-concentrating growth program being promoted by the experts at the World Trade Organization, the World Bank, and the International Monetary Fund, who make global commercial competitiveness the top priority. Unfortunately, dollars are not democratic. The poor do not have equal opportunity in this kind of world, and localities are pitted against each another. The next great cultural development must put the interests of all people first by letting local communities and households set priorities. A useful guiding principle can be found in the concept of *Pareto optimality*, which is the ideal point at which development stops, that being when no one can get richer without making someone else poorer.

Our long-run self-interest demands that we diffuse social power and reduce the scale of culture to manageable human proportions. We can begin this essential evolutionary correction by moving now to construct public policies that will strengthen the political and economic powers of households, local

The Mondragón Cooperatives

A successful, highly democratic, and economically just cultural system has been operating quietly in northern Spain since the 1950s (Morrison 1991, Whyte and Whyte 1988). Stubbornly independent Basques have created an integrated regional society of some 250,000 people, based on a system of numerous small-scale, worker-owned cooperatives centered on the town of Mondragón. Each Mondragón cooperative is limited in size to no more than 500 members, who each have an equal vote in management decisions. There are no giant, remotely owned corporations. The scale limit is crucial, because the Basques have learned that it is almost impossible for larger production units to remain truly democratic. Likewise, the pay scale normally increases by no more than a factor of six from top to bottom, which both rewards hard work and sets a ceiling on executive pay. Everyone shares in annual profits, and a proportion goes to support local community projects and the Basque cultural heritage.

Mondragón cooperatives manufacture world-class computerized robots and a wide range of exported industrial goods and consumer durables. They also run their own consumer co-ops and cooperative banking, social insurance, education, and child care services that respond directly to the needs of local people. The Mondragón mission statement makes employment, community, equity, education, and environment the primary objectives, and Basque cultural autonomy is a key to their achievement. The Basques are a unique people, who claim to be descendants of the Ice Age peoples who produced the great paintings on the cave walls at Lascaux and Altamira 30,000 years ago. In fact, their language and genetic roots do connect them with the most ancient Europeans. The Basques have learned that general welfare and domestic tranquility can best be achieved when everyone is allowed to manage the human, cultural, and natural resources that produce wealth.

This example shows how localization processes are actually being implemented in a particular region. The Basques are attempting to maintain high degrees of local cultural autonomy based on economic self-reliance. They are using industrial technology and capitalist economics within an integrated network of worker-owned, small-scale corporate business enterprises that strive to be highly democratic and egalitarian while supporting households and local communities. Cooperative enterprises may also help dampen the negative human impact of long-wave capitalist economic cycles in particular regions (Booth 1987).

and regional communities, and noncommercial institutional structures, including voluntary associations. We need to abandon the goal of perpetual economic growth as an end in itself and focus instead on the design of our cultural systems in order to truly democratize social power. We need to focus on allocation rather than production. The incentives for destabilizing wealth concentration can be reduced by progressive tax laws that promote philanthropy. Corporate welfare can be channeled to small businesses. Corporations that misuse their power or engage in criminal conduct can be dechartered. Tax laws that reward mergers and speculative finance can be eliminated. Perhaps most importantly, we must deny anonymity to anyone with massive power. The public must have full information about power networks and the ways power is used.

The commercial culture's two unresolved interconnected problems—impoverishing concentrations of social power and the impossibility of perpetual growth in a finite world—are both exaggerated by increases in scale. A more humane culture would use market forces to reward equitable and sustainable allocations of material prosperity. Democratic processes could bring both scale and power under control. Local and regional markets designed to draw on locally owned and managed resources could enhance every community's potential for self-reliance—much like domestic-scale indigenous cultures that based their success on maintaining a permanent stake in particular places. Local residents would shift their finance capital out of remote mutual funds and foreign corporations into local enterprises in which investors have a direct, permanent stake. The efficiencies that local, small-scale enterprises gain by reducing the need for transportation costs, advertising, large CEO salaries, and ever-larger shareholder profits might offset the scale advantages that remote giant enterprises now enjoy. As energy costs rise and as the human costs of global business become more apparent, small-scale alternatives will become more attractive, and people will choose to bring their capital home. Many communities are already experimenting with local currencies and reviving regional produce markets. An energizing positive feedback will begin as citizens become increasingly disillusioned with remote and unresponsive political systems and turn to their own local and regional governments for solutions. Economic crises in the global system will only speed this inevitable cultural development process.

SUMMARY

The most fundamental issue facing humanity is this: How can a global commercial culture based on perpetual growth and inequality survive in a finite world? Truly successful cultural adaptation demands a long-term balance between available resources and consumption. In theory, there are measurable limits beyond which cultures cannot expand without degrading their resources and threatening their own existence. Industrial systems that rely primarily on fossil fuels will necessarily be a short-lived phenomenon lasting a few centuries at best. By contrast, cultural systems designed for lower levels of consumption can maintain a balance with renewable sources of solar energy and thus could exist for millions of years.

The ominous possibility exists that critical carrying-capacity limits may already have been exceeded, given the present structure of the commercial culture. Whether or not human-induced global warming is already underway, people now clearly have the capability to disrupt the life-support systems of the planet in a way that would have been inconceivable a mere 200 years ago. Food production systems are being strained in many areas of the world; unless distribution systems and consumption patterns can be modified, it is unlikely that even the most optimistic technological solutions will prevent Malthusian crises.

There are alternative solutions to create a more secure human future. Our comparative analysis of cultural systems from an anthropological culture-scale perspective suggests that an equitable and secure world needs to combine the best features of domestic-, political-, and commercial-scale cultural patterns. Social justice and preservation of the biosphere will require effective management by highly autonomous local communities, democratic regional governments, and fully representative global institutions.

STUDY QUESTIONS

1. In what sense can cultural development be called a mixed blessing that both solves problems and creates new ones? Use specific examples from each level of culture scale.

2. What are the problems with using increasing cultural control over nature and human reproductive success as measures of greater human adaptability? Refer to consumer biomass, biodiversity, and resource depletion.

3. What is the basis for the optimism of resource economists and futurist planners who argue that there are no limits to the availability of resources?

4. Compare the Club of Rome *Limits to Growth* study and the *Global 2000* report, referring to basic assumptions, methods, and conclusions.

5. Discuss the dynamics of global warming, referring to the greenhouse effect, greenhouse gases, fossil fuels, carbon cycle, carbon sinks, sea-level rise, and thermal expansion. What degree of warming and sea-level rise is predicted over the next century?

6. Why is there uncertainty about the rate and pace of global climate and sea-level changes? Why do some challenge the consensus view?

7. What are the likely consequences of global warming?

8. Why is it difficult to apply a carrying-capacity model to the global system? What variables need to be considered in setting a global maximum for human population? What different estimates have been proposed?

9. Critique the Malthusian model of food production and population growth. Refer to natural and cultural checks on population, diminishing returns, and absolute limits on food production.

10. What evidence is there that global food production systems may already be overextended? What factors set absolute limits on food production?

11. Distinguish between predominantly technological approaches to world problems and those that are more broadly cultural. Provide specific examples.

12. What is the argument in favor of the devolution of political and economic power as a solution to world problems?

SUGGESTED READING

BARNEY, GERALD O. (ED.). 1977–1980. *The Global 2000 Report to the President of the United States*, 3 vols. New York: Pergamon Press. A study of global trends and predictions to the year 2000, commissioned by President Carter in 1977.

BROWN, LESTER R. (ED.). 1984–. *State of the World* (annual). New York and London: Norton. Annual surveys of global conditions and prospects covering such issues as food, health, and economics.

DURNING, ALAN THEIN. 1992. *How Much Is Enough? The Consumer Society and the Future of the Earth.* The Worldwatch Environmental Alert Series. New York and London: Norton. Argues that people in the richest countries must reduce their consumption of resources.

IPCC (INTERGOVERNMENTAL PANEL ON CLIMATE CHANGE). 1991. *Climate Change: The IPCC Response Strategies.* Washington, D.C., and Covelo, Calif.: Island Press. Presents the findings of an international panel assembled by the United Nations in 1988 to examine the long-range issue of global climate change.

KOHR, LEOPOLD. 1978. *The Breakdown of Nations.* Reprint. New York: Dutton. Economist Kohr's argument that global problems are primarily a result of nations being too large.

KOTLER, NEIL G. (ED.). 1990. *Sharing Innovation: Global Perspectives on Food, Agriculture, and Rural Development.* Washington and London: Smithsonian Institution Press. The proceedings of a conference on the world food problem sponsored by the Smithsonian Institution in 1989, exploring the technological limits to production.

MEADOWS, DONELLA H., DENNIS L. MEADOWS, JORGEN RANDERS, AND WILLIAM W. BEHRENS, III. 1972. *The Limits to Growth.* New York: Universe. The first widely publicized computer simulation of the global system, designed to diagnose problems and seek solutions.

SINGER, S. FRED (ED.). 1989. *Global Climate Change: Human and Natural Influences.* New York: Paragon House. An overview of the climate change issue by a distinguished panel of specialists.

Topical Glossary

CULTURAL ECOLOGY

adaptation The long-term cultural process of maintaining a balance between population levels and natural resources within a given environment.

agricultural intensification Changes in farming technology, such as shortened fallow periods, use of fertilizers, new crops, or irrigation, in order to produce more food per year in a given area, often at greater energy cost.

agricultural involution Geertz's concept of a labor-intensive agricultural system that provides an incentive for population growth.

band A group of twenty-five to fifty people that camp and forage together.

carrying capacity The number of people who could, in theory, be supported indefinitely in a given environment with a given technology and culture.

cash cropping The raising of crops for market sale rather than for domestic consumption.

deficit production The situation in which more calories are expended in food production than are produced for human food.

diminishing returns A decline in output for each increase in effort that accompanies an attempt to increase total production beyond a certain point. Overhunting often produces diminishing returns.

ecocide The degradation of an ecosystem.

energy subsidy The use of fossil fuels to increase food production above the rate that could be sustained through use of renewable energy sources.

factory farming Commercial agriculture based on fossil-fuel energy subsidies, mechanization, pesticides, chemical fertilizers, and large-scale monocropping.

forest fallow system A system of cultivation in which soil nutrients are restored by allowing the forest to regrow.

fuel revolution The large-scale adoption of fossil fuels such as coal and oil.

genocide The extermination of a human population.

Green Revolution Dramatic increases in agricultural production from genetically engineered hybrid grains that produce high yields in return for high inputs of chemical fertilizers and pesticides.

high-yield variety High-yield plant varieties developed by selective breeding as part of the Green Revolution.

immiseration Malthusian impoverishment, a declining standard of living attributed to continuous population growth on a limited-resource base.

marginal returns The increase in the total output produced by the additional input; in subsistence production, the additional amount above what was produced the previous year, resulting from the increased effort.

monocrop farming Growing one plant species, sometimes only a single variety, often in very large continuous stands.

selective female infanticide According to cultural materialist theory, a cultural pattern in which infant girls are selectively killed or neglected in favor of boys, who will become hunters and warriors.

slash and burn A farming technique in which forest is cleared and burned to enrich the soil for planting; a forest fallow system depending on forest regrowth.

subsistence intensification Technological innovations that produce more food from the same land area but often require increased effort.

transhumance Seasonal movement of livestock herds to maintain optimum grazing conditions; often involves altitudinal shifts.

utilitarianism The use of economic profit, direct material advantage, or physical welfare, such as food and shelter, as an explanation for cultural practices.

ECONOMIC SYSTEMS

bilateral development assistance Aid that is given directly from one country to another and that may be given under conditions that favor the donor.

bride-service The cultural expectation that a newly married husband will perform certain tasks for his in-laws.

bride-wealth   Goods, often livestock, that are transferred from the family of the groom to the family of the bride in order to legitimize the marriage and the children of the couple.

capital   Marx's term for land and tools as the means of production; also refers generally to accumulated wealth used for productive purposes.

capital accumulation   Expanding wealth and the means of production that can be devoted to further production.

capitalist production   A mode of production in which a few people control the means of production and purchase the labor of those who could not otherwise support themselves.

cash cropping   The raising of crops for market sale rather than for domestic consumption.

closed corporate community   Communally organized peasants who exclude outsiders and limit the acquisition of wealth and power by their own members.

commercialization   The production and maintenance of private profit-making business enterprise.

commodities   Basic goods that are produced for their exchange value in a market economy to generate profit to be accumulated as capital.

core   The wealthy industrial countries at the center of the world system where the recipients of unequal exchange reside.

debt bondage   An exploitive economic relationship that is managed to keep individuals in virtually perpetual indebtedness.

deferred exchange   A form of trade in which gift giving is reciprocated with a return gift at a later time, thus providing an excuse for maintaining contacts and establishing alliances between potentially hostile groups.

deindustrialization   The replacement of factory employment with service sector employment in formerly industrial countries as production jobs are moved to low-wage countries.

disembodied economy   The concept of an economy as something that can be understood apart from the rest of society and culture, especially with a capitalist mode of production.

embedded economy   An economy that can only be observed and understood within the context of the social, political, and religious systems of the culture.

estate   Property held in common by a descent group, perhaps including territory, sacred sites, and ceremonies.

exchange value   The value of goods when used as commodities.

exploitation   Unjust use of someone to differentially benefit another, especially when one social class is deprived of basic necessities while the elites live in luxury.

factory farming   Commercial agriculture based on fossil fuel energy subsidies, mechanization, pesticides, chemical fertilizers, and large-scale monocropping.

feudalism   A political system in which village farmers occupy lands owned by local lords to whom they owe loyalty, rent, and service.

financialization   A cultural process involving the flow of finance capital, money, and securities, rather than the actual production and distribution of goods and services.

generalized reciprocity   The distribution of goods and services by direct sharing. It is assumed that in the long run giving and receiving balances out, but no accounts are maintained.

gross domestic product (GDP)   The total output of goods and services produced within a country, by monetary value.

gross national product (GNP)   The total output of a country's goods and services, by monetary value; includes profits from foreign activities.

hacienda   A Latin American agricultural estate with dependent laborers that produced for local rather than global markets and was designed to maintain the social status and lifestyle of the *hacendado* landowner.

household   A social unit that shares domestic activities such as food production, cooking, eating, and sleeping, often under one roof, and is usually based on the nuclear or extended family.

invisible hand   The capitalist belief that market forces, operating through supply and demand, will lead to continuous economic growth and benefit everyone.

kin-ordered production   A mode of production organized at the domestic or kinship level and producing primarily for domestic use rather than exchange.

limited good   A belief often found in peasant communities that total wealth is limited and that anyone who acquires too much is taking away from others. This is a justification for wealth leveling.

minifundia   Tiny landholdings of the Latin American peasantry.

multilateral development assistance   Aid that is donated by several countries and channeled through a single international agency such that it can be free of political favoritism.

national income   All wages, salaries, and profits received by the members of a country, calculated by subtracting various indirect taxes from NNP (net national product).

official development assistance (ODA)   Aid given by a government for development purposes, including both direct gifts and low-rate loans.

oligopoly   Concentrated economic power when a market is dominated by only a few producers—like a monopoly, which is controlled by a single producer.

patron   A Spanish term for someone who extends credits or goods to a client who is kept in a debt relationship.

peasantry   Village farmers who provide most of their own subsistence but who must pay taxes and are politically and often, to some extent, economically dependent on the central state government.

periphery   Capital-poor areas that supply raw materials and labor to the core; this area was integrated into the early capitalist world system through conquest and coercion.

political economy   A cultural pattern in which centralized political authority intervenes in the production and distribution of goods and services.

redistribution   A form of exchange in which goods, such as foodstuffs, are concentrated and then given out under the control of a central political authority.

social class   A group of people in a stratified society, such as elites and commoners, who share a similar level of access to resources, power, and privilege.

specialist   An individual who provides goods and services to elites in hierarchically organized societies. Such a specialist does not produce his or her own food but is supported from the surplus that is politically extracted by central authorities.

staple economy   The state-controlled production, storage, and distribution of subsistence staples, such as potatoes and maize in the Inca case, to support nonfood-producing specialist groups and to provide emergency aid.

structural adjustments   Austerity measures designed to increase foreign exchange through increased exports.

structure   The social, economic, and political organization of a culture, which is shaped by the technological base, or infrastructure, according to Harris' cultural materialist theory.

subsistence economy   Production and distribution carried on at the local community level, primarily for local consumption.

surplus   Subsistence production that exceeds the needs of the producer households and that is extracted by political leaders to support nonfood-producing specialists.

tributary production   A mode of production in which products are extracted as surplus from a self-supporting peasantry and used to support the state.

unequal exchange   Market-based exchanges in which one party is consistently able to accumulate a disproportionate share of the profit or wealth.

unlimited good   The belief in continuous economic growth often used to justify wealth inequality.

use value   The value of goods produced for domestic consumption, usually within a kin-ordered mode of production.

utilitarianism   The use of economic profit, direct material advantage, or physical welfare such as food and shelter, as an explanation for cultural practices.

wealth economy   The state-controlled production, storage, and distribution of wealth objects that support the status hierarchy.

wealth-leveling device   Any cultural means, such as ritual feasting, used to redistribute wealth within a community and thereby reduce inequality.

world system   An international hierarchy of diverse societies and cultures integrated into a single economic system based on unequal exchange that allows wealth to accumulate in the core.

GENERAL CULTURAL ANTHROPOLOGY

acculturation   Culture change brought about by contact between peoples with different cultures. Usually refers to the loss of traditional culture when the members of domestic-scale cultures adopt elements of commercial-scale cultures.

assimilation   Ethnocide without genocide; the loss of distinctive cultural traits as a population surrenders its autonomy and is absorbed into a dominant society and culture.

bipedalism   Walking upright on two legs.

central place   A settlement that serves as the focus of a regional communication network.

commercial-scale culture   A cultural system organized by impersonal market exchanges, commercial enterprises, contracts, and money, and potentially encompassing the entire world.

cultural relativism   Understanding other cultures by their own categories, which are assumed to be valid and worthy of respect.

culture   Socially transmitted, often symbolic, information that shapes human behavior and that regulates human society so that people can successfully maintain themselves and reproduce. Culture has mental, behavioral, and material aspects; it is patterned and provides a model for proper behavior.

culture scale   Order-of-magnitude differences among cultures on various socioeconomic dimensions, based on different modes of organizing social power.

domestic-scale culture   A cultural system characterized by small, kinship-based societies, often with only 500 people, in which households organize production and distribution.

emic   Cultural meanings derived from inside a given culture and presumed to be unique to that culture.

ethnocentrism   Evaluating other cultures from the perspective of one's own presumably superior culture.

ethnographic method   Reliance on direct participant observation, key informants, and informal interviews as a data-collecting technique.

ethnographic present   An arbitrary time period when the process of culture change is ignored in order to describe a given culture as if it were a stable system.

etic   Cultural meanings as translated for cross-cultural comparison.

folk-urban continuum   Redfield's concept of a gradual distinction between the Little Tradition culture of rural commoners and the Great Tradition culture of the urban elites in a political-scale culture.

functionalism   The assumption that particular cultural traits may have a role in maintaining the culture.

genealogical method   Tracing the marriage and family relationships among people as a basis for identifying cultural patterns in a community.

genocide   The extermination of a human population.

hominid   A member of the human family, distinct from the great apes.

inclusive fitness   A sociobiological concept referring to the degree to which individuals are successful in passing on a high proportion of their genes to succeeding generations.

key informant   A member of the host culture who helps the anthropologist learn about the culture.

law of cultural differentiation   A statement of the cultural relativity of cognitive ability or basic intelligence. It assumes that no single culture-bound test can adequately test cognitive ability because different cultures produce different cognitive abilities in individuals.

multilinear evolution   Steward's theory that, given similar conditions, cultures can develop independently along similar lines. For example, he argued that irrigation agriculture led to state organization several times.

participant intervention   A form of culture change in which those in control become members of the system they seek to change.

participant observation   Field method in which the observer shares in community activities.

political-scale culture   A cultural system characterized by centrally organized societies with thousands or millions of members and energy-intensive production directed by political rulers.

sapienization   The production and maintenance of human beings, human societies, and human cultures, based on social power organized at the household, or domestic, level.

selective female infanticide   According to cultural materialist theory, a cultural pattern in which infant girls are selectively killed or neglected in favor of boys, who will become hunters and warriors.

society   An interacting, intermarrying population sharing a common culture.

KINSHIP AND SOCIAL ORGANIZATION

achieved status   Social position based on a person's demonstrated personal abilities apart from social status ascribed at birth.

affine   A relative by marriage.

age-class system   A system in which individuals of similar age are placed in a named group and moved as a unit through the culturally defined stages of life. Specific rituals mark each change in age status.

age grade   A culturally defined stage of an age-class system such as childhood, adolescence, parenthood, and old age.

agnatic   Kin who are related through male links.

ascribed status   The social status that one is born into; includes gender, birth order, lineage, clan affiliation, and connection with elite ancestors.

band   A group of twenty-five to fifty people who camp and forage together.

bride-service   The cultural expectation that a newly married husband will perform certain tasks for his in-laws.

bride-wealth   Goods, often livestock, that are transferred from the family of the groom to the family of the bride in order to legitimize the marriage and the children of the couple.

caste An endogamous, ranked, occupationally defined group, known as *jati* in India.

clan A named group claiming descent from a common but often remote ancestor and sharing a joint estate.

cognatic line A descent line that is traced to a common ancestor and that need not rely on exclusively male or female links.

consanguine A relative by culturally recognized descent from a common ancestor; sometimes called a "blood" relative.

cross-cousin The son or daughter of one's mother's brother or father's sister, and often considered to be in a marriageable category.

descent group A social group based on genealogical connections to a common ancestor.

ethnic group A dependent, culturally distinct population that forms part of a larger state or empire and that was formally autonomous.

exogamy Marriage outside a culturally defined group.

extended family A joint household based on a parent family and one or more families of its married children.

filiation A parent–child relationship link used as a basis for descent-group membership.

genitor The biological father of a child.

gerontocracy An age hierarchy that is controlled or dominated by the oldest age groups.

household A social unit that shares domestic activities such as food production, cooking, eating, and sleeping, often under one roof, and is usually based on the nuclear or extended family.

hypergamy Marriage to someone of higher rank. For example, Hindu women may marry men of a higher subcaste.

hypogamy Marriage to someone of lower rank.

kinship terminology An ego-centered system of terms that specifies genealogical relationships of consanguinity and affinity in reference to a given individual.

levirate A cultural pattern in which a woman marries a brother of her deceased husband.

male supremacy complex A functionally interrelated series of presumably male-centered traits, including patrilocality, polygyny, inequitable sexual division of labor, male domination of headmanship and shamanism, and ritual subordination of women.

matrilocality Residence near the wife's kin, normally near her parents.

moiety One part of a two-part social division.

nation A people with a common language, culture, and territory and who claim a common identity.

nuclear family The primary family unit of mother, father, and dependent children.

pater The culturally legitimate, or sociological, father of a child.

patrilineage A lineage based on descent traced through a line of men to a common male ancestor and sharing a joint estate.

patrilineal descent Descent traced through a line of men to a male ancestor.

patrilocal band A theoretical form of band organization based on exogamy and patrilocal residence.

patrilocality A cultural preference for a newly married couple to live near the husband's parents or patrilineal relatives.

polygyny A form of marriage in which a man may have more than one wife.

primogeniture Preferential treatment to a couple's first-born offspring or oldest surviving child; may be a basis for establishing social rank.

rank Social position in a status hierarchy.

section system A social division into four (sections) or eight (subsections) intermarrying, named groups, which summarize social relationships. Members of each group must marry only members of one other specific group.

segmentary lineage system A system in which complementary opposition and genealogical principles of unilineal descent are used by residential groups as a basis for political mobilization in the absence of centralized political leadership.

social class A group of people in a stratified society, such as elites and commoners, who share a similar level of access to resources, power, and privilege.

social power An individual's ability to get what he or she wants, even when others might object.

social status A position that an individual occupies within a social system; defined by age, gender, kinship relationships, or other cultural criteria and involving specific behavioral expectations.

social stratification A ranking of social statuses such that the individuals of a society belong to different groups having differential access to resources, power, and privileges.

structure The social, economic, and political organization of a culture, which is shaped by the technological base, or infrastructure, according to Harris' cultural materialist theory.

unilineal descent group   Membership based on descent traced through a line of ancestors of one sex to a common ancestor.

LANGUAGES AND LINGUISTICS

cognates   Related words found in more than one language and that were derived from a common proto-language.

glottochronology   A method of estimating the relative date at which related languages separated from a common ancestral language, by calculating the percentage of cognates shared between the related languages.

phoneme   The minimal unit of sound that carries meaning and is recognized as distinctive by the speakers of a given language.

Sapir-Whorf hypothesis   Suggests that one's view of the world is shaped by language, such that the speakers of different languages may live in different perceptual worlds.

POLITICAL SYSTEMS

acephalous   A political system without central authority or permanent leaders.

agromanagerial despotism   Wittfogel's explanation for the rise of the Mesopotamian state, arguing that the first rulers controlled irrigation and agriculture.

aristocracy   A political system in which a small, privileged elite rule.

bigman   A self-made leader in a small-scale culture. His position is temporary, depending on personal ability and consent of his followers.

circumscription   Carneiro's explanation for the development of political centralization—that villagers may be forced to surrender their autonomy if they are unable to move away from authorities because of geographic barriers or neighboring societies.

city-states   Political-scale cultures based on relatively self-sufficient city-states, drawing their primary support from their immediate surroundings.

complementary opposition   A situation in which people assume a group identity in political opposition to another group at the same level.

cultural autonomy   Self-determination by a cultural group.

direct rule   The use of European colonial administrators to control a native community at the local level.

ethnocide   The forced destruction of a cultural system.

feuding   Chronic intergroup conflict that exists between communities in the absence of centralized political authority. It may involve a cycle of revenge raids and killing that is difficult to break.

gerontocracy   An age hierarchy that is controlled or dominated by the oldest age groups.

Great Tradition   The culture of the elite in a state-organized society with a written tradition that is not fully shared by nonliterate, village-level commoners.

headman   A political leader who coordinates group activities and is a village spokesman but who serves only with the consent of the community and has no coercive power.

idealist   A policy position that advocates cultural autonomy for indigenous peoples as a basic human right.

indigenous   Peoples who are the original inhabitants of a territory and who seek to maintain political control over their resources and their domestic-scale cultural heritage.

indirect rule   The situation in which European colonial administrators appointed local natives to serve as mediating officials, or chiefs, to help them control local communities.

integration   The absorption of a formerly autonomous people into a dominant state society, with the possible retention of ethnic identity.

internal colony   A territory within a state containing an indigenous population that is denied the right of self-determination.

liturgical government   The use of ritually prescribed interpersonal relations and religious, moral authority as a primary means of social control in a state-level society.

male supremacy complex   A functionally interrelated series of presumably male-centered traits, including patrilocality, polygyny, inequitable sexual division of labor, male domination of headmanship and shamanism, and ritual subordination of women.

monumental architecture   Large-scale permanent structures, such as temples, palaces, or tombs, that require large labor forces and central planning.

political economy   A cultural pattern in which centralized political authority intervenes in the production and distribution of goods and services.

politicization   The production and maintenance of political power.

realist   A policy position that maintains that indigenous peoples must surrender their political and economic autonomy and be integrated into dominant state societies.

redistribution   A form of exchange in which goods, such as foodstuffs, are concentrated and then distributed under the control of a central political authority.

reverse dominance hierarchy   System whereby the members of a village or community intentionally limit the power of leaders, keeping them subservient to the group will.

segmentary lineage system   A system in which complementary opposition and genealogical principles of unilineal descent are used by residential groups as a basis for political mobilization in the absence of centralized political leadership.

self-determination   The right of any people to freely determine its own cultural, political, and economic future.

social class   A group of people in a stratified society, such as elites and commoners, who share a similar level of access to resources, power, and privilege.

social stratification   A ranking of social statuses such that the individuals of a society belong to different groups having differential access to resources, power, and privileges.

specialist   An individual who provides goods and services to elites in hierarchically organized societies. Such a specialist does not produce his or her own food but is supported from the surplus that is politically extracted by central authorities.

uncontrolled frontier   A tribal territory that is invaded by colonists from a state-organized society but where the government chooses not to regulate the actions of the colonists.

village-states   Political-scale cultures based on an urban administrative and ceremonial center, drawing their support from peasant villages scattered over a vast region.

RELIGION, RITUAL, AND COSMOLOGY

ancestor worship   A religious system based on reverence for specific ancestors and sometimes involving shrines, rituals, and sacrifice.

animism   A belief in spirits that occupy plants, animals, and people. Spirits are supernatural and normally invisible but may transform into different forms. Animism is considered by cultural evolutionists to be the simplest and earliest form of religion.

animistic thinking   The soul concept used by tribal individuals as an intellectual explanation of life, death, and dream experiences, part of Tylor's theory of animism as the origin of religion.

collective representations   Ideas, or thoughts, and emotions common to a society as a whole, especially in reference to the supernatural.

complementary opposition   A structural principle in which pairs of opposites, such as males and females, form a logical larger whole.

cosmogony   An ideological system that seeks to explain the origin of everything: people, nature, and the universe.

cosmology   An ideological system that explains the order and meaning of the universe and people's places within it.

cultural hegemony   Dominant influence by elites over the cultural symbols and beliefs that influence human behavior.

filial piety   *Hsiao*, the ritual obligation of children to respect their ancestors, and especially the duty of sons to care for shrines of their partrilineal ancestors.

Great Tradition   The culture of the elite in a state-organized society with a written tradition that is not fully shared by nonliterate, village-level commoners.

impurity   Low ritual status attributed to association or contact with polluting biological events or products.

law of participation   The assumption that a thing can participate in or be part of two or more things at once; identified by Lévy-Bruhl as the principle underlying his concept of prelogical thought.

law of sympathy   Frazer's explanation for the logic underlying magic, sorcery, and shamanism. He thought that tribal peoples believed that anything ever connected with a person, such as hair or blood, could be manipulated to influence that person.

liminal phase   An ambiguous phase of ritual transition in which one is on the threshold between two states.

Little Tradition   Ritual beliefs and practices followed by nonliterate commoners, especially rural villagers who are part of a larger state-level society.

liturgical government   The use of ritually prescribed interpersonal relations and religious, moral authority as a primary means of social control in a state-level society.

mana   An impersonal supernatural force thought to reside in particular people and objects. In the Pacific islands, *mana* is the basis of chiefly power.

myth   A narrative that recounts the activities of supernatural beings. Often acted out in ritual, myths encapsulate a culture's cosmology and cosmogony and provide justification for culturally prescribed behavior.

mythical thought   Lévi-Strauss' term for the thinking underlying myth and magic; logically similar to scientific thought but based on the science of the concrete and used to serve aesthetic purposes and to solve existential problems.

natural symbols   Inherent qualities of specific plants and animals used as signs or metaphors for issues that concern people.

polytheism   A religious system based on belief in many gods or deities.

prelogical thinking   Lévy-Bruhl's characterization of the collective representations of tribal peoples, which he thought reflected concrete thought and a mystic reality unique to domestic-scale cultures.

purity   Ritually superior status; a category in logical opposition to impurity.

rite of passage   A ritual marking culturally significant changes in an individual's life cycle, such as birth, puberty, marriage, old age, and death.

science of the concrete   Thought based on perceptions and signs, images, and events, as opposed to formal science based on concepts.

shaman   A part-time religious specialist with special skills for dealing with the spirit world; may help his community by healing, by divination, and by directing supernatural powers against enemies.

shamanic state of consciousness   (SSC) An interpretation of the shamanic trance phenomenon that distinguishes it from the altered state of consciousness of schizophrenics. A shaman may enter and leave the SSC at will, remains aware of his surroundings, and uses the SSC for socially beneficial purposes.

superstructure   The mental, ideological, or belief systems, as expressed in the religion, myth, and rituals of a culture. According to Harris' cultural materialist theory, superstructure is shaped by the structure.

symbol   Anything with a culturally defined meaning.

tabu   Actions that are forbidden under the sanction of supernatural punishment. *Tabus* may be imposed by chiefs and are supported by chiefly *mana*.

theocracy   State government based on religious authority or divine guidance. The Chinese emperor was the highest civil and religious leader.

totem   In Australia, specific animals, plants, natural phenomena, or other objects that originate in the Dreaming and are the spiritual progenitors of aboriginal descent groups. Elsewhere refers to any cultural association between specific natural objects and human social groups.

Bibliography

AABY, PETER. 1977. "What Are We Fighting For? 'Progress' or 'Cultural Autonomy'?" In *Cultural Imperialism and Cultural Identity,* edited by Carola Sanbacka, pp. 61–76. Transactions of the Finnish Anthropological Society, No. 2. Helsinki: Finnish Anthropological Society.

ADAMS, RICHARD N. 1988. *The Eighth Day: Social Evolution as the Self-Organization of Energy.* Austin: University of Texas Press.

ADAMS, ROBERT McC. 1981. *Heartland of Cities: Surveys of Ancient Settlement and Land Use on the Central Floodplain of the Euphrates.* Chicago and London: University of Chicago Press.

ADAMS, ROBERT McC. 1982. "Property Rights and Functional Tenure in Mesopotamian Rural Communities." In *Societies and Languages of the Ancient Near East: Studies in Honour of I. M. Diakonoff,* pp. 1–14. Warminster, Eng.: Aris & Phillips.

AHMED, LEILA. 1982. "Western Ethnocentrism and Perceptions of the Harem." *Feminist Studies* 8(3):521–534.

ALBERT, BRUCE. 1985. "Temps du Sang, Temps des Cendres. Représentations de la Maladie, Système Rituel et Espace Politique chez les Yanomami du Sud-est (Amazonie Bresilienne)." Ph.D. dissertation, Université de Paris X (Nanterre).

ALERS, J. OSCAR. 1971. "Well Being." In *Peasants, Power, and Applied Social Change: Vicos as a Model,* edited by Henry Dobyns, Paul Doughty, and Harold Lasswell, pp. 115–136. Beverly Hills, Calif., and London: Sage.

ALKIRE, WILLIAM H. 1965. *Lamotrek Atoll and Inter-Island Socioeconomic Ties.* Studies in Anthropology, no. 5. Urbana: University of Illinois Press.

ALLCHIN, BRIDGET, AND F. RAYMOND ALLCHIN. 1982. *The Rise of Civilization in India and Pakistan.* Cambridge, Eng.: Cambridge University Press.

ALLCHIN, F. RAYMOND. 1982. "The Legacy of the Indus Civilization." In *Harappan Civilization: A Contemporary Perspective,* edited by Gregory Possehl, pp. 325–333. New Delhi: Oxford and IBH.

ALVA, WALTER. 1990. "New Tomb of Royal Splendor." *National Geographic* 117(6):2–15.

AMAZONIA INDIGENA. 1981. "Pronunciamiento Sobre el Projecto Especial Pichis-Palcazu." *Amazonia Indigena* 1(3):3–5.

AMBROSE, STANLEY H. 1984. "The Introduction of Pastoral Adaptations to the Highlands of East Africa." In *From Hunters to Farmers: The Causes and Consequences of Food Production in Africa,* edited by J. Desmond Clark and Steven Brandt, pp. 212–239. Berkeley: University of California Press.

AMERICAN PSYCHIATRIC ASSOCIATION (APA). 1980. *Diagnostic and Statistical Manual of Mental Disorders,* 3rd ed. Washington, D.C.: American Psychiatric Association.

AMMERMAN, ALBERT J., AND L. L. CAVALLI-SFORZA. 1984. *The Neolithic Transition and the Genetics of Populations in Europe.* Princeton, N.J.: Princeton University Press.

ANDERSON, RICHARD L. 1990. *Calliope's Sisters: A Comparative Study of Philosophies of Art.* New York: Prentice-Hall.

ANTHROPOLOGICAL INSTITUTE OF GREAT BRITAIN AND IRELAND. 1903. "A Plea for the Scientific Study of the Native Laws and Customs of South Africa: A Memorial Addressed by the Anthropological Institute and the Folklore Society to H.M. Secretary of State for the Colonies; and Subsequent Correspondence." *Man* 3(37):70–74.

ANZAAS (Australia and New Zealand Association for the Advancement of Science). 1914. "Welfare of Aborigines Committee." Report of the Fourteenth Meeting of the Australasian Association for the Advancement of Science, 450–452.

ARENS, W. 1979. *The Man Eating Myth: Anthropology and Anthropophagy.* New York: Oxford University Press.

ARENSBERG, CONRAD M., AND ARTHUR H. NIEHOFF. 1964. *Introducing Social Change: A Manual for Americans Overseas.* Chicago: Aldine.

ARNOLD, JEANNE E. 1993. "Labor and the Rise of Complex Hunter-Gatherers." *Journal of Anthropological Archaeology* 12(1):75–119.

ASCHER, MARCIA, AND ROBERT A. ASCHER. 1981. *Code of the Quipu: Study in Media, Mathematics, and Culture.* Ann Arbor: University of Michigan Press.

ASHTON, T. S. 1969. *The Industrial Revolution 1760–1830.* London: Oxford University Press.

ASIMOV, ISAAC. 1971. "The End." *Penthouse* (January).

BAILEY, ROBERT C., G. HEAD, M. JENIKE, B. OWEN, R. RECHTMAN, AND E. ZECHENTER. 1989. "Hunting and Gathering in Tropical Rain Forest: Is It Possible?" *American Anthropologist* 91(1):59–82.

BARNET, RICHARD J., AND JOHN CAVANAGH. 1994. *Global Dreams: Imperial Corporations and the New World Order.* New York: Simon & Schuster.

BARNETT, HAROLD, AND CHANDLER MORSE. 1963. *Scarcity and Growth: The Economics of Natural Resource Availability.* Baltimore: Johns Hopkins University Press.

BARNEY, GERALD O. (ED.). 1977–1980. *The Global 2000 Report to the President of the United States,* 3 vols. New York: Pergamon Press.

BATEMAN, JOHN. 1883. *The Great Landowners of Great Britain and Ireland,* 4th ed. London: Harrison.

BAUER, BRIAN S. 1996. "Legitimization of the State in Inca Myth and Ritual." *American Anthropologist* 98(2):327–337.

BEACH, WILLIAM W., AND GARETH DAVIS. 1998. "The Institutional Setting of Economic Growth." In *1998 Index of*

Economic Freedom, edited by Bryan T. Johnson, Kim R. Holmes, and Melanie Kirkpatrick, pp. 1–10. Washington, D.C., and New York: The Heritage Foundation and Dow Jones & Co.

BEAGLEHOLE, ERNEST. 1954. "Cultural Factors in Economic and Social Change." *International Labour Review* 69(5): 415–432.

BEARD, CHARLES A. 1913. *An Economic Interpretation of the Constitution of the United States.* New York: Macmillan.

BEHRENS, CLIFFORD A. 1986. "Shipibo Food Categorization and Preference: Relationships Between Indigenous and Western Dietary Concepts." *American Anthropologist* 88(3): 647–658.

BEIDELMAN, T. O. 1966. "The Ox and Nuer Sacrifice: Some Freudian Hypotheses About Nuer Symbolism." *Man* 1(4): 453–467.

BEIDELMAN, T. O. (ED.). 1971. "Nuer Priest and Prophets: Charisma, Authority, and Power Among the Nuer." In *The Translation of Culture: Essays to E. E. Evans-Pritchard*, pp. 375–415. London: Tavistock.

BELAUNDE-TERRY, FERNANDO. 1965. *Peru's Own Conquest.* Lima: American Studies Press.

BELL, DIANE. 1983. *Daughters of the Dreaming.* Sydney: McPhee Gribble/Allen & Unwin.

BELL, DIANE. 1987. "Aboriginal Women and the Religious Experience." In *Traditional Aboriginal Society: A Reader*, edited by W. H. Edwards, pp. 237–256. South Melbourne: Macmillan.

BELLWOOD, PETER S. 1985. *Prehistory of the Indo-Malaysian Archipelago.* New York and Sydney: Academic.

BENEDICT, RUTH. 1934. *Patterns of Culture.* Boston: Houghton Mifflin.

BERGMAN, ROLAND W. 1974. "Shipibo Subsistence in the Upper Amazon Rainforest." Ph.D. dissertation, Department of Geography, University of Wisconsin–Madison. Ann Arbor, Mich.: University Microfilms.

BERLIN, BRENT. 1972. "Speculations on the Growth of Ethnobotanical Nomenclature." *Language in Society* 1:51–86.

BERLIN, BRENT, AND ELOIS ANN BERLIN. 1983. "Adaptation and Ethnozoological Classification: Theoretical Implications of Animal Resources and Diet of the Aguaruna and Huambisa." In *Adaptive Responses of Native Amazonians*, edited by Raymond Hames and William Vickers, pp. 301–325. New York: Academic Press.

BERLIN, BRENT, DENNIS E. BREEDLOVE, AND PETER H. RAVEN. 1973. "General Principles of Classification and Nomenclature in Folk Biology." *American Anthropologist* 75(1):214–242.

BERLIN, BRENT, AND PAUL KAY. 1969. *Basic Color Terms: Their Universality and Evolution.* Berkeley and Los Angeles: University of California Press.

BERN, JOHN. 1979. "Ideology and Domination: Toward a Reconstruction of Australian Aboriginal Social Formation." *Oceania* 50(2):118–132.

BERNARDI, BERNARDO. 1985. *Age Class Systems: Social Institutions and Polities Based on Age.* Cambridge, Eng.: Cambridge University Press.

BERREMAN, GERALD. 1960. "Caste in India and the United States." *American Journal of Sociology* 66:120–127.

BERREMAN, GERALD D. 1979. *Caste and Other Inequities: Essays on Inequality.* Meerut, Uttar Pradesh, India: Ved Prakash Vatuk, Folklore Institute.

BERRY, J. W., AND S. H. IRVINE. 1986. "Brocolage: Savages Do It Daily." In *Practical Intelligence: Nature and Origins of Competence in the Everyday World*, edited by Robert Sternberg and Richard Wagner, pp. 271–306. Cambridge, Eng.: Cambridge University Press.

BICKERTON, DEREK. 1990. *Language and Species.* Chicago and London: University of Chicago Press.

BIRD-DAVID, NURIT. 1992. "Beyond 'The Original Affluent Society': A Culturalist Reformulation." *Current Anthropology* 33(1):25–47.

BIRDSELL, JOSEPH B. 1957. "Some Population Problems Involving Pleistocene Man." *Cold Spring Harbor Symposium on Quantitative Biology* 22:47–70.

BIRDSELL, JOSEPH B. 1973. "A Basic Demographic Unit." *Current Anthropology* 14(4):337–350.

BLUESTONE, BARRY, AND BENNETT HARRISON. 1982. *The Deindustrialization of America.* New York: Basic Books.

BOAS, FRANZ. 1911. *The Mind of Primitive Man.* New York: Macmillan.

BOCQUET-APPEL, JEAN-PIERRE, AND CLAUDE MASSET. 1981. "Farewell to Paleodemography." *Journal of Human Evolution* 11:321–333.

BODLEY, JOHN H. 1970. "Campa Socio-Economic Adaptation." Ph.D. dissertation, University of Oregon. Ann Arbor, Mich.: University Microfilms.

BODLEY, JOHN H. 1972a. "A Transformative Movement Among the Campa of Eastern Peru." *Anthropos* 67:220–228.

BODLEY, JOHN H. 1972b. *Tribal Survival in the Amazon: The Campa Case.* IWGIA (International Work Group for Indigenous Affairs) Document, no. 5. Copenhagen: IWGIA.

BODLEY, JOHN H. 1973. "Deferred Exchange Among the Campa Indians." *Anthropos* 68:589–596.

BODLEY, JOHN H. 1975. *Victims of Progress.* Menlo Park, Calif.: Cummings.

BODLEY, JOHN H. 1976. *Anthropology and Contemporary Human Problems.* Menlo Park, Calif.: Cummings.

BODLEY, JOHN H. 1981a. "Deferred Exchange Among the Campa: A Reconsideration." In *Networks of the Past: Regional Interaction in Archaeology*, edited by Peter Francis, F. J. Kense, and P. G. Duke, pp. 49–59. Calgary: University of Calgary Archaeological Association.

BODLEY, JOHN H. 1981b. "Inequality: An Energetic Approach." In *Social Inequality: Comparative and Developmental Approaches*, edited by Gerald Berreman, pp. 183–197. New York: Academic Press.

BODLEY, JOHN H. 1988. *Tribal Peoples and Development Issues: A Global Overview.* Mountain View, Calif.: Mayfield.

BODLEY, JOHN H. 1990. *Victims of Progress*, 3rd ed. Mountain View, Calif.: Mayfield.

BODLEY, JOHN H. 1996. *Anthropology and Contemporary Human Problems*, 3rd ed. Mountain View, Calif.: Mayfield.

BODLEY, JOHN H. 1999. *Victims of Progress*, 4th ed. Mountain View, Calif.: Mayfield.

BODLEY, JOHN H., AND FOLEY BENSON. 1979. *Cultural Ecology of Amazonian Palms.* Reports of Investigations, no. 56. Laboratory of Anthropology, Washington State University.

BODMER, W., AND LUIGI CAVALLI-SFORZA. 1970. "Intelligence and Race." *Scientific American* 223:19–29.

BOEHM, CHRISTOPHER. 1993. "Egalitarian Behavior and Reverse Dominance Hierarchy." *Current Anthropology* 34(3): 227–254.

BOOTH, CHARLES. 1892–1903. *Life and Labour of the People in London.* London and New York: Macmillan.

BOOTH, DOUGLAS E. 1987. *Regional Long Waves, Uneven Growth, and the Cooperative Alternative.* New York: Praeger.

BORGSTROM, GEORG. 1965. *The Hungry Planet,* 2nd ed. New York: Macmillan.

BOSERUP, ESTER. 1965. *The Conditions of Economic Growth.* Chicago: Aldine.

BOSERUP, ESTER. 1970. *Women's Role in Economic Development.* London: Allen & Unwin.

BOSTER, J. 1983. "A Comparison of the Diversity of Jivaroan Gardens with That of the Tropical Forest." *Human Ecology* 11(1):47–68.

BOURLIERE, FRANÇOIS, AND M. HADLEY. 1983. "Present-Day Savannas: An Overview." In *Ecosystems of the World 13: Tropical Savannas,* edited by François Bourliere, pp. 1–17. New York: Elsevier.

BOWDLER, S. 1977. "The Coastal Colonisation of Australia." In *Sunda and Sahul: Prehistoric Studies in Southeast Asia, Melanesia and Australia,* edited by J. Allen, J. Golson, and R. Jones, pp. 205–246. London: Academic Press.

BOYD, ROBERT, AND PETER J. RICHERSON. 1985. *Culture and the Evolutionary Process.* Chicago and London: University of Chicago Press.

BRAIDWOOD, ROBERT J., AND BRUCE HOWE. 1960. *Prehistoric Investigations in Iraqi Kurdistan.* Studies in Ancient Oriental Civilization, no. 31. Chicago: University of Chicago Press.

BRANDEIS, LOUIS D. 1914. *Other People's Money and How the Bankers Use It.* New York: Frederick A. Stokes.

BROWN, BARTON MCCAUL. 1987. "Population Estimation from Floor Area: A Restudy of 'Naroll's Constant.'" *Behavior Science Research* 21(1–4):1–49.

BROWN, CECIL H. 1977. "Folk Botanical Life-Forms: Their Universality and Growth." *American Anthropologist* 79(2): 317–342.

BROWN, CECIL H. 1979a. "Folk Zoological Life-Forms: Their Universality and Growth." *American Anthropologist* 81(4): 791–817.

BROWN, CECIL H. 1979b. "Growth and Development of Folk Botanical Life Forms in the Mayan Language Family." *American Anthropologist* 6(2):366–385.

BROWN, DONALD E. 1991. *Human Universals.* Philadelphia: Temple University Press.

BROWN, HARRISON. 1956. "Technological Denudation." In *Man's Role in Changing the Face of the Earth,* edited by William Thomas, Jr., pp. 1023–1032. Chicago: University of Chicago Press.

BROWN, J. LARRY, AND ERNESTO POLLITT. 1996. "Malnutrition, Poverty and Intellectual Development." *Scientific American* 274(2):38–43.

BROWN, LESTER R. 1987. "Sustaining World Agriculture." In *State of the World 1987,* edited by Lester Brown et al., pp. 122–138. New York and London: Norton.

BROWN, LESTER R. 1989. "Reexamining the World Food Prospect." In *State of the World 1987,* edited by Lester Brown et al., pp. 41–58. New York and London: Norton.

BROWN, LESTER R. 1994. "Facing Food Insecurity." In *State of the World 1994: A Worldwatch Institute Report on Progress Toward a Sustainable Society,* edited by Lester Brown et al., pp. 177–197. New York: Norton.

BROWN, LESTER R., AND SANDRA POSTEL. 1987. "Thresholds of Change." In *State of the World 1987,* edited by Lester Brown et al., pp. 3–19. New York and London: Norton.

BROWN, MICHAEL F. 1984. "The Role of Words in Aguaruna Hunting Magic." *American Ethnologist* 11(3):545–558.

BRUSH, STEPHEN B. 1976. "Man's Use of an Andean Ecosystem." *Human Ecology* 4(2):147–166.

BRUSH, STEPHEN B., HEATH J. CARNEY, AND ZOSIMO HUAMAN. 1981. "Dynamics of Andean Potato Agriculture." *Economic Botany* 35(1):70–88.

BUELL, RAYMOND L. 1928. *The Native Problem in Africa,* vol. 1. New York: Macmillan.

BUHLER, G. 1886. "The Laws of Manu." In *The Sacred Books of the East,* edited by F. M. Muller. Oxford, Eng.: Clarendon Press.

BUNSEN, C. C. J. 1854. *Outlines of the Philosophy of Universal History Applied to Language and Religion,* 2 vols. London: Longman.

BURBANK, VICTORIA KATHERINE. 1994. *Fighting Women: Anger and Aggression in Aboriginal Australia.* Berkeley: University of California Press.

BURGER, RICHARD L., AND NIKOLAAS J. VAN DER MERWE. 1990. "Maize and the Origins of Highland Chavin Civilization: An Isotopic Perspective." *American Anthropologist* 92(1): 85–95.

BURNELL, ARTHUR COKE, AND EDWARD W. HOPKINS (EDS.). 1884. *The Ordinances of Manu.* London: Trubner.

BURTON, JOHN W. 1980. "Women and Men in Marriage: Some Atuot Texts (Southern Sudan)." *Anthropos* 75:710–720.

BURTON, JOHN W. 1981. "Ethnicity on the Hoof: On the Economics of Nuer Identity." *Ethnology* 20(2):157–162.

CANNON, WALTER B. 1942. "'Voodoo' Death." *American Anthropologist* 44(2):169–181.

CARNEIRO, ROBERT L. 1960. "Slash-and-Burn Agriculture: A Closer Look at Its Implications for Settlement Patterns." In *Men and Cultures: Selected Papers of the International Congress of Anthropological and Ethnological Sciences,* edited by A. Wallace, pp. 229–234. Philadelphia: University of Pennsylvania Press.

CARNEIRO, ROBERT. 1978a. "The Knowledge and Use of Rain Forest Trees by the Kuikuru Indians of Central Brazil." In *The Nature and Status of Ethnobotany.* Anthropological Papers, no. 67, edited by R. Ford, pp. 210–216. Ann Arbor: Museum of Anthropology, University of Michigan.

CARNEIRO, ROBERT L. 1978b. "Political Expansion as an Expression of the Principle of Competitive Exclusion." In *Origins of the State: The Anthropology of Political Evolution,* edited by R. Cohen and E. R. Service, pp. 205–223. Philadelphia: Institute for the Study of Human Issues.

CARNEIRO, ROBERT L. 1981. "The Chiefdom: Precursor of the State." In *The Transition to Statehood in the New World,* edited by Grant Jones and Robert Kautz, pp. 37–79. Cambridge, Eng.: Cambridge University Press.

CARNEIRO, ROBERT L. 1983. "The Cultivation of Manioc Among the Kuikuru of the Upper Xingu." In *Adaptive Responses of Native Amazonians,* edited by Raymond Hames and William Vickers, pp. 65–111. New York: Academic Press.

CARNEIRO, ROBERT L., AND STEPHEN F. TOBIAS. 1963. "The Application of Scale Analysis to the Study of Cultural Evolution." *Transaction of the New York Academy of Sciences* (ser. 2) 26:196–207.

CAVALLI-SFORZA, LUIGI LUCA, AND FRANCESCO CAVALLI-SFORZA. 1995. *The Great Human Diasporas: The History of Diversity and Evolution.* Reading, Mass.: Addison-Wesley.

CAVALLI-SFORZA, LUIGI LUCA, AND M. FELDMAN. 1981. *Cultural Transmission and Evolution.* Princeton, N.J.: Princeton University Press.

CAVALLI-SFORZA, LUIGI LUCA, PAOLO MENOZZI, AND ALBERTO PIAZZA. 1994. *The History and Geography of Human Genes.* Princeton, N.J.: Princeton University Press.

CAWTE, JOHN. 1974. *Medicine Is the Law: Studies in Psychiatric Anthropology of Australian Tribal Societies.* Honolulu: University Press of Hawaii.

CAWTE, JOHN E. 1976. "Malgri: A Culture-Bound Syndrome." In *Culture-Bound Syndromes, Ethnopsychiatry, and Alternate Therapies.* Vol. 4 of *Mental Health Research in Asia and the Pacific,* edited by William Lebra, pp. 22–31. Honolulu: University Press of Hawaii.

CGIAR (CONSULTATIVE GROUP ON INTERNATIONAL AGRICULTURAL RESEARCH). 1980. *Consultative Group on International Development.* Washington, D.C.: CGIAR.

CHADWICK, SIR EDWIN. 1842. *Report . . . on an Inquiry Into the Sanitary Conditions of the Labouring Population of Great Britain.* London.

CHAGNON, NAPOLEON A. 1968a. *Yanomamo: The Fierce People.* New York: Holt, Rinehart & Winston.

CHAGNON, NAPOLEON A. 1968b. "Yanomamo Social Organization and Warfare." In *War: The Anthropology of Armed Conflict and Aggression,* edited by Morton Fried, Marvin Harris, and Robert Murphy, pp. 109–159. Garden City, N.Y.: Doubleday.

CHAGNON, NAPOLEON A. 1979. "Is Reproductive Success Equal in Egalitarian Societies?" In *Evolutionary Biology and Human Social Behavior: An Anthropological Perspective,* edited by Napoleon Chagnon and William Irons, pp. 374–401. North Scituate, Mass.: Duxbury Press.

CHAGNON, NAPOLEON A. 1983. *Yanomamo: The Fierce People,* 3rd ed. New York: Holt, Rinehart & Winston.

CHAGNON, NAPOLEON A. 1988. "Life Histories, Blood Revenge, and Warfare in a Tribal Population." *Science* 239(4843): 985–992.

CHAGNON, NAPOLEON. 1992. *The Yanomamo,* 4th ed. New York: Holt, Rinehart & Winston.

CHAI, CH'U, AND WINBERG CHAI. 1967. "Introduction." In *Li Chi: Book of Rites,* vol. 1, translated by James Legge, pp. xxiii–lxxxiv. New Hyde Park, N.Y.: University Books.

CHANDLER, ALFRED D., JR. 1977. *The Visible Hand: The Managerial Revolution in American Business.* Cambridge, Mass., and London: The Belknap Press of Harvard University Press.

CHANDLER, ROBERT F., JR. 1990. "Thoughts on the Global Issues of Food, Population, and the Environment." In *Sharing Innovation: Global Perspectives on Food, Agriculture, and Rural Development,* edited by Neil Kotler, pp. 169–185. Washington, D.C., and London: Smithsonian Institution Press.

CHANG, KWANG-CHIH. 1980. *Shang Civilization.* New Haven, Conn., and London: Yale University Press.

CHANG, KWANG-CHIH. 1983. *Art, Myth, and Ritual: The Path to Political Authority in Ancient China.* Cambridge, Mass.: Harvard University Press.

CHANG, KWANG-CHIH. 1986. *The Archaeology of Ancient China,* 4th ed. New Haven, Conn.: Yale University Press.

CHANG, T. T. 1983. "The Origin and Early Culture of the Cereal Grains and Food Legumes." In *The Origins of Chinese Civilization,* edited by D. N. Keightley, pp. 65–94. Berkeley: University of California Press.

CHAO, KANG. 1986. *Man and Land in Chinese History: An Economic Analysis.* Stanford, Calif.: Stanford University Press.

CIBA FOUNDATION. 1977. *Health and Disease in Tribal Societies.* CIBA Foundation Symposium 49, pp. 49–67. Amsterdam: Elsevier/Excerpta Medica/North-Holland.

CICERONE, RALPH J. 1989. "Methane in the Atmosphere." In *Global Climate Change: Human and Natural Influences,* edited by S. Fred Singer, pp. 91–112. New York: Paragon House.

CLAESSEN, HENRY J. M., AND PETER SKALNIK (EDS.). 1978. "The Early State: Theories and Hypotheses." In *The Early State,* pp. 3–29. The Hague, Paris, and New York: Mouton.

CLARK, GROVER. 1936. *The Balance Sheets of Imperialism: Facts and Figures on Colonies.* New York: Columbia University Press.

CLARK, J. DESMOND. 1984. "Prehistoric Cultural Continuity and Economic Change in the Central Sudan in the Early Holocene." In *From Hunters to Farmers: The Causes and Consequences of Food Production in Africa,* edited by J. Desmond Clark and Steven Brandt, pp. 113–126. Berkeley: University of California Press.

CLASTRES, PIERRE. 1977. *Society Against the State: The Leader as Servant and the Humane Uses of Power Among the Indians of the Americas.* New York: Urizen Books.

CLEAVE, T. L. 1974. *The Saccharine Disease.* Bristol, Eng.: John Wright.

CODRINGTON, R. H. 1981. *The Melanesians.* Oxford, Eng.: Clarendon Press.

COHEN, LEONARD A. 1987. "Diet and Cancer." *Scientific American* 257(5):42–48.

COHEN, MARK NATHAN. 1989. *Health and the Rise of Civilization.* New Haven, Conn., and London: Yale University Press.

COHEN, YEHUDI (ED.). 1974. *Man in Adaptation,* 2nd ed. Chicago: Aldine.

COLBY, GERARD, AND CHARLOTTE DENNETT. 1995. *Thy Will Be Done: The Conquest of the Amazon: Nelson Rockefeller in the Age of Oil.* New York: HarperCollins, HarperPerennial.

COLCHESTER, MARCUS. 1984. "Rethinking Stone Age Economics: Some Speculations Concerning the Pre-Columbian Yanoama Economy." *Human Ecology* 12(3):291–314.

COLE, H. S. D. (ED.). 1973. *Models of Doom.* New York: Universe.

COLLIER, JANE FISHBURNE. 1988. *Marriage and Inequality in Classless Societies.* Stanford, Calif.: Stanford University Press.

COLLIER, PETER, AND DAVID HOROWITZ. 1976. *The Rockefellers: An American Dynasty.* New York: Holt, Rinehart & Winston.

CONRAD, GEOFFREY W. 1981. "Cultural Materialism, Split Inheritance, and the Expansion of Ancient Peruvian Empires." *American Antiquity* 46:3–26.

CONRAD, GEOFFREY W., AND ARTHUR A. DEMAREST. 1984. *Religion and Empire: The Dynamics of Aztec and Inca Expansionism.* Cambridge, Eng.: Cambridge University Press.

COOK, EARL. 1971. "The Flow of Energy in an Industrial Society." *Scientific American* 224(3):134–144.

CORRIS, PETER. 1968. *Aborigines and Europeans in Western Victoria.* Occasional Papers in Aboriginal Studies, no. 12, Ethnohistory Series, no. 1. Canberra: Australian Institute of Aboriginal Studies.

COUGHENOUR, M. B., J. E. ELLIS, D. M. SWIFT, D. L. COPPOCK, K. GALVIN, J. T. MCCABE, AND T. C. HART. 1985. "Energy Extraction and Use in a Nomadic Pastoral Ecosystem." *Science* 230(4726):619–625.

COWLISHAW, GILLIAN. 1978. "Infanticide in Aboriginal Australia." *Oceania* 48(4):262–283.

CROSBY, ALFRED W. 1986. *Biological Imperialism: The Biological Expansion of Europe, 900–1900.* Cambridge, Eng.: Cambridge University Press.

CROSSON, PIERRE R., AND NORMAN J. ROSENBERG. 1989. "Strategies for Agriculture." *Scientific American* 261(3): 128–135.

CUMBERLAND, KENNETH BRAILEY. 1956. *Southwest Pacific: A Geography of Australia, New Zealand and Their Pacific Neighborhoods.* London: Methuen.

DAHL, GUDREN, AND ANDERS HJORT. 1976. *Having Herds: Pastoral Herd Growth and Household Economy.* Stockholm Studies in Social Anthropology, no. 2. Stockholm: Department of Social Anthropology, University of Stockholm.

DALES, GEORGE F. 1964. "The Mythical Massacre at Mohenjo-Daro." *Expedition* 6(3):36–43.

DALES, GEORGE F. 1965. "Civilization and Floods in the Indus Valley." *Expedition* 7(4):10–19.

DALES, GEORGE F. 1966. "The Decline of the Harappans." *Scientific American* 214(5):92–100.

DALES, GEORGE F. 1982. "Mohenjodaro Miscellany: Some Unpublished, Forgotten, or Misinterpreted Features." In *Harappan Civilization: A Contemporary Perspective,* edited by Gregory Possehl, pp. 97–106. New Delhi: Oxford and IBH.

DALES, G. F., AND R. L. RAIKES. 1968. "The Mohenjo–Daro Floods: A Rejoinder." *American Anthropologist* 70(5):957–961.

D'ALTROY, TERENCE N., AND TIMOTHY K. EARLE. 1985. "Staple Finance, Wealth Finance, and Storage in the Inka Political Economy." *Current Anthropology* 26(2):187–206.

D'ANS, ANDRÉ-MARCEL. 1972. "Les Tribus Indigènes du Parc National du Manu." *Proceedings of the 39th International Americanists Congress* 4:95–100.

D'ANS, ANDRÉ-MARCEL. 1981. "Encounter in Peru." In *Is God an American? An Anthropological Perspective on the Missionary Work of the Summer Institute of Linguistics,* edited by Søren Hvalkof and Peter Aaby, pp. 145–162. Copenhagen and London: IWGIA and Survival International.

DAVIS, SHELTON H. 1976. "The Yanomamo: Ethnographic Images and Anthropological Responsibilities." In *The Geological Imperative: Anthropology and Development in the Amazon Basin of South America,* edited by Shelton Davis and Robert Mathews, pp. 7–23. Cambridge, Mass.: Anthropology Resource Center.

DAVIS, SHELTON H. 1977. *Victims of the Miracle: Development and the Indians of Brazil.* Cambridge, Eng.: Cambridge University Press.

DEFOREST, ROBERT W., AND LAWRENCE VEILLER (EDS.). 1903. *The Tenement House Problem: Including the Report of the New York State Tenement House Commission of 1900.* 2 vols. New York: Macmillan.

DENEVAN, WILLIAM. 1976. *The Native Population of the Americas in 1492.* Madison: University of Wisconsin Press.

DENNETT, GLENN, AND JOHN CONNELL. 1988. "Acculturation and Health in the Highlands of Papua New Guinea." *Current Anthropology* 29(2):273–299.

DEWHURST, J. FREDERIC (ED.). 1947. *America's Needs and Resources: A Twentieth Century Fund Survey Which Includes Estimates for 1950 and 1969.* New York: Twentieth Century Fund.

DIAMOND, STANLEY. 1968. "The Search for the Primitive." In *The Concept of the Primitive,* edited by Ashley Montagu, pp. 99–147. New York: Free Press.

DICKENS, CHARLES. (1852–1853) 1953. *Bleak House.* Garden City, N.Y.: The Literary Guild of America.

DICKSON, F. P. 1981. *Australian Stone Hatchets: A Study in Design and Dynamics.* Sydney: Academic Press.

DIVALE, WILLIAM, AND MARVIN HARRIS. 1976. "Population, Warfare and the Male Supremacist Complex." *American Anthropologist* 78(3):521–538.

DOBYNS, HENRY E., AND PAUL L. DOUGHTY. 1976. *Peru: A Cultural History.* New York: Oxford University Press.

DOBYNS, HENRY F., PAUL. L. DOUGHTY, AND HAROLD D. LASSWELL (EDS.). 1971. *Peasants, Power, and Applied Social Change: Vicos as a Model.* Beverly Hills, Calif., and London: Sage.

DOLE, GERTRUDE. 1964. "Shamanism and Political Control Among the Kuikuru." In *Beitrage zur Völkerkunde Sudamerikas Festgabe für Herbert Baldus zum 65. Geburtstag,* edited by Hans Becher, pp. 53–62. *Völkerkundliche Abhandlungen,* Vol. 1, Des Niedersächsischen Landesmuseum.

DOLE, GERTRUDE. 1978. "The Use of Manioc Among the Kuikuru: Some Implications." In *The Nature and Status of Ethnobotany.* Anthropological Papers, no. 67, edited by R. Ford, pp. 217–247. Ann Arbor: Museum of Anthropology, University of Michigan.

DOMHOFF, G. WILLIAM. 1967. *Who Rules America?* Englewood Cliffs, N.J.: Prentice-Hall.

DOMHOFF, G. WILLIAM. 1983. *Who Rules America Now? A View for the '80s.* Englewood Cliffs, N.J.: Prentice-Hall.

DOUGHTY, PAUL L. Forthcoming. "Ending Serfdom in Peru: The Struggle for Land and Freedom in Vicos." In *Contemporary Cultures and Societies of Latin America,* edited by Dwight B. Heath. Prospect Heights, Ill.: Wavland Press.

DOUGLAS, MARY. 1966. *Purity and Danger: An Analysis of Concepts of Pollution and Taboo.* New York: Praeger.

DOW, JAMES. 1986. "Universal Aspects of Symbolic Healing: A Theoretical Synthesis." *American Anthropologist* 88(1): 56–69.

DULL, JACK L. 1990. "The Evolution of Government in China." In *Heritage of China: Contemporary Perspectives on Chinese Civilization,* edited by Paul Ropp, pp. 55–85. Berkeley: University of California Press.

DUMONT, LOUIS. 1970. *Homo Hierarchicus: An Essay on the Caste System.* Chicago: University of Chicago Press.

DURHAM, WILLIAM H. 1979. *Scarcity and Survival in Central America: Ecological Origins of the Soccer War.* Stanford, Calif.: Stanford University Press.

DURHAM, WILLIAM H. 1991. *Coevolution: Genes, Culture, and Human Diversity.* Stanford, Calif.: Stanford University Press.

DURHAM, WILLIAM H. 1995. "Political Ecology and Environmental Destruction in Latin America." In *The Social Causes of Environmental Destruction in Latin America,* edited by Michael Painter and William H. Durham, pp. 249–264. Ann Arbor: University of Michigan Press.

DUSSEL, ENRIQUE. 1975. "Bartolome de Las Casas." *Encyclopaedia Britannica* 10:684–686.

DYE, THOMAS R. 1983. *Who's Running America? The Reagan Years.* Englewood Cliffs, N.J.: Prentice-Hall.

DYSON-HUDSON, RADA, AND NEVILLE DYSON-HUDSON. 1969. "Subsistence Herding in Uganda." *Scientific American* 220(2): 76–89.

EARLE, TIMOTHY. 1978. *Economic and Social Organization of a Complex Chiefdom: The Halelea District, Kaua'i, Hawaii.* Anthropological Papers, no. 63. Ann Arbor: Museum of Anthropology, University of Michigan.

EARLE, TIMOTHY. 1987. "Specialization and the Production of Wealth: Hawaiian Chiefdoms and the Inka Empire." In *Specialization, Exchange, and Complex Societies,* edited by Elizabeth Brumfiel and Timothy Earle, pp. 64–75. Cambridge, Eng.: Cambridge University Press.

EARLS, JOHN, AND IRENE SILVERBLATT. 1978. "La Realidad Fisica y Social en la Cosmologia Andina." *Proceedings of the International Congress of Americanists* 42(4):299–325.

EASTMAN, LLOYD E. 1988. *Family, Fields, and Ancestors: Constancy and Change in China's Social and Economic History, 1550–1949.* New York: Oxford University Press.

EASTWELL, HARRY D. 1982. "Voodoo Death and the Mechanisms for Dispatch of the Dying in East Arnhem, Australia." *American Anthropologist* 84(1):5–18.

EBREY, PATRICIA. 1990. "Women, Marriage, and the Family in Chinese History." In *Heritage of China: Contemporary Perspectives on Chinese Civilization,* edited by Paul Ropp, pp. 197–223. Berkeley: University of California Press.

ECK, DIANA L. 1985. *Darsan: Seeing the Divine Image in India.* Chambersburg, Pa.: Anima Books.

EDGERTON, LYNNE T. 1991. *The Rising Tide: Global Warming and World Sea Levels.* Washington, D.C., and Covelo, Calif.: Island Press.

EDGERTON, ROBERT B. 1992. *Sick Societies: Challenging the Myth of Primitive Harmony.* New York: Free Press.

EHRENBERG, RICHARD. 1928. *Capital and Finance in the Age of the Renaissance: A Study of the Fuggers and Their Connections.* New York: Harcourt, Brace.

EHRLICH, PAUL. 1968. *The Population Bomb.* New York: Ballantine Books.

EISENBURG, J., AND R. THORINGTON, JR. 1973. "A Preliminary Analysis of a Neotropical Mammal Fauna." *Biotropica* 5(3): 150–161.

EKELUND, ROBERT B., JR., AND ROBERT F. HEBERT. 1983. *A History of Economic Theory and Method,* 2nd ed. New York: McGraw-Hill.

ELKIN, A. P. 1933. "Wanted: A Positive Policy." *Sydney Morning Herald,* Oct. 13, p. 6.

ELKIN, A. P. 1934. "Anthropology and the Future of the Australian Aborigines." *Oceania* 5(1):1–18.

ENGELS, FRIEDRICH. 1973. *The Condition of the Working Class in England.* Moscow: Progress.

ERDOSY, GEORGE. 1988. *Urbanization in Early Historic India.* BAR International Series 430. Oxford, Eng.: Oxford University Press.

ESTES, RALPH. 1996. *Tyranny of the Bottom Line: Why Corporations Make Good People Do Bad Things.* San Francisco: Berrett-Kohler.

EVANS-PRITCHARD, E. E. 1940. *The Nuer: A Description of the Modes of Livelihood and Political Institutions of a Nilotic People.* New York and Oxford, Eng.: Oxford University Press.

EVANS-PRITCHARD, E. E. 1951. *Kinship and Marriage Among the Nuer.* Oxford, Eng.: Oxford University Press.

EVANS-PRITCHARD, E. E. 1953. "The Nuer Conception of Spirit in Its Relation to the Social Order." *American Anthropologist* 55(2, pt.1):201–214.

FAIRSERVIS, WALTER A., JR. 1967. "The Origin, Character, and Decline of an Early Civilization." *American Museum Novitates* 2302:1–48.

FEDER, ERNEST. 1978. *Strawberry Imperialism: An Enquiry into the Mechanisms of Dependency in Mexican Agriculture.* The Hague: Institute of Social Studies.

FEDERALIST PAPERS (Alexander Hamilton, James Madison, John Jay, papers No. 1–85, originally published 1787–1788, numerous editions have been republished).

FEHER, JOSEPH. 1969. *Hawaii: A Pictorial History.* Bernice P. Bishop Museum Special Publication, no. 58. Honolulu: Bishop Museum Press.

FEI, HSIAO-TUNG, AND CHIH-I CHANG. 1945. *Earthbound China: A Study of Rural Economy in Yunnan.* Chicago: University of Chicago Press.

FERGUSON, R. BRIAN. 1995. *Yanomami Warfare: A Political History.* Santa Fe: School of American Research Press.

FERGUSON, R. BRIAN, AND NEIL L. WHITEHEAD (EDS.). 1992. *War in the Tribal Zone: Expanding States and Indigenous Warfare.* Santa Fe: School of American Research Press.

FEUERWERKER, ALBERT. 1990. "Chinese Economic History in Comparative Perspective." In *Heritage of China: Contemporary Perspectives on Chinese Civilization,* edited by Paul Ropp, pp. 224–241. Berkeley: University of California Press.

FIELD, C. R. 1985. "The Importance to Rendille Subsistence Pastoralists of Sheep and Goats in Northern Kenya." In *Small Ruminants in African Agriculture,* edited by R. T. Wilson and D. Bourzat, pp. 188–197. Addis Ababa, Ethiopia: International Livestock Centre for Africa.

FIRTH, RAYMOND. [1936] 1957. *We the Tikopia: A Sociological Study of Kinship in Primitive Polynesia,* 2nd ed. New York: Barnes & Noble.

FIRTH, RAYMOND. [1940] 1967. "The Work of the Gods." In *Tikopia,* 2nd ed. London: Athlone Press.

FIRTH, RAYMOND. [1965] 1975. *Primitive Polynesian Economy.* New York: Norton.

FITTKAU, E., AND H. KLINGE. 1973. "On Biomass and Trophic Structure of the Central Amazonian Rain Forest Ecosystem." *Biotropica* 5(1):2–14.

FLANNERY, KENT V. 1965. "The Ecology of Early Food Production in Mesopotamia." *Science* 147(3663):1247–1256.

FLANNERY, KENT V. 1972a. "The Cultural Evolution of Civilizations." *Annual Review of Ecology and Systematics* 3:399–426.

FLANNERY, KENT V. 1972b. "The Origins of the Village as a Settlement Type in Mesoamerica and the Near East: A Comparative Study." In *Man, Settlement and Urbanism,* edited by P. J. Ucko, R. Tringham, and G. W. Dimbleby, pp. 25–53. London: Duckworth.

FLOOD, JOSEPHINE. 1980. *The Moth Eaters.* Atlantic Highlands, N.J.: Humanities Press.

FLOOD, JOSEPHINE. 1983. *Archaeology of the Dreamtime.* Honolulu: University of Hawaii Press.

FLOWERS, NANCY M. 1983. "Seasonal Factors in Subsistence, Nutrition, and Child Growth in a Central Brazilian Indian Community." In *Adaptive Responses of Native Amazonians,* edited by Raymond Hames and William Vickers, pp. 357–390. New York: Academic Press.

FLYNN, JOHN T. 1941. *Men of Wealth: The Story of Twelve Significant Fortunes from the Renaissance to the Present Day.* New York: Simon & Schuster.

FOSTER, GEORGE M. 1965. "Peasant Society and the Image of Limited Good." *American Anthropologist* 67(2):293–315.

FOSTER, GEORGE M. 1969. *Applied Anthropology.* Boston: Little, Brown.

FOUNDATION DIRECTORY. 1998. Vol. 20. New York: Columbia University Press.

FOUTS, ROGER S. 1994. "Transmission of a Human Gestural Language in a Chimpanzee Mother–Infant Relationship." In *The Ethological Roots of Culture,* edited by R. A. Gardner et al., pp. 257–270. Dordrecht, Boston, and London: Kluwer Academic.

FRANK, ANDRÉ GUNDER. 1967. *Capitalism and Underdevelopment in Latin America.* New York: Monthly Review Press.

FRANKE, RICHARD W., AND BARBARA H. CHASIN. 1989. *Kerala: Radical Reform as Development in an Indian State.* Food First Development Report No. 6. San Francisco: The Institute for Food and Development Policy.

FRAZER, JAMES G. 1990 [1890] 1900. *The Golden Bough,* 3 vols. London: Macmillan.

FRAZER, SIR JAMES. 1910. *Totemism and Exogamy,* 4 vols. London: Macmillan.

FREED, STANLEY A., AND RUTH S. FREED. 1981. "Sacred Cows and Water Buffalo in India: The Uses of Ethnography." *Current Anthropology* 22(5):483–490.

FREEDMAN, MAURICE. 1966. *Chinese Lineage and Society: Fukien and Kwangtung.* London School of Economics, Monographs on Social Anthropology, no. 33. London: Athlone Press.

FREEDMAN, MAURICE. 1979. *The Study of Chinese Society.* Stanford, Calif.: Stanford University Press.

FRIED, MORTON H. 1983. "Tribe to State or State to Tribe in Ancient China." In *The Origins of Chinese Civilization,* edited by D. N. Keightley, pp. 467–493. Berkeley: University of California Press.

GALATY, JOHN G. 1982. "Being 'Maasai'; Being 'People-of-Cattle': Ethnic Shifters in East Africa." *American Ethnologist* 9(1):1–20.

GALE, FAY (ED.). 1983. *We Are Bosses Our-Selves: The Status and Role of Aboriginal Women Today.* Canberra: Australian Institute of Aboriginal Studies.

GARDNER, R. ALLEN, AND BEATRIX T. GARDNER. 1994a. "Development of Phrases in the Utterances of Children and Cross-Fostered Chimpanzees." In *The Ethological Roots of Culture,* edited by R. A. Gardner et al., pp. 223–255. Dordrecht, Boston, and London: Kluwer Academic Press.

GARDNER, R. ALLEN, AND BEATRIX T. GARDNER. 1994b. "Ethological Roots of Language." In *The Ethological Roots of Culture,* edited by R. A. Gardner et al., pp. 199–222. Dordrecht, Boston, and London: Kluwer Academic Press.

GATES, BILL, WITH NATHAN MYHRVOLD AND PETER RINEARSON. 1996. *The Road Ahead,* 2nd ed. New York and London: Penguin Books.

GEERTZ, CLIFFORD. 1963. *Agricultural Involution: The Process of Ecological Change in Indonesia.* Berkeley: University of California Press.

GEIST, VALERIUS. 1994. "Culture and Its Biological Origins: A View from Ethnology, Epigenesis and Design." In *The Ethological Roots of Culture,* edited by R. A. Gardner et al., pp. 441–459. Dordrecht, Boston, and London: Kluwer Academic Press.

GELB, I. J. 1965. "The Ancient Mesopotamian Ration System." *Journal of Near Eastern Studies* 24(3):230–243.

GEMINI CONSULTING. 1998. *World Wealth Report 1998.* New York: Gemini Consulting.

GENNEP, ARNOLD L. VAN. 1909. *Les Rites de Passage.* Paris: E. Nourry.

GEORGE, SUSAN. 1992. *The Debt Boomerang: How Third World Debt Harms Us All.* Boulder, Colo.: Westview Press.

GIBSON, MCGUIRE. 1976. "By Stage and Cycle to Sumer." In *The Legacy of Sumer.* Vol. 4 of *Bibliotheca Mesopotamia,* edited by Denise Schmandt-Besserat, pp. 51–58. Malibu, Calif.: Undena Publications.

GILDER, GEORGE. 1981. *Wealth and Poverty.* New York: Basic Books.

GIVEN-WILSON, C. 1991. "Wealth and Credit, Public and Private: The Earls of Arundel 1306–1397." *The English Historical Review* 418:1–26.

GLADWIN, THOMAS. 1970. *East Is a Big Bird.* Cambridge, Mass.: Harvard University Press.

GLICKMAN, MAURICE. 1972. "The Nuer and the Dinka: A Further Note." *Man* 7(4):586–594.

GLUCKMAN, MAX. 1956. *Custom and Conflict in Africa.* New York: Barnes & Noble.

GODELIER, MAURICE. 1975. "Modes of Production, Kinship, and Demographic Structures." In *Marxist Analyses and Social Anthropology,* edited by Maurice Bloch, pp. 3–27. New York: Wiley.

GOLDMAN, IRVING. 1970. *Ancient Polynesian Society.* Chicago and London: University of Chicago Press.

GOLDSTEIN, JOSHUA S. 1988. *Long Waves: Prosperity and War in the Modern Age.* New Haven, Conn., and London: Yale University Press.

GOODALL, J. 1986. *The Chimpanzees of Gombe.* Cambridge, Mass.: Belknap Press.

GOODENOUGH, WARD HUNT. 1963. *Cooperation in Change: An Anthropological Approach to Community Development.* New York: Wiley.

GOODENOUGH, WARD H. 1965. "Yankee Kinship Terminology: A Problem in Componential Analysis." Part 2. *American Anthropologist* 67(5):259–287.

GOODLAND, ROBERT. 1982. *Tribal Peoples and Economic Development: Human Ecological Considerations.* Washington, D.C.: International Bank for Reconstruction and Development/World Bank.

GOODY, JACK. 1976. *Production and Reproduction: A Comparative Study of the Domestic Domain.* Cambridge, Eng.: Cambridge University Press.

GORHAM, KAFKA, AND NEELAKANTAN. 1998. "The Forbes 400: The Richest People in America." *Forbes* 162(8):165–428.

GOSH, A. 1982. "Deurbanization of the Harappan Civilization." In *Harappan Civilization: A Contemporary Perspective,* edited by George Possehl, pp. 321–324. New Delhi: Oxford and IBH.

GOULD, RICHARD A. 1969. "Subsistence Behavior Among the Western Desert Aborigines of Australia." *Oceania* 39(4):253–273.

GOULD, RICHARD A. 1970. *Spears and Spear-Throwers of the Western Desert Aborigines of Australia.* American Museum Novitates, no. 2403. New York: American Museum of Natural History.

GOULD, RICHARD A. 1980. *Living Archaeology.* Cambridge, Eng.: Cambridge University Press.

GOULD, RICHARD A. 1981. "Comparative Ecology of Food-Sharing in Australia and Northwest California." In *Omnivorous Primates: Gathering and Hunting in Human Evolution,* edited by Robert Harding and Geza Teleki, pp. 422–454. New York: Columbia University Press.

GOULD, STEPHEN JAY. 1981. *The Mismeasure of Man.* New York: Norton.

GOULDING, MICHAEL. 1980. *The Fishes and the Forest: Explorations in Amazonian Natural History.* Berkeley: University of California Press.

GRAEDEL, THOMAS E., AND PAUL. J. CRUTZEN. 1989. "The Changing Atmosphere." *Scientific American* 261(3):58–68.

GRAINGER, A. 1980. "The State of the World's Forests." *Ecologist* 10(1):6–54.

GRAY, ANDREW. N.d. *Freedom and Territory: Slavery in the Peruvian Amazon.* Unpublished manuscript.

GRAY, ANDREW. 1987. "IWGIA Report on the ILO Meeting of Experts to Discuss the Revision of Convention 107 Geneva, 1–10 September, 1986." In *IWGIA Yearbook 1986: Indigenous Peoples and Human Rights,* pp. 73–92. Copenhagen: IWGIA.

GRAY, ANDREW. 1990. "The ILO Meeting at the UN, Geneva, June 1989: Report on International Labour Organisation Revision of Convention 107." In *IWGIA Yearbook 1989,* pp. 173–191. Copenhagen: IWGIA.

GREAT BRITAIN BOARD OF TRADE. 1909. *Statistical Abstracts for the Several British Colonies, Possessions, and Protectorates in Each Year from 1894 to 1908,* no. 46. London: His Majesty's Stationery Office.

GREGORIO, DAVID I., STEPHEN J. WALSH, AND DEBORAH PATURZO. 1997. "The Effects of Occupation-Based Social Position on Mortality in a Large American Cohort." *American Journal of Public Health* 87(9):1472–1475.

GRONOWICZ, ANTHONY. 1998. *Race and Class Politics in New York City Before the Civil War.* Boston: Northeastern University Press.

GROSS, DANIEL R. 1975. "Protein Capture and Cultural Development in the Amazon Basin." *American Anthropologist* 77(3):526–549.

GROSS, DANIEL R., AND BARBARA A. UNDERWOOD. 1971. "Technological Change and Caloric Costs: Sisal Agriculture." *American Anthropologist* 73(2):725–740.

GROSSMAN, RICHARD L., AND FRANK T. ADAMS. 1996. "Exercising Power over Corporations Through State Charters." In *The Case Against the Global Economy and for a Turn Toward the Local,* edited by Jerry Mander and Edward Goldsmith, pp. 374–389. San Francisco: Sierra Club Books.

GUDSCHINSKY, SARAH C. 1956. "The ABC's of Lexicostatistics (Glottochronology)." *Word* 12:175–210.

HADINGHAM, EVAN. 1987. *Lines to the Mountain Gods: Nazca and the Mysteries of Peru.* New York: Random House.

HAILEY, WILLIAM MALCOLM. 1950. *Native Administration in the British African Territories. Part One, East Africa: Uganda, Kenya, Tanganyika.* Colonial Office. London: His Majesty's Stationery Office.

HALLPIKE, C. R. 1979. *The Foundations of Primitive Thought.* Oxford, Eng.: Clarendon Press.

HALLPIKE, C. R. 1986. *The Principles of Social Evolution.* Oxford, Eng.: Clarendon Press.

HAMES, RAYMOND. 1987. "Game Conservation or Efficient Hunting?" In *The Question of the Commons: The Cultural Ecology of Communal Resources,* edited by Bonnie McCoy and James Acheson, pp. 92–107. Tucson: University of Arizona Press.

HAMILTON, ANNETTE. 1979. "A Comment on Arthur Hippler's Paper 'Culture and Personality Perspective of the Yolngu of Northeastern Arnhem Land: Part 1.'" *Mankind* 12(2):164–169.

HAMMACK, DAVID C. 1982. *Power and Society: Greater New York at the Turn of the Century.* New York: Russell Sage Foundation.

HANDY, E. S. C., AND E. G. HANDY. 1972. *The Native Planters in Old Hawaii: Their Life, Lore, and Environments.* Bernice P. Bishop Museum bull. 233. Honolulu: Bishop Museum Press.

HANKS, LUCIEN M. 1972. *Rice and Men: Agricultural Ecology in Southeast Asia.* Chicago: Aldine.

HARDIN, GARRETT. 1968. "The Tragedy of the Commons." *Science* 162(3859):1243–1248.

HARNER, M. J. 1980. *The Way of the Shaman.* New York: Harper & Row.

HARRIS, MARVIN. 1965. "The Myth of the Sacred Cow." In *Man, Culture, and Animals,* edited by A. P. Vayda and A. Leeds, pp. 217–228. Washington, D.C.: American Association for the Advancement of Science.

HARRIS, MARVIN. 1966. "The Cultural Ecology of India's Sacred Cattle." *Current Anthropology* 7(1):51–59.

HARRIS, MARVIN. 1971a. "A Comment on Heston: An Approach to the Sacred Cow of India." *Current Anthropology* 12(2):199–201.

HARRIS, MARVIN. 1971b. *Culture, Man, and Nature: An Introduction to General Anthropology.* New York: Crowell.

HARRIS, MARVIN. 1974. *Cows, Pigs, Wars, and Witches: The Riddles of Culture*. New York: Random House.

HARRIS, MARVIN. 1981. *America Now: The Anthropology of a Changing Culture*. New York: Simon & Schuster.

HARRIS, MARVIN. 1984. "A Cultural Materialist Theory of Band and Village Warfare: The Yanomamo Test." In *Warfare, Culture, and Environment*, edited by R. Brian Ferguson, pp. 111–140. New York: Academic Press.

HARRIS, MARVIN. 1985. *Good to Eat: Riddles of Food and Culture*. New York: Simon & Schuster.

HARRIS, MARVIN. 1988. *Culture, People, Nature: An Introduction to General Anthropology*, 5th ed. New York: Harper & Row.

HARTMANN, BETSY, AND JAMES K. BOYCE. 1983. *A Quiet Violence: View from a Bangladesh Village*. San Francisco: Institute for Food and Development Policy.

HASLUCK, PAUL M. 1953. "The Future of the Australian Aborigine." Twenty-ninth Meeting of the Australian and New Zealand Association for the Advancement of Science, Sydney. *Australian and New Zealand Association for the Advancement of Science* 29:155–165.

HASSAN, FEKRI A. 1981. *Demographic Archaeology*. New York: Academic Press.

HASTORF, CHRISTINE A. 1993. *Agriculture and the Onset of Political Inequality Before the Inka*. Cambridge, Eng.: Cambridge University Press.

HAWKES, JAMES F., AND KRISTEN O'CONNELL. 1981. "Affluent Hunters? Some Comments in Light of the Alyawarra Case." *American Anthropologist* 83(3):622–626.

HAYDEN, BRIAN. 1977. "Stone Tool Functions in the Western Desert." In *Stone Tools as Cultural Markers: Change, Evolution and Complexity*, edited by R. V. S. Wright, pp. 178–188. Prehistory and Material Culture Series, no. 12. Canberra: Australian Institute of Aboriginal Studies.

HEADLAND, THOMAS N., KENNETH L. PIKE, AND MARVIN HARRIS. 1990. *Emics and Etics: The Insider/Outsider Debate*. Newbury Park, Calif.: Sage.

HECKER, HOWARD M. 1982. "Domestication Revisited: Its Implications for Faunal Analysis." *Journal of Field Archaeology* 9:217–236.

HEILBRONER, ROBERT, AND LESTER C. THUROW. 1987. *Economics Explained*. Englewood Cliffs, N.J.: Prentice-Hall.

HEMMING, JOHN. 1978. *Red Gold: The Conquest of the Brazilian Indians*. Cambridge, Mass.: Harvard University Press.

HENRY, JULES. 1963. *Culture Against Man*. New York: Random House.

HERRNSTEIN, RICHARD J. 1971. "IQ." *Atlantic Monthly* (September):43–64.

HERRNSTEIN, RICHARD J., AND CHARLES MURRAY. 1994. *The Bell Curve: Intelligence and Class Structure in American Life*. New York: Free Press.

HERSKOVITS, MELVILLE J. 1926. "The Cattle Complex in East Africa." *American Anthropologist* 28(1):230–272, 28(2):361–388, 28(3):494–528, 28(4):633–664.

HESTON, ALAN. 1971. "An Approach to the Sacred Cow of India." *Current Anthropology* 12(2):191–197.

HEYERDAHL, THOR. 1952. *American Indians in the Pacific: The Theory Behind the Kon-Tiki Expedition*. London: Allen & Unwin.

HIATT, L. R. 1984a. *Aboriginal Landowners: Contemporary Issues in the Determination of Traditional Aboriginal Land Ownership*. Oceania Monograph, no. 27. Sydney: University of Sydney.

HIATT, L. R. 1984b. "Your Mother-in-Law Is Poison." *Man* 19(2):183–198.

HIATT, L. R. 1987. "Aboriginal Political Life." In *Traditional Aboriginal Society*, edited by W. H. Edwards, pp. 174–188. South Melbourne: Macmillan.

HILL, KIM, AND A. MAGDALENA HURTADO. 1996. *Ache Life History: The Ecology and Demography of a Foraging People*. New York: Aldine.

HIPPLER, ARTHUR. 1977. "Cultural Evolution: Some Hypotheses Concerning the Significance of Cognitive and Affective Interpenetration During Latency." *Journal of Psychohistory* 4(4):419–460.

HIPPLER, ARTHUR. 1978. "Culture and Personality Perspective of the Yolngu of Northeastern Arnhem Land: Part 1. Early Socialization." *Journal of Psychological Anthropology* 1(2):221–244.

HIPPLER, ARTHUR. 1981. "The Yolngu and Cultural Relativism: A Response to Reser." *American Anthropologist* 83(2):393–397.

HOBEN, ALLAN. 1982. "Anthropologists and Development." *Annual Review of Anthropology* 11:349–375.

HOEBEL, E. ADAMSON. 1968. *The Law of Primitive Man*. New York: Atheneum.

HOMER-DIXON, THOMAS F. 1991. "On the Threshold: Environmental Changes as Causes of Acute Conflict." *International Security* 16(2):76–116.

HOMEWOOD, K. M., AND W. A. RODGERS. 1984. "Pastoralism and Conservation." *Human Ecology* 12(4):431–441.

HOPKINS, DIANE E. 1985. "The Peruvian Agrarian Reform: Dissent from Below." *Human Organization* 44(1):18–32.

HOUSE OF COMMONS. 1837. *Report from the Select Committee on Aborigines (British Settlements)*. Imperial Blue Book, no. 7, 425. British Parliamentary Papers.

HOWARD, ALAN. 1967. "Polynesian Origins and Migrations: A Review of Two Centuries of Speculation and Theory." In *Polynesian Culture History: Essays in Honor of Kenneth P. Emory*, edited by Genevieve Highland, Roland Force, Alan Howard, Marion Kelly, and Yosihiko Sinoto, pp. 45–101. Bernice P. Bishop Museum Special Publication, no. 56. Honolulu: Bishop Museum Press.

HSU, FRANCIS L. K. 1963. *Clan, Caste, and Club*. Princeton, N.J.: Van Nostrand.

HSU, FRANCIS L. K. (ED.). 1972. "American Core Value and National Character." In *Psychological Anthropology*, pp. 240–262. Cambridge, Mass.: Schenkman.

HSU, FRANCIS L. K. 1981. *Americans and Chinese: Passage to Difference*. Honolulu: University Press of Hawaii.

HUBERT, M. KING. 1969. "Energy Resources." In *Resources and Man*, edited by National Academy of Sciences, pp. 157–242. San Francisco: Freeman.

HUEY, JOHN. 1993. "The World's Best Brand." *Fortune*, May 31, pp. 44–54.

HUNN, EUGENE. 1985. "The Utilitarian Factor in Folk Biological Classification." In *Directions in Cognitive Anthropology*, edited by Janet Dougherty, pp. 117–140. Urbana and Chicago: University of Illinois Press.

HUTTON, J. H. 1963. *Caste in India: Its Nature, Function, and Origins*, 4th ed. London: Oxford University Press.

HVALKOF, S., AND ANDREW GRAY. 1990. "Inscription and Titling of Native Communities in the Ucayali Department." In *Supervision Report on Land Titling Project, Peruvian Amazon*. Report to IWGIA, Copenhagen.

HYSLOP, JOHN. 1984. *The Inka Road System*. New York: Academic Press.

II, JOHN PAPA. 1983. *Fragments of Hawaiian History*. Bernice P. Bishop Museum Special Publication, no. 70. Honolulu: Bishop Museum Press.

ILR (INTERNATIONAL LABOUR REVIEW). 1951. "Reports and Enquiries: First Session of ILO Committee of Experts on Indigenous Labour." *International Labour Review* 64(1): 61–84.

ILR (INTERNATIONAL LABOUR REVIEW). 1954. "Reports and Enquiries: The Second Session of the ILO Committee of Experts on Indigenous Labour." *International Labour Review* 70(5):418–441.

ILYATJARI, NGANYINTJA. 1983. "Women and Land Rights: The Pitjantjatjara Land Claims." In *We Are Bosses Our-Selves: The Status and Role of Aboriginal Women Today*, edited by Fay Gale, pp. 55–61. Canberra: Australian Institute of Aboriginal Studies.

INFORMATION PLEASE ALMANAC ATLAS AND YEARBOOK 1967. 1966. New York: Simon & Schuster.

IPCC (INTERGOVERNMENTAL PANEL ON CLIMATE CHANGE). 1991. *Climate Change: The IPCC Response Strategies*. Washington, D.C., and Covelo, Calif.: Island Press.

IRVINE, S. H., AND J. W. BERRY. 1988. "The Abilities of Mankind: A Revaluation." In *Human Abilities in Cultural Context*, edited by S. H. Irvine and J. W. Berry, pp. 3–59. Cambridge, Eng.: Cambridge University Press.

ISBELL, WILLIAM H. 1978. "Environmental Perturbations and the Origin of the Andean State." In *Social Anthropology: Beyond Subsistence and Dating*, edited by Charles Redman, Mary Jane Berman, Edward Curtin, William Langhorne, Jr., Nina Versaggi, and Jeffery Wanser, pp. 303–313. New York: Academic Press.

IWGIA (INTERNATIONAL WORKGROUP FOR INDIGENOUS AFFAIRS). 1987. *IWGIA Yearbook 1986: Indigenous Peoples and Human Rights*. Copenhagen: IWGIA.

JACOBSEN, THORKILD. 1976. *The Treasures of Darkness: A History of Mesopotamian Religion*. New Haven, Conn., and London: Yale University Press.

JACOBSEN, THORKILD, AND ROBERT McC. ADAMS. 1958. "Salt and Silt in Ancient Mesopotamian Agriculture." *Science* 128 (3334):1251–1258.

JACOBSON, DORANNE. 1982. "Purdah and the Hindu Family in Central India." In *Separate Worlds: Studies of Purdah in South Asia*, edited by Hanna Papanek and Gail Minault, pp. 81–109. Delhi: Chanakya Publications.

JACOBSON, JODI L. 1989. "Abandoning Homelands." In *State of the World 1987*, edited by Lester Brown et al., pp. 59–76. New York and London: Norton.

JAHER, FREDERIC COPLE. 1972. "Nineteenth-Century Elites in Boston and New York." *Journal of Social History* 6(1): 32–77.

JAHER, FREDERIC COPLE. 1982. *The Urban Establishment: Upper Strata in Boston, New York, Charleston, Chicago, and Los Angeles*. Urbana: University of Illinois Press.

JANSEN, EIRIK G. 1986. *Rural Bangladesh: Competition for Scarce Resources*. Oslo: Universitetsforlaget, Norwegian University Press.

JENSEN, ARTHUR. 1969. "How Much Can We Boost I.Q. and Scholastic Achievement?" *Harvard Educational Review* 29: 1–123.

JOHANNES, ROBERT E. 1981. *Words of the Lagoon: Fishing and Marine Lore in the Palau District of Micronesia*. Berkeley: University of California Press.

JOHNSON, ALLEN. 1975. "Time Allocation in a Machiguenga Community." *Ethnology* 14(3):301–310.

JOHNSON, ALLEN. 1983. "Machiguenga Gardens." In *Adaptive Responses of Native Amazonians*, edited by Raymond Hames and William Vickers, pp. 29–63. New York: Academic Press.

JOHNSON, ALLEN. 1985. "In Search of the Affluent Society." In *Anthropology: Contemporary Perspectives*, edited by David Hunter and Phillip Whitten, pp. 201–206. Boston: Little, Brown. (Reprinted from *Human Nature*, September 1978.)

JOHNSON, ALLEN, AND CLIFFORD A. BEHRENS. 1982. "Nutritional Criteria in Machiguenga Food Production Decisions: A Linear-Programming Analysis." *Human Ecology* 10(2): 167–189.

JOHNSON, BRYAN T., KIM R. HOLMES, AND MELANIE KIRKPATRICK (EDS.). 1998. *Index of Economic Freedom*. Washington, D.C., and New York: The Heritage Foundation and Dow Jones.

JOHNSON, GREGORY ALAN. 1973. *Local Exchange and Early State Development in Southwestern Iran*. Anthropological Papers, no. 51. Ann Arbor: Museum of Anthropology, University of Michigan.

JONES, ALICE HANSON. 1977. *American Colonial Wealth: Documents and Methods*. 3 Vols. New York: Arno Press.

JONES, ALICE HANSON. 1980. *Wealth of a Nation to Be: The American Colonies on the Eve of the Revolution*. New York: Columbia University Press.

JONES, P. D., T. M. L. WIGLEY, AND P. B. WRIGHT. 1986. "Global Temperature Variations Between 1861 and 1984." *Nature* 322(6078):430–434.

JONES, RHYS, AND BETTY MEEHAN. 1978. "Anbarra Concept of Colour." In *Australian Aboriginal Concepts*, edited by L. R. Hiatt, pp. 20–39. Canberra: Australian Institute of Aboriginal Studies.

JULIEN, CATHERINE J. 1982. "Inka Decimal Administration in the Lake Titicaca Region." In *The Inca and Aztec States 1400–1800*, edited by George Collier, Renato Rosaldo, and John Wirth, pp. 119–151. New York: Academic Press.

KAHN, HERMAN, AND ANTHONY J. WIENER. 1967. *The Year 2000: A Framework for Speculation on the Next Thirty-Three Years*. New York: Macmillan.

KAMIN, LEON J. 1995. "Behind the Curve." *Scientific American* 272(2):99–103.

KAPLAN, DAVID. 1960. "The Law of Cultural Dominance." In *Evolution and Culture*, edited by Marshall Sahlins and Elman Service, pp. 69–92. Ann Arbor: University of Michigan Press.

KATZ, SOLOMON H., AND MARY M. VOIGT. 1986. "Bread and Beer: The Early Use of Cereals in the Human Diet." *Expedition* 28(2):23–34.

KAY, PAUL, AND WILLETT KEMPTON. 1984. "What Is the Sapir-Whorf Hypothesis?" *American Anthropologist* 86(1):65–79.

KEATINGE, RICHARD W. 1981. "The Nature and Role of Religious Diffusion in the Early Stages of State Formation: An Example from Peruvian Prehistory." In *The Transition to Statehood in the New World,* edited by Grant Jones and Robert Kautz, pp. 172–187. Cambridge, Eng.: Cambridge University Press.

KEATS, DAPHNE M., AND JOHN A. KEATS. 1988. "Human Assessment in Australia." In *Human Abilities in Cultural Context,* edited by S. H. Irvine and J. W. Berry, pp. 283–298. Cambridge, Eng.: Cambridge University Press.

KEENLEYSIDE, H. L. 1950. "Critical Mineral Shortages." In *Proceedings of the United Nations Scientific Conference on the Conservation and Utilization of Resources,* pp. 38–46, August–September 1949, Lake Success, N.Y.: United Nations.

KEIGHTLEY, DAVID N. 1990. "Early Civilization in China: Reflections on How It Became Chinese." In *Heritage of China: Contemporary Perspectives on Chinese Civilization,* edited by Paul Ropp, pp. 15–54. Berkeley: University of California Press.

KELLOGG, WILLIAM W. 1989. "Carbon Dioxide and Climate Changes: Implications for Mankind's Future." In *Global Climate Change: Human and Natural Influences,* edited by S. Fred Singer, pp. 37–65. New York: Paragon House.

KELLY, RAYMOND C. 1985. *The Nuer Conquest: The Structure and Development of an Expansionist System.* Ann Arbor: University of Michigan Press.

KENCHINGTON, RICHARD. 1985. "Coral-Reef Ecosystems: A Sustainable Resource." *Nature & Resources* 21(2):18–27.

KENNEDY, KENNETH A. R. 1982. "Skulls, Aryans and Flowing Drains: The Interface of Archaeology and Skeletal Biology in the Study of the Harappan Civilization." In *Harappan Civilization: A Contemporary Perspective,* edited by Gregory Possehl, pp. 289–295. New Delhi: Oxford and IBH.

KEYFITZ, NATHAN. 1989. "The Growing Human Population." *Scientific American* 261(3):119–126.

KING, F. H. 1911. *Farmers of Forty Centuries or Permanent Agriculture in China, Korea and Japan.* Madison, Wis.: Mrs. F. H. King.

KIRCH, PATRICK VINTON. 1985. *Feathered Gods and Fishhooks: An Introduction to Hawaiian Archaeology and Prehistory.* Honolulu: University of Hawaii Press.

KIRCH, PATRICK VINTON, AND DOUGLAS E. YEN. 1982. *Tikopia: The Prehistory and Ecology of a Polynesian Outlier.* Bernice P. Bishop Museum, bull. 238. Honolulu: Bishop Museum Press.

KLICH, L. Z. 1988. "Aboriginal Cognition and Psychological Nescience." In *Human Abilities in Cultural Context,* edited by S. H. Irvine and J. W. Berry, pp. 427–452. Cambridge, Eng.: Cambridge University Press.

KNUDSON, KENNETH E. 1970. "Resource Fluctuation, Productivity, and Social Organization on Micronesian Coral Islands." Ph.D. dissertation, University of Oregon.

KOHR, LEOPOLD. 1978. *The Breakdown of Nations.* New York: Dutton.

KONDRATIEFF, NIKOLAIR. 1984. *The Long Wave Cycle.* New York: Richardson & Snyder.

KORTEN, DAVID C. 1996. *When Corporations Rule the World.* West Hartford, Conn.: Kumarian Press; and San Francisco: Berrett-Koehler.

KOSSE, KRISZTINA. 1990. "Group Size and Societal Complexity: Thresholds in the Long-Term Memory." *Journal of Anthropological Archaeology* 9(3):275–303.

KRAMER, SAMUEL NOAH. 1963. *The Sumerians: Their History, Culture, and Character.* Chicago: University of Chicago Press.

KRANTZ, GROVER S. 1978. *Interproximal Attrition and Modern Dental Crowding.* Occasional Papers in Method and Theory in California Archaeology, no. 2, pp. 35–41. Society for California Archaeology.

KRANTZ, GROVER S. 1980. *Climatic Races and Descent Groups.* North Quincy, Mass.: Christopher.

KROEBER, A. L. 1948. *Anthropology.* New York: Harcourt, Brace & World.

KUPER, ADAM. 1982. "Lineage Theory: A Critical Retrospect." *Annual Review of Anthropology* 11:71–95.

LA LONE, DARRELL E. 1982. "The Inca as a Nonmarket Economy: Supply on Command Versus Supply and Demand." In *Contexts for Prehistoric Exchange,* edited by Jonathon Ericson and Timothy K. Earle, pp. 291–316. New York: Academic Press.

LAMBRICK, H. T. 1967. "The Indus Flood-Plain and the 'Indus' Civilization." *Geographical Journal* 133(4):483–495.

LANDSBERG, HANS H. 1964. *Natural Resources in America's Future: Patterns of Requirements and Availabilities 1960–2000.* Baltimore: Johns Hopkins University Press.

LANDSBERG, HELMUT E. 1989. "Where Do We Stand with the CO_2 Greenhouse Effect Problem?" In *Global Climate Change: Human and Natural Influences,* edited by S. Fred Singer, pp. 87–89. New York: Paragon House.

LANE-FOX PITT-RIVERS, A. H. 1882. "Anniversary Address to the Anthropological Institute of Great Britain and Ireland." *Journal of the Royal Anthropological Institute* 11(4):488–509.

LANNING, EDWARD P. 1967. *Peru Before the Incas.* Englewood Cliffs, N.J.: Prentice-Hall.

LAPPE, FRANCES MOORE, JOSEPH COLLINS, AND CARRY FOWLER. 1979. *Food First: Beyond the Myth of Scarcity.* New York: Ballantine Books.

LAPPE, FRANCES MOORE, JOSEPH COLLINS, AND DAVID KINLEY. 1981. *Aid as Obstacle: Twenty Questions About Our Foreign Aid and the Hungry.* San Francisco: Institute for Food and Development Policy.

LAPPE, FRANCES MOORE, RACHEL SCHURMAN, AND KEVIN DANAHER. 1987. *Betraying the National Interest.* New York: Grove Press.

LARICK, ROY. 1986. "Age Grading and Ethnicity in the Style of Loikop (Samburu) Spears." *World Archaeology* 18(2):269–283.

LARRICK, JAMES W., JAMES A. YOST, JON KAPLAN, GARLAND KING, AND JOHN MAYHALL. 1979. "Patterns of Health and Disease Among the Waorani Indians of Eastern Ecuador." *Medical Anthropology* 3(2):147–189.

LASCH, CHRISTOPHER. 1995. *The Revolt of the Elites and the Betrayal of Democracy.* New York: Norton.

LATHRAP, DONALD W. 1970. *The Upper Amazon.* New York: Praeger.

LATHRAP, DONALD W. 1977. "Our Father the Cayman, Our Mother the Gourd: Spinden Revisited, or a Unitary Model for the Emergence of Agriculture in the New World." In *Origins of Agriculture,* edited by C. A. Reed, pp. 713–751. The Hague: Mouton.

LEE, RICHARD B. 1981. "Is There a Foraging Mode of Production?" *Canadian Journal of Anthropology* 2(1):13–19.

LEE, RICHARD, AND IRVEN DEVORE (EDS.). 1968. "Problems in the Study of Hunters and Gatherers." In *Man the Hunter,* pp. 3–12. Chicago: Aldine.

LEFROY, ARCHDEACON. 1912. *The Future of Australian Aborigines.* Report of the Thirteenth Meeting of the Australasian Association for the Advancement of Science, Sydney, pp. 453–454.

LEGGE, JAMES. 1967. *Li Chi: Book of Rites,* 2 vols. New Hyde Park, N.Y.: University Books.

LEVISON, M., R. G. WARD, AND J. W. WEBB. 1973. *The Settlement of Polynesia: A Computer Simulation.* Minneapolis: University of Minnesota Press.

LÉVI-STRAUSS, CLAUDE. 1944. "The Social and Psychological Aspects of Chieftainship in a Primitive Tribe: The Nambikuara of Northwestern Matto Grosso." *Transactions of the New York Academy of Sciences* 7:16–32.

LÉVI-STRAUSS, CLAUDE. [1949] 1969. *The Elementary Structures of Kinship.* Boston: Beacon Press.

LÉVI-STRAUSS, CLAUDE. 1963. *Totemism.* Boston: Beacon Press.

LÉVI-STRAUSS, CLAUDE. 1966. *The Savage Mind.* Chicago: University of Chicago Press.

LÉVI-STRAUSS, CLAUDE. 1969. *The Raw and the Cooked: Introduction to a Science of Mythology 1.* New York: Harper & Row.

LÉVI-STRAUSS, CLAUDE. 1973. *From Honey to Ashes: Introduction to a Science of Mythology 2.* New York: Harper & Row.

LÉVI-STRAUSS, CLAUDE. 1978. *The Origin of Table Manners: Introduction to a Science of Mythology 3.* New York: Harper & Row.

LEVY, REUBEN. 1962. *The Social Structure of Islam.* London: Cambridge University Press.

LÉVY-BRUHL, LUCIEN. [1922] 1923. *Primitive Mentality.* New York: Macmillan.

LÉVY-BRUHL, LUCIEN. 1926. *How Natives Think [Les Fonctions Mentales dans les Sociétés Inférieures].* New York: Knopf.

LEWIS, BERNARD. 1960. *The Arabs in History.* New York: Harper Torchbooks.

LEWIS, D. 1976. "Observations on Route-Finding and Spatial Orientation Among the Aboriginal Peoples of the Western Desert Region of Central Australia." *Oceania* 46(4):249–282.

LEWIS, OSCAR. 1959. *Five Families: Mexican Case Studies in the Culture of Poverty.* New York: Basic Books.

LEWIS, OSCAR. 1966a. "The Culture of Poverty." *Scientific American* 215(4):19–25.

LEWIS, OSCAR. 1966b. *La Vida: A Puerto Rican Family in the Culture of Poverty—San Juan and New York.* New York: Random House.

LINDENBAUM, SHIRLEY. 1987. "Loaves and Fishes in Bangladesh." In *Food and Evolution: Toward a Theory of Human Food Habits,* edited by Marvin Harris and Eric Ross, pp. 427–443. Philadelphia: Temple University Press.

LITTLE, MICHAEL A., AND GEORGE E. B. MORREN, JR. 1976. *Ecology, Energetics, and Human Variability.* Dubuque, Iowa: Brown.

LIZOT, JACQUES. 1977. "Population, Resources and Warfare Among the Yanomami." *Man* 12(3/4):497–517.

LIZOT, JACQUES. 1985. *Tales of the Yanomami: Daily Life in the Venezuelan Forest.* Cambridge, Eng.: Cambridge University Press.

LOBEL, PHIL S. 1978. "Gilbertese and Ellice Islander Names for Fishes and Other Organisms." *Micronesica* 14(2):177–197.

LOUNSBURY, FLOYD G. 1964. "A Formal Account of the Crow- and Omaha-Type Kinship Terminologies." In *Explorations in Cultural Anthropology,* edited by Ward Goodenough, pp. 351–393. New York: McGraw-Hill.

LOURANDOS, HARRY. 1985. "Intensification and Australian Prehistory." In *Prehistoric Hunter-Gatherers: The Emergence of Cultural Complexity,* edited by Douglas Price and James A. Brown, pp. 385–423. New York: Academic Press.

LOURANDOS, HARRY. 1987. "Pleistocene Australia: Peopling a Continent." In *The Pleistocene Old World: Regional Perspectives,* edited by Olga Soffer, pp. 147–165. New York: Plenum.

LOZOFF, BETSY, AND GARY M. BRITTENHAM. 1977. "Field Methods for the Assessment of Health and Disease in Pre-Agricultural Societies." In *Health and Disease in Tribal Societies,* pp. 49–67. CIBA Foundation Symposium, no. 49. Amsterdam: Elsevier/Excerpta Medica/North-Holland.

LUTEN, DANIEL B. 1974. "United States Requirements." In *Energy, the Environment, and Human Health,* edited by A. Finkel, pp. 17–33. Acton, Mass.: Publishing Sciences Group.

LYONS, WILLIAM H. 1995. "Sleepy in Sarnath: Forager Time Storage and Food Resources of Semiarid Regions." Paper presented at the 49th Annual Northwest Anthropological Conference, Moscow, Idaho.

MAISELS, CHARLES KEITH. 1990. *The Emergence of Civilization: From Hunting and Gathering to Agriculture, Cities, and the State in the Near East.* London and New York: Routledge.

MALINOWSKI, BRONISLAW. 1929. "Practical Anthropology." *Africa* 2(1):22–38.

MALINOWSKI, BRONISLAW. 1944. *A Scientific Theory of Culture.* Chapel Hill: University of North Carolina Press.

MALO, DAVID. 1951. *Hawaiian Antiquities,* 2nd ed. Bernice P. Bishop Museum Special Publication, no. 2. Honolulu: Bernice P. Bishop Museum.

MALTHUS, THOMAS R. [1798, 1807] 1895. *An Essay on the Principle of Population.* New York: Macmillan.

MANDER, JERRY. 1996. "The Rules of Corporate Behavior." In *The Case Against the Global Economy and for a Turn Toward the Local,* edited by Jerry Mander and Edward Goldsmith, pp. 309–322. San Francisco: Sierra Club Books.

MANN, MICHAEL. 1986. *The Sources of Social Power,* Vol. 1, *A History of Power from the Beginning to AD 1760.* Cambridge, Eng.: Cambridge University Press.

MANNERS, ROBERT A. 1956. "Functionalism, Realpolitik, and

Anthropology in Under-Developed Areas." *America Indigena* 16(1):7–33.

MANNHEIM, BRUCE. 1991. *The Language of the Inka Since the European Invasion.* Austin: University of Texas Press.

MARKS, JONATHAN. 1995. "Egalitarianism and Human Biodiversity." *Anthropology Newsletter* 36(9):20.

MARSH, GEORGE PERKINS. 1864. *Man and Nature: Physical Geography as Modified by Human Action.* New York: Scribner.

MARTIN, P. S. 1967. "Prehistoric Overkill." In *Pleistocene Extinctions,* edited by P. S. Martin and H. E. Wright, Jr., pp. 75–120. New Haven, Conn.: Yale University Press.

MARX, KARL, AND FRIEDRICH ENGELS. 1967. *The Communist Manifesto.* London: Penguin Books.

MAYER, ADRIAN C. 1970. *Caste and Kinship in Central India: A Village and Its Region.* Berkeley and Los Angeles: University of California Press.

MAYHEW, BRUCE H., AND PAUL T. SCHOLLAERT. 1980a. "Social Morphology of Pareto's Economic Elite." *Social Forces* 59(1): 25–43.

MAYHEW, BRUCE H., AND PAUL T. SCHOLLAERT. 1980b. "The Concentration of Wealth: A Sociological Model." *Sociological Focus* 13(1):1–35.

MAYHEW, HENRY. 1861–62. *London Labour and the London Poor,* 4 vols. London: Griffin, Bohn. (Reprinted 1968. New York: Dover.)

MCARTHUR, MARGARET. 1960. "Food Consumption and Dietary Levels of Groups of Aborigines Living on Naturally Occurring Foods." In *Records of the American-Australian Scientific Expedition to Arnhem Land.* Vol. 2 of *Anthropology and Nutrition,* edited by Charles Mountford, pp. 90–135. Melbourne: Melbourne University Press.

MCCARTHY, F. D., AND MARGARET MCARTHUR. 1960. "The Food Quest and Time Factor in Aboriginal Economic Life." In *Records of the American-Australian Scientific Expedition to Arnhem Land.* Vol. 2 of *Anthropology and Nutrition,* edited by Charles Mountford, pp. 145–194. Melbourne: Melbourne University Press.

MCCAY, BONNIE J., AND JAMES M. ACHESON (EDS.). 1987. *The Question of the Commons: The Culture and Ecology of Communal Resources.* Tucson: University of Arizona Press.

MCCLOSKEY, DONALD N. 1976. "English Open Fields as Behavior Towards Risk." *Research in Economic History* 1: 124–170.

MCCOY, JOHN. 1970. "Chinese Kin Terms of Reference and Address." In *Family and Kinship in Chinese Society,* edited by Maurice Freedman, pp. 209–226. Stanford, Calif.: Stanford University Press.

MCDONALD, DAVID. 1977. "Food Taboos: A Primitive Environmental Protection Agency (South America)." *Anthropos* 72: 734–748.

MCDONALD, FORREST. 1958. *We the People: The Economic Origins of the Constitution.* Chicago: University of Chicago Press.

MCDONALD, FORREST. 1979. *E. Pluribus Unum: The Formation of the American Republic,* 2nd ed. Indianapolis, Ind.: Liberty Press.

MCDONALD, FORREST. 1985. *Novus Ordo Seclorum: The Intellectual Origins of the Constitution.* Lawrence: University Press of Kansas.

MCGREW, W. C. 1992. *Chimpanzee Material Culture.* Cambridge, Eng.: Cambridge University Press.

MCNEIL, WILLIAM H. 1987. *A History of the Human Community: Prehistory to the Present.* Englewood Cliffs, N.J.: Prentice-Hall.

MEAD, MARGARET. 1942. *And Keep Your Powder Dry: An Anthropologist Looks at America.* New York: Morrow.

MEAD, MARGARET. 1961. *New Lives for Old.* New York: New American Library.

MEADOWS, DONELLA H., DENNIS L. MEADOWS, AND JORGEN RANDERS. 1992. *Beyond the Limits: Confronting Global Collapse, Envisioning a Sustainable Future.* Post Mills, Vt.: Chelsea Green.

MEADOWS, DONELLA H., DENNIS L. MEADOWS, JORGEN RANDERS, AND WILLIAM W. BEHRENS III. 1972. *The Limits to Growth.* New York: Universe.

MEEHAN, BETTY. 1982. "Ten Fish for One Man: Some Anbarra Attitudes Towards Food and Health." In *Body, Land and Spirit: Health and Healing in Aboriginal Society,* edited by Janice Reid, pp. 96–120. St. Lucia: University of Queensland Press.

MEGGERS, BETTY J. 1954. "Environmental Limitation on the Development of Culture." *American Anthropologist* 56(5, pt. 1):801–824.

MEGGERS, BETTY J. 1971. *Amazonia: Man and Culture in a Counterfeit Paradise.* Arlington Heights, Ill.: AHM.

MEILLASSOUX, CLAUDE. 1981. *Maidens, Meal and Money: Capitalism and the Domestic Community.* Cambridge, Eng.: Cambridge University Press.

MELLAART, J. 1967. *Çatal Hüyük: A Neolithic Town in Anatolia.* London: Thames & Hudson.

MERRILEES, D. 1968. "Man the Destroyer: Late Quaternary Changes in the Australian Marsupial Fauna." *Journal of the Royal Society of Western Australia* 51:1–24.

MESAROVIC, MIHAJLO, AND EDUARD PESTEL. 1974. *Mankind at the Turning Point: The Second Report of the Club of Rome.* New York: New American Library.

MICHAEL, FRANZ. 1964. "State and Society in Nineteenth-Century China." In *Modern China,* edited by Albert Feuerwerker, pp. 57–69. Englewood Cliffs, N.J.: Prentice-Hall.

MIGLIAZZA, ERNEST C. 1982. "Linguistic Prehistory and the Refuge Model in Amazonia." In *Biological Diversification in the Tropics,* edited by Ghillean Prance, pp. 497–519. New York: Columbia University Press.

MILLER, DANIEL. 1985. "Ideology and the Harappan Civilization." *Journal of Anthropological Archaeology* 4:34–71.

MILLER, EDWARD, AND JOHN HATCHER. 1995. *Medieval England: Towns, Commerce and Crafts 1086–1348.* London and New York: Longman.

MILLER, SOLOMON. 1967. "Hacienda to Plantation in Northern Peru: The Processes of Proletarianization of a Tenant Farmer Society." In *Contemporary Change in Traditional Societies.* Vol. 3, *Mexican and Peruvian Communities,* edited by Julian Steward, pp. 133–225. Urbana: University of Illinois Press.

MILLS, C. WRIGHT. 1956. *The Power Elite.* New York: Oxford University Press.

MINER, HORACE M. 1955. "Planning for the Acculturation of Isolated Tribes." *Proceedings of the 31st International Congress of Americanists* 1:441–446.

MINTZ, SIDNEY W. 1985. *Sweetness and Power: The Place of Sugar in Modern History*. New York: Viking Press/Penguin Books.

MINTZ, SIDNEY W., AND ERIC R. WOLF. 1957. "Haciendas and Plantations in Middle America and the Antilles." *Social and Economic Studies* 6:380–412.

MONTAGU, ASHLEY. 1972. "Sociogenic Brain Damage." *American Anthropologist* 74(5):1045–1061.

MOORE, ANDREW M. T. 1983. "The First Farmers in the Levant." In *The Hilly Flanks and Beyond: Essays on the Prehistory of Southwestern Asia*, pp. 91–111. Studies in Ancient Oriental Civilization, no. 36. Chicago: Oriental Institute, University of Chicago.

MORGAN, DAN. 1979. *Merchants of Grain*. New York: Viking Press.

MORGAN, LEWIS HENRY. 1851. *League of the Ho-de-no-sau-nee, or Iroquois*. Rochester, N.Y.: Sage.

MORGAN, LEWIS HENRY. 1877. *Ancient Society*. New York: Holt.

MORRIS, CRAIG, AND DONALD E. THOMPSON. 1985. *Huanaco Pampa: An Inca City and Its Hinterland*. London: Thames & Hudson.

MORRISON, ROY. 1991. *We Build the Road as We Travel*. Philadelphia: New Society Publishers.

MOSELEY, MICHAEL EDWARD. 1975. *The Maritime Foundations of Andean Civilization*. Menlo Park, Calif.: Cummings.

MOSELEY, MICHAEL E., AND K. C. DAY (EDS.). 1980. *Chan Chan: The Desert City and Its Hinterland*. Albuquerque: University of New Mexico Press.

MOSELEY, MICHAEL E., AND CAROL J. MACKEY. 1973. "Chan Chan, Peru's Ancient City of Kings." *National Geographic* 143(3):318–345.

MOUNTFORD, CHARLES P. 1965. *Ayers Rock: Its People, Their Beliefs, and Their Art*. Honolulu: East-West Center Press.

MUNN, NANCY D. 1969. "The Effectiveness of Symbols in Murngin Rite and Ritual." In *Forms of Symbolic Action: Proceedings of the 1969 Annual Spring Meeting of the American Ethnological Society*, edited by Robert Spencer, pp. 178–207. Seattle and London: American Ethnological Society.

MUNN, NANCY D. 1973. *Walbiri Iconography: Graphic Representation and Cultural Symbolism in a Central Australian Society*. Ithaca, N.Y., and London: Cornell University Press.

MURAL, MARY, FLORENCE PEN, AND CAREY D. MILLER. 1958. *Some Tropical South Pacific Island Foods: Description, History, Use, Composition, and Nutritive Value*. Hawaii Agricultural Experiment Station, bull. 110. Honolulu: University of Hawaii Press.

MURDOCK, GEORGE P. 1949. *Social Structure*. New York: Macmillan.

MURDOCK, GEORGE P. 1981. *Atlas of World Cultures*. Pittsburgh: University of Pittsburgh Press.

MURPHY, ROBERT F. 1957. "Intergroup Hostility and Social Cohesion." *American Anthropologist* 58:414–434.

MURPHY, ROBERT F. 1960. *Headhunter's Heritage*. Berkeley: University of California Press.

MURPHY, YOLANDA, AND ROBERT F. MURPHY. 1974. *Women of the Forest*. New York and London: Columbia University Press.

MURRA, JOHN V. 1960. "Rite and Crop in the Inca State." In *Culture in History: Essays in Honor of Paul Radin*, edited by Stanley Diamond, pp. 393–407. New York: Columbia University Press.

MURRA, J. V. 1972. "'El Control Vertical' de un Maximo de Pisos Ecologicos en la Economia de las Sociedades Andinas." In *Vista de la Provincia de Leon de Huanuco (1562)*, Vol. 2, edited by Inigo Ortiz de Zuniga, pp. 429–476. Huanuco, Peru: Universidad Hermillo Valdizan.

MYERS, FRED R. 1980. "The Cultural Basis of Politics in Pintupi Life." *Mankind* 12(3):197–214.

NAROLL, RAOUL. 1962. "Floor Area and Settlement Population." *American Antiquity* 27(4):587–589.

NASH, JUNE. 1989. *From Tank Town to High Tech: The Clash of Community and Industrial Cycles*. Albany: State University of New York Press.

NASH, JUNE. 1994. "Global Integration and Subsistence Insecurity." *American Anthropologist* 96(1):7–30.

NATIONAL CENTER FOR HEALTH STATISTICS. 1998. *Health, United States, 1998*. Washington, D.C.: U.S. Government Printing Office.

NATIONAL PROVISIONER. 1990a. *National Provisioner* 202(2)

NATIONAL PROVISIONER. 1990b. *National Provisioner* 202(9).

NATIONAL RESEARCH COUNCIL, COMMITTEE ON MINERAL RESOURCES AND THE ENVIRONMENT. 1975. *Mineral Resources and the Environment*. Washington, D.C.: National Academy of Sciences.

NEEL, JAMES V. 1970. "Lessons from a 'Primitive' People." *Science* 170(3960):815–822.

NEWCOMER, PETER J. 1972. "The Nuer Are Dinka: An Essay on Origins and Environmental Determinism." *Man* 7(1):5–11.

NEWMAN, KATHERINE S. 1988. *Falling from Grace: The Experience of Downward Mobility in the American Middle Class*. New York: Free Press.

NEWMAN, KATHERINE S. 1993. *Declining Fortunes: The Withering of the American Dream*. New York: Basic Books.

NIETSCHMANN, BERNARD. 1988. "Third World Colonial Expansion: Indonesia, Disguised Invasion of Indigenous Nations." In *Tribal Peoples and Development Issues: A Global Overview*, edited by John H. Bodley, pp. 191–207. Mountain View, Calif.: Mayfield.

NISSEN, HANS J. 1986. "The Archaic Texts from Uruk." *World Archaeology* 17(3):317–334.

NOBLE, DAVID F. 1993. *Progress Without People: In Defense of Luddism*. Chicago: Keer.

NOLL, RICHARD. 1984. "The Context of Schizophrenia and Shamanism." *American Ethnologist* 11(1):191–192.

OCHOLLA-AYAYO, A. B. C. 1979. "Marriage and Cattle Exchange Among the Nilotic Luo." *Paideuma* 25:173–193.

O'CONNELL, JAMES F., AND KRISTEN HAWKES. 1981. "Alyawara Plant Use and Optimal Foraging Theory." In *Hunter-Gatherer Foraging Strategies*, edited by B. Winterhalder and E. A. Smith, pp. 99–125. Chicago: University of Chicago Press.

ODUM, HOWARD T. 1971. *Environment, Power, and Society*. New York: Wiley Inter-Science.

OLIVER, DOUGLAS L. 1989. *Oceania: The Native Cultures of Australia and the Pacific Islands*, 2 vols. Honolulu: University of Hawaii Press.

ONERN (OFICINA NACIONAL DE EVALUACIÓN DE RECURSOS NA-
TURALES). 1968. *Inventario, Evaluación e Integración de los
Recursos Naturales de la Zona del Rio Tambo-Gran Pajonal.*
Lima: ONERN.

ORLOVE, BENJAMIN S. 1987. "Stability and Change in Highland Andean Dietary Patterns." In *Food and Evolution: Toward a Theory of Human Food Habits,* edited by Marvin
Harris and Eric Ross, pp. 481–515. Philadelphia: Temple
University Press.

ORWIN, C. S., AND C. S. ORWIN. 1967. *The Open Fields.* Oxford,
Eng.: Clarendon Press.

PALMER, INGRID. 1972. *Science and Agricultural Production.*
Geneva: UN Research Institute for Social Development.

PAPANEK, HANNA. 1982. "Purdah: Separate Worlds and Symbolic Shelter." In *Separate Worlds: Studies of Purdah in
South Asia,* edited by Hanna Papanek and Gail Minault, pp.
3–53. Delhi: Chanakya.

PARKINSON, C. NORTHCOTE. 1957. *Parkinson's Law and Other
Studies in Administration.* Boston: Houghton Mifflin.

PARRY, JONATHAN P. 1979. *Caste and Kinship in Kangra.* London: Routledge & Kegan Paul.

PERKINS, DWIGHT H. 1969. *Agricultural Development in China
1368–1968.* Chicago: Aldine.

PERRY, W. J. 1923. *The Children of the Sun.* London: Methuen.

PESSEN, EDWARD. 1971. "The Egalitarian Myth and the American Social Reality: Wealth, Mobility, and Equality in the
'Era of the Common Man.'" *The American Historical Review*
76(4):989–1034.

PESSEN, EDWARD. 1973. *Riches, Class, and Power Before the
Civil War.* Lexington, Mass.: Heath.

PETERS, LARRY G., AND DOUGLASS PRICE-WILLIAMS. 1980. "Towards an Experiential Analysis of Shamanism." *American
Ethnologist* 7(3):397–418.

PETERSON, NICOLAS. 1986. *Australian Territorial Organization.* Oceania Monograph, no. 30. Sydney: University of
Sydney.

PHILLIPS, KEVIN. 1994. *Arrogant Capital: Washington, Wall
Street, and the Frustration of American Politics.* Boston: Little, Brown.

PHILLIPSON, DAVID W. 1985. *African Archaeology.* Cambridge,
Eng.: Cambridge University Press.

PIETRASZEK, GREG. 1990. "Cattlemen Face Future Competition with Confidence." *National Provisioner* 202(12):
5–8.

PIKE, KENNETH L. 1954. *Language in Relation to a Unified Theory of the Structure of Human Behavior,* vol. 1. The Hague:
Mouton.

POLANYI, KARL. 1977. *The Livelihood of Man.* New York: Academic Press.

PORTEUS, S. D. 1917. "Mental Tests with Delinquents and Australian Aboriginal Children." *Psychological Review* 24(1):
32–42. (Reprinted in *The Psychology of Aboriginal Australians,* edited by G. E. Kearney, P. R. de Lacey, and G. R.
Davidson, pp. 29–37. Sydney: Wiley, 1973.)

PORTEUS, S. D. 1931. *The Psychology of a Primitive People.*
London: E. Arnold.

POSPISIL, LEOPOLD. 1972. *The Ethnology of Law.* Addison-
Wesley Module in Anthropology, no. 12. Reading, Mass.:
Addison-Wesley.

POSSEHL, GREGORY L. 1967. "The Mohenjo-Daro Floods: A
Reply." *American Anthropologist* 69(1):32–40.

POSSEHL, GREGORY L. 1977. "The End of a State and Conti-
nuity of a Tradition: A Discussion of the Late Harappa." In
Realm and Region in Traditional India, edited by Richard
Fox, pp. 234–254. Program in Comparative Studies on
Southern Asia, Duke University. Monograph and Occa-
sional Papers Series, Monograph no. 14. Durham, N.C.

PRICE, A. G. 1950. *White Settlers and Native Peoples.* London:
Cambridge University Press.

PRICE, WESTON ANDREW. 1945. *Nutrition and Physical Degen-
eration: A Comparison of Primitive and Modern Diets and
Their Effects.* Redlands, Calif.: Weston Price.

PYLE, TOM. 1964. *Pocantico: Fifty Years on the Rockefeller Domain.* New York: Duell, Sloan & Pearce.

QUILTER, JEFFREY, AND TERRY STOCKER. 1983. "Subsistence
Economies and the Origins of Andean Complex Societies."
American Anthropologist 85(3):545–562.

RADCLIFFE-BROWN, A. R. 1913. "Three Tribes of Western Australia." *Journal of the Royal Anthropological Institute* 43:
143–195.

RADCLIFFE-BROWN, A. R. 1918. "Notes on the Social Organization of Australian Tribes." *Journal of the Royal Anthropological Institute* 48:222–253.

RADCLIFFE-BROWN, A. R. 1929. "The Sociological Theory of
Totemism." Proceedings of the Fourth Pacific Science Congress. (Reprinted in *Structure and Function in Primitive Society,* edited by A. R. Radcliffe-Brown, pp. 117–132. New
York: Free Press, 1965.)

RADCLIFFE-BROWN, A. R. 1941. "The Study of Kinship Systems." *Journal of the Royal Anthropological Institute.* (Reprinted in *Structure and Function in Primitive Society,* edited
by A. R. Radcliffe-Brown, pp. 49–89. New York: Free Press,
1965.)

RADCLIFFE-BROWN, A. R. 1958. Presidential Address to Section E. South African Association for the Advancement of
Science, July 1928. (In *Method in Social Anthropology: Selected Essays by A. R. Radcliffe-Brown,* edited by M. N. Srinivas. Chicago: University of Chicago Press.)

RADIN, PAUL. 1971. *The World of Primitive Man.* New York:
Dutton.

RAIKES, ROBERT L. 1964. "The End of the Ancient Cities of the
Indus." *American Anthropologist* 66(2):284–299.

RAIKES, ROBERT L. 1965. "The Mohenjo-Daro Floods." *Antiquity* 38(155):196–203.

RAMOS, ALCIDA R. 1987. "Reflecting on the Yanomami: Eth-
nograpic Images and the Pursuit of the Exotic." *Cultural
Anthropology* 2(3):284–304.

RANDALL, ROBERT A., AND EUGENE S. HUNN. 1984. "Do Life-
Forms Evolve or Do Uses for Life? Some Doubts About
Brown's Universals Hypotheses." *American Ethnologist* 1(2):
329–349.

RAO, S. R. 1982. "New Light on the Post-Urban (Late Harap-
pan) Phase of the Indus Civilization in India." In *Harappan
Civilization: A Contemporary Perspective,* edited by Gregory
Possehl, pp. 353–359. New Delhi: Oxford and IBH.

RAPPAPORT, ROY A. 1977a. "Maladaptation in Social Systems."
In *The Evolution of Social Systems,* edited by J. Friedman
and M. J. Rowlands, pp. 49–71. London: Duckworth.

RAPPAPORT, ROY A. 1977b. "Normative Models of Adaptive Processes: A Response to Anne Whyte." In *The Evolution of Social Systems,* edited by J. Friedman and M. J. Rowlands, pp. 79–87. London: Duckworth.

RAWSKI, EVELYN S. 1987. "Popular Culture in China." In *Tradition and Creativity: Essays on East Asian Civilization,* edited by Ching-I Tu, pp. 41–65. New Brunswick, N.J., and Oxford, Eng.: Transaction Books.

READ, C. H. 1901. "Presidential Address." *Journal of the Royal Anthropological Institute* 31:14–15.

REDFIELD, ROBERT. 1941. *The Folk Culture of Yucatan.* Chicago: University of Chicago Press.

REDFIELD, ROBERT. 1947. "The Folk Society." *American Journal of Sociology* 52(4):295–298.

REDFIELD, ROBERT, RALPH LINTON, AND MELVILLE J. HERSKOVITS. 1936. "Memorandum for the Study of Acculturation." *American Anthropologist* 38(1):149–152.

REDMAN, CHARLES L. 1978a. "Mesopotamian Urban Ecology: The Systemic Context of the Emergence of Urbanism." In *Social Archaeology: Beyond Subsistence and Dating,* edited by Charles Redman, Mary Jane Berman, Edward Curtin, William Langhorne, Jr., Nina Versaggi, and Jeffery Wanser, pp. 329–347. New York: Academic Press.

REDMAN, CHARLES L. 1978b. *The Rise of Civilization: From Early Farmers to Urban Society in the Ancient Near East.* San Francisco: Freeman.

REEVES, ROSSER. 1961. *Reality in Advertising.* New York: Knopf.

REICH, ROBERT B. 1992. *The Work of Nations.* New York: Vintage Books/Random House.

REICHEL-DOLMATOFF, GERARDO. 1971. *Amazonian Cosmos: The Sexual and Religious Symbolism of the Tukano Indians.* Chicago: University of Chicago Press.

REICHEL-DOLMATOFF, GERARDO. 1976. "Cosmology as Ecological Analysis: A View from the Rain Forest." *Man* 11(3):307–318.

RENFREW, COLIN. 1989. "The Origins of Indo-European Languages." *Scientific American* 261(4):106–114.

RESER, JOSEPH. 1981. "Australian Aboriginal Man's Inhumanity to Man: A Case of Cultural Distortion." *American Anthropologist* 83(2):387–393.

RIBEIRO, DARCY. 1957. *Culturas e Linguas Indigenas do Brasil.* Separata de Educação e Ciencias Soçais, no. 6. Rio de Janeiro: Centro Brasileiro de Pesquisas Educaçionais.

RICHARDS, PAUL W. 1973. "The Tropical Rain Forest." *Scientific American* 229(6):58–67.

RIIS, JACOB A. 1904. *How the Other Half Lives: Studies Among the Tenements of New York.* New York: Scribner.

RIVIERE, PETER. 1969. *Marriage Among the Trio: A Principle of Social Organization.* Oxford, Eng.: Clarendon Press.

ROBERTS, RICHARD G., RHYS JONES, AND M. A. SMITH. 1990. "Thermoluminescence Dating of a 50,000-Year-Old Human Occupation Site in Northern Australia." *Nature* 345:153–156.

ROCHESTER, ANN. 1936. *Rulers of America: A Study of Finance Capital.* New York: International.

RODSETH, LARS, RICHARD W. WRANGHAM, ALISA M. HARRIGAN, BARBARA B. SMUTS. 1991. "The Human Community as a Primate Society." *Current Anthropology* 32(3):221–254.

ROE, PETER G. 1982. *The Cosmic Zygote: Cosmology in the Amazon Basin.* New Brunswick, N.J.: Rutgers University Press.

ROGERS, ALISON. 1993. "Billionaires: The World's 101 Richest People." *Fortune,* June 28, pp. 36–66.

ROSS, JANE BENNETT. 1984. "Effects of Contact on Revenge Hostilities Among the Achuara Jivaro." In *Warfare, Culture, and Environment,* edited by R. Brian Ferguson, pp. 83–109. New York: Academic Press.

ROSS, W. MCGREGOR. 1927. *Kenya from Within: A Short Political History.* London: Allen & Unwin.

ROSTOW, W. W. 1960. *The Process of Economic Growth.* New York: Norton.

ROWE, JOHN H. 1982. "Inca Policies and Institutions Relating to the Cultural Unification of the Empire." In *The Inca and Aztec States 1400–1800,* edited by George Collier, Renato Rosaldo, and John Wirth, pp. 93–118. New York: Academic Press.

ROWLAND, F. SHERWOOD. 1989. "Chlorofluorocarbons, Stratospheric Ozone, and the Antarctic 'Ozone Hole.'" In *Global Climate Change: Human and Natural Influences,* edited by S. Fred Singer, pp. 113–155. New York: Paragon House.

ROY, MANISHA. 1975. *Bengali Women.* Chicago and London: University of Chicago Press.

RUBINSTEIN, DON. 1978. "Native Place-Names and Geographic Systems of Fais, Caroline Islands." *Micronesica* 14(1):69–82.

RUHLEN, MERRITT. 1987. *A Guide to the World's Languages,* Vol. 1, *Classification.* Stanford, Calif.: Stanford University Press.

SAFINA, CARL. 1995. "The World's Imperiled Fish." *Scientific American* 273(4):46–53.

SAHLINS, MARSHALL. 1958. *Social Stratification in Polynesia.* Seattle: University of Washington Press.

SAHLINS, MARSHALL. 1961. "The Segmentary Lineage: An Organization of Predatory Expansion." *American Anthropologist* 63(2, pt. 1):322–345.

SAHLINS, MARSHALL. 1963. "Poor Man, Rich Man, Big-Man, Chief: Political Types in Melanesia and Polynesia." *Comparative Studies in Society and History* 5:285–303.

SAHLINS, MARSHALL. 1965. "On the Ideology and Composition of Descent Groups." *Man* 65 (July/August):104–107.

SAHLINS, MARSHALL. 1968. "Notes on the Original Affluent Society." In *Man the Hunter,* edited by Richard Lee and Irven DeVore, pp. 85–89. Chicago: Aldine.

SAHLINS, MARSHALL. 1972. *Stone Age Economics.* Chicago: Aldine.

SAHLINS, MARSHALL. 1976a. "Colors and Cultures." *Semiotica* 16:1–22.

SAHLINS, MARSHALL. 1976b. *Culture and Practical Reason.* Chicago and London: University of Chicago Press.

SAHLINS, MARSHALL. 1976c. *The Use and Abuse of Biology: An Anthropological Critique of Sociobiology.* Ann Arbor: University of Michigan Press.

SAHLINS, MARSHALL. 1996. "The Sadness of Sweetness: The Native Anthropology of Western Cosmology." *Current Anthropology* 37(3):395–428.

SAHLINS, MARSHALL, AND ELMAN SERVICE (EDS.). *Evolution and Culture.* Ann Arbor: University of Michigan Press.

SAMUELSON, PAUL A. 1964. *Economics: Introductory Analysis.* New York: McGraw-Hill.

SCHATTENBURG, PATRICIA. 1976. "Food and Cultivar Preservation in Micronesian Voyaging." Miscellaneous Work

Papers. *University of Hawaii Pacific Islands Program* 1: 25–51.

SCHEPER-HUGHES, NANCY. 1992. *Death Without Weeping: The Violence of Everyday Life in Brazil.* Berkeley: University of California Press.

SCHMANDT-BESSERAT, DENISE. 1982. "The Emergence of Recording." *American Anthropologist* 84(4):871–878.

SCHNEIDER, STEPHEN H. 1989. "The Changing Climate." *Scientific American* 261(3):70–79.

SCHWARTZBERG, JOSEPH E. 1977. "The Evolution of Regional Power Configurations in the Indian Subcontinent." In *Realm and Region in Traditional India,* edited by Richard Fox, pp. 197–233. Monograph and Occasional Papers Series, Monograph no. 14. Durham, N.C.: Program in Comparative Studies on Southern Asia, Duke University.

SEEBOHM, FREDERIC. 1905. *The English Village Community Examined in Its Relations to the Manorial and Tribal Systems and to the Common or Open Field System of Husbandry: An Essay in Economic History.* London: Longmans, Green.

SEN, AMARTYA. 1981. *Poverty and Famines: An Essay on Entitlement and Deprivation.* Oxford, Eng.: Clarendon Press.

SERVICE, ELMAN R. 1960. "The Law of Evolutionary Potential." In *Evolution and Culture,* edited by Marshall Sahlins and Elman Service, pp. 93–122. Ann Arbor: University of Michigan Press.

SERVICE, ELMAN. 1962. *Primitive Social Organization.* New York: Random House.

SERVICE, ELMAN R. 1975. *Origins of the State and Civilization: The Process of Cultural Evolution.* New York: Norton.

SEWELL, TOM. 1992. *The World Grain Trade.* New York: Woodhead-Faulkner.

SHALER, NATHANIEL S. 1905. *Man and the Earth.* New York: Duffield.

SHAMASASTRY, R. (TRANS.). 1960. *Kautilya's Arthasastra.* Mysore, India: Mysore.

SHAPIRO, WARREN. 1981. *Miwuyt Marriage: The Cultural Anthropology of Affinity in Northeast Arnhem Land.* Philadelphia: Institute for the Study of Human Issues.

SHWEDER, RICHARD A. 1982. "On Savages and Other Children." *American Anthropologist* 84(2):354–366.

SILVERMAN, JULIAN. 1967. "Shamans and Acute Schizophrenia." *American Anthropologist* 69(1):21–31.

SIMOONS, FREDERICK J. 1979. "Questions in the Sacred Cow Controversy." *Current Anthropology* 20(3):467–476.

SINDIGA, ISAAC. 1987. "Fertility Control and Population Growth Among the Maasai." *Human Ecology* 15(1):53–66.

SISKIND, JANET. 1973. *To Hunt in the Morning.* London: Oxford University Press.

SKINNER, G. WILLIAM. 1964. "Marketing and Social Structure in Rural China (Part 1)." *Journal of Asian Studies* 24(1):3–43.

SKLAIR, LESLIE. 1991. *Sociology of the Global System.* Baltimore: Johns Hopkins University Press.

SLURINK, POUWELL. 1994. "Causes of Our Complete Dependence on Culture." In *The Ethological Roots of Culture,* edited by R. A. Gardner et al., pp. 461–474. Dordrecht, Boston, and London: Kluwer Academic Press.

SMITH, ADAM. 1776. *An Inquiry into the Nature and Causes of the Wealth of Nations,* Vol. 1. London: Strahan & Cadell.

SMITH, ANDREW B. 1984. "Origins of the Neolithic in the Sahara." In *From Hunters to Farmers: The Causes and Conse-* quences of Food Production in Africa, edited by J. Desmond Clark and Steven Brandt, pp. 84–92. Berkeley: University of California Press.

SMITH, G. ELLIOT. 1928. *In the Beginning: The Origin of Civilization.* New York: Morrow.

SMITH, RICHARD CHASE. 1977. *The Amuesha-Yanachaga Project, Peru: Ecology and Ethnicity in the Central Jungle of Peru.* Survival International Document 3. London: Survival International.

SMITH, WILBERFORCE. 1894. "The Teeth of Ten Sioux Indians." *Journal of the Royal Anthropological Institute* 24: 109–116.

SOLTOW, LEE. 1975. *Men and Wealth in the United States 1850–1870.* New Haven, Conn.: and London: Yale University Press.

SOLTOW, LEE. 1989. *Distribution of Wealth and Income in the United States in 1798.* Pittsburgh: University of Pittsburgh Press.

SOUTHALL, AIDAN. 1976. "Nuer and Dinka Are People: Ecology, Ethnicity and Logical Possibility." *Man* 11:463–491.

SPENCER, CHARLES S. 1990. "On the Tempo and Mode of State Formation: Neoevolutionism Reconsidered." *Journal of Anthropological Archaeology* 9(1):1–30.

SPENCER, HERBERT. 1967. *The Evolution of Society: Selections from Herbert Spencer's Principles of Sociology,* edited by Robert Carneiro. Chicago: University of Chicago Press.

SPENCER, PAUL. 1965. *The Samburu: A Study of Gerontocracy in a Nomadic Tribe.* Berkeley: University of California Press.

SPENCER, PAUL. 1988. *The Maasai of Matapato: A Study of Rituals of Rebellion.* Bloomington and Indianapolis: Indiana University Press.

SPOKESMAN REVIEW. 1991. "Biggest Beef Packer Put on Auction Block." *Spokesman Review,* February 29.

SRINIVAS, M. N. 1959. "The Dominant Caste in Rampura." *American Anthropologist* 61(1):1–16.

STEIN, GIL. 1986. "Herding Strategies at Neolithic Gritille: The Use of Animal Bone Remains to Reconstruct Ancient Economic Systems." *Expedition* 28(2):35–42.

STEINHART, JOHN S., AND CAROL E. STEINHART. 1974. "Energy Use in the U.S. Food System." *Science* 184 (4134): 307–316.

STEWARD, JULIAN H. 1936. "The Economic and Social Basis of Primitive Bands." In *Essays in Anthropology in Honor of Alfred Louis Kroeber,* pp. 331–350. Berkeley: University of California Press.

STEWARD, JULIAN H. 1955. *Theory of Culture Change.* Urbana: University of Illinois Press.

STOKEN, DICK. 1993. *The Great Cycle: Predicting and Profiting from Crowd Behavior, the Kondratieff Wave, and Long-Term Cycles.* Chicago: Probus.

STONE, LINDA. 1997. *Kinship and Gender: An Introduction.* Boulder, Colo.: Westview Press.

STONE, LINDA, AND CAROLINE JAMES. 1995. "Dowry, Bride-Burning, and Female Power in India." *Women's Studies International Forum* 18(2):125–134.

STOVER, LEON N., AND TAKEKO KAWAI STOVER. 1976. *China: An Anthropological Perspective.* Pacific Palisades, Calif.: Goodyear.

SWANSON, G. E. 1960. *The Birth of the Gods.* Ann Arbor: University of Michigan Press.

SWENSON, SALLY, AND JEREMY NARBY. 1986. "The Pichis–Palcazu Special Project in Peru—a Consortium of International Lenders." *Cultural Survival Quarterly* 10(1):19–24.

TAAGEPERA, REIN. 1978a. "Size and Duration of Empires: Systematics of Size." *Social Science Research* 7:108–127.

TAAGEPERA, REIN. 1978b. "Size and Duration of Empires: Growth-Decline Curves, 3000 to 600 B.C.." *Social Science Research* 7:180–196.

TAAGEPERA, REIN. 1997. "Expansion and Contraction Patterns of Large Polities: Context for Russia." *International Studies Quarterly* 41:475–504.

TAINTER, JOSEPH A. 1988. *The Collapse of Complex Societies.* Cambridge, Eng.: Cambridge University Press.

TAMBIAH, STANLEY JEYARAJA. 1985. *Culture, Thought, and Social Action: An Anthropological Perspective.* Cambridge, Mass., and London: Harvard University Press.

THOMAS, NICHOLAS. 1989. "The Force of Ethnology." *Current Anthropology* 30(1):27–41.

THOMAS, VERL M. 1986. *Beef Cattle Production: An Integrated Approach.* Philadelphia: Lea & Febiger.

THOMSON, DONALD F. 1938. *Recommendations of Policy in Native Affairs in the Northern Territory of Australia,* no. 56.-F.2945. Canberra: Parliament of the Commonwealth of Australia.

THUROW, LESTER C. 1996. *The Future of Capitalism: How Today's Economic Forces Shape Tomorrow's World.* New York: Morrow.

TINDALE, NORMAN B. 1974. *Aboriginal Tribes of Australia: Their Terrain, Environmental Controls, Distribution, Limits, and Proper Names.* Berkeley: University of California Press.

TINDALE, NORMAN B. 1981. "Desert Aborigines and the Southern Coastal Peoples: Some Comparisons." In *Ecological Biogeography of Australia,* vol. 3, pt. 6, edited by Allen Keast, pp. 1853–1884. *Monographiae Biologicae,* vol. 41. The Hague: Dr. W. Junk.

TOCQUEVILLE, ALEXIS DE. 1835–40. *Democracy in America* (original *De la démocratie*), various editions.

TODD, IAN A. 1976. *Çatal Hüyük in Perspective.* Menlo Park, Calif.: Cummings.

TOMASELLO, MICHAEL. 1994. "The Question of Chimpanzee Culture." In *Chimpanzee Culture,* edited by Richard W. Wrangham, Frans B. M. de Waal, and W. C. McGrew, pp. 301–317. Cambridge, Mass.: Harvard University Press.

TOTH, JAMES. 1992. "Doubts About Growth: The Town of Carlisle in Transition." *Urban Anthropology* 21(1):2–44.

TOWNSEND, ROBERT M. 1993. *The Medieval Village Economy: A Study of the Pareto Mapping in General Equilibrium Models.* Princeton, N.J.: Princeton University Press.

TROWELL, HUGH C. 1954. "Kwashiorkor." *Scientific American* 191(6):46–50.

TURNER II, CHRISTY G. 1989. "Teeth and Prehistory in Asia." *Scientific American* 260(2):88–96.

TYLOR, EDWARD B. 1871. *Primitive Culture.* London: Murray.

TYLOR, EDWARD B. 1875. "Anthropology." *Encyclopaedia Britannica,* Vol. 1.

UNITED NATIONS. 1959. *International Labour Organisation Convention (No. 107) Concerning the Protection and Integration of Indigenous and Other Tribal and Semi-Tribal Populations in Independent Countries.* United Nations Treaty Series, no. 4738. New York: United Nations.

UNITED NATIONS. 1968a. *Statistical Yearbook 1967.* New York: United Nations.

UNITED NATIONS. 1968b. *Yearbook of National Accounts Statistics 1967.* New York: United Nations.

UNITED NATIONS, DEPARTMENT OF ECONOMIC AND SOCIAL AFFAIRS. 1963. *Report on the World Social Situation.* New York: United Nations.

UNITED NATIONS, DEPARTMENT OF ECONOMIC AND SOCIAL AFFAIRS. 1975. *1974 Report on the World Social Situation.* New York: United Nations.

UNITED NATIONS, DEPARTMENT OF SOCIAL AFFAIRS. 1952. *Preliminary Report on the World Situation: With Special Reference to Standards of Living,* E/CN.5/267/rev.1. New York: United Nations.

UNITED STATES, AID (AGENCY FOR INTERNATIONAL DEVELOPMENT). 1985. *Blueprint for Development: The Strategic Plan of the Agency for International Development.* Washington, D.C.: Government Printing Office.

UNITED STATES CONGRESS. 1974. Nomination of Nelson A. Rockefeller to be Vice President of the United States. Hearings Before the Committee on the Judiciary, House of Representatives, Ninety-Third Congress. Serial No. 45.

URTON, GARY. 1981. *At the Crossroads of the Earth and Sky: An Andean Cosmology.* Austin: University of Texas Press.

U.S. DEPARTMENT OF COMMERCE, BUREAU OF THE CENSUS. 1990. *Statistical Abstract of the United States: 1990,* 110th ed. Washington, D.C.: Government Printing Office.

VALENTINE, CHARLES A. 1968. *Culture and Poverty: Critique and Counter-Proposals.* Chicago and London: University of Chicago Press.

VALENTINE, CHARLES A. 1971. "The 'Culture of Poverty': Its Scientific Significance and Its Implications for Action." In *The Culture of Poverty: A Critique,* edited by Eleanor Burke Leacock, pp. 193–225. New York: Simon & Schuster.

VALENTINE, CHARLES A., ET AL., 1969. "Culture and Poverty: Critique and Counterproposals." *Current Anthropology* 10(2/3):181–201.

VAN SCHENDEL, WILLEM. 1981. *Peasant Mobility: The Odds of Life in Rural Bangladesh.* Assen: Van Gorcum.

VARESE, STEFANO. 1972. "Inter-Ethnic Relations in the Selva of Peru." In *The Situation of the Indian in South America,* edited by W. Dostal, pp. 115–139. Geneva: World Council of Churches.

VATUK, SYLVIA. 1982. "Purdah Revisited: A Comparison of Hindu and Muslim Interpretations of the Cultural Meaning of Purdah in South Asia." In *Separate Worlds: Studies of Purdah in South Asia,* edited by Hanna Papanek and Gail Minault, pp. 54–78. Delhi: Chanakya.

VERDON, MICHEL. 1982. "Where Have All Their Lineages Gone? Cattle and Descent Among the Nuer." *American Anthropologist* 84(3):566–579.

VER STEEG, CLARENCE L. 1954. *Robert Morris Revolutionary Financier.* Philadelphia: University of Philadelphia Press.

VITOUSEK, PETER M., PAUL R. EHRLICH, ANNE H. EHRLICH, AND PAMELA A. MATSON. 1986. "Human Appropriation of the Products of Photosynthesis." *BioScience* 36(6):368–373.

VOIGT, MARY. 1987. "Relative and Absolute Chronologies for Iran Between 6500 and 3500 BC." In *Chronologies in the Near East,* edited by O. Aurenche, J. Evin, and F. Hours, pp. 615–646. BAR International Series 379(ii). Oxford, Eng.: BAR.

WAKE, CHARLES STANILAND. 1872. "The Mental Conditions of Primitive Man as Exemplified by the Australian Aborigine." *Journal of the Royal Anthropological Institute* 1:78–84.

DE WALL, FRANS. 1982. *Chimpanzee Politics: Power and Sex Among Apes.* London: Jonathan Cape.

WALLACE, ANTHONY F. C. 1978. *Rockdale: The Growth of an American Village in the Early Industrial Revolution.* New York: Knopf.

WALLERSTEIN, IMMANUEL. 1974. *The Modern World-System: Capitalist Agriculture and the Origins of the European World-Economy in the Sixteenth Century.* New York: Academic Press.

WALLERSTEIN, IMMANUEL. 1990. "Culture as the Ideological Battleground of the Modern World-System." *Theory, Culture & Society* 7:31–55.

WALL STREET 20TH CENTURY. 1960. *A Republication of the Yale Daily News' Wall Street 1955.* New Haven, Conn.: Yale Daily News.

WALSH, J., AND R. GANNON. 1967. *Time Is Short and the Water Rises.* Camden, N.J.: Nelson.

WARNER, W. L. 1958. *A Black Civilization.* New York: Harper.

WCED (WORLD COMMISSION ON ENVIRONMENT AND DEVELOPMENT). 1987. *Our Common Future.* Oxford, Eng.: Oxford University Press.

WEAVER, THOMAS. 1985. "Anthropology as a Policy Science: Part II, Development and Training." *Human Organization* 44(3):197–205.

WEBER, MAX. [1904–1905] 1930. *The Protestant Ethic and the Spirit of Capitalism.* New York: Scribner.

WEBSTER, DAVID. 1981. "Late Pleistocene Extinction and Human Predation; A Critical Overview." In *Omnivorous Primates: Gathering and Hunting in Human Evolution,* edited by Robert Harding and Geza Teleki, pp. 556–595. New York: Columbia University Press.

WEI-MING, TU. 1990. "The Confucian Tradition in Chinese History." In *Heritage of China: Contemporary Perspectives on Chinese Civilization,* edited by Paul Ropp, pp. 112–137. Berkeley: University of California Press.

WEISS, GERALD. 1975. *Campa Cosmology: The World of a Forest Tribe in South America.* Anthropological Papers, no. 52(5). New York: American Museum of Natural History.

WENDORF, FRED, AND ROMUALD SCHILD. 1984. "The Emergence of Food Production in the Egyptian Sahara." In *From Hunters to Farmers: The Causes and Consequences of Food Production in Africa,* edited by J. Desmond Clark and Steven Brandt, pp. 93–101. Berkeley: University of California Press.

WERNER, DENNIS. 1983. "Why Do the Mekranoti Trek?" In *Adaptive Responses of Native Amazonians,* edited by Raymond Hames and William Vickers, pp. 225–238. New York: Academic Press.

WESTERMARK, EDWARD. 1922. *The History of Human Marriage,* 5th ed. New York: Allerton Book Co.

WESTERN, DAVID, AND VIRGINIA FINCH. 1986. "Cattle and Pastoralism: Survival and Production in Arid Lands." *Human Ecology* 14(1):77–94.

WHEATLEY, PAUL. 1971. *The Pivot of the Four Quarters: A Preliminary Enquiry into the Origins and Character of the Ancient Chinese City.* Chicago: Aldine.

WHEELER, JANE C. 1984. "On the Origin and Early Development of Camelid Pastoralism in the Andes." In *Animals and Archaeology,* vol. 3, edited by Juliet Clatton-Brock and Caroline Grigson, pp. 395–410. BAR International Series, no. 202. Oxford, Eng.: BAR.

WHITE, J. PETER, AND JAMES F. O'CONNELL. 1982. *Prehistory of Australia, New Guinea and Sahul.* New York: Academic Press.

WHITE, LESLIE A. 1949. *The Science of Culture.* New York: Grove Press.

WHYTE, WILLIAM FOOTE, AND KATHLEEN KING WHYTE. 1988. *Making Mondragon: The Growth and Dynamics of the Worker Cooperative Complex.* Ithaca, NY: ILR Press.

WILKINSON, RICHARD G. 1996. *Unhealthy Societies: The Afflictions of Inequality.* London and New York: Routledge.

WILKINSON, RICHARD G. 1997. "Comment: Income, Inequality, and Social Cohesion." *American Journal of Public Health* 87(9):1504–1506.

WILLIAMS, NANCY M. 1986. *The Yolngu and Their Land: A System of Land Tenure and the Fight for Its Recognition.* Stanford, Calif.: Stanford University Press.

WILSON, ALLAN C., AND REBECCA L. CANN. 1992. "The Recent African Genesis of Humans: Genetic Studies Reveal That an African Woman of 200,000 Years Ago Was Our Common Ancestor." *Scientific American* 266(April):68–73.

WILSON, EDWARD O. 1989. "Threats to Biodiversity." *Scientific American* 261(3):108–116.

WILSON, EDWARD O., AND FRANCES M. PETER (EDS.). 1988. *Biodiversity.* Washington, D.C.: National Academy Press.

WILSON, PETER J. 1988. *The Domestication of the Human Species.* New Haven, Conn., and London: Yale University Press.

WISE, MARY RUTH, EUGENE E. LOOS, AND PATRICIA DAVIS. 1977. "Filosofiá y Métodos del Instituto Linguistico de Verano." *Proceedings of the 42nd International Americanists Congress* 2:499–525.

WITTFOGEL, KARL A. 1957. *Oriental Despotism: A Study of Total Power.* New Haven, Conn.: Yale University Press.

WOLF, ARTHUR P. 1968. "Adopt a Daughter-in-Law, Marry a Sister: A Chinese Solution to the Problem of the Incest Taboo." *American Anthropologist* 70(5):864–874.

WOLF, ARTHUR P. (ED.). 1974. "Gods, Ghosts, and Ancestors." In *Religion and Ritual in Chinese Society,* pp. 131–182. Stanford, Calif.: Stanford University Press.

WOLF, ARTHUR P. 1995. *Sexual Attraction and Childhood Association: A Chinese Brief for Edward Westermarck.* Stanford, Calif.: Stanford University Press.

WOLF, ERIC R. 1955. "Types of Latin American Peasantry." *American Anthropologist* 57(3, pt.1):452–471.

WOLF, ERIC R. 1957. "Closed Corporate Peasant Communities in Mesoamerica and Central Java." *Southwestern Journal of Anthropology* 13(1):1–18.

WOLF, ERIC R. 1969. *Peasant Wars of the Twentieth Century.* New York: Harper & Row.

WOLF, ERIC R. 1982. *Europe and the People Without History.* Berkeley: University of California Press.

WOLF, MARGERY. 1968. *The House of Lim: A Study of a Chinese Farm Family.* New York: Appleton-Century-Crofts.

WOLF, STEWARD, AND JOHN G. BRUHN. 1993. *The Power of Clan: The Influence of Human Relationships on Heart Disease*. New Brunswick, N.J., and London: Transaction Books.

WOODBURN, JAMES. 1982. "Egalitarian Societies." *Man* 17(3): 431–451.

WOOD JONES, FREDERIC. 1928. "The Claims of the Australian Aborigine." *Report of the Eighteenth Australasian Association for the Advancement of Science* 18:497–519.

WOODRUFF, WILLIAM. 1966. *The Impact of Western Man*. London: Macmillan.

WOOLLEY, SIR LEONARD. 1982. *Ur "of the Chaldees."* London: Herbert Press.

World Almanac and Book of Facts. 1998. Mahwah, N.J.: World Almanac Books.

WORLD BANK. 1988–1995. *World Development Report*. New York: Oxford University Press.

WRIGHT, ARTHUR F. 1977. "The Cosmology of the Chinese City." In *The City in Late Imperial China*, edited by G. William Skinner, pp. 33–73. Stanford, Calif.: Stanford University Press.

WRIGHT, HENRY T. 1969. *The Administration of Rural Production in an Early Mesopotamian Town*. Anthropological Papers, no. 38. Ann Arbor: Museum of Anthropology, University of Michigan.

WRIGHT, JOHN W. 1990. *The Universal Almanac*. Kansas City, Mo.: Andrews & McMeel.

YALMAN, NUR. 1963. "On the Purity of Women in the Castes of Ceylon and Malabar." *Journal of the Royal Anthropological Institute* 93:25–58.

YDE, JENS. 1965. *Material Culture of the Waiwai*. National-museets Skrifter. Ethnografisk Roekke 10. Copenhagen: National Museum.

YENGOYAN, ARAM A. 1981. "Infanticide and Birth Order: An Empirical Analysis of Preferential Female Infanticide Among Australian Aboriginal Populations." In *The Perception of Evolution: Essays Honoring Joseph B. Birdsell*, edited by Larry Mai, Eugenia Shanklin, and Robert Sussman, pp. 255–273. Anthropology UCLA, vol. 7, nos. 1 and 2. Los Angeles: Department of Anthropology, University of California.

YOFFEE, NORMAN. 1988a. "The Collapse of Ancient Mesopotamian States and Civilization." In *The Collapse of Ancient States and Civilizations*, edited by Norman Yoffee and George Cowgill, pp. 44–68. Tucson: University of Arizona Press.

YOFFEE, NORMAN. 1988b. "Orienting Collapse." In *The Collapse of Ancient States and Civilizations*, edited by Norman Yoffee and George Cowgill, pp. 1–19. Tucson: University of Arizona Press.

ZUIDEMA, R. TOM. 1990. *Inca Civilization in Cuzco*. Austin: University of Texas Press.

Credits

PHOTOS

Chapter 2   p. 29 top, courtesy Barry S. Hewlett; p. 29 bottom, Animals Animals/ © Hans and Judy Beste; p. 35, courtesy Barry S. Hewlett; p. 39 Baldwin Spencer Collection No 751. Reproduced courtesy Museum Victoria; p. 43, Neg. # 298390, courtesy Department of Library Services, American Museum of Natural History; p. 44, © Irven DeVore/Anthro-Photo.

Chapter 3   p. 56, The Rainforest Action Network; p. 74, courtesy of Jesus Ignacio Cardoza.

Chapter 4   p. 90, courtesy Robert J. Blumenschine; p. 94, courtesy Elliot M. Fratkin; p. 108, © J. F. E. Bross/Anthro-Photo; p. 116, © Smucker/Anthro-Photo.

Chapter 5   p. 124, © Margaret Thompson, 1974/Anthro-Photo; p. 140, © Napoleon Chagnon/Anthro-Photo; p. 143, © SEF/Art Resource, NY.

Chapter 6   p. 159, courtesy Barry S. Hewlett; p. 161 top, courtesy of the Bernice P. Bishop Museum, Hawaii; p. 161 bottom, © The Field Museum, Neg. # A100920; p. 164, courtesy Barry S. Hewlett; p. 175, © Miki Akiyoshi/Pacific Stock; p. 178, courtesy of the Bernice P. Bishop Museum, Hawaii.

Chapter 7   p. 195, drawings by Eliza McFadden from *Plato Prehistorian* by Mary Settegast, published by the Lindisfarne Press, 1986. Used by permission of Lindisfarne Books, Hudson, NY 12534; pp. 196, 197, Gregory Johnson, Hunter College; p. 199 top, © George Gerster/Comstock; p. 199B, University of Pennsylvania Museum (neg. # S8-139326); p. 200, Courtesy German Archaeology Institute, Division Baghdad; pp. 205, 207, Negs. 36787, 330282, courtesy Department of Library Services, American Museum of Natural History.

Chapter 8   p. 219, courtesy Peter J. Mehringer; p. 227, © Wally McNamee/Woodfin Camp & Associates; p. 234, © Audrey Topping/Photo Researchers, Inc.

Chapter 9   p. 256, Harappan Archaeological Research Project, Project Director Richard H. Meadows; p. 265, © S. Nagendra/Photo Researchers, Inc.; p. 270, © Mimi Nichter/Anthro-Photo; p. 272, © Paolo Koch/Photo Researchers, Inc.; p. 274, © Nancy D'Antonio/Photo Researchers, Inc.

Chapter 10   p. 284, © Paolo Koch/Photo Researchers, Inc.; p. 287, © DDB Stock Photo.

Chapter 11   p. 302, © Joel Gordon 1981; pp. 306, 311, 313, © Corbis-Bettmann.

Chapter 12   p. 351, © Corbis-Bettmann; p. 342, courtesy of Tim McCabe; p. 355, © UPI/Corbis-Bettmann.

Chapter 13   p. 365, © Betty B. Derig/Photo Researchers, Inc.; p. 374, © Susan Meiselas/Magnum Photos, Inc.; p. 386, courtesy Christine Eber with appreciation to Maria Arias Pérez and Manuel Cura; p. 390 top, © Bernard Wolff/Magnum Photos, Inc; p. 390 bottom, courtesy Dr. Paul Doughty.

Chapter 14   p. 401, © Karl Lumholtz, 1902, *Among Cannibals*, New York: Charles Scribners; p. 403, courtesy of The Peabody Essex Museum, Salem, Massachusetts; p. 406, The Granger Collection, New York; p. 411, courtesy of Belinda Wright.

Chapter 15   p. 427, © Jeffrey Lepore/Photo Researchers, Inc.; p. 434, The Rainforest Action Network, p. 438, Copyright © 1995, Decisions Investments Corp. Reprinted with the permission of Decisions Investments Corp. and Biosphere 2 Center, Inc., Archives Department, Biosphere 2, photo by Gil Kenny.

TEXT AND ILLUSTRATIONS

Chapter 3   p. 62, Gertrude Dole, "The Use of Manioc Among the Kuikuru: Some Implications," Michigan Museum of Anthropology, *Anthropological Papers* 67:217–247; p. 80, Roe, Peter, *Cosmic Zygote*. Copyright © 1982 by Rutgers, The State University. Reprinted by permission of Rutgers University Press.

Chapter 4   p. 98, Ochollo-Ayayo, A.B.C., "Marriage and Cattle Exchange Among the Nilotic Luo, 1979. *Paideuma* 25: 173–193. Used with permission of the publisher; p. 106, 112, From E. E. Evans-Pritchard, *The Nuer: A Description of the Modes of Livelihood and Political Institutions of a Nilotic People*, Oxford University Press, 1940. By permission of Oxford University Press; p. 113, "Being Maasai, Being People of Cattle: Ethnic Shifters in East Africa" by John G. Galatay. Reproduced by permission of the American Anthropological Association from *American Ethnologist* 9:1, February 1982. Not for further reproduction; p. 114, Paul Spencer, *The Maasai of Matapato: A Study of Rituals of Rebellion*, Indiana University Press, 1988.

473

Index

Page numbers in italics indicate figures or tables; page numbers in boldface indicate definitions.